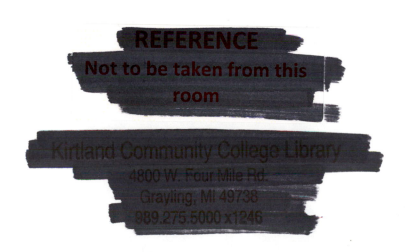

SALEM HEALTH

Psychology & Behavioral Health

SALEM HEALTH

Psychology & Behavioral Health

Volume 1
Ability tests – Community psychology

Editor

Paul Moglia, PhD
South Nassau Communities Hospital
Oceanside, NY

SALEM PRESS
A Division of EBSCO Information Services, Inc.
IPSWICH, MASSACHUSETTS

GREY HOUSE PUBLISHING

∞The paper used in these volumes conforms to the American National Standard for Permanence of Paper for Printed Library Materials, Z39.48 1992 (R1997).

Some of the updated and revised essays in this work originally appeared in *Magill's Encyclopedia of Social Science: Psychology*, edited by Nancy A. Piotrowski, PhD (2003) and *Magill's Survey of Social Science: Psychology*, edited by Frank N. Magill (1993).

Publisher's Cataloging-In-Publication Data
(Prepared by The Donohue Group, Inc.)

Psychology & behavioral health / editor, Paul Moglia, PhD. – Fourth edition.

5 volumes : illustrations ; cm. -- (Salem health)

At head of title: Salem health.
Previously published as: Psychology & mental health.
Includes bibliographical references and index.
Contents: Volume 1. Ability tests-Community psychology -- volume 2. Comorbidity-Health psychology -- volume 3. Hearing-Parental alienation syndrome -- volume 4. Parenting styles-Sleep -- volume 5. Sleep apnea-Philip Zimbardo; Appendixes; Indexes.
ISBN: 978-1-61925-543-2 (5-volume set)
ISBN: 978-1-61925-810-5 (vol.1)
ISBN: 978-1-61925-811-2 (vol.2)
ISBN: 978-1-61925-812-9 (vol.3)
ISBN: 978-1-61925-813-6 (vol.4)
ISBN: 978-1-61925-814-3 (vol.5)

1. Psychology, Applied--Encyclopedias. 2. Mental health--Encyclopedias. 3. Mental illness--Encyclopedias. 4. Medicine and psychology--Encyclopedias. I. Moglia, Paul. II. Title: Psychology and behavioral health III. Title: Salem health IV. Series: Salem health (Pasadena, Calif.)

BF636 .P86 2015
150.3

First Printing
Printed in the United States of America

PUBLISHER'S NOTE

This is the fourth edition of *Psychology & Behavioral Health*, previously called *Psychology & Mental Health*. It remains a valuable addition to the Salem Health series, which includes *Magill's Medical Guide; Addictions & Substance Abuse; Complementary & Alternative Medicine; Infectious Diseases & Conditions; Genetics; Cancer;* and coming soon, *Adolescent Health & Wellness*. This five-volume set covers not only the history of the field and the core aspects of behaviorism, cognitive psychology, and psychoanalytic psychology, but also diagnoses, disorders, treatment, assessment, and notable individuals in the field.

This new edition includes 690 articles. Of the nearly 100 brand new articles, many address how culture, ethnicity, and gender affect psychological theory and beliefs. They include *Bad Boy Appeal, Electronic Media and Psychological Impact, Exercise Addiction, Memory Enhancement, Reality TV,* and *Sports Psychology*. The new topics also include *Dog Psychology, DSM-V Controversies, Hoarding, Luminosity,* and *Toxic Environments and Human Development*.

Every previously published entry has been reviewed, and the vast majority have been updated. All articles include a helpful list of sources for Further Study. The work includes five appendixes and two indexes.

Organization and Format

Entries in *Psychology & Behavioral Health* range from one to eight pages in length. Every entry begins with Type of Psychology; Abstract; and Key Concepts. When appropriate, dates when theories were first presented are provided, and biographical entries include the Identity and Birth/Death of the subject.

The text of each article offers a clear and concise discussion of the topic. Subheads appear frequently. Mental disorder entries include cause, diagnosis, treatment and impact. Theory entries include origin, history and current status. Organization entries include history and functions. Assessment entries include development and application. Biographical entries include the individual's life, career and contributions. All terminology is explained and most bibliographic listings have been thoughtfully annotated by the author, whose name appears at the end of the entry. Lastly is a helpful list of cross references to other articles within *Psychology & Behavioral Health*.

Resources and Indexes

A complete Table of Contents appears at the beginning of each volume. Appendixes and Indexes appear at the end of volume five.

Appendixes:

- Glossary – more than 600 clearly-defined terms relevant to the fields of psychology and behavioral health
- Bibliography – books, journals and articles, organized in 33 categories from Aggression to Testing, and most with valuable annotations
- Web Site Directory – more than 50 annotated web site listings of major psychological associations and organizations
- Mediagraphy – 150 films and television shows with mental health themes and characters, all with detailed descriptions
- Organizations and support groups – 150 organizations grouped by North American, Specialties, International and Specific Disorders plus dozens of hotlines

Indexes:

- Category Index groups all articles in this 5-volume set into 60 categories from Abnormality models to Women's psychology
- Subject Index alphabetically lists all the significant people, places and concepts covered in this set

Acknowledgments

Salem Press gratefully acknowledges Paul Moglia, PhD, editor of this edition, whose introduction to the work follows this Publisher's Note. Salem Press also thanks the work of many contributors, whose names and affiliations follow Dr. Moglia's introduction.

EDITOR'S INTRODUCTION

People fascinate people. We seem programmed, genetically, societally, both, to be consumed with who we are, why we developed the way we did, what is our purpose, what is important to us, who is important to us, where are we going, what makes people bad, difficult, hurtful. What makes the good, good; how did they get that way? How is it that some overcome remarkable obstacles in life and even triumph? How is it others are crushed by the weight of remarkably similar circumstances? Every human inquiry from physics to politics, from economics to art, from dance to architecture, provides ways to see and understand what it is to be human, and how to influence that process.

Psychology, a social science, is soft. It lacks the rigor and rules of mathematics, itself more language than science. It lacks the precision of engineering. Unlike chemistry experiments, psychology's experiments are really just quasi-experiments. Its methods of learning how we learn, how cognition, emotion, consciousness, and even how a conscience comes to be, have far less surety and intellectual satisfaction than so many other branches of human inquiry. A point guard knows in the release whether the basket is good. An engineer knows why a bridge will hold. A musicologist knows why a concerto works or doesn't. (And just how they know is a fascinating area of psychology.) Psychology and the other social sciences study a complex thing: what makes us who we are. The social sciences use a remarkable range of study tools, approaches, methods, statistics and other analytical tools. In spite of this, the *study of the psyche* (the etymology of psychology) will always leave us intellectually hungry.

For me, the uncertainty is welcome. Psychological investigation and the information it yields is humbling and grounding. It promotes caution and excitement at the same time. Understanding who we are, how do we make meaning as individuals who always exist within a group context, and how we learn to gratify and fulfill ourselves, is an awe-inspiring quest. Psychology is just one of many languages spoken along the road to more accurate and complete understanding of our own nature as species and our natures as individuals. But psychology is also the primary language spoken in these five volumes.

We present you with almost 700 stories (aka topics) told in this language. Our authors update what we have learned since the last time *Psychology & Mental Health* appeared. We give you what we believe you will be interested in now. We retain the historical foundations of psychology, its history and systems of differing thoughts and methods. Some of these progress one from the other; some have been synthesized, yielding sums greater than their parts. Some are simply incompatible with each other, challenging us with the epistemological conundrum of holding two contradictory beliefs that both seem true. We have also retained overviews of the giants in the field, some of whom could not legally call themselves psychologists today, as all states limit use of the title by statute. We have also added to this list of luminaries, those we believe you will want to know more about.

We never escape biology. How we come to think, create, love and hate, fundamentally resides in how our biological selves developed. Did we achieve all the potential locked in the marriage of the chromosomal halves that gave birth to us, and mysteriously, not someone else? How does the human brain make sense of visual images? How is it our ears make sense of the limited range of syllables our voices can make, and turn them into expressive and receptive language, and do the same with not just one language but thousands? How is it nutrition and physical movement play such determinative roles in how well we function and feel, or how poorly? We speak to this in the many entries that cover psychobiology, the biological bases of human behavior and humanity.

We include entries that focus on individual growth, how we become who we are, the enigmatic process of individual development which is paradoxically only possible in the context and safe surroundings of others, of family, tribe, culture, nation, ethnicity, and race. Our scholars discuss how intelligence develops, how we measure it, what happens when it fails to develop the "right" way, and how it relates to other cognitive processes like creativity, emotionality, and intuition.

Most people live in families, even the majority of homeless people live with their homeless family members. We provide multiple entries on the relationship between parents and children, the nature of family itself, its dynamics, its social psychological roles, and the ways psychology and allied health disciplines (psychiatry, social work, pastoral counseling, and marriage and family therapy for example) work with families to promote its optimal functioning and growth.

We present hundreds of clinical articles that collectively may prove the most beneficial to those like you who have picked up this work. Authored by psychologists, allied clinicians, social science researchers, and academic scholars, their efforts aim to inform you about some aspect of human behavior that troubles you or someone you care about. The overviews are current, the latest in clinical and psychotherapeutic thinking, and explain what we know about causes, courses, and treatments. And every author provides suggestions about where else to look for more and what you will find there if you do. Our writers do not offer treatment here. This is not a five-volume self-help series. Our writers do offer information, ways to understand the problem, and what treating the person troubled means.

By now, it is old and repetitive news that the industry of health care, approaching one-fifth the US gross national product, is changing. We are in the middle of a swarm of efforts and endeavors that speak to cost-effectiveness, clinical outcomes and efficiencies, patient-centered medical homes, teletherapy, meaningful use, evidence-based treatments, and new business models to deliver clinical care, including care of the mind and emotions. Our fourth edition's name change from *Mental Health* to *Behavioral Health* reflects the jargon of our day, suggesting that treatment is about behavioral change, change that can and must be measured if clinicians are to know (along with their patients, clients, consumers, customers) that our work is helping, and what exactly it is helping with. I am not convinced that the mystery and majesty of the human person and what promotes health in him and her will fit congruently in the ways we are now trying to understand. The phenomenology of humanity may not be able to genuflect to the canon of science and its truly wondrous methods.

I have envisioned the principal users of *Psychology & Behavioral Health* will be from one of two groups. The first will be those with an academic interest, students completing course assignments. If we have done our jobs well and lived up to our responsibility, you should find what you need somewhere among our pages, or at least find good guidance on where more specific information lies.

The second group will be those who worry about some psychological or clinical issue, disorder, condition or diagnosis that they or someone they care about has. Again, if we have done our jobs correctly, one or more of our clinical scholars will speak to you, explain to you, encourage you, and tell you, 'now that you know this, here are other places to look.' Life is marked by unfair and unjust challenges. If our work helps you manage them better in some way, we are grateful for the opportunity to serve.

I too am grateful to those who have helped make my participation in this enterprise possible. Alexandra Sabrina Blanchard, an honors psychology major from Pace University in New York City, readily came to my aide in completing professionally and competently the many tasks I sent her way. My son, Michael, recently of Stony Brook University, read every article submitted to me. He did so with a critical and discerning eye for readability, internal logic, prosody, and syntax. I thank Melissa Rose, editorial assistant at Grey House, who blended cheerfulness and thoroughness at all times in every phase of this project and who was in contact with every contributor. Neither Grey House nor I could have had a better liaison. I also am grateful to Grey House's capable Vice President, Editorial, Laura Mars, who offered me the chance to wear my editor's hat once more and without whose wise and experienced counsel, *Psychology & Behavioral Health* could have well ended up in the weeds along with my hat. Finally, I am grateful to Jean Ann and our children, Jenna, Michael, and Briana Frances for patiently supporting my absence as I manned this helm.

Paul Moglia, PhD
Glen Cove, New York

CONTRIBUTORS

Christopher M. Aanstoos
University of West Georgia

Faith Abalos-Marino
South Nassau Communities Hospital

Norman Abeles
Michigan State University

Steven C. Abell
Loyola College of Chicago

Richard Adler
University of Michigan-Dearborn

C. Emmanuel Ahia
Rider University

Saima Ahmed
South Nassau Communities Hospital,

Mark B. Alcorn
University of Northern Colorado

Charles N. Alexander
Maharishi International University

Jeffery B. Allen
University of Mississippi

Tara Anthony
Syracuse University

Jamie D. Aten
University of Southern Mississippi

Richard P. Atkinson
Fort Hays State University

Bryan C. Auday
Gordon College

Stephen M. Auerbach
Virginia Commonwealth University

Buffie Longmire Avital
National Development and Research Institutes, Inc., and Public Health Solutions

Dana K. Bagwell
Memory Health and Fitness Institute

Bruce E. Bailey
Stephen F. Austin University

Carl L. Bankston III
Tulane University

Sandra Barrueco
The Catholic University of America

Karen Barto-Sisamout
University of Arizona

Roy F. Baumeister
Florida State University

Stephen R. H. Beach
University of Georgia

Donald G. Beal
Eastern Kentucky University

Alan J. Beauchamp
Northern Michigan University

Brett L. Beck
Bloomsbury University

Susan E. Beers
Sweet Briar College

Tanja Bekhuis
TCB Research

Michael S. Bendele
Indiana University-Purdue University, Fort Wayne

Alvin K. Benson
Utah Valley State College

Professor Jacquelyn H. Berry
State University of New York at New Paltz

Krishna Bhaskarabhatla
Saint Joseph's Regional Medical Center, Mount Sinai School of Medicine

Virginiae Blackmon
Fort Hays, Texas

Cathy J. Bogart
Avila University

Professor Laurie Bonjo
State University of New York at New Paltz

Lyn T. Boulter
Catawba College

Professor Mary M. Brabeck
New York University

Barbara E. Brackney
Eastern Michigan University

Nyla R. Branscombe
University of Kansas

Lillian J. Breckenridge
Oral Roberts University

Barbara A. Bremer
Pennsylvania State University, Harrisburg

Christiane Brems
University of Alaska

Bruce Bridgeman
University of California, Santa Cruz

T. L. Brink
Crafton Hills College

Victor K. Broderick
Ferris State University

David W. Brokaw
Azusa Pacific University

Leonie J. Brooks
Towson University

Gayle L. Brosnan-Watters
Vanguard University of Southern California

Dennis Bull
Dallas Theological Seminary

Michael A. Buratovich
Spring Arbor University

John T. Burns
Bethany College

Daniel Busso
Harvard Graduate School of Education

Joan Bartczak Cannon
University of Lowell

Mary E. Carey
University of Oklahoma

Russell N. Carney
Missouri State University

Christine M. Carroll
American Medical Writers Association

Jack Carter
University of New Orleans

Karen Chapman-Novakofski
University of Illinois

Paul J. Chara, Jr.
Northwestern College

Garvin Chastain
Boise State University

Philip Cheng
Sleep Disorders Center, Henry Ford Health System

Kausalya Chennapragada
Saint Joseph's Regional Medical Center, Mount Sinai School of Medicine

Judith M. Chertoff
Baltimore-Washington Institute for Psychoanalysis

Rebecca M. Chesire
University of Hawaii—Manoa

Grace E. Cho
St. Olaf College

Maryalice Citera
State University of New York at New Paltz

Ruth Melanie Colwill
Brown University

Richard G. Cormack
Ventura, California

Salvatore Cullari
Lebanon Valley College

Michael Daly
Florida State University Trinity College Dublin

Elizabeth W. Davies
University of St. Francis

Kenneth G. DeBono
Union College

Everett J. Delahanty, Jr.
Manhattanville College

Patricia J. Deldin
University of Michigan

Jack Demick
Suffolk University

James R. Deni
Appalachian State University

Ryan M. Denney
University of Southern Mississippi

Karen M. Derr
Airport Marina Counseling Service

Thomas E. DeWolfe
Hampden-Sydney College

M. Casey Diana
Arizona State University

Kenneth Dill
South Nassau Communities Hospital

Amber D. Dillon
Illinois Emergency Management Agency (IEMA)

Ronna F. Dillon
Southern Illinois University

Duane L. Dobbert
Florida Gulf Coast University

Stefan C. Dombrowski
Rider University

George Domino
University of Arizona

Roger A. Drake
Western State College of Colorado

Robert J. Drummond
University of North Florida

Dana S. Dunn
Moravian College

Christopher A. Duva
Eastern Oregon University

Patricia Stanfill Edens
Global Oncology SP

Ted Eilders
American Psychological Association

Russell Eisenman
McNeese State University

David G. Elmes
Washington and Lee University

John W. Engel
University of Hawaii at Manoa

Carolyn Zerbe Enns
Cornell College

Charles H. Evans
LaGrange College

Lawrence A. Fehr
Widener University

Leonard Feinberg
Iona College

Julie A. Felender
Fullerton College

Ellen C. Flannery-Schroeder
University of the Sciences in Philadelphia

Robert Flatley
Kutztown University

John H. Fleming
University of Minnesota-Minneapolis

Anthony J. Fonseca
Nicholls State University

Karen Anding Fontenot
Louisiana State University

Michael J. Fontenot
Southern University at Baton Rouge

Katherine A. Fowler
Emory University

Margaret M. Frailey
American Association of Counseling and Development

Robin Franck
Southwestern College

Cynthia McPherson Frantz
Amherst College

Donna Frick-Horbury
Appalachian State University

Lisa Friedenberg
University of North Carolina at Asheville

Jerome Frieman
Kansas State University

Jim Fultz
Northern Illinois University

R. G. Gaddis
Gardner-Webb University

Judi Garland
Wilmington Family Counseling Service

Judith L. Gay
Chestnut Hill College

Hannah L. Geller
Kingsboro Psychiatric Center, John Jay College of Criminal Justice

J. Ronald Gentile
State University of New York at Buffalo

Alan K. Gibson
Southern California College

Kimberly Glazier
Yeshiva University

Virginia L. Goetsch
West Virginia University

Doyle R. Goff
Lee College

Jennifer Goldschmied
University of Michigan

Ursula Goldsmith
Louisiana State University

Sanford Golin
University of Pittsburgh

Diane C. Gooding
University of Wisconsin-Madison

Charles A. Gramlich
Xavier University of Louisiana

Jeff Greenberg
University of Arizona

Laurence Grimm
University of Illinois at Chicago

Lonnie J. Guralnick
Western Oregon State College

Regan A. R. Gurung
University of Wisconsin, Green Bay

Elizabeth Haase
The New York Hospital

Irwin Halfond
McKendree University

Stephen Hampe
Capella University

Ruth T. Hannon
Bridgewater State College

Jo-Ida C. Hanson
University of Minnesota

Phyllis A. Heath
Central Michigan University

Joanne Hedgespeth
Pepperdine University Graduate School of Education and Psychology

Daniel Heimowitz
National Psychological Association for Psychoanalysis

Carol A. Heintzelman
Millersville University

Jean S. Helgeson
Collin County Community College

Katherine M. Helm
Lewis University

James Taylor Henderson
Wingate College

Lindsey L. Henninger
Burr Ridge, Illinois

Oliver W. Hill, Jr.
Virginia State University

Peter C. Hill
Grove City College

Robert A. Hock
Xavier University

David Wason Hollar, Jr.
Rockingham Community College

Brynda Holton
St. Mary's College of Maryland

Sigmund Hsiao
University of Arizona

Timothy L. Hubbard
Eastern Oregon State College

Mary Hurd
East Tennessee State University

Loring J. Ingraham
George Washington University

Tiffany A. Ito
University of Southern California

Stanley D. Ivie
Educational Leadership

Jay W. Jackson
Indiana University-Purdue University, Fort Wayne

Shelley A. Jackson
Texas A&M University-Corpus Christi

Robert Jensen
California State University, Sacramento

Bruce E. Johansen
University of Nebraska at Omaha

Barbara E. Johnson
University of South Carolina, Aiken

Craig Johnson
Syracuse University

Eugene R. Johnson
Central Washington University

Mark E. Johnson
University of Alaska

Robert D. Johnson
Arkansas State University

Kelly M. Jordan
University of Minnesota

Jonathan Kahane
Springfield College

Laura Kamptner
California State University, San Bernardino

Anne M. W. Kelly
Dakota Wesleyan University

Ing-Wei Khor
Discovery Institute of Medical Education

William B. King
Edison Community College

Terry J. Knapp
University of Nevada, Las Vegas

Felicitas Kort
New York, NY

Gabrielle Kowalski
Cardinal Stritch University

Robin M. Kowalski
Clemson University

Carol A. Kusché
Seattle Psychoanalytic Society and Institute

George T. Ladd
Rhode Island College

Daniel Lalande
Université Laval

Kristin E. Landfield
Alliant International University

R. Eric Landrum
Boise State University

Kevin T. Larkin
West Virginia University

Ellen Lavelle
Teikyo Western University

Richard Lettieri
Los Angeles Psychoanalytic Society and Institute

Melanie E. Leuty
University of Southern Mississippi

Leon Lewis
Appalachian State University

Thomas Tandy Lewis
St. Cloud State University

Scott O. Lilienfeld
Emory College

Gary T. Long
University of North Carolina at Charlotte

Martha Oehmke Loustaunau
New Mexico State University

Anna Lowe
Loyola University Chicago

Heather L. Lucas
Seattle Pacific University

Arthur J. Lurigio
Loyola University

Lesley D. Lutes
East Carolina University

Adam Lynn
Riverdale, NY

Nancy E. Macdonald
University of South Carolina at Sumter

Robin MacFarlane
New York, NY

Salvador Macias III
University of South Carolina at Sumter

Susan Mackey-Kallis
Villanova University

Paul D. Mageli
Kenmore, New York

Muhammad Usman Majeed
Rockville Centre, New York

Amy Marcus-Newhall
Occidental College
University of Southern California

Richard D. McAnulty
University of North Carolina at Charlotte

Deborah R. McDonald
New Mexico State University

David S. McDougal
Plymouth State College of the University System of New Hampshire

Lata K. McGinn
Yeshiva University

Sharon McLennon Wier
Concordia College

Richard L. McWhorter
Prairie View A&M University

Linda Mealey
College of St. Benedict

Bernard Mergen
George Washington University

Michael R. Meyers
Pfeiffer University

William M. Miley
The Richard Stockton College of New Jersey

Laurence Miller
Western Washington University

Norman Miller
University of Southern California

Rowland Miller
Sam Houston State University

Todd Miller
University of St. Thomas

Randall L. Milstein
Oregon State University

Andrew Minigan
Harvard Graduate School of Education

Briana Moglia
The University at Albany

Eugenia Moglia
Glen Cove, NY

Michael Moglia
Glen Cove, NY

Paul Moglia
South Nassau Communities Hospital

Robin Kamienny Montvilo
Rhode Island College

Martin Mrazik
University of Alberta

Brian Mullen
Syracuse University

Karen D. Multon
University of Missouri-Columbia

Debra L. Murphy
Huston-Tillotson College

Michelle Murphy
Pasadena, California

Steven Nakisher
Centerpiece Consulting

Donald J. Nash
Colorado State University-Lamar

Elizabeth M. McGhee Nelson
Christian Brothers University

John W. Nichols
Tulsa Junior College

Janet Nicol
University of Arizona

Steve A. Nida
Franklin University

Elizabeth M. Nielson
John Jay College of Criminal Justice

Annette O'Connor
La Salle University

Cynthia O'Dell
Indiana University Northwest

Amy L. Odum
University of New Hampshire

Janine T. Ogden
Marist College

Nancy Oley
City University of New York, Medgar Evers College

Ayn Embar-Seddon O'Reilly
Capella University

Dawn Ortiz
Milan, NY

Kimberly Ortiz
Alliant International University

Don R. Osborn
Bellarmine College

Randall E. Osborne
Phillips University

Gerard O'Sullivan
Felician College

Melissa Otero
Westchester Medical Center, New York Medical College

Ronghua Ouyang
Kennesaw State University

Linda J. Palm
Edison Community College

Beverly B. Palmer
California State University, Dominguez Hills

Robert J. Paradowski
Rochester Institute of Technology

Crystal L. Park
University of Connecticut

Allan D. Pass
National Behavioral Science Consultants

Elyssa Pearlstein
University of Michigan

Catalina Pérez
The Catholic University of America

Christina Hamme Peterson
Rider University

Vicky Phares
University of South Florida

Nancy A. Piotrowski
Capella University and University of California, Berkeley

Patricia Pitta
St. John's University

Anthony R. Pratkanis
University of California, Santa Cruz

Frank J. Prerost
Midwestern University

Debra S. Preston
University of North Carolina at Pembroke

Judith Primavera
Fairfield University

Jean Prokott
Winona State University

R. Christopher Qualls
Emory and Henry College

Christopher Rager
Pasadena, California

Timothy S. Rampey
Victoria College

Lillian M. Range
Our Lady of Holy Cross College

F. Wayne Reno
Mt. Vernon Nazarene College

Paul August Rentz
South Dakota State University

Wendy E. S. Repovich
Eastern Washington University

Ronald G. Ribble
University of Texas at San Antonio

Richard J. Ricard
Texas A&M University

Betty Richardson
Southern Illinois University at Edwardsville

Cheryl A. Rickabaugh
University of Redlands

Loretta A. Rieser-Danner
Pennsylvania State University, Ogontz

Gina Riley-Daly
City University of New York, Hunter College

Jaclyn Rodriguez
Occidental College

Michael D. Roe
Seattle Pacific University

René R. Roth
University of Western Ontario, Canada

Elizabeth Rothstein
Jericho, NY

Lauren Ruvo
Harvard University Graduate School of Education

Daniel Sachau
Mankato State University

Denise S. St. Cyr
New Hampshire Technical College

James D. St. James
Millikin University

Frank A. Salamone
Iona College

David Sands
Maharishi International University

John Santelli
Fairleigh Dickinson University

Anthony C. Santucci
Manhattanville College

Linda Sapanski Smith
Great Neck, NY

Tulsi B. Saral
University of Houston-Clear Lake

Elizabeth D. Schafer
Loachapoka, Alabama

Rosemary Scheirer
Chestnut Hill College

Rebecca Lovell Scott
College of Health Sciences

Pennie S. Seibert
Boise State University

Felicisima C. Serafica
Ohio State University

Manoj Sharma
University of Nebraska at Omaha

Matthew J. Sharps
California State University, Fresno

Michael F. Shaughnessy
Eastern New Mexico University

June Shepherd
Eastern New Mexico University

Margaret Sheridon
Boston Children's Hospital, Harvard Medical School

Bonnie S. Sherman
St. Olaf College

R. Baird Shuman
University of Illinois at Urbana-Champaign

Harold I. Siegel
Rutgers University

Marilyn N. Silva
California State University, Hayward

Sanford S. Singer
University of Dayton

Virginia Slaughter
University of Queensland

Lesley A. Slavin
Virginia Commonwealth University

Stephanie Smith
Indiana University Northwest

Janet A. Sniezek
University of Illinois at Urbana- Champaign

Sheldon Solomon
Skidmore College

Frank J. Sparzo
Ball State University

Gerald Sperrazzo
University of San Diego

Michael D. Spiegler
Providence College

Mark Stanton
Azusa Pacific University

Sharon Wallace Stark
Monmouth University

Michael A. Steele
Wilkes University

Polly D. Steenhagen
Delaware State University

Stephanie Stein
Central Washington University

Joseph E. Steinmetz
Indiana University Bloomington

Faye B. Steuer
College of Charleston

Glenn Ellen Starr Stilling
Appalachian State University

Lloyd K. Stires
Indiana University of Pennsylvania

William M. Struthers
Wheaton College

John D. Sweetland
Point Lookout, NY

Molly Sweetland
South Nassau Communities Hospital

Kathleen A. Tallent
University of Wisconsin-Madison

Laura Tahir
New York, NY

Richard G. Tedeschi
University of North Carolina at Charlotte

Janice Tedford
Gordon College

Linda R. Tennison
College of Saint Benedict/Saint John's University

April D. Thames
Alliant International University

Thomas J. Thieman
College of St. Catherine

Susan E. Thomas
Indiana University, South Bend

Harry A. Tiemann, Jr.
Mesa State College

Derise E. Tolliver
DePaul University

James T. Trent
Middle Tennessee State University

Marlene E. Turner
San Jose State University

John V. Urbas
Kennesaw State College

Susana P. Urbina
University of North Florida

Eugenia M. Valentine
Xavier University of Louisiana

Mary Moore Vandendorpe
Lewis University

Anju Varanasi
South Nassau Communities Hospital

Lois Veltum
University of North Dakota

Scott R. Vrana
Purdue University

John F. Wakefield
University of North Alabama

Elaine F. Walker
Emory University

Mary L. Wandrei
Marquette University

Daniel L. Wann
Murray State University

Jennifer A. Sanders Wann
Murray, Kentucky

Allyson Washburn
Institute on Aging/Jewish Home

T. Steuart Watson
Mississippi State University

Ann L. Weber
University of North Carolina at Asheville

Marcia J. Weiss
Point Park College

Robin A. Wells
Eastern New Mexico University

George I. Whitehead III
Salisbury State University

Edward R. Whitson
State University of New York, College at Genesco

Jeremy Wicks
Centerpiece Consulting

Michael Wierzbicki
Marquette University

April Michele Williams
Drury University

Bradley R. A. Wilson
University of Cincinnati

Gregory L. Wilson
Washington State University

Edward J. Wisniewski
University of North Carolina at Greensboro

Stephen L. Wolfe
University of California, Davis

Karen Wolford
State University of New York at Oswego

Jing Wu
Soochow University, China

Edelgard Wulfert
State University of New York at Albany

Susan J. Wurtzburg
University of Utah

Frederic Wynn
County College of Morris

Geetha Yadav
Bio-Rad Laboratories, Inc.

George B. Yancey
Emporia State University

Daniel L. Yazak
Montana State University-Billings

Debra Zehner
Wilkes University

Ling-Yi Zhou
University of St. Francis

Thomas G. Zimmerman
South Nassau Communities Hospital

COMPLETE LIST OF CONTENTS

VOLUME 1

VOLUME 2

VOLUME 3

VOLUME 4

VOLUME 5

Ability tests

Date: 1890's forward
Type of psychology: Learning

Ability testing assesses the capabilities of people, typically measuring qualities such as intelligence. Exactly what is measured and how, as well as what test results mean, have been the subject of debate.

Key Concepts:

- Ability
- Intelligence
- Intelligence quotient (IQ)
- Nature vs nurture
- Psychometrics
- Testing

INTRODUCTION

Whatever intelligence may be, the first scientific attempts to measure it were conducted by French psychologist and physician Alfred Binet. From 1894 until his death, Binet was director of the psychology laboratory at the Sorbonne. Between 1905 and 1911, Binet and his colleague Théodore Simon devised a series of tests that became the basis for tests in many areas. The Stanford, Herring, and Kuhlmann tests are among the revisions to Binet and Simon's tests. Binet, unlike many of his contemporaries in psychology, was interested in how normal minds work, rather than in mental illness. It was his goal to discover inherent intelligence, apart from any educational influence.

Binet came to develop his tests through observation of his daughters. He was interested in how they solved problems that he set for them. Binet noted the existence of individual differences and the fact that not all thought processes use the same operational path. Binet argued that lack of ability in specific fields was not a mental illness. There were also, he noted, different types of memory. This discovery led to his work with Simon on achievement levels for "normal" children.

Binet's first test, carried out in 1905, asked children to follow commands, copy patterns, name objects, and put things in order or arrange them properly. He administered the test to students in Paris. His standard was based on his data. Thus, if 70 percent of a certain age group succeeded on a given task, those who passed at that level were at that mental age level. It was Binet who introduced the term "intelligence quotient,"

Intelligence quotient or IQ. IQ is the ratio of mental age to chronological age, with 100 being average. For example, an eight-year-old who succeeds on the ten-year-olds' test would have an IQ of 10/8 100, or 125. Soon there was a widespread enthusiasm for testing and finding IQ scores. A number of measures were introduced. The US Army used tests to sort out recruits in World War I. The tests assessed general knowledge rather than ability on specific tasks.

Binet's tests required modifications. The first, and perhaps most famous, was the Stanford-Binet test developed in 1916 by Lewis Terman. It was immediately put to use by various educational, government, and other agencies. This test is mainly based on verbal ability and uses an IQ. Terman worked to overcome the limitations of the age-scale principle of testing.He wanted to measure the full range of intelligence. There were two major shortcomings of Binet's scales in measuring adult intelligence. First, an older person's score became meaningless when divided by his or her chronological age. Terman assigned the chronological age of fifteen to everyone over sixteen. Another major defect in Binet's scales was the absence of test items to test and measure high intelligence. Terman added such items, assigning them mental age levels up to twenty-two. This enabled him to measure IQs of older children and young adults.

There were additional revisions of the Stanford-Binet test. In 1937, for example, Terman and Maude Merrill published a revision of the test based on the same principles as the 1916 examination. However, they improved the selection of items and method of standardization. Merrill published another revision in 1959. These revisions have found wide acceptance, also serving as models for other individual IQ tests and as a means for checking their scales.

The Wechsler scale, introduced in 1939, includes both verbal and performance measures. These scores compare an individual's intelligence with those of others of the same age to yield an IQ score. The Wechsler-Bellevue adult scale uses a derived IQ to measure the intelligence of people between the ages of seven and seventy, comparing each person's scores with standards for his or her age group. Wechsler produced two other scales, the Wechsler Intelligence Scale for Children-Third Edition, published in 1949, designed for children age five to fifteen, and the Wechsler Adult Intelligence Scale, published in 1955, for people from sixteen to sixty-four, including a special standardization for people age sixty to seventy-five.

Originally, IQ tests were individual tests, not group tests. However, as the military and other large organizations became involved in testing, large-scale tests were given. Individual tests tend to be more accurate, because an individual examiner is more likely to note the mood of a test taker in a one-to-one setting than in the more typical group setting. Individual tests are more likely to be administered to those who are thought to be either gifted or intellectually disabled. Group tests are more common in educational and military settings. Originally, all intelligence tests were individual tests, meaning that they were given in a one-to-one situation.

There is a good deal of dispute regarding the nature of intelligence and whether it can be measured in a quantitative fashion. Additionally, since the 1930s, there have been a number of virulent disputes regarding the role of genetics in determining IQ, often termed the nature-nurture debate.

Most psychologists concede that because environments are never uniform and the expression of genes is elastic, the argument for one or the other element as the sole determination of intelligence is somewhat flawed. Thus, intelligence, whatever it may be, is a function of both nature and nurture, of environment and genetic makeup.

Twin studies estimating environmental effects put genetic factors pertaining to "intelligence" at somewhere below 50 percent. However, wide variation exists according to the particular characteristic of intelligence under study. Indeed, later views of intelligence hold that many different abilities make up intelligence. The question for those who seek to measure intelligence, the process of psychometrics, is how to measure specific and general intelligence. Researchers note that there are many skills involved in both academic and professional success. For example, spatial intelligence is related to success in mathematics, science, engineering, architecture, and related fields, while it is not as important in literature or music

PSYCHOMETRICS

A number of theories of intelligence exist: psychological measurement, often called psychometrics; cognitive psychology, the merger of cognitive psychology with conceptualism; and biologic science, which considers the neural bases of intelligence. Psychometric theories have been most concerned with the quantification of intelligence and its parts. Psychometricians generally seek to understand the structure of intelligence, that is, the forms it may take and the relationship between any parts it may have. These theories are tested through paper-and-pencil tests. These tests include analogies, classifications, and series completions.

The psychological model on which these tests are based states that intelligence is made up of abilities that mental tests measure. Each test score is based on a weighted composite of scores taken from the underlying abilities. The mathematical model is additive and assumes that less of one type of ability can be compensated for by more of another ability.

Charles Spearman, who put forth the first psychometric theory, published his first major article on intelligence in 1904. Spearman noted that people who do well on one mental ability test generally do well on others and, conversely, those who do poorly on one test tend to do poorly on others. Spearman's factor analysis enabled him to posit that there are two major factors underlying intelligence. The first and more important factor is the "general factor," or g. The second factor is that which is specifically related to each particular test. Spearman was not sure what g was, but he did posit that it was "mental energy."

L. L. Thurstone disagreed with both Spearman's theory and with his isolation of a single factor of general intelligence. Thurstone argued that Spearman's misapplication of his factor method led him to find just one factor, the g factor. He argued that there are seven primary mental abilities underlying intelligence: verbal comprehension, verbal fluency, number, spatial visualization, inductive reasoning, memory, and perceptual speed.

Psychologists such as Philip E. Vernon and Raymond B. Cattell argued that in some senses both Thurstone and Spearman were correct. Their reasoning is that abilities are arranged in a hierarchy. General ability, or *g*, is at the summit. The other abilities relate to ever more specific tasks as a person descends the hierarchy. Cattell went on to suggest that there are two major categories of abilities, fluid and crystallized. Fluid abilities, reasoning and problem solving, are measured by tests such as the analogies, classifications, and series completions. Crystallized abilities, derived from fluid abilities, include vocabulary, general information, and knowledge about specific fields. Most psychologists agreed that a broader subdivision of abilities was needed than was provided by Spearman, but not all of them agreed that the subdivision should be hierarchical. Other psychologists disagreed with the hierarchical ordering of abilities. The structure-of-intellect theory devised by J. P. Guilford, for example, postulated 120 abilities. He later increased the number to 150.

In general, it was becoming obvious to many that there were problems with psychometric theory. The number of factors had gone from 1 to more than 150. There was no satisfactory explanation given for any of these factors that explained overall intelligence.

TWIN STUDIES

Twin studies use two methods to measure the effect of nature and nurture on overall intelligence. The first method examines identical twins reared apart, and the second looks at the differences between identical twins reared together and fraternal twins reared together. Identical, or monozygotic, twins are not totally identical, because they have had different experiences and are unique social and cultural products. Fraternal twins are formed from two different fertilized eggs, just as normal siblings are. Unrelated children reared together are also studied.

Although most identical twins studied show a 50 to 80 percent genetic contribution to intelligence, a closer examination reveals identical pairs with up to a twenty-point difference in IQ scores. This occurs when the environment is drastically different. The closeness of most identical twins is a result of nature and nurture; that is, the twins being raised in similar settings.

It has been reasonably obvious that many of the skills measured by IQ tests can be taught just as any other skills can be taught. If these skills can be taught, then at least part of what is measured by ability tests, including IQ tests, is learned and not inherent.

SPECIFIC ABILITY TESTS

Among the more common ability tests are the School and College Ability Test (SCAT) and the Sequential Test of Educational Progress (STEP). The SCAT measures specific abilities in verbal and quantitative areas. It is used to make general, overall decisions about level and pace of instruction. The SCAT focuses on aptitude, not specific educational goals. The STEP battery measures actual achievement in reading, written language, and mathematics. STEP measures actual mastery and is, therefore, useful in indicating skills a student is ready to master.

Both SCAT and STEP testing can be used for in-grade-level or above-grade-level testing. In-grade-level testing provides information compared with others in the same grade, while above-grade-level testing indicates probable success or failure compared with those in higher grades.

SCAT assesses both verbal and mathematical reasoning abilities, using verbal analogies and quantitative comparison items. STEP mathematics computation measures a broad variety of computational skills, including operations (with whole numbers, fractions, and percentages) to evaluation of formulas and manipulations with exponents. STEP mathematics basic concepts measures knowledge of various concepts, including those involving numbers and operations; measurement and geometry; relations, functions, and graphs; and proofs. It also includes knowledge of probability and statistics, mathematical sentences, sets and mathematical systems, and application. STEP reading measures the capacity to read and appreciate a multiplicity of written materials. STEP English expression measures the aptitude to assess the accuracy and efficiency of sentences by requiring the student to perceive mistakes in grammar and usage or to decide among rewordings of sentences.

The SAT Reasoning Test is a widely used aptitude test that attempts to measure both intelligence and ability to undertake college studies. There are verbal and mathematical components to the test. The mean score on each test is 500, and each has a standard deviation of 100. The test was standardized on a group of ten thousand students in 1941. However, when scores dropped in the 1990s, with a verbal mean of 422 and a mathematical mean of 474, there was a readjustment of means. Educators attributed these lower scores of the student population to television and to deterioration in home and school situations.

CONTROVERSIES

IQ and other ability tests have been widely criticized, especially since the 1960s. These controversies have centered on the Eurocentric nature of the tests; namely, they have been designed primarily for use with white, middle-class children. The tests, therefore, have drawn fire from critics for being culture-bound. Some have seen them as unfair to African Americans, Latinos, and members of other minority groups. However, attempts to create culturally neutral tests have failed, and the tests have withstood court challenges. In Parents in Action on Special Education (PASE) v. Hannon (1980), a US District Court case involving Chicago schools, it was settled that the tests were not culturally biased and could be used to place children in special education courses.

These concerns over cultural bias, however, have raised another, related issue. That issue goes to the heart of IQ testing and concerns exactly what the tests measure. Critics argue that the tests do not measure mental abilities. The tests, they say, do not show how children arrive at their answers, only whether they are right or wrong. Knowing how a child arrives at an answer would better allow evaluators to gauge intelligence, for those who arrive at a right answer by guessing are not necessarily more intelligent than those who get the wrong answer but whose reasoning is sound. Additionally, people from different cultural backgrounds have different but equally valid ways of approaching problems. Westernized tests do not take these skills into account.

Moreover, there is still a debate concerning the relative impact of nature and nurture on intelligence. Those who hold for the predominant role of heredity have used comparative test results to argue for the dominant role of genetic differences among the various ethnic groups. In the early 1970s, the published research of Nobel Prize–winning physicist William Shockley of Stanford University and educational psychologist Arthur R. Jensen of the University of California concluded that heredity accounts for most differences in intelligence among different racial groups. This conclusion caused a great controversy, matched by the publication of *The Bell Curve* (1994) by Richard Herrnstein and Charles Murray, which came to much the same conclusions: Intelligence is primarily inherited, and there are different levels of intelligence among races.

Another controversy regards the tendency of most tests to take a holistic approach to intelligence. The Stanford-Binet test, for example, sees intelligence as a unified trait. In the minds of many critics, IQ tests are designed to measure a particular type of ability defined by the predominant class. Tests are culturally biased, so scores do not reflect an objective universal pattern of intelligence. Intelligence, they argue, is a social construct. Guilford devised a 180-factor model of intelligence, which classified each intellectual task according to three dimensions: content, mental operation, and product. This theory is the predecessor to Howard Gardner's theory of multiple intelligence, developed since 1985.

Because of the influence of those social scientists who have argued for the influence of cultural differences, the tests are not the only basis for evaluating intellectual performance. There is a much greater awareness on the part of most psychologists of motivational and cultural factors in the role of development.

RESPONSE TO CRITICISM

Intelligence tests seek to measure intellectual potential by using novel items, forcing test takers to think on the spot. The point is to avoid tapping factual knowledge. It is understood by psychologists that people come from different backgrounds, so it is difficult if not impossible to find items that are totally novel. Therefore, test makers require test takers to use relatively common knowledge. It is impossible to control for all of a test taker's prior knowledge. Therefore, intelligence scores represent a blend of potential and knowledge.

IQ tests have reliability correlations in the range of 0.90 and above, which is higher than most other psychological tests. This fact does not mean that variations in motivation or anxiety do not lead to misleading scores. IQ tests are also valid when used to predict success in academic work. They are, therefore, great predictors of school success, but they are not good for predicting other types of success. People have acquired the belief that these tests measure a general sense of mental ability, when they actually focus on abstract reasoning and verbal fluency, the type of skills needed for academic success. They do not measure either social or practical intelligence. IQ tests do not stabilize until adulthood, and even then, they can change. There is a high correlation between high IQ scores and being in a prestigious occupation. Specific success in any given occupation, however, cannot be predicted in a meaningful way.

IQ tests not only are stable, reliable, and valid but also predict academic success and occupational status. They are one good measure of giftedness and can be used with measures of creativity to aid recognition of this type of intelligence. They can also be used to identify which children should be placed in remedial classes.

CONCLUSION

It is essential to note that no psychological test should be used in isolation, whether that test is diagnostic of psychological and behavioral problems or of ability. Each test result needs to be compared with and used in conjunction with results from other tests. Trained psychologists need to evaluate the test results in context, whether these are diagnostic tests, intelligence tests, tests for evaluating emotional depression, or personality tests.

Much progress has been made since the era of the dominance of psychometric theories. Then, the study of intelligence was dominated by investigations of individual differences in people's test scores. Lee Cronbach, a major figure in testing, bewailed the segregation of those who study individual differences and those who seek regularities in human behavior. He made his plea for a union of these studies in an address to the American Psychological Association in 1957. His call helped lead to the development of cognitive theories of intelligence.

Use of cognitive theories has aided in interpreting the results of ability tests, for they give an understanding of the processes underlying intelligence. These processes allow an evaluator to understand why someone may do poorly on various tests. It may not simply be a matter of poor reasoning, for example, that leads to poor performance on an analogies test. It may be that the student does not understand the words in the analogies. The different interpretations may lead to different recommendations. Someone who is good at reasoning but does not understand basic vocabulary requires an intervention that is different from that needed for someone who is a poor reasoner.

For cognitive psychologists, intelligence is a combination of a set of mental representations and a set of processes that can operate on them. Thus, ability tests based on these principles have sought to measure the speed of various types of thinking. There is, moreover, an assumption that processes are executed in a serial fashion. There are a number of cognitive theories of intelligence, but all of them assume a mental process working on a mental representation.

A number of cognitive theories of intelligence have evolved. Among them is that of Earl B. Hunt, Nancy Frost, and Clifford E. Lunneborg. In 1973, they demonstrated that psychometrics and cognitive modeling could be combined. They started with tests that experimental psychologists used to study perception, learning, and memory. Individual differences in these tests were related to patterns of individual differences in IQ scores. They concluded that the basic cognitive process could be the basic components of intelligence.

Other developments led psychologists to begin with the psychometric tests themselves and to investigate the cognitive components of the skills tested on the tests. When these basic components were isolated, they could be evaluated and tested in isolation to compute their relationship with intelligence. This was done for information processing and computer modeling. Computer modeling, such as that of Allen Newell and Herbert Simon, uses a means-ends analysis to determine how close a problem is to a solution. Newell and Simon proposed a general theory of problem solving.

There are a number of psychologists who hold that information processing is parallel rather than serial. They argue that the brain processes information simultaneously, not in a serial fashion. It has proved difficult to construct ability tests to test this hypothesis. Moreover, the fact that intelligence differs from one culture to another, as Michael E. Cole has argued, has been ignored in psychometric tests. Additionally, psychometric tests are not good indicators of job performance.

BIBLIOGRAPHY

Binet, Alfred, and Théodore Simon. *The Development of Intelligence in Children*. 1916. Reprint. Salem, NH: Ayer, 1983. Print.

Fish, Jefferson M., ed. *Race and Intelligence: Separating Science from Myth.* Mahwah, NJ: Erlbaum, 2002. Print.Green, Anthony. Exploring Language Assessment and Testing: Language in Action. New York: Routledge, 2014. Print.

Gregory, Robert J. *Psychological Testing: History, Principles, and Applications*. London: Pearson, 2014. Print.

Herrnstein, Richard, and Charles Murray. *The Bell Curve*. New York: Simon, 1996. Print.

Lynn, Richard. *The Global Bell Curve: Race, IQ, and Inequality Worldwide*. Augusta, GA: Washington Summit, 2008. Print.

Minton, Henry L. *Lewis M. Terman: Pioneer in Psychological Testing*. New York: NYUP, 1988. Print.

Murdoch, Stephen. *IQ: A Smart History of a Failed Idea*. Hoboken, NJ: Wiley, 2007. Print.

Naglieri, Jack A., and Sam Goldstein, eds. *Practitioner's Guide to Assessing Intelligence and Achievement*. Hoboken, NJ: Wiley, 2009. Print.

Plomin, Robert, et al. *Behavioral Genetics in the Postgenomic Era.* Washington, DC: APA, 2003. Print.

Shaffer, David R., and Katherine Kipp. *Developmental Psychology: Childhood and Adolescence*. Belmont, CA: Cengage, 2014. Print.

Urbina, Susana. *Essentials of Psychological Testing*. Hoboken, NJ: Wiley, 2014. Digital file.

Frank A. Salamone

SEE ALSO: Assessment; Binet, Alfred; Career and personnel testing; Career Occupational Preference System (COPS); Cognitive Abilities Test (CogAT); College entrance examinations; Creativity and intelligence; Emotional intelligence; General Aptitude Test Battery (GATB); Human resource training and development; Intelligence; Intelligence Quotient (IQ); Intelligence tests; Interest inventories; Kuder Occupational Interest Survey (KOIS); Multiple intelligences; Peabody Individual Achievement Test (PIAT); Race and intelligence; Stanford-Binet Test; Strong Interest Inventory (SII); Testing: Historical perspectives; Wechsler Intelligence Scale for Children-Third Edition (WISC-III).

Abnormality
Biomedical models

TYPE OF PSYCHOLOGY: Psychopathy

Biomedical models of abnormality examine the roles of medical, neurological, and biochemical factors in creating psychological disturbances. Psychologists have come to realize that many disturbances have a significant biomedical component or are, in some cases, primarily organic. This had led to the development of more effective biomedical therapies, such as drug therapies, for these disorders.

KEY CONCEPTS:

- Antidepressant drugs
- Antipsychotic drugs
- Biogenic amines
- Cerebrospinal fluid
- Differential diagnosis
- Limbic system
- Neurotransmitter
- Tranquilizers

INTRODUCTION

The study of biomedical bases for mental illnesses and their treatment is called biological psychiatry or biopsychiatry. A basic premise of biopsychiatry is that psychiatric symptoms occur in many conditions—some psychological and some medical.

Inherent in this viewpoint is a different outlook on mental illness. Faced with a patient who is lethargic, has lost his or her appetite, cannot sleep normally, and feels sad, traditional psychotherapists may diagnose the patient as having one of the depressive disorders. Usually, the diagnostic bias is that this illness is psychological in origin and calls for treatment with psychotherapy. Biopsychiatrists, however, see depression not as a diagnosis but as a symptom of the patient's condition. The task of diagnosing, of finding the underlying illness, remains to be done.

After examining the patient and performing a battery of medical tests, the biopsychiatrist may also conclude that the condition is a primary mood disorder. Further tests may reveal whether it is caused by life stresses, in which case psychotherapy is appropriate, or by biochemical imbalances in the brain, in which case drug therapy—perhaps in concert with psychotherapy—is appropriate. The medical tests may indicate that the depression is secondary to a medical condition, such as Addison's disease or cancer of the pancreas, in which case medical treatment of the primary condition is needed.

PHYSIOLOGICAL BASES OF PSYCHIATRIC CONDITIONS

An important distinction must be made between psychiatric conditions resulting from the psychological stress of having a serious illness and psychiatric conditions resulting from chemical imbalances or endocrine disturbances produced by an illness. For example, the knowledge that a person has pancreatic cancer can certainly lead to depression. This is a primary mood disorder that can be treated with psychotherapy. According to biopsychiatrist Mark Gold, however, depression occurs secondarily to pancreatic cancer in up to three-quarters of patients who have the disease and may precede physical symptoms by many years. In such a case, psychotherapy not only would be pointless but also would actually put the patient's life at risk if it delayed diagnosis of the underlying cancer.

According to Gold, there are at least seventy-five medical diseases that can produce psychiatric symptoms. Among these are endocrine disorders, including diseases of the thyroid, adrenal, and parathyroid glands; disorders of the blood and cardiovascular system; infectious diseases, such as hepatitis and syphilis; vitamin deficiency diseases caused by insufficient niacin or folic acid; temporal-lobe and psychomotor epilepsies; drug abuse and side effects of prescription drugs; head injury; brain tumors and other cancers; neurodegenerative diseases such as Alzheimer's, Huntington's, and Parkinson's diseases; multiple sclerosis; stroke; poisoning by toxic chemicals, such as metals or insecticides; respiratory disorders; and mineral imbalances.

After medical illnesses are ruled out, the psychiatric symptoms can be attributed to a primary psychological disorder. This is not to say that biomedical factors are unimportant. Compelling evidence indicates that the more severe psychotic disorders are caused by biochemical imbalances in the brain.

GENETIC PREDISPOSITIONS AND BIOCHEMICAL IMBALANCES

The evidence of genetic predispositions for schizophrenia, major depressive disorder, and bipolar disorder is strong. The function of genes is to regulate biochemical activity within cells, which implies that these disorders are caused by biochemical abnormalities.

Research suggests that schizophrenia, in most cases, results from an abnormality in the dopamine neurotransmitter system in the brain. All drugs that effectively treat schizophrenia block the action of dopamine, and the more powerfully they do so, the more therapeutically effective they are. Furthermore, overdoses of drugs, such as amphetamines, that strongly stimulate the dopamine system often cause a schizophrenia-like psychosis. Finally, studies show that, in certain areas of the brain in schizophrenic patients, tissues are abnormally sensitive to dopamine.

In major depressive disorders, the biogenic amine theory is strongly supported. Biogenic amines, among which are dopamine, norepinephrine, and serotonin, are neurotransmitters in the brain that are concentrated in the limbic system, which regulates emotional responses. Biogenic amines were originally implicated by the observation that drugs that deplete them in the brain, such as reserpine, frequently cause depression, whereas drugs that stimulate them, such as amphetamines, cause euphoria. Studies of cerebrospinal fluid have revealed abnormalities in the biochemical activity of these amines in some depressed patients. In many suicidally depressed patients, for example, serotonin activity in the brain is unusually low. In other depressed patients, norepinephrine or dopamine activity is deficient. These patients often respond well to antidepressant medications, which increase the activity of the biogenic amine neurotransmitter systems.

Less severe neurotic emotional disturbances may also have biochemical explanations in some patients. Research suggests that mild or moderate depressions often result from learned helplessness, a condition in which people have learned that their behavior is ineffective in controlling reinforcing or punishing consequences. Experiments show that this produces depletion of norepinephrine in the brain, as do other psychological stressors that cause depression. These patients also are sometimes helped by antidepressant drugs.

Finally, many anxiety disorders may result from biochemical imbalances in the brain. Drugs that alleviate anxiety, such as chlordiazepoxide (Librium) and diazepam (Valium), have powerful effects on a brain neurotransmitter called gamma-aminobutyric acid (GABA), as do other tranquilizers, such as alcohol and barbiturates. GABA is an inhibitory neurotransmitter that acts to keep brain activity from running away with itself, so to speak. When GABA is prevented from acting, the result is agitation, seizures, and death. Positron emission tomography (PET) scans of the brains of people suffering from panic attacks show that they have abnormally high activity in a part of the limbic system called the parahippocampal gyrus, an effect that might be caused by a GABA deficiency there.

IMPROVING DIAGNOSIS AND CARE

Understanding the biomedical factors that cause illnesses with psychiatric symptoms leads directly to improved diagnoses and subsequent patient care. Numerous studies have shown that psychiatric disorders are misdiagnosed between 25 and 50 percent of the time, the most persistent bias being toward diagnosing medical problems as psychological illnesses. A study published in 1981 by Richard Hall and colleagues found that, of one hundred psychiatric patients admitted consecutively to a state hospital, eighty had a physical illness that required medical treatment but had not been diagnosed in preadmission screening. In twenty-eight of these patients, proper medical treatment resulted in rapid and dramatic clearing of their psychiatric symptoms. In another eighteen patients, medical treatment resulted in substantial improvement of their psychiatric conditions. In an earlier study, Hall and colleagues found that 10 percent of psychiatric outpatients—those whose conditions were not severe enough to require hospitalization—had medical disorders that caused or contributed to their psychiatric illnesses.

Psychiatric symptoms are often among the earliest warning signs of dangerous, even life-threatening, medical illnesses. Therefore, proper physical evaluation and differential diagnosis, especially of patients with psychiatric symptoms not obviously of psychological origin, is critical. In other cases, psychiatric illnesses result from biochemical imbalances in the brain. In any case, patients and therapists alike must be wary of uncritically accepting after-the-fact psychological explanations. A psychological bias can all too easily become a self-fulfilling prophecy, to the detriment of the patient's health and well-being.

Hall and colleagues found that a medical workup consisting of psychiatric and physical examinations, complete blood-chemistry analysis, urinalysis and urine drug screening, an electrocardiogram (EKG), and an electroencephalogram (EEG) successfully identified more than 90 percent of the medical illnesses present in their sample of one hundred psychiatric patients. The authors recommend that such a workup be done routinely for all patients admitted to psychiatric hospitals.

E. Fuller Torrey makes similar recommendations for patients admitted to psychiatric hospitals because of schizophrenia. He recommends that a thorough examination include a careful and complete medical history and mental-status examination, with assistance from family members and friends if necessary. Physical and neurological examinations are also recommended. A blood count, blood-chemical screen, and urinalysis should be done to reveal conditions such as anemia, metal poisoning, endocrine or metabolic imbalances, syphilis, and drug abuse. A computed tomography (CT) scan may be necessary to clarify suspicions of brain abnormalities. Some doctors recommend that a CT scan be done routinely to detect conditions such as brain tumors, neurodegenerative diseases, subdural hematomas (bleeding into the brain resulting from head injuries), viral encephalitis, and other conditions that might be missed on initial neurological screening. Torrey also recommends a routine examination of cerebrospinal fluid obtained by lumbar puncture, which can reveal viral infections, brain injury, and biochemical abnormalities in the brain, and a routine electroencephalogram, which can reveal abnormal electrical activity in the brain caused by infections, inflammations, head injury, or epilepsy.

If any medical disorder is discovered, it should be treated appropriately. If this does not result in clearing the psychiatric symptoms, Torrey recommends that antipsychotic medications be given. If the initial drug trial is unsuccessful, then the dosage may have to be adjusted or another drug tried, because a patient's response to medication can be quite idiosyncratic. About 5 percent of patients react adversely to medication, in which case, it may have to be discontinued.

Biopsychiatrist Gold makes parallel recommendations for patients with depressive and anxiety disorders. In patients who have depressive symptoms, tests for thyroid function are particularly important. Perhaps 10 to 15 percent of depressed patients test positive for thyroid disorder. Hypothyroidism, especially before the disease is fully developed, may present only psychiatric, particularly depressive, symptoms. Thyroid disorders may be indicated by depression, mania, or psychosis. Blood and urine screens for drug abuse are also indicated for patients with depression.

Patients who are found to have a primary mood disorder may be candidates for antidepressant drug therapy. Because responses to these medications are highly idiosyncratic, careful monitoring of patients is required. Blood tests can determine whether the drug has reached an ideally effective concentration in the body.

In some cases, even biological depressions can be treated without drugs. Seasonal affective disorder (SAD), also called winter depression, may be treated with exposure to full-spectrum lights that mimic sunlight. Studies suggest that this alters activity in the pineal gland, which secretes melatonin, a hormone that has mood-altering effects. Similarly, some depressions may result from biological rhythms that are out of synchronization. Exposure to light is often helpful in such cases.

In anxious patients, tests for endocrine function, especially hyperthyroidism, are called for, as are tests of the cardiovascular system and tests for drug abuse. In patients in whom no primary medical disorder is identified, the use of antianxiety medications may be indicated. Patients on medication should be closely monitored. Psychotherapy, such as behavior therapy for avoidant behaviors engendered by panic attacks and phobias, is also indicated.

As the public becomes more knowledgeable about the biomedical factors in psychiatric illnesses, malpractice lawsuits against therapists who misdiagnose these illnesses or who misapply psychotherapy and psychoactive drug therapy have become more common. This suggests that mental health providers may have to become more medically sophisticated and rely more on medical testing for the purpose of the differential diagnosis of illnesses presenting psychiatric symptoms.

HISTORY OF PSYCHIATRIC CARE

Theories of abnormal behavior have existed since prehistoric times. At first, these centered on supernatural forces. Behavior disturbances were thought to result from invasion by evil spirits. Treatment was likely to consist of trephination—the practice of drilling a hole in the skull to allow malevolent spirits to escape.

In the fourth century BCE, the Greek physician Hippocrates proposed the first rudimentary biomedical theory. He proposed that illnesses, including mental illnesses, resulted from imbalances in vital bodily fluids. His break with supernatural explanations resulted in more humane treatment of the mentally ill. However, by medieval times, theories of abnormality had reverted to demonology. Mental illness was often attributed to demoniac possession, and "treatment" was sometimes little less than torture.

The Renaissance, with its revival of learning and interest in nature, initially saw little change in this attitude. People whose behavior was considered peculiar were often accused of witchcraft or of conspiring with the devil. As knowledge of the human organism increased, however, superstitions again gave way to speculation that " insanity" resulted from physical illness or injury. The mentally ill were consigned to asylums where, it was hoped, they would be treated by physicians. In most cases, however, asylums were essentially prisons, and medical treatment, when available, was rarely effective.

Two historical movements were responsible for restoring humane treatment to the mentally ill. The first was a moral reform movement ushered in by such individuals as Philippe Pinel in France, William Tuke in England, and Dorothea Dix in the United States.

The second was continuing research in chemistry, biology, and medicine. By the nineteenth century, the brain had become recognized as the seat of human reasoning and emotion. Once thought to be a place of supernatural happenings, the brain was finally revealed to be an organ not unlike the liver. Like the liver, the brain is subject to organic disturbances, and the result of these is similarly predictable—namely, psychological abnormalities. Discovery of diseases, such as advanced syphilis, that cause brain deterioration and are characterized by psychological symptoms supported this organic model.

By the mid-twentieth century, little reasonable doubt remained that some psychological disturbances have biomedical causes. Interest centered especially on schizophrenia, major depressive disorder, and bipolar disorder. Genetic studies strongly indicated that organic factors existed in each of these illnesses, and research was directed toward finding the biomedical fault and effecting a cure.

Paradoxically, effective treatments were found before medical understanding of the disorders was achieved. Therapeutic drugs were developed first for schizophrenia, then for depression, and finally for anxiety. These drugs proved to be important research tools, leading directly to discovery of neurotransmitter systems in the brain and helping elucidate the biochemical nature of brain functioning. Much neuroscience research is still motivated by the desire for a better biomedical understanding of psychological disorders, which will ultimately lead to more effective treatments and patient care for these conditions.

BIBLIOGRAPHY

Breedlove, S. Marc, Mark R. Rosenzweig, and Neil V. Watson. *Biological Psychology: An Introduction to Behavioral, Cognitive, and Clinical Neuroscience*. 7th ed. Sunderland, MA: Sinauer, 2013. Print.

Deacon, Brett J. "The Biomedical Model of Mental Disorder: A Critical Analysis of Its Validity, Utility, and Effects on Psychotherapy Research." *Clinical Psychology Review* 33.7 (2013): 846–61. Academic Search Premier. Web. 10 Feb. 2014.

DeVries, A. Courtney, and Randy J. Nelson, eds. *Current Directions in Biopsychology*. Boston: Pearson, 2009. Print.

Dowd, Sheila M., and Philip G. Janicak. *Integrating Psychological and Biological Therapies*. Philadelphia: Wolters, 2009. Print.

Gerrig, Richard J. *Psychology and Life*. Boston: Pearson, 2013. Print.

Gotlib, Ian H., and Constance L. Hammen, eds. *Handbook of Depression*. 2d ed. New York: Guilford, 2009. Print.

Torrey, E. Fuller. *Surviving Schizophrenia: A Family Manual*. 6th ed. New York: Collins, 2013. Print.

Willner, Paul. *Depression: A Psychobiological Synthesis*. New York: Wiley, 1985. Print.

Zvolensky, Michael J., and Jasper A. J. Smits, eds. *Anxiety in Health Behaviors and Physical Illness*. New York: Springer, 2008. Print.

William B. King

See Also: Abnormality: Legal models; Abnormality: Psychological models; Antianxiety medications; Antidepressant medications; Antipsychotic medications; Anxiety disorders; Bipolar disorder; Depression; Mental illness: Historical concepts; Neurons; Schizohprenia: Background, types, and symptoms; Szhizophrenia: Theoretical explanations; Seasonal affective disorder.

Abnormality
Legal models

Type of psychology: Psychopathology

The law assumes rationality. Abnormality, a departure from rationality, includes the incapacity to have criminal intent (insanity) and the inability to understand legal responsibilities (incompetence). The trend is toward a more restricted use of these exemptions from rational expectations and the expansion of procedural safeguards against their abuse.

Key Concepts

- American Law Institute (ALI) rule
- Civil commitment
- Guilty but mentally ill verdict
- Incompetency
- Insanity
- M'Naghten rule
- *parens patriae*
- Police power

INTRODUCTION

In the United States, three broadly based legal principles and their elaboration by judicial interpretation (case law) and by legislatures (statutory law) reflect the law's core assumptions about normal and abnormal behavior. These principles are rationality, the protection of the incompetent, and protection of the public from the dangerous.

The first of these principles is rationality. The normal person is, the law assumes, sufficiently rational that the individual can base his or her choices and actions on a consideration of possible consequences, of benefits and costs. In the civil law, two people making a contract or agreement are expected to be competent to understand its terms. In the criminal law, a destructive act is deemed much worse and punishable if it is intentional and deliberate. Concern about motivation extends through the normal range of illegal acts, and offenses resulting from malice (that is, intentional offenses) are generally dealt with more harshly than those that result from mere negligence. Under the civil law, those incapable of understanding simple business transactions with ordinary prudence may be deemed incompetent. Under the criminal law, in a principle that dates to Roman times, persons who are deprived of understanding are considered incapable of intent and the corresponding guilty mind (mens rea). According to the 1843 M'Naghten rule (named for Daniel M'Naghten, also spelled McNaughton), if the accused is laboring under such a defect of reason from a disease of the mind as not to know the nature and quality of the act he or she was doing, or if he or she did understand the act's nature and quality but did not know that the act was wrong, then this accused person is "insane" and cannot be found guilty.

The second principle deals with the state's duty to protect those who cannot protect themselves, in this case the mentally incompetent. The doctrine of parens patriae as early as 1324 authorized King Edward II of England to protect the lands and profits of "idiots" and "lunatics." Under this doctrine, the state may appoint a guardian for the harmless but helpless mentally ill—that is, those incapable of managing their ordinary business affairs. Because mentally incompetent people cannot make an informed decision about their need for treatment, the protection of the state allows the commitment of such people to hospitals, regardless of their own wishes.

The third principle that has been applied to the abnormal is the police power of the state. Inherent in the very concept of a state is a duty to protect its citizens from danger to their personal safety or property. This includes the right to remove from society those abnormal people who are dangerous and to segregate them in institutions. In the United States, the laws of all fifty states authorize the restraint and custody of persons displaying aberrant behaviors that may be dangerous to themselves or others.

These principles of law, all based on logically derived exemptions from assumptions concerning rational intent and understanding, have changed slowly in response to influences from the public and from the mental health professions. In institutionalization decisions, the parens patriae power of the state became more widely used beginning in the mid-nineteenth century as judges and the public became more accepting of the mental health enterprise. Hospitals were considered protective, nonstressful environments where the harmless insane would be safe.

The insanity exemption from legal responsibility also has been adjusted and modified. The central concern of the professionals was that insanity under the strict

M'Naghten rule included only the small minority of offenders who had no understanding whatsoever that their offense was unlawful, the sort of offender who shot the victim thinking he was a tree. An offender could be mentally ill by psychiatric standards but still be considered sane. As a response to these criticisms, new legal tests that expanded the meaning of insanity were somewhat experimentally adopted by a few courts. The irresistible impulse rule, stating that a person would not be considered responsible if driven by an impulse so strong it would have occurred had there been "a policeman at his elbow," supplemented the M'Naghten rule in some states.

In *United States v. Durham* (1954), the U.S. Court of Appeals for the District of Columbia created through its decision an even simpler rule: Insanity involves simply the illegal act being "the product of mental disease or defect." This Durham rule was quickly attacked for turning over a legal decision better left to juries to mental health professionals, some of whom seemed to consider virtually all deviancy a disease. The same court rejected the Durham rule in *United States v. Brawner* (1972). The federal courts, along with twenty-six states, adopted a rule proposed by the American Law Institute (the ALI rule) that seemed to incorporate aspects of each of the preceding rules:

A person is not responsible for criminal conduct if at the time of such conduct as a result of mental disease or defect he lacks substantial capacity to appreciate the wrongfulness of his conduct or to conform his conduct to the requirements of the law.

In endorsing an illness-caused inability to conform to the requirements of law as a standard for insanity, the ALI rule encouraged a definition that extended the parameters of insanity beyond those used to describe obviously disoriented people and not incidentally continued a major diagnostic role for the mental health professional.

PSYCHIATRIC SCIENCE AND LEGAL TRADITION

The legal model assumed that most people are rational in that they can foresee the immediate consequences of their decisions. Those incompetent to comprehend a legal proceeding, those unable to care for themselves, or those unable to understand the wrongfulness of a criminal act must be treated differently. Abnormality in the legal sense was any condition that involved the incapacity to make rational decisions with an awareness of the consequences. There was a sharp dividing line between "normality" and the rare condition of abnormality.

As research into psychology and psychiatry progressed, more discriminating, accurate, and sensitive appraisals of abnormal individuals became possible. In practice, the concept of mental illness proved to be an elastic one, with boundaries that could easily be expanded to include new conditions. Mental health experts looked for the causes behind the behavior of the mentally ill, such as childhood emotional trauma or chemical imbalances within the body. In contrast to the legal model, which interpreted such unwanted or inadequate human behavior as bad decisions willfully undertaken, the mental illness model implied that this behavior was caused by events in the past and beyond the individual's control.

CRITICISM AND DOUBTS

The least restricted use of psychiatric standards by the legal profession occurred in the 1950s and 1960s, when faith in the potential of the science of psychiatry appeared unbounded. The ALI rule, which by the 1960s was used in federal courts throughout the United States, premised an underlying condition of mental illness manifested by a lack of control as insanity, a phrase that could easily encompass a wide range of conditions. However, the expansion of conditions that were viewed as insanity caused a backlash of sorts. In the latter part of the twentieth century, the role of psychiatric decision making in the law diminished, with the adoption of procedural safeguards and a return to more restricted legal definitions of insanity.

In the 1960s and 1970s, psychiatrist Thomas Szasz argued that mental illnesses were little more than metaphors for problems in living, myths that were used harmfully to deprive individuals of their feelings of responsibility. Erving Goffman charged that institutionalization was not a health-restoring, protective sanctuary but rather a degrading, dependency-producing process. John Monahan reviewed research that suggested that the prediction of dangerousness, a primary reason for commitment to institutions, even under the best conditions involved more failures than successes.

Public criticism of psychiatric influence on the law heightened after the use of the insanity defense in some prominent cases. Especially influential was the acquittal by reason of insanity of presidential assailant John Hinckley in 1982. Hinckley's act had many of the characteristics of one resulting from mental illness. An aimless wanderer who had been diagnosed as schizophrenic, he shot and wounded President Ronald Reagan under the fantastic assumption that this would win admiration from and a date with an actor he had never met. He was committed to a mental hospital after his trial. Nevertheless, his crime seemed premeditated and particularly heinous. The possibility that he might someday be "cured" and released struck many as outrageous. In other well-publicized cases, it was argued, often unsuccessfully, that otherwise criminal behavior resulted from such events as contamination by excessive television viewing, premenstrual syndrome (PMS), or hyperglycemia from eating sugary snack cakes. It appeared to many ordinary citizens that apparent mental illness could be used to excuse practically any type of crime or, alternatively, to have almost anyone involuntarily committed to a mental institution.

PROCEDURAL AND DEFINITIONAL ADJUSTMENT

As a result of such criticisms, civil commitment decisions were subject to increasing procedural safeguards According to the illness model, such decisions should be left to the doctors, the experts who could diagnose the patient as "sick" and pronounce the patient "cured." However, civil commitment was less oriented toward treatment and more like incarceration in prison, depriving the mental patient of many freedoms. Increasingly, the legal system began to focus on commitment to a mental hospital in terms of the freedoms denied rather than health benefits conferred. Reasons for such enforced hospitalization were narrowed. Laws and judges demanded that the disability had to be grave and the inability to care for the self life-threatening before the *parens patriae* powers of the state could be invoked. "Dangerousness" increasingly meant dangers that were imminent, such as suicide or physical violence against others. Emergency detention, a loose procedure invoked during an emotional crisis, became limited in time to a few days.

In *Wyatt v. Stickney* (1971), the Supreme Court held that institutionalized mental patients must be actively treated. Also, in the landmark decision of *Addington v. Texas* (1979), the Supreme Court decreed that civil commitment required a formal hearing, adversarial in nature. In such a hearing, the prospective patient should be permitted counsel and the cross-examination of witnesses. The state must demonstrate clear and convincing evidence of the need for such commitment.

The legislatures of most states enacted legislation requiring that inpatient hospitalization be employed only as a last resort. Such "least restrictive alternative" laws compelled judges to consider placement of the mentally ill outside hospitals whenever possible. Increasingly, patients who continued to take their medication were permitted to live under supervision in the community.

In a similar vein, the rules concerning the determination of legal incompetency were tightened in the last decades of the twentieth century. Ordinary citizens are required to make many important decisions in matters such as handling everyday purchases, willing property to heirs, selecting and consenting to medical treatments, and standing trial for an alleged offense. Each situation requires a certain level of comprehension and an ability to appraise the benefits and risks. The mere diagnosis of schizophrenia or mental retardation came to be regarded as insufficient evidence of incompetence in any legal situation. Instead, legal tests for incompetence focused on the presence or absence of decision-making skills demanded in specific situations.

Procedural and definitional changes in evaluating a defendant's competence to stand trial, or adjudicative competence, offers a case in point. Such competence demands that defendants in criminal trials possess the ability to understand the charges against them, the nature of a court, the role of the participants (judge, prosecutor, defense lawyer, and jury), and the consequences of being found guilty or innocent. Throughout the earlier part of the twentieth century, defendants who had been diagnosed as psychotic might be automatically considered to lack such understanding and be institutionalized for an indefinite period. By the 1980s and 1990s, the specific required understandings were being investigated, often by psychologists. Tests were developed that quantitatively measured defendants' capacity to understand courtroom procedures. Procedural safeguards were developed against using such incompetence as a pretext for indefinite hospitalization. The Supreme Court ruled in *Jackson v. Indiana* (1972) that confinement of defendants incompetent to stand trial could last only for the limited period necessary to determine whether competence could be restored. If competence was restored, defendants should stand trial; if not, they must be formally committed or released.

Similar trends occurred in criminal law, where definitions of insanity narrowed and the conditions under which an insanity defense could be employed were restricted. The insanity defense is employed in only about 1 percent of criminal cases, and most contested attempts to employ this defense fail. Many cases involve defendants so clearly impaired that they are uncontested by the prosecution, and most defendants decreed insane spend many years in mental hospitals. However, because of a very few, highly publicized cases such as that of Hinckley, public opinion moved sharply to a concern that the insanity defense was a convenient loophole permitting wealthy defendants to escape punishment by having themselves declared "mentally ill." Closing this loophole became of public concern.

In 1984, Congress enacted the Insanity Defense Reform Act, which removed the "inability to conform to the requirements of law" phrase from the definition of insanity and returned to the narrower "inability to appreciate the wrongfulness of one's acts" of the M'Naghten rule. This act further specified that an insanity defense could be considered only in cases of a severe mental illness. The Insanity Defense Reform Act applied to the federal courts. The scope of the insanity defense was reduced by at least twelve states in another way. These states added a "guilty but mentally ill" alternative to strict M'Naghten rule insanity. Under this alternative, mentally ill but not "insane" defendants might serve part of their sentence in a hospital rather than a prison. Only institutional placement, not the length of the sentence, would be affected by the presence of mental illness or its cure. The presumption was that juries, with an alternative way to treat a defendant with an obvious mental illness, would reserve insanity verdicts for only the most extreme cases.

PSYCHOLOGY IN THE SERVICE OF LAW

The era of the law's enchantment with the science of abnormal psychology has ended. Forensic psychologists and psychiatrists remain important to the law's functioning, but their psychological concepts and perspectives have receded in importance as legal safeguards have reduced their discretion in determining who is legally insane. The law's allegiance to its assumption of a rational citizen who makes rational decisions endures. Necessary exceptions to this rule also endure. Citizens incompetent to make legal decisions or unable to determine the difference between right and wrong continue to be treated as special cases. In 2002, the U.S. Supreme Court ruled that it was unconstitutional to execute intellectually disabled murderers. Forensic scientists are essential in examining these conditions and in applying the legal rules to individual cases, but they function within the legal framework as servants of the law.

BIBLIOGRAPHY

Bartol, Curt R., and Anne M. Bartol. *Psychology and Law: Theory, Research, and Application*. 3d ed. Belmont, CA: Thomson/Wadsworth, 2004. Print.

Borum, R. "Improving the Clinical Practice of Violence Risk Assessment." *American Psychologist* 51 (1996): 945–56. Print.

Davison, Gerald C., and John M. Neale. *Abnormal Psychology.* 10th ed. New York: Wiley, 2006. Print.

Elliot, Carl. *The Rules of Insanity: Moral Responsibility and the Mentally Ill Offender*. Albany: State U of New York P, 2000. Print.

Frederick, Richard I., Richart L. DeMier, Martha S. Smith, and Karin Towers. *Examinations of Competency to Stand Trial: Foundations in Mental Health Case Law*. Sarasota, FL: Professional Resource, 2014. Print.

Gaylin, Willard. *The Killing of Bonnie Garland*. New York: Penguin, 1995. Print.

Greene, Edie, et al. *Wrightsman's Psychology and the Legal System*. 7th ed. Belmont, CA: Thomson/Wadsworth, 2011. Print.

Kapardis, Andreas. *Psychology and Law: A Critical Introduction*. New York: Cambridge UP, 2014. Print.

Melton, Gary B., et al. *Psychological Evaluations for the Courts: A Handbook for Mental Health Professionals and Lawyers*. 3d ed. New York: Guilford, 2007. Print.

Stredny, Rebecca V., Amber L. S. Parker, and Ashley Engels Dibble. "Evaluator Agreement in Placement Recommendations for Insanity Acquittees." *Behavioral Sciences and the Law* 30.3 (2012): 297–307. Academic Search Premier. Web. 10 Feb. 2014.

Thomas E. DeWolfe

See Also: Abnormality: Biomedical models; Abnormality: Psychological models; Insanity defense; Law and psychology.

Abnormality
Psychological models

Type of psychology: Psychopathology; Psychotherapy

Abnormal behavior is typically defined as behavior that is harmful to the self or others or that is dysfunctional. Three models of abnormality stress medical or biological roots; psychological aspects, such as unconscious conflicts, inappropriate learning, blocking of full development, or maladaptive thoughts; and social and cultural context.

Key Concepts

- Behavioral model
- Cognitive model
- Humanistic model
- Medical model
- Psychoanalytical model
- Sociocultural model

INTRODUCTION

Prehistoric humans believed that evil spirits, witchcraft, the full moon, or other supernatural forces caused mental disorders. In modern times, people have more naturalistic ideas. The models of abnormality can be divided into three types: medical, psychological, and cultural. Medical models hold that mental disorders take on a psychological appearance, but the underlying problems are physical in nature. Psychological models hold that mental disorders are caused and then maintained by a person's past and present life experiences, which can result in inner conflicts, learned responses that are problematic, blocked efforts to grow and achieve self-actualization, or pessimistic, distorted thinking. Cultural models emphasize the sociocultural context of stress.

Medical or biological models of abnormality stem back to the Greek physician Hippocrates, who proposed that psychological disorders are caused by body-fluid imbalances. The Greeks believed that the uterus could move around a woman's body, attaching itself at different places and causing the symptoms of hysteria, a disorder in which a person has physical symptoms without the usual organic causes.

The medical model gained support when people realized that some bizarre behaviors were due to brain damage and other identifiable physical causes. For example, people with scars in certain areas of the brain may have seizures. Also, people who contract the sexually transmitted disease syphilis, which is caused by microorganisms, can develop aberrant behavior ten to twenty years after the initial infection. Syphilis moves through the body and attacks different organs, sometimes the brain.

In modern times, biological researchers use modern research techniques to explore the brain chemistries of mentally disturbed people. They suspect that changes in the workings of neurotransmitters may contribute to many psychological disorders. For example, depression can be associated with abnormally low levels of norepinephrine and serotonin.

The medical model of abnormality is pervasive and can been seen in the language that is often used to describe mental problems. In this language, a patient is "diagnosed" with a mental disorder. This "illness" needs "treatment" that might include hospitalization and therapy to relieve symptoms and produce a cure.

The medical model ushered in humane treatment for people who hitherto had been persecuted as agents of the devil. Some of the resulting advances in treatment for psychological problems include antipsychotic medication, which can reduce hallucinations and help a person with schizophrenia avoid hospitalization; lithium, which can moderate the debilitating mood extremes of bipolar disorder; antidepressants, which can relieve the chronic pain of depression; and antianxiety drugs, which can relieve the acute stress of anxiety disorders. These kinds of advances help many people in their day-to-day lives.

Also, the medical model has focused research attention on the genetic inheritance of mental illness. One way to study the genetic basis of behavior is to compare identical twins and nontwins. An identical twin of a schizophrenic person who was adopted into an entirely different family and has never met the other twin is twice as likely to be schizophrenic as is a person identified randomly from the general population. Another way to study the genetic basis of behavior is to compare adopted children to their adoptive parents and to their biological parents. Using these types of research, scientists have implicated heredity in a number of mental disorders, including schizophrenia, depression, and alcoholism.

However, it may not be appropriate to view all psychological disorders in medical terms. Some disorders can be directly tied to life experiences. Also, the medical model has promoted the idea that people who behave abnormally are not responsible for their actions. They are mentally sick, therefore not in control of themselves. Some people disagree with this notion. *In The Myth of Mental Illness* (1961), American psychiatrist Thomas Szasz argued that mental illness is a socially defined, relative concept that is used to cast aside people who are different. In 1987, Szasz charged psychologists, psychiatrists, and other mental health professionals with being too quick to guard society's norms and values and too slow to take care of the people who are in some way different. Further, Szasz claimed that the label "sick" invites those with problems to become passively dependent on doctors and drugs rather than relying on their own inner strengths.

PSYCHOLOGICAL MODELS OF ABNORMALITY

The psychological model of abnormality also stems from ancient Greece. In the second century CE, the Greek physician Galen described a patient whose symptoms were caused either by an inflammation of the uterus or by something about which she was troubled but that she was not willing to discuss. He tested these two hypotheses and concluded that the patient's problem was psychological in origin.

The psychological model gained support when French physician Jean-Martin Charcot used hypnosis to distinguish hysterical paralysis (that is, paralysis with no organic cause) from neurologically based paralysis. When Charcot hypnotized patients, those with hysterical paralysis were able to use their supposedly paralyzed body part. One of Charcot's students, Austrian physician Sigmund Freud, expanded this approach. Freud and others believed that mental disorders usually begin with a traumatic event in childhood and can be treated with psychotherapy, a form of "talking cure." Four main psychological models of abnormality evolved: psychoanalytic, behavioral, humanistic, and cognitive.

Psychoanalytic Model. A psychoanalytic model, stemming from Freud's work, emphasizes the role of parental influences, unconscious conflicts, guilt, frustration, and an array of defense mechanisms that people use, unconsciously, to ward off trauma. According to this view, people develop psychological problems when they have inner conflicts intense enough to overwhelm their normal defenses.

Freud thought that all people have some aspects of their personality that are innate and self-preserving (the id), some aspects of their personality that are learned rules or conscience (the superego), and some aspects of their personality that are realistic (the ego). For example, the id of a person who is hungry wants to eat immediately, in any manner, regardless of the time or social conventions. However, it may be time to meet with the supervisor for an important review. The superego insists on meeting with the supervisor right now, for as long as necessary. The ego may be able to balance personal needs and society's requirements by, for example, bringing bagels for everyone to the meeting with the supervisor. People must somehow harmonize the instinctual and unreasoning desires of the id, the moral and restrictive demands of the superego, and the rational and realistic requirements of the ego.

Conflicts between the id, ego, and superego may lead to unpleasant and anxious feelings. People develop defense mechanisms to handle these feelings. Defense mechanisms can alleviate anxiety by staving off the conscious awareness of conflicts that would be too painful to acknowledge. A psychoanalytic view is that everyone uses defense mechanisms, and abnormality is simply the result of overblown defense mechanisms.

Some of the most prominent defense mechanisms are repression, regression, displacement, reaction formation, sublimation, and projection. In repression, an unconscious wish is prevented from being fulfilled and is instead channelled into the formation of a symptom, such as a tic or stutter. In regression, a person reverts to activities and feelings of a younger age. For example, a toddler who reclaims his old discarded bottle when a new baby sister comes on the scene is regressing. In displacement, a person has strong feelings toward one person but feels for some reason unable to express them. Subsequently, she finds herself expressing these feelings toward a safer person. For example, a person who is extremely angry with her boss at work may keep these feelings to herself until she gets home but then find herself angry with her husband, children, and pets.

In reaction formation, people have very strong feelings that are somehow unacceptable, and they react in the opposite way. For example, a person who is campaigning against adult bookstores in the community may be secretly fascinated with pornography. In sublimation, a person rechannels energy, typically sexual energy, into socially acceptable outlets. For example, a woman who is attracted to the young men in swimsuits at the pool may decide to swim one hundred laps. In projection, people notice in others traits or behaviors that are too painful to admit in themselves. For example, a person who is very irritated by his friend's whining may have whining tendencies himself that he cannot admit. All defense mechanisms are unconscious ways to ward off mental trauma.

The psychoanalytic model opened up areas for discussion that were previously taboo and helped people understand that some of their motivations are outside their own awareness. For example, dissociative disorders occur when a person's thoughts and feelings are dissociated, or separated, from conscious awareness by memory loss or a change in identity. In dissociative identity disorder, formerly termed multiple personality disorder, the individual alternates between an original or primary personality and one or more secondary or subordinate personalities. A psychoanalytic model would see dissociative identity disorder as stemming from massive repression to ward off unacceptable impulses, particularly those of a sexual nature. These yearnings increase during adolescence and adulthood, until the person finally expresses them, often in a guilt-inducing sexual act. Then, normal forms of repression are ineffective in blocking out this guilt, so the person blocks the acts and related thoughts entirely from consciousness by developing a new identity for the dissociated bad part of self.

The psychoanalytic model views all human behavior as a product of mental or psychological causes, though the cause may not be obvious to an outside observer, or even to the person performing the behavior. Indeed, the model views all human behavior as abnormal to a greater or lesser extent. It emphasizes that abnormality is a question of degree and kind, rather than presence or absence, in the human psyche. Psychoanalytic influence on the modern perspective of abnormality has been enormous. Freudian concepts, such as Freudian slips and unconscious motivation, are so well known that they are now part of ordinary language and culture. However, the psychoanalytic model has been criticized because it is not verifiable, because it gives complex explanations when simple and straightforward ones are sufficient, because it cannot be proven wrong (lacks disconfirmability), and because it was based mainly on a relatively small number of upper-middle-class European patients and on Freud himself. Freud believed that the model was perfectly verifiable, however, because when the mental cause of a symptom was found and explained to a patient, the symptom disappeared. The fact that the model produced clinical results seemed to validate it—although, those results and the model itself may have been far more culturally specific than Freud was willing to admit.

Behavioral Model. A behavioral, or social learning, model—stemming from the work of American psychologists such as John B. Watson and B. F. Skinner—emphasizes the role of environment in developing abnormal behavior. According to this model, people acquire abnormal behavior in the same ways they acquire normal behavior, by learning from rewards and punishments they either experience directly or observe happening to someone else. Their perceptions, expectations, values, and role models further influence what they learn. In this view, a person engaging in abnormal behavior has a different reinforcement history from that of others.

The behavioral model of abnormality stresses classical conditioning, operant conditioning, and modeling. In classical conditioning, a child might hear a very loud sound immediately after entering the elevator. Thereafter, this child might develop a phobia of elevators and other enclosed spaces. In operant conditioning, a mother might give the child a cookie to keep him quiet. Soon, the child will notice that when he is noisy and bothersome, his mother gives him cookies and will develop a pattern of temper tantrums and other conduct disorders. In modeling, the person might notice that her mother is very afraid of spiders. Soon, she might develop a phobia of spiders and other small creatures.

The behavioral model advocates a careful investigation of the environmental conditions in which people display abnormal behavior. Behaviorists pay special attention to situational stimuli, or triggers, that elicit abnormal behavior and to the typical consequences that follow abnormal behavior. Behaviorists search for factors that reinforce or encourage the repetition of abnormal behaviors.

The behavioral model helped people realize how fears become associated with specific situations and the role that reinforcement plays in the origin and maintenance of inappropriate behaviors. However, this model ignores the evidence of genetic and biological factors playing a role in some disorders. Further, many people find it difficult to accept the view of human behavior as simply a set of responses to environmental stimuli. They argue that human beings have free will and the ability to choose their situations, as well as how they will react.

Humanistic Model. A humanistic model, stemming from the work of American psychologist Carl R. Rogers and others, emphasizes that mental disorders arise when people are blocked in their efforts to grow and achieve self-actualization. According to this view, the self-concept is all-important, and people have personal responsibility for their actions and the power to plan and choose their behaviors and feelings.

The humanistic model stresses that humans are basically good and have tremendous potential for personal growth. Left to their own devices, people will strive for self-actualization. However, people can run into roadblocks. Problems will arise if people are prevented from satisfying their basic needs or are forced to live up to the expectations of others. When this happens, people lose sight of their own goals and develop distorted self-perceptions. They feel threatened and insecure and are unable to accept their own feelings and experiences.

In this model, losing touch with one's own feelings, goals, and perceptions forms the basis of abnormality. For example, parents may withhold their love and approval unless a young person conforms to their standards. In this case, the parents are offering conditional positive regard. This causes children to worry about such things as, "What if I do not do as well on the next test?" "What if I do not score in the next game?" and "What if I forget to clean my room?" In this example, the child may develop generalized anxiety disorder, which includes chronically high levels of anxiety. What the child needs for full development of maximum potential, according to the humanistic view, is unconditional positive regard.

American psychologist Abraham Maslow and other humanistic theorists stress that all human activity is normal, natural, rational, and sensible when viewed from the perspective of the person who is performing the behavior. According to this model, abnormality is a myth. All abnormal behavior would make sense if it the world could be seen through the eyes of the person behaving abnormally.

The humanistic model has made useful contributions to the practice of psychotherapy and to the study of consciousness. However, the humanistic model restricts attention to immediate conscious experience, failing to recognize the importance of unconscious motivation, reinforcement contingencies, future expectations, biological and genetic factors, and situational influences. Further, contrary to the optimistic, self-actualizing view of people, much of human history has been marked by wars, violence, and individual repression.

Cognitive Model. A cognitive model, stemming from the work of American psychologists Albert Ellis and Donald Meichenbaum, American psychiatrist Aaron T. Beck, and others, finds the roots of abnormal behavior in the way people think about and perceive the world. People who distort or misinterpret their experiences, the intentions of those around them, and the kind of world where they live are bound to act abnormally.

The cognitive model views human beings as thinking organisms that decide how to behave, so abnormal behavior is based on false assumptions or unrealistic views of situations. For example, Sally Smith might react to getting fired from work by actively searching for a new job. Sue Smith, in contrast, might react to getting fired from work by believing that this tragedy is the worst possible thing that could have happened, something that is really awful. Sue is more likely than Sally to become anxious, not because of the event that happened but because of what she believes about this event. In the cognitive model of abnormality, Sue's irrational thinking about the event (getting fired), not the event itself, caused her abnormal behavior.

Beck proposed that depressed people have negative schemas about themselves and life events. Their reasoning errors cause cognitive distortions. One cognitive distortion is drawing conclusions out of context, while ignoring other relevant information. Another cognitive distortion is overgeneralizing, drawing a general rule from one or just a few isolated incidents and applying the conclusion broadly to unrelated situations. A third cognitive distortion is dwelling on negative details while ignoring positive aspects. A fourth cognitive distortion is thinking in an "all-or-nothing" way. People who think this way categorize experiences as either completely good or completely bad, rather than somewhere in between the two extremes. A fifth cognitive distortion is having automatic thoughts, negative ideas that emerge quickly, spontaneously, and seemingly without voluntary control.

The cognitive and behavioral models are sometimes linked and have stimulated a wealth of empirical knowledge. The cognitive model has been criticized for focusing too much on cognitive processes and not enough on root causes. Some also see it as too mechanistic.

The cognitive model proposes that maladaptive thinking causes psychological disorders. In contrast, the psychoanalytic model proposes that unconscious conflicts cause psychological disorders; the humanistic model proposes that blocking of full development causes psychological disorders; and the behavioral model proposes that inappropriate conditioning causes psychological disorders. These psychological models of abnormality stress the psychological variables that play a role in abnormal behavior.

Sociocultural Models of Abnormality. A sociocultural model of abnormality emphasizes the social and cultural context, going so far as to suggest that abnormality is a direct function of society's criteria and definitions for appropriate behavior. In this model, abnormality is social, not medical or psychological. For example, the early Greeks revered people who heard voices that no one else heard, because they interpreted this phenomenon as evidence of divine prophecy. In the Middle Ages, some Europeans tortured or killed people who heard voices, because they interpreted this same proclivity as evidence of demonic possession or witchcraft. In modern Western culture, doctors treat those who hear voices with medicine and psychotherapy, because the phenomenon is viewed as a symptom of schizophrenia.

Social and cultural context can influence the kinds of stresses people experience, the kinds of disorders they are likely to develop, and the treatment they are likely to receive. Particularly impressive evidence for a social perspective is a well-known 1973 study by American psychologist David L. Rosenhan. Rosenhan arranged for eight normal people, including himself, to arrive at eight different psychiatric hospitals under assumed names and to complain of hearing voices repeating innocuous words such as "empty," "meaningless," and "thud." These pseudopatients responded truthfully to all other questions except their names. Because of this single symptom, the hospital staff diagnosed all eight as schizophrenic or manic-depressive and hospitalized them.

Although the pseudopatients immediately ceased reporting that they heard voices and asked to be released, the hospitals kept them from seven to fifty-two days, with an average of nineteen days. When discharged, seven of the eight were diagnosed with schizophrenia "in remission," which implies that they were still schizophrenic but simply did not show signs of the illness at the time of release. The hospital staff, noticing that these people took notes, wrote hospital chart entries such as "engages in writing behaviors." No staff member detected that the pseudopatients were normal people, though many regular patients suspected as much. The context in which these pseudopatients behaved (a psychiatric hospital) controlled the way in which others interpreted their behavior.

Particularly impressive evidence for a cultural perspective comes from the fact that different types of disorders appear in different cultures. Bulimia nervosa, which involves binge eating followed by purging, primarily strikes middle- and upper-class women in Western cultures. In such cultures, women may feel particular pressure to be thin and have negatively distorted images of their own bodies. Amok, a brief period of brooding followed by a violent outburst that often results in murder, strikes Navajo men and men in Malaysia, Papua New Guinea, the Philippines, Polynesia, and Puerto Rico. In these cultures, this disorder is frequently triggered by a perceived insult.

Pibloktoq, a brief period of extreme excitement that is often followed by seizures and coma lasting up to twelve hours, strikes people in Arctic and Subarctic Eskimo communities. The person may tear off his or her clothing, break furniture, shout obscenities, eat feces, and engage in other acts that are later forgotten. As researchers examine the frequency and types of disorders that occur in different societies, they note some sharp differences not only between societies but also within societies as a function of the decade being examined and the age and gender of the individuals being studied.

The sociocultural model of abnormality points out that other models fail to take into account cultural variations in accepted behavior patterns. Understanding cross-cultural perspectives on abnormality helps in better framing questions about human behavior and interpretations of data. Poverty and discrimination can cause psychological problems. Understanding the context of the abnormal behavior is essential.

The medical, psychological, and sociocultural models of abnormality represent profoundly different ways of explaining and thus treating people's problems. They cannot be combined in a simple way, because they often contradict one another. For example, a biological model asserts that depression is due to biochemistry. The treatment, therefore, is medicine to correct the imbalance. In contrast, a behavioral model asserts that depression is learned. The treatment, therefore, is changing the rewards and punishments in the environment, so the person unlearns old, bad habits and learns new, healthy habits.

One attempt to integrate the different models of abnormality is called the diathesis-stress model of abnormality. It proposes that people develop disorders if they have a biological weakness (diathesis) that predisposes them to the disorder when they encounter certain environmental conditions (stress). The diathesis-stress approach is often used to explain the development of some forms of cancer, which also seem to be caused by a biological predisposition coupled with certain environmental conditions. According to this model, some people have a predisposition that makes them vulnerable to a disorder such as schizophrenia. They do not develop schizophrenia, however, unless they experience particularly stressful environmental conditions.

It is unlikely that any single model can explain all disorders. It is more probable that each of the modern perspectives explains certain disorders and that any single abnormal behavior has multiple causes.

BIBLIOGRAPHY

Alloy, Lauren B., Neil S. Jacobson, and Joan Acocella. *Abnormal Psychology: Current Perspectives*. 9th ed. Boston: McGraw, 2005. Print.

American Psychiatric Association. *Diagnostic and Statistical Manual of Mental Disorders: DSM-5*. Washington, DC: APA, 2000. Print.

Carlson, Janet F., and Bernard C. Beins, eds. *Personality and Abnormal Psychology*. New York: Facts On File, 2012. Print.

Engler, Barbara. *Personality Theories: An Introduction.* 9th ed. Belmont: Wadsworth, 2014. Print.

Gotlib, Ian H., and Constance L. Hammen. *Psychological Aspects of Depression: Toward a Cognitive-Interpersonal Integration*. New York: Wiley, 1992. Print.

Gottesman, Irving I. *Schizophrenia Genesis: The Origins of Madness*. New York: Freeman, 1991. Print.

Maksimov, Aleksei. *Encyclopedia of Abnormal Psychology.* New York: Nova Science, 2012. eBook Collection (EBSCOhost). Web. 19 May 2014.

Osborne, Randall E., David V. Perkins, and Joan Lafuze. *Case Analyses for Abnormal Psychology: Learning to Look beyond the Symptoms.* Hoboken: Taylor, 2013. eBook Collection (EBSCOhost). Web. 19 May 2014.

Plante, Thomas G. *Abnormal Psychology across the Ages.* Santa Barbara: Praeger, 2013. eBook Collection (EBSCOhost). Web. 19 May 2014.

Plante, Thomas G., ed. *Mental Disorders of the New Millennium.* 3 vols. Westport.: Praeger, 2006. Print.

Rosenhan, David L. "On Being Sane in Insane Places." *Science* 179 (1973): 250–58. Print.

Sue, David, Derald Sue, and Stanley Sue. *Understanding Abnormal Behavior.* 10th ed. Boston: Houghton, 2011. Print.

Lillian M. Range

See Also: Abnormality; Biomedical models; Behavioral assessment; Borderline personality disorder; Ellis, Albert; Feminist psychotherapy; Histronic personality disorder; Narcissistic personality disorder; Personality disorders; Psychoanalytic psychology; Psychosexual development; Rogers, Carl R.

Achievement motivation

Type of psychology: Motivation

The study of achievement motivation examines crucial ingredients in the accomplishment of desirable goals. Studies have included a wide variety of domains, providing new insights into academic achievement, economic and other work-related achievement, gender and ethnic differences regarding achievement orientation, and individual personality differences.

Key Concepts

- Academic success
- Achievement need
- Expectancy-value theory
- Explanatory style theory
- Extrinsic motivation
- Goal orientation
- Instrinsic motivation
- Locus of control
- Trait theory

INTRODUCTION

Achievement motivation can be understood simply as the tendency to strive for success or to attain a desirable goal. Embedded within this definition are a number of important implications. First, it is suggested that achievement motivation involves an inclination on the part of the individual. Historically, this has included a consideration of the individual's personality and how that personality influences a motivational state, given the presence of certain environmental factors. Since the 1980s, the focus of achievement motivation research has shifted from individual differences in personality to the cognitive, situational, and contextual determinants of achievement. Second, achievement usually involves a task-oriented behavior that can be evaluated. Third, the task orientation usually involves some standard of excellence that may be either internally or externally imposed.

Henry A. Murray, in his influential book *Explorations in Personality* (1938), conceived of personality as a series of needs that involve a "readiness to respond" in certain ways under specific conditions. One of these is the need for achievement. He defined the need as a desire or tendency to "overcome obstacles, to exercise power, to strive to achieve something difficult as well as and as quickly as possible." Thus, achievement is a generalized need. Like many later motivational theorists, Murray argued that the pleasure of achievement is not in attaining the goal but rather in developing and exercising skills. In other words, it is the process that provides the motivation for achievement.

David McClelland and his many associates at Harvard University furthered the idea of needs in several decades' worth of work in learned needs theory. McClelland argued that people, regardless of culture or gender, are driven by three motives: achievement, affiliation, and influence. The need for achievement is characterized by the wish to find solutions to problems, master complex tasks, set goals, and obtain feedback on one's level of success. McClelland proposed that these needs were socially acquired or learned.

John Atkinson, who collaborated with McClelland in some early work, developed a distinctively cognitive theory of achievement motivation that still retained the basic ideas of McClelland's theory—that people select and work toward goals because they have an underlying need to achieve. Atkinson made two important additions. First, he argued that the achievement motive is determined by two opposing inclinations: a tendency to approach success and a tendency to avoid failure. The first tendency is manifested by engaging in achievement-oriented activities, while the second tendency is manifested by not engaging in such activities. Second, Atkinson suggested that these two fundamental needs interact with expectations (the perceived probability of success or failure of the action) and values (the degree of pride in accomplishment versus the degree of shame in failure).

Several modifications were subsequently offered by Atkinson and others. For example, an important distinction between extrinsic motivation (engagement in a task for an external reward, such as a school grade or a pay raise) and intrinsic motivation (engagement in a task as a pleasure in its own right, with some standard of performance as a goal in itself) was developed to explain why some people may still engage in achievement activities, such as attending school or accepting a demanding job, even when their tendency to avoid failure is greater than their tendency to seek success.

Bernard Weiner's *Explanatory Style Theory* (1972) developed out of the observation that people have different explanations for success and failure. He postulates in the book that success and failure at achievement tasks may be attributed to any of four factors: ability, effort, task difficulty, and luck. These four factors can be classified along two dimensions: locus of control (internal versus external) and stability (stable versus unstable). Internals believe that their successes and failures result from their own actions. Whether they succeed or fail, they attribute the outcome to their ability or to the effort they expended. Externals, in contrast, tend to believe that success or failure is beyond their control. They succeed because they had an easy task or were lucky. They fail because they had a difficult task or were unlucky.

In Self-Theories (1999), Carol Dweck and her associates suggest that differences in achievement can be understood through the implicit theories that people have about the origins of their competency. People who adopt a performance orientation tend to attribute their successes and failures to unchanging personal traits such as ability. They also tend to pursue extrinsic rewards. People who adopt a mastery orientation tend to focus less on ability and more on the process of overcoming obstacles and solving problems. They tend to find internal rewards very appealing and seek out and enjoy the challenge posed by difficult tasks.

PRACTICAL ACHIEVEMENT

Achievement motivation is an important psychological concept, and it is useful in explaining why some people are more successful in attaining goals than are others. In general, people with a higher need for achievement, people with a more internal locus of control, and people who pursue mastery goals tend to do better than their performance-oriented, external-locus-of-control, low-achievement-need counterparts.

McClelland, Dweck, Weiner, and their associates have studied the relationship between achievement motivation and academic and vocational performance. Their conclusions are remarkably similar: High achievement motivation is generally a desirable trait that leads to more successful performance. Students who are higher in achievement motivation maintain higher grades, enjoy school and academic challenges more, and show greater persistence than students with low achievement motivation. In business, it appears that entrepreneurs require a high need for achievement to function successfully.

One of the most interesting applications in the study of achievement motivation has involved gender differences. Women and men may experience achievement motivation in considerably different ways. Most of the research conducted by McClelland and Atkinson during the 1950s and 1960s was with men only, in part on the basis of the belief that men need success and women need approval. With women's changing roles in society, however, the study of achievement motivation in women has flourished since the late 1960s.

Early research indicated that women evince less need for achievement than do men. One explanation was derived from Atkinson's expectancy value model, which suggested that women fear success out of concern for the negative social consequences they may experience if they achieve too much. An example would be a girl who lets her boyfriend win when they play tennis. In part, she may be concerned about his feelings, but she may also believe that she will be better accepted (by him and others) if she loses.

While it is clear that some people, especially some women, may not find as much delight in winning as do others, subsequent research has suggested that some of the original conclusions may have been overstated. In fact, in terms of Janet Spence and Robert Helmreich's three-factor model of achievement motivation, it appears that the structure of men's and women's achievement motives are more similar than they are different. When sex differences do emerge, women tend to be slightly higher than men in work orientation, while men seem to be slightly higher in mastery and considerably higher in competitiveness.

Another interesting application has centered on ethnic differences in achievement. It has commonly been noted that children from ethnic minority groups perform much lower than average in a variety of achievement-oriented measures. These findings are frequently presented in terms of "deficits." The central comparison group is middle-class white students. Much of this work is confounded by a failure to consider socioeconomic status. When ethnicity and socioeconomic status are investigated in the same study, social class is a far better predictor of achievement than is ethnicity. Further research suggests that encouraging ethnic minority children of low socioeconomic status to pursue mastery goals leads to improvements in academic success.

McClelland also attempted to demonstrate the potential benefits of increasing achievement motivation in certain populations. Through various educational programs, increasing achievement motivation has helped raise the standard of living for the poor, has helped in the control of alcoholism, and has helped make business management more effective. McCelland also developed, with apparent success, an elaborate program designed to increase achievement motivation among businesspeople, especially in developing nations.

HISTORIC ACHIEVEMENT

The study of achievement motivation grew out of two separate perspectives in the study of personality. The first perspective is the psychoanalytic tradition of Sigmund Freud. Murray was a committed Freudian in his theory of personality, stressing an unconscious dynamic interaction of three personality components: the id, the ego, and the superego. Psychoanalytic thought stresses the similarity of motives among all people by focusing on these driving forces from the unconscious domain of the personality. Murray's contribution to the psychoanalytic tradition is the concept of need, which is understood as an entity that unconsciously organizes one's perception of and one's action orientation toward the world. One of these needs is the need for achievement.

The second major perspective is the trait, or dispositional, tradition in personality theory. This perspective assumes that there are measurable individual differences between people in terms of their needs and motives; that these individual differences are relatively stable over time and manifest themselves in a wide variety of behaviors; and that motives (including the achievement motive), as dispositions within people, provide the basis of behavior. Thus, the emphasis within the trait tradition is on individuals' differences of motives. The psychoanalytic and trait approaches intersect in Murray's theory, which is one reason that theory is so important in psychology.

In addition, developments in industrial and postindustrial twentieth century societies made the time ripe for the study of achievement. McClelland suggested that achievement motivation may explain economic differences between societies. In his book *The Achieving Society* (1961), McClelland attempts to predict the economic growth of twenty-three countries from 1929 to 1950 on the basis of images of achievement found in children's stories published in those countries between 1920 and 1929. He found that those societies that emphasized achievement through children's stories generally experienced greater economic growth. Although direct cause-and-effect relationships could not be established in a study such as this, subsequent research using experimental studies provided some support for McClelland's position.

Finally, developments in academic achievement testing and vocational performance testing since the early part of the twentieth century have provided a natural setting for measuring attainment in these domains. As more and more tests were developed, and as they became increasingly sophisticated in measuring achievement, it became readily apparent that a conceptual model of achievement was necessary.

BIBLIOGRAPHY

Atkinson, John William, and D. Birch. *An Introduction to Motivation*. 2d ed. New York: Van Nostrand, 1978. Print.

Atkinson, John William, and Joel O. Raynor, eds. *Motivation and Achievement*. New York: Halsted, 1974. Print.

Cohen, Ronald Jay, Mark E. Swerdlik, and Edward Sturman. *Psychological Testing and Assessment: An Introduction to Tests and Measurement*. New York: McGraw, 2013. Print.

DeCharms, Richard. *Enhancing Motivation in the Classroom*. New York: Irvington, 1976. Print.

Dweck, Carol S. *Self-Theories: Their Role in Motivation, Personality, and Development.* Philadelphia: Psychology, 1999. Print.

Heckhausen, Jutta, and Heinz Heckhausen. *Motivation and Action.* New York: Cambridge UP, 2008. Print.

McClelland, David. *Human Motivation.* New York: Cambridge UP, 1987. Print.

Olsson, Filip M., ed. *New Developments in the Psychology of Motivation.* New York: Nova, 2008. Print.

Ormrod, Jeanne Ellis. *Educational Psychology: Developing Learners.* Boston: Pearson, 2014. Print.

Ryan, Richard M. *The Oxford Handbook of Human Motivation.* New York: Oxford UP, 2012. Print.

Spence, Janet T., ed. *Achievement and Achievement Motives: Psychological and Sociological Approaches.* San Francisco: Freeman, 1983. Print.

Sweeney, Camille, and Josh Gosfield. *The Art of Doing: How Superachievers Do What They Do and How They Do It So Well.* New York: Penguin, 2013. Print.

Peter C. Hill; updated by Cynthia O'Dell

See Also: Birth order and personality; Coaching; Giftedness; Leadership; Motivation; Motivation: intrinsic and extrinsic; Murray, Henry A.; Personality theory; Personology: Henry A. Murray; Sports psychology; Work motivation.

Addictive personality and behaviors

Type of psychology: Psychopathology

There are many types of personalities and personality features associated with problems related to addictive behavior. No single personality type or disorder exists alone in this relationship. Furthermore, personality and addictive behavior may influence each other: Personality may cause some addictive behavior, and some addictive behavior may encourage the development of certain personality features or even personality disorders.

Key Concepts

- Addiction
- Compulsion
- Generalization
- Obession
- Personality
- Self-regulation
- Symptom

INTRODUCTION

Addiction is a condition in which individuals engage in habitual behaviors or use of substances in a way that is maladaptive and causes them harm or distress. Fascination with the idea of an addictive personality and related behavior dates to 950 BCE, to the works of Homer, the Greek poet, and perhaps before that to the writings of Laozi, a Chinese philosopher and imperial adviser. These men studied human nature and wrote about the uncontrollable allure of certain desires, which led to behaviors that were likely to cause personal and cultural destruction. Thus, these two writers were exploring the realm of personality: the intellectual, emotional, interpersonal, and intrapersonal structure of an individual that is exhibited through consistent patterns of thinking, worldview, self-view, and behavior.

Some researchers have asked whether a single psychological predisposition or a multilevel series of complications is involved in the addictive personality or whether virtually any personality is vulnerable to addiction. Researchers administering personality tests to individuals with addictive behavior problems have found a variety of notable personality traits. Sometimes these traits precede the addiction, and sometimes they seem to be caused by or exacerbated by the addiction. These findings are highly controversial and have fueled many heated discussions.

Symptoms, or indications of a problem, with personality are varied. For some individuals with addictive behavior problems, aggressive energy and antiauthority issues seem to be at the core of their personality. Indulgence in the addictive behavior is accompanied by the release of aggressive impulses, resulting in a feeling of euphoria. This feeling of relief is then associated with the outlet used, and it seduces the user to attempt a duplication of the original process, thus reexperiencing the euphoria.

Inadequate self-esteem is a psychological predisposition thought to be a common source of imperceptible pain, and the inability to handle the pain can lead to a desire to find an outlet to reduce the pain. In fact, according to research by Zhanshen Chen, socially based pain can last longer than physical pain and, in effect, do more damage. Thus, as a risk factor to addiction, pain suffered because of self-esteem issues is a substantial consideration. Some individuals with addictive behavior problems want to control the pain but lack the necessary social, psychological, and biological tools to do so. Other symptoms that may be identified early enough to allow preventive measures to be taken include poor impulse control; intolerance and low frustration level, leading to a need for control; and rigidity and extremes in action and thoughts.

Behavior with addictive characteristics may involve alcohol and other drugs, food, work, sex, gambling, exercise, video-game playing, television watching, and even Internet-related behavior. Online gaming, role-playing, and sexual interactions based on the Internet have addictive features. However, these behaviors must receive much greater study before they can be recognized as actual addictions. The notion of an addictive personality developed in the twentieth century partially because some individuals displayed more than one behavior with addictive characteristics or, when one addictive behavior was given up, one quickly replaced it. Some have seen this process of substitution as a form of generalization in which behaviors form an addictive behavior pattern. Problems such as manipulation, denial of responsibility, displacement of emotions, and general dishonesty in lifestyle may provoke this process. In general, however, the addictive process can be periodic, cyclic, sporadic, or continuous, depending on a person's life patterns, resources, and basic personality. In fact, research indicates that any personality can become addicted.

PERSONALITY THEORIES

Different personality theories present conflicting ideas about addiction, adding to the controversy surrounding this topic. Psychoanalysts believe that addiction is a result of unconscious conflicts and of fixation on the pleasure principle, which states that one's energy in life is directed toward reducing pain and that one's innate drives control one's actions. Although some neo-Freudians disagree with the cause of pain, most agree with the basic concept. Social learning and behavioral psychologists believe that an addictive personality is molded through shaping—the slow and continual development of a behavior—with continuous reinforcement along the way, based on the mores prevalent in an individual's society. The need to be accepted becomes a person's driving force.

Cognitive psychologists hold that an addictive personality is formulated by the way a person receives, processes, stores, and retrieves sensory information. Also important is the nature of the attributes the person ascribes to the addictive substances or behaviors; those ascribing more power, whether it is there or not, may be at higher risk. An individual may develop very positive expectancies for what the behavior can do for them, whether or not their attributions and beliefs are true. If the substance or behavior produces a positive effect, then the person is likely to repeat the process so that the effect can be duplicated. In essence, people become addicted to the pleasurable results of the substance before they become addicted to the particular path taken to achieve them.

Humanistic psychologists concentrate on the present, focusing on the fact that people have choices, yet many people do not know how to make proper ones because of trauma experienced during youth. To the humanist, the idea of the family is important, particularly how love was expressed and experienced, because through love, people can believe in themselves enough to be able to make positive choices.

The proponents of trait theory contend that people are born with certain tendencies and preferences of action, which may or may not be genetic; the evidence is inconclusive. Trait theorists seem to agree, however, that society and the family have a strong influence on people and that some people are predisposed toward compulsive behavior from an early age.

Biological studies have been conducted to explore the suspected link between addictive behavior and genes, substance use disorders suggesting that, at least in part, a tendency toward addiction may be inherited. Studies suggest that certain people may inherit impaired neurological homeostasis, which is partly corrected by their addiction. The sons of fathers with alcohol dependence have a higher "body sway" (the degree to which a person sways when standing upright with the eyes closed) than do sons of men without alcohol dependence; "body sway" decreases when the sons are intoxicated. Sons of men with alcohol dependence have a higher rate of addiction than daughters do, no matter which parent reared the children.

People with "familial essential tremor," an inherited disorder, have less tremor when drinking and have a higher rate of alcohol dependence. Also, while alcohol-dependent people do not have higher levels of arousal at rest, they become more aroused when stressed, as measured by heart rate, and are slower to return to rest.

The majority of controlled scientific studies on genetics have been conducted on the alcoholic population. Consequently, the studies are inconclusive when discussing addiction and any related personality problems overall. However, the studies do add evidence to the possible link between biology and behavior.

SELF-REGULATION

Research seems to indicate that addiction is a multilevel problem with complex roots in psychology, sociology, biology, and genetics. Among the symptoms of addictive behavior are tendencies toward excessiveness, compulsion, and obsessions. Compulsions are impulses that are difficult to resist, while obsessions are compelling ideas or feelings that are usually somewhat irrational. These tendencies have prompted many to wonder about the existence of an addictive personality.

For some, this tendency can be traced back to childhood and used as a warning sign. If the tendency is identified in advance, efforts can be made to alter the child's first impulse and slowly, over time and with much positive reinforcement, show the child alternative, acceptable behavior. When the child can be taught to achieve self-regulation in a positive way, within acceptable social limits, there is a better chance for positive achievement as an outcome. Self-regulation is a process whereby individuals manage their feelings, reactions, and thoughts in response to internal and external events. In a culture where excessiveness is common, however, teaching balance and self-regulation can be difficult. This is because immediate gratification may be promoted and reinforced in such a culture.

Whether addictive behavior is learned for survival, passed on genetically, or is an intricate combination of both, apparently, a set of personal features can predispose a person toward addiction, or, at the least, can place a person in a high-risk group. If these symptoms can be identified early enough, the chance to teach potential addicts the path toward balance increases, and the compulsive lifestyle can be decreased or channeled in a healthy way.

ADDICTION TREATMENTS

Addictions and the victims of addictions have been studied and described at least since the beginning of written language, and probably since humanity first communicated by storytelling. As such, many treatments and related self-help efforts have developed over the years. In 1935, in Ohio, Robert Smith and William Wilson organized Alcoholics Anonymous (AA). AA is not a formal program of treatment but instead a self-help resource consisting of a group of people with alcohol problems who are in various stages of recovery, from those desiring to quit to those who have achieved very long-term abstinence from alcohol. It is a program in which most individuals work through a series of steps as they make progress in their recovery.

The value of AA is world renowned. The organization is considered by most professionals and nonprofessionals who have contact with it to be one of the more far-reaching recovery resources in the world, in terms of the many ways in which it may help its attendees. The twelve-step program, an idea that AA started, transcends the boundaries of alcohol problems and has been applied to many addictions. AA is run by people recovering from alcohol problems who desire to remain abstinent. They are primarily nonprofessionals who simply seek to help other individuals who desire to quit. However, not until the early 1970s did addiction gain national and international attention through significant progress based on research funded by the US government.

In 1971, the National Institute on Alcohol Abuse and Alcoholism conducted research that showed addiction to be threatening American society. Afterward, a concentrated effort was made to study individuals addicted to alcohol and other drugs, with an attempt to find symptoms that could predict individuals at high risk for developing such problems. The federally funded studies would ostensibly find ways to help prevent and reduce the tremendous health, social, and economic consequences of addiction in the United States. Assessing dependence potential and discovering vulnerability or high-risk factors through demographic characteristics, psychological status, and individual drug history became the focus of studies. The funding of these studies became a critical component in the fight to better understand addiction. As a result, many promising treatments became available for individuals and families seeking help for problems with addiction and behaviors with addictive features. Treatment goals also expanded to address not only those with a desire to quit but also those who want to cut down on their use or prevent use altogether. Such approaches include cognitive behavioral treatments focusing on relapse prevention, readiness-to-change treatments such as motivational interviewing, programs for adolescents such as multisystemic family therapy, harm-reduction strategies focused on reducing the risks and problems associated with substance use while also potentially reducing use, and a wide variety of pharmacological approaches involving the use of prescription medications to stave off addictions.

Internationally, studies indicate that technologically advanced societies seem to give rise to more kinds of dependency than do more slowly developing countries, a fact which could help researchers focus on some societal misconceptions of overall health. For example, in the United States and some other similarly advanced societies, there exists a tendency toward instant gratification. People who are tense are advised to take a pill. People who are lonely can call a certain number for conversation. People who are bored might have an alcoholic drink. People who are unhappy might eat. Ideally, societies, governments, and researchers will unite to unveil all possible symptoms of addiction, to identify those at high risk for addiction, and to employ successful recovery methods.

BIBLIOGRAPHY

Anderson, Robert E., Gordon E. Barnes, and Robert P. Murray. "Psychometric Properties and Long-Term Predictive Validity of the Addiction-Prone Personality (APP) Scale." *Personality and Individual Differences* 50.5 (2011): 651–56. Academic Search Complete. Web. 13 Feb. 2014.

Khantzian, Edward J. *Treating Addiction as a Human Process*. Northvale, NJ: Aronson, 1999. Print.

McNeece, C. A., and D. M. DiNitto. *Chemical Dependency: A Systems Approach*. 4th ed. Needham Heights, MA: Allyn, 2012. Print.

Mulé, S. Joseph, ed. *Behavior in Excess: An Examination of the Volitional Disorders*. New York: Free, 1981. Print.

Orford, Jim. *Excessive Appetites: A Psychological View of Addictions*. 2nd ed. New York: Wiley, 2001. Print.

Thombs, Dennis L., and Cynthia J. Osborn. *Introduction to Addictive Behaviors*. New York: Guilford, 2013. Print.

Twerski, Abraham J. *Addictive Thinking: Understanding Self-Deception*. 2nd ed. Center City, MN: Hazelden, 1997. Print.Wilson, Bill. Alcoholics Anonymous. 3rd ed. New York: Alcoholics Anonymous, 1999. Print.

Frederic Wynn; Updated by Nancy Piotrowski

See Also: Alcohol dependence and abuse; Codependency; Coping: Social support; Hunger; Motivation; Obesity; Self-esteem; Substance use disorders.

Adler, Alfred

Born: February 7, 1870, in Penzing, Austria
Died: May 28, 1937, in Aberdeen, Scotland
Identity: Jewish Austrian psychoanalyst
Type of psychology: Psychopathology

Adler posited the inferiority complex as a source for understanding human motivation and founded the school of individual psychology.

Alfred Adler was born in a suburb of Vienna into a middle-class Jewish family. He began his medical career as an ophthalmologist, then became a general practitioner, and finally became a psychiatrist in 1907. He had become interested in the manner in which people overcome organ inferiorities and compensate for them. His work came to the attention of Sigmund Freud, and Adler became a member of Freud's inner circle.

At first, Adler's work was in agreement with Freud's general doctrines. However, Adler began to launch out in his own direction. He wrote a paper concerning what he termed an aggression instinct. Adler then followed that paper with one on children's inferiority complexes, arguing that Freud's notions of infantile sexuality should be treated more as metaphorical than as factual.

In spite of their differences, Freud chose Adler as president of the Viennese Analytic Society and coeditor of the organization's newsletter. However, Adler continued to attack Freud's ideas, resigning with a number of his supporters to form the Society for Free Psychoanalysis in 1911. In 1912, this group became the Society for Individual Psychology.

Adler's experiences during World War I turned his concerns to social interest. He became convinced that to survive, humans had to undergo reform, and that individual psychology had a major role to play in that change. Adler turned increasingly to social projects, including clinics affiliated with state schools and the training of teachers. A 1926 lecture tour led to a visiting position at the Long Island College of Medicine. Adler and his family left Austria in 1934.

Adler gave many different names to the single drive that he believed motivated human behavior. He originally termed it an aggressive drive. He later came to term it the striving for perfection, a notion close to Abraham Maslow's theory of self-actualization. The term "aggression drive," first used for the drive, referred to humans' frustration when their needs are blocked. People compensate for this frustration, and Adler argued that personalities could be explained by the manner in which they accomplish this compensation.

Adler offered an alternative to Freud's sexual theory of human development. His theory of personality was grounded in holistic empiricism. He sought to discern social practices as well as innate influences. His concern for social interests led him to look at cultural factors in personality development. Adler died at Aberdeen, Scotland, where he was giving a series of lectures at the university, on May 28, 1937.

BIBLIOGRAPHY

Handlbauer, Bernard. *The Freud-Adler Controversy.* Rockport, Mass.: Oneworld, 1998. A history of the growing rift between Adler and Freud.

Kottman, Terry. *Partners in Play: An Adlerian Approach to Play Therapy.* Alexandria, Va.: American Counseling, 1995. Applies Adler's theories of drives to the use of play in psychotherapy.

Savage, Allan Maurice, and Sheldon William Nicholl. *Faith, Hope, and Charity as Character Traits in Adler's Individual Psychology: With Related Essays in Spirituality and Phenomenology.* Lanham, Md.: University Press of America, 2003. Study of the role of religion and religious tropes in Adler's psychological theory.

Frank Salamone

See Also: Adlerian psychotherapy; Aggression; Aggression: Reduction and control; Cognitive therapy; Freud, Sigmund; Humanistic psychology; Individual psychology: Alfred Adler; Play therapy.

Adlerian psychotherapy

Type of psychology: Psychotherapy

Adlerian psychotherapy is a set of therapeutic and assessment techniques developed by Alfred Adler and followers of his school of individual psychology. This approach can be seen as a precursor of later forms of brief, humanistic, empathic, and cognitive psychotherapy.

Key Concepts

- Early recollections
- Individual psychology
- Inferiority
- Organ dialect
- Private logic
- Transference

INTRODUCTION

Alfred Adler's individual psychology, his approach to psychotherapy, starts with the assumption that all people suffer from a feeling of inferiority. Though most people outgrow this complex by developing healthy compensations through their career, family, and friends, many individuals turn inward and attempt to compensate with a private logic. This is a personal and unconscious "fictional" way of understanding self and reality to assuage feelings of inferiority. Reliance on private logic, however, impairs the individual's ability to cope.

The concept of private logic underlies Adler's understanding of psychopathology. Each disorder represents a different manifestation of private logic. For example, schizophrenics cope with the inferiority complex by believing their own private logic so thoroughly that they separate from external reality and live in a delusional world in which they are intensely talented and important. The schizophrenic's neologisms (invented words) can be seen as evidence of creativity. On the other hand, the critical auditory hallucinations often experienced by schizophrenics can be understood as their inability to master their internal worlds.

An obsessive-compulsive patient has focused attention exclusively on some private issue of no real objective importance; in the person's private logic, however, the issue has great importance, which may confer on the person him- or herself some special status. A paranoid person's private logic allows the person to believe that he or she is the most important person in the world—why else would the Mafia, CIA, or Martians, for example, persecute the person?

Adler was a general practitioner before he became a psychiatrist. As a result, he saw all sorts of patients, most of whom did not define their various diseases and problems as mental. Psychosomatic, hypochondriacal, and somatoform patients illustrate what Adler called organ dialect, in which their bodies' problems reflect their dysfunctional approaches to life. Such physical disorders (real or imagined) mitigate feelings of inferiority by serving as an excuse for failure or a plea for sympathy.

Depressed patients suffer from low self-esteem, which may include feelings of hopelessness, helplessness, and guilt. The private logic of such a patient may be inadequate to lift the patient out of the inferiority complex. Some depressed patients even seem to rely on their own suffering as a sham sense of merit: "I suffer, therefore I am worthy." Personality disorders, delinquency, and crime may spring from the attempt to overcome feelings of inferiority through defiance and a facade of toughness rather than by making meaningful contributions to society. Prostitutes and chemically dependent individuals have unresolved inferiority complexes coupled with ambivalent attitudes toward dependency.

What unifies people with different kinds of mental disorders, according to Adler, is that their private logic gives them a mistaken understanding of themselves and the world. They persist in their dysfunctional behaviors and attitudes to preserve their sham sense of self-esteem, but at the price of effective coping. When Adler set out to diagnose a patient, he was less interested in labeling that patient with a specific disorder than he was in reaching a deeper understanding of who the patient was: It is not so important what disease the person has, but what kind of person has the disease. Therefore, Adler's approach to diagnosis was more qualitative than quantitative, more tailored to the individual situation than systematic and structured. However, Adler had an arsenal of a half dozen techniques that he employed regularly.

DIAGNOSTIC TECHNIQUES

Adler's first diagnostic technique was to observe the patient's body language. This included not only the organ dialect of the presenting (physical) problem but also all sorts of nonverbal behavior: how the patient walked into the room, how he or she wiggled or slouched in the seat, the kind of handshake, the degree of eye contact, and so on. Adler once said that one can learn more from patients in a minute of watching them as if they were mimes (and ignoring anything they say) than one can in an hour of listening to them.

A second approach was the use of direct and specific questions, not only about the manifest symptoms but also about the patient's background. Because Adler was convinced that the formative stage of personality development is the first six years of life, he was most interested in asking about early childhood (relations with parents, siblings, teachers, and others), as well as the patient's lifetime history of medical problems. Adler believed that people are purposive creatures and that mental disorders (and possibly physical disorders as well) are means to the end of assuaging feelings of inferiority; he would sometimes directly ask his patients: "If you were cured of this disorder, what would happen to you?" The answer could reveal what the patient most feared—sometimes that he or she would have higher expectations of his or her own performance in the areas of interpersonal relations and career.

During his ten-year association with Sigmund Freud, Adler learned to use dreams as a way of exploring a patient's unconscious. He believed that dreams were ways in which the patient rehearsed coping for waking life. The behavior of the dreamer reflected his or her real-life coping patterns and private logic.

One diagnostic technique that originated with Adler was the use of early recollections. Asking a patient to recall early experiences is a projective technique facilitated by the question "What is the farthest back that your memory can go?" Adler realized that such recollections would be hazy on the facts, but they would provide excellent vehicles for expressing the patient's private logic. Such recollections, like the patient's dreams or works of art, could be made the instruments of projective techniques, because they were rich with the markings of the patient's personality. Additionally, the patient's current mood would color the mood of the recollection, and conflicts currently on the patient's mind would be projected into the story. As the patient improved over the course of his or her psychotherapy, the early recollections would become more positive in tone, reflecting more effective coping strategies.

Adler's own character is evident from the earliest recollection of his childhood. Young Alfred was lying in bed, very ill, and overheard the doctor out in the hall telling his father that Alfred would not make it through the night. Adler recalls that he resolved to live and prove the doctor wrong, and eventually to become a doctor himself and fight death. The memory shows Adler's tremendous willpower as well as a desire to overcome suffering.

THERAPY TECHNIQUES

The first step in Adlerian psychotherapy was to use diagnostic techniques to comprehend the patient's underlying private logic. The next step was to use empathy to develop the patient's trust. (This was not to be allowed to evolve into a transference, or the transferring of emotions that a patient feels about other people onto the therapist treating the patient. Adler regarded transference as a childish dependency that would lengthen therapy and delay progress.) Then, patients would be led to identify their own guiding private logic and to realize that it was dysfunctional. This might be accomplished through various techniques, including direct confrontation of the patient's misfocusing, abstractness, closed-mindedness, or excessive self-expectations. The last stage of therapy was the cultivation of the patient's social interest. It involved encouraging the patient to venture forth into interpersonal relations and the world of work, emerging from the protective shell of the private logic and into the normal world's challenges.

Unlike Freudian psychoanalysis, Adler's approach to psychotherapy was directive. In addition to direct confrontation, Adler sometimes attempted to shake up the patient's guarded structure of private logic by answering with the unexpected. When one patient called him at home at three o'clock in the morning to report some trivial symptom, she ended by apologizing for awakening him; Adler responded that he had been sitting by his telephone awaiting her call. She thus gained the insight that she was behaving like a pampered child. Another patient was obsessed with the idea that he had contracted syphilis. He had compulsively sought the attention of many physicians around Vienna, all of whom had reported no evidence of the disease. Adler immediately agreed with the patient that he did, indeed, have the dreaded disease, thus pushing the patient to accept the validity of the previous diagnoses.

A variant of this technique was developed by one of Adler's protégés, Rudolf Dreikurs, who became one of the foremost apostles of individual psychology in the United States. Dreikurs used antisuggestion, urging patients who complained of an uncontrollable urge to give in to it and even practice it.

Unlike practitioners of classical psychoanalysis, Adler believed that therapy should be brief. Progress should be apparent in weeks, and termination should be possible in less than a year. Even after their sessions have ended, patients often continue to progress on their own. Unlike the humanistic and emotional therapies of the 1960s, Adlerian psychotherapy tries not to provoke abreaction (the expression of repressed emotions or thoughts) but to build the patient's capacity for self-control.

CASE STUDIES

Case studies of diagnosis and counseling with three very different patients can illustrate Adlerian techniques.

Jay. Jay, age forty, had a psychophysiologic disorder (an ulcer) and was mildly depressed. He attributed his problems to organizational changes at the small firm where he had worked for a dozen years. An outstanding engineer with an earned doctorate, an MBA., and numerous patents, Jay was convinced that his own efforts had helped the company grow and survive. As vice president for research and development, Jay advocated several new projects to get the firm's sales moving again; however, the other major figures in the company largely ignored Jay's plans and lurched from one budget-cutting scheme to another. Jay reported, "I am working eighty-hour weeks and worrying about the company all the time, but I just can't get things moving."

Jay's body language included averting his gaze and slouching, which he attributed to Vietnam War wounds. On direct questioning, he said that he was an only child: His father, fifty-five when Jay was born, wanted no children and resented the "accident" of Jay's conception, while his mother wanted more children and had to be satisfied with one son. Jay found that his mother was extremely encouraging and loving, perhaps spoiling Jay somewhat, while his father tended to ignore him except when some major accomplishment got his father's attention. Jay's guiding private logic was "I must work hard and accomplish something great; then I will get attention." This drove Jay to earn his degrees, invent new products, and work hard at the company. His frustration came from the fact that the old formula was not working in his changing corporate culture.

Jay was most angry at his company's chief executive officer (CEO) and board of directors, whom he regarded as intellectually inferior to him. The CEO was an incredibly charming (and handsome) MBA from the sales division who rejected most of Jay's suggestions for new products but had few ideas of his own. Jay admitted feeling envious of the CEO's sustained popularity, "especially considering that he has been running the company into the ground for seven years."

The earliest childhood recollection that Jay produced was that he was watching his mother use the toilet, sitting down on the bowl with the seat up, and that Jay was telling her that it was dangerous to do it that way. When the therapist encouraged Jay to ask his parents what had really happened, Jay found out that he was toilet trained early, and because he would urinate on the floor (through the crack between the seat and the bowl), his mother encouraged him to sit down on the bowl. His mother recalled that Jay then developed a fear of falling backward into the toilet. The interesting thing about Jay's recollection is that he inverted his role with his mother's: He was the one warning her of the danger. Although a Freudian would say something about the Oedipus complex or anal fixation here, Adlerians are more concerned with the power quality of the interpersonal relations. Jay saw himself as the one who pointed out the danger; he was also very frustrated when the parental figures (the CEO and members of the board of directors) failed to heed his warnings.

Jay's ulcer was a badge of merit, like his earned degrees or patents ("Look at how much I have suffered for this company!"). Sacrifice and success had been Jay's strategy for winning the attention of his "parents," but now that strategy was not working, so he had become depressed.

An intelligent man, Jay rapidly gained insight into his private logic. After four sessions, he had the following dream: "I am going through one of my rental houses, and I discover a room that I did not remember before—a living room that looked so comfortable, I just wanted to sit and read for pleasure." Jay enjoyed the dream and agreed that it reflected his ongoing resolution of his problem. The dream represented new possibilities in Jay's life: a more mellow lifestyle in which he saw less need to push himself on the fast track to maintain his self-esteem.

Jay terminated after eight sessions, having made plans to seek a position with another firm. After two years in the new position, Jay reported that he made almost as much money, had slightly less status, worked half as many hours, but had twice as much enjoyment. His ulcer and depression had not recurred.

Dan. Dan was also a forty-year-old engineer when he began counseling. He met most, though not all, of the criteria for narcissistic personality disorder (which is characterized by a grandiose sense of self, lack of empathy, and other criteria). Although a brilliant computer programmer, Dan had never obtained a college degree. He had never remained with one company for more than a year, and most of his work history had been with "job shops" or as an independent consultant. The presenting problem for Dan was that he had gotten his girlfriend pregnant, and he was ambivalent about getting married and becoming a father.

Direct questioning revealed that Dan was the third of four children. His grandfather had been a famous politician, his father was an attorney, and an older brother was an accomplished (and very wealthy) surgeon. Dan directly denied feeling inferior to these male family members, for he was convinced that he was smarter than any of them and had a broader range of knowledge. Dan's private logic worked something like this: "Everyone else needs to get a degree and work in one career line for twenty years to be a success; I don't have to, because I am more brilliant than anyone else. Finishing my education or sticking with one company would be an admission that I am not more brilliant."

During the first few sessions, Dan used big words and attempted to impress the therapist with his knowledge of psychology. Although Dan claimed an inability to come up with an early recollection, he was able to remember a dream: "I am at a new restaurant, and I am given a table next to the kitchen; although the waiters go back and forth, they ignore me. Finally, I am given the check and realize that I do not have enough money." After much resistance and intellectualization, Dan agreed that the dream exposed his dissatisfaction with his life: the fear that the honors and accomplishments of the other men in his family would pass him by and that he would be unable to achieve as much.

The cultivation of Dan's social interest took eight months, but it did progress. He accepted a position (which he initially thought to be beneath his talents) offering stable employment and advancement. He married his pregnant girlfriend and reported himself to be satisfied with his role of father, although he found his wife to be a little too "naggy." He did not try so hard to impress people with his intelligence.

Alicia. Alicia, a sixty-four-year-old widow of fifteen years, went into therapy complaining of depression and suicidal thoughts. Her feeling of inferiority was expressed primarily as helplessness and ruminations of guilt. Direct questioning and discussion engendered by dreams indicated that she still blamed herself for her husband's fatal heart attack ("I cooked food that was too rich"), for her son's accidental death ("I encouraged him to follow his heart and become a pilot"), and for her daughter's upcoming marriage to a former priest ("I did not instill enough religion in her"). The function of her depressive illness was that her daughter was talking about delaying her marriage until her mother got better.

Her earliest recollection was that her parents would punish her for wetting the bed by making her sit in a tub of cold water; once, when her parents were out of the house, she wet the bed. When her parents returned they found her sitting in a tub of cold water, telling herself "You sit there." This consolidated the identification of her private logic: "I am responsible for things that go wrong, and I must punish myself when things go wrong."

Alicia developed the insight that her private logic was dysfunctional and her own depression was a manipulative, though effective, way of reacting to her daughter's forthcoming marriage. The facilitation of social interest in this case focused on getting Alicia out of the enmeshed relationship with her daughter and more involved with activities outside the home, such as religion and charity work.

UNIQUE CONTRIBUTIONS

Most of Sigmund Freud's patients were "hysterical" women (with what would now be called somatoform or dissociative reactions) from the middle and upper classes of Viennese society. Most of Adler's patients were from the poor and working classes; they were not as articulate as were Freud's patients, so Adler had to assume a more directive stance. Adler remained in general medical practice, treating all kinds of physical illnesses and injuries as well as mental problems. Although he probably saw more patients in any given month than Freud saw in his professional lifetime, the brevity of Adler's counseling may have given the impression that he had only a superficial understanding of their problems.

Adler, like Josef Breuer, Carl Jung, and Otto Rank, broke with Freud and came up with an alternative to psychoanalysis. He redefined Freud's use of dreams and interpretation of patient resistance as a reaction against the threat to the private logic that assuages inferiority feeling. Adler rejected transference as an artificial by-product of therapy and as a license for the patient to continue infantile behavior. He redefined the unconscious not as a repository of sexual energy, but as the limitations of consciousness to understand one's own private logic.

Adler's emphasis on empathy and appreciating the uniqueness of each individual patient can be seen as a precursor to the humanistic approaches (such as that of Carl R. Rogers) that surfaced in the 1950s and 1960s. Adler's focus on the patient's private logic and coping strategies was echoed in the growth during the 1970s and 1980s of the cognitive approach (exemplified by Aaron T. Beck and Albert Ellis).

Some of Adler's ideas have been challenged by modern research. The correlation between birth order and personality, for example, is lower than Adler believed. Adler's notion that healthy people have no need to dream has been challenged by evidence from sleep laboratories that all people dream several times a night, though they might not remember their dreams. Nevertheless, Adler's specific techniques of diagnosis and therapy are useful tools that eclectic therapists often add to their collection.

BIBLIOGRAPHY

Adler, Alfred. *The Individual Psychology of Alfred Adler.* Ed. Heinz L. Ansbacher and Rowena R. Ansbacher. New York: Harper, 1977. Print.

Adler, Alfred. *Superiority and Social Interest.* Ed. Heinz L. Ansbacher and Rowena R. Ansbacher. Evanston, IL: Northwestern UP, 1964. Print.

Carlson, Jon, and Michael P. Maniacci. *Alfred Adler Revisited.* Hoboken, NJ: Taylor, 2011. Print.

Dinkmeyer, Don C., and W. L. Pew. *Adlerian Counseling and Psychotherapy.* 2d ed. Columbus, OH: Merrill, 1987. Print.

Dreikurs, Rudolf. *Fundamentals of Adlerian Psychology.* 1950. Reprint. Chicago: Adler Institute, 1989. Print.

Grey, Loren. *Alfred Adler: The Forgotten Prophet.* Westport, CT: Praeger, 1998. Print.

Mozak, Harold H., and Michael Maniacci. *A Primer of Adlerian Psychology: The Analytic-Behavioral-Cognitive Psychology of Alfred Adler.* Chicago: Brunner, 1999. Print.

Oberst, Ursula E. *Adlerian Psychotherapy: An Advanced Approach to Individual Psychology.* New York: Routledge, 2014. Digital file.

Sommers-Flanagan, John, and Rita Sommers-Flanagan. *Counseling and Psychotherapy Theories in Context and Practice: Skills, Strategies, and Techniques.* Hoboken, NJ: Wiley, 2012. Digital file.

Watts, Richard E., ed. *Adlerian, Cognitive, and Constructivist Therapies: An Integrative Dialogue.* New York: Springer, 2003. Print.

T. L. Brink

SEE ALSO: Abnormality: Psychological models; Birth order and personality; Clinical interviewing, testing, and observation; Cognitive therapy; Depression; Dreams; Hypochondriasis, conversion, and somatization; Individual psychology: Alfred Adler; Psychoanalysis; Psychoanalytic psychology; Psychotherapy: Goals and techniques; Obsessive-compulsive disorder.

Adolescence
Cognitive skills

TYPE OF PSYCHOLOGY: Developmental psychology

Adolescence brings the potential for logical and theoretical reasoning, systematic problem solving, and acquisition of abstract concepts; adolescent cognitive skills are reflected in social and personality development as well as in learning and problem-solving behavior.

KEY CONCEPTS

- Concrete operations stage
- Developmental approach
- Egocentrism
- Formal operations stage

- Hypothetical-deductive reasoning
- Imaginary audience
- Information-processing approach
- Personal fable
- Psychometric approach

INTRODUCTION

Psychologists approach the study of adolescent cognitive skills from three perspectives: the psychometric, the developmental, and the information-processing. The psychometric approach focuses on defining and measuring intellectual skills. Psychometric research typically involves studies of performance on intelligence tests. The developmental approach seeks to identify the types of cognitive skills that are unique to the adolescent years. This approach has been heavily influenced by the cognitive stage theory of Swiss psychologist Jean Piaget. The information-processing approach examines the characteristics of memory and problem solving. It views adolescent cognitive skills as parameters that determine how the brain stores and analyzes information.

PSYCHOMETRIC APPROACH

In the psychometric view, adolescence is a period of cognitive stability. Intelligence quotient (IQ) scores show little change during adolescence. Although IQ scores often fluctuate during early childhood, scores generally stabilize about age eight. It is common to find temporary periods of instability in IQ scores after age eight, such as at the onset of puberty or during other stressful times, but dramatic and long-term score changes are rare. According to this perspective, adolescence does not bring significant changes in cognitive skills.

Theory and research on cognitive skills began with the development of modern intelligence tests, such as Alfred Binet's 1916 test; however, the intelligence-testing, or psychometric, approach has contributed little to an understanding of adolescent cognitive skills. Intelligence tests are best suited to the study of individual differences, or how people compare to others of their age. It is difficult to use intelligence testing to compare and contrast cognitive skills at different ages.

Intelligence tests also are used to study the stability of intellectual level and the likelihood it will change in later years. Research indicates, however, that intelligence test scores in adolescence generally are similar to scores during childhood, although scores may fluctuate during childhood as a function of changes in factors such as diet, socioeconomic status, and education. Again, the psychometric approach seems poorly suited to the study of adolescent cognitive skills.

DEVELOPMENTAL APPROACH

The developmental approach seeks to identify the cognitive skills of adolescence and to contrast them with the skills found at other ages. This approach addresses both the qualities of thought and the process of change. In 1958, Piaget and his coworker Barbel Inhelder published *The Growth of Logical Thinking from Childhood Through Adolescence*, a detailed account of his four stages of cognitive development. In addition to proposing that specific cognitive skills emerge in each stage, Piaget proposed that the move from one stage to the next is largely maturational.

This statement may be confusing. Clearly, sixteen-year-olds must "know more" than eight-year-olds, and adolescents have the capacity to learn school subjects beyond the grasp of elementary school children. The psychometric approach, however, is not designed to contrast the nature of cognitive skills at different ages. Intelligence tests are scored by comparing a specific person to other people of the same age. A score of 100 at age eight means that a person performs similarly to the average eight-year-old; a score of 100 at age eighteen means that a person performs similarly to the average eighteen-year-old. IQ score is expected to remain the same if the person matures at a relatively normal rate.

Two of Piaget's stages are of particular importance to the study of adolescence: the concrete operational stage (ages seven to twelve) and the formal operational stage (age twelve and up). During the concrete operational stage, children acquire basic logical concepts such as equivalence, seriation, and part-whole relations. Children also master reversibility, a skill allowing them mentally to restore a changed object or situation to its original state. With reversibility, children can recognize that a small glass of juice poured into a taller and thinner glass may look like more juice but is actually the same amount. During concrete operations, children can think logically as long as their reasoning is in reference to tangible objects.

The formal operational stage follows the concrete operational stage and is the final stage of cognition, according to Piaget. Beginning at adolescence, thinking becomes more logical, more abstract, more hypothetical, and more systematic. Unlike their concrete operational counterparts, formal thinkers can study ideologies, generate a variety of possible outcomes to an action, and systematically evaluate alternative approaches to a problem. Formal thinkers also are better able to adopt a new course of action when a particular strategy proves unsuccessful. In the Piagetian model, adolescents are compared to scientists as they use hypothetical-deductive reasoning to solve problems. Although children during the concrete operational stage would solve problems by trial and error, adolescents could be expected to develop hypotheses and then systematically conclude which path is best to follow to solve the problem.

INFORMATION-PROCESSING APPROACH

The information-processing approach provides additional information about these contrasts between children and adolescents. According to John Flavell, cognitive growth is the acquisition of increasingly sophisticated and efficient problem-solving skills. For example, adolescents can hold more information in memory than can children, which enhances their ability to solve complex problems. Improvements in memory reflect more than changes in capacity: Adolescents are better able to develop associations between words and ideas, which in turn facilitates remembering them. Part of their improvement is a result of the fact that adolescents know more than children. Adolescents also are better able to think abstractly and develop hypotheses.

These skills in part reflect improvements in generalization, identifying similarities between previous situations and new ones. Changes in thinking and hypothesizing also enable adolescents to generate a wider variety of problem-solving strategies, which also enhances their performance. Finally, adolescents know more about the nature of thought and memory. This metacognition, or ability to "think about thinking," increases the planning in their problem-solving behavior.

Information-processing research has helped explain some of the inconsistencies that appear in Piagetian research. According to Piagetian theory, people are located within particular cognitive stages and will reason at those levels of maturity in all problem-solving situations. Why, then, do most people show features of several stages, depending on the type of problem presented? According to information-processing research, variability in performance across different problem types is to be expected. The more one knows, the easier it is to use efficient cognitive processes. People will appear more cognitively mature performing tasks about which they are knowledgeable.

APPLICATION OF RESEARCH

The research on adolescent thinking has been applied to the study of learning, personality, and social behavior during adolescence. For example, research on adolescent cognition has influenced the development of both curricula and teaching methods at the middle-school and high-school levels. As individuals who are entering the stage of formal thinking, adolescents are better equipped to handle abstract topics such as geometry and physics. Their emerging ability to consider systematically the effects of several factors when solving a problem make adolescents good candidates for laboratory science courses.

Some applications of research on adolescent cognitive skills are the subject of much debate, however; ability tracking is a case in point. Psychometric research indicates that intellectual functioning becomes relatively stable in preadolescence. From this point onward, children continue to perform at the same level relative to their age mates on standardized measures such as IQ tests. The stability of test performance has been used to support the creation and maintenance of ability "tracks" beginning in the middle school years.

Proponents of tracking maintain that ability grouping or tracking enables teachers to challenge more able students without frustrating less capable students. Opponents of tracking maintain that less able students benefit from both the academic challenges and the competent role models provided by superior students in ungrouped classrooms. In fact, critics of tracking charge that the level at which performance stabilizes actually results from subtle differences in how teachers interact with their students, differences often based on inaccurate assumptions about student potential. Perhaps students with low test scores, many of whom are poor or minority students, perform poorly in part because people expect them to be less capable.

ADOLESCENTS AND SOCIAL COGNITION

Although Piaget primarily limited his research of adolescent reasoning to mathematical and scientific concepts, he did consider the role that formal operations play in the adolescent's social life. David Elkind continued research in this area by noting that features of formal thinking are reflected in adolescent personality characteristics. According to Elkind, the ability to think abstractly and hypothetically enables adolescents to develop their own idealistic, theoretical views of the world. The ability to distinguish between reality and theory, however, can lead to disillusionment and the recognition that adolescents' idols have "feet of clay." Elkind identified an adolescent egocentrism that he equates with the heightened self-consciousness of adolescence. This egocentrism demonstrates itself in two types of social thinking—personal fable and imaginary audience.

In personal fable, young adolescents see themselves as unique and special. Personal fable may lead adolescents to take unnecessary risks because they believe they are so different from others: "I can drink and drive." "Only other people get pregnant." Personal fable also makes adolescents believe that no one else can understand how they feel or offer any useful suggestions: "No one has ever had a problem like mine." In imaginary audience, adolescents believe that "everyone" is watching them. Elkind sees this self-consciousness as an application of hypothetical thinking: "If my characteristics are so obvious to me, they must also be obvious to everyone else."

Cognitive changes also affect social behavior by inducing changes in social cognitive development. Social cognition refers to an individual's understanding of people and of interactions between people. According to Piaget, changes in cognition are reflected in the way people think about themselves and others. The thinking of preadolescents (seven to eleven years old) begins to focus less on the obvious features of objects, events, and people. They are better able to translate patterns of behavior into psychological characteristics, such as concluding that a particular person is "nice" or "rude." They become less egocentric, better able to appreciate that people have different points of view. It is not surprising, then, that they are better able to see the world from the perspective of another person. As they enter formal operations (eleven or twelve years and older), adolescents are able to think in more logical and abstract ways. These changes are reflected in their ability to describe people in abstract terms, such as "cooperative" or "uncoordinated," and compare people along psychological dimensions.

Robert Selman has observed that changes in social cognition occur in stages that closely parallel Piaget's stages of cognitive development. According to Selman's research, most concrete operational preadolescents (ages ten to twelve) recognize the existence of different points of view. Many of them, however, have difficulty evaluating conflicting perspectives or understanding how perspectives relate to membership in different social groups. As adolescents become more fully formal operational (twelve to fifteen years and older), they become able to understand the relationship between other people's perspectives and their membership in social systems. For example, the difference between two people's points of view may reflect their membership in different racial or ethnic groups. Progress through Selman's stages also is influenced by social experiences. In other words, it is possible for a person to mature intellectually and to become less egocentric without becoming skillful at adopting others' points of view.

FORMAL OPERATIONS CONTROVERSY

Piaget believed that formal operational thought, entered between eleven and fifteen years of age, was the fourth and final stage of cognitive development, although he did hold that adults are quantitatively more knowledgeable than adolescents. Some experts argue that young adults demonstrate a fifth, postformal stage that is different from adolescent thinking. Postformal thought is characterized by an understanding that the correct answer to a problem requires reflective thinking that may vary from one situation to another. Truth is viewed as an ongoing, never-ending process. Critics of this view argue that research evidence is lacking to document this as a qualitatively more advanced stage than formal operational thought.

Research has called into question the link between adolescence and the stage of formal operational thought. It is estimated that only one in three young adolescents is a formal operational thinker. Many adolescents think in ways characteristic of concrete operations or use formal thinking only part of the time. In fact, even many adults have not mastered formal operations. Critics argue that individual differences and cultural experiences may play a greater role in determining formal operations than Piaget envisioned.

Piagetian theory has been notoriously difficult to evaluate. Research indicates that performance on Piagetian tasks depends on understanding the instructions, being able to attend to the relevant aspects of the problems, and being interested in the problems themselves. Adolescents who perform best on formal operational tasks are often those with interests in the natural sciences—an unlikely finding if cognitive change is largely maturational.

Adolescents who do use formal operations may experience development in two phases, one early and the other during late adolescence. The initial stage is primarily assimilation and involves incorporating new information into existing knowledge. Rather than using hypothetical-deductive thinking, adolescents at this point may simply be consolidating their concrete operational thinking. They tend to perceive their world in subjective and idealistic terms. During the later phase, adolescents are more likely to accommodate, restoring intellectual balance after a cognitive upheaval occurs.

Although the popularity of Piagetian theory has declined, it remains one of the most influential theories in developmental psychology. In fact, it was Piagetian theory that led information-processing psychologists to become interested in cognitive development. In summation, understanding adolescent cognitive skills requires some familiarity with all perspectives, in spite of their respective weaknesses. Each has made a unique historical contribution to current views of cognition.

BIBLIOGRAPHY

Byrnes, James P. *Minds, Brains, and Learning: Understanding of the Psychological and Educational Relevance of Neuroscientific Research*. New York: Guilford, 2001. Print.

Elkind, David. *The Child's Reality: Three Developmental Themes*. Hillsdale, NJ: Erlbaum, 1978. Print.

Flavell, John, Patricia H. Miller, and Scott Miller. *Cognitive Development*. 4th ed. Englewood Cliffs, NJ: Prentice, 2002. Print.

Ginsburg, Herbert, and Sylvia Opper. *Piaget's Theory of Intellectual Development*. 3rd ed. Englewood Cliffs, NJ: Prentice, 1988. Print.

Halpenny, Ann Marie. *Introducing Piaget: A Guide for Practitioners and Students in Early Years Education*. London: Routledge, 2014.Print.

Kuhn, D. "Adolescence: Adolescent Thought Processes." *Encyclopedia of Psychology*. Ed. Alan E. Kazdin. New York: Oxford UP, 2000. Print.

Mitchell, Peter, and Fenja Ziegler. *Fundamentals of Developmental Psychology.* New York: Psychology, 2013. Print.

Mooney, Carol Garhart. *Theories of Childhood: An Introduction to Dewey, Montessori, Erikson, Piaget, and Vygotsky.* St. Paul, MN: Redleaf, 2013. Print.

Muuss, R. E. "Social Cognition: Robert Selman's Theory of Role Taking." *Adolescence* 17.67 (1982): 499–525. Print.

Pruitt, David B., ed. *Your Adolescent: Emotional, Behavioral, and Cognitive Development from Early Adolescence Through the Teen Years*. New York: Harper, 2000. Print.

Sokol, Bryan W., Frederick M. E. Grouzet, and Ulrich Mueller. *Self-Regulation and Autonomy: Social and Developmental Dimensions of Human Conduct*. New York: Cambridge UP, 2013. Print.

Lisa Friedenberg; updated by Lillian J. Breckenridge

SEE ALSO: Adolescence: Cross-cultural patterns; Adolescence: Sexuality; Cognitive ability: Gender differences; Cognitive development: Jean Piaget; Cognitive psychology; Developmental psychology; Identity crises; Intelligence tests; Learning; Problem-solving stages; Problem-solving strategies; Social perception; Teenage suicide; Teenagers' mental health; Violence by children and teenagers.

Adolescence
Cross-cultural patterns

TYPE OF PSYCHOLOGY: Developmental psychology; Multicultural psychology

Adolescence, generally considered to be the years between the ages of twelve and eighteen, is a time of rapid development and confusion, both physically and emotionally. Adolescence is viewed differently in different cultures; although certain characteristics seem to be widespread, they are not necessarily universal.

KEY CONCEPTS

- Formal operations
- Gender role orientation
- Identity crisis
- Rites of passage
- Self-esteem

INTRODUCTION

Adolescence is a time of rapid and difficult changes unlike any other period in a human's life. Both physical development and cognitive development enter dramatic new stages. The physical changes of puberty signal the onset of sexuality; cognitive abilities progress to the sophistication needed for mathematics and complex word use. Social relationships outside the family become much more important than before. American psychologist and educator G. Stanley Hall is remembered most for his "storm and stress" theory on adolescent development. Hall suggested that adolescence is a time of conflict with parents, mood swings, and engaging in risky behaviors. However recent research suggests that many adolescents continue to seek out their families for social support. The interdependence model suggests that successful navigation of adolescent development is through steady increases in freedom and responsibility. When presented with this consistency, adolescents are less likely to rebel. However, adolescence is still widely regarded as the most turbulent period of life and a time in which adolescents restlessly seek their own identity (psychoanalyst Erik H. Erikson referred to the process as the identity crisis stage of development).

Both psychological and general Western cultural views of adolescence reflect the way this period is perceived in Western society. Two of the most widely discussed psychological models of adolescence—Jean Piaget's cognitive stage of formal operations and Erikson's view of the identity crisis—exemplify this Western orientation. Piaget's model of the stages of cognitive development (beginning in infancy), in particular, has been studied cross-culturally; that is, researchers have explored whether the stages apply equally well to various cultures. It has been found that the stages do not universally occur in the order that Piaget suggested.

RITES OF PASSAGE

Historically, the idea of adolescence as a separate stage is a relatively new idea. Before the mid-nineteenth century, in fact, a person was simply considered to pass from childhood to adulthood. Historically, and in different cultures, there have been various types of initiation rituals or rites of passage to mark this transition. In contemporary American society, one event that typically occurs in adolescence that could be considered such a rite of passage is learning to drive. This event embodies some of the complexities of modern society in that learning to drive symbolizes a new autonomy, yet the adolescent is still dependent on a parent or parents: The parents usually own the first car the adolescent drives, they often pay the necessary insurance, and they set restrictions such as curfews.

Many tribal cultures have puberty rituals that reflect the way puberty is viewed in the culture. The Arapesh, a society in New Guinea, have a ceremony at a girl's first menstruation in which a menstrual hut is built for her; she is rubbed with stinging nettles by the older women, and she fasts for a number of days. Among the Mano of Liberia, boys participated in a pubertal ceremony in which they underwent a symbolic death, complete with chicken's blood to make it seem as if they had been punctured by a spear. The Pueblo Indians' traditional puberty ceremony for boys involves whipping, a largely ceremonial event in which no blood is drawn. During the initiation, children are supposed to be very frightened; they are not ashamed to cry aloud. Taking a psychoanalytical approach to studying male initiation ceremonies across cultures, John Whiting, Richard Kluckholm, and Albert Anthony noted that, in some cultures, mother and newborn infant share a bed exclusively for a year or more after childbirth. They concluded that such societies are more likely to have a ceremony of transition from boyhood to manhood, with the ritual helping to sever the boy's emotional bond with his mother. In various cultures, hazing, harsh endurance tests, and genital operations have all been performed in the name of initiation protocol.

Cultural attitudes and expectations of adolescence, as well as adolescent behaviors and skills, show both similarities and differences in different cultures. Much has been learned about this by studying the conflicts and difficulties experienced by adolescents of minorities and adolescents whose families have immigrated to the United States. These youths often have conflicting role models (or worse, no effective role models). The experiences of Asian American youths from Southeast Asia have been discussed by J. F. Nidorf. Living in the United States, the youth feels that he or she must develop autonomy from parents to attain a personal identity and sense of worth. Yet the parents believe that the adolescent should remain "indefinitely in a position of mutual interdependence with family members" and that a sense of self-worth comes from subordinating one's own needs and assuming greater responsibility for the needs of other family members. In other words, the adolescent hears that one should "become a success in the United States, but find a way to do it without becoming an American." In another example, in traditional Chinese families, dating, as practiced in the United States, does (or did) not exist. As B. L. Sung puts it, in China, teenagers are kept "under wraps" until they are married; in the United States, they are "titillated."

ADOLESCENCE IN ISRAEL

Among the cultures in which various aspects of childhood and adolescent development have been studied are Israel and Japan. The Israeli kibbutz is a collective settlement, either agricultural or industrial. The profits that are generated supply the members' basic needs as well as medical and social services. Approaches to child rearing vary among kibbutzim; children are often reared as much by other supervising adults and by the community as a whole as by their biological parents. Traditionally, adults have their own living quarters, but children often live separately from their parents in special children's housing (this is by no means true of all kibbutzim). Cooking and dining are communal activities.

Psychoanalyst Edith Buxbaum practiced in Israel in 1965–66 at Oranim, the child guidance clinic of the kibbutzim; she wrote of her experiences there in "Problems of Kibbutz Children" in *Troubled Children in a Troubled World* (1970). She noted that behavior considered to be delinquent was not usually reported as such, but that it occurred in connection with other symptoms. The peer group has a very strong influence on kibbutz adolescents (as on kibbutz children of all ages), in part because the children are together so much of the time. The peer group is as much a consistent factor in a child's life as are the child's parents; the group is together from infancy until graduation from high school. The group is a primary source of security as well as of rules and demands. From about the age of ten, children are often given work to do on the adult farm, and shirking one's duty is looked on very unfavorably by the peer group.

Although adolescence in most cultures is a time of belonging to groups, they are most frequently voluntary groups. This is not true of kibbutz adolescents, Buxbaum points out, and she compares the general attitude of loyalty and helpfulness among teenagers there to that among students at institutions such as boarding schools. In most adolescent groups, the voluntary aspect gives the group much of its character; it leads to a sense of assertion and rebelliousness. This rebellious quality is largely missing from the kibbutz adolescent group; here, individual rebellion must be directed against the group itself. In its extreme cases, rebellion may cause an adolescent or young adult to leave the kibbutz altogether—often for a different kibbutz.

Possibly the biggest rite of passage for a person reared on a kibbutz occurs at the end, not the beginning, of adolescence. At the age of eighteen, both men and women leave the kibbutz temporarily to perform Israel's compulsory military service. For some, this will be their first extensive experience with the "outside" world. Some who leave do not return, although leaving can involve challenges caused in part by a lack of preparedness for living outside the kibbutz. The purpose of kibbutz upbringing and education is primarily to help children reach their potential while preparing them for life on the kibbutz. It is not necessarily designed to promote success in the wider society, since the kibbutz prefers that young people return.

ADOLESCENCE IN JAPAN

In Japan, only been since the 1950s has the concept of an adolescent, or teenager, in the Western sense, become popular. Its arrival has largely been attributable to Western, especially American, influences, and to an increase in affluence. Historically, a young person passed from childhood to adulthood. There is no real Japanese-language equivalent for the word "teenager." High school students are commonly referred to as children (young people age seven or eight through fourteen are called shonen, and those fifteen to twenty-four are called seinen). The skepticism and questioning attitude toward society that have come to be associated with late adolescence also came to Japan relatively recently, and typical Japanese adolescent rebellions pale in comparison with Western proportions and standards.

Japanese adolescents associate mostly with same-sex friends, tending to associate with people their own age (as opposed to spending time with their elders) much more than previous generations have. The changes wrought by technological advances have increased the importance of the nuclear family structure in Japan, although adolescents spend most of their time outside of school with their friends. The family's primary demand on the adolescent is for academic achievement. Students spend several hours a day on homework. Values such as diligence, endurance, dedication, and the willingness and ability to choose a difficult task play important roles in education. Socialization is also very important in Japanese culture, generally much more so than in American society.

A 1984 study that looked at self-concept and gender role development in Japan concluded that major inequalities exist between girls' and boys' levels of self-esteem, which proved to be considerably lower in girls. An even greater discrepancy was found in gender roles, self-concepts, and perceived gender role norms. Girls are much more conditioned to conform to traditional gender role expectations. Educational institutions demand, either explicitly or implicitly, that students—especially girls—conform to traditional gender role stereotypes. In a 1989 study of Japanese and German students' own perceptions of socialization and gender, it was noted that the Japanese students reported significantly more parental acceptance and parental control than their German counterparts. Traditional gender role orientations were also more apparent in Japanese students.

PSYCHOLOGY AND ANTHROPOLOGY

The study of behavior in different cultures has traditionally been the province of anthropology and sociology rather than psychology. A few psychological theorists in the 1960s, however, did begin to question psychology's nearly total reliance on Western cultural values for its models of normality and abnormality, noting, for example, the similarities between symptoms of "madness" and types of religious experiences such as shamanistic trances.

One of the first widely read works dealing with adolescence in a non-Western society was anthropologist Margaret Mead's *Coming of Age in Samoa* (1928). Causing something of a sensation when it first appeared, the book described puberty and adolescence in a simple Pacific island culture (her study focused only on girls). Mead's methodology and findings have since been reexamined and called into question by such researchers as Derek Freeman, who wrote a 1983 volume intended to "right the wrongs" committed by Mead and present a more accurate picture of traditional Samoan society. Nevertheless, her work, flawed though it may have been, was influential in focusing interest on other societies' approaches to life stages and to sexuality.

The study of adolescence in American society began in earnest in the 1950s, an era of postwar prosperity in which teenagers as a group had increasing visibility and mobility, attributable in part to the automobile. There was a growth of behavior labeled juvenile delinquency—illegal antisocial behavior, including gang activity—that caused concern among sociologists, law-enforcement agencies, and parents alike. The image of rebellious teenagers riding motorcycles and listening to rock and roll caught the public imagination and became the fodder for many motion pictures.

In many cultures, adolescence is a time of strong peer-group attachments. Moreover, cognitive abilities reach new levels of sophistication (Piaget's "formal operations" stage). Therefore, as adolescents are being formally or informally initiated into the ways of adulthood, they are also able to question those ways; the types of questions asked, the satisfaction with traditional answers, and the levels of actual rebellion that occur vary from culture to culture and from time to time. Similarly, the skills and behaviors necessary for success in a society vary, depending on the society's complexity and stratification. In technological societies, such as those in the United States and Japan, formal education becomes tremendously important. Whatever the needs of a particular society, however, the period of adolescence is a critical time for learning what the necessary skills are and discovering one's ability to acquire them.

BIBLIOGRAPHY

Alsaker, Françoise D., August Flammer, and Nancy Bodmer, eds. *The Adolescent Experience: European and American Adolescents in the 1990s*. Hillsdale, NJ: Erlbaum, 1999. Print.

Barnouw, Victor. *Culture and Personality.* 4th ed. Belmont, CA: Wadsworth, 1985. Print.

Brown, Lyn Mikel, and Carol Gilligan. Meeting at the Crossroads: *Women's Psychology and Girls' Development*. New York: Ballantine, 1993. Print.

Buxbaum, Edith. *Troubled Children in a Troubled World.* New York: International UP, 1970. Print.

Feldman, S. Shirley, and Glen R. Elliott, eds. *At the Threshold: The Developing Adolescent*. Cambridge, MA: Harvard UP, 1993. Print.

Freeman, Derek. *Margaret Mead and Samoa*. Cambridge, MA: Harvard UP, 1983. Print.

Fukuzawa, Rebecca, and Gerald K. Letendre. *Intense Years: How Japanese Adolescents Balance School, Family, and Friends.* New York: Routledge, 2001. Print.

Hays, Danica G., and Bradley T. Erford. *Developing Multicultural Counseling Competence: A Systems Approach.* Boston: Pearson, 2014. Print.

Hewlett, Bonnie L. *Adolescent Identity: Evolutionary, Cultural, and Developmental Perspectives.* London: Routledge, 2013. Print.

San Antonio, Donna Marie. *Adolescent Lives in Transition: How Social Class Influences the Adjustment to Middle School*. Albany: State U of NY P, 2004. Print.

Schousboe, Ivy, and Ditte Winther-Lindqvist. *Children's Play and Development: Cultural-Historical Perspectives*. New York: Springer, 2013. Print.

Tatum, Beverly D."Why Are All the Black Kids Sitting Together in the Cafeteria?" and *Other Conversations about Race*. New York: Basic, 1997. Print.

White, Merry. *The Japanese Educational Challenge.* New York: Free, 1987. Print.

Denise S. St. Cyr; updated by Buffie Longmire Avital

See Also: Adolescence: Cognitive skills; Adolescence: Sexuality; Cross-cultural psychology; Cultural competence; Culture and diagnosis; Culture-bound syndromes; Identity crises; Juvenile delinquency; Teenage suicide; Teenagers' mental health; Violence by children and teenagers.

Adolescence
Sexuality

Type of psychology: Developmental psychology

Adolescent sexuality examines the physical, psychological, and behavioral changes that occur as individuals leave childhood, acquire sexual maturity, and incorporate the various aspects of sexuality into their identity.

Key Concepts
- Contraception
- Development of sexual identity
- Levels of sexual activity
- Psychological effects
- Puberty

INTRODUCTION
Perhaps no single event during the adolescent years has as dramatic or widespread effects as the realization of sexuality. The lives of both male and female adolescents become wrapped in this new dimension. Adolescence is a time of sexual exploration and experimentation, of sexual fantasies and realities, and of incorporating sexuality into one's identity. These processes determine adolescents' comfort with their own emerging sexuality as well as with that of others. Adolescents are also beginning to be involved in intimate relationships, a context in which sexual activity often occurs.

In the twenty-first century, many of the milestones by which adulthood is defined and measured—full-time employment, economic independence, domestic partnership/marriage, and childbearing—are attained at later ages in people's lives than they were in earlier generations, while puberty begins at earlier ages. Therefore, adolescents face many years between the onset of puberty, fertility, and the natural intensification of sexual feelings, and committed relationships and economic independence. As a result, young people have sexual intercourse earlier in life, and there is a greater percentage of adolescents who are sexually experimenting at every age level, a greater number of acts of premarital intercourse, and a greater number of sexual partners before marriage.

PHYSICAL CHANGES
Adolescence is the life stage between childhood and adulthood. Its age limits are not clearly specified, but it extends roughly from age twelve to the late teens, when physical growth is nearly complete. Puberty, a term often confused with adolescence, occurs at the end of childhood and lasts from two to four years. It is the period of adolescence during which an individual reaches sexual maturity.

Human beings grow most rapidly at two times during their lives: before they are six months old and again during adolescence. The second period of accelerated growth is often referred to as the adolescent growth spurt. Adolescents grow both in height and weight, with the increase in height occurring first. As they gain weight, the amount and distribution of fat in their bodies change, and the proportion of bone and muscle tissue increases. In girls, the adolescent growth spurt usually begins between the ages of nine and eleven and reaches a peak at an average of twelve and a half years. Then growth slows and usually ceases completely between the ages of fifteen and eighteen. The growth spurt in boys generally begins about two years later than it does in girls and lasts for a longer time. It begins between the ages of eleven and fourteen, reaches a peak at about age fifteen, and slowly declines until the age of nineteen or twenty.

The teenager's body grows at differing rates, so that at times adolescents look a bit awkward. Big feet and long legs are the early signs of a changing body, but even these changes do not occur at the same time. First the hands and feet grow, then the arms and legs; only later do the shoulders and chest grow to fit the rest of the developing body. Changes in body proportion become obvious. The trunk widens in the hips and shoulders, and the waistline narrows. Boys tend to broaden mostly in the shoulders, girls in the hips.

Puberty is chiefly characterized by sexual development. Sexual development can be best understood by examining the maturation of primary and secondary sex characteristics. Primary sex characteristics are the physiological features of the sex organs. For men, these organs are the penis and the testes; for women, they are the ovaries, uterus, clitoris, and vagina. Secondary sex characteristics are not directly related to the sexual organs but nevertheless distinguish a man from a woman. Examples of secondary sex characteristics are the male beard and the female breasts.

In girls, the onset of breast development is usually, but not always, the first sign that puberty has begun. This typically occurs between the ages of ten and eleven, but can occur as late as ages thirteen and fourteen. There is simultaneous development of the uterus and vagina, with enlargement of the labia and clitoris.

Menarche (the first menstrual period), although perhaps the most dramatic and symbolic sign of a girl's changing status, occurs relatively late in puberty, after the growth spurt has reached its peak velocity. The first menstrual periods tend to be irregular, and ovulation (the release of a mature egg) does not usually begin until a year or so after menarche. Age at menarche has decreased as body weight has increased, with girls on average reaching menarche at ten and a half to eleven years of age.

The first noticeable change in boys is usually growth of the testes and scrotum. The growth of the genitals begins, on average, about the age of twelve and is completed, on average, by about the age of fifteen. Boys generally become capable of ejaculation about a year after the penis begins to grow. These first emissions may occur as a result of nocturnal emissions, the ejaculation of semen during sleep. Nocturnal emissions are a normal phase of development and are frequently caused by sexual excitation in dreams or by some type of physical condition, such as a full bladder or even pressure from pajamas.

As adolescents develop more adult bodies, their interest in sexual behavior increases sharply. They must learn the necessary behavior to satisfy that interest, and they must face the issue of a mature gender identity. This includes the expression of sexual needs and feelings and the acceptance or rejection of gender roles.

The onset of dating and the beginning of physical intimacies with the opposite sex can provoke frustration and anxiety. As this unfamiliar territory is explored, the adolescent is often poorly informed and overly self-conscious. Conflicting sexual values and messages are frequently encountered, accentuating the problem of integrating sexual drives with other aspects of the personality.

PSYCHOLOGICAL ADJUSTMENT

Adolescents are acutely aware of the rapid changes taking place in their bodies. How they react to such changes greatly affects how they evaluate themselves; it is in this manner that physical and psychological development are related.

Physical changes may cause psychological discomfort. Adolescents are particularly concerned about whether they are the "right" shape or size and whether they measure up to the "ideal" adolescent. Rapid growth, awkwardness, acne, voice changes, menarche, and other developments may produce emotional distress. Therefore, it is not surprising that the timing of physical and sexual maturity may have an important influence on psychosocial adjustment. Adolescents are generally concerned about anything that sets them apart from their peers. Being either the first or last to go through puberty can cause considerable self-consciousness.

In general, boys who mature early have a distinct advantage over those who mature late. They tend to be more poised, easygoing, and good-natured. They are taller, heavier, and more muscular than other boys their age. They are also more likely to excel in sports, achieve greater popularity, and become school leaders. The ideal form for men in American society, as represented by the media, is that of the postpubescent male. Therefore, early entry into puberty draws boys closer to the male "ideal." In contrast, late-maturing boys not only are smaller and less developed than others in their age group but also are not as interested in dating. When they do become interested in girls, they often lack social skills; they are more likely to feel inadequate, anxious, and self-conscious. These personality characteristics tend to persist into early adulthood, although they may become less marked and often disappear as time goes by.

For girls, early maturation appears to be a mixed blessing. Girls who mature early grow taller, develop breasts, and go through menarche as much as six years before some of their peers. Their larger size and more adult physique may make them feel conspicuous and awkward, while at the same time they may be popular with boys and experience more dating opportunities. They also may have to deal with parents and other caregivers who have reacted to their early sexual development by being overly restrictive. The beauty ideal for women in American society, as portrayed by the media, is that of a prepubescent female. Changes in body fat related to puberty thus may lead to body image problems, as entry into puberty increases the distance from the beauty ideal just as girls become most interested in it. As with boys, the consequences of early and late maturation decrease over time. However, either early or late start of menarche seems significantly more difficult to deal with than more typical timing.

SEXUAL BEHAVIOR

Sexual maturation has other psychological consequences. In particular, patterns of sexual behavior change tremendously with the arrival of sexual maturity. As adolescents' bodies become more adult, their interest in sexual behavior increases sharply; as they explore their sexual identities, they develop a sexual script, or a stereotyped pattern for how individuals should behave sexually.

The sexual script for boys is frequently different from the sexual script for girls. As a result, boys and girls generally think differently about sex. This discrepancy can cause problems and confusion for adolescents as they struggle with their sexual identities. For boys, the focus of sexuality may be sexual conquest, to the point that young men who are nonexploitative or inexperienced may be labeled with negative terms such as "sissy." Boys are more likely than girls to see intercourse as a way of establishing their maturity and of achieving social status. As a consequence, boys are more likely to have sex with someone who is a relative stranger, to have more sexual partners, and to disassociate sex from love and emotional intimacy.

Female adolescents are much more likely than male adolescents to link sexual intercourse with love. The quality of the relationship between a girl and her partner is a very important factor. Most women would agree that sexual intercourse is acceptable if the two people are in love and is not acceptable if they are not in a romantic relationship. Consequently, women are less likely than men to list pleasure, pleasing their partner, and relieving sexual tension as reasons for having sex.

During latter part of the twentieth century, attitudes toward sexual activity began to change dramatically. Views regarding premarital sex, extramarital sex, and specific sexual acts are probably more open and permissive in the twenty-first century than they have been at any other time in recent history. Young people are exposed to sexual stimuli on television and the Internet and in magazines and motion pictures to a greater extent than ever before. Effective methods of birth control have lessened the fear of pregnancy. All these changes have given the adolescent more freedom. At the same time, the rise of acquired immunodeficiency syndrome (AIDS) in the late 1970s, the sharp increases in AIDS cases among heterosexual teenagers in the 1990s, and the increased concern over antibiotic-resistant gonorrhea and other sexually transmitted diseases have produced more conflict, since guidelines for "appropriate behavior" are less clear-cut than they were in the past. In some families, the divergence between adolescent and parental standards of sexual morality is great.

Research specifically directed toward the exploration of adolescent sexuality was not seriously undertaken until the 1950s and 1960s. Even then, the few studies that were conducted handled the topic delicately and focused on attitudes rather than behavior. When behavior was emphasized, age at first intercourse was generally selected as the major variable. Later studies have been more detailed and expansive; however, a paucity of research in this area still exists.

In *Facing Facts* (1995), Debra W. Haffner categorizes adolescent sexuality into three stages; early, middle, and late. In early adolescence (ages nine to thirteen for girls, eleven to fifteen for boys) experimenting with sexual behavior is common, although sexual intercourse is usually limited. A 1994 national telephone survey of ninth- to twelfth-grade students found that nearly all had engaged in kissing; more than 70 percent had engaged in touching above the waist and more than 50 percent below the waist; 15 percent had engaged in mutual masturbation. This time period is characterized by the beginning of the process of separating from the family and becoming more influenced by peers. During middle adolescence (thirteen to sixteen for girls, fourteen to seventeen for boys) sexual experimentation is common, and many adolescents first have intercourse during this stage of life. Some 50 percent of ninth- through twelfth-grade students report having had sexual intercourse, with percentages from 38 percent of ninth-graders to 65 percent of twelfth-graders. A slightly higher percentage of young men than young women reported having had sexual intercourse. In late adolescence (women sixteen and older; men seventeen and older), the process of physical maturation is complete. There is autonomy from family as well as from the peer group as adult roles are defined. Sexuality often becomes associated with commitment and planning for the future.

Awareness of sexual orientation often emerges in adolescence. A study, conducted by Margaret Rosario and her colleagues, of fourteen- to twenty-one-year-old lesbian, gay, and bisexual youths reports that the average age at which girls were certain of being gay was approximately 16, and the average age for boys was 14.6, with the majority reporting a history of sexual activity with both sexes.

Boys appear to initiate intercourse earlier than girls, but girls catch up by the late teens. The timing of puberty is important for boys, while for girls, social controls exert a greater influence than the onset of puberty. Girls who are academically engaged, with higher self-esteem, and with interests outside the dating culture are more likely to delay the onset of sexual activity. For both boys and girls, dual-parent families, higher socioeconomic status, parental supervision, and a close relationship with parents are all associated with delayed onset of sexual activity.

Contraceptive use among adolescents continues to increase. Two-thirds of adolescents report using some method of contraceptive, usually condoms, the first time they have sexual intercourse. The older they are at first intercourse, the more likely they are to use a contraceptive. Programs that improve teen access to contraceptives have not produced increased rates of sexual activity but do increase condom use.

Social concerns such as teenage pregnancy, sexually transmitted diseases, and sex education have focused attention on the need to clearly understand the dynamics of adolescent sexuality. This awareness should continue to encourage broader perspectives for the study of teenage sexual behavior and produce detailed knowledge of adolescent sexuality.

BIBLIOGRAPHY

Alan Guttmacher Institute. *Sex and America's Teenagers.* New York: Author, 1994. Print.

Columbia University Health Education Program. *The Go Ask Alice Book of Answers: A Guide to Good Physical, Sexual, and Emotional Health*. New York: Owl, 1998. Print.

Gilmore, Karen, and Pamela Meersand. *Normal Child and Adolescent Development: A Psychodynamic Primer.* Washington, DC: American Psychiatric, 2014. Print.

Haffner, Debra W. *Beyond the Big Talk: Every Parent's Guide to Raising Sexually Healthy Teens—From Middle School to High School, and Beyond.* New York: Newmarket, 2001. Print.

Kerig, Patricia, Marc S. Schulz, and Stuart T. Hauser. *Adolescence and Beyond: Family Processes and Development*. New York: Oxford UP, 2012. Print.

Libby, Roger W. *The Naked Truth about Sex: A Guide to Intelligent Sexual Choices for Teenagers and TwentySomethings.* Topanga, CA: Freedom, 2006. Print.

Madaras, Lynda, with Area Madaras. *The "What's Happening to My Body?" Book for Boys*. 3d rev. ed. New York: Newmarket, 2007. Print.

Madaras, Lynda, with Area Madaras. *The "What's Happening to My Body?" Book for Girls*. 3d rev. ed. New York: Newmarket, 2007. Print.

Paludi, Michele Antoinette. *The Psychology of Love.* Santa Barbara, CA: Praeger, 2012. Print.

Slap, Gail B., ed. *Adolescent Medicine*. Philadelphia: Mosby, 2008. Print.

Doyle R. Goff; updated by Cythia O'Dell

See Also: Adolescence: Cognitive skills; Adolescence: Cross-cultural patterns; Child abuse; Drives; Gender identity formation; Gender roles and gender role conflicts; Homosexuality; Identity crises; Psychosexual development; Sex hormones and motivation; Sexual behavior patterns; Teenagers' mental health; Violence and sexuality in the media.

Adrenal gland

Type of psychology: Biological bases of behavior

The paired adrenal glands, situated above the kidneys, are each divided into two portions, a cortex and a medulla. The cortex produces steroid hormones, involved in the control of metabolism, inflammation, and other important processes; the medulla produces the amino acid–derived catecholamines, which are thought to be important in brain behavior.

Key Concepts

- Affective disorders
- Endocrine gland
- Hormone
- Protein
- Receptor
- Steroid hormone
- Target organ

INTRODUCTION

The adrenal glands are a pair of triangular endocrine glands, one lying on top of each of the kidneys. These glands secrete several hormones that are essential to life in that they regulate the body's metabolism of fats, carbohydrates, and proteins; help maintain appropriate amounts of body fluids, thus participating in blood-pressure regulation; fight the effects of stress and injury on the body; participate in the immune response; and function in nerve-impulse transmission and brain function.

Endocrine glands produce one or more hormones and secrete them into the blood so that they can serve as intercellular messengers. In contrast, exocrine glands secrete their chemical products through ducts (such as the kidney, pancreas, or stomach). Hormones themselves are trace chemicals—present in tiny amounts—that act as extracellular messengers, controlling body processes in target organs far from the endocrine gland that produced them. A target organ is one that responds to a hormone by changing its biological capabilities.

ADRENAL CORTICOSTEROIDS

The adrenal gland is divided into an outer cortex and an inner medulla. The cortex produces about three dozen hormones, all fatlike steroids. These adrenal corticosteroids are divided into two main groups, glucocorticoids and mineralocorticoids; the adrenal cortex also produces steroid sex hormones. Glucocorticoids, whose production is controlled mostly by the pituitary gland through the adrenocorticotropic hormone (ACTH), mediate the ways in which the body breaks down and uses fats, carbohydrates, and proteins. The most abundant and potent of these hormones is cortisol (hydrocortisone). In times of stress (such as injury, extreme temperature change, illness, surgery, or ingestion of toxic chemicals), ACTH will stimulate production of glucocorticoids. The glucocorticoids also have tremendous ability as anti-inflammatory agents, fighting inflammation caused by arthritis and allergic reactions. For this reason, they are used medically to combat allergy, asthma, and arthritis. In some instances, overdosage of glucocorticoids can cause abnormal mental behavior.

The second major group of adrenal corticosteroids is the mineralocorticoids. These hormones control the body's salt levels (sodium and chloride ions), which are important to the maintenance of body water balance and to the cellular import and export of both nutrients and wastes. If too much sodium chloride is retained in blood and tissues, the total fluid volume in the blood vessels increases and produces high blood pressure. Mineralocorticoids also control potassium levels, which is important because this ion is essential to nerve-impulse transport. The main mineralocorticoid, aldosterone, interacts with a kidney protein called renin to maintain appropriate blood volume by controlling the rate of salt and water excretion. Diseases of underproduction or overproduction of adrenal steroids, including the sex hormones, can have serious consequences.

The adrenal steroids all act by forming complexes with special receptor proteins in target organs, transporting hormone-receptor complexes to cell nuclei, and stimulating the production of key cell proteins by interaction with the hereditary material (gene derepression) in cell nuclei. Proteins are amino acid polymers that have many biological functions, including acting as enzymes (biological catalysts) and hormone receptors. Receptors are proteins that interact with a specific hormone to enable it to carry out messenger functions in target organs.

The adrenal medulla—which arises from fetal nervous tissue—produces amino-acid-derived hormones called catecholamines, stores them, and releases them on receiving an appropriate signal. The main catecholamines are epinephrine (adrenaline), norepinephrine (noradrenaline), and dopamine. These chemicals are linked with the nervous system in several ways. First, epinephrine and norepinephrine are hormones that control the fight-or-flight responses that enable the body to respond to emergencies by anger or fear reactions. Such responses are partly attributable to linkage between the adrenal medulla and the sympathetic nervous system, which can produce the signals that cause release of catecholamines in times of stress.

Such release has many useful effects, including the dilation of eye pupils to allow better sight; elevation of the blood pressure and increasing of the heartbeat to allow better transport of energy-producing food; release of energy reserves of sugar from the liver and muscles; and contraction of blood vessels near the skin, to minimize bleeding if wounds should occur. Epinephrine, norepinephrine, and dopamine also heighten the reactions of the central nervous system, acting as neurotransmitters in different parts of the brain and evoking responses needed for fight, flight, and normal brain function.

These actions of catecholamines can be harmful, as is evidenced in a disease called pheochromocytoma, in which adrenal medullary hormones are overproduced because of tumors of the medulla or the sympathetic nervous system. Afflicted persons exhibit symptoms that include high blood pressure, heart palpitations, nervousness, anxiety, and neurotic symptoms. Abnormalities of catecholamine levels are implicated in a primary fashion in many psychological disorders. Catecholamine actions, like those of steroid hormones (a hormone that is a fatlike chemical derived from cholesterol), involve specific receptors; however, catecholamine-related processes do not involve hormone-receptor interactions with the hereditary material. Rather, they use a "second messenger" mechanism in which already-existing proteins are activated.

RELATIONSHIP TO MENTAL DISORDERS

Mental illness is frequently divided into two basic types: organic and functional. Organic mental illness is a consequence of a known disease, such as diabetes or a tumor of the adrenal gland, that alters the structure of the brain or its ability to function correctly or that produces a malfunction of some other part of the nervous system. Cure of organic mental illness may involve surgery or other methods that eradicate the causative disease. In contrast, the exact basis for functional mental illness has often evaded understanding and has long been viewed as deriving from operational flaws of mental function. Among the most widely publicized mental disorders are schizophrenia and bipolar disorder(also known as manic-depressive disorder).

Relatively clear understanding has begun to develop for bipolar disorder, wherein afflicted persons alternate rapidly between an excessively happy (manic) state and a severely depressed (depressive) state. The alternation is so severe that it renders patients unable to cope with the world around them. Understanding this disorder begins with consideration of the function and malfunction of the human nervous system, composed of a central computer—the brain—and a network of neuron wires—nerves—that communicate with the rest of the body via nerve impulses. When nerve impulses pass through the nervous system correctly, they allow recognition of and appropriate response to the world. Malfunction of nerve-impulse generation and passage through the nerves or brain is believed to produce some functional mental illnesses.

Nerve cells (neurons) are separated from one another by minute synaptic gaps, and the passage of nerve impulses through a nerve requires the impulses to cross thousands of such gaps. Nerve-impulse transport across synaptic gaps is mediated by biochemicals called neurotransmitters. The best known of these is acetylcholine, which acts in cholinergic nerves. The dysfunction of cholinergic nerves, via disruption of acetylcholine action, is believed to be a major component of functional mental disease. This belief derives partly from observation of impaired mental function in people exposed to nerve gases and insecticides that act by disrupting acetylcholine production and use.

Other neurotransmitters associated with mental disorders include catecholamines and chemicals called indoleamines. The main catecholamine neurotransmitters are the adrenal medulla hormones epinephrine, norepinephrine, and dopamine. The catecholamines control nerve-impulse transmission by adrenergic portions of the nervous system. The indoleamines (especially serotonin act in neurons related to sleep and sensory perception.

ROLE IN DEPRESSION

Some theories of depression and mania have arisen from the catecholamine (actually, norepinephrine) hypothesis of Joseph Schildkraut and others. This hypothesis proposes that depression is attributable to suboptimum production or utilization of norepinephrine (decreased noradrenergic activity) and that mania arises from increased noradrenergic activity. Acceptance of this theory has led to the examination of norepinephrine levels in normal and mental disease states; use of observed levels of the neurotransmitter to explain how existing drugs, electric shock, and other psychiatric treatments affect functional mental illness; choice of new therapeutic drugs on the basis of their effects on norepinephrine levels; and study of the effects of other catecholamines and related biogenic amines.

These efforts have demonstrated that dopamine, a catecholamine cousin of norepinephrine, is implicated in central nervous system dysfunction. It was observed that several important tranquilizers (among them reserpine) decreased both norepinephrine and dopamine levels. Consequently, the catecholamine hypothesis has expanded to include dopamine. In fact, low levels of dopamine have been shown to be more intimately involved in depression than are low epinephrine levels.

The biogenic indoleamine serotonin was next implicated in depression, because it is also depleted by tranquilizers such as reserpine. It was then shown that the action of therapeutic drugs called tricyclic antidepressants is also related mostly to alteration of serotonin levels. Because of this, an indoleamine (serotonin) corollary was added to the catecholamine hypothesis of affective disease.

In 1972, David Janowsky and coworkers at Vanderbilt University's psychiatry department proposed a new hypothesis of affective disease. Their hypothesis focused on the cholinergic neurotransmitter acetylcholine but expanded the conceptual basis for functional mental illness. Unlike preceding concepts, it recognized the importance of interaction between the various systems participating in nerve-impulse transmission and suggested that the affective state of any individual represents a balance between adrenergic and cholinergic activity. Furthermore, the hypothesis proposed depression as a disease of relative cholinergic predominance, while mania was said to be attributable to relative adrenergic predominance.

THERAPEUTIC DRUGS

Until the advent of the catecholamine (and later indoleamine) hypothesis of affective mental disorder and the realization of the adrenal medullary involvement in psychiatric disorders, the primary treatments attempted for functional mental disease included procedures such as lobotomy, electroconvulsive (shock) therapy, and insulin coma. These procedures are now viewed as being imprecise at best, though some use of each has persisted, most often as part of mixed psychotherapy (which incorporates them alongside psychoanalysis and treatment with psychotherapeutic drugs) or therapy involving patients who are extremely difficult to treat.

Much of the basis for use of such drugs evolved from examinations of therapeutic drugs to determine their ability to alter catecholamine and indoleamine levels. Among the first psychotherapeutic drugs were the tricyclic antidepressants, organic chemicals that affected catecholamine and serotonin levels. Another useful family of these drugs is a group of chemicals called monoamine oxidase inhibitors (MAOIs). MAOIs prevent biological modification of catecholamines by the enzyme monoamine oxidase, prolonging their presence in the body. In addition, the importance of lithium-containing chemicals in fighting functional mental illness is also believed to be attributable to a mechanism that includes alterations of catecholamine and indoleamine concentrations in the nervous system.

CONTRIBUTIONS

The developing understanding of the role of the adrenal medulla in both normal and pathological processes in the nervous system has led to a more complete understanding of the basis for the utility of major tranquilizers in treatment of the severely mentally ill. It has also enabled better differentiation of schizophrenia from affective disorders—functional mental disorders associated with emotions or feelings—and led to explanations of the causes of the psychogenic manifestations of many illegal addictive drugs. Understanding of the adrenal gland has also led to the discovery of additional neurotransmitter chemicals that promise better understanding of the nervous system. Furthermore, examination of the steroid hormones of the adrenal cortex has shown that those hormones can produce some psychopathology.

BIBLIOGRAPHY

"Adrenal Gland Disorders." *National Institute of Child Health and Human Development.* National Institutes of Health, 3 Apr. 2013. Web. 19 Feb. 2014.

"Adrenal Insufficiency Fact Sheet." *Hormone Health Network. Endocrine Society,* Aug. 2010. Web. 19 Feb. 2014.

Janowsky, David S., et al. "Neurochemistry of Depression and Mania." *Depression and Mania.* Ed. Anastasios Georgotas and Robert Cancro. New York: Elsevier, 1988. Print.

Janowsky, David S., M. Khaled el-Yousef, John M. Davis, and H. Joseph Sekerke. "A Cholinergic-Adrenergic Hypothesis of Mania and Depression." *Lancet* 2 (September, 1972): 632–35. Print.

Lehninger, Albert L. *Lehninger Principles of Biochemistry.* 5th ed. New York: Freeman, 2008. Print.

Linos, Dimitrios, and Jon A. van Heerden, eds. *Adrenal Glands: Diagnostic Aspects and Surgical Therapy.* New York: Springer, 2005. Print.

Valenstein, Elliot S. *Great and Desperate Cures: The Rise and Decline of Psychosurgery and Other Radical Treatments for Mental Illness.* New York: Basic, 1986. Print.

Derived from: "Adrenal gland." *Psychology and Mental Health.* Salem Press. 2009.

Sanford S. Singer

See Also: Antidepressant medications; Antipsychotic medications; Bipolar disorder; Brain structure; Depression; Endocrine system; Gonads; Hormones and behavior; Nervous system; Pituitary gland; Psychosurgery; Seasonal affective disorder; Sex hormones and motivation; Shock therapy; Stress: Physiological responses; Synaptic transmission; Thyroid gland.

Adult ADHD

Type of psychology: Biological bases of human behavior; Clinical; Cognition; Counseling; Developmental; Psychopathology; Psychotherapy; School

Attention deficit/hyperactivity disorder in adulthood is often underdiagnosed and erroneously assumed to be a childhood condition. But adult ADHD also requires identification and assessment and frequently involves medication, counseling, and management issues. As society has become more complex and technologically sophisticated, it is imperative to have a keen understanding of adult attention deficit disorder and related problems such as hyperactivity and impulsivity.

Key Concepts

- Attention deficit disorder
- Hyperactivity
- Impulsivity
- Test of Variables of Attention (TOVA)

- Medication
- Management

INTRODUCTION

The construct of attention deficit disorder with or without hyperactivity, and with or without impulsivity, has been with us for decades. Quite often, this diagnosis is reserved for school children as their learning requires attention, concentration, and freedom from distractibility for extended periods of time. Some children seem to have grown out" of attention deficit disorder, or the difficulties have abated when they have graduated to a college which allows them to take the classes they want during the time periods they prefer. Many adolescents have simply learned to cope with their attention deficit disorder, while others have remained on medication. Some college students do seek accommodations and modifications and adults may seek counseling to cope with a problematic disorder which interferes with their learning.

The latest edition of the *Diagnostic and Statistical Manual of Mental Disorders* (DSM-5) discusses ADHD and reviews diagnostic features, prevalence, development and course, risk and prognostic factors, gender related diagnostic issues, culture-related diagnostic issues, and differential diagnosis. The general public is keenly aware of attention deficit disorder, and there is consensus that this condition does exist and interferes with learning.

The concept of attention deficit disorder, with or without hyperactivity and/or impulsivity, has been accepted for many years. Many children received identification, medication, and accommodations and modifications in the public schools. Many of these individuals either learn to cope with this disorder, but others, for whatever reason, continue into adulthood attempting to cope with the signs and symptoms of adult ADHD.

As children and adults enter adulthood, the demands of a full time job and perhaps a full time relationship become problematic. Parenting is another realm which requires patience, compassion, empathy, warmth, and prioritization. For the adult with ADHD, some of these skills are in short supply. Further, some adults with ADHD may be involved in auto accidents and other difficulties working with machines and other electrical and mechanical devices. Marriages often end in divorce as the individual with ADHD fails to provide the proper attention to his or her mate, spouse, or loved one.

DIAGNOSIS

The DSM-5 provides the criteria for ADHD. For inattention, the individual must manifest five of the nine criteria relative to inattention (six of nine needed in childhood and adolescence) and five of the nine criteria for hyperactivity and impulsivity (six of nine needed in childhood and adolescence). Hyperactivity and impulsivity are not separated in the DSM-5. Further, the clinician establishes the severity (mild, moderate, or severe) and specifies if it is a combined presentation (predominately inattentive or predominately hyperactive/impulsive).

TREATMENT

Adults with ADHD are often keenly aware of their limitations surrounding attention span and impulsive behavior. They may have sublimated their energy if they participate in sports, jogging, or other activities which provide an outlet for their energy. Without an outlet, others may simply cause consternation to those around them in the work or familial environment.

COUNSELING ISSUES

The adult with ADHD may be frustrated and exasperated as he or she may have believed that ADHD problems would resolve themselves upon reaching adulthood. If they are college students, they may need to request accommodations and modifications from a disabilities service office. In terms of differential diagnosis, the adult student may need further testing for a learning disability inasmuch as while they may have received a medical diagnosis of ADHD, psychoeducational assessment may not have been done and a learning disability in reading, spelling, written expression, or mathematics may not have been identified. Thus, the adult with ADHD has further adjustment to make and may need additional consultation and assistance as he or she progresses through college.

Interpersonal issues may also be problematic as the expectations for sexual and interpersonal intimacy may be different than the expectation of an adolescent.

Often, an individual with adult ADHD will also present with low frustration tolerance, irritability, and/or mood lability. These may present in the work environment, home environment, or academic environment.

LATE IDENTIFICATION

If the individual has not been previously diagnosed with ADHD, a comprehensive workup is appropriate. There are several computerized tests such as the Test of Variables of Attention (TOVA) which can specify if the attentional problems are in the visual or auditory realm or both. Further, the TOVA can differentiate between impulsivity, hyperactivity, and inattention.

MEDICATION

Some adults with ADHD are maintained on a dosage of medication which may meet their needs and allow them to function well in the work and familial environment. Often the dosage needs to be titrated as the individual ages and as expectations change regarding work and family demands. Traffic violations and automobile accidents are more likely to occur if the individual is not on medication or has forgotten to take medication. In some instances, ongoing physical examinations and blood/urine analysis is recommended in order to rule out other difficulties and for general optimal functioning.

MISDIAGNOSIS

Often individuals with adult attention deficit disorder that have not been diagnosed in childhood or adolescence are incorrectly diagnosed. It may be problematic for adult psychiatrists to correctly diagnose adult ADHD and signs and symptoms of ADHD may be confused with borderline personality disorders or narcissism. However, adult ADHD individuals do not engage in the self-injurious behavior or extreme ambivalence seen with personality disorders.

PROGNOSIS

With medication, counseling, and educative therapy, the individual with adult ADHD can live a potentially happy life, using skills and coping strategies to assist them with their occupation and interpersonal relationships. Supportive counseling is obviously an additional benefit. Activities which require sustained attention for long periods of time may be problematic and the individual should be encouraged to break attentional tasks into smaller components and be aware that others may be perturbed by inattentive behaviors which could be construed as being negligent of or ignoring other individuals.

BIBLIOGRAPHY

American Psychiatric Association. (2013). *Diagnostic and Statistical Manual of Mental Disorders*. (5th ed.). Washington, DC: Author.

www.strattera.com Includes an Adult Self-Report Screener, symptoms, and side effects of certain medications.

www.neuropl.us. Contains resources for online training for attention, focusing and concentration.

alothealthy.com/conditions/adult-adhd--1161. Emphasizes the importance of counseling and coping skills.

www.hellolife.net Features a natural approach with products that can be purchased online.

http://www.audible.com/pd/Science-Technology/Driven-to-Distraction-Audiobook. An excellent book that has become a classic in the field and is available for purchase online.

www.chadd.org. Contains multiple resources and is likely the most comprehensive source on ADHD.

Michael Shaughnessy

See Also: Attention Deficit Hyperactivity Disorder; Attention; Inattention; Hyperactivity; Impulsivity; Defiance.

Advertising

Type of psychology: Cognition; Motivation; Social psychology

Advertising is a psychological process of persuasion through attitude change. Advertisers create change in consumer beliefs, emotions, and intentions to act in regard to their products. Effective advertising draws on knowledge of narrative script, information processing, miscomprehension, psychological appeals, classical conditioning, and subliminal messages.

Key Concepts

- Attitude
- Classical conditioning
- Encoding
- Information processing
- Miscomprehension
- Narrative script
- Needs
- Persuasion
- Psychological appeal
- Subliminal advertising

INTRODUCTION

Advertising is a process of persuading an audience to buy products, contract services, or support a candidate or issue. Advertising creates a reality for the consumer—both the image of the product, company, or candidate and the need for a product or service. Advertisements try to change consumer attitudes toward a product, company, or candidate. Attitudes consist of three components: belief, affect (emotion), and intention to act. The ultimate goal of the advertiser is to persuade the consumer to act—to buy the product, support the candidate or company, or use the service.

Advertising is one form of mass communication. A classified ad from around 1000 b.c.e. offered a reward (a gold coin) to anyone finding and returning a runaway slave. Johannes Gutenberg, an inventor and metallurgist, invented movable type in the fifteenth century, which allowed for the printed mass communication of advertising. The Industrial Revolution of the nineteenth century cultivated commercialism and transportation of national publications, including a large number of magazines. Advertising proliferated on radio after 1920, on television after 1945, and on the Internet starting in the mid-1990s.

Psychologists study advertising as a form of communication in the context of cognition and psycholinguistics. Consumers "read" advertisements, whether in print, on television, or online, similarly to the way they read books. Therefore, one way to examine how consumers understand and react to advertisements is by researching comprehension of narrative scripts. For advertisements to effectively change consumer attitudes, their message must be understood. Psychologists study how consumers process the information in the advertisement. Sometimes information processing leads to miscomprehension which, often unintentionally, can create in the consumer false ideas about the product.

From a more social cognitive and humanistic perspective, psychologists look at the appeals advertisers make to human needs. Advertisements associate basic needs and natural responses to those needs with their products. Advertisers classically condition consumers to respond to their products as they would to any stimulus naturally satisfying a need. Sometimes these associations are not consciously made.

NARRATIVE SCRIPT

The first step in changing consumer attitudes toward an advertised product is to persuade the consumer that the informational content of the advertisement is true. One way advertisers create belief in the consumer is to follow a narrative script, a simple plot such as a child might hear when a parent reads a story.

The narrative script is a knowledge structure composed of exposition, complication, and resolution. The exposition introduces the characters and settings of the story. The complication is a developing problem. The resolution is the solution to the problem. Many advertisements take the form of the narrative script to facilitate comprehension and belief. For example, John, Jane, and their daughter Judy are playing at the park (exposition). While swinging, Judy falls on the ground, scraping her knee (complication). Jane soothes Judy and dresses her wound by applying a plastic bandage coated with an antibacterial agent (resolution). The consumer is comfortable with the narrative script as an understandable and entertaining format. The advertiser is able to hold the audience's attention. The resolution is associated with the product (bandages).

INFORMATION PROCESSING

The consumer's belief in the advertisement is affected by how the consumer processes the information presented in it. There are eight stages of information processing involved in the comprehension of advertisements. The belief component of the consumer's attitude toward the product can be formed or modified at any stage. The first stage is exposure. The consumer must have the opportunity to perceive the advertisement. The second stage is attention. The consumer may pay attention to part or all of an advertisement. The third stage is comprehension. The consumer must understand the information in the ad. The fourth stage is evaluation. The consumer assesses the information presented in the ad. The fifth stage is encoding. The consumer encodes, or saves, the advertised information in long-term memory. Later, the sixth stage, retrieval, can occur: The consumer retrieves the encoded information. The seventh stage is decision. The consumer decides to buy (or not buy) the advertised product. The final stage is the action of buying the product.

MISCOMPREHENSION

Advertisers may persuade consumers to buy their product by intentionally inducing miscomprehension. The basis of the miscomprehension is the tendency for people to encode inferences, or interpretations, of stated advertising claims. Therefore, the consumer later remembers inferences made, but not explicitly stated, about a product. At no point is the advertiser presenting false information. However, the advertisement is structured in a way that induces the consumer to draw a specific inference. An advertisement might use hedge words such as "may" or "could." For example, pain reliever Brand A "may help" prevent heart attacks.

Other advertisements contain elliptical comparatives. In an elliptical comparison, the standard that something is being compared to is intentionally left out. The consumer naturally completes the comparison with the most logical standard. However, the true standard might not be the most logical. For example, cereal Brand A "gives you more." More what? A logical standard might be "more vitamins." The true standard might be "more heartburn." An advertisement might imply causation when in actuality the relationship is correlational. Juxtaposing two imperative statements implies that the first statement leads to, or causes, the next statement: Buy tire Brand A. Drive safely.

PSYCHOLOGICAL APPEALS

Advertisers use psychological appeals directed to basic human needs. Abraham Maslow, the American humanist psychologist who developed a hierarchy of needs in the 1960s, theorized that all humans have needs that must be met to achieve self-fulfillment. The most basic are the physiological needs, such as food, water, and shelter. People also need basic feelings: feeling secure, that they belong, and that they are loved, as well as feelings of self-esteem. The final need is self-actualization, the highest form of self-fulfillment. Advertisements may focus on any one, or combinations, of these needs.

Psychological appeals in advertising influence the emotional component of people's attitudes. The advertised product is associated with positive emotions such as fun, love, belonging, warmth, excitement, and satisfaction. Advertisements can also be based on fear: The advertisers try to convince consumers that there will be negative consequences if they do not buy their product, focusing on the need for safety. For example, buying any tire other than the one advertised will increase the risk of an automobile accident. Advertisements also appeal to the human need for self-esteem, which is heightened through power and success. An ad may aim to associate the product with the consumer being the best or having the most.

CLASSICAL CONDITIONING

Russian physiologist Ivan Petrovich Pavlov discovered the process of classical conditioning in the early twentieth century. An unconditioned stimulus (US) produces naturally an unconditioned response (UR). For example, the image of a baby may naturally produce pleasant, even maternal or paternal, feelings. In classical conditioning, the unconditioned stimulus is paired with a neutral stimulus (one that does not normally produce the unconditioned response). For example, a can of soda (neutral stimulus) can be paired with a picture of a baby (unconditioned stimulus). With several pairings, the neutral stimulus will become the conditioned stimulus, eliciting the unconditioned response without the actual association with the unconditioned stimulus. Once conditioning occurs, the unconditioned response becomes the conditioned response (CR).

Thus, the can of soda becomes the conditioned stimulus when it alone produces pleasant feelings (conditioned response). Advertisers use classical conditioning to associate a product with a stimulus that elicits the desired responses (belief in the product, positive emotions about the product, intent to buy the product) in the consumer. While shopping, a consumer sees the advertised can of soda, associates it with positive feelings, and therefore is more likely to purchase this brand of soda.

SUBLIMINAL ADVERTISING

Stimuli that are subliminal are below the threshold of conscious perception. Consumers are not normally aware of subliminal stimuli unless they consciously look for them. For example, an image on a product package may contain the shape of sexual organs. There is some weak evidence that subliminal messages in advertising may positively affect the emotional quality of consumer attitudes toward a product. However, there is no evidence that subliminal messages affect consumer behavior toward a product.

BIBLIOGRAPHY

Benoit, William L., and Pamela J. Benoit. *Persuasive Messages: The Process of Influence*. Malden: Blackwell, 2008. Print.

Cialdini, Robert B. *Influence: Science and Practice*. 5th ed. Boston: Pearson Education, 2009. Print.

Cialdini, Robert B. *Influence: The Psychology of Persuasion*. Rev. ed. New York: Collins, 2007. Print.

Day, Nancy. *Advertising: Information or Manipulation?* Berkeley Heights: Enslow, 1999. Print.

Harris, Richard J., and Fred W. Sanborn. *A Cognitive Psychology of Mass Communication*. 6th ed. New York: Routledge, 2014. Print.

Heath, Robert. *Seducing the Subconscious: The Psychology of Emotional Influence in Advertising*.

Chichester: Wiley-Blackwell, 2012. Print.
Hogan, Kevin. *The Psychology of Persuasion: How to Persuade Others to Your Way of Thinking*. Gretna: Pelican, 1996. Print.
Maddock, Richard C., and Richard L. Fulton. *Marketing to the Mind*. Westport: Greenwood, 1996. Print.
Mills, Harry A. *Artful Persuasion: How to Command Attention, Change Minds, and Influence People*. New York: AMACOM, 2000. Print.
Pradeep, A. K. *Mind Men: How Neuromarketing Advances Are Transforming Advertising*. Hoboken: Wiley, 2014. Print.
Pratkanis, Anthony R., and Elliot Aronson. *The Age of Propaganda: The Everyday Use and Abuse of Persuasion*. Rev. ed. New York: Freeman, 2007. Print.
Schumann, David W., and Esther Thurson, eds. *Advertising and the World Wide Web*. Hillsdale: Erlbaum, 1999. Print.
Sugarman, Joseph, Dick Hafer, and Ron Hugher. *Triggers: How to Use the Psychological Triggers of Selling to Motivate, Persuade, and Influence*. Las Vegas: Delstar, 1999. Print.

Elizabeth M. McGhee Nelson

See Also: Attention; Attitude formation and change; Concept formation; Conditioning; Consumer psychology; Drives; Emotions; Media psychology; Motication; Motivation: Intrinsic and extrinsic; Pavlovian conditioning; Reinforcement; Hierarchy of needs.

Affiliation and friendship

Type of psychology: Personality; Social psychology

Affiliation is the tendency to seek the company of others. People are motivated and instinctually driven to affiliate for several reasons. Friendship is an important close relationship based on affiliation, attraction, and intimacy.

Key Concepts

- Affliation
- Attraction
- Communal relationship
- Complementarity
- Consensual validation
- Exchange relationship
- Propinquity
- Proselytize
- Social comparison

INTRODUCTION

Affiliation is the desire or tendency to be with others of one's own kind. Many animal species affiliate, collecting in groups to migrate or search for food. Human affiliation is not controlled simply by instinct but is affected by specific motives. One motivation for affiliation is fear: people seek the company of others when they are anxious or frightened. The presence of others may have a calming or reassuring influence. In 1959, research by social psychologist Stanley Schachter indicated that fear inducement leads to a preference for the company of others. Further work confirmed that frightened individuals prefer the company of others who are similarly frightened to the companionship of strangers. This preference for similar others suggests that affiliation is a source of information as well as reassurance.

SOCIAL COMPARISON THEORY

The value of obtaining information through affiliating with others is suggested by social comparison theory. Social comparison is the process of comparing oneself with others in determining how to behave. According to Leon Festinger, who developed social comparison theory in 1954, all people have beliefs and place importance on the validity of their beliefs. Some beliefs can be verified objectively by consulting a reference such as a dictionary or a standard such as a yardstick. Others are subjective beliefs and cannot be verified objectively. In such cases, people look for consensual validation—the verification of subjective beliefs by obtaining a consensus among other people—to verify their beliefs. The less sure people are of the correctness of a belief, the more they rely on social comparison as a source of verification. The greater number of people there are who agree with one's opinion about something, the more correct one feels in holding that opinion.

INFLUENCES ON AFFILIATION

Beyond easing fear and satisfying the need for information or social comparison, mere affiliation with others is not usually a satisfactory form of interaction. Most people form specific attractions to other individuals rather than experiencing mere satisfaction with belonging to a group. These attractions usually develop into friendship, love, and other forms of intimacy. Interpersonal attraction—the experience of preferring to interact with specific others—is influenced by several factors. An important situational or circumstantial factor in attraction is propinquity, which refers to the proximity or nearness of other persons. Research by Festinger and his colleagues confirmed that people are more likely to form friendships with those who live nearby, especially if they have frequent accidental contact with them.

Further research by social psychologist Robert Zajonc indicated that propinquity increases attraction because it increases familiarity. Zajonc found that research subjects expressed greater liking for a variety of stimuli merely because they had been exposed to those stimuli more frequently than to others. The more familiar a person is, the more predictable that person seems to be. People are reassured by predictability and feel more strongly attracted to those who are familiar and reliable in this regard.

Another important factor in affiliation is physical attractiveness. A common stereotype about people who are considered physically attractive is that they are good and valuable in other ways. For example, physically attractive people are often assumed to be intelligent, competent, and socially successful. Attraction to physically attractive persons is somewhat modified by the fear of rejection. Consequently, most people use a matching principle in choosing friends and partners: They select others who match their own levels of physical attractiveness and other qualities.

Matching implies the importance of similarity. Similarity of attitudes, values, and background is a powerful influence on interpersonal attraction. People are more likely to become friends if they have common interests, goals, and pastimes. Similar values and commitments are helpful in establishing trust between two people. Over time, they choose to spend more time together, and this strengthens their relationship.

Another factor in interpersonal attraction is complementarity, defined as the possession of qualities that complete or fulfill another's needs and abilities. Research has failed to confirm that "opposites attract," since attraction appears to grow stronger with similarities, not differences, between two people. There is some evidence, however, that people with complementary traits and needs will form stronger relationships. For example, a person who enjoys talking will have a compatible relationship with a friend or partner who enjoys listening. Their needs are different but not opposite—they complement each other.

FRIENDSHIP

Friendship begins as a relationship of social exchange. Exchange relationships involve giving and returning favors and other resources, with a short-term emphasis on maintaining fairness or equity. For example, early in a relationship, if one person does a favor for a friend, the friend returns it in kind. Over time, close friendships involve shifting away from an exchange basis to a communal basis. In a communal relationship, partners see their friendship as a common investment and contribute to it for their mutual benefit. For example, if one person gives a gift to a good friend, he or she does not expect repayment in kind. The gift represents an investment in their long-term friendship, rather than a short-term exchange.

Friendship also depends on intimate communication. Friends engage in self-disclosure and reveal personal information to one another. In the early stages of friendship, this is reciprocated immediately: one person's revelation or confidence is exchanged for the other's. As friendship develops, immediate reciprocity is not necessary; long-term relationships involve expectations of future responses. According to psychologist Robert Sternberg, friendship is characterized by two experiences: intimacy and commitment. Friends confide in one another, trust one another, and maintain their friendship through investment and effort.

COMFORT IN A GROUP

Theories of affiliation explain why the presence of others can be a source of comfort. In Schachter's classic 1959 research on fear and affiliation, university women volunteered to participate in a psychological experiment. After they were assembled, an experimenter in medical attire deceived them by explaining that their participation would involve the administration of electrical shock. Half the subjects were told to expect extremely painful shocks, while the others were assured that the shocks would produce a painless, ticklish sensation. In both conditions, the subjects were asked to indicate where they preferred to wait while the electrical equipment was set up. Each could indicate whether she preferred to wait alone in a private room, preferred to wait in a large room with other subjects, or had no preference.

The cover story about electrical shock was a deception; no shocks were administered. The fear of painful shock, however, influenced the subjects' preferences: Those who expected painful shocks preferred to wait with other subjects, while those who expected painless shocks expressed no preference. Schachter concluded that, as the saying goes, "misery loves company." In a later study, subjects were given the choice of waiting with other people who were not research subjects. In this study, subjects who feared shock expressed specific preference for others who also feared shock: misery loves miserable company.

The social comparison theory of affiliation explains the appeal of group membership. People join groups such as clubs, organizations, and churches to support one another in common beliefs or activities and to provide one another with information. Groups can also be a source of pressure to conform. One reason individuals feel pressured to conform with group behavior is that they assume the group has better information than they have. This is termed informational influence. Cohesive groups—those with strong member loyalty and commitment to membership—can also influence members to agree in the absence of information. When a member conforms with the group because he or she does not want to violate the group's standards or norms, he or she has been subjected to normative influence.

FACTORS IN FRIENDSHIP

Studies of interpersonal attraction and friendship have documented the power of circumstances such as propinquity. In their 1950 book *Social Pressures in Informal Groups*, Festinger, Schachter, and Kurt Back reported the friendship preferences of married students living in university housing. Festinger and his colleagues found that the students and their families were most likely to form friendships with others who lived nearby and with whom they had regular contact. Propinquity was a more powerful determinant of friendship than common background or academic major. Propinquity appears to act as an initial filter in social relationships: nearness and contact determine the people an individual meets, after which other factors may affect interpersonal attraction.

The findings of Festinger and his colleagues can be applied by judiciously choosing living quarters and location. People who wish to be popular should choose to live where they will have the greatest amount of contact with others: on the ground floor of a high-rise building, near an exit or stairwell, or near common facilities such as a laundry room. Zajonc's research on the power of exposure confirms that merely having frequent contact with others is sufficient to predispose them to liking.

Mere exposure does not appear to sustain relationships over time. Once people have interacted, their likelihood of having future interactions depends on factors such as physical attractiveness and similarity to one another. Further, the quality of their communication must improve over time as they engage in greater self-disclosure. As friends move from a tit-for-tat exchange to a communal relationship in which they both invest time and resources, their friendship will develop more strongly and satisfactorily.

LOVE

Research on love has identified a distinction between passionate love and companionate love. Passionate love involves intense, short-lived emotions and sexual attraction. In contrast, companionate love is calmer, more stable, and based on trust. Companionate love is strong friendship. Researchers argue that if passionate love lasts, it will eventually transform into companionate love.

Researcher Zick Rubin developed a scale to measure love and liking. He found that statements of love involved attachment, intimacy, and caring. Statements of liking involved positive regard, judgments of similarity, trust, respect, and affection. Liking or friendship is not simply a weaker form of love but a distinctive combination of feelings, beliefs, and behaviors. Rubin found that most dating couples had strong feelings of both love and liking for each other; however, follow-up research confirmed that the best predictor of whether partners were still together later was how much they had liked—not loved—each other. Liking and friendship form a solid basis for love and other relationships that is not easily altered or forgotten.

RESEARCH

Much early research on affiliation and friendship developed from an interest in social groups. After World War II, social scientists were interested in identifying the attitudes and processes that unify people and motivate their allegiances. Social comparison theory helps to explain a broad range of behavior, including friendship choices, group membership, and proselytizing. Festinger suggested that group membership is helpful when one's beliefs have been challenged or disproved. Like-minded fellow members will be equally motivated to rationalize the challenge. In their 1956 book *When Prophecy Fails*, Festinger, Henry Riecken, and Schachter document the experience of two groups of contemporary persons who had attested to a belief that the world would end in a disastrous flood. One group was able to gather and meet to await the end, while the other individuals, mostly college students, were scattered and could not assemble. When the world did not end as predicted, only those in the group context were able to rationalize their predicament, and they proceeded to proselytize, spreading the word to "converts." Meanwhile, the scattered members, unable to rationalize their surprise, lost faith in the prophecy and left the larger group.

Friendship and love are challenging topics to study since they cannot be re-created in a laboratory setting. Studies of personal relationships are difficult to conduct in natural settings; if people know that others are observing while they talk or date, they behave differently or leave the scene. Natural or field studies are also less conclusive than laboratory research, since the factors that have produced the feelings or actions that can be observed are not always clear.

Friendship has not been as popular a topic in relationships research as romantic love, marriage, and sexual relationships. Some research has identified gender differences in friendship: Women communicate their feelings and experiences with other women, while men's friendships involve common or shared activities. Developmental psychologists have also identified some age differences: Children are less discriminating about friendship, identifying someone as a friend who is merely a playmate; adults have more complex ideas about friendship forms and standards.

As research on close relationships has gained acceptance, work in communication studies has contributed to the findings of social psychologists. Consequently, more has been learned about the development and maintenance of friendship as well as the initial attractions and bonds that encourage people's ties to others and reasons, such as neglect, for friendships ending. Studies consider friendships at various life stages, including middle and old age. Cultural changes affect relationship patterns, particularly by shaping people's attitudes and motivations regarding affiliations. Modern examples of how culture affects affiliation include reality television programs that test alliances formed specifically for those competitions and the fact that some adolescents and young adults have "friends with benefits," with whom they are intimate but not romantic.

Twenty-first-century psychology researchers studied childhood and adolescent friendships to gain new insights into the dynamics of those relationships. Psychologists focused on specific factors, motivating adolescents to develop and maintain friendships which had not been scientifically evaluated. Carnegie Mellon University researcher Vicki S. Helgeson and colleagues investigated how chronic health concerns affected friends. They studied relationships formed by healthy teenagers with diabetic girls and boys. The teenagers rated their friendships with individuals with similar or contrasting health status and from the same or opposite gender based on such issues as emotional support and conflict, specifying what they found appealing or not about those relationships. The researchers determined that health concerns did not significantly alter friendship patterns, although diabetic girls might desire more emotional support and appreciate more similar friends than their healthy peers would.

At the University of Missouri–Columbia, Amanda J. Rose evaluated survey responses by eight hundred female and male middle school students. The survey questioned students regarding their friendships, whether they divulged information about their problems, and if they had been anxious or depressed. The researchers determined that girls who shared their worries with friends benefited from strengthening those relationships but suffered emotional stress and depression if they fixated on problems too long, overanalyzing them and internalizing blame. Girls often became overwhelmed, concentrating emotions and energy on their problems instead of pursuing healthier endeavors. Rose referred to this dwelling behavior as corumination. Divulging their problems also enhanced friendships between boys. However, most boys did not experience similar psychological distress, perhaps because they did not blame themselves but accused others and external factors for causing conflicts in their lives.

DIGITIZED AFFILIATION

By the early twenty-first century, digital technology altered how many people met and chose to pursue friendships and relationships or seek affiliation with groups. Although traditional psychological factors continued to shape social patterns, new technologies offered ways other than propinquity for people to encounter and contact others who shared interests or appealed to them. The Internet expanded people's awareness of, and immediate access to, other cultures despite physical distances. Communication technology—especially cell phones, Blackberries, and iPhones—provided people the ability to contact friends, either vocally or by texting and e-mail, regardless of location or time. These communication forms often affected social relationships: people sometimes focused on texting and responding to electronic messages rather than interacting with people around them. Researchers have considered the psychological impact of the interference of digital communication with school, work, or sleep.

People formed affiliations by participating in virtual chat boards, support groups, or other Internet forums. Many people joined Internet dating sites to meet potential romantic partners in their communities or elsewhere. Some people designed avatars to represent them when gaming online or responding to blogs to communicate with virtual friends. The anonymity of the Internet enabled people to portray themselves, often deceptively, in ways they might be unable to in non-Internet affiliations. Abrupt familiarity often quickened the formation of friendships and sometimes presented emotional and, occasionally, physical dangers.

Social networking sites, including MySpace and Facebook, transformed how people perceived friendships. Created in 2004, Facebook initially formed communities of university students before eventually allowing other users to join. Most users of social networks chose to share their profile and information, including their romantic status, publicly instead of activating privacy settings. Each member acquired links to friends; in this case the concept of a friend was anybody the member approved who had requested to be a friend. Although most members had friends who were acquaintances, relatives, or friends of friends, other members acquired friends with whom they had no previous affiliation.

Researchers recognize the value of digital data available on social networking websites as useful for psychological analysis of affiliation and friendship connections. Protocol for studying humans participating in online social networks is vague; institutions sponsoring research have established various demands for psychology researchers, including requiring some researchers to acquire site or member permission. Researchers could study Facebook members' public information to evaluate existing theories concerning popularity, self-esteem, identity, and relationships. For example, researchers at Harvard University and the University of California, Los Angeles used Facebook data to test a theory by Georg Simmel about triadic closure. Simmel hypothesized about friendships forming among an individual's friends but was unable to acquire data to analyze his premise.

S. Shyam Sundar, of the Pennsylvania State University Media Effects Research Laboratory, studied how Facebook members' friend quantities shape people's opinions of those members' possible psychological strengths or flaws. Eliot R. Smith, an Indiana University psychological and brain sciences specialist, secured a National Science Foundation grant to use Facebook data to interpret the processes involved in romances developing between strangers.

BIBLIOGRAPHY

Comer, Ronald, and Elizabeth Gould. *Psychology around Us*. 2nd ed. Hoboken: Wiley, 2013. Print.

Deaux, Kay, and Mark Snyder. *The Oxford Handbook of Personality and Social Psychology.* New York: Oxford UP, 2012. Print.

Ellison, Nicole B., Charles Steinfield, and Cliff Lampe. "The Benefits of Facebook 'Friends': Social Capital and College Students' Use of Online Social Network Sites." *Journal of Computer-Mediated Communication* 12.4 (2007): 1143–68. Print.

Gackenbach, Jayne, ed. *Psychology and the Internet: Intrapersonal, Interpersonal, and Transpersonal Implications*. 2nd ed. Amsterdam: Academic, 2007. Print.

Harré, Rom, and Fathali M. Moghaddam, eds. *The Psychology of Friendship and Enmity.* Santa Barbara: Praeger, 2013. Print.

Harvey, John H., and Ann L. Weber. *Odyssey of the Heart: Close Relationships in the Twenty-First Century.* 2d ed. Mahwah: Erlbaum, 2002. Print.

Helgeson, Vicki S., Kerry A. Reynolds, Adam Shestak, and Stephanie Wei. "Brief Report: Friendships of Adolescents with and without Diabetes." *Journal of Pediatric Psychology* 31.2 (2006): 194–99. Print.

Hendrick, Clyde, and Susan S. Hendrick, eds. *Close Relationships: A Sourcebook.* Thousand Oaks: Sage, 2000. Print.

Ling, Rich. "Life in the Nomos: Stress, Emotional Maintenance, and Coordination via the Mobile Telephone in Intact Families." *The Cell Phone Reader: Essays in Social Transformation.* Ed. Anandam Kavoori and Noah Arceneaux. New York: Lang, 2006. 61–84. Print.

Mackey, Eleanor Race, and Annette M. La Greca. "Adolescents' Eating, Exercise, and Weight Control Behaviors: Does Peer Crowd Affiliation Play a Role?" *Journal of Pediatric Psychology* 32.1 (2007): 13–23. Print.

Rose, Amanda J., Wendy Carlson, and Erika M. Waller. "Prospective Associations of Co-Rumination with Friendship and Emotional Adjustment: Considering the Socioemotional Trade-Offs of Co-Rumination."

Developmental Psychology 43.4 (2007): 1019–31. Print.

Taylor, Shelley E. "Tend and Befriend: Biobehavioral Bases of Affiliation under Stress." *Current Directions in Psychological Science* 15.6 (2006): 273–277. Print.

Valkenburg, Patti M., Jochen Peter, and Alexander P. Schouten. "Friend Networking Sites and Their Relationship to Adolescents' Well-Being and Social Self-Esteem." *CyberPsychology and Behavior* 9.5 (2006): 584–590. Print.

Affiliation motive

Type of psychology: Motivation

The affiliation motive is the tendency for individuals within a society to form groups or associations that are recognized components of the society's cultures. Affiliation may be based on cooperation, friendship, mutual interests, age, sex, protection, acquisition of physical resources, or social pressures to conform; affiliations transcend the usual kinship organizational structures of most societies.

Key Concepts

- Afflilation
- Aggregation
- Altruism
- Association
- Caste
- Dominance hierarchy
- Drive
- Incentive
- Kinship

INTRODUCTION

Social behavior is a characteristic of animals with highly developed nervous systems, in particular the vertebrates (mammals, birds, reptiles, amphibians, and fish) and the invertebrate social insects (ants and termites). In all these species, there are behaviors that are exclusively instinctive (endogenous); however, in mammals and birds, the process of learning from environmental experiences (exogenous behaviors) becomes pronounced. In mammalian and bird species, complex social interactions have evolved in which individuals aggregate and work together for the benefit of the group as a whole.

Such highly social species form aggregations composed of both males and females. These aggregations usually are either migratory, as the individuals of the aggregate search for food, or territorial, in areas of abundant food supply. Aggregation can be defined as a grouping of members of a species for mutual protection and acquisition of resources. Social aggregation is thus designed to find food for the sustenance of the group, to reproduce, and to protect the group members from predators. Single individuals or very small groups generally have more difficulty in finding food and in defending themselves than do large groups. This easily can be seen in birds or cattle, which flock or herd, respectively, at the approach of a predator.

DOMINANCE HIERARCHIES

Within such aggregates or societies, male and female associations develop; both associations are based on dominance hierarchies. Association can be defined as an accepted social organization into which individuals affiliate based on common interests for the attainment of the society's cultural goals.

A dominance hierarchy, or pecking order, is a precisely ranked ordering of individuals from most dominant to most subordinate. Dominance hierarchies are important features of practically all mammalian and avian (bird) societies. They are dynamic social structures that are constantly changing because of continual interactions, encounters, and conflicts between individuals and groups of individuals. Several less powerful males may cooperate to usurp the power of the dominant male, for example. Young males or females usually start at the bottom of a dominance hierarchy and gradually work their way up the scale of dominance. Older individuals, as they weaken, generally fall down the dominance scale because of intergroup competition. The overall format of the dominance hierarchy guarantees the best territory, the most mates, the most abundant and best food supply, and the best protection from predators for the most dominant individuals. The most subordinate individuals usually have the worst territory, few if any mates, poor nutrition, and great susceptibility to predation.

Such dominance hierarchies permeate human societies, although their presence is often subtle within the context of extremely complex social and cultural systems. Human societies, whether primarily technological, agricultural, or hunting, consist of institutions, organizations, religions, clubs, and other groups with which individuals are affiliated. To some extent, many of these groups serve the same purposes as groups in other animal societies: food assimilation, reproduction, and protection from predators, enemies, or other "undesirable" people. Human societies, however, employ unique rationales for individual affiliation. Affiliation is defined as the joining of an individual to a group of individuals, many of whom may be unrelated, based on such things as cooperation, mutual interests, friendship, age, gender, and protection.

The affiliation motive behind an individual's joining a particular group lies within all these factors. Nevertheless, lurking beneath these factors are some very basic sociobiological principles. It is to the individual's advantage to affiliate with other individuals. Through interactions with others, one can assert one's position within the existing dominance hierarchy, thereby gaining recognition for oneself not only in terms of dominance relationships but also in terms of meeting the society's views of acceptable behavior. Outcasts and other individuals who fail to affiliate within the accepted social institutions are frowned on by their peers and are subject to prejudicial treatment and perhaps social exclusion. Antisocial behavior is strongly discouraged and is punished in many societies.

The dominance hierarchy is, without question, a major evolutionary adaptation for the survival of social animal species. In every association of individuals, the dominance hierarchy is expressed in the power structure of the group, as well as in peer pressure aimed at forcing all societal members to conform. Conformity means affiliation with acceptable societal groups and submission to the dominance hierarchy.

SOCIAL MOTIVES

An individual's drive, or motivation, to affiliate with other individuals may be attributable to common interests or characteristics, but often this drive is tempered by social pressures to conform to the stability of the existing dominance structure. In many instances, the motivation to affiliate is influenced by societal incentives—a motivating force or system of rewards that is presented to people if they behave or successfully perform specified tasks according to the norms of society. Affiliation with some groups may bring prestige, a better standard of living, and other benefits. Such affiliations usually are easier when kinship with group members exists. (Kinship is the primary social organizing force in many human and animal societies, based on the relatedness of individuals.) Otherwise, the individual may have to make certain sacrifices.

Human social groups include organizations such as elitist country clubs, social clubs, sport-related clubs, special-interest groups (gem clubs, astronomy clubs), professionally related organizations, women's clubs, men's clubs, teen groups, elderly groups, churches, volunteer rescue squads and fire departments, and sports teams. Even youth gangs, mobsters, and hate groups fall within such categories. Affiliation is a social behavior in which practically everyone participates in some way, either willingly or unwillingly.

One phenomenon of affiliation behavior that is prevalent in numerous groups is altruism, an unselfish contribution on the part of an individual for others even if they are not genetically related to the individual. Altruism occurs in numerous species, although it usually occurs between related individuals. Humans exhibit an unusual level of altruism even toward unrelated individuals. There is some philosophical debate over whether such behavior in humans is truly unselfish. A number of investigators seek other underlying motives in such behavior and dismiss the notion that people help others purely out of a sense of caring. For example, up until extremely recently on the evolutionary calendar, humans lived in clans and were related to every other human with whom they came in contact.

Affiliation motives, therefore, are based on mutual interest and characteristics between people, altruistic behavior, and peer pressure associated with existing social dominance hierarchies. Affiliation is an important component of the stable structuring of society. It is of major concern in specific cases when individuals are barred from groups because of intelligence, family background, political affiliation, religious beliefs, race, or personal wealth.

STUDY OF AFFILIATION

Affiliation is a major subject of study for psychologists, sociologists, and sociocultural anthropologists. A critical behavior in the formation of the complex societies that characterize mammalian and bird species, it is very pronounced in human societies. Psychologists and anthropologists study group associations in many different human societies, comparing the characteristics of these different groups to ascertain the importance of affiliation and other group interactions in the development of the individual, the development of culture, and the evolution of human civilization. Studies are also made of group behaviors in primates and other closely related species to arrive at the sequence of evolutionary events leading to group adaptations.

Affiliation motives and drives reveal the psychological background of various individuals and, as a result, enable the researcher to understand differences between people in achievement of goals. Such knowledge can be of great value in uncovering the psychological and physical blocks that prevent some people from reaching their maximum intellectual and physical potential. Dominance hierarchies, while representing a central, structured component of practically all societies, are stumbling blocks to many people. Understanding how they operate can be of great use in assisting the smooth, nonviolent interaction of differing peoples. It also can be used to unravel the roots of antisocial behavior.

CULTURAL DIFFERENCES AND SIMILARITIES

Social and cultural anthropologists have studied the structure and organization of hundreds of different societies throughout the world. These societies exhibit many of the same social processes and patterns of organized behavior. They all exhibit dominance hierarchies, acceptable rules of individual and group behavior, and strong orderliness based on kinship. Some such societies (Hindu, for example) relegate their members to separate castes, permanent divisions based on genetic inheritance and particular trades. In advanced technological societies, large populations, fast-paced lifestyles, and high regional mobility result in social structures based less on kinship and more on other factors, such as mutual interests, age, gender, and race.

The study of social groups and affiliation motives for such groups provides an informative analysis of human social evolution within the context of rapidly changing societies. The psychological impact of such changes on the individual and on the group as a whole can provide an understanding of societal problems such as crime, social inequality, and intergroup tensions. Underlying all these situations is the natural biological tendency for individuals to aggregate for the common good of all members, thereby reducing the chance of danger to individual members. Humans, like all animals, have a need to interact and associate with other members of their own species. The drive to affiliate is related to the need for acceptance and the subsequent goals of recognition, power, protection, and mating.

MOTIVATIONAL THEORIES

Societal pressures to conform and to affiliate are great. Numerous psychologists have propounded theories describing the psychological bases behind an individual's motives to affiliate with other individuals. These theories are in agreement as to the goals of affiliation—objectives such as friendship, mutual interests, mating, acquiring food, and ensuring protection. These theories differ, however, in the psychological mechanisms behind the affiliation motive.

Among the most famous of these motivational theories is one that comes from the work of the psychoanalytical pioneer Sigmund Freud. Freud proposed that all motivational drives within an individual center on two principal components of the individual psyche: the libido and the Eros instinct. The libido is an aspect of one's psychological makeup whose prime focus is sexual reproduction, whereas the Eros instinct is one's inner need to survive. The libido could actually be seen as a component of Eros, which would then be the need to survive and to reproduce. Influenced by Darwinian evolutionary theory, Freud for much of his career maintained that all motives, including the affiliation motive, are aimed at satisfying one's sexual and survival needs. In his later work, however, he discovered a new instinct, Thanatos, or the death drive, which he described as self-directed aggression resulting from an inability to channel aggression outward at others and a consequent need to redirect it against the self.

The analytical psychologists Kurt Goldstein and Abraham Maslow maintained that an individual's psyche organizes itself about a tiered arrangement of personal needs and goals. These tiers include basic bodily needs such as food and protection, the need to be loved, and " self-actualization."According to their theories, different individuals focus on different aspects of these psychological needs. They further maintained that one's psychological needs all emerge from the need for self-actualization, the need to be recognized as an important member of society. Psychological disorders were believed to occur as a result of conflicts within these inner needs.

Other theories of social involvement and motivation include those of Carl Jung and Alfred Adler. Jung concentrates on individuals as being introverts or extroverts. Adler concentrates on inferior people overcompensating to become superior, with inferiority complexes arising when inferior individuals choose socially unacceptable means of becoming superior. All these theories and others employ many of the same basic concepts. They generally center on basic instinctive desires (sexuality, food acquisition, protection from danger) and the need for recognition (dominance, personal achievement). Consequently, they reflect the biological basis of behavior that has evolved in animals over the past few hundred million years.

ROLE OF SOCIOBIOLOGY

The psychological theories of motivation and the cultural manifestations of association and affiliation fall within the domain of sociobiology, a branch of biological thought advanced by numerous behaviorists and analytical psychologists that has been considerably refined and compellingly presented by Harvard University entomologist Edward O. Wilson. The motive of individual affiliation in any animal society, including human society, is the achievement of personal and group needs, which essentially boil down to views of survival and reproduction similar to those expressed by Freud.

Psychology and animal behavior have isolated the basis of affiliation and of behavior as one's instinctive needs as a living organism. This rationale stems from the fact that humans are animals and are the products of billions of years of evolutionary change on Earth. The nature of all life is to survive and to reproduce. Therefore, the activities of all organisms are centered on the achievement of these goals. In sociobiological theory, animal behavior and animal societies are driving forces in the survival, reproduction, and evolution of any given animal species. This theory has produced much controversy and debate; however, there is considerable evidence supporting it.

Affiliation is one of the foci of social behavior. Animals have a need to associate with other individuals of their own species. In so doing, they ensure their own safety and enhance their own reproductive potential. An individual's behavior is directed toward these ends. Another sociobiological viewpoint is that of the "selfish gene," a concept developed by modern molecular biologists and advanced by Richard Dawkins in his 1976 book of that name. The selfish gene concept maintains that evolution occurs at the level of the gene and that individual organisms are the means by which genetic information is copied and transmitted to future generations. All aspects of the organism and populations of organisms are geared to this end. Biochemical changes within an individual's nervous and endocrine systems facilitate such motivations. The physiology of motivation is an object of intense study.

BIBLIOGRAPHY

Carter, C. Sue, I. Izja Lederhendler, and Brian Kirkpatrick, eds. *The Integrative Neurobiology of Affiliation*. Cambridge: MIT P, 1999. Print.

Chagnon, Napoleon A. *Yanomamo: The Fierce People*. 5th ed. Belmont: Wadsworth, 1996. Print.

Eidse, Faith, and Nina Sichel, eds. *Unrooted Childhoods: Memoirs of Growing Up Global*. Yarmouth: Intercultural, 2004. Print.

Hall, Edward Twitchell. *The Hidden Dimension*. 1966. Reprint. New York: Anchor, 1990. Print.

Hill, Craig A. "Affiliation Motivation." *Handbook of Individual Differences in Social Behavior*. Ed. Mark R. Leary and Rick H. Hoyle. New York: Guilford, 2009. 410–25. Print.

Manning, Aubrey, and Marion Stamp Dawkins. *An Introduction to Animal Behavior*. 6th ed. New York: Cambridge UP, 2012. Print.

Skinner, B. F. *Science and Human Behavior*. 1953. Reprint. Delray: Classics of Medicine Library, 2000. Print.

Vela-McConnell, James A. *Who Is My Neighbor? Social Affinity in a Modern World*. Albany: State U of New York P, 1999. Print.

David Wason Hollar, Jr.

See Also: Achievement motivation; Adler, Alfred; Adlerian psychotherapy; Afflilation and friendship; Aggression; Freud, Sigmund; Groups; Motivation; Self; Self-actualization; Social identity theory; Social networks; Social perception.

African Americans and mental health

Type of psychology: Multicultural psychology; Psychopathology; Psychotherapy

The study of the mental health of African Americans has frequently been influenced by negative and stereotypic views of this population. The diagnosis and treatment of mental health problems among African Americans has evolved from practices based on dysfunctional and deficient models to ones based on an acceptance and understanding of this population's cultural differences.

Key Concepts

- African American
- Black
- Colored
- Dysfunctional, deficient, and different models
- Eugenics
- Jim Crow laws

- Multiculturalism
- Negro
- Psychometrics
- Racial identity

INTRODUCTION

According to the 2010 US Census, 13.6 percent of the United States population—just over 42 million people—identify themselves as African American (including more than 3 million African Americans of mixed race). The majority of black people in the United States are descendants of African slaves. In the past, African Americans were actively oppressed and discriminated against, which affected the way in which mental illnesses in members of this group were viewed, diagnosed, and treated.

The first Africans arrived in Virginia in 1619 as indentured servants. However, the system of indentured servitude did not last for Africans after the profits to be had from slave trading became apparent. As more Europeans settled in the colonies, the demand for a cheap labor force increased. From the mid-seventeenth through the eighteenth centuries, more than 6 million people were forcibly removed from Africa and sold as slaves. The slave trade was outlawed in the United States in 1808 but continued illegally. Slavery officially ended in 1865; however, Jim Crow laws in the South introduced *de jure* segregation in public facilities. Through the efforts of the twentieth-century civil rights movement, Jim Crow laws were gradually repealed. From 1965 to 1968, President Lyndon B. Johnson signed into law several bills, including the Civil Rights Act and the Voting Rights Act, that prohibited discrimination against African Americans in housing, education, employment, and voting.

An awareness of the legacy of discrimination and ongoing racism is critical to understanding African American mental health issues. The years of slavery and discrimination, as well as continuing prejudice against people of color in American society, have had a lasting impact on the mental health of African Americans.

For much of American history, African Americans were referred to as "negroes" and "colored." The black community began to reject these terms during the civil rights movement. In the 1960s and 1970s, African Americans adopted the terms "Afro-American" and "black" to describe themselves, in celebration of their rich heritage and to promote the idea that having black skin was a positive rather than a negative characteristic. In the 1980s, many blacks began to embrace the term "African American." For the 2010 US Census, the terms "black" and "African American" were used to describe this group, and these terms have come to be used interchangeably. The evolution of this terminology is often viewed as evidence of the black community's embracing a positive racial identity. Racial identity refers to the recognition and acceptance of one's self as a racial being in a society that often discriminates based on racial group membership. A positive black racial identity has been found to protect individuals against some of the negative consequences of racism, and it is viewed a positive indicator of mental health.

Photo: iStock

HISTORICAL OVERVIEW

Early models of mental health were not sensitive to cultural differences and often stereotyped blacks as being morally and intellectually inferior. Blacks were seen as inherently dysfunctional. Later models saw blacks as culturally deficient, which suggested that acculturation to mainstream white culture would "cure" them. Modern models of mental health embrace the differences model, which promotes acceptance of cultural differences and seeks to incorporate a more culturally sensitive view in the diagnosis and treatment of mental illnesses. This model examines how social, cultural, political, and economic factors affect mental illness. This mental health model has ushered in psychology's fourth force, multiculturalism.

Early examples of the "culturally deficient" model's influence on mental health diagnoses include the psychological disorder drapetomania. This disorder, which affected only slaves, was defined as "the disease causing Negroes to run away" from their owners. The treatment for this disorder, once it was determined that the disease had progressed to the stage of actually running away, as opposed to the mere desire to do so, was more frequent whipping. Further treatment guidelines included keeping slaves in a submissive state and treating them like children.

The study of African Americans' mental health was often obscured by questionable methodology. For example, in a nineteenth-century study of black rates of insanity, the data were manipulated to demonstrate that blacks in the North had higher rates of insanity than blacks in the South did. The conclusion was that freedom drove blacks crazy. Much of the early knowledge of blacks' mental health came from slave owners' accounts. Early twentieth-century studies of mental illness among blacks relied on severely mentally ill, hospitalized patients. Findings based on a limited number of hospitalized blacks were used to make broad generalizations about the entire population of African Americans. These studies were also used to support the view that mental illness occurred at higher rates among blacks than whites. At the time these studies were performed, the field of psychiatry had not developed a standardized method for diagnoses or specific diagnostic categories.

Sir Francis Galton was a nineteenth-century psychometrician and eugenicist. He studied racial differences on intelligence tests. In Galton's time, psychometrics was the field concerned with developing tests to measure personality traits, intellectual ability, and psychological attitudes. Eugenicists believed that the lighter-skinned white race was genetically, intellectually, and morally superior to darker-skinned races. Galton claimed that those with African ancestry were significantly below Anglo-Saxons in the normal frequency distribution of general mental ability. Early proponents of eugenics supported sterilization and selective breeding of blacks to decrease and control their numbers in the population. The thinking was that through selective breeding, eugenicists could reduce the intellectual inferiority of blacks, which was thought to contribute to immoral behavior, and that sterilization would prevent any increase in the number of blacks in the population, which would weaken the national gene pool. Eugenics was often used as an attempt to defend racism on the basis of science. Racial differences on tests of intelligence were often used to justify the disproportional placement of black children in special education courses. Although ethnic differences on tests of intelligence continue to be controversial areas of study, it is generally accepted that racial or ethnic performance differences on tests of intelligence are caused by environmental factors such as nutrition, access to quality education, richness of the early home environment, and other environmental factors.

By the mid-1970s, diagnostic criteria for mental disorders had been established and helped scientists develop more objective research methodologies. The National Institute of Mental Health conducted the Epidemiologic Catchment Area (ECA) program (1980–85), the largest study of mental illness of its kind up to that time. The program examined the incidence and prevalence of various types of mental illness among different populations. The study found that there was little variation in psychological disorders and rates of substance abuse by race. These findings have been replicated multiple times.

CONTRIBUTING SOCIOECONOMIC FACTORS

Various social, political, and economic factors significantly affect what types of mental distress are experienced by African Americans. Although the majority of African Americans are not poor, a significant number fall below the government's official poverty line. Some 24 percent of African American families live in poverty, compared with 13 percent of families in the United States as a whole, and 8 percent of non-Hispanic white Americans. Rates of unemployment are also higher among African Americans than among whites. Higher rates of mental illness are correlated with lower socioeconomic status, higher rates of violence, and lower attention paid to mental health treatment. Blacks have higher rates of divorce, separation, and never-married status when compared with other ethnic groups. Black children are more likely to live in households headed by a woman, which are more likely to be poor or experience continual economic hardship. More than 20 percent of blacks do not have health insurance, although most blacks are employed. Black men have higher incarceration rates than any other ethnic group, and African Americans are disproportionately represented among the homeless population (40 percent of the homeless are black). These demographic conditions significantly affect rates of mental illness within the population.

African Americans underutilize mental health services. Only one-third of African Americans with a mental illness get care. The percentage of African Americans receiving care is half that of non-Hispanic whites. Because of the historic negative treatment of blacks by medical and mental health professionals, many blacks are reluctant to seek professional treatment for mental disorders. African Americans are more likely to use emergency services or seek services from their primary care physicians than from a mental health professional, and they typically seek care after the mental illness has reached a crisis point. An increase in the number of African American mental health professionals could positively affect the scientific study of this group, its utilization rates of existing mental health services, and how this population deals with mental health issues.

CURRENT RATES OF MENTAL ILLNESS

Rates of mental illness among African Americans are similar to those among whites; however, differences exist for specific mental illnesses. For example, African Americans are less likely than other races to suffer from major depression and have lower rates of suicide, except for young black men (ages thirteen to twenty-four), among whom suicide rates are rising. Simple phobias and somatization are more common in blacks (15 percent) than in whites (9 percent). Compared with the general population, African Americans are more likely to be exposed to violence, which affects the rates at which they are affected by post-traumatic stress disorder and depression.

African American youths have lower rates of tobacco, alcohol, and other illicit drug use than either whites or Hispanics do. However, when African American youths abuse substances, they are more likely to suffer negative social consequences (such as expulsion from school) than members of other ethnic groups.

BIASES AND DISPARITIES

When compared with whites who exhibit the same symptoms, African Americans are more likely to be diagnosed with schizophrenia. Blacks are also more likely than whites to be improperly diagnosed when suffering from affective disorders such as depression.

African Americans have higher rates of diabetes, stroke, obesity, and cardiac disease than other ethnic groups. These medical conditions have been linked to genetic factors as well as the high levels of stress often experienced by this population. African Americans also have a lower life expectancy (75.1 years in 2010) when compared with white Americans (78.9 years).

BIBLIOGRAPHY

Belgrave, Faye Z., and Kevin W. Allison. *African American Psychology: From Africa to America.* 2nd ed. Los Angeles: Sage, 2009. Print.

Cross, William E., Jr. *Shades of Black: Diversity in African American Identity.* Philadelphia: Temple UP, 1991. Print.

David, E. J. R., ed. *Internalized Oppression: The Psychology of Marginalized Groups.* New York: Springer, 2013. Print.

Guthrie, Robert V. *Even the Rat Was White: A Historical View of Psychology.* New York: Harper & Row, 1976. Print.

Hill, Nancy E., Tammy L. Mann, and Hiram E. Fitzgerald. *African American Children and Mental Health*. Santa Barbara: Praeger, 2011. Print.

McAdoo, Harriette Pipes. *Black Families.* 4th ed. Thousand Oaks: Sage , 2007. Print.

Neville, Helen A., and Jessica M. Walters. "Contextualizing Black Americans' Health." *Counseling American Minorities*. Ed. Donald Atkinson. 6th ed. New York: McGraw-Hill, 2004. Print.

Tatum, Beverly D. "Why Are All the Black Kids Sitting Together in the Cafeteria?" *and Other Conversations about Race*. New York: Basic, 1997. Print.

Katherine M. Helm

See Also: Abnormality: Biomedical models; Abnormality: Psychological models; Biracial heritage and mental health; Cross-cultural psychology; Culture and diagnosis; Genetics and mental health; Homelessness: Psychological causes and effects; Intelligence tests; Multicultural psychology; Race and intelligence; Racism; Scientific methods; Violence: Psychological causes and effects.

Ageism

Type of psychology: Developmental psychology

Ageism refers to prejudice and discrimination directed toward people because they are elderly. These negative attitudes and perceptions affect the ways that individuals and society treat the elderly and may determine people's own reactions to growing older.

Key Concepts

- Discrimination
- Gerontophobia
- Negative ageism
- Positive ageism
- Prejudice
- Prevalence
- Stereotyping

INTRODUCTION

The term ageism was coined by Robert Butler, the first director of the National Institute on Aging. Like racism and sexism, ageism involves prejudice and discrimination directed toward a specific segment of the population. When someone claims that African Americans are inferior to whites or that females are less intelligent than males, the listener usually realizes that racist and sexist attitudes are being presented. Many persons, however, will accept the notion that the aged are senile, asexual, inflexible, poverty-stricken, and incapable of learning, without recognizing the prejudicial nature of such statements. In most instances, the stereotypical elderly person is viewed negatively; the prevailing attitude in the United States is that young is good and old is inferior. According to sociologist Erdman Palmore, ageism differs from racism and sexism in two major ways: All people become targets of ageism if they live long enough, and people are often not aware that ageism exists.

Surveys and other research indicate that ageist attitudes are widely held in American culture. Any attitude must be learned, and there are many sources available in American society. On television and in motion pictures, there are comparatively few older characters. The few older persons portrayed are typically depicted as either bumbling, forgetful souls who beget laughter and ridicule (negative ageism) or saintly paragons of virtue who possess great wisdom (positive ageism). Neither portrayal is realistic. In actuality, these are stereotypes that correspond to the attributes most commonly assumed to apply to old persons. Magazines and television present innumerable images of healthy, attractive young adults laughing, exercising, dancing, playing sports, and generally having a good time. It is not surprising that children begin to associate youth with goodness and old age with decrepitude.

The media also report cases of elderly persons who are found living in isolation, abandoned by relatives, and who are so poor that they resort to eating things such as cat food. Such cases are news precisely because of their rarity. There are destitute older persons, but reports produced by the federal government indicate that the percentage of aged persons (those above sixty-five years of age) below the official poverty line is actually less than the impoverished percentage of the general population. The elderly poor tend to be persons who have been impoverished for most of their lives. According to Palmore, a minority of the elderly are actually lonely and deserted by relatives; surveys indicate that most older persons live within a thirty-minute drive of at least one child and have frequent contact with offspring. Also, fewer than 10 percent of those over the age of sixty-five report that they do not have enough friends. Only about 5 percent of the aged are in nursing homes at any one time.

AGE AND AGEISM

Children and others hear many jokes told about the aged. Analysis indicates that these jokes are usually derogatory and concern topics such as sexual behavior, physical ailments, and cognitive deficits. As is the case with ethnic jokes, whether the jokes are funny depends on the listener. People seldom laughs at jokes that ridicule their own social group, unless they are told by other members of that group; persons who are racist or ageist, however, will find these jokes amusing and perhaps perceive them as being accurate.

Another factor in the ubiquity of ageism is that there may be less contact with the elderly in modern life than there was in the past. Families are more mobile today, and the extended family, in which several generations live in the same dwelling, is much less common. Many youngsters grow up in nuclear families without interacting extensively with aged persons; those with such limited contact are very likely to believe the ageist notions presented by others or by the media. In contrast, persons who have close relationships with several older individuals usually realize that most aged individuals are healthy and productive.

A 2000 study by Melinda Kennedy and Robin Montvilo indicated that children who have close contact with older adults on a regular basis are more likely to view the elderly in a positive manner than are children who have infrequent contact with the elderly. Degree of daily contact in adults did not seem to influence attitudes toward the elderly. Education to improve attitudes toward aging and the elderly therefore appears more useful in the young.

Ageism is not restricted to young persons or the uneducated. Ageist attitudes are often maintained even into old age. Ironically, this means that some older people may be prejudiced against their own age group. Resolution of this dilemma often focuses on these individuals' refusal to label themselves as "old" or "elderly." Age identification studies typically find that the majority of persons over the age of sixty-five identify themselves as being "middle-aged." Even among subjects over eighty years of age, there is a considerable percentage (10 to 30 percent) who deny that they are "old." This denial allows the aging person to maintain ageist beliefs. Conversely, ageism may contribute to the denial. If one believes that old persons are all senile, and one is obviously not senile oneself, then it follows that one must not be old.

PHYSICIANS AND AGEISM

Research suggests that ageist attitudes have been prevalent even among physicians and other professionals. Until the late twentieth century, geriatrics, the branch of medicine that deals with disorders and diseases of the aged, was not a popular specialty among doctors. Robert Butler's *Why Survive? Being Old in America* (1975), demonstrates that the elderly have been given very low priority by physicians. In part, this is because physicians are paid more by private health insurers than they are by Medicare, the government health insurance program for people aged sixty-five and older. Additionally, younger adults are seen as having fewer health problems and taking less time to treat.

Less thorough physical examinations are given to older patients. Psychiatrists and clinical psychologists report very little contact with aged clients and may be prone to believe that older persons cannot really suffer from the same mental disorders that younger clients do or believe that they need to be treated with medication as a quick fix. Senility (an ambiguous term that is not a clinical diagnosis) is not a normal aspect of aging. Alzheimer's disease and other organic brain syndromes afflict only a small proportion of the aged.

Most cases of confusion and disorientation in the aged are produced by drug intoxication or poor blood circulation to the brain. Nevertheless, such patients may be viewed as suffering from irreversible disorders and given little professional attention other than medication, which often exacerbates the symptoms. In spite of the negative stereotypes associated with aging, by the beginning of the twenty-first century, many physicians were going into geriatrics to meet the increasing demand occasioned by the aging of baby boomers born in the middle of the twentieth century.

SOCIAL POLICY AND AGEISM

Varying beliefs and attitudes concerning the aging process have existed throughout the history of Western civilization. Indeed, in the Old Testament, longevity is granted to those who are faithful to God, and the elders are viewed as a source of great wisdom. Contemporary views toward aging, which typically are much more negative, have been influenced significantly by social policies. In an attempt to help end the Great Depression, the federal government initiated the Old Age and Survivors' Program (Social Security) in 1935 to encourage retirement and reduce unemployment among younger workers. This program was intended to help support people though the last three to four years of their lives. Medicare and Medicaid began in the mid-1960s. These measures served to identify older Americans as a homogeneous group of persons in need of special aid from the rest of society; old age thus became a distinct stage of development.

As mentioned previously, studies have found that the aged, as a group, are as well off financially as the general population (although often living on fixed incomes). Nevertheless, most states and the federal government grant tax relief in various forms to all aged citizens, rich and poor. Many businesses such as pharmacies, restaurants, and hotels give discounts to elderly customers. Some banks offer higher interest rates on savings and free checking to "senior citizens." Despite the fact that such practices might seem discriminatory against the young, there is little public protest. The general acceptance of these policies may be based on the mistaken belief that most aged persons are living in or near poverty.

Older persons often confront ageist attitudes when trying to obtain or continue employment. Widely held perceptions about the aged include the beliefs that they cannot learn new skills, miss many workdays because of illness, are prone to work-related accidents, and work significantly more slowly than do younger workers. Each of these notions is inaccurate, according to Palmore. Research involving a variety of occupations has determined that older persons are productive employees who actually have fewer accidents at work and miss fewer workdays than do younger workers. Although motor responses are slowed with age, most workers increase their productivity as a result of increased experience. Learning new skills does usually require slightly more time for older workers, but they can, and do, learn.

Despite these research findings, many employers have discriminated against older applicants and have refused to hire them because of their advanced age. In response, the US Congress passed the Age Discrimination in Employment Act (1967; ADEA), which outlaws age discrimination in hiring practices and sets seventy years as the age of mandatory retirement for most occupations. Fortunately, many companies have begun to realize the efficacy of older workers and have encouraged them to become employees. The "McMasters Program," established by the McDonald's fast-food restaurant chain, is one example of a business welcoming older applicants.

GERONTOPHOBIA

Gerontophobia—a fear of the elderly or of the aging process—is closely related to ageism. Believing that the aged are decrepit, lonely, and likely to be senile makes one fear growing older. Many companies produce products that play on this fear; indeed, these businesses have a financial stake in perpetuating gerontophobia. Commercial advertisements bombard consumers with messages indicating that to be old is to be ugly, and Americans spend enormous sums of money trying to look younger through cosmetic surgery, hair dye, "wrinkle removers," and so on. People are even encouraged by friends to try to look young. Many gerontologists, however, view these efforts as costly and futile; these procedures can alter one's appearance, but they do not stop or retard the aging process.

Gerontophobia may also reflect the association often made between old age and death. In the past, many babies and young persons died of infectious and communicable diseases. Infant mortality is much lower today, and life expectancy has increased dramatically. Therefore, death in old age is typical, and this fact may well increase the fear of growing old that many persons experience.

Ironically, holding ageist views may adversely affect one's own aging. Indeed, many psychologists think that beliefs or expectations may be self-fulfilling. More simply put, an expectation may affect one's behavior so that, eventually, one acts in accordance with the expectation. A common example involves sexual behavior. An ageist view persists that older persons are no longer sexually viable. Males, especially, seem to accept this notion and to worry about their sexual performance. If, for example, a sixty-year-old man does experience an inability to achieve orgasm during intercourse, he may attribute this "failure" to aging; he may then be extremely anxious during his next sexual episode. This anxiety may cause further sexual problems and preclude orgasm. Believing that he is now too old for sex, the man may even terminate coital activity. In contrast, if he attributes his initial problem to stress or some other transitory variable, then his future sexual behavior may be unimpeded, especially in a society that now has anti-impotence drugs such as Viagra available.

CHANGES IN AGEISM SINCE 1960

The late 1960s were years of tremendous political and social unrest, as numerous minority groups clamored for greater power and fairer treatment. The aged had been delineated as a special-interest group with distinct needs. As the aged began to be defined solely by their age, a group consciousness began to emerge. Older persons, as a group, are more interested in politics and more likely to vote than are their younger counterparts. Politicians became aware of and became more sensitive to elderly issues. Out of this milieu, Robert Butler helped make these concerns salient by inventing the term "ageism."

Ageism has been heightened by medical advances, as the concomitant increased life expectancy enjoyed in technologically advanced societies has altered views about aging. The life expectancy in the United States was more than seventy-eight years in 2011. Social Security and Medicare are thus available to people for more than a dozen years on the average. This places a financial strain on society and makes the elderly seem a burden.

As a higher percentage of people now live into old age, death has become increasingly associated with growing old. Without doubt, the fear of death causes some people to shun the elderly and to view them as being "different from us." To admit that one is old is tantamount to confronting one's own mortality squarely. Many gerontologists and sociologists argue that the United States is a death-denying society. Death is a taboo topic in most circles; the majority of deaths in the United States occur in institutions. The denial and fear of death may encourage ageist notions.

Palmore has developed a survey instrument consisting of twenty items to assess the types and prevalence of ageism in the United States today. The most frequent types of ageism found using this tool have been disrespect for older people and assumptions made about ailments and frailty caused by age. In an initial study, 77 percent of the elderly assessed reported having experienced ageism. This tool may be used to help reduce the prevalence of ageism in society by allowing it to be identified and by educating those in need.

Ageism may decline in the near future, simply because the median age of Americans is increasing. The baby boomers, a large and influential segment of society, are aging, and their impact is likely to be substantial. People in this age group have dramatically changed society as they have developed. When they were children, more schools had to be built, and education was emphasized. Their adolescence produced a rebellious period in the late 1960s and a lowering of the voting age. As young adults, they touched off a boom in construction, as many new houses were needed. As the baby boomers become senior citizens, their sheer numbers may cause a shift toward more positive attitudes toward the elderly. Also, more aged persons are maintaining good health and active lifestyles than in the past. This trend will undoubtedly help counteract stereotypical ideas about the infirmities of the elderly.

BIBLIOGRAPHY

Achenbaum, W. A. "Societal Perceptions of Aging and the Aged." *Handbook of Aging and the Social Sciences*. Ed. Robert H. Binstock and Linda George. 7th ed. Amsterdam: Elsevier/Academic, 2011. Print.

Birren, James E., and K. Warner Schaie, eds. *Handbook of the Psychology of Aging*. 7th ed. Boston: Elsevier Academic, 2011. Print.

Butler, Robert N. "Ageism." *The Encyclopedia of Aging*. Ed. G. Maddox. 2nd ed. New York: Springer, 1995. Print.

Butler, Robert N. *Why Survive? Being Old in America*. New York: Harper & Row, 1975. Print.

Ferraro, Kenneth F. "The Gerontological Imagination." Gerontology: *Perspectives and Issues*. New York: Springer, 1990. Print.

Friedan, Betty. *The Fountain of Age*. New York: Simon, 2006. Print.

Gullette, Margaret Morganroth. *Agewise: Fighting the New Ageism in America*. Chicago: U of Chicago P, 2011. Print.

Kennedy, Melinda J., and Robin Kamienny Montvilo. "Effects of Age and Contact on Attitudes toward Aging and the Elderly." *Gerontologist* 40 (2000): 147. Print.

Nelson, Todd D., ed. Ageism: Stereotyping and Prejudice against Older Persons. Cambridge: MIT P, 2002. Print.

Oberleder, Muriel. *Avoid the Aging Trap*. Washington, DC: Acropolis, 1982. Print.

Palmore, Erdman. *Ageism: Negative and Positive*. 2nd ed. New York: Springer, 1999. Print.

Charles H. Evans; updated by Robin Kamienny Montvilo

SEE ALSO: Aging: Cognitive changes; Aging: Physical changes; Aging: Theories; Alzheimer's disease; Elder abuse; Elders' mental health; Prejudice; Prejudice reduction; Racism; Retirement; Sexism

Aggression

TYPE OF PSYCHOLOGY: Biological bases of behavior; Emotion; Personality; Psychopathology

Aggression is an emotional response to frustration that often leads to angry and destructive actions directed against individuals, animals, or such organizations as corporate bureaucracies, social and religious groups, or governments.

KEY CONCEPTS

- Anger
- Defensive aggression
- Frustration
- Hostility
- Offensive aggression
- Predatory aggression
- Regression
- Social immaturity
- Socialization
- Stress
- Tantrum

INTRODUCTION

Aggression, as the term is applied to humans, occurs as an emotional reaction to dissatisfactions and stress, and it can result in behaviors that society considers antagonistic and destructive. The term as used in common parlance has broad meanings and applications. In psychological parlance, however, aggression generally refers to an unreasonable hostility directed against situations with which people must cope or think they must cope. On a simple and relatively harmless level, people may demonstrate momentary aggressive behavior if they experience common frustrations such as missing a bus, perhaps reacting momentarily by stamping their foot on the ground or mouthing an oath subvocally. The moment passes, and no one is hurt by this sort of aggression, which most people demonstrate with fair frequency as they deal with frustration in their daily lives.

People with tattered self-images may direct their aggression toward themselves, possibly in the form of expressing or thinking disparaging things about themselves or, in extreme cases, harming themselves physically, even to the point of suicide. Such internalized forms of aggression may remain pent up for years in people who bear their frustrations silently. Such frustrations may eventually erupt into dangerous behavior directed at others, leading to assaults, verbal or physical abuse, and, in the most extreme cases, to massacres. Such was the case when Timothy McVeigh blew up the Alfred P. Murrah Federal Building in Oklahoma City on April 19, 1995, as an act of civil protest, killing 167 people, none of whom he knew.

Infants and young children make their needs known and have them met by crying or screaming, which usually brings them attention from whoever is caring for them. Older children, basing their actions on these early behaviors, may attempt to have their needs met by having tantrums, or uncontrolled fits of rage, in an effort to achieve their ends. In some instances, adults who are frustrated, through regression to the behaviors of infancy or early childhood, have tantrums that, while disconcerting, frequently fail to succeed in anything more than emphasizing their social immaturity. Socialization demands that people learn how to control their overt expressions of rage and hostility.

TYPES OF AGGRESSION

Hugh Wagner, a behavioral psychologist concerned with the biology of aggression, has identified three types: offensive aggression, defensive aggression and predatory aggression. Offensive aggression occurs when the aggressor initiates aggressive behavior against one or more nonaggressors. The response to offensive aggression is likely to be defensive aggression that generally takes the form of self-defense.

Predatory aggression differs from offensive or defensive aggression, although it is basically a form of offensive aggression. It is characterized by, for example, such phenomena as the lurking of predatory animals that make themselves as inconspicuous as possible until their prey is within striking distance. They then pounce on the prey with the intention of killing it as quickly as they can so that they can eat it. Among humans, hunters are examples of predatory aggressors, although not all contemporary hunters consume their prey.

BIOLOGICAL ROOTS OF AGGRESSION

Although aggressive acts are usually triggered by environmental factors, laboratory research suggests that aggression has biological roots. Various experiments point to the fact that the three basic types of aggression are controlled by different mechanisms in the midbrain. It has been demonstrated in laboratory animals that offensive aggression has intimate connections to neurons in the ventral tegmental area of the midbrain. When lesions occur in this section of the brain, offensive aggression decreases markedly or disappears altogether, although defensive and predatory aggression are not affected.

Conversely, when parts of the anterior hypothalamus are stimulated, offensive behavior increases and attack may ensue. The brain appears in these experiments to be programmed in such a way that defensive aggression is controlled by the periaqueductal gray matter (PAG) found in the midbrain. So specialized are the neural activities of the midbrain that defensive aggression involving perceived threats emanates from a different part of the brain than does defensive aggression that involves an actual attack. Acid-based amino neurons from the medial hypothalamus are known to trigger defensive aggression.

Alcoholic intake often intensifies aggressive behavior, because alcohol reduces the inhibitions that the cerebral cortex controls while stimulating the neural pathways between the medial hypothalamus and the PAG. Although alcohol does not increase aggressive behavior in all humans, many people react aggressively when they consume alcoholic beverages.

AGGRESSION AND BODY CHEMISTRY

In most species, including humans, males are more aggressive than females. This is thought to be because of the testosterone levels present in varying degrees in males. The higher the testosterone level, the more aggressive the male. Aggressive behavior that threatens the welfare of the species is often controlled in humans by medication that reduces the testosterone levels and pacifies aggressive males.

It is notable that young males tend to be considerably more aggressive than older males, presumably because as men age, their testosterone levels decrease considerably. Prisons are filled with young males unable to control their aggressions sufficiently to stay out of trouble with the law. Many of these prisoners mellow into relatively benign older men not because prison has reformed them but because their body chemistry has undergone significant changes through the years.

At one time, aggressive behavior was controlled by electric shock therapy (which is used at present in some extreme cases) or by the more drastic surgical procedure known as lobotomy. Lobotomies often left people in virtually catatonic states from which they could never emerge. Drugs and psychiatric treatment have replaced most of the more devastating procedures of the nineteenth and twentieth centuries.

ROAD RAGE AND AIR RAGE

Two of the most common forms of offensive aggression in contemporary society are road rage and air rage. Road rage, which generally occurs on crowded, multilane highways or freeways, is often experienced by otherwise civilized individuals who, when behind the wheel of a car that weighs well over a ton, are transformed into irrational monsters. If someone cuts them off in traffic, drives slowly in the lane ahead of them, or commits some other perceived roadway insult, perpetrators of road rage may bump the rear of the car ahead of them, pass the car and shoot at the offending driver, or force the offending driver off the road and onto the shoulder, where a fight, a stabbing, or a shooting may occur.

Air rage is somewhat different. Some people who have been flying for long periods in cramped conditions, often passing through several time zones, may suffer from disorientation. Often, this feeling is intensified by the consumption of alcohol before or during the flight. Such people, if refused another drink or if asked to return to their seats and buckle their seat belts, may strike out at flight attendants or at fellow passengers.

AGGRESSION IN ANIMALS

Although humans exhibit aggression in its most subtle and complicated forms, other species of animals also manifest aggressive behaviors. Most animals will fight if they are attacked because self-defense and self-preservation are inherent in most species. Within their own social constructs, some animals will attack those outside their group, even those of the same species, although few animals turn on their own species to nearly the extent that humans do. Carnivorous animals exhibit aggressiveness in preying on other animals as food sources, the large overpowering the small, the swift overtaking the slow, the strong killing and consuming the weak. Most animals also aggressively defend the areas in which they forage and build their nests or dens.

The less aggressive species of animals, notably poultry, cattle, and fish, have been domesticated by humans as sources of food. More aggressive animals are sometimes used in sports such as bullfighting or cockfighting. In these instances, the animals are taught aggressive behaviors that are not instinctive to most of them. They are trained to perform, and satisfactory performance on their part is rooted in aggression.

AGGRESSION AND PROCREATION

Aggressive behavior in nearly all species is rooted in sexuality. The male is usually more aggressive than the female. The sexual act is fundamentally an act of male aggression. Males during their sexual prime maintain the high levels of testosterone that assure the continuance of their species but that also result in aggressive, sometimes antisocial behavior.

The offensive aggression of one species, such as the predatory birds that feed on newborn turtles in the Galápagos Islands, evokes defensive aggressive behavior on the parts of those seeking to protect their young and to ensure the continuance of their species. The species that demonstrates defensive aggression in a situation of this sort may demonstrate offensive aggression in pursuing and attacking a weaker species. All of these aggressions among nonhumans are, in the final analysis, directed at preserving the species.

CAN HUMAN AGGRESSION BE CONTROLLED?

Aggression is so inherent in nearly every species that it is doubtful that it can ever be fully controlled, nor would it necessarily be desirable to control it. When aggression among humans reaches the point of threatening the social fabric, however, steps must be taken to control or, at least, to redirect it. The adolescent male who wants to beat everyone up probably is suffering from extreme anger. It may be possible to redirect this anger, which is a form of energy, into more socially acceptable channels. It may also be possible to control elements in the environment—home life, being bullied at school, being rejected by peers—in such ways as to reduce the anger and resentment that have led to aggressive behavior.

The management of aggression through psychotherapy and medication may prove effective. Aggressive individuals, however, may resist treatments that could succeed in controlling the socially unacceptable aggressive behavior in which they engage. Attempts to control aggression often run counter to the very nature of human beings as they pass through the various developmental stages of their lives.

BIBLIOGRAPHY

Anderson, Daniel R., et al. *Early Childhood Television Viewing and Adolescent Behavior.* Boston: Blackwell, 2001. The five coauthors of this valuable study seek to explore the roots of aggression in teenagers in terms of their exposure to violence through television viewing in their formative years.

Archer, John, and Kevin Browne. *Human Aggression: Naturalistic Approaches*. New York: Routledge, 1989. The approach is that of the social psychologist who is much concerned with environmental factors affecting aggression. A worthwhile book for the beginner.

Blanchard, Robert J., and Caroline D. Blanchard, eds. *Advances in the Study of Aggression.* New York: Academic Press, 1984. Dan Olweus's chapter, "Development of Stable Aggressive Reaction Patterns in Males," and John Paul Scott's chapter, "Advances in Aggression Research: The Future," are particularly compelling. The book as a whole is well constructed, although it may be more appropriate to those experienced in the field than to beginners.

Englander, E. K. *Understanding Violence*. Mahwah, N.J.: Lawrence Erlbaum, 1997. Presents a panoramic view of violence and human aggression, condensing effectively the major research in the field over the past half century.

Feshbach, Seymour, and Jolanta Zagrodzka, eds. *Aggression: Biological, Developmental, and Social Perspectives*. New York: Plenum, 1997. This comprehensive collection, although somewhat specialized, covers the two major factors in aggression (the biological roots and social determinants) thoroughly and accurately, interpreting recent research in the field extremely well.

Hoffer, Eric. *The True Believer: Thoughts on the Nature of Mass Movements.* New York: Harper & Row, 1951. One of the most compelling accounts of mass movements and their relation to aggressive behavior in individuals.

Lesko, Wayne A., ed. *Readings in Social Psychology: General, Classic, and Contemporary Selections.* 7th ed. Boston: Pearson/Allyn & Bacon, 2009. The discussion of aggression is clear and forthright. This resource is a desirable starting point for those who are not experienced in the field.

Lorenz, Konrad. *On Aggression.* Translated by Marjorie Kerr Wilson. Reprint. New York: Routledge, 2002. This classic and revolutionary study posits a killer instinct in both animals and humankind.

Scott, John Paul. *Aggression*. Chicago: University of Chicago Press, 1958. Although it is somewhat outdated, this book remains especially valuable for its discussion of the physiology of aggression and of the social causes of aggression. The book is well written and easily understandable for those who are new to the field.

Wagner, Hugh. *The Psychobiology of Human Motivation*. New York: Routledge, 1999. This resource explores productively possible biological origins of the three types of aggression: offensive, defensive, and predatory.

R. Baird Shuman

See also: Aggression: Reduction and control; Air rage; Alcohol dependence and abuse; Anger; Battered woman syndrome; Conduct disorder; Defense reactions: Species specific; Domestic violence; Elder abuse; Emotions; Fight-or-flight response; Hormones and behavior; Impulse control disorders; Inhibitory and excitatory impulses; Jealousy; Lobotomy; Misbehavior; Psychotic disorders; Road rage; Shock therapy; Stress: Behavioral and psychological responses; Violence and sexuality in the media; Violence by children and teenagers.

Aggression
Reduction and control

Type of psychology: Social psychology

Aggressive behavior has been a problem for humans since before the beginning of recorded history. Psychologists have developed many theories of aggression, and there are many different ideas as to how—or whether—aggression might be controlled.

KEY CONCEPTS

- Anger
- Defensive aggression
- Frustration
- Hostility
- Offensive aggression
- Predatory aggression
- Regression
- Social immaturity
- Socialization
- Stress
- Tantrum

INTRODUCTION

Aggression has been humankind's steady companion throughout history—in life, literature, and art. Many hypotheses have been suggested by psychologists and other scientists concerning the nature of aggression; some have suggested that it is learned behavior, others that it is an innate, genetically inherited drive. The fields of ethology and sociology have mustered evidence to support the evolutionary (genetic) basis of aggression. Theories based on these viewpoints hold that at some point in humankind's past, aggressiveness was an adaptive trait—that is, aggression helped ensure the survival of the individual who possessed that quality, thereby enabling the aggressive trait to be passed on to future generations. Social psychologists, on the other hand, have studied the effects of modeling aggressive behavior. When children, for example, have been exposed to aggressive behavior modeled (acted out or demonstrated in some way) by others, they have shown an increase in aggressive behavior. In other words, the children observe and learn the behavior. Albert Bandura's social learning theory describes this concept of aggression.

The frustration-aggression hypothesis, as described by John Dollard, holds that both violence and aggression are the result of being frustrated in an attempt to reach a goal. When basic needs have been thwarted, aggression appears. As Leonard Berkowitz states in *Roots of Aggression* (1969), "If a person is aggressive, he has been frustrated. If a person is frustrated, he has become aggressive." Negative environmental factors are also believed by many to have a major impact on aggression. Studies have found links, for example, between the number of violent crimes and air temperature. Overcrowding and economic hard times are also associated with higher crime rates. These studies tend to support negative affect theory, which holds that exposure to stimuli that create discomfort leads to aggression.

The amount of hope a person holds for the possibility of reducing or controlling aggression depends, to some extent, on the theory of aggression that the individual believes to be most accurate. If aggressive behavior is an integral part of the genetic makeup of the human species, the outlook is not nearly as promising as it is if aggression is primarily a behavior learned from others and reinforced by certain rewards. In the former case, aggressive actions can perhaps be controlled by societal strictures, but the aggressive instinct will always remain within. In the latter case, decreasing the modeling of aggression or increasing the modeling of and rewards for nonaggressive behavior could conceivably produce effective results. Different studies have produced different results concerning the effectiveness of various attempts to reduce aggressive behavior.

Another complication in understanding and controlling aggression is that different people will react very differently when in similar circumstances. When frustrated, some people will react aggressively, while others will become withdrawn and depressed. Depression itself can lead to aggression, however, and this type of delayed aggression can produce seemingly unpredictable acts of violence. Psychologists simply do not have all the answers to why some people react aggressively and others do not when faced with identical predicaments.

TREATMENT TECHNIQUES

Psychologists Matthew McKay, Martha Davis, and Patrick Fanning adapted Donald Meichenbaum's concept of stress inoculation training to produce one technique that allows aggressive people to control their own aggressive behavior. McKay and his colleagues present simple, concise, step-by-step directions to deal with aggression. Because aggression is often fueled by emotional distress, they offer a technique of "covert assertion" through the development of two separate skills: thought interruption and thought substitution. When becoming angry or frustrated, the potential aggressor thinks of the word "stop" or some other interrupting device. The void suddenly created is then filled with a reserve of previously prepared positive, nonaggressive thoughts. This technique can be mastered, these psychologist maintain, if it is practiced conscientiously throughout the day for three days to a week.

The creation of an aggression stimulants structure gives those who are compelled to be negatively aggressive the opportunity to take a personal inventory of who (or what) the targets of their aggression are, what the feelings associated with those people are, and what would occur if a plan of "attack" against them were to be put into action. This type of analysis lends itself well to self-accountability; it allows people to "own" the problem and to believe that it can be controlled if they choose to control it. It also allows, through its identification of specific targets and imaging of the act of aggression, a global perspective on what can otherwise seem a very fragmented problem.

Aggression in the work environment can be damaging and disruptive both for individuals and for organizations. In a 1987 article in the *Journal of Occupational Psychology*, Philip L. Storms and Paul E. Spector claim that high frustration levels of organizational employees were positively related to interpersonal aggression, sabotage, and withdrawal. Suggestions for dealing with aggression in the workplace have included such strategies as training courses and the use of humor to defuse tensions. Diane Lamplugh notes that aggression in this arena can range from whispered innuendo to harassment to violence. She maintains that a training course that focuses on tension control, relaxation techniques, customer-relations orientation, assertiveness practice, aggression-centered discussions, and self-defense training can be helpful. She also states that support from management in identifying problem areas and formulating guidelines for staff support is crucial. William A. Kahn promotes humor as a means for organizational members to make statements about themselves, their groups, or their organization. Humor, he notes, is a nonthreatening vehicle that allows people to say things that might otherwise insult or offend coworkers, thereby making them defensive and threatening working relationships.

Written or unwritten laws, rules, and codes of conduct are established in an attempt to curb unacceptably aggressive behavior. A company may terminate an employee who does not adhere to certain standards of behavior; athletes are benched for aggression or violence. Society as a whole formulates laws to control its members' aggressive behavior. When individuals act in ways that are damagingly aggressive to other people or to the property of others, law-enforcement agencies step in to safeguard the population. Perpetrators are fined or sentenced to prison terms.

Studies disagree as to the most effective means of rehabilitating offenders, but many studies do suggest that rehabilitation is possible. One avenue that is frequently explored is the use of various techniques founded in behaviorism. In *Psychological Approaches to Crime and Its Correction* (1984), edited by Irving Jacks and Steven G. Cox, Stanley V. Kruschwitz investigates the effectiveness of using a voluntary token reinforcement procedure to change the behavior of inmates who are difficult to manage. In the same volume, Albert F. Scheckenbach makes an argument for behavior modification as it relates to adult offenders. Modeling positive behaviors and holding group discussions have been found at least somewhat effective in rehabilitating juvenile delinquents, as has the development of behavioral contracts. John Lochman and his colleagues, using what they called an anger coping mechanism, explored cognitive behavioral techniques for reducing aggression in eleven-year-old boys. The boys treated with this procedure showed vast improvements—a reduction of disruptive classroom behavior and an increase in perceived social competence. Such techniques, used with young people, might reduce their high-risk status for later difficulties.

THEORETICAL EXPLANATIONS

Acts of aggression have been central in human history, myth, literature, and even religion. In the biblical account, for example, humankind has barely come into existence when Cain kills his brother Abel. Almost as old are questions concerning the causes of aggression and the debate over how to control it.

Sigmund Freud saw aggression as the result of struggles within the psyche of the individual. He believed that the tension produced in the struggle between the life instinct and the death instinct creates outward aggression. Alfred Adler, another psychodynamic theorist, stated that aggression represents the most general human striving and is a necessity of life; its underlying principle is self-assertion. Humanistic theorist Rollo May notes that attention to aggression has nearly universally focused on its negative aspects. In *Power and Innocence* (1972), May writes that "we have been terrified of aggression, and we assume— delusion though it is—that we can better control it if we center all our attention on its destructive aspects as though that's all there is."

It was first the behaviorist school, then the proponents of social learning theory (such as Albert Bandura), who explored ways to reduce and control aggression. The frustration-aggression hypothesis, for example, was developed in the 1930s. Behaviorists tended to approach aggressive behavior in terms of stimuli, responses, and reinforcement. In a general sense, any approaches that seek to punish unacceptably aggressive behavior or to reward positive behavior are related to the behavioral view. Bandura and other social learning theorists found that in some situations, children would respond to viewing aggressive acts by performing aggressive acts themselves. The implications of this have been widely argued and debated; one aspect concerns the effects of viewing violence in the media. Viewing violence on television and in films has been linked to increased aggressive behavior in some studies, although because of the nature of the types of studies most often performed, it can be difficult to draw incontestable cause-and-effect relationships.

CONTROLLING AGGRESSION

The debate over whether aggression is learned, innate, or both (and, if both, over the relative importance of the two aspects) is not likely to end soon. Debates over how to control aggression will also continue. As in many areas of psychology, bridging the gap between the theoretical and the practical is difficult.

Researchers in the behavioral and social learning schools have developed numerous methods of controlling aggression. Interventions to control aggression can be made at the individual and group levels. Individuals can learn to control their aggression through relaxation training, self-control training, communication skills training, contingency management, and psychotherapy. These techniques vary in the extent that they involve and rely on others. Relaxation training involves breathing techniques or meditation. Self-control training involves rational restructuring, cognitive self-instruction, and stress inoculation. It basically teaches people to make verbal statements to themselves reminding them to think first and respond in a less aggressive manner. It has been proven to work. Communication skills training focuses on methods of negotiation and conflict resolution. Contingency management involves the use of rewards for desired behavior and nonphysical punishment for undesired behaviors. Psychotherapy tries to find the root of the person's problem with aggression.

Group interventions, done in small groups, involve skill training as well as values, character, and moral education. Skills training educates people on how to use procedures such as modeling, behavioral rehearsal, and feedback on performance to manage their aggression. It has been shown to be effective. The other interventions typically take place in a school setting. All three seek to teach prosocial behavior to children and differ in the extent to which they teach students or let them discover on their own. Moral education teaches morality, and character education uses a series of lessons to foster prosocial character traits. Values clarification involves students in activities that help them identify and choose values.

In addition to these behavioral methods of controlling aggression, there are control methods based on biological or societal causes of aggression. These methods examine biological factors such as serotonin, hormones, and genetics and can involve pharmaceuticals as well as behavior therapy. Studies have found correlations, for example, between aggressiveness and high levels of norepinephrine and low levels of serotonin, two important neurotransmitters, although the significance of such chemical findings remains to be ascertained. The biological approach to fighting aggression involves the fields of neuroanatomy, neurochemistry, neuroendocrinology, genetics, and psychopathology. Another approach looks for an underlying mental condition such as a personality disorder. If the aggression is a symptom of such a disorder, then control of it becomes a matter of treating the mental condition. If the aggression occurs in a particular environment—bullying in a school, aggression or domestic violence in a family, fights in bars, or even war in the political arena—the efforts to control aggression take on a much wider approach, looking at societal and economic factors as well.

BIBLIOGRAPHY

Berkowitz, Leonard, ed. *Roots of Aggression*. New York: Atherton, 1969. Print.

Cavell, Timothy A., and Kenya T. Malcolm, eds. *Anger, Aggression, and Interventions for Interpersonal Violence*. Mahwah: Erlbaum, 2007. Print.

Forgas, Joseph P., Arie W. Kruglanski, and Kipling D. Williams, eds. *The Psychology of Social Conflict and Aggression*. New York: Psychology, 2011. Print.

Hewstone, Miles, Wolfgang Stroebe, and Klaus Jonas. *An Introduction to Social Psychology*. 5th ed. Chichester: Wiley, 2012. Print.

Hudley, Cynthia. *You Did That on Purpose: Understanding and Changing Children's Aggression*. New Haven: Yale UP, 2008. Print.

Krahé, Barbara. *The Social Psychology of Aggression*. 2nd ed. New York: Psychology, 2013. Print.

Martinez, Manuela, ed. *Prevention and Control of Aggression and the Impact on Its Victims*. New York: Kluwer Academic, 2001. Print.

May, Rollo. *Power and Innocence*. New York: Norton, 1998. Print.

Nelson, Randy J. *Biology of Aggression*. New York: Oxford UP, 2006. Print.

Simmons, Rachel. *Odd Girl Out: The Hidden Culture of Aggression in Girls.* San Diego: Harcourt, 2002. Print.

Denise S. St. Cyr

See Also: Adler, Alfred; Aggression; Anger; Bandura, Albert; Bullying; Child abuse; Domestic violence; Elder abuse; Freud, Sigmund; Genetics and mental health; Impulse control disorders; Instinct theory; May, Rollo; Media exposure and mental health; Psychoanalytic psychology and personality: Sigmund Freud; Violence and sexuality in the media; Violence by children and teenagers; Violence: Psychological causes and effects.

Aging
Cognitive changes

Type of psychology: Cognition; Intelligence and intelligence testing; Language; Learning; Memory; Psychopathology; Sensation and perception

Behavioral scientists have become increasingly interested in studying the cognitive changes that occur in the elderly over time. These studies have been conducted to assist individuals in their adjustment to aging as well as to unlock the secrets of the aging process itself.

Key Concepts

- Attention
- Cognition
- Environmental influences
- Informationa processing
- Learning
- Long-term memory
- Mild cognitive impairment (MCI)
- Pacing of instruction
- Sensioriperceptual changes
- Short-term memory

INTRODUCTION

Cognitive changes refer to those changes that occur in overall mental functions and operations. Cognition encompasses all mental operations and functions, including attention, intelligence, memory, language and speech, perception, learning, concept formation, thought, problem solving, spatial and time orientation, and motor/behavior control. Psychologists have worked hard to define and measure various areas of cognitive functioning, even though there has been no consensus about these areas. Understanding the progression of cognitive functioning requires an understanding of brain structure and those human functions emanating from the brain and its fullest human potential, the mind. There is considerable debate within the scientific community about what type of cognitive functions actually exist as well as the nature of the mental mechanisms that are necessary to understand cognitive functioning.

There is a common belief that cognitive abilities decline markedly in older individuals. More and more, however, this idea is being shown to be exaggerated. Studies have shown that the diminution of cognitive skills with age may not be significant, especially before the age of about seventy-five. Aging has been found to have different effects on long-term memory and short-term memory processes. The capacity of short-term memory (which is quite limited in all age groups) remains essentially the same for older people. Long-term memory, however, does show a decline. This decline can be minimized by various strategies; the use of mnemonic devices is very effective, as is taking extra time in learning and remembering.

Both biological and environmental factors have been studied in regard to aging and cognition. An environment that induces apathy or depression has been found to have a lowering effect on cognitive abilities. Environments that provide stimuli to interest the individual can reduce cognitive decline. Moreover, at least one study has found that providing challenging stimuli can even reverse cognitive decline. There is a tremendous range of aging effects from individual to individual, with some showing virtually no changes and others showing serious deterioration of functions. It should be noted that this discussion concerns cognition in healthy individuals; diseases such as Alzheimer's disease and Parkinson's disease and events such as strokes (cardiovascular accidents) have effects on memory that are considered separately from the normal effects of aging.

Common age-related stereotypes suggest that older adults are slower at performing many tasks and have poorer memories than when they were younger. Other stereotypes suggest that increased knowledge and wisdom come with age. Scientific evidence indicates that as people age, their mental processes become less efficient, but at the same time, they gain growth and experience, which are useful in solving complex problems.

Contemporary research on cognitive changes caused by aging emphasizes the information-processing capabilities of individuals as reflected in memory capacities. Memory is a basic psychological function on which higher-level psychological processes such as speech, learning, concept formation, and problem solving are based. Lester Sdorow describes the brain's information-processing capacities as the human being's active acquisition of information about the world. Sensory stimuli are transmitted to the brain, where replicas of the external world are stored briefly in the sensory registry (one second for visual stimuli and four seconds for auditory memory). Information is then transferred to short-term memory for about twenty seconds, unless it is actively rehearsed, then into long-term memory, where it is potentially retained for a lifetime.

INFORMATION PROCESSING AND MEMORY

Information processing is a view of cognitive development that is based on the premise that complex cognitive skills develop as the product of the integration of a hierarchy of more basic skills obtained through life experience and learning. According to this view, fundamental skills are mastered and form the foundation for more and more complex skills.

Information-processing theories emerged as psychologists began to draw comparisons between the way computers operate and the way humans use logic and rules about the world as they develop. Humans use these rules for processing information. New rules may be added and old rules modified throughout childhood and adulthood as more information is obtained from interactions with the world and life experiences. The cognitive changes that occur throughout adult life, as more useful and accurate rules are learned, are every bit as important as the cognitive advances that occurred during childhood, as long as the basic rules acquired in childhood were not distorted by aberrant experiences. Each advance refines the ability to process information. Elizabeth F. Loftus points out that the terms "cognition" and "information processing" have supplanted the term "thinking" among contemporary cognitive scientists. Similar efforts have been made to redefine other human abilities such as problem solving (by Herbert Simon) and intelligence (by Robert Sternberg) to describe greater specificity of function.

Researchers have spent much time and effort defining and redefining memory constructs, although theorists remain in the early stages of understanding memory. Much debate has focused on naturalistic versus laboratory methodologies, with few resolutions as to how the results of both can contribute to a permanent knowledge base of memory.

The mediation school of thought suggests theoretical mechanisms of encoding, retention, and retrieval to explain memory functioning. Consequently, concerted efforts have been made to attribute memory changes across the life span to the specific deterioration of such mechanisms. Researchers continue to debate the importance, even existence, of such constructs. Similarly, the dichotomy of long-term versus short-term memory continues to be debated. To test the empirical validity of such theories, constructs must be able to be disproved if false, and these metaphorical constructs have proved difficult or impossible to test because of their abstract nature.

The greatest controversy in memory research focuses on laboratory versus naturalistic experiments; some researchers, such as Mahzarin R. Banaji and Robert G. Crowder, state that naturalistic experiments have yielded no new principles and no new methods of memory research and should be abandoned. Others, such as H. P. Bahrick, however, claim that the naturalistic approach has provided in ten years what the laboratory has not in a hundred years. Banaji and Crowder criticize naturalistic experiments for their lack of control and thus their lack of generalizability. Yet confining a study to a specific population in a contrived laboratory setting does not seem to generalize any further. S. J. Ceci and Urie Bronfenbrenner emphasize the need to focus on the process of understanding, whatever that process might be. As Endel Tulving notes, the polemics that have ensued from this debate are not going to advance the science of memory. He concludes that there is no reason to believe that there is only one correct way of studying memory.

INFORMATION PROCESSING IN THE ELDERLY

Learning, memory, and attention are all aspects of cognition. Learning is the acquisition of information, skills, and knowledge measured by improvement in responses. Memory involves retaining and retrieving information for later use. Attention is the mechanism by which individuals process information. Cognition is how sensory input is transformed, stored, and retrieved from memory.

Major stages of information-processing models of learning and memory include memory registration (input), memory storage (retention), and memory retrieval (processing of input for response). Attention is a major component of registration in that focusing on stimuli and processing of information begin at this stage. Environmental influences, age-related sensoriperceptual changes, and pacing of instruction affect the processing of information.

Environmental influences can produce negative responses from the elderly because older adults are less comfortable in unfamiliar settings and with unfamiliar people and have difficulty performing multiple tasks. Additionally, the ability to block out extraneous information and to focus on multiple instructions decreases with age.

Sensoriperceptual changes include age-related vision deficits such as altered color perception as a result of yellowing of the eye lens, difficulty seeing at various distances as a result of presbyopia, difficulty adjusting from light to dark, and decreased peripheral vision and depth perception. Sensorineural hearing loss affects the ability to hear high-frequency sounds and consonants and hinders communication. Also, excessive noise interferes with the ability to hear in the elderly.

Pacing of instruction includes both the time it takes to present and the amount of information presented. With age, there is slowing of physiological and psychological responses. Reaction time increases. Studies have shown that the elderly learn more efficiently when they are able to learn and respond at their own pace. The total number of brain cells in the healthy elderly decreases only slightly, but a lifetime of activity causes the cells to be less efficient than they once were because of decreased blood flow and other physiological changes. Decreases in cognitive function are likely because of these deficiencies. The amount of decrease varies widely, however, ranging from insignificant to troublesome.

STUDIES IN AGE-RELATED COGNITION

In examining cognitive changes in aging populations, aside from the theoretical debates, researchers have reported that cognitive processes progressively decline as chronological age advances. Studies have tended to describe the cognitive declines as gradual and general, rather than being attributable to discrete cognitive losses in specific areas of functioning.

Several studies have supported the existence of age-related cognitive decline, while other studies dispute the severity of such declines. Research interest is increasing in the areas of identifying factors related to cognitive decline and interventions to abate them. Under the direction of Ronald C. Petersen and Michael Grundman, the National Institute on Aging is studying whether daily doses of vitamin E or donepezil can prevent those with mild cognitive impairment from developing Alzheimer's disease. Vitamin E is also being researched in conjunction with B vitamins. A 2005 study found that healthy people who consumed more than 400 micrograms of the B vitamin folate (the recommended daily amount for adults) cut their risk of developing Alzheimer's in half. Gingko biloba, the so-called memory herb, appears to help slow cognitive decline for some people in the early stages of Alzheimer's. Research studies making this claim have been criticized, however, and further studies are necessary. Other studies are investigating cholinesterase inhibitors and anti-inflammatory agents as a means to slow the progression of mild cognitive impairment.

Psychologists who studied memory change identified diminished memory capacity in the elderly as attributable to a number of processes, such as slowed semantic access and a reduced ability to make categorical judgments. Other researchers concluded that older subjects were slower in mental operations but were not less accurate. Some researchers hypothesized that slower speed tied up processing functions, resulting in apparent memory impairment. Still others hypothesized that older adults have more trouble with active memory tasks because of increased competition for a share of memory processing resources, whereas others linked the aged's poor performance on working memory tasks to an actual deficiency in processing resources. Finally, some researchers concluded that older adults might simply have less mental energy to perform memory tasks. These studies accept gradual memory decline, or a slowing of processing, as a normal by-product of aging.

There are some who believe that mild cognitive impairment is a neurological disorder. This belief stems from the identification of atrophy of the left medial lobe and small medial temporal lobe, low parietal/temporal perfusion, and asymmetry of the brain as revealed by computed tomography. One study identified those with small hippocampi as prone to developing Alzheimer's disease. Additionally, electroencephalogram tracings of the brains of patients with mild cognitive impairment and patients with Alzheimer's disease showed similarities.

R. A. Hock, B. A. Futrell, and B. A. Grismer studied eighty-two elderly people, from sixty to ninety-nine years of age, who were living independently in the community. These normal adults were tested on a battery of eight tasks that were selected to reflect cognitive functioning, particularly measuring primary and secondary memory, memory for nonverbal material, span of attention, the capacity to divide attention between competing sources of stimulation, and two motor tasks requiring psychomotor integrity. This study found a gradual, progressive decline in cognitive functioning but found that the decline did not reach statistically significant levels. The decline was general, suggesting that it may have been a function of reduced attention rather than more discrete losses. This finding appears to be consistent with the notion that crystallized intellectual or abstract processes are well maintained across time. There were suggestions that speed of information processing is a sensitive measure of the aging process.

It is possible, however, that the tasks selected for this study did not discriminate between younger and older aging adults because the tasks may be more reliable for assessing brain injuries and psychologically impaired persons, who were not included in the population studied. Consequently, further studies on the same cognitive tasks with impaired aged adults would be necessary to see if the same relationships and conclusions would apply. Individuals with impaired cognitive functioning offer a unique opportunity to determine whether the brain continues to show the same propensity to function as a unitary, global system as is observed with individuals who experience the normal aging process.

Although the brain does exhibit localization of functions, with specialization of certain brain cells for specific functions, its overall mode of operation is as a total unit. The brain has an exceptional capacity to compensate for the loss of some specific functions and continue the rest of its mental operations. This capacity or flexibility in brain function has been termed equipotentiation. Further studies of individuals with brain impairments will help to show how the brain attempts to carry out its overall functions when more specific impairments have been sustained. When cognitive disorders result in faulty information processing, actual observable changes may occur in a person's daily behavior. The previously neat person, for example, may neglect personal hygiene. The person who previously exhibited exceptional verbal abilities may speak in a socially inappropriate manner. The staid conservative businessperson may act impulsively, make unreasonable decisions about personal finances, and show impaired social judgment.

MILD COGNITIVE IMPAIRMENT

Studies of cognitive changes across the life span must distinguish between normal gradual change in the elderly and change that is associated with disordered functioning. Studies must also respect the complexity of the human brain. Morton Hunt notes that cognitive scientists have concluded that there may be 100 billion neurons in the interior of the brain. Each of these neurons may be interconnected to hundreds of others by anywhere from one thousand to ten thousand synapses, or relay points. This may enable the average healthy person to accumulate five hundred times as much information as is contained in the entire Encyclopedia Britannica, or 100 trillion bits of information. The circuitry in one human brain is probably sixty times the complexity of the entire United States telephone system. Given this complexity, even the daily estimated loss of 100,000 brain cells from the aging process may leave human beings capable of sound cognitive functioning well into old age.

The most frequent cognitive complaint made by and about the elderly is loss of memory, especially short-term memory. Researchers are finding that staying active and engaged in a challenging activity requiring mental concentration, such as learning a new language, taking music lessons, doing crossword puzzles, playing games such as chess, or reading books, may help to combat or slow the onset of dementia and keep the mind alert. Not everyone loses the same skills at the same time, but by the eighties, nearly everyone has experienced some cognitive loss. A study in the late 1990s by Gerald E. McClearn of the Center for Developmental and Health Genetics at Pennsylvania State University examined the influence of genes on aspects of cognition in the elderly. Using 240 sets of twins averaging eighty-three years of age, the twins were tested for verbal meaning, figure logic, block design, and picture memory. Genetic inheritance accounted for 55 percent of the individual differences in ability, a result similar to that of middle-aged people. The study concluded that the relative influence of genetics and environment (half and half) extends into advanced age, contrary to the commonly held belief that environmental influences increase throughout the life span as genetic influences decrease.

MILD COGNITIVE IMPAIRMENT

Cognitive impairment, mild is a term used to describe isolated memory loss without changes in activities of daily living. There is some support for the theory that mild cognitive impairment represents a transitional stage between normal aging and Alzheimer's disease and may be a precursor to Alzheimer's disease. However, a significant proportion of patients with mild cognitive impairment do not progress to Alzheimer's disease. One research study followed a group of mildly cognitively impaired patients and reported they developed Alzheimer's disease at a rate of 10 to 15 percent per year, while individuals without mild cognitive impairment developed Alzheimer's disease at a rate of 1 to 2 percent per year. Individuals who have a memory problem but do not meet clinical criteria for Alzheimer's disease are considered to have mild cognitive impairment with memory loss. One study supported that those who carried the gene apolipoprotein E-4 (APOE-4) were more likely to develop Alzheimer's disease. Studies involving molecular brain activity have contributed to understanding normal and abnormal memory activities. Another study linked poor performance on a memory test that provided cues to help participants at time of recall as indicating a cognitive decline. There is no cure for mild cognitive impairment. However, treatment of coexisting conditions such as depression and high blood pressure can help cognition. Also donepezil (Aricept) has been used to try to slow the progression of mild cognitive impairment to Alzheimer's disease. Awareness and early identification are important in management of mild cognitive impairment.

Paul Baltes notes that it used to be considered common knowledge that cognitive abilities decline with age, but this view has become highly debatable. When the effects of disease and injury are separated out in studies of the healthy elderly, no drastic decline in cognitive ability is found. This conclusion may be one reason that studies of cognition and aging have begun to make a distinction regarding intelligence. The distinction is between crystallized intelligence, involving the accumulation of facts and knowledge, which holds up with age, and fluid intelligence, which is the rapid processing of new information, a function that appears particularly associated with the young, and vulnerable to the effects of age or disease. Studies of neurologically healthy aging adults have revealed no consistent evidence of a reduced ability to learn. Studies have further shown that very little practice may be required to substantially improve an elderly person's ability to perform some cognitive tasks, reflecting a motivational factor. Studies of mentally active persons in their eighties have concluded that loss of cognitive ability stemmed more from intellectual apathy or boredom than from actual physical deterioration.

John Darley and his colleagues concluded that on average, the decline of intellectual capability with age is slight and probably does not occur before age seventy-five. When declines do occur, they do not occur equally across cognitive functions. Vocabulary and verbal skills may actually improve with age, whereas skills involving spatial visualization and deductive reasoning are more likely to diminish. In general, verbal skills and accumulated knowledge are maintained with aging, while tasks that require quick responses are more susceptible to aging.

BIBLIOGRAPHY

Bahrick, H. P. "A Speedy Recovery from Bankruptcy for Ecological Memory Research." *American Psychologist* 46.1 (1991): 76–77. Print.

Banaji, Mahzarin R., and Robert G. Crowder. "The Bankruptcy of Everyday Memory." *American Psychologist* 44.9 (1989): 1185–93. Print.

Birren, James E., and K. Warner Schaie, eds. *Handbook of the Psychology of Aging.* Burlington: Academic, 2011. Digital file.

Ceci, S. J., and Urie Bronfenbrenner. "On the Demise of Everyday Memory." *American Psychologist* 46.1 (1991): 27–31. Print.

Craik, Fergus I. M., and Timothy Salthouse, eds. *The Handbook of Aging and Cognition.* 3rd ed. New York: Psychology, 2007. Print.

Lear, Martha Weinman. *Where Did I Leave My Glasses? The What, When, and Why of "Normal" Memory Loss.* New York: Wellness Central, 2008. Print.

Loftus, Elizabeth F. *Memory: Surprising New Insights into How We Remember and Why We Forget.* Reading: Addison-Wesley, 1980. Print.

Nuland, Sherwin B. *The Art of Aging: A Doctor's Prescription for Well-Being.* New York: Random, 2007. Print.

Park, Denise, and Norbert Schwarz, eds. *Cognitive Aging: A Primer.* New York: Psychology, 2012. Print.

Petersen, Ronald C. "Mild Cognitive Impairment or Questionable Dementia?" *Archives of Neurology* 57 (2000): 643–644. Print.

Shah, Yogesh, Eric Tangalos, and Ronald C. Petersen. "Mild Cognitive Impairment: When Is It a Precursor to Alzheimer's Disease?" *Geriatrics* 55 (2000): 62–67. Print.

Smith, Glenn E., and Mark W. Bondi. *Mild Cognitive Impairment and Dementia: Definitions, Diagnosis, and Treatment.* New York: Oxford UP, 2013. Print.

Weil, Andrew. *Healthy Aging: A Lifelong Guide to Your Physical and Spiritual Well-Being.* New York: Knopf, 2005. Print.

Robert A. Hock, updated by Sharon Wallace Stark and Marcia J. Weiss

See Also: Ageism; Aging: Physical changes; Aging: Theories; Bronfenbrennar, Urie; Cognitive maps; Coping: Terminal illness; Dementia; Elder abuse; Elders' mental health; Forgetting and forgetfulness; Long-term memory; Memory; Memory: Physiology; Memory storage; Parkinson's disease; Short-term memory.

Aging
Physical changes

TYPE OF PSYCHOLOGY: Developmental psychology

Physical aging involves a process of change. This change proceeds at different rates among individuals, as well as in different ways within various systems in the same people.

KEY CONCEPTS

- Arthritis
- Gerontology
- Immune system
- Life expectancy
- Life span
- Metabolism
- Osteoporosis
- Reaction time

INTRODUCTION

The human life span (the length of time people may live under optimal conditions) is about 120 years. Although this figure has not changed over the last century, life expectancy has. The amount of time an American baby can be expected to live has increased from under sixty years if born in 1900 to nearly seventy-nine years if born in 2010, according to a 2013 report by the Centers for Disease Control and Prevention. As people have begun to live longer, they have become aware of many changes that occur as they age. The scientists who study aging are called gerontologists. It is known that predictable changes occur in the body as it gets older. Some are easily noticed, such as graying or thinning hair and wrinkles. Other changes, such as a tendency toward rising blood pressure, are not visible.

In general, research on aging has emphasized losses. More recently, increased interest in the aging process has stimulated physiological, sociological, and psychological research on aging. Although many physiological variables show major losses with advancing age, it is important, when looking at the average, to note that there is substantial variability at all ages throughout life. Scientists have found that some changes in blood pressure and cholesterol levels that had originally been interpreted as age specific are common in industrial societies but not in agricultural ones.

IN BODY SYSTEMS WITH AGE

One of the major physical changes that occurs with age is an increase in reaction time. As one gets older, it takes longer to respond to a stimulus. This increased reaction time is due to a number of factors, including changes in sensory function, an increased concern for accuracy, a slower response (often due to arthritis), and a slowing of transmission of neural impulses. This slowdown in the transmission of impulses through the nervous system is due in large part to demyelinization. As the axons lose their fatty covering (myelin sheath), saltatory conduction is impaired, and slowing of the neural impulse occurs.

Advancing age is associated with progressive impairments in the capacity to metabolize glucose. Again, there is substantial variability in the results for successive age groups, with many older individuals metabolizing glucose as well as their younger counterparts. The carbohydrate intolerance of aging may carry substantial risk, even in the absence of disease. Attempts have been made to determine which components of the age-associated alterations in carbohydrate intolerance are related to aging itself and which components might be related to diet, exercise, or medications. It is thought that factors such as physical fitness may decrease the likelihood of carbohydrate intolerance with advancing age. Metabolism also begins to slow at around age twenty-five. For each decade thereafter, the number of calories required to maintain one's weight drops by at least 2 percent. Muscle mass gradually shrinks, so older people tend to have more body fat than they did when they were younger.

Aging is also associated with a decline in bone density in both men and women, but primarily women. Osteoporosis, a condition in which the bones become dangerously thin and fragile, is a major problem for the elderly. Bone mass reaches its peak in the thirties for both men and women and then begins to drop by about 1 percent per year. Brittle bones are the major cause of the fractures, particularly in the vertebrae and hips, that cripple many of the elderly. A number of studies suggest that bone loss can be reduced in advanced age by adherence to moderate exercise programs, in addition to adequate calcium intake throughout life. Drugs such as calcitonin-salmon (Miacalcin) and alendronate sodium (Fosamax) have been developed to treat osteoporosis.

Arthritis (inflammation of the joints) is one of the common complaints of middle-aged and elderly adults.

Osteoarthritis is the type that most commonly develops with age. It leads to stiffening of the joints, along with pain. As a result, people may tend to exhibit decreased mobility and slowing of their responses. Arthritis has long been treated with corticosteroids. Pain is often treated using nonsteroidal anti-inflammatory drugs (NSAIDs). Recent research has focused on the use of glucosamine and chondroitin to treat arthritis. Joint replacement is available as an option to treat advanced arthritis.

The senses of the elderly and the associated organs also go through changes. Taste diminishes as the nose loses its sense of smell. Odors account for most of the overall sensation of flavors, so taste is lost as a function of loss of smell. Loss of taste can lead to lack of appetite and to serious nutritional deficiencies.

Hearing also fades, particularly in the high-frequency range, resulting in presbycusis. This high-frequency hearing loss with age begins at age twelve, and involves a loss of fifty cycles per second per year (beginning with a maximum frequency of twenty thousand cycles per second). Pathological hearing loss also is found as people age and often seems to relate to exposure to noise pollution. As a result, it has been seen more commonly in men (as a result of participation in wars and noisy work environments) and is expected to increase in frequency in the future as a result of the use of loud electronic equipment and headphones. Pathological hearing loss is of great concern to gerontologists and geriatricians because it is often denied by the elderly, who then do not seek treatment and often develop interpersonal isolation and paranoid behavior as a result.

Vision changes also commonly occur with age. Beginning at about age forty, people become aware that they have difficulty reading and seeing close up. By the age of forty-five, a majority of adults wear glasses or contact lenses to correct for presbyopia (farsightedness that develops with age). Other visual disturbances that may occur with advancing age include cataracts (opacity of the lens of the eye) and glaucoma (increasing intraocular pressure). Additionally, the elderly lose the ability to see color at the shorter wavelengths, so that violet and navy come to be seen as black.

As adults get older, they also become less sensitive to pressure and therefore more likely to develop bedsores or skin ulcerations. Temperature regulation also becomes impaired, so that the elderly are often too hot or too cold. Sense of balance is also less precise, so presbystasis (lack of sense of balance with age) occurs, making falls more likely. Changes occur in the skin: The topmost layer, or epidermis, becomes dry, whereas the middle layer, or dermis, becomes thin and less elastic. Along with loss of fat from the underlying subcutaneous layer, these changes cause the skin to sag and become wrinkled.

There are other physiological changes that accompany aging. For example, the immune system starts to decline in young adulthood. The white blood cells that fight off invaders such as viruses and bacteria lose some of their effectiveness as a person gets older. Antibody production in people over the age of sixty-five is less than 10 percent of what it was in adolescence. As a result, the older adult is much more susceptible to illness than the adolescent or young adult. Thus, the elderly are advised to get flu and pneumonia shots to help keep themselves healthy.

The respiratory system undergoes many changes with age. There is a reduction in breathing efficiency because the lungs no longer expand to take in as much air. In fact, lungs lose, on the average, 30 to 50 percent of their maximum breathing capacity between ages thirty and eighty. The uptake of oxygen in the lungs is diminished, so less oxygen is carried by the blood, which has health ramifications since oxygen is necessary for the synthesis of amino acids and fatty acids and for the production of energy.

THEORIES OF AGING

Virtually all systems of the body, including the cardiovascular, circulatory, endocrine, excretory, and gastrointestinal systems, show changes with age. Several theories on aging attempt to explain the aging process. The aging of cells is a complex process that scientists still do not completely understand. There are genetic theories, as well as nongenetic and physiological ones. Genetic and nongenetic theories of aging both explain aging at the cellular or molecular level.

Genetic theories assume that a problem occurs in cell formation with age. This problem occurs at the level of the ribonucleic acid (RNA) or deoxyribonucleic acid (DNA). Error theory is the genetic theory best supported by evidence, and it assumes that aging is most likely to occur as a result of a change in RNA.

Nongenetic theories assume that cell formation occurs normally with age but that something interferes with cell functioning as one ages. Wear-and-tear theory and accumulation theory are two of the best-supported nongenetic theories. The buildup of free radicals in the cell (which fits accumulation theory) has led to the popular use of antioxidants (nutritional supplements) to try to slow the aging process.

Physiological theories assume that aging occurs at the molar level—the level of tissues, organs, or systems. These theories attribute aging to a breakdown in the integration and function of systems. Evidence indicates support for some genetic, nongenetic, and physiological theories, indicating that each may play a role in bringing about the physical changes of aging.

TRENDS IN AGING

The number of elderly people in the United States increased rapidly in the second half of the twentieth century and the first decade of the twenty-first. Americans are living longer than ever before. According to a 2011 report by the Administration on Aging, a division of the US Department of Health and Human Services, by 2030 there will be as many as 72 million Americans age sixty-five or older. This demographic is projected to make up 19.3 percent of the population, up from about 13 percent in 2010.

One popular misconception disputed by recent research is the idea that aging means inevitable physical and sexual failure. Although some changes necessarily occur, many of the problems associated with old age fall into the category of secondary aging. Such problems are not the result of age but of abuse and disuse, which often can be controlled by the individual. Researchers have found that people wear out faster from disuse than they wear out from overuse. This also applies to sexuality.

Studies from the time of Alfred Kinsey's work in the 1940s and 1950s to the early twenty-first century show that sexual interest and activity decrease with age, but the drop varies greatly among individuals. Psychologist Marion Perlmutter reported that one of the best predictors of continued sexual intercourse is past sexual enjoyment and frequency. People who have never enjoyed sexuality much may consider age a good reason to give up sex.

Psychosocial factors have been studied, and they sometimes reveal how older men and women feel about the physical changes happening to their bodies. It is important that family members and members of the helping professions, along with the elderly themselves, come to understand that the physical changes that occur with passing time produce needs that are real and that elderly people are not simply trying to make demands for attention. Elderly people must be allowed to retain their dignity and to remain as active and independent as possible. No one, at whatever age, likes to be helpless or to be perceived as helpless. As a result of helplessness, researchers find lowered self-esteem, health problems, depression, and sometimes death.

Several lines of research on psychosocial factors and health focus on the idea of social support. Empirical research has found consistent relationships between social support and various indicators of health and well-being. Social networks and support are persistent conditions that affect the mortality of older people. Support-disrupting life events have specific negative effects on both mortality and morbidity. The positive effects of social support have been demonstrated by means of intervention studies. Most of the intervention has involved supportive behaviors by health care professionals. Positive effects include increased rate and completeness of recovery from injuries, a smaller number of heart attacks, decreased incidence of cancer, and fewer physical illnesses.

STUDIES ON AGING

Important early studies of aging were performed in the 1950s, including the Human Aging Study, conducted by the National Institute of Mental Health; the Duke Longitudinal Studies, done by the Center for the Study of Aging and Human Development at Duke University; and the Baltimore Longitudinal Study of Aging. These pioneering studies and hundreds of others have benefited from growing federal support.

The Human Genome Project (especially Project Chronos) is among studies important in the field of aging. These studies continue to investigate the changes that take place in aging, as well as attempting to find ways to stop or delay these changes. In contemporary society, many people reaching one hundred years of age (centenarians) continue to function very well, showing minimal physical change with age. As these people are studied in projects such as Chronos, perhaps humankind will find an answer to the biological changes in aging, as well as finding ways to delay such changes.

BIBLIOGRAPHY

Administration on Aging. "A Profile of Older Americans: 2011." *Administration on Aging*. Department of Health and Human Services, 2011. Web. 21 Feb. 2014.

Birren, James E., and K. Warner Schaie, eds. *Handbook of the Psychology of Aging*. 6th ed. Boston: Elsevier, 2011. Digital file.

Centers for Disease Control and Prevention. "Life Expectancy." CDC. *Centers for Disease Control and Prevention*, 21 Nov. 2013. Web. 21 Feb. 2014.

Hoyer, William J., and Paul A. Roodin. *Adult Development and Aging*. 5th ed. Boston: McGraw-Hill, 2003. Print.

Masoro, Edward J., and Steven N. Austad, eds. *Handbook of the Biology of Aging*. 6th ed. Boston: Elsevier, 2006. Print.

Morgan, Leslie A., and Suzanne R. Kunkel. *Aging, Society, and the Life Course*. 4th ed. New York: Springer, 2011. Print.

Schaie, K. Warner, and Sherry L. Willis. *Adult Development and Aging*. 5th ed. Upper Saddle River: Prentice Hall, 2002. Print.

Whitbourne, Susan Krauss. *Adult Development and Aging: Biopsychosocial Perspectives*. 3d ed. Hoboken: Wiley, 2008. Print.

Whitbourne, Susan Krauss, and Martin Sliwinski, eds. *The Wiley-Blackwell Handbook of Adulthood and Aging*. Malden: Wiley, 2012. Print.

Deborah R. McDonald; updated by Robin Kamienny Montvilo

See Also: Ageism; Aging: Cognitive changes; Aging: Theories; Alzheimer's disease; Death and dying; Dementia; Elder abuse; Elders' mental health; Hearing; Kinsey, Alfred; Memory: Physiology; Pain; Pain management; Parkinson's disease; Stress: Physiological responses; Stress-related diseases; Visual system.

Aging
Theories

Type of psychology: Developmental psychology

Aging is an entropic (energy-disorder) phenomenon that is exhibited by most multicellular organisms. Two major theories—the free radical theory and the genetic programming theory—have been suggested to explain the mechanisms of aging. Although each theory emphasizes different aspects of the aging process, they almost certainly are interrelated.

Key Concepts

- Antioxidant
- Entropy
- Free radical theory
- Genetic programming theory
- Longevity

INTRODUCTION

The aging process occurs in all living organisms, although it is most pronounced in vertebrate animals, animals having a cartilaginous, bony endoskeleton, an efficient heart, and a highly developed nervous system. It is part of the basic sequence of animal development from conception to reproductive maturity to death. It follows the second law of thermodynamics, a physical principle of the entire universe that maintains that the disorder (entropy) of the universe is constantly increasing because of the dissipation of energy and the gradual transfer of energy from system to system. Living organisms age because of the inefficiency of the chemical reactions within their cells, thereby creating disorder as is evidenced by breakdowns in physiological rhythms (for example, nerve cell functioning, blood pressure changes, and reduced kidney filtration) and physical structure (for example, bone deformations, muscle weakness, and hair loss). The second law of thermodynamics maintains that no machine is 100 percent efficient; therefore, energy will be lost continuously with accompanying decay of the system, or body.

PHYSIOLOGICAL AGING

In humans and other mammalian species, the process of aging follows a very predictable pattern. An individual is conceived by the union of genetic information from the mother via an egg and the father via sperm, thereby producing a single-celled zygote. By the connected processes of mitosis (chromosome duplication followed by separation) and cytokinesis (cell division), the zygote divides into two cells, which later divide to make four cells, then eight cells, and so on until an individual composed of approximately 100 trillion cells is produced. Very early in development (for example, a few hundred cells), different cells in various locations begin to specialize, or differentiate, by hormonally initiated changes in gene expression within these cells, thereby giving rise to specialized structures such as nerves, muscle, skin, bone, eyes, and fingers.

After the individual organism is fully developed and can survive in the environment on its own, it will either exit the mother's body or hatch from a protective egg case, or shell. Subsequent juvenile development will include brain neuronal changes (plasticity) as a result of learning and social interactions, and physiological changes, leading to sexual maturity, or adulthood. Development up to adulthood does technically constitute aging, although there is little evidence of physiological decay.

Various hormones, particularly steroid hormones, are prominent during a person's sexual stage, when the individual is capable of sexual reproduction. Individuals are at their physical peak during the reproductive period. At the end of the critical reproductive period (menopause in women), the degenerative physical effects of true aging become very evident and accelerate with time as the individual becomes older. In a biological sense, the purpose of an organism is to reproduce and continue the transfer of genetic information. By age fifty or so, both men and women should have achieved this objective, and estrogen (in women) and testosterone (in men) begin a more rapid decline. Consequently, the individual organism begins a progressive deterioration after age fifty or so toward death, thereby making room in the environment for its descendants. This is a harsh, but real, view of an organism's life. The key to understanding why deteriorative aging occurs lies in the hormones, chemicals, and cellular changes that are present in the organism just before this stage.

Among the physical changes of aging that are evident very early are heart and respiratory changes. On birth, the average human newborn has a pulse of 120 heartbeats per minute, a breathing rate of forty to forty-five breaths per minute, and a blood pressure of 60/30. These data indicate a very high metabolic rate in individuals during early development. As humans age, both pulse and breathing rates decrease, whereas blood pressure increases. The average healthy adult has a pulse of approximately 60 to 80 heartbeats per minute, a breathing rate of approximately eight to twelve breaths per minute, and a blood pressure somewhere around 120/70. Neuronal plasticity of the brain and, therefore, learning peak during the early reproductive years and decline around the age of forty-five to fifty. Most physiological processes undergo a steady decline from age twenty or so, with steeper declines occurring near age fifty, although large individual variation exists.

THEORIES OF AGING

When an organism dies, the electrical activity of billions of brain neurons ceases, along with cessation of heart and respiratory muscle contractions. In more than 80 percent of human deaths by "natural causes," however, the exact cause of death cannot be determined. The physiological causes of aging and death remain poorly understood, although more than three hundred theories have been proposed to explain the process. Of all the theories proposed, two—the free radical theory and the genetic programming theory—have withstood vigorous testing and continue to be widely studied. Although each theory emphasizes different aspects of cellular aging, they are complementary and both may be correct in their combined interpretations.

Free Radical Theory. The role of free radicals in cell damage and aging was first proposed by Denham Harman in 1972. The free radical theory of aging maintains that the degenerative events that occur within the cell and the entire organism during aging are caused by the toxic effects of oxidizing free radical molecules. Free radicals are molecules that have a free extra electron per molecule that can be donated to another molecule. As a result, free radicals are highly reactive with most substances that they encounter. Their chemical reaction with a recipient molecule may affect the structure and function of that molecule so that it does not function properly. In a living cell, such an event could have disastrous consequences. The deoxyribonucleic acid (DNA) nucleotide sequence of any gene could be mutated, or altered, by a free radical, thereby altering the structure or function of the protein encoded by that gene and affecting all cellular functions controlled by that specific protein. If the protein is essential for the cell's survival, the result could be cellular death or cellular transformation to the cancerous state.

Free radicals such as superoxide, hydroxyl radical, and hydrogen peroxide are naturally produced as by-products of the cell's metabolic activities. The cells of most living organisms produce antioxidant enzymes such as catalase, glutathione peroxidase, and superoxide dismutase to scavenge and inactivate free radicals wherever they occur. No such capture operation is 100 percent efficient, however. Some free radicals react with cellular molecules; the accumulated effects of these reactions over time may be responsible for cellular aging. Antioxidants, such as vitamins C and E, block free radicals and are suggested for prolonging life. These antioxidant chemicals are frequently cited as the basis of claims for the benefits of consuming a diet rich in fruit and vegetables. However, antioxidant supplementation has not yet been proven to extend life. Although phenybutylnitrone was shown to produce about a 10 percent extension of the life span in animals, the results of this experiment have not been reproduced. Of all the theories of aging, Harman's free-radical theory has the most consistent experimental support. However some models demonstrate that increased oxidative stress has no effect on life span. Thus, more data are needed to decisively determine the role of free radicals in aging.

Genetic Programming Theory. The genetic programming theory of aging maintains that the cells of all living organisms contain genes that encode signaling protein hormones. These hormones, when produced, elicit aging-related changes within the cells at specific times during the organism's development, including death. Another viewpoint within this theory is that the cells of various tissues within living organisms are programmed to die after undergoing a specified number of genetically encoded divisions. Some studies in gene theory suggest it is the altering of genes over time that causes aging. In addition, because observations of older people demonstrate an increase of mutated genes, it is also theorized that gene mutations over time cause aging. Indeed, cancer is often the result of mutations. Molecular biology underlies the more recent theories on aging. Cells keep dividing until they can no longer divide and then they simply die. Embryonic cells divide much more than cells from adults. Hence, this theory proposes that cell division holds the key to the mechanics of human aging. Other nonbiological theories of aging include disengagement, activity, selectivity, and continuity theories. Additional biological theories include telomere, reproductive-cell cycle, wear-and-tear, evolutionary, accumulative-waste, autoimmune, aging-clock, and cross-linkage theories.

APPLYING THEORIES TO HEALTH AND DISEASE

By the start of the twenty-first century, researchers in laboratories throughout the world had begun actively investigating the mechanisms of the aging process. The problem was being tackled from many different perspectives, including biochemical, genetic, physiological, gerontological, psychological, and sociological approaches. The topic is of particular interest in countries such as the United States, where the overall population is becoming progressively older. Although much of the research has been devoted to medical care for the elderly, many scientists have begun exploring the biochemistry of aging with hopes of understanding the process and possibly slowing or reversing it.

The two principal theories of aging (senescence), when combined, provide a very good working model for attacking the aging problem. The free radical theory of aging provides the cause, and the genetic programming theory provides an overall developmental view of the phenomenon. There can be no question that there are certain genes within all living cells that in a step-by-step manner control the sequential development of the entire organism. At the same time, free radical molecules are constantly being produced within body cells, and these same cells are being exposed to mutagenic (mutation-causing) radiation and chemicals. These substances will cause accumulated cellular damage over time, even with the body's combined defenses of antioxidant enzymes, immune system cells, and kidney filtration of impurities from blood. These defenses work extremely well up to the end of the individual's reproductive period; then, they decline rapidly, almost as if they were programmed to do so.

Recent studies have shown that calorie restriction, which limits the intake of energy, reduces free radicals and increases the life span of rodents. Severely reducing calories by restricting the number of meals and fasting has been shown to suppress the development of various diseases and to increase the longevity of life in rodents by 30 to 40 percent. However, severely reducing calories by 50 percent or more resulted in death. In addition, for caloric restriction, which lengthens the time between cell divisions, to be beneficial, it must be started early in life because age, at the molecular level, is counted as the number of cell doublings. Drug companies have begun searching for methods to mimic the beneficial effects of caloric restriction without severely limiting food intake.

Among humans, several unusual pathologies are of interest to scientists who research aging. Among these is the disease called progeria, a condition in which the aging process is greatly accelerated. The aging process is also emphasized in acquired immunodeficiency syndrome (AIDS) and the genetic disorder called autoimmune deficiency syndrome. In both situations, an individual's entire immune system is rendered useless, thereby leaving the individual's body defenseless against the continuous onslaught of usually harmless bacteria, viruses, and mutations.

Cancer is one of the leading causes of death, and the incidence of cancer increases as people age. Cancer is essentially a disease of uncontrolled cell growth, which interferes with the normal functions of the body. There are several dozen types of cancer, based on the affected tissues, site of the cancer in the tissue, and cell type that is affected. Causes of cancers are believed to be both genetically and environmentally defined; that is, some people are genetically more susceptible to environmental insults than others. Scientists believe that all cancers begin with one cell that becomes damaged and is not stopped from dividing and creating new damaged cells.

An important scientific discovery has been the identification of certain genes involved in the development of cancerous cells: the proto-oncogenes and the tumor-suppressor genes. How cancer relates to death is complex and continues to be debated. Until more research is completed, it will not be known with certainty whether aging-related changes in cells and their systems make them more susceptible to cancer, or whether advancing time just allows more genetic hits to accumulate and produce cancerous cells.

The process of aging is difficult to measure, describe, or quantify, although it is a process that every organism experiences. Aging is a focus of many sciences, including physiology, chemistry, biochemistry, and genetics. As a scientific process, aging must have a beginning and an end, a substrate and a product, and a reason for the metabolic change; however, the scientific process of aging is not yet understood.

PSYCHOLOGICAL PERSPECTIVE

The process of aging occurs within all living organisms. Theories describing the mechanisms of aging are of relevance to psychology because the aging process is a developmental process that encompasses all bodily systems, including the brain and central nervous system. Aging is a fundamental focal point of consciousness, religious beliefs, and social structure. Simply, people are afraid of dying. As a result, aging is incorporated into human religions, behavior, and culture. Society stresses youthfulness, so humans go to great lengths and expense to reverse the effects of aging with skin creams, baldness cures or coverups, clothing, bodybuilding, cosmetic injections, and plastic surgery. Psychologists have found that negative stereotypes about aging can actually shorten life and that people who have a positive perception of aging live seven and a half years longer than those who have a negative view.

Psychology is a phenomenon of intelligent living organisms, and living organisms are complex entities consisting of intricate chemical reactions. These biochemical reactions, which are responsible for all aspects of life, follow the fundamental physical and chemical properties of the universe. One of these physical processes is the second law of thermodynamics, which maintains that any system loses energy because of inefficiency and therefore becomes more disordered, or entropic. Therefore, aging is an entropic process for the entire universe. Living organisms do undergo a building process during early development that is antientropic; however, after a certain time, specifically the end of the reproductive period, entropy takes over and accelerates. All aspects of the living animal, including the brain, deteriorate.

The free radical and the genetic programming theories of aging have provided scientists with greater insights into the mechanisms of the aging process. These theories also give researchers ideas for attacking aging as a disease that can be treated. Although the so-called fountain of youth represents wishful thinking, research on aging realistically can lead to the prolongation of human life and improvement of the quality of human life. Aging research may help eliminate or treat maladies such as heart disease, Alzheimer's disease, cancer, and general aging-related declines in most bodily functions.

One factor that permeates human biology in terms of aging, disease, and abnormal psychological behavior is stress. Research has repeatedly linked stress with accelerated aging, increased susceptibility to many diseases (including cancer), decreased mental agility and memory, and insanity. Indeed, scientific research demonstrates that stress speeds the aging process by harming DNA. The rise in the human population and continuing technological growth have been paralleled by a rapid increase in individual stress levels; stress-related diseases such as heart disease, stroke, and cancer; acts of violence, devastating wars, torture, exploitation, and destruction of human life; and the use of alcohol and illegal drugs in an attempt to relieve stress. Reevaluation of the way that one treats fellow humans, a slowing of the fast-paced society, major social reforms, and medical advances in the treatment of stress all will be needed for decreasing stress, a major killer and contributor to the aging process.

Advances in biochemical and genetic medical research probably will produce the means for extending life within the twenty-first century. Regardless of whether human longevity is extended, aging will continue. As it does, researchers will continue to study how and why people age and the consequences of aging for both the individual and the community.

BIBLIOGRAPHY

Arking, Robert. *Biology of Aging: Observations and Principles.* New York: Oxford UP, 2006. Print.

Baudisch, Annette. *Inevitable Aging? Contributions to Evolutionary-Demographic Theory.* New York: Springer, 2008. Print.

Bergtson, Vern L., and K. Warner Schaie, eds. *Handbook of Theories of Aging.* 2nd ed. New York: Springer, 2008. Print.

Birren, James E., and K. Warner Schaie, eds. *Handbook of the Psychology of Aging*. Burlington: Elsevier, 2011. Digital file.

Erber, Joan T. *Aging and Older Adulthood*. 3rd ed. Malden: Wiley, 2013. Print.

Lewin, Benjamin. *Genes*. 9th ed. New York: Oxford UP, 2007. Print.

Masoro, Edward J., and Steven N. Austad, eds. *Handbook of the Biology of Aging*. 6th ed. San Diego: Academic, 2005. Print.

Morgan, Leslie A., and Suzanne R. Kunkel. *Aging, Society, and the Life Course*. 4th ed. New York: Springer, 2011. Print.

David Wason Hollar, Jr.; updated by Karen Chapman-Novakofski and M. Casey Diana

See Also: Ageism; Aging: Cognitive changes; Aging: Physical changes; Alzheimer's disease; Brain structure; Coping: Chronic illness; Coping: Terminal illness; Death and dying; Dementia; Elders' mental health; Endocrine system; Genetics and mental health; Neuropsychology; Parkinson's disease; Quality of life; Stress: Physiological responses; Stress-related diseases.

Agoraphobia and panic disorders

Type of psychology: Psychopathology

Panic disorders such as agoraphobia are characterized by severe anxiety attacks coupled with avoidance of a wide range of situations. Considerable progress has been made toward understanding their causes and treatment..

Key Concepts

- Depersonalization
- Derealization
- Fear of fear
- Flooding
- Habituation
- Hyperventilation
- Mitral valve prolapse syndrome
- Palpitations
- Paresthesia
- Social phobia

INTRODUCTION

Panic disorder is a condition characterized by frequent panic attacks—that is, intense surges of anxiety. These attacks of anxiety often occur unexpectedly or "out of the blue"; the individual frequently is unable to identify an external trigger for them. Between attacks, the patient often ruminates about the possibility of additional attacks.

Panic attacks tend to be accompanied by a number of physical symptoms. Hyperventilation—overly rapid or deep breathing—is common, as are choking and smothering sensations, dizziness, faintness, and paresthesias—sensations of numbness and tingling, particularly in the extremities. Other common symptoms during panic attacks are sweating, trembling, nausea, abdominal distress, hot or cold flashes, accelerated heart rate, chest pain, and heart palpitations. Not surprisingly, many individuals who are having a panic attack believe that they are experiencing a heart attack.

Panic attacks are also frequently characterized by a number of psychological symptoms, of which depersonalization and derealization are among the most common. Depersonalization is marked by feelings of unreality regarding oneself or one's body—sensations of being disconnected from oneself or of watching oneself as an outside observer. Derealization refers to feelings of unreality concerning the external world; objects or people may seem somehow strange or unfamiliar. Also common during panic attacks are fears of dying (for example, from a heart attack or stroke), losing one's mind, or performing embarrassing behaviors (such as screaming uncontrollably).

The difficulties of many patients with panic disorder do not end here, however; many, but not all, of these patients develop an often debilitating syndrome known as agoraphobia. Agoraphobia is a fear of situations in which escape is difficult, inconvenient, or potentially embarrassing, or in which assistance might not be readily available. Specifically, what appears to occur is that many panic patients, dreading the possibility of a future attack, begin to fear and (in many cases) avoid situations that might precipitate such an attack. The situations and locations feared or avoided by agoraphobics are extremely varied, but they include public transportation, open spaces, shopping malls, supermarkets, large social gatherings, elevators, driving in heavy traffic, passing over bridges or through tunnels, standing in long lines, and sitting in crowded theaters or churches.

In mild cases, agoraphobics may experience moderate discomfort while traveling or shopping alone and may avoid those situations in only certain cases. In severe cases, agoraphobics may be unwilling to leave the house unaccompanied. The fears of an agoraphobic are generally alleviated by the presence of another individual, particularly one close to the patient, probably because this person could provide help in the event of an emergency, such as a heart attack.

The prevalence of panic disorder with agoraphobia in the general population of the United States has been estimated to be approximately 5 percent; an additional 2 percent of Americans have been estimated to have panic disorder without agoraphobia. Thus, panic disorder is relatively common, and it is perhaps the most frequent reason individuals seek outpatient psychiatric care. In addition, isolated panic attacks occur frequently among individuals in the general population. G. Ron Norton and his colleagues, for example, have found that approximately 34 percent of college students experience occasional panic attacks.

Panic disorder and agoraphobia have been reported to occur more frequently among women than men, although this difference is probably more marked for agoraphobia than for panic disorder. In addition, the prevalence of panic disorder appears to decline with age; its frequency has generally been reported to be highest among individuals under thirty and lowest among individuals over sixty-five. The course of panic disorder tends to be chronic but fluctuating. In other words, its symptoms often persist for many years, but they typically wax and wane depending on the level of life stress and other factors.

In addition, panic disorder patients appear to have elevated rates of several medical conditions. A subset of these patients, for example, has been reported to have mitral valve prolapse syndrome, a condition in which the heart's mitral valve bulges into the atrium. Because this syndrome results in physical symptoms such as palpitations and chest pain, it may be a risk factor for panic disorder in some individuals. In addition, a subset of panic patients appear to have disturbances of the vestibular system, an apparatus in the inner ear responsible for maintaining balance. As dizziness is a common symptom of panic attacks, vestibular dysfunction may be an important precipitant of some panic attacks.

A number of psychiatric conditions are commonly found among patients with panic disorder and agoraphobia. Depression is a particularly frequent complication of both syndromes; in many cases, it probably results from the distress produced by panic attacks and the constriction of activities produced by agoraphobia. This depression may have tragic consequences; panic disorder patients have been reported to be at greatly increased risk for suicide compared with individuals in the general population. In addition, many panic disorder patients turn to alcohol or other substances to alleviate their anxiety. Also commonly associated with panic disorder is social phobia, a condition characterized by fears of the possible scrutiny or criticism of others. Like patients with panic disorder, many social phobics experience panic attacks. Nevertheless, in social phobia these attacks are almost invariably triggered by situations in which the patient is the perceived focus of others' attention.

POSSIBLE CAUSES

A variety of models have been proposed for the causation of panic disorder and agoraphobia. Early explanations tended to focus largely or exclusively on physiological factors. In the 1960s, Donald Klein and his colleagues reported that panic disorder improved following administration of imipramine, a drug traditionally used to treat depression, whereas more sustained and long-lasting (generalized) anxiety did not. Based on this finding, Klein and his coworkers argued that panic is biologically distinct from other forms of anxiety. Although Klein's observation was important, it should be noted that making inferences about the nature of a disorder from the treatment of that disorder is logically flawed: A condition's treatment bears no necessary implications for its cause (for example, one would not be justified in concluding that headaches are caused by a lack of aspirin).

Nevertheless, it seems likely that physiological factors play an important role in panic disorder. Identical twins (who share all the same genes) with panic disorder are more likely than are fraternal twins (who share only half of their genes, on average) to have co-twins with panic disorder, suggesting that genetic factors play at least some role in this disorder. It is not known, however, whether these genetic factors predispose a person to panic disorder per se or to anxiety in general.

There is evidence that the locus coeruleus, a structure in the pons (which is located at the back of the brain), is overactive during panic attacks. The locus coeruleus is a major center for norepinephrine, a chemical transmitter in the nervous system that appears to play a major role in the genesis of arousal and anxiety. Finally, it has been found that many patients with panic disorder, unlike those without the condition, develop panic attacks following infusion of certain substances, such as sodium lactate and caffeine. It is possible, however, that this is simply attributable to greater arousal on the part of panic disorder patients; the infusion of these substances may provoke attacks in these patients because they are already on the verge of panicking.

Many subsequent models of the causation of panic disorder have attempted to move beyond physiological abnormalities to examine how panic disorder patients react to and construe their environment. One of the most influential of these might be termed the "fear of fear" model. According to Dianne Chambless, Alan Goldstein, and other proponents of this model, individuals who are afraid of their own anxiety are particularly prone to the development of panic disorder. During frightening experiences, this fear of fear can spiral into a panic attack.

A more recent theory of panic disorder is the cognitive model of David Clark, Aaron T. Beck, and other researchers. According to this model, panic attacks result from the catastrophic misinterpretation of unusual or unexpected bodily sensations. In other words, panic attacks may occur when a physical symptom (such as rapid heartbeat or dizziness) is misinterpreted as presaging a disastrous outcome (heart attack or stroke). Interestingly, many of the physical symptoms of anxiety, such a rapid heartbeat, can themselves be exacerbated by anxiety, as anyone who has felt his or her heart race uncontrollably while giving a speech can attest. Thus, the misinterpretation of certain physical sensations may set in motion a cycle in which these sensations progressively increase in intensity, giving rise to further misinterpretations and ultimately culminating in a panic attack. The cognitive model is also consistent with the evidence, mentioned earlier, that some panic patients have physiological abnormalities, such as mitral valve prolapse and vestibular dysfunction. These abnormalities might be chronically misinterpreted by some individuals as indicative of serious consequences, and thereby provide a repeated trigger for panic attacks.

There is good evidence that many cases of panic disorder and agoraphobia are treatable by means of either medication or psychotherapy. Imipramine, as well as several other antidepressant drugs, appears to ameliorate the symptoms of these syndromes. It is not clear, however, whether these drugs actually exert their impact on panic or whether they instead work by alleviating the depressive symptoms so common to these patients. Alleviating depressive symptoms may then provide agoraphobics with the energy and confidence needed to confront previously avoided situations.

Panic disorder and agoraphobia also are amenable to interventions involving confrontation with feared situations. For example, many panic patients improve following flooding, a technique involving prolonged and intense exposure to feared stimuli. In the case of panic disorder, patients typically are exposed, in graduated fashion, to increasingly anxiety-producing situations. Patients are encouraged to remain in the situation until their anxiety subsides.

The efficacy of flooding and related treatments for panic disorder and agoraphobia can be explained in at least two ways. One possibility is that flooding works by a process known as habituation. Habituation is a process in which physiological or psychological responses decline in intensity with repeated stimulation. For example, many parachute jumpers find that their anxiety reactions gradually decrease with each succeeding jump; habituation may be the basis of this phenomenon. A second possibility is that flooding works by means of the cognitive model. That is, prolonged exposure to feared stimuli may demonstrate to patients that these stimuli are not as dangerous as they had believed.

HISTORY

The term "panic" derives from the Greek god Pan, who let out a terrifying scream whenever he was awakened by passersby. Most of the earliest accounts of panic attacks emphasized their physiological nature. In 1871, Jacob DaCosta described a syndrome he termed irritable heart, which was characterized by palpitations, shortness of breath, dizziness, and other symptoms now recognized as typical of panic disorder. DaCosta observed this condition both in Civil War soldiers and in individuals not involved in military combat. Irritable heart syndrome became a frequent diagnosis among anxiety-stricken soldiers in the Franco-Prussian and Boer Wars. Other early names for this syndrome were effort syndrome and neurocirculatory asthenia; again, both of these terms emphasized overexertion of the heart and circulatory system as the principal causes of panic symptoms.

At approximately the same time, Sigmund Freud was describing a syndrome he called anxiety neurosis. Freud noted that this neurosis could occur in a diffuse, long-lasting form (what later would be called generalized anxiety) or in sudden, discrete attacks marked by symptoms such as excessive heartbeat and respiration (what later would be called panic disorder). In contrast to DaCosta and other writers of this period, Freud emphasized unconscious psychological factors as the primary determinants of panic disorder. According to Freud, anxiety attacks resulted from a massive damming up (repression) of sexual impulses. In his later writings, Freud revised his position to assert that anxiety served as a signal to the individual that impulses needed to be repressed. According to this later view, anxiety (including panic) is a cause, rather than a result, of repression and functions as a defense mechanism to ward off trauma. Although many psychologists did not concur with Freud's conjectures, by World War II, there was increasing appreciation that many of the panic reactions seen among soldiers were largely of psychogenic origin.

The term "agoraphobia" stems from the Greek agora, meaning marketplace. As noted earlier, however, although agoraphobics fear marketplaces and similar situations, their fears tend to be extremely varied. "Agoraphobia" was coined by Alexander Westphal in 1871, who observed that many patients experienced anxiety while walking across open spaces or deserted streets. Interestingly, Moritz Benedikt had observed a similar syndrome in 1870; he labeled it Platzschwindel (dizziness in public places), a term that presaged findings of vestibular dysfunction in some of these patients.

Panic disorder and agoraphobia are recognized as two different, although often overlapping, conditions; however, professional opinion has vacillated on this point. In the third edition of the American Psychiatric Association's *Diagnostic and Statistical Manual of Mental Disorders* (DSM-III, 1980), for example, panic disorder and agoraphobia were listed as separate disorders. Then, in DSM-IV (1994), the two were specifically linked in three diagnoses: panic disorder with agoraphobia, panic disorder without agoraphobia, and agoraphobia with no history of panic disorder. In DSM-5 (2013), the pendulum of professional consensus swung back the other way, with the two again being listed as separate disorders, in recognition of the sizable number of individuals with agoraphobia who do not experience panic attacks.

BIBLIOGRAPHY

Bandelow, Borwin, Katharina Domschke, and David S. Baldwin. *Panic Disorder and Agoraphobia.* New York: Oxford UP, 2014. Print.

Barlow, David H. *Anxiety and Its Disorders.* 2nd ed. New York: Guilford, 2002. Print.

Bourne, Edmund J. *The Anxiety and Phobia Workbook.* 5th ed. Oakland: New Harbinger, 2011. Print.

Chambless, Dianne L., and Alan J. Goldstein, eds. *Agoraphobia: Multiple Perspectives on Theory and Treatment.* New York: Wiley, 1982. Print.

Lader, Malcolm H., and Thomas W. Uhde. *Anxiety, Panic, and Phobias.* 2nd ed. Abingdon: Health, 2006. Print.

Mathews, Andrew M., Michael G. Gelder, and Derek W. Johnston. *Agoraphobia: Nature and Treatment.* New York: Guilford, 1981. Print.

North, Carol S., and Sean H. Yutzy. "Panic Disorder and Phobias." *Goodwin and Guze's Psychiatric Diagnosis.* 6th ed. New York: Oxford UP, 2010. Print.

Sanfelippo, Augustin J., ed. *Panic Disorders: New Research.* New York: Nova Biomedical, 2006. Print.

Walker, John R., G. Ron Norton, and Colin A. Ross, eds. Panic Disorder and Agoraphobia: *A Comprehensive Guide for the Practitioner.* Pacific Grove: Brooks/Cole, 1991. Print.

Scott O. Lilienfeld

SEE ALSO: Antianxiety medications; Antidepressant medications; Anxiety disorders; Cognitive therapy; Depression; Diagnosis; Emotions; Phobias; Stress: Behavioral and psychological responses; Stress: Theories;

Air rage

DATE: 1990s forward

TYPE OF PSYCHOLOGY: Emotion; Social psychology; Stress

Air rage is a general term that describes unacceptable passenger behavior on aircraft. Many causes of air rage have been documented; these include alcohol and drugs, stress, mental illness, and even decompression sickness. Treatments and preventions vary according to the causes.

KEY CONCEPTS

- Aggression
- Alcohol
- Mental illness
- Stress
- Substance abuse

INTRODUCTION

The term "air rage" was coined by a newspaper reporter in the 1990s to describe abnormal, aberrant, or abusive airline passenger behavior that could potentially interfere with the ability of the cabin or flight crew to perform their duties and thereby endanger the crew and other passengers or prevent the safe operation of the aircraft. The phenomenon has been increasing steadily since the late 1970s, when airlines were deregulated and the increase in the number of passengers made flights more crowded and created more delays. Incidences of passengers exhibiting abnormal, aberrant, or abusive behavior on aircraft or while embarking or deplaning have gradually increased. In some ways, the term "air rage" is a misnomer, because although it describes passengers who become enraged and act out, it also is used to describe incidents in which passengers become erratic or combative for reasons other than rage. Before the September 11, 2001, terrorist attacks on the World Trade Center and the Pentagon, hijacking was often considered a form of air rage, but it is now clearly recognized that hijacking is a planned, purposeful attack, whereas air rage is not.

The very environment in which air rage occurs contributes to it. The airplane is an enclosed space with nowhere for the angry, upset, or ill passenger to go or any place to which the threatened passengers or crew can escape.

CAUSES

Although many passengers expect a relaxing, quick trip on an airplane, the reality of modern air travel can be stressful, with flight delays, long lines at security stations and ticket counters, and crowded, uncomfortable seating. The "classic" cases of air rage occur when passengers become stressed and irritated to a breaking point, resulting in violent, abusive behavior.

Alcohol is estimated to play a role in 50 to 75 percent of reported air rage incidents. Alcohol is served in airport bars and on flights and is usually free to first-class passengers. The body requires oxygen to metabolize alcohol, and the reduced oxygen levels at altitude cause people consuming one or two drinks to become more intoxicated than they would at sea level. Incidents have been reported in which intoxicated passengers, after their requests for additional alcohol were refused by flight attendants, became enraged and assaulted crew members and other passengers.

Prescription and illegal drugs can also be causes of air rage incidents. There have been cases in which people with psychotic disorders left their prescription medications in their checked baggage or had them confiscated by security and then suffered psychotic episodes on their flights. Passengers under the influence of illegal drugs such as lysergic acid diethylamide (LSD) and phencyclidine (PCP) have threatened the safety of their flights with combative, erratic behavior. Nicotine is also a drug, and approximately 9 percent of air rage cases involve passengers trying to smoke on airplanes, where smoking is prohibited.

Undiagnosed mental illnesses have contributed to instances of air rage. Passengers who variously threatened to blow up aircraft, attempted to kill flight crews, or took over the cockpit and tried to steer the aircraft into the ground were later diagnosed with conditions such as depression, bipolar disorder, or severe anxiety. One passenger, on a flight home from a scuba diving trip in the Caribbean, became severely depressed and attempted suicide on the aircraft. Later it was found that his mental condition was caused by decompression sickness, a result of the scuba diving. Approximately 22 percent of air rage incidents involve mental illness or instability.

PREVENTION

It is very difficult to predict where or when air rage will occur or to identify an individual who might be an air rage perpetrator, and a number of proposals have been made to reduce or prevent incidences of air rage. One is for airlines to have a zero tolerance policy toward air rage and prosecute cases of air rage more stringently. Another is to limit or remove alcohol from flights and to prevent intoxicated passengers from boarding aircraft. A few airlines based in countries outside the United States have nicotine gum, pills, and patches available for the use of passengers who are smokers.

Several airlines have begun training their flight crews in how to deal with angry passengers with the goal of preventing incidents before they happen. German airlines allow their crews to carry handcuffs to restrain passengers if necessary. One international aviation agency has requested that closed circuit cameras be installed in the cabins of aircraft so that the flight crew can monitor any disruptive activities in the cabin from the security of the flight deck.

Information and education may also help passengers. Some passengers get upset by delays that they do not understand, so if airlines supply passengers with updates and information on flight conditions and delays, this could help prevent dissatisfaction from turning into rage. In addition, helping travelers understand that they should bring essential medications on board rather than check them in their luggage would ensure that these medications are available to passengers during flight if necessary.

BIBLIOGRAPHY

Akgeyik, Tekin. "Air Rage: Violence toward Cabin Crew." *Review of Business Research* 11.3 (2011): 68–73. Print.

Anonymous and Andrew R. Thomas. *Air Rage: Crisis in the Skies.* Amherst: Prometheus, 2001. Print.
Bor, Robert, ed. *Passenger Behavior.* Burlington: Ashgate, 2003. Print.
Celetano, Ted. *Combating Air Rage.* Bloomington: Authorhouse, 2001. Print.
Dahlberg, Angela. *Air Rage: The Underestimated Safety Risk.* Burlington: Ashgate, 2001. Print.
Gawthrop, Mary. "Psychological Aspects of Travel." *Practice Nurse* 40.4 (2010): 30–34. Print.
Fairechild, Diana. *Jet Smarter: The Air Traveler's Rx.* New York: Flyana, 2003. Print.

Polly D. Steenhagen

See Also: Aggression; Aggression: Reduction and control; Alcohol dependence and abuse; Anger; Nicotine dependence; Road rage.

Albee, George W.

Born: December 20, 1921
Birthplace: St. Mary's, Pennsylvania
Died: July 8, 2006
Place of death: Longboat Key, Florida
Type of psychology: Social psychology

Albee was a pioneer in the study of the psychology of prevention of mental illness.

George W. Albee graduated from Bethany College in West Virginia with a bachelor's degree in psychology in 1943. After serving in the US Army for three years during World War II, he attended the University of Pittsburgh and earned his doctorate in psychology in 1949. Between 1951 and 1953, Albee served as an assistant executive secretary for the American Psychological Association. In 1954, he accepted a position as an associate professor of psychology at Case Western Reserve University in Cleveland, Ohio.

During the 1950s and 1960s, Albee authored groundbreaking studies in the field of social psychology showing that psychologists would never cure psychiatric disorders by treating one patient at a time. He believed that not only biological disorders but also societal and environmental factors, including racism, sexism, poverty, child abuse, and any other condition that allowed the exploitation of individuals, were responsible for promoting mental illness. Because there are too few qualified practitioners to treat the enormous number of mental and emotional disorders on an individual basis, Albee concluded that the most effective and humane way to reduce mental illness is by primary prevention brought about by social changes. Just as preventive medicine lowers the risk that a person may experience an illness or injury later in life, preventive social change can allow each person the resources and freedom to cope successfully with life's challenges.

Under President Dwight D. Eisenhower, Albee served as the director of the Task Force on Manpower of the Joint Commission on Mental Illness and Health in 1957. His report on the shortage of mental health providers in the United States led to the development of community mental health centers. In 1971, he accepted a position as professor of psychology at the University of Vermont. In 1975, he established the Vermont Conference on the Primary Prevention of Psychopathology (VCPPP), one of the leading forums in the world for discussion and dissemination of information on all aspects of preventive psychopathology.

In 1975, Albee received the Distinguished Professional Contribution Award from the American Psychological Association. From 1977 to 1978, he served under President Jimmy Carter as coordinator of the Task Panel on Prevention for the President's Commission on Mental Health. During his distinguished career, Albee published more than two hundred articles and book chapters about mental illness prevention. He retired in 1992 and died from liver cancer in 2006.

BIBLIOGRAPHY

Kendler, Kenneth S. *Genes, Environment, and Psychopathology.* New York: Guilford, 2006. Print.
Kessler, Marc, Stephen E. Goldston, and Justin M. Joffe, eds. *The Present and Future of Prevention: In Honor of George W. Albee.* Thousand Oaks: Sage, 1992. Print.
Melchert, Timothy P. *Foundations of Professional Psychology.* Waltham: Elsevier, 2011. Print.
Simonton, Dean Keith. *Great Psychologists and Their Times: Scientific Insights into Psychology's History.* Washington: American Psychological Association, 2002. Print.
U'Ren, Richard. Social Perspective: *The Missing Element in Mental Health Practice.* Toronto: U of Toronto P, 2011. Print.
Vera, Elizabeth, ed. *The Oxford Handbook of Prevention in Counseling Psychology.* New York: Oxford UP, 2013. Print.

Alvin K. Benson

See Also: Child abuse; Psychopathology; Racism; Sexism

Alcohol dependence and abuse

Type of psychology: Psychopathology

Alcohol dependence is a psychiatric disorder characterized by a maladaptive pattern of alcohol use involving serious behavioral and physical consequences and that may, in its most severe form, result in death.

Key Concepts

- Cerebral cortex
- Cirrhosis
- Delirium tremens
- Harm reduction
- Neuritis
- Psychosis
- Relapse prevention
- Wernicke-Korsakoff syndrome

INTRODUCTION

Pure ethyl alcohol is a colorless, mild-smelling liquid that boils at 79 degrees Celsius and evaporates quickly at room temperature. It is made either by fermentation of grain mashed and suspended in water or fruit juice followed by the distillation (boiling) of the beer or wine that is produced or by chemical synthesis from the petrochemical ethylene. Ethyl alcohol—usually simply called alcohol—has many uses, including the sterilization of surgical instruments and inclusion in the fuel gasohol; it is the liquid in which many medicines are dissolved, it serves as the main component of perfumes and colognes, and it is used in the manufacture of many useful chemicals. The best-known use of alcohol, however, is in alcoholic beverages, viewed by many as recreational beverages because of the mood-altering properties of the alcohol they contain.

It is believed that alcoholic beverages have been made since prehistoric times. The oldest records of widespread brewing of beer and production of wine have been found in what were ancient Babylon and Egypt. According to historians, the main reason for the preparation of alcoholic beverages by early civilizations was alcohol's antimicrobial properties that kept grape juice and other food sources from spoiling. Drinking sparing amounts of fermented beverages was also thought to prevent illnesses that people contracted from contaminated drinking water or from other unfermented beverages.

The misuse of alcoholic beverages has occurred since their discovery; however, it became widespread during the Middle Ages when the art of distillation became more universal and producing hard liquors containing five to ten times the alcohol of beer and wine made it easier to reach alcoholic euphoria and stupor. A 2012 Gallup poll reported that equal numbers of men and women in the United States claimed to consume alcoholic beverages, although men claimed to have more drinks on average than women. At any given time, 5 percent of all drinkers polled qualify for a diagnosis of alcohol dependence. People who misuse alcohol to the point of severe physical consequences and conditions such as alcohol dependence are often called alcoholics. They may exhibit problems with controlling their use of alcohol, despite its severe negative consequences on their health, behavior, daily functioning, time management, and relationships.

Continued drinking over a long period of time, despite alcohol dependence, affects many of the organs in the body such as the brain, where related alcohol induced mental disorders include delirium tremens (also known as the DTs), acute alcoholic hallucinations, and Wernicke-Korsakoff syndrome. The DTs are a response to severe alcohol withdrawal that includes anxiety attacks, confusion, depression, delirium, tremor, terrifying hallucinations, and other symptoms of psychosis. Psychosis is a severe mental state characterized by partial or complete withdrawal from reality. Wernicke-Korsakoff syndrome is a degenerative brain disorder caused by a lack of thiamine, often produced by alcohol abuse, that causes disorientation, impaired long-term memory, and the production of false perceptions to fill or make sense of memory gaps. It is a two-stage disease, with Wernicke's encephalopathy being the acute phase and Korsakoff's amnesic syndrome being the chronic phase. Both the DTs and Wernicke-Korsakoff syndrome may be accompanied by physical debility that can require hospitalization.

Alcoholic neuritis will develop when alcohol is the sole food consumed. In addition, alcohol dependence can lead to liver damage (causing cirrhosis, a potentially lethal condition), kidney damage, and damage to the heart and the pancreas. Cirrhosis is a chronic liver disease characterized by the destruction of liver cells and their replacement by nonfunctional tissue. This ultimately causes blocked blood circulation, liver failure, and death. Furthermore, the National Institute on Alcohol Abuse and Alcoholism reported in 2010 that alcohol dependence, combined with excessive cigarette smoking, greatly enhances the incidence of cancer of the mouth, throat, liver, and breast.

There is no clear physical explanation for or cause of the development of alcohol dependence. The National Institute of Health reported in 2014 that research suggests that alcohol dependence develops as the result of a genetic predisposition, although it is unknown which genes are responsible. Numerous studies point to other factors such as an individual's perceived social problems and psychological stress as contributors to alcohol dependence.

There is also no known cure for alcohol dependence. However, for the majority of individuals entering treatment, some benefit regardless of treatment orientations or treatment goals. Depending on the level of functioning of the individual before entering treatment for alcohol use disorders, rates of complete abstinence from drinking for one year following treatment may range from 20 to 65 percent. Abstinence is only one treatment goal, however; relapse prevention and harm reduction approaches also are sometimes employed.

In relapse prevention, the goal is to have people manage high-risk situations and lapses during which they are more likely to drink so that they do not turn into extended relapses or full-blown returns to pretreatment drinking. In harm reduction approaches, the goal might be to have patients refrain from drinking in risky situations, such as while driving or while taking medication, or to decrease the frequency or amount consumed rather than quit drinking altogether. This latter approach is used to achieve some progress toward more adaptive behavior when, for whatever reasons, a client might not wish to abstain completely or might not be able to do so.

The recognition of alcohol dependence as a medical problem has led to the opening of many alcohol-rehabilitation treatment centers, where psychiatric treatment, medication, and physical therapy in various combinations provide valuable treatments. Furthermore, many experts believe that Alcoholics Anonymous (AA) programs are effective deterrents to a return to maladaptive alcohol use.

CHANGING ATTITUDES

As pointed out by Andrew M. Mecca, before 1935 alcohol dependence was perceived mainly as criminal behavior that merited punishment. Around 1935, the problem began to be identified as a disease. Crucial to the successful treatment of alcohol dependence was the advent of Alcoholics Anonymous (AA), which was founded in that year. This organization operates on the premise that abstinence is the best course of treatment for alcohol dependence and achieving sobriety.

The methodology of Alcoholics Anonymous is psychosocial. It brings individuals with alcohol problems to the realization that they cannot use any amount of alcoholic beverages without succumbing to alcohol dependence. It identifies the need for help from a higher power, and it develops a support group of people with the same condition. As stated by Mecca, "Alcoholics Anonymous never pronounces the disease cured. . . . [I]t is arrested." Alcoholics Anonymous estimated that as of January 2014, membership had grown to over 2 million members and the organization was represented in over 170 countries. Members of AA achieve results ranging from discrete periods of sobriety (usually lasting for longer periods as membership in the organization continues) to lifelong sobriety. A liability of relying solely on Alcoholics Anonymous for treatment, according to many experts, is the lack of medical, psychiatric, and trained psychosocial counseling. This is especially true for individuals whose addiction to alcohol occurs concurrently with other disorders such as depression, anxiety, or post-traumatic stress disorder.

In addition to abstinence and therapeutic interventions, there are also medical options available to individuals who suffer from alcohol dependence. One drug, which was first discovered in the 1920s, is disulfiram (brand names Antabuse and Antabus), which, if alcohol is used in conjunction with it, produces immediate and unpleasant physical reactions such as vomiting, cold sweats, and increased heart rate. Citrated calcium carbimide (brand name Temposil) is also used to treat alcoholism and produces a similar physical reaction. Normally, alcohol dehydrogenase converts alcohol to the toxic chemical acetaldehyde. Aldehyde dehydrogenase then quickly converts acetaldehyde to acetic acid, the main biological fuel of the body. Abstem and Antabuse turn off aldehyde dehydrogenase. This causes acetaldehyde buildup in the body when alcohol is consumed, quickly leading to violent headache, flushing, nausea, dizziness, heart palpitation, and vertigo. A nine-year study published in 2006 in the journal Alcoholism: Clinical and Experimental Research found that the incorporation of Antabuse and Temposil into the outpatient treatment plan of 180 alcoholics resulted in a 50 percent rate of abstinence among participants. Neither drug should be given without a doctor's supervision or without the alcoholic's knowledge because of the serious danger the drugs pose when combined with alcohol.

Another medication used in the treatment of alcohol dependence is naltrexone, which is a once-daily pill that works with brain receptors in order to reduce cravings for alcohol. Unlike Antabuse and Temposil, which are used to promote abstinence from alcohol, naltrexone has been effectively used to reduce the frequency of drinking as well as the severity of relapse to drinking. In 2010, the Federal Drug Administration (FDA) approved an injectable, extended release form of naltrexone that is given monthly in a physician's office.

Photo: iStock

Tranquilizers and related sedative hypnotics may also be used to treat alcohol dependence. However, this must also be done with great care and under a doctor's supervision because many of these drugs have addictive properties. In addition, sedatives, when combined with alcohol, can be fatal.

The value of engaging in therapy to treat alcohol dependence has been identified by various sources. David H. Knott, in his book *Alcohol Problems: Diagnosis and Treatment* (1986), points out that while a psychotherapist cannot perform miracles, psychotherapy can be very valuable in helping the alcoholic patient by identifying factors leading to "destructive use of alcohol," exploring and helping rectify problems associated with alcohol abstinence, providing emotional support that helps many patients rebuild their lives, and interfacing in referring patients to Alcoholics Anonymous and other long-term support efforts. The psychotherapist also has irreplaceable experience with psychoactive therapeutic drugs, behavioral modification techniques, and identifying whether a given individual requires inpatient treatment.

Knott also points out the importance of behavioral modification as a cornerstone of alcohol psychotherapy and makes it clear that a wide variety of choices are available to alcoholics desiring psychosocial help. An interesting point made by A. E. Bennett in *Alcoholism and the Brain* (1977) is that autopsy and a variety of sophisticated medical techniques, including computed tomography (CT) scans, identify atrophy of the cerebral cortex of the brain in many alcoholics. This damage is viewed as a factor in the inability of alcoholics to stop drinking, as well as in loss of motor skills and eventual development of serious conditions such as Wernicke-Korsakoff syndrome.

TREATING AN EPIDEMIC

The excessive use of alcoholic beverages, with resultant alcohol dependence, has occurred for many centuries. Modern efforts to deal with alcohol dependence are often considered to have begun in the early twentieth century, with the activities of the American temperance movement that culminated with Prohibition and the ratification of the Eighteenth Amendment. The idea behind Prohibition was that making liquor "impossible to get" would force sobriety on the nation. The measure turned out to be self-defeating, however, and several sources point out that it actually increased the incidence of alcohol dependence in the country. It was repealed in 1933.

The next effort to combat alcohol dependence was the psychosocial approach of Alcoholics Anonymous, which was founded in 1935. Other efforts and treatment methodologies that have been used to combat alcoholism include psychiatric counseling, alcohol rehabilitation centers, family counseling, and alcohol management programs in the workplace. These options—alone or in various combinations—have had considerable success, especially when combined with alcohol dependence therapy; however, it has not yet been possible to stem the tide of increasing alcohol dependence or to cure the disease. Instead, these techniques succeed in arresting the disease perhaps because the basis for alcohol dependence is not clearly understood by those attempting to eradicate it. One hope for curing alcohol dependence is ongoing research into the biochemistry, pharmacology, and physiology of alcohol dependence.

BIBLIOGRAPHY

Bennett, Abram Elting. *Alcoholism and the Brain.* New York: Stratton Intercontinental Medical, 1977. Print.

Connors, Gerard Joseph, Dennis M. Donovan, and Carlo DiClemente. *Substance Abuse and the Stages of Change: Slecting and Planning Interventions*. 2nd ed. New York: Guilford, 2013. Print.

Cox, W. Miles, ed. *The Treatment and Prevention of Alcohol Problems: A Resource Manual.* Orlando.: Academic, 1987. Print.

Fletcher, Anne M., and Frederick B. Glasser. *Sober for Good: New Solutions for Drinking Problems—Advice from Those Who Have Succeeded*. Boston: Houghton Mifflin, 2001. Print.

Hester, Reid K., and William R. Miller, eds. *Handbook of Alcoholism Treatment Approaches: Effective Alternatives.* 3rd ed. Boston: Allyn & Bacon, 2003. Print.

Kaufmann, Christopher N., Lian-Yu Chen, Roas M. Crum, and Ramin Majtabai. "Treatment Seeking and Barriers to Treatment for Alcohol Use in Persons with Alcohol Use Disorders and Comorbid Mood or Anxiety Disorders." *Social Psychiatry and Psychiatric Epidemiology.* (2013). Print.

Knapp, Caroline. *Drinking: A Love Story.* New York: Bantam Dell, 2005. Print.

Knott, David H. *Alcohol Problems: Diagnosis and Treatment.* New York: Pergamon, 1986. Print.

Ludwig, Fabian, et al."Self-Efficacy as a Predictor of Outcome After Residential Treatment Programs for Alcohol Dependence: Simply Ask the Patient One Question!" *Alcoholism: Clinical & Experimental Research* 37:4 (2013): 663–7. Print.

Mecca, Andrew M. *Alcoholism in America: A Modern Perspective.* Belvedere: California Health Research Foundation, 1980. Print.

Ramchandani, V. A., J. Umhau, F. J. Pavon, et al. "A Genetic Determinant of the Striatal Dopamine Response to Alcohol in Men." *Molecular Psychiatry* 16.8 (2011): 809–17. Print.

Tracy, Sarah W. *Alcoholism in America: From Reconstruction to Prohibition.* Baltimore: Johns Hopkins UP, 2007. Print.

Sanford S. Singer; updated by Nancy A. Piotrowski

See Also: Addictive personality and behaviors; Battered woman syndrome; Brain structure; Codependency; Coping: Social support; Group therapy; Hallucinations; Motivation; Optimal arousal theory; Pain management; Psychotic disorders; Self-esteem; Self-help groups; Substance use disorders; Support groups

Allport, Gordon

Born: November 11, 1897
Birthplace: Montezuma, Indiana
Died: October 9, 1967
Place of death: Cambridge, Massachusetts
Type of psychology: Personality; Social psychology

Allport rejected behaviorism and studied personality and the self, as well as practical aspects of social psychology such as the functioning of values, rumor, and prejudice. He promoted a humanistic psychology.

Gordon Allport was the youngest of four boys in a midwestern family. His father was a physician; an elder brother, Floyd, became an important figure in social psychology. Allport received a BA from Harvard University in 1919, taught English in Turkey for a year, and received a PhD from Harvard in 1922. For the next two years, he studied in Germany and England, making contacts that would influence him for a lifetime. He returned to spend the rest of his life teaching and conducting research at Harvard, except during a four-year hiatus from 1926 to 1930 spent at Dartmouth College.

Influenced heavily by his European studies, he was one of the few successfully to resist both behaviorism and psychoanalysis as defining schools of thought.

One of Allport's mentors was the German psychologist William Stern, whose personalistic psychology was seen by Allport as a step toward his own idiographic method (a study of the individual, as opposed to the study of the group, which is labeled nomothetic). Allport claimed that the closest counterpart of Stern's system of thought in the United States was the self psychology of Mary W. Calkins, a student of William James. Allport left a rich store of ideas about the personality and the self, or the ego, which he finally designated as the proprium.

In 1937, Allport published his major work, *Personality: A Psychological Interpretation*. He introduced the concept of functional autonomy and gave prominent mention to Alfred Adler, the psychoanalyst who first stressed social variables. In 1955, he published *Becoming: Basic Considerations for a Psychology of Personality.* In this work, he first introduced the term "proprium," addressing the question of whether the concept of self is necessary, and, making note of valid criticisms, opted for a bare minimum of self functions.

In a 1961 revision of *Personality* titled *Pattern and Growth in Personality,* Allport elaborated on the concept of the proprium but followed his 1937 scheme of presenting the aspects of the self in a developmental context. He also enlarged his thinking on the mature person. His best-known and most popular work, *The Nature of Prejudice* (1954), represents a practical area in which he was interested. He also published focused studies of religion, expressive movement, social attitudes, rumor, and radio.

BIBLIOGRAPHY

Deaux, Kay, and Mark Snyder, eds. *The Oxford Handbook of Personality and Social Psychology*. New York: Oxford UP, 2012. Print.

Evans, Richard I. *Gordon Allport: The Man and His Ideas.* New York: Praeger, 1981. Print.

Hewstone, Miles, Wolfgang Stroebe, and Klaus Jonas, eds. *An Introduction to Social Psychology.* 5th ed. Chichester: Wiley, 2012. Print.

Monte, Christopher. "Gordon W. Allport: Humanistic Trait and Self Theory." *Beneath the Mask: An Introduction to Theories of Personality.* Ed. Christopher F. Monte and Robert N. Sollod. 7th ed. Hoboken: Wiley, 2003. Print.

Nicholson, Ian A. M. *Inventing Personality: Gordon Allport and the Science of Selfhood.* Washington: American Psychological Association, 2003. Print.

Sheehy, Noel. *Fifty Key Thinkers in Psychology.* New York: Routledge, 2013.

Everett J. Delahanty, Jr.

See Also: Adler, Alfred; Humanistic psychology; Humanistic trait models: Gordon Allport; Individual psychology: Alfred Adler; Personality theory; Prejudice; Prejudice reduction.

Altered states of consciousness

Type of psychology: Addiction, Behavioral medicine, Biological bases of human behavior, Clinical, Cognitive, Counseling, Social

An altered state of consciousness can be defined as a process that alters the state of awareness or awakeness. Many things can produce an altered state of consciousness, including sleep, psychoactive drugs, hypnosis, and meditation. The activity of the brain during an altered state of consciousness can be measured by the use of an electroencephalogram.

Key concepts:

- Electroencephalogram
- Sleep
- Psychoactive Drugs
- Hypnosis
- Meditation

INTRODUCTION

Consciousness can be defined as a subjective awareness of internal and external events. It can also be defined as a state of awakeness. Consciousness involves focus, as many times in the human experience, we choose to focus on different thoughts, sensations, and experiences. An altered state of consciousness can be defined as a process that effects or alters the state of awareness or awakeness. This altered state can be psychological, physiological, or induced; and can include sleep, illegal and prescription drug use, meditation, and hypnosis.

The activity of the brain during an altered state of consciousness can be measured by an electroencephalogram (or EEG). EEG's track and record brain wave patterns, and are usually used by neurologists. By reading these patterns, neurologists can identify brain state and/or brain abnormalities. Alpha waves denote activity and wakefulness. Theta waves are seen in periods of deep relaxation. Delta waves are slow, large brain waves and indicate a particular stage of sleep.

SLEEP

Sleep is a physiological change in one's level of awareness. In sleep, one's consciousness shifts as electrical and neuronal activity in the brain changes.

There are five stages of sleep, each with its own altered state of awareness. Stage 1 through 4 are known as NREM (non-rapid eye movement) stages; while Stage 5 is considered REM (rapid eye movement) sleep.

In Stage 1 sleep, an individual is in a deep state of relaxation, but can hear everything that is going on around them. EEG readings will show theta waves, which are slow in frequency and large in amplitude. During stage 1, an individual may experience what is called a hypnic jerk, which is an involuntary muscle twitch. Many people perceive a sense of free falling during a hypnic jerk.

Stage 2 is categorized as a state of sleep in which the brain is in an altered state, yet is still sensitive and can be woken up by loud noises. K complex sleep spindles (which are sudden, sharp leaps in EEG wave readings) are seen during any abrupt awakening due to noise or other environmental changes in the room.

Stage 3 and 4 are the deeper states of sleep. If woken up during a stage 3 or 4 sleep, an individual may feel disorientated. Delta waves usually show up in stage 3 sleep, signifying an altered state of consciousness. During stages 3 and 4 of sleep, breathing, heart rate, and blood pressure all decline.

Stage 5 sleep is REM sleep. REM sleep is also called paradoxical sleep, because EEG readings during REM sleep resemble a period of awakeness. Physiologically during REM sleep, increases in heart rate, blood pressure, and metabolism are observed. Rapid, rolling eye movements take place, along with twitching in fingers and toes. The large muscles of the body experience sleep paralysis, and penile erection may occur.

REM sleep usually, but not always, includes a high level of dream sleep. There are many theories as to why we may dream, including Freud's *Wish Fulfillment Theory* (1900) and Hobson & McCarley's *Activation Synthesis Theory* (1977). Freud's *Wish Fulfillment Theory* posits that dreams function to fulfill the unexpressed personal wishes and thoughts of an individual. *Activation Synthesis Theory* hypothesizes that dreaming is only a function of rapid cell activity in the brain. Many researchers also feel that dreaming may be important for memory consolidation.

Researchers generally believe that sleep has two main functions. One is a restoration function, while the other is an evolutionary function. The restoration function of sleep suggests that sleep provides downtime for the ever-active brain. It also creates a space for humans to rest and recover physically from their daily activities. The evolutionary function of sleep may be an adaptive response to the perceived dangers of the night. Our ancestors needed to stay sheltered in the night to protect themselves from nocturnal animals and other environmental hazards. Thus, we may be evolutionarily predisposed to sleep during the night.

PSYCHOACTIVE DRUGS

Psychoactive drugs affect mental and behavioral process in an individual, leading to an altered state of consciousness. Drugs disrupt the neurotransmitter transmission process in the brain. Neurotransmitters are chemicals released by neurons, or brain cells; examples of major neurotransmitters include serotonin, dopamine, and gamma amino butyric acid (GABA). Addiction to drugs becomes an issue, as the individual drug user may become physically and psychologically dependent on a specific drug.

Depressants are a class of drugs that slow down the ongoing activity in the nervous system. Types of depressants include alcohol, tranquilizers, and barbiturates. Alcohol works on the GABA and dopamine systems in the brain. Alcohol increases feelings of sluggishness, reduces overall reaction time, and tends to decrease one's self-awareness. In low doses, tranquilizers and barbiturates may increase relaxation; but in high doses, concentration is lost, memory becomes impaired, and speech may become slurred.

Stimulants tend to increase nervous system activity. Types of stimulants include caffeine, nicotine, amphetamines, and cocaine. These drugs tend to increase alertness and feelings of pleasure, and work directly on the brain's dopamine system. Those who use stimulants may report higher heart and blood pressure rates, as well as a lower appetite.

Opiates such as heroin and morphine depress nervous system activity, and increase levels of dopamine in the brain. Use of opiates tends to reduce anxiety and elevate mood. They also lower sensitivity to pain. Opiates have powerful addictive qualities, and can cause confusion, drowsiness, nausea, and decreased respiration.

Hallucinogens alter one's perception of reality, and tend to effect the secretion of serotonin in the brain.

Some users of lysergic acid diethylamide (LSD) report blendings of sensory experiences, including being able to taste colors, and hear textures. Psychologically, this phenomenon is known as synesthesia. Flashbacks, intense feelings of panic, and depression have also been reported. Marijuana is a more common hallucinogen that tends to lower anxiety, increase sensory sensitivity, and increase feelings of wellbeing. Side effects of marijuana include panic, loss of concentration, decreased motor coordination, and decreased visual tracking ability.

HYPNOSIS

Hypnosis is an altered state of consciousness that produces a heightened state of suggestibility in a willing participant. It is usually performed by a trained hypnotist or psychologist, and has been used as a tool for smoking cessation, weight loss, and pain relief. It has also been used clinically to decrease levels of anxiety, depression, and post-traumatic stress disorder. When a person is hypnotized, they arrive at a deep state of relaxation. The hypnotist may then ask the individual to focus on an object, image, or the hypnotist's voice. After a while, the hypnotist may make a suggestion regarding the individuals' feelings or perceptions. This suggestion stays with them as they exit the hypnotic state and go about their day, thus changing behavior and automatic responses to nicotine, food, pain, or stress. Not all individuals are highly hypnotizable. Current research states that approximately two thirds of individuals will respond to hypnosis as a therapeutic technique.

There are two major theories that focus on what happens during hypnosis. Hilgard's (1977) dissociation theory states that hypnosis really is an altered state of consciousness. Specifically, Hilgard explains that during hypnosis, the mind divides into two states. One level of consciousness voluntarily agrees to behave under the suggestion of the hypnotist in a state of deep relaxation, while the other level is in a hidden observer state. The hidden observer state is aware of all that is happening, yet still follows the commands of the hypnotist. Response set theory (Kirsch, 2000), states that hypnosis is not an altered state of consciousness at all. Instead, the individual being hypnotized is just displaying a high level of willingness when responding to a hypnotists' suggestion.

MEDITATION

Meditation can also produce an altered state of consciousness. Meditation relies on a level of deep relaxation, and the focus is on clearing the mind of intrusive thoughts. Meditation allows an escape from the automaticity of everyday life, and has its roots in Eastern philosophy. Most individuals who meditate rely on a mantra, or repeated word, phrase, or prayer. After meditation, users report an expanded state of awareness, and a better ability to effectively self-reflect. Meditation has been shown to have several health benefits, including lowering blood pressure, heart rate, and respiration rate. Many individuals who meditate also report stronger immune function, as well as lower levels of stress and anxiety.

BIBLIOGRAPHY

American Society of Clinical Hypnosis (n.d.) Retrieved from http://www.asch.net/.

Largest U.S. organization of professional clinicians who use hypnosis in their practice. ASCH provides training, workshops, certifications, and support for hypnotists and those interested in hypnosis.

Kabat – Zinn, J. (2011). *Mindfulness For Beginners: Reclaiming the Present Moment – and Your Life.* Louisville, CO: Sounds True Publishers.

Gives an overview on the importance of meditation for health and well being, also includes beginning reflections and practices from leading meditation researcher Kabat –Zinn.

Julien, R.M. (1995). *A Primer of Drug Action: A Concise, Nontechnical Guide to the Actions, Uses, and Side Effects of Psychoactive Drugs.* (7th ed.). New York: Henry Holt & Company.

A clinical book on the effects of psychoactive drugs on the brain. Includes a chapter on psychopharmaceutical and non-psychopharmaceutical drug treatment of major psychological disorders.

Morin, C.M. (Ed.) & Espie, C.A. (Ed.). (2012). *The Oxford Handbook of Sleep and Sleep Disorders.* New York: Oxford University Press. Provides a comprehensive overview of current research on sleep, sleep stages, and sleep disorders.

Pastorino, E. & Doyle – Portillo, S. (2011). *Consciousness: Wide Awake, In a Daze, or Dreaming? In What is Psychology?* (pp. 143 – 186). Belmont, CA: Wadsworth.

A basic overview of altered states of consciousness. Includes sections on sleep, meditation, dreaming, hypnosis, and psychoactive drug use.

Gina Riley

Altruism, cooperation, and empathy

Type of psychology: Biological bases of behavior; Social psychology

Altruism and cooperation are types of prosocial behavior. Empathy involves identification with another, and it leads to increased prosocial behavior.

Key Concepts
- Altruism
- Cooperation
- Egoistic motivation
- Empathy
- Prosocial behavior

INTRODUCTION

Social psychologists, like other social scientists and social philosophers, have long been intrigued by what is called the "altruism paradox." The altruism paradox arises from the fact that individuals sometimes engage in self-sacrificial acts that benefit another. This contradicts the assumption made in most theories of motivation that individuals engage only in behavior that is beneficial to themselves. There are two basic ways to resolve the altruism paradox. One way is to try to identify the perhaps subtle self-benefits from helping that motivate seemingly altruistic prosocial behavior—behavior intended to benefit another. The second way is to assert that individuals do engage in behavior that benefits others, irrespective of any benefit to the self. Theories and research on prosocial behavior

THEORIES OF EGOISTIC MOTIVATION

Theories of egoistic motivation for helping assume that some form of self-benefit motivates individuals to act prosocially. The self-benefits from helping are most easily recognizable in the case of cooperation. Cooperation is a type of prosocial behavior in which the self-benefit is the same as the benefit to the person helped: individuals mutually benefit by achieving a common goal. An individual's self-interest is often best served by cooperating with others because, without cooperation, the individual may be unable to achieve a desirable goal. Selfishness, then, may prompt cooperation; if it does, the motivation to act prosocially is egoistic, not altruistic. The benefit to the other is a by-product of acting prosocially to benefit the self.

Theories of egoistic motivation for helping point out that cooperation is not the only type of prosocial behavior that can be mutually beneficial for both the persons giving and receiving help. The self-benefit for the person giving help also can be different from the benefit for the person receiving help. This principle forms the basis of the arousal-reduction explanation for helping developed by Jane Allyn Piliavin and her colleagues. Their theory proposes that individuals experience aversive physiological arousal when they encounter another person in need. One way to reduce this aversive arousal is to help the person in need, because alleviating the other's need terminates the stimulus causing the bystander's own distress. Thus, the theory proposes that bystanders will help as a way to reduce their own aversive arousal. The persons giving and receiving help benefit in different ways, but it is important to recognize that the egoistic desire to reduce aversive arousal motivates the bystander's helping, not unselfish regard for the other's welfare.

Other theories of egoistic motivation for helping propose that prosocial behavior can be based on factors different from the arousal caused by witnessing another's suffering. For example, the negative state relief explanation for helping developed by Robert Cialdini and his colleagues in the 1970s proposes that temporary depression or sorrow can motivate helping as way to dispel the negative mood state. This negative state, it is reasoned, produces helping because people learn through socialization that feelings of personal satisfaction accompany the performance of good deeds. Helping, therefore, occurs as a way to lift the spirits of the temporarily depressed individual. An important implication of this theory is that even affective states that are not caused by witnessing another's suffering can produce helping. A personal failure, thinking about a sad event, or watching a sad motion picture all can prompt helping as a way to relieve the negative mood state. Benefiting a person in need occurs as a way to benefit the self by dispelling a negative mood.

Additional theories of egoistic motivation for helping propose that many forms of selfishness can lead to helping. For example, motives to maintain a positive mood state, avoid guilt for failing to help, and gain social approval have been suggested to promote prosocial behavior.

In general, theories of egoistic motivation for helping resolve the altruism paradox by proposing some form of self-benefit that motivates seemingly self-sacrificial behavior. In contrast, theories of altruistic motivation for helping propose that individuals do engage in behavior that benefits another, irrespective of any benefit to themselves. Such theories generally concur in assuming that empathy—an identification with another produced by similarity or attachment—is an important source of altruistic motivation, if it exists.

EMPATHY-ALTRUISM HYPOTHESIS

Conceptions of empathy, however, vary greatly. Although all assume that empathy involves identification with another, different approaches emphasize the cognitive, affective, or behavioral components of empathy, or some combination of each. In the study of the possibility of genuine human altruism, empathy is typically conceived as an emotional response to another's suffering that is characterized by feelings of sympathy, compassion, tenderness, and the like. The suggestion that this emotional response leads to prosocial behavior motivated by unselfish concern for the other's welfare has come to be called the "empathy-altruism hypothesis."

The research efforts of C. Daniel Batson and his colleagues beginning in the 1980s are largely responsible for the advancement of the empathy-altruism hypothesis from a theoretical possibility to a plausible explanation for some, but certainly not all, prosocial behavior. Through their efforts, empathy has been shown to be an emotional response to another's suffering that is distinct from aversive arousal or temporary depression and that leads to motivation to help that is different from egoistic motivation to reduce aversive arousal or to relieve negative mood. A major challenge is to determine whether empathy leads to motivation to help that is different from all possible egoistic motives for acting prosocially.

PROSOCIAL MOTIVATIONS

The study of prosocial behavior has led to important insights into the determinants of the amount and the type of help that an individual provides to another when given the opportunity. Individuals often act apathetically or even antisocially toward one another because they lack sufficient incentives for acting prosocially. Competitive relationships involve situations in which one individual's gain is incurred at another individual's expense, so self-interest is best served by exploiting the other. Competitive relationships therefore often lead to antagonism and antisocial behavior. If it is possible to change the reward structure, however, this behavior can be changed. Instituting a superordinate goal, defined as a shared goal that can be achieved only through cooperation among individuals, reduces the antisocial behavior and increases the prosocial behavior of individuals in formerly competitive relationships. Prosocial behavior can be increased simply by making it more rewarding for individuals to act positively toward one another and less rewarding for them to act negatively toward one another. Researchers study how religion encourages a shared prosociality to assist others, including strangers, finding that people vary in their response to sacrifice and conform with group expectations to maintain their reputation by proving spirituality and commitment to religious ideas and practices.

Prosocial behavior can be increased by a variety of explicit material rewards (for example, money) or social rewards (for example, praise), but it also can occur in the absence of explicit rewards. For example, a bystander is often likely to intervene in an emergency when the emergency is unambiguous and there are no other potential helpers present. Research on the bystander effect, the phenomenon in which the presence of others decreases helping, has revealed several factors that contribute to the lack of responsiveness of large groups of bystanders. These factors include increased uncertainty about the need for help, potential embarrassment about offering help, and diffusion of the responsibility for helping. The absence of these factors, however, is insufficient for explaining the responsive behavior of a single witness to an emergency. If there are no material or social rewards for helping, and no punishments for not helping, why would an anonymous witness to an emergency stop to help?

One way to explain bystander intervention in the absence of explicit rewards for helping is to acknowledge that a victim's current state can affect the bystander's own state. Interestingly, the capacity to be affected by another's current state appears to be inborn. Even newborn babies respond emotionally to signs of distress in others. They often cry when they hear other babies cry. Adults also become more physiologically and emotionally aroused when exposed to another in need. The theory that arousal reduction serves as motivation for helping builds on the fact that people do respond emotionally to another's need. As the theory would predict, there is considerable evidence that people help rapidly and more vigorously the greater the arousal they experience in emergency situations. Intense crises, such as the September 11, 2001, terrorist attacks in the United States, provoke large-scale altruism responses as people, often in shock, strive to regain a sense of community, security, and ensured survival.

There may be innate sources of motivation to help in emergencies, but much prosocial behavior occurs in nonemergency situations. The motivation to help in nonemergency situations is often assumed to result from socialization.In general, children become more helpful as they grow older. Developmental theories of prosocial motivations suggest that children's helpfulness is first encouraged by material rewards, later by social rewards, and finally by self-rewards produced by the internalization of social norms advocating helpfulness. The ability to reward oneself for helping leads the socialized individual to act prosocially even in the absence of explicit material or social rewards, because helping is accompanied by the positive feelings that become associated with doing good deeds during socialization. Helping thus acquires reinforcing properties and becomes particularly likely to occur when individuals are in need of reinforcement. It is well known that people self-indulge when they are saddened or depressed. People often treat themselves to a favorite dessert, a shopping trip, or a television show when they are sad, because self-indulgence relieves depression. Developmental theories of prosocial motivation would suggest that socialized individuals also use acting helpfully as a form of self-indulgence. Consistent with this suggestion, and with the prediction of the negative state relief explanation for helping, adults often act more prosocially when they are temporarily saddened than when they are in a neutral mood.

EGOISTIC MOTIVATIONS

Given that there are both innate and socialized sources of motivation to help, it may seem curious that people do not always act prosocially. Egoistic theories of motivation to help, however, point out an important exception to the rule that people will help others to benefit themselves: helping will occur only if it is a relatively noncostly, gratifying way to benefit the self. Thus, if helping is a more costly behavior than putting the victim's suffering out of sight and out of mind by leaving the scene, helping should not occur. Similarly, temporarily saddened individuals facing the prospects of large costs and small rewards for helping would not be expected to help because it would not be perceived as gratifying overall. Helping would be expected to occur only when the self-benefits of helping outweigh the costs. Egoistic theories of motivation for helping therefore provide a way to explain not only why people do help but also why they do not.

A problem for egoistic theories of motivation for helping is to explain the effects of feeling empathy (sympathy, compassion) on helping a person in need. Heightened empathy leads to increased prosocial behavior across a wide variety of both emergency and nonemergency situations. Furthermore, research testing the empathy-altruism hypothesis suggests that empathy does not lead to any of the more common types of egoistic motivation for helping. If the empathy-altruism hypothesis is valid, unselfish motives, as well as selfish ones, must be included in theories of why people act prosocially.

EMERGENCE OF SOCIAL PSYCHOLOGY

Social psychology emerged as a distinct field of psychology after World War II, during the years in which behaviorism was the dominant theoretical perspective in psychology. Initially, social psychologists devoted little attention to the study of prosocial behavior, perhaps because it was assumed that the general determinants of individual behavior would also apply to interpersonal behavior, as behaviorist theory would dictate. During the 1950s, some research on prosocial behavior was initiated. This research tended to focus on cooperation, however, to the exclusion of other forms of prosocial behavior. Behaviorist principles were often applied to determine, for example, if rewarding cooperation made it more likely to occur and competition less likely to occur.

In 1964, a troubling murder captured the attention of social psychologists and spurred interest in studying emergency intervention and other forms of prosocial behavior. In March of that year, a young woman named Kitty Genovese was attacked on the street near her home late at night. The attack continued for more than an hour and her screams woke many of her neighbors, but none of them left their homes to help her. Interest in the behavior of the unresponsive bystanders during this attack prompted social psychologists to investigate factors that lead people not to intervene in emergencies. This research led to demonstration of the bystander effect and revealed a number of factors that contribute to the unresponsiveness of groups of bystanders who witness an emergency.

Research on bystander intervention also revealed that certain circumstances make it quite likely for a bystander to offer help. The decline of behaviorism by the early 1970s provided a climate in which researchers could explore the effects of internal motives as well as external reinforcers on helping. Several influential egoistic theories of motivation for helping were developed during the 1970s. By the end of the decade, these theories had clearly displaced earlier behaviorist theories as prominent explanations for prosocial behavior.

STUDY OF EMPATHY

Another trend to develop in the 1970s was the study of the effects of empathy on helping. By the 1980s, several theorists were proposing that empathy for a person in need leads to genuinely altruistic motivation for helping. Research during the 1980s quite consistently showed that empathy leads to helping even in situations in which egoistic motivation would not be expected to lead to help. Demonstrating that humans are capable of transcending selfishness and acting out of concern for another's welfare would have profound implications for psychological theories of motivation and views of human nature. It would be necessary to acknowledge that human behavior can be influenced by unselfish motives as well as by selfish ones.

INTERDISCIPLINARY AND BIOLOGICAL RESEARCH

In the early twenty-first century, prosocial research benefited from interdisciplinary approaches. Experts in various fields, ranging from genetics to economics, supplemented psychologists' work in previous decades. Researchers sought answers to such questions as whether any genes could be linked to altruistic behavior or to shaping prosocial behavior. They used evolutionary psychology methodology to study altruism. Some scholars applied game theory, posing hypothetical dilemmas, to assess altruism and cooperation behavior according to which choices are beneficial to the altruistic players and recipients of generosity or assistance.

In addition to these academic analyses, advances in medical technology and cognitive neuroscience enabled scientists to use brain scans and computer simulations to seek biological bases for altruism. A 2007 *Nature Neuroscience* article reported that scientists at Duke University Medical Center conducted brain scans with fMRI of forty-five test subjects while they interacted with a computerized game, either playing directly or observing the computer playing, to acquire money to donate to charities. An fMRI study at the University of Oregon differentiated between pure altruism and actions that gave participants what researchers referred to as a "warm glow." Nineteen women played a game in which they made donations to a food bank. In the game, altruism was voluntary or mandatory when government assistance funded that charity with the players' taxes.

By early 2007, Duke neuroscientist Scott A. Huettel and his colleagues hypothesized that altruistic thoughts were associated with the brain's posterior superior temporal sulcus, which became most active in subjects who exhibited the greatest selflessness and generosity to donate funds. Participants also answered a survey regarding their altruism, but scientists emphasized that measuring altruistic behavior with interviews might be skewed by subjects providing exaggerated responses. Researchers theorized that people's attitudes and perceptions instigate altruism instead of their behavior and stated that altruism research might aid scientific comprehension of antisocial or autistic people.

A 2007 National Institute of Mental Health study suggested that people's recognition of fear in others' expressions motivated altruistic responses. Many test participants responded to fearful faces by offering to give money and assist perceived victims. In the study's report, Abigail Marsh hypothesized that amygdala deficiencies in brains might prevent people from detecting fear and hindering their ability to be empathetic and altruistic.

Researchers have investigated possible health benefits from altruism, examining how helpfulness and empathy are associated with endorphins and opiates being released, which might reinforce immune systems, quicken healing, and extend life spans. Some scientists have studied the role of the hormone oxytocin with altruism and whether it might cause helpful behavior or be produced because of generosity. Likewise, studies conducted in the late 2000s found that dopamine and serotonin, which are responsible for a person's feelings of pleasure, were associated with prosocial behaviors that avoid inflicting harm.

Psychology and neurobiology researchers such as Barbara Oakley have also begun to examine pathological altruism, which is often characterized by unintended harm, rather than benefit, to the recipient and may be harmful to the giver as well. Pathological altruism has been linked to such phenomena as survivor's guilt, codependency, and battered person syndrome.

BIBLIOGRAPHY

Batson, C. Daniel. *Altruism in Humans.* New York: Oxford UP, 2011. Print.

Dawkins, Richard. *The Selfish Gene*. Oxford: Oxford UP, 2006. Print.

Dovidio, John F., Jane Allyn Piliavin, David A. Schroeder, and Louis A. Penner. *The Social Psychology of Prosocial Behavior.* Mahwah: Erlbaum, 2007. Print.

Dugatkin, Lee Alan. *The Altruism Equation: Seven Scientists Search for the Origins of Goodness.* Princeton: Princeton UP, 2011. Digital file.

Dunbar, Robin, Ian MacDonald, and Louise Barrett, eds. *The Oxford Handbook of Evolutionary Psychology.* Oxford: Oxford UP, 2009. Print.

Harbaugh, William T., Ulrich Mayr, and Daniel Burghart. "Neural Response to Taxation and Voluntary Giving Reveal Motives to Charitable Donations." *Science* 316.5831 (2007): 1622–25. Print.

Henrich, Natalie S., and Joseph Henrich. *Why Humans Cooperate: A Cultural and Evolutionary Explanation.* Oxford: Oxford UP, 2007. Print.

Kottler, Jeffrey A. *Doing Good: Passion and Commitment for Helping Others.* Philadelphia: Brunner, 2000. Print.

Norenzayan, Ara, and Azim F. Shariff. "The Origin and Evolution of Religious Prosociality." *Science* 322.5898 (2008): 58–62. Print.

Oakley, Barbara, Ariel Knafo, Guruprasad Madhavan, and David Sloan Wilson, eds. *Pathological Altruism.* New York: Oxford UP, 2012. Print.

Post, Stephen G., ed. *Altruism and Health: Perspectives from Empirical Research.* Oxford: Oxford UP, 2007. Print.

Sober, Elliott, and David Sloan Wilson. *Unto Others: The Evolution and Psychology of Unselfish Behavior.* Cambridge: Harvard UP, 2003. Print.

Sussman, Robert W., and C. Robert Cloninger, eds. *Origins of Altruism and Cooperation.* New York: Springer, 2011. Print.

Jim Fultz; updated by Elizabeth D. Schafer

SEE ALSO: Afflilation and friendship; Attraction theories; Bystander intervention; Cooperation, competition, and negotiation; Help-seeking; Helping; Love; Motivation; Motivation: Intrinsic and extrinsic; Women's psychology: Carol Gilligan.

Alzheimer's disease

TYPE OF PSYCHOLOGY: Cognition; Memory; Psychopathology

Alzheimer's disease is the most frequent cause of dementia, or the loss of cognitive and social abilities to the degree that it interferes with activities of daily living. It is an irreversible and gradual brain disorder that sometimes occurs with aging.

KEY CONCEPTS

- Activities of daily living (ADLs)
- Cognitive function
- Cognitive impairment
- Dementia
- Memory loss
- Motor function
- Neurofibrillary fibers
- Plaques

INTRODUCTION

Alzheimer's disease and dementia are not normal parts of aging. Alzheimer's is caused by diseases that affect the brain, such as genetic, immunologic, and vascular abnormalities. A defect in connections between the brain's cells causes gradual death of brain cells. Alzheimer's disease advances progressively, from mild forgetfulness to a severe loss of mental function. It results in memory loss, behavior and personality changes, deterioration in thinking abilities, difficulty speaking (aphasia), declining motor function (apraxia), and disability recognizing objects (agnosia).

Forgetfulness, forgetting, and loss of concentration are early symptoms that may not be readily identified because they are considered normal signs of aging. Forgetfulness and loss of concentration may also result from use of drugs or alcohol, depression, fatigue, grief, physical illness, impaired vision, or hearing loss. The symptoms of Alzheimer's disease usually occur after sixty years of age but may occur as early as forty. Symptoms often begin with recent memory loss, confusion, poor judgment, and personality changes. In later stages of the disease, activities of daily living (ADLs) such as dressing and eating are affected. Eventually, those with Alzheimer's disease are completely dependent on others for ADLs. They become so debilitated that they become bedridden, at which time, other physical problems develop. Seizures may occur late in Alzheimer's disease.

PREVALENCE AND IMPACT

Alzheimer's disease accounts for 50 to 75 percent of all dementias. Its prevalence increases from 1 percent at age sixty-five to between 20 and 35 percent by age eighty-five. On average, those with the disease may live from eight to twenty years following diagnosis. According to the World Health Organization (WHO), the number of people worldwide aged sixty-five and older will reach 1.2 billion by 2025 and will exceed 2 billion by 2050. Of these, an estimated 22 million individuals will be afflicted with Alzheimer's disease worldwide. The Alzheimer's Association speculates that if a cure is not found, Alzheimer's will be diagnosed in 14 million Americans by the middle of the twenty-first century.

A study done in 1998 revealed that African Americans

and Latinos might have a higher overall risk of Alzheimer's disease. Socioeconomic status, health care, level of education, and culture may also influence the diagnosis of Alzheimer's. Another study in 1998 estimated that the annual economic burden created by the cost of caring for a patient with mild Alzheimer's is $18,000; for a patient with moderate Alzheimer's, $30,000; and for a patient with severe Alzheimer's, $36,000. More than half of Alzheimer's patients are cared for at home, with almost 75 percent of their care provided by family and friends. In 2002, the Alzheimer's Association estimated that approximately $33 billion is lost annually by American businesses as a result of the disease. Time taken by caregivers of people with the disease accounts for $26 billion, and $7 billion is spent for health issues and long-term care related to the disease. Additionally, Alzheimer's disease costs the United States more than $100 billion annually.

HISTORY

Alzheimer's disease is named after a German physician, Alois Alzheimer, who in 1906 found plaques and neurofibrillary tangles in the brain of a mentally disturbed woman. Today, these plaques and tangles in the brain are considered hallmarks of the disease.

There is also evidence that Greeks and Romans recognized the disease, as there are writings dating from their time that appear to describe symptoms of Alzheimer's disease. In the sixteenth century, playwright and poet William Shakespeare wrote that old age is a "second childishness and mere oblivion." In the past, terms such as "senility" and "hardening of the arteries" were commonly used to describe dementia. Until recently, Alzheimer's disease was considered an inevitable consequence of aging. Researchers began discovering more

DSM-IV-TR CRITERIA FOR DEMENTIA OF THE ALZHEIMER'S TYPE

Development of multiple cognitive deficits manifested by both memory impairment (impaired ability to learn new information or recall previously learned information) and one or more of the following cognitive disturbances:

- aphasia (language disturbance)
- apraxia (impaired ability to carry out motor activities despite intact motor function)
- agnosia (failure to recognize or identify objects despite intact sensory function)
- disturbance in executive functioning (planning, organizing, sequencing, abstracting)

Cognitive deficits each cause significant impairment in social or occupational functioning and represent significant decline from previous level of functioning

Course characterized by gradual onset and continuing cognitive decline

Cognitive deficits not due to any of the following:

- other central nervous system conditions causing progressive deficits in memory and cognition (such as cerebrovascular disease, Parkinson's disease, Huntington's disease, subdural hematoma, normal-pressure hydrocephalus, brain tumor)
- systemic conditions known to cause dementia (such as hypothyroidism, vitamin B or folic acid deficiency, niacin deficiency, hypercalcemia, neurosyphilis, HIV infection)
- substance-induced conditions

Deficits do not occur exclusively during course of a delirium

Disturbance not better accounted for by another Axis I disorder (such as Major Depressive Episode, Schizophrenia)

Code based on presence or absence of clinically significant behavioral disturbance:

- Without Behavioral Disturbance (DSM code 294.10): Cognitive disturbance not accompanied by any clinically significant behavioral disturbance
- With Behavioral Disturbance (DSM code 294.11): Cognitive disturbance accompanied by clinically significant behavioral disturbance (such as wandering, agitation)

Specify with Early Onset (onset at age sixty-five years or younger) or with Late Onset (onset after age sixty-five) about the disease in the last quarter of the twentieth century.

RISK FACTORS

The major risk factors for Alzheimer's disease are age and family history. Other possible risk factors include a serious head injury and lower socioeconomic status. There is speculation that genetics, environmental influences, weight, educational level, blood pressure, and blood cholesterol levels are factors that may increase the risk for the disease.

CAUSES

There are no definitive causes of Alzheimer's disease. Some possibilities that have been identified include lesions caused by plaque, inflammation in brain cells, oxidative stress effects on brain cells, genetic factors, beta-amyloid protein and senile plaques, tau protein and neurofibrillary tangles, estrogen effects on brain neurotransmitters, dysfunction in brain cell communication, autoimmune responses, viruses, and vessel anomalies.

PLAQUE

In Alzheimer's disease, plaques develop in the areas of the brain that regulate memory and other cognitive functions. These plaques are deposits of beta-amyloid (a protein fragment from a larger protein called amyloid precursor protein, or APP) intermingled with portions of neurons and with nonnerve cells such as microglia (cells that surround and digest damaged cells or foreign substances) and astrocytes (glial cells that support and nourish neurons). Plaques are found in the spaces between the brain's nerve cells. Researchers do not know whether amyloid plaques cause the disease or are a by-product of the disease process.

Alzheimer's disease consists of abnormal collections of twisted threads found inside nerve cells. The chief component is a protein called tau. In the central nervous system, tau proteins bind and stabilize brain cells' support structure by forming tubules that guide nutrients and molecules from the cells to the ends of the axon. Tau normally holds together connector pieces of the tubule tracks. In Alzheimer's disease, tau threads twist around each other and form neurofibrillary tangles. Support to the cell is lost, causing cell death and leading to dementia.

GENETIC FACTORS

Two types of Alzheimer's disease have been identified: familial Alzheimer's disease (FAD), which follows an inheritance pattern, and sporadic Alzheimer's disease. Alzheimer's may exhibit early onset (younger than sixty-five years) or late onset (sixty-five years and older). Only 5 to 10 percent of Alzheimer's cases are early onset. Some forms of early-onset Alzheimer's are inherited and often progress faster than late-onset Alzheimer's. The evidence for a genetic basis of at least some forms of the disease as well as variations in risk associated with ethnic differences—late-onset Alzheimer's disease appears more common among those of Chinese ancestry—has resulted in greater research focus on identifying the roles of specific genes in these patients. In addition to variations within the tau gene that may increase risk, certain polymorphisms in inflammatory genes such as those encoding tumor necrosis factor may also contribute to the genetic risk.

ESTROGEN

Estrogen use has been associated with a decreased risk of Alzheimer's disease and enhanced cognitive functioning. Its antioxidant and anti-inflammatory effects enhance the growth process of neurons for memory function. This has created intense interest in the relationship between estrogen, memory, and cognitive function in humans.

AUTOIMMUNE SYSTEM

The body's immune system may attack its own tissues and produce antibodies against essential cells. Some researchers postulate that aging neurons in the brain trigger an autoimmune response that causes Alzheimer's disease. Antibodies have been identified in the brains of those with Alzheimer's.

VIRUSES

No evidence has yet been found that viruses, either "conventional" or "slow viruses" such as those associated with simian virus (SV) 40, are responsible for forms of Alzheimer's disease. However, persons with certain alleles of eukaryotic transcription initiation factors (EIF2AK2) targeted by herpes simplex virus have been shown to be at increased risk of developing Alzheimer's. The significance of these findings remains uncertain.

GROWTH FACTORS

Some researchers believe that a decline in growth factors or an increase in factors that are toxic to neuronal cells causes Alzheimer's disease. Researchers are investigating introducing naturally occurring nerve growth factor (NGF) into the brain to stimulate brain cell growth in rats.

CHEMICAL DEFICIENCIES

The brains of those with Alzheimer's disease have lower levels of neurotransmitters responsible for cognitive functions and behavior. Acetylcholine is a neurotransmitter that is found in lower levels in the Alzheimer's brain than in normally functioning brains. Scientists have seen slight, temporary cognitive improvement in Alzheimer's patients when their acetylcholine levels have been increased.

METALS

Concern over the possible association of metals such as aluminum being associated with Alzheimer's disease began in the 1980's, when persons accidentally exposed to aluminum during dialysis developed a form of dementia. In addition, aluminum and zinc have been found in the brain tissue of people with Alzheimer's or with some forms of dementia. However, no evidence has been found linking exposure to these metals in small quantities to development of disease, and it is now believed that their presence is a secondary result of the ubiquitous nature of these metals in the environment.

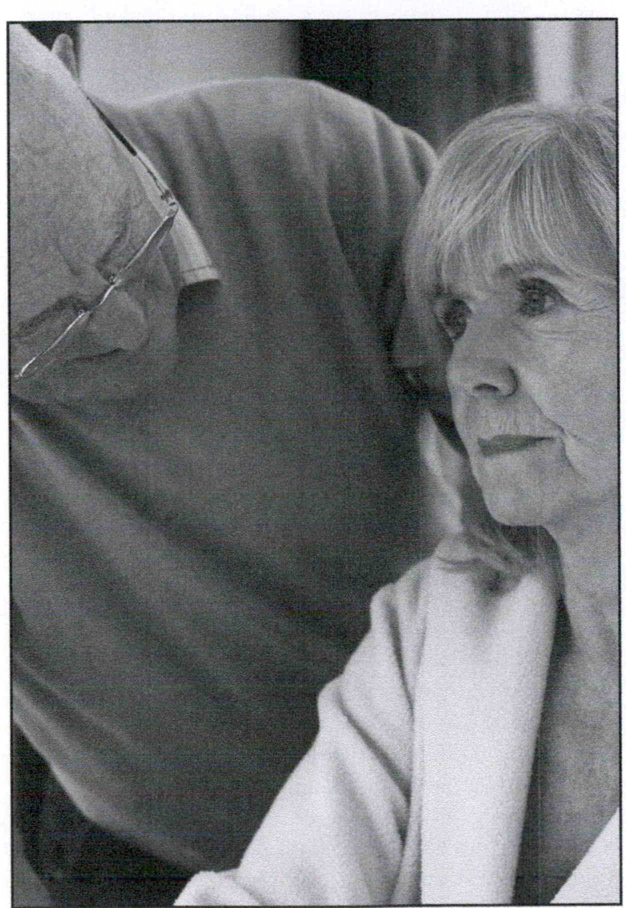

Photo: iStock

DIAGNOSIS

Historically, criteria used in diagnosing Alzheimer's disease have been largely directed at changes in behavior as well as alterations in mental functions of the patient; however, these methods did not clearly delineate Alzheimer's disease from other, sometimes treatable forms of dementia. Diagnostic criteria for Alzheimer's included dementia and a medical history and physical and mental examinations consistent with the disease. Brain imaging computed tomography (CT) or magnetic resonance imaging (MRI) might also indicate brain atrophy.

A medical history is used to provide information about mental or physical conditions, prescription drugs, and family health history. A physical examination evaluates nutritional status, blood pressure, and pulse. A neurological examination evaluates for neurological disorders. The Mini-Mental State Examination (MMSE) and Addenbrooke's Cognitive Examination (ACE) are instruments used to evaluate Alzheimer's disease.

Blood and urine tests evaluate for other causes of dementia. Psychiatric evaluation assesses mood and emotional factors that mimic dementia. A neuropsychological assessment evaluates memory, sense of time and place, and ability to understand, communicate, and do simple calculations.

MRI and CT scans of the brain assess for the possibility of other potential causes of dementia, such as stroke, Huntington's disease, or Parkinson's disease.

Tests have been developed that measure the levels of Alzheimer's-associated proteins in the cerebrospinal fluid (CSF) of patients. High levels of the protein tau in CSF, particularly when this finding accompanies measurements of low levels of the beta-amyloid protein, represents a positive diagnosis of the disease. Early diagnosis of Alzheimer's is important to determine the proper treatment and to detect underlying diseases such as depression, drug interactions, vitamin deficiencies, or endocrine problems. These diseases may be reversible if detected early. A definitive diagnosis of Alzheimer's disease can be confirmed only on autopsy.

FOUR STAGES OF ALZHEIMER'S DISEASE

Early stage Alzheimer's disease is recognized when a person exhibits recent memory loss, mild aphasia, avoidance of the unfamiliar, difficulty writing, and the need to be reminded to perform ADLs such as dressing, washing, brushing the teeth, and combing the hair. Apathy and depression are common.

Middle stage Alzheimer's is recognized when a person exhibits routine recent memory loss, moderate aphasia, a tendency to get lost in familiar surroundings, repetitive actions, apraxia, mood and behavior disturbances, and the need for reminders and help with ADLs.

Late stage Alzheimer's is recognized when a person misidentifies familiar people and places, is bradykinesic (exhibits slowness of movement and general muscle rigidity), frequently falls, has more frequent mood and behavior disturbances, and needs help with all ADLs.

Terminal stage Alzheimer's is recognized when a person has no association to the past or present, is mute or enunciates few coherent words, is oblivious to surroundings, has little spontaneous movement, is dysphagic (has difficulty swallowing), exhibits passive mood and behavior, and needs total care.

The American Psychiatric Association's *Diagnostic and Statistical Manual of Mental Disorders* (4th ed., 1994, DSM-IV) divides Alzheimer's into subtypes that represent the predominant features of the clinical presentation: with delirium, with delusions, with depressed mood, and uncomplicated. "With behavioral disturbance" can also be used to indicate the presence of difficulties such as wandering or combativeness.

TREATMENT

The principal goal of treatment is to slow the progression of Alzheimer's disease, provide a safe environment, maintain function as long as possible, and provide emotional support for the patient and family through social services and support groups. However, the treatment of dementia varies according to the stage of the disease and is focused on management of symptoms because no cure exists. Medical professionals must educate the patient and family about Alzheimer's disease, its course, ramifications, and treatment options. Treatment includes both patients and caregivers. In early stages of Alzheimer's, patients and their families may need counseling to deal with a sense of loss; be made aware of support groups, respite care, and other social services that are available to them; and be introduced to legal considerations in making decisions about future care needs such as medical and financial powers of attorney and a living will. As more supervision is required, caregivers need to be aware of physical dangers that can result from memory loss, such as fires from unattended stoves or burning cigarettes; malnutrition from forgetting to eat and difficulty swallowing; increased risk for falls related to confusion, disorientation, and declining motor function; and issues with driving related to poor motor and cognitive function. Caregivers should also be aware of the patient's finances to assist in paying and recording bills, and planning for future care needs. During late stage Alzheimer's, the family may need assistance in preparing for the patient's death. Hospice care should be discussed, as it provides for physical care and comfort for the patient and emotional support for the family.

PHARMACEUTICAL THERAPY

Pharmaceutical agents used to slow the progression of Alzheimer's disease include acetylcholinesterase inhibitors (tacrine, donepezil, rivastigmine, and galantamine). These agents block the breakdown of neurotransmitters in the brain and are used to lessen symptoms of mild to moderate Alzheimer's. Their action extends cognitive function and improves behavioral symptoms for twelve months up to two years. Estrogen has been associated with a decreased risk of Alzheimer's and enhanced cognitive functioning. Its antioxidant and anti-inflammatory effects enhance the growth processes of neurons for memory function. Herbal remedies such as ginkgo biloba have been shown to provide no benefit to patients. In the absence of agitation or combativeness, the best treatment remains reassurance and distraction. Delusions and hallucinations accompanied by agitation and combativeness can be treated with low doses of antipsychotic or antidepressant medications. Medications may also be used to control wandering, anxiety, insomnia, and depression.

COMPLICATIONS

People with Alzheimer's disease do not die from the disease but rather from complications that result from it. The most common cause of death in Alzheimer's is pneumonia. Difficulty swallowing increases the risk of inhaling foods and liquids into the lungs, which then may cause aspiration and pneumonia. The risk for falling is increased by disorientation, confusion, and declining motor function. Falls can lead to fractures and head injuries. Surgical intervention and immobilization also present risks for additional life-threatening complications in the elderly. Memory loss may result in fires from unattended stoves or burning cigarettes, or malnutrition from forgetting to eat.

PREVENTION

Studies have supported that regular use of nonsteroidal anti-inflammatory drugs (NSAIDs) such as ibuprofen (Advil, Motrin, Nuprin), naproxen sodium (Aleve), and indomethacin (Indocin) may reduce Alzheimer's disease risk by 30 to 60 percent. Moderate exercise by the elderly as well as activities that stimulate brain activity seem to have some effect in delaying the possible onset of Alzheimer's. The significance of these findings is uncertain.

RESEARCH FOR THE FUTURE

The National Institutes of Health's Alzheimer's Disease Prevention Initiative was organized to investigate pharmacological interventions and to identify factors that will assist in early recognition of Alzheimer's disease and delay its development. A collaborative association with federal and private agencies has allowed for diverse investigations that include biologic and epidemiologic research, instrument development to identify high-risk individuals and facilitate clinical trials, and research into alternate strategies to treat behavioral disturbances in Alzheimer's patients.

New drugs to reduce symptoms of Alzheimer's disease are being studied in clinical trials. Other research is being done to identify factors related to patients' and caregivers' coping and stress, as well as support mechanisms in dealing with the progressive nature of Alzheimer's.

BIBLIOGRAPHY

Karlin, Nancy, J., Paul A. Bell, and Jody L. Noah. "Long-Term Consequences of the Alzheimer's Caregiver Role: A Qualitative Analysis." *American Journal of Alzheimer's Disease* (May/June, 2001): 177-182. Examines caregivers' adaptation to their role, caregiver burden and coping, social support issues, and positive and negative experiences created by unplanned changes brought on by Alzheimer's disease.

Mace, M., and P. Rabins. *The Thirty-six-Hour Day: A Family Guide to Caring for Persons with Alzheimer Disease, Related Dementing Illnesses, and Memory Loss in Later Life*. Baltimore: Johns Hopkins University Press, 1999. Discusses what dementia is, physical and psychological problems, effects on caregivers, financial and legal issues, and long-range care planning for those with Alzheimer's disease.

Powell, L., and K. Courtice. *Alzheimer's Disease: A Guide for Families and Caregivers*. 3d ed. Cambridge, Mass.: Perseus, 2002. Provides information about early signs, tests, diagnosis, and treatment research for Alzheimer's disease. Also provides insight into the emotional aspects experienced by caregivers, with advice on communication, safety, and long-term care issues for those with Alzheimer's.

Sell, Colleen. *A Cup of Comfort for Families Touched by Alzheimer's*. Avon, Mass.: Adams Media, 2008. A collection of first-person accounts describing how families cope with loved ones who have Alzheimer's disease.

Smith, Patricia, Mary Mitchell Kenan, and Mark Edwin Kunik. *Alzheimer's for Dummies*. Hoboken, N.J.: Wiley, 2004. One of a series of explanatory works, the book provides an extensive "lay" summary of causes, care, and management of the disease.

Terry, R., R. Katzman, K. Bick, and S. Sisodia. *Alzheimer Disease*. 2d ed. Philadelphia: Lippincott, Williams & Wilkins, 1999. An in-depth review of hereditary links, signs and symptoms, diagnosis, and treatment for Alzheimer's disease.

Wolfe, Michael. "Shutting Down Alzheimer's." *Scientific American* 294 (May, 2006): 72-79. Summary of the latest research into Alzheimer's disease, as well as prospects for detection and treatment.

Sharon Wallace Stark; updated by Richard Adler

See Also: Aging: Cognitive changes; Aging: Physical changes; Assisted living; Brain structure; Coping: Chronic illness; Coping: Terminal illness; Dementia; Elder abuse; Elders' mental health; Forgetting and forgetfulness; Genetics and mental health; Hospice; Parkinson's disease; Quality of life

American Psychiatric Association

Date: Founded in 1844

Type of psychology: Origin and definition of psychology; Psychotherapy

The Association of Medical Superintendents of American Institutions for the Insane, established in 1844, changed its name to the American Medico-Psychological Association in 1893 and to the American Psychiatric Association in 1921. It oversaw the transformation of psychiatry into

a professionalized occupation during the nineteenth and early twentieth centuries.

Key Concepts
- Bloodletting
- Chemical intervention
- Drug therapy
- Hydrotherapy
- Political appointments
- Psychiatric nursing
- Psychiatric social work

INTRODUCTION

The Association of Medical Superintendents of American Institutions for the Insane (also known as the Superintendents' Association), grandparent of the American Psychiatric Association (APA), was established in 1844. At the time, there were twenty-four mental hospitals in the United States and two in Canada. The first of these was founded in Philadelphia, where Benjamin Rush, the acknowledged father of psychiatry in the United States, was instrumental in its establishment. Rush wrote the first psychiatric textbook, *Medical Inquiries and Observations upon Diseases of the Mind* (1812), which was the dominant textbook in the field for the next seven decades. He explored such methods of treating mental illness as bloodletting, control of diet, exercise, hydrotherapy, chemical intervention, diversion, and travel. He called for the humane treatment of mental patients.

Two other mental hospitals existed in the United States before 1800, the Eastern State Hospital in Williamsburg, Virginia, and Spring Grove Hospital in Catonsville, Maryland. During the nation's colonial period and long afterward, the care of the mentally ill fell largely to their families. In extreme cases that threatened community safety, however, public officials ordered people they considered dangerous confined, often holding them in prisons, sometimes chained to the walls or the floor. Disturbed people who did not have relatives to look after them were expelled from communities. If they stayed on, they might be put in the stocks and publicly whipped, after which they were forced to leave.

As mental hospitals were established, they received many more applications than they could accommodate. Horace Mann, who conducted a legislative survey in 1829, identified 289 mentally disabled people in Massachusetts, of whom 138 were in almshouses, 141 confined in jails or treated at home, and a mere 10 cared for in mental hospitals. Mann's survey provided the impetus for the construction of the Worcester State Hospital in 1833. This institution became a model for other such institutions elsewhere in the country.

EARLY MEDICAL SCHOOLS AND SOCIETIES

In eighteenth-century America, men could practice medicine simply by declaring themselves to be physicians. Many medical doctors received their training through apprenticeships provided by other doctors. Of thirty-five hundred physicians in the country during the 1700s, about four hundred had received formal training, usually gained by study in European medical schools. By 1840, about 35 percent of the physicians in New England had formal training.

Small medical schools existed in the United States during the eighteenth century, notably those established at the College of Philadelphia in 1756, King's College—now Columbia University—in New York City in 1767, Harvard University in 1782, and Dartmouth Medical School in 1797. These, however, were limited operations with meager faculties and few students.

In the 1820s, laws were passed permitting medical societies to establish standards for licensing physicians and to grant licenses. Such documents, however, were not required for those who wished to practice medicine, although unlicensed physicians were banned from suing in court to collect unpaid medical bills. At this time, no organization existed for physicians who specialized in treating the mentally ill.

In 1844, John M. Galt, a physician and grandnephew of James Galt—the first administrator of Eastern State Hospital in Williamsburg, Virginia—helped establish what would become the American Psychiatric Association (APA). Twenty-five years old at the time, Galt met in Philadelphia with twelve other superintendents of mental hospitals. The impetus for this meeting came partially from the establishment, in 1841, of the British Association of Medical Officers of Lunatic Asylums (later the Royal Society of Psychiatrists), which emphasized the need for superintendents of mental hospitals to share ideas about the management, treatment, and care of the mentally ill.

Superintendents of mental hospitals from Maine to Virginia were present at the Philadelphia meeting, which began on October 16, 1844, and continued for four days. Thomas Story Kirkbride, superintendent of the Philadelphia Hospital for the Insane, organized the conference and entertained the delegates in his residence on the grounds of the Philadelphia Hospital. As a result of this meeting, the Association of Medical Superintendents of American Institutions for the Insane was established. Samuel B. Woodward was elected president and Samuel White, the oldest of the thirteen delegates, vice president.

EARLY OBJECTIVES OF THE ASSOCIATION

A widely distributed circular stated the objectives of the Superintendents' Association, urging administrators of mental hospitals to communicate to share the results of their administrative experiences. This circular suggested that administrators should gather statistical information about mental illness and assist one another in finding ways to improve the treatment of the mentally ill.

To facilitate communication, it was decided that the organization should meet regularly. The second meeting was held in Washington, DC, beginning on May 10, 1846. Ten superintendents who had not attended the first meeting were present for the second meeting, along with the thirteen original delegates. It was decided that subsequent meetings should be held in May, a time of year when travel was relatively easy. Membership was open to the medical superintendents of any incorporated or legally constituted institutions for the insane, and, where there was no medical superintendent because of different organizational patterns, the regular medical officer of such institutions might attend the scheduled meetings.

Between 1844 and 1860, meetings were held every year except 1845 and 1847. Meeting places were varied and included Philadelphia; Boston; Washington, DC; Baltimore; Cincinnati; Quebec; Utica, New York; New York City; and Lexington, Kentucky. With rare exceptions, annual meetings have been held every May since the 1860s.

EARLY INITIATIVES

As the Superintendents' Association grew in size, it also grew in strength and influence. At its 1851 meeting, it set standards for the construction of mental hospitals, emphasizing such matters as ideal size, location, fire safety, and overall design. From its 1866 meeting came guidelines urging every state to provide facilities for the care of the mentally ill. Large states were to be divided into districts within which mental patients might be housed in residential facilities. The association called for those considered mentally ill but curable and those considered incurable to reside together. It called on states to construct hospitals for the insane following closely the recommendations of its 1851 meeting.

In 1868, the association set forth twenty-one legal constraints relating to mental patients, emphasizing individual rights and dignity and designed for the protection of those with mental disorders. It had earlier condemned political appointments of superintendents of mental hospitals, demanding instead that the best person be appointed.

REORGANIZATION

Despite its influence, the Superintendents' Association never had a large membership. Fewer than thirty delegates attended most of its annual meetings, although the fiftieth-anniversary meeting in 1894 drew about one hundred delegates. At this time, the organization lacked a constitution and was run by a president, a vice president, and a secretary-treasurer.

Fourteen years earlier, the association had abolished its committees. In 1892, it established eight new committees that dealt with a broad range of mental disorders and related matters. It adopted its first constitution, which established a governing council and three levels of membership: active, associate, and honorary. The proceedings of the meetings were to be published in a journal called Transactions. The following year, as the organization prepared for its fiftieth anniversary, it was renamed the American Medico-Psychological Association (AMPA), a name it retained until 1920. In 1921, the organization became the American Psychiatric Association.

THE TWENTIETH CENTURY

The twenty-seven years of AMPA's existence were marked by phenomenal growth in modern psychiatry, impelled by the influence of such leading European theorists as Sigmund Freud, Alfred Adler, and Carl Jung. The association had earlier suggested guidelines for the training of psychiatrists. During this time, the field of child psychiatry came into being, and such fields as psychiatric social work and psychiatric nursing were established.

The American Medical Association (AMA) had long sought to have the associations serving psychiatry join it, but it took until 1930 for the AMA to form a committee on mental health. This committee suggested an increased emphasis on psychiatry in medical schools, as well as on issues relating to the mentally ill and to legal aspects of their care and treatment.

Psychiatry received a boost during and immediately after World War II, when many enlisted men or returning veterans experienced psychiatric conditions caused by the stress of combat. During the late 1940s, two APA leaders, William Menninger and Daniel Blain, helped establish new programs and obtained funding to strengthen the association. More advances in treating the mentally ill, particularly through drug therapy, occurred in the last half of the twentieth century than had been made in the preceding three centuries.

During the directorship of Blain, from 1948 to 1958, the APA moved into handsome headquarters at 1700 18th Street NW, in Washington, DC, where a permanent staff ran the now-flourishing organization. Under Walter E. Barton's directorship, from 1963 to 1974, the permanent staff grew from 48 to 116 persons. The APA Museum was constructed and the headquarters building was renovated and expanded.

Following Barton as medical director was Melvin Sabshin, who assumed office on September 1, 1974. He founded the American Psychiatric Press and set about raising funds for the construction of the twelve-story headquarters building at 1400 K Street NW, in Washington, DC, that was needed to serve an ever-increasing membership, which had spiraled from 5,856 members in 1950 to 18,407 members by 1970 and to 37,000 members by the early twenty-first century.

Now headquartered in Arlington, Virginia, the organization continues to grow and contribute significantly to its medical subspecialty as well as the broader spectrum of mental health professions, especially through publication of its influential *Diagnostic and Statistical Manual of Mental Disorders* (DSM), first published in 1952 and in its fifth edition since 2013. The APA also has a notable impact on legislation regarding the mentally ill and is influential in directing the course of psychiatric training and licensure throughout the United States and Canada.

BIBLIOGRAPHY

Barton, Walter E. *The History and Influence of the American Psychiatric Association.* Washington, DC: American Psychiatric, 1987. Print.

Bordley, J. B., and A. M. Harvey. *Two Centuries of American Medicine, 1776–1976.* Philadelphia: Saunders, 1976. Print.

De Young, Mary. *Madness: An American History of Mental Illness and Its Treatment.* Jefferson: McFarland, 2010. Print.

Drescher, Jack, and Joseph P. Merlino, eds. *American Psychiatry and Homosexuality: An Oral History.* New York: Harrington Park, 2007. Print.

Grob, Gerald N. *Mental Illness and American Society, 1875–1940.* Princeton: Princeton UP, 1983. Print.

Hall, J. K., Gregory Zilboorg, and Henry A. Bunker, eds. *One Hundred Years of American Psychiatry.* New York: Columbia UP, 1944. Print.

Hirshbein, Laura. "The American Psychiatric Association and the History of Psychiatry." *History of Psychiatry* 22.3 (2011): 302–14. Print.

Kenrick, Douglas T., Steven L. Neuberg, and Robert B. Cialdini, eds. *Social Psychology: Unraveling the Mystery.* 3rd ed. Boston: Allyn, 2005. Print.

Kolb, Lawrence C. *Modern Clinical Psychology.* 11th ed. Philadelphia: Saunders, 1982. Print.

McGovern, Constance M. *Masters of Madness: Social Origins of the American Psychiatric Profession.* Hanover: UP of New England, 1985. Print.

Sabshin, Melvin. *Changing American Psychiatry: A Personal Perspective.* Washington, DC: American Psychiatric, 2008. Print.

R. Baird Shuman

SEE ALSO: American Psychological Association; *Diagnostic and Statistical Manual of Mental Disorders* (DSM); Psychology: Fields of specialization; Psychology: History.

American Psychological Association

DATE: Founded in 1892
TYPE OF PSYCHOLOGY: All

The American Psychological Association is the largest national organization of psychologists in the United States, that in 2011 represented the interests of over 84,000 members, including students, professors, practitioners, policy makers, and citizens who bring psychology to the American public and the larger international community.

KEY CONCEPTS

- Advocacy
- Directorates
- Divisions
- Lobbying
- Policy
- Practice

INTRODUCTION

The American Psychological Association (APA) is a professional organization that represents the interests of psychologists and psychological science in the United States and is headquartered in Washington, DC. It is also in close proximity to many other professional organizations and governmental bodies such as the National Institutes of Health, the Institute of Medicine, and the National Science Foundation.

The APA has the mission of advancing psychology as a scientific discipline and as a profession. It promotes psychology as a science, as an area of clinical practice, as a field and tool of education, and as a matter of public policy and interest. Additionally, it maintains a mission of promoting human welfare and health through the work of psychologists. These goals are addressed in several ways. For instance, the APA encourages the continuing development of psychology as a field by forging new and better research methodologies. Similarly, the APA fosters high standards of achievement, education, ethics, and general conduct among psychologists. Finally, it increases the dissemination and use of psychological knowledge through collegial communications and communications with the public at large.

The APA also engages in advocacy, on behalf of its members and their interests. It does this by fostering ethical standards among its members and also by taking positions on important public issues, especially those that are the subject of governmental decisions and debates. In some cases, this might include lobbying, encouraging members to contact governmental representatives or particular organizations, informing them of positions taken by the organization as a whole, or letting key officials know their constituents' wishes. APA members also participate in various decision-making and policy-making groups that influence laws and guidelines regarding health care, education, and scientific conduct.

Members may also influence clinical practice by participating on boards of psychology that oversee the profession of psychology in each state. In the larger organization of the APA, structured subgroups are devoted to specific activities and areas of psychology to achieve similar tasks. One type of subgroup, the directorate, is devoted to a branch of psychology related to science, practice, public interest, or education. A second type of subgroup, with a special relationship to the directorates, is the division, a group designated to advance specific topical areas in psychology. Together, the directorates and divisions of the APA help inform both the association's membership and the public at large about special events, themes, or decisions of importance to the discipline.

HISTORY AND STRUCTURE

The APA is managed by a formal set of bylaws and by a constitution. It is membership driven, meaning individuals who are members of the organization vote to determine how it will adapt to contemporary social problems or needs for organizational development.

The bylaws of the APA provide an outline of the structure of the organization and describe this structure as including a central office with a chief executive officer, standing boards and committees, officers, a council of representatives, and a board of directors. The organization is also characterized by divisions, each of which has special interests in particular areas of psychological science, or the study of specific types of behavior. The relative size of the membership in each division determines the voting power and influence of the division within the organization.

The majority of the work completed by the APA as a whole is performed by volunteer members. These members, elected or appointed by division members or the council, volunteer their time and energy to take on special projects and develop proposals for conferences, publications, or special projects; inform other members of important issues; and set strategic plans for the different areas of psychology in the organization. The organization is supported in part by membership dues and by money it makes through other means. These other means include an annual convention for the membership and the development and sale of books and professional journals.

As an organization, the APA is diverse. Its divisions are numerous and developed out of basic academic needs to have special discussion groups on specific topics in psychology, around relevant social issues, and around relevant professional issues. In some cases, the divisions developed from organizational societies within the APA. The first divisions focused on different types of basic psychological science. As the APA developed, it added divisions representing more specialized branches of psychological work that grew from the earlier basic areas. Further development resulted in the emergence of numerous groups focusing on specific types of practitioners, populations, and settings. The divisions reveal the maturation process of psychology as a professional discipline, as it grew from a concern with basic science to attend to education, practice, and public policy.

FUNCTIONS

To understand some strategies the organization uses to reach its goals, it is helpful to take a closer look at each of the four major directorates of the APA: the Science Directorate, the Education Directorate, the Practice Directorate, and the Public Interest Directorate. Each has unique targets for change in terms of how the APA interacts with its members and the public at large.

The Science Directorate has a particular interest in advancing the study of psychology through such endeavors as encouraging career development in the area of psychological science. Such work happens at all levels, from encouraging science students in their precollege years to think about psychology as a field of choice to attracting midcareer professionals who are thinking about a blended career where psychology plays a role. It may take the form of public announcements, for instance, disseminating new psychological research findings on important social problems such as Alzheimer's disease, why beeping mechanical sounds might distract military personnel, or pain relief in individuals with chronic health problems, or it might take the form of outreach, such as psychologists going into school systems and talking about their work with interested students in science classes. Another important role the Science Directorate plays is informing the members of the APA about policy and governmental regulation changes that have the potential to affect the work of psychological science. Such topics might include rules about how animal or human research is conducted, plans for how tax dollars are distributed for research, or rules related to how data must be preserved.

The Education Directorate focuses on matters related to formal education. This includes issues involving training psychologists, such as graduate education programs, program accreditation, and continuing professional education. Additionally, the directorate focuses its activities on psychology curricula for undergraduates and younger students. For instance, the Education Directorate has an interest in gifted education and also advances efforts to engage young minds with interest in the field by making psychology more accessible to them. Finally, the Education Directorate encourages advocacy on the topic of education in general and also as it specifically relates to psychology.

The Practice Directorate plays the important role of helping professionals who provide psychological services get the information they need. For instance, this directorate provides tips on how to be an advocate of psychology as a profession and information on licensing and service provision for psychologists in independent practice. It also provides information to individuals in the community who might be seeking psychological help or assistance. During the months following the September 11, 2001, terrorist attacks, for instance, the Practice Directorate provided, among other things, public education materials geared toward helping children to cope with the aftereffects of terrorism, a disaster response network for psychologists to volunteer much-needed services, and an advice column written for psychologists to help them cope and maintain their own resilience during such professionally demanding times.

Finally, the Public Interest Directorate facilitates the interface between psychology and public policy. Highlighting the needs of special populations and psychology's ability to better address those needs has been an important focus of the Public Interest Directorate. Aging, children, youth, families, gender, disability, human immunodeficiency virus (HIV) and acquired immunodeficiency syndrome (AIDS), sexual orientation, and ethnic and racial health disparities are just some of the areas where the Public Interest Directorate has concentrated its efforts. As with the other directorates, these efforts have taken the form of press releases, the provision of educational materials, and conferences to bring issues of policy to public attention.

As a whole, the directorates form the basic foci for the APA in terms of how it interacts with its members and the general public. Their dynamic natures allow them to shift in response to pressing social issues and foster beneficial growth within the organization.

BIBLIOGRAPHY

Dewsbury, Donald A., ed. *Unification Through Division: Histories of the Divisions of the American Psychological Association*. 5 vols. Washington, DC: American Psychological Association, 1996–2000. Print.

"Divisions of the APA." *American Psychological Association*. American Psychological Association, 2014. Web. 4 February 2014.

Dodgen, Daniel, Raymond D. Fowler, and Carol Williams-Nickelson. "Getting Involved in Professional Organizations: A Gateway to Career Advancement." *The Portable Mentor: Expert Guide to a Successful Career in Psychology.* Ed. Mitchell J. Prinstein. New York: Springer, 2013. 257–67. Print.

Kimble, Gregory A., Michael Wertheimer, and Charlotte White, eds. *Portraits of Pioneers in Psychology.* Washington, DC: American Psychological Association,

1991. Print.

Norcross, John C., and Christie P. Karpiak. "Clinical Psychologists in the 2010s: 50 Years of the APA Division of Clinical Psychology." *Clinical Psychology: Science and Practice* 19.1 (2012): 1–12. Print.

Pickren, Wade E., and Donald A. Dewsbury, eds. *Evolving Perspectives on the History of Psychology.* Washington, DC: American Psychological Association, 2002. Print.

Puente, Antonio E., Janet Matthews, and Matthew Brewer, eds. *Teaching Psychology in America: A History.* Washington, DC: American Psychological Association, 1992. Print.

Reiber, Robert W., and Kurt Salzinger, eds. *Psychology: Theoretical-Historical Perspectives.* 2nd ed. Washington, DC: American Psychological Association, 1998. Print.

Wright, Rogers, and Nicholas Cummings, eds. *The Practice of Psychology: The Battle for Professionalism.* Phoenix: Zeig, Tucker & Theisen, 2001. Print.

Nancy A. Piotrowski

See Also: American Psychiatric Association; Psychology: Fields of specialization; Research ethics.

Amnesia and fugue

Type of psychology: Psychopathology

The inability to totally or partially recall or identify a past experience is called amnesia. A fugue is an extensive escape from life's problems that involves an amnesiac state and actual flight from familiar surroundings. During a fugue, a new partial or entire identity may be assumed. Both fugue and amnesia involve dissociation.

Key Concepts

- Behavioral explanation
- Continous amnesia
- Dissociation
- Dissociative disorders
- Generalized amnesia
- Localized amnesia
- Psychodynamic explanation
- Psychogenic explanation
- Selective amnesia

INTRODUCTION

Amnesia involves the failure to recall a past experience, often because of an anxiety that is associated with the situation. Fugue states take place when a person retreats from life's difficulties by entering an amnesiac state and leaving familiar surroundings. During a fugue state, a person may assume a new partial or whole personality. Although amnesia may be caused by organic brain pathology, attempts to cope with anxiety can also produce amnesia and fugue. Dissociation involves the ability of the human mind to split from conscious awareness. Through dissociation, a person can avoid anxiety and difficulty in managing life stresses. When stress and anxiety overwhelm a person, the mind may dissociate from a conscious awareness of the troubling situations. When this takes place, the individual loses memory of the event and may physically leave the stressful situation through a fugue state.

Amnesia and fugue are two of the dissociative disorders recognized by the American Psychiatric Association. The dissociative disorders are methods of avoiding anxiety through the process of pathological dissociation. In addition to amnesia and fugue, the dissociative disorders include dissociative identity disorder (formerly known as multiple personality disorder) and depersonalization disorder. In the former, a person develops a number of alter identities. Depersonalization disorder involves a process in which individuals suddenly feel that their bodies or senses of self have changed dramatically.

AMNESIA TYPES

Another term for dissociative amnesia is psychogenic amnesia. This term conveys the concept that the amnesia is not due to organic brain pathology. Individuals developing psychogenic or dissociative amnesia often encounter a traumatic event or extreme stress that overloads their coping abilities. Four different types of psychogenic or dissociative amnesia can be identified. Localized amnesia is seen when a person cannot remember anything about a specific event. This is often seen after a person experiences a traumatic event, such as a serious accident, and then does not recall what happened. The second type of amnesia is called selective amnesia and occurs when only some parts of a certain time period are forgotten. Infrequently, generalized amnesia takes place and the person forgets his or her entire life history. The fourth type of dissociative amnesia is the continuous type. This form of amnesia is seen when a person does not remember anything beyond a certain point in the past.

DIAGNOSIS

Reliable data on the prevalence of dissociative disorders are lacking, but it appears that women are diagnosed with the dissociative disorders at a rate five times that of men. To make the diagnosis of dissociative amnesia, a doctor must identify a disturbance in memory that involves the appearance of one or more episodes of inability to recall important personal information that is usually of a traumatic or stressful nature. This memory loss must be too extensive to be explained by ordinary forgetfulness. When people develop dissociative amnesia, they may not be able to remember their own names or the identities of relatives, but they retain a number of significant abilities. In psychogenic or dissociative amnesia, basic habits and skills remain intact. Thus, the person is still able to read a book, drive a car, and recognize familiar objects. The memories that are lost revolve around life events and autobiographical information.

The diagnosis of dissociative fugue requires sudden unexpected travel away from home or the customary place of work. Together with this travel, the person is unable to recall the past. During the fugue, the person shows confusion about personal identity or assumes a new one. The person's activities at the time of the fugue can vary extensively, from short-term involvement in new interests to traveling to distant locations and assuming a new identity and work roles. The fugue can last for days, weeks, or even years. At some point, the individual will leave the fugue state and be in a strange place without awareness of the events that took place during the dissociative period. When a fugue state is taking place, the person appears normal to others and can complete complex tasks. Usually, the activities selected by the person are typical of a different lifestyle from the previous one.

The diagnosis of dissociative amnesia and fugue can be controversial, because it often depends on self-reports. The possibility that a person is faking the symptoms must be considered. Objective diagnostic measures for these disorders do not exist. The possibility of malingering or fabricating the symptoms must be considered in arriving at a diagnosis of dissociative amnesia and fugue.

When diagnosing dissociative amnesia and fugue, a number of other disorders and conditions have to be excluded. A number of medical conditions, such as vitamin deficiency, head trauma, carbon monoxide poisoning, and herpes encephalitis, can produce similar symptoms. Amnesia can also be found in conjunction with alcoholism and the use of other drugs.

POSSIBLE CAUSES

Normal dissociation is often differentiated from pathological dissociation. Normal dissociation can be an adaptive way to handle a traumatic incident. It is commonly seen as a reaction to war and civilian disasters. In normal dissociation, the person's perception of the traumatic experience is temporarily dulled or removed from the conscious mind. Pathological dissociation is an extreme reaction of splitting the anxiety-provoking situation from consciousness.

There exist a limited number of research studies that seek to explain the causes of dissociation in certain individuals and predict which people are vulnerable to the development of dissociative amnesia or fugue during periods of trauma or overwhelming stress. The psychodynamic explanation emphasizes the use of repression as a defense against conscious awareness of the stressful or traumatic event. Entire chunks of the person's identity or past experiences are split from the conscious mind as a way to avoid painful memories or conflicts. According to this explanation, some individuals are vulnerable to the use of dissociation because of their early childhood experiences of trauma or abuse. With the early experience of abuse, the child learns to repress the memories or engage in a process of self-hypnosis. The hypnotic state permits the child to escape the stress associated with the abuse or neglect. The abused child feels a sense of powerlessness in the face of repeated abuse and splits from this conscious awareness. This isolation of the stressful event leads to the development of different memory processes from those found in normal child development.

A behavioral explanation for the likely development of dissociation as a means to cope with stressful events focuses on the rewarding aspects of dissociative symptoms. The child learns to role-play and engage in selective attention to recognize certain environmental cues that provide rewards. Stressful circumstances are blocked out and disturbing thoughts ignored. Eventually, this process expands into a tendency to assume new roles and block out stressful situations.

The dissociative disorders appear to be influenced by sociocultural factors that depend on social attitudes and cultural norms. Acceptance and toleration of the symptoms associated with dissociative disorders depend on prevailing societal attitudes. Over time, cultures vary in the acceptance of dissociative symptoms and the manifestation of amnesia and fugue states. For example, historical reports of spirit possession can be interpreted as the experience of a fugue state.

TREATMENT

The symptoms associated with dissociative amnesia and fugue usually spontaneously disappear over time. As the experience of stress begins to lessen, the amnesia and fugue often disappear. When providing treatment for these individuals, it is important that caregivers provide a safe environment that removes them from the possible sources of stress. Some people are hospitalized for this reason. The institutional setting allows them to regain comfort away from the traumatizing or stress-producing situation. Occasionally the lost memories can be retrieved through the use of specific medications. One such medication is sodium amytal, which can be used during an interview process that attempts to restore the lost memories. Hypnosis is also used as a means to put the person in a receptive state for questions that may overcome the amnesia.

Hypnosis is also used in the treatment of fugue states. The goal when using hypnosis is to access important memories that may have triggered the fugue. Medications are sometimes used with patients who have a history of fugue. Antianxiety medications called benzodiazepines have been used with individuals showing dissociative fugue. The medication helps to alleviate the feelings of worry and apprehension.

Because amnesia does not typically interfere with a person's daily functioning, few specific complaints about the lack of memory take place. Individuals may complain about other psychological symptoms, but not the amnesia. Consequently, treatment often does not focus on the lost memories. Some of the associated symptoms that occur with amnesia include depression and stress due to a fugue state. Treatment is often directed toward alleviating the depression and teaching a person stress management techniques.

BIBLIOGRAPHY

"Dissociative Disorders." *Mayo Clinic*. Mayo Foundation, 3 Mar. 2011. Web. 21 Feb. 2014.

Dorahy, Martin L., and Rafaële J. C. Huntjens. "Memory and Attentional Processes in Dissociative Identity Disorder: A Review of the Empirical Literature." *Traumatic Dissociation: Neurobiology and Treatment*. Ed. Eric Vermetten, Martin J. Dorahy, and David Spiegel. Washington, DC: American Psychiatric, 2007. Print.

Lewis, D., et al. "Objective Documentation of Child Abuse and Dissociation in Twelve Murderers." *American Journal of Psychiatry* 154 (1997): 1703–10. Print.

Lowenstein, R. "Psychogenic Amnesia and Psychogenic Fugue." *Review of Psychiatry*. Ed. A. Tasman and S. Goldfinger. New York: American Psychiatric, 1991. Print.

Lynn, S., and J. Rhue, eds. *Dissociation: Clinical and Theoretical Perspectives*. New York: Guilford, 1994. Print.

"Memory Loss." MedlinePlus. *US National Library of Medicine*, 16 Feb. 2012. Web. 21 Feb. 2014.

Michelson, L., and W. Ray. *Handbook of Dissociation: Theoretical, Empirical, and Clinical Perspectives*. New York: Plenum, 1996. Print.

Putnam, F. *Dissociation in Children and Adolescents*. New York: Guilford, 1997. Print.

Rieber, Robert W. *The Bifurcation of the Self: The History and Theory of Dissociation and Its Disorders*. New York: Springer, 2006. Print.

Sadovsky, R. "Evaluation of Patients with Transient Global Amnesia." *American Family Physician* 57 (1998): 2237–38. Print.

Tulving, Endel. "What Is Episodic Memory?" *Current Directions in Psychological Science* 2 (1993): 67–70. Print.

Tutkun, H., V. Sar, L. Yargic, and T. Ozpulat. "Frequency of Dissociative Disorders among Psychiatric Inpatients in a Turkish University Clinic." *American Journal of Psychiatry* 155 (1998): 800–805. Print.

Wieland, Sandra. *Dissociation in Traumatized Children and Adolescents: Theory and Clinical Interventions*. New York: Routledge, 2010. Print.

Frank J. Prerost

See Also: Antianxiety medications; Aphasias; Brain damage; Brain structure; Child abuse; Dissociative disorders; Forgetting and forgetfulness; Long-term memory; Memory; Memory: Animal research; Memory: Empirical studies; Memory: Physiology; Memory: Sensory; Memory storage; Short-term memory; Split-brain studies.

Analytic psychology
Jacques Lacan

Type of psychology: Personality

Jacques Lacan, a pioneering psychoanalyst who emphasized the relationship between language and the unconscious, radically reinterpreted Freud in the light of philosophy and structuralist linguistics. Lacan's theories of the unconscious (that it is "structured like a language") and the mirror phase significantly reshaped the discourse of psychoanalysis and cultural theory.

KEY CONCEPTS

- Desire
- Falsifying character of the ego
- Imaginary
- Imaginary misidentification/ *méconnaissance jouissance*
- Lack/ *manque*
- Mirror stage
- object little o/ *objet petit a*
- Real
- Symbolic

INTRODUCTION

According to Freudian psychoanalysis, desire is biological and driven by sexual force or libido. Jacques Lacan (1901–81), however, regards desire as a drive to regain an original ontological unity that can never be achieved because of the psychic split resulting from what he called the "mirror stage" as well as the Freudian Oedipal phase. Desire emerges from this split or lack, which it tries, continually, to fill. Desire expresses itself through language.

Lacan believed that his form of psychoanalysis was not a departure from, but a return to, the original principles of Freudian analysis. Lacan's readers have long complained about the difficulty of his prose, which is characterized by a seeming lack of linearity and an often impenetrable style. Many of Lacan's commentators have likened his discursive style to a rebus or puzzle, designed to communicate the idea that no truth about psychic life can ever be wholly and fully expressed through language, because the psyche is always split against itself, and language is the result of absence and difference.

THE MIRROR STAGE

Central to Lacanian psychoanalysis is the celebrated mirror stage. Lacan argues that a child's ego begins to emerge only between the ages of six and eighteen months, when the child first sees its own reflection in a mirror. This experience is illusory, according to Lacan, because the child's actual experience of its own body is never that of a clearly delineated whole in the child's full control, so that the reflection seems to have a wholeness and mastery that the actual child lacks. Lacan's observations on the mirror stage relied heavily on the earlier work of the American psychologist and philosopher James Mark Baldwin.

Desire emerges from the perceived distance between the actual or lived experience of the child's own body and the reflection it first sees in the mirror. The child envies the perfection of the mirror image or the mirroring response of its parents, says Lacan, and this lack, or manque, is permanent, because there will always be a gap or existential distance between the subjective experience of the body and the complete image in the mirror, or the apparent wholeness of others.

Desire begins at the mirror stage in the psychic development of the young child. The apparent completeness of the reflected image gives the otherwise helpless child a sense of mastery over its own body, but this sense of self-mastery is as illusory as it is frustrating. Lacan urged his fellow psychoanalysts to reassess their focus on the patient's ego and turn their attention back to the unconscious because of what he termed "the falsifying character of the ego." Lacan argued that psychoanalysis should return to Freud and abandon its fascination with the ultimately untrustworthy ego of the patient.

Lacan believed that his theory of the mirror stage answered two fundamental questions raised by Freud's 1914 essay "On Narcissism": what "psychical action" takes place to bring the ego into being? and if we are not narcissists from the earliest stages of life, what causes narcissism to emerge? According to Lacan, the mechanism of the mirror stage answers both of these questions.

THE OEDIPUS COMPLEX

Lacan, like Sigmund Freud, believed that individuals are socialized by passing through the three stages of the Oedipus complex: seduction, the primal scene, and the castration phase, the last of which Lacan reconfigured as the Father's "No." In the so-called seduction phase, the child is attracted to the original object of desire, which is the body of the mother. In the primal scene, or primal stage, the child witnesses the father having sexual intercourse with the mother, and this is followed by the castration phase, wherein the father restricts the child's access to the mother under threat of castration. The law of the father, or Father's "No," causes the child to redirect desire from the mother to what Lacan calls the "Other"—a hypothetical "place" in the unconscious that allows the individual to later project desire onto other persons—other, that is, than the mother.

Lacan holds that there are three registers in the subject's psychosexual development: the imaginary, the symbolic, and the real. These correspond—somewhat—to the Freudian oral, anal, and genital stages and are related, indirectly, to the three stages of the Oedipus complex.

At the level of the imaginary, the pre-Oedipal infant

inhabits a world without clear subject-object distinctions. The child thinks that it is coextensive with the mother's body. While the child perceives the mother's body as nurturing and pleasurable, it also entertains fantasies that the mother's body might overwhelm and destroy it. This yields alternating fantasies of incorporation and assault, whereby the child is both blissful in its identification with the body of the mother and frightfully aggressive toward it. At this stage in its development, the child inhabits a world of images. The mirror stage is the most important moment of imaginary misidentification, or *méconnaissance*.

It is the father who disrupts the closed dyadic relationship between mother and child, according to Lacan. The father signifies what Lacan calls the law, or the law of the father, which is always, in the first instance, the incest taboo. The child's intensely libidinal relationship with its mother's body is opened to the wider world of family and society by the figure of the father. The father's appearance divides the child from the mother's body and drives the child's desire for its mother into the unconscious. Therefore the law and unconscious desire for the mother emerge at the same time, according to Lacanian psychoanalysis.

The child's experience of the father's presence is also its first experience of sexual difference, and with it comes the dim awareness that there is someone else other than the mother in its world. The Father's "No" deflects the child's desire from the mother to the Other. Lacan identified the Other as a hypothetical place in the unconscious that can be projected onto human counterparts by subjects. Lacan held that the Other is never fully grasped because the nature of desire is such that its object is always beyond its reach.

LANGUAGE AND THE SYMBOLIC

This is the point at which the child enters the register of the symbolic. It is at this stage, according to Lacan, that the child also enters into the language system. Absence, lack, and separation characterize the language system, according to Lacan, because language names things that are not immediately present (signifieds) and substitutes words (signifiers) for them. This is also the beginning of socialization, says Lacan. Just as the child realizes that sexual identity is the result of an originary difference between mother and father, it comes to grasp that language itself is an unending chain of differences, and that the terms of language are what they are only by excluding one another. Signs always presuppose the absence of the objects they signify—an insight that Lacan inherited from structuralist anthropology and linguistics.

The loss of the precious object that is the mother's body drives desire to seek its satisfaction in incomplete or partial objects, none of which can ever fully satisfy the longing bred by the loss of the maternal body. People try vainly to settle for substitute objects, or what Lacan calls the object little o (to distinguish it from the capital O in Other). Lacan's thinking was heavily influenced by structuralist thinkers such as the anthropologist Claude Lévi-Strauss and linguists Ferdinand de Saussure and Roman Jakobson. Lacan's chief claim, based on his readings of Saussure and Jakobson, is that the unconscious is "structured like a language." Lacan refashioned Freud's terminology of psychic condensation and displacement by translating them into what Lacan believed to be their equivalent rhetorical terms: metaphor and metonymy. Metaphor works by condensing two separate images into a single symbol through substitution, while metonymy operates by association—using a part to represent the whole (such as "crown" for "king") or using contiguous elements (such as "sea" and "boat").

The presence of the father teaches the child that it must assume a predefined social and familial role over which it exercises no control—a role that is defined by the sexual difference between mother and father, the exclusion of the child from the sexual relationship that exists between the mother and the father, and the child's relinquishment of the earlier and intense bonds that existed between itself and the mother's body. This situation of absence, exclusion, and difference is symbolized by the phallus, a universal signifier or metonymic presence that indicates the fundamental lack or absence that lies at the heart of being itself—the *manque à être*, as Lacan calls it.

THE REAL AND *JOUISSANCE*

Finally, Lacan posits a register called the real—not the empirical world but rather the ineffable realm of constancy beyond the field of speech. According to Lacan, the reality that is given to consciousness is no more and no less than an amalgam of the imaginary (the specular and imagistic world of the rationalizing ego, with all of its self-delusions, defenses, and falsifications) and the symbolic (the meaningful social world of language). Lacan resists defining the real in any explicit or easily codifiable way. In his later work in the 1960s, Lacan discussed the register of the real in the light of his work on *jouissance*, a term that is loosely translated as "enjoyment" but that is much more complex.

According to Lacan, *jouissance* is any experience that is too much for the organism to bear. More often than not, it is experienced as suffering—an unbearable pain that is experienced as a kind of satisfaction by the unconscious drives. According to Lacan, this is what lies at the heart of the Freudian repetition compulsion—namely, an unconscious, and unconsciously satisfying, wish to suffer. Healthy human life is about the regulation of jouissance. Children's bodies are prone to overexcitation and overstimulation because they are full of *jouissance*, which is slowly drained from the body of the child after its encounter with the law of the father and its entry into the register of the symbolic. Portions of *jouissance* linked to especially intense bodily memories from childhood can become "caught" or centered in the body and manifest as symptoms. Lacan reconfigured Freud's theory of castration by redefining it as the loss of jouissance from the body. More broadly, Lacan says that the entry into language itself is castration because it introduces the idea of lack or absence into the world.

LACANIAN CLINICAL PRACTICE

For Lacan, human subjects construct themselves through language. One of the chief goals of Lacanian clinical practice is to create a space wherein the patient can experience and release jouissance through speech without the disintegration of the sense of self. The analyst will then determine where a patient lies on a diagnostic continuum—neurotic (obsessional or hysteric), perverse, or psychotic.

Psychotic patients, according to Lacanian analysis, are most greatly disconnected at the level of language, or the symbolic. The Lacanian analyst works with the disjointed speech of the psychotic to allow him or her to live within and to express, through language, the world of signifiers without significant discontinuity.

The perverse patient, on the other hand, is often drawn to a fetish object. The fetish object is a compliant one, and it allows the patient to experience jouissance without having to relive the experience of castration that was attendant on the Father's "No." The perverse patient engages in an act of substitution, whereby a complicit object grants a sense of release—a real or simulated experience of jouissance—while allowing him or her to avoid the painful sense of separation from the Other, or the presymbolic mother.

The obsessional neurotic fears loss of control. Obsessional neurotics struggle to control and contain the upwelling of desire and the accompanying experience of jouissance. The obsessional neurotic speaks the language of mastery and order and attempts to exercise control well beyond his or her purview. The analyst is sensitive to dichotomizing tendencies in the patient's speech (order and disorder, right and wrong). According to Lacan, the patient's fantasy is that the upwelling of jouissance will alienate those around him or her and leave havoc in its wake. The analyst works with the obsessional neurotic to help the patient meet his or her needs without limiting defenses—to experience and speak desire without the fear of losing self-control.

Hysterics experience a deep and debilitating sense of lack that leads to a feeling of alienation from the Other. Once the hysteric obtains the imaginary object of the mother's desire, he or she wishes to be rid of it—sometimes almost violently. The goal of Lacanian analysis when working with hysterics is to move them beyond the dichotomy of having/not having to help them to achieve satisfactory levels of comfort with themselves and to find a neutral space where the sense of lack is not all-consuming.

THE CASE OF AIMÉE

Lacan's early work on paranoia dealt with the case of a patient he called Aimée (Marguerite Anzieu) who was arrested by the Paris police in the attempted stabbing of a famous actress, Huguette Duflos. Lacan first encountered Aimée in 1931 at Sainte-Anne's Hospital, where he had begun his clinical training as a *légiste medicale*, or forensic psychiatrist, four years earlier. Lacan's patient, the subject of numerous press accounts and much public speculation, came to believe that her young son was about to be murdered by Duflos. One night Aimée attended a play that featured the famous Parisian actress and suddenly lunged from the crowd of theatergoers, brandishing a knife. Aimée was promptly arrested and given over to Lacan's care.

Lacan conducted an exhaustive number of analytic interviews with Aimée. Lacan was able to reconstruct the trajectory of Aimée's descent into what he termed "self-punishment paranoia." Aimée both feared and admired Duflos, and she came to believe that the actress—really her ideal image of the actress—posed a danger to her and to her young child. Duflos's ideal image was the object of Aimée's intense hatred as well as her excessive fascination, writes Lacan, and in attacking Duflos, the deluded woman was really punishing herself.

In one especially striking memory, Aimée recalled (falsely) reading an article in a newspaper in which the actress allegedly told an interviewer that she was planning to kill Aimée and her young son. Aimée therefore regarded her attack on Duflos as an act of preemptive self-defense based on a misrecognition. Aimée finally found the real punishment she unconsciously craved (her jouissance) in her public humiliation, arrest, and confinement.

Lacan was struck by the relationship between memory (or, in this case, false memory) and identity. One sees in Lacan's early analysis of Aimée many of the most significant elements of his psychoanalytic theory, including the mirror stage, the imaginary, jouissance and its role in paranoia, and the power of misidentification.

Lacan's detailed analysis of the case of Aimée in his 1932 doctoral thesis, *De la psychose paranoiaque dans les rapports avec la personnalité* (Paranoid psychosis and its relations to the personality), laid the groundwork for much of his later work on the nature of identity, the genesis of narcissism, the power of the image, and the fundamentally social character of personality. From 1933 onward, Lacan was known as a specialist in the diagnosis and treatment of paranoia. His densely textured doctoral dissertation was widely circulated among artists and poets identified with the Surrealist movement, and Lacan wrote regularly for *Minotaure*, a Surrealist review published between 1933 and 1939 by Albert Skira. Many of Lacan's interpreters regard his work with philosopher Alexandre Kojève as a theoretical turning point and the genesis of his thinking on the psychological significance of lack, loss, and absence.

In 1936, Lacan presented his paper "Le stade du miroir" (the mirror stage) at the fourteenth International Psychoanalytical Congress, held at Marienbad in August of 1936 under the chairmanship of the preeminent British psychoanalyst Ernest Jones. It is in this seminal essay, since lost, that Lacan outlined his theory of the mirror stage. His theory of self-mastery through mimicry, in which the young child responds to its prematuration or defenselessness by identifying with images outside itself, was influenced by the anthropological insights of Roger Caillois.

Lacan's radical revision of psychoanalysis, which he regarded as a return to Freud, led to his eventual ejection from the Société Française de Psychanalyse (SFP) in 1963. Lacan founded a new school, first called the École Française de Psychanalyse and then later the École Freudienne de Paris (EFP). Lacan dissolved the EFP in 1980 and died a year later, leaving behind a body of work that continues to influence psychoanalytic studies, philosophy, and literary and cultural theory.

BIBLIOGRAPHY

Bracher, Mark, and Ellie Ragland-Sullivan. *Lacan and the Subject of Language*. London: Routledge, 2014. Digital file.

Dor, Joël. *Introduction to the Reading of Lacan: The Unconscious Structured Like a Language*. Ed. Judith Feher-Gurewich and Susan Fairfield. New York: Other, 2004. Print.

Evans, Dylan. *An Introductory Dictionary of Lacanian Psychoanalysis*. New York: Routledge, 1996. Print.

Fink, Bruce. *A Clinical Introduction to Lacanian Psychoanalysis: Theory and Technique*. Cambridge: Harvard UP, 1999. Print.

Fink, Bruce. *Fundamentals of Psychoanalytic Technique: A Lacanian Approach for Practitioners*. New York: Norton, 2007. Print.

Gallop, Jane. *Reading Lacan*. Ithaca: Cornell UP, 1985. Print.

Lacan, Jacques. *Écrits: A Selection*. Trans. Bruce Fink. New York: Norton, 2004. Print.

Leader, Darian, and Judy Groves. *Introducing Lacan*. Rev. ed. London: Icon, 2010. Print.

Miller, Michael J. *Lacanian Psychotherapy: Theory and Practical Applications*. New York: Routledge, 2011. Digital file.

Muller, John P., and William J. Richardson. *Lacan and Language: A Reader's Guide to Écrits*. 1982. New York: International UP, 1994. Print.

Parker, Ian. *Lacanian Psychoanalysis: Revolutions in Subjectivity*. London: Routledge, 2011. Digital file.

Shepherdson, Charles. Lacan and the Limits of Language. New York: Fordham UP, 2008. Print.

Gerard O'Sullivan

See Also: Children's mental health; Fetishes; Lacan, Jacques; Langauge; Linguistics; Oedipus complex; Psychoanalytic psychology; Psychoanalytic psychology and personality: Sigmund Freud.

Analytic psychology
Carl Jung

Type of psychology: Personality

Jungian analytical psychology is one of the most complex theories of personality. It attempts to improve on Sigmund Freud's work by deemphasizing sexual instincts and the abnormal side of human nature. Three of its more significant contributions are the notions of psychological types, the concept of the collective unconscious, and the depiction of the unconscious self as the most critical structure within the psyche.

Key Concepts

- Anima and animus
- Archetypes
- Collective unconcious
- Conscious ego
- Persona
- Personal unconcious
- Self
- Shadow

INTRODUCTION

Carl Jung founded analytical psychology, perhaps the most complex major theory of personality. This theory includes the presentation and analysis of concepts and principles based on numerous disciplines within the arts and sciences. Because this complexity is combined with Jung's often-awkward writing, the task of mastering his theory is a challenge even for experts in the field of personality. His key contribution was taking the study of psychology beyond the claims made by Sigmund Freud. Jung's emphasis on adult development and personality types and his willingness to break with strict Freudian teachings were major contributions within the history of psychology in general and personality in particular.

Jung's theory can best be understood by examining the key structures he proposes and the dynamics of personality. Jung divides the personality, or psyche,into three levels: at the conscious level, there is the ego. The conscious ego lies at the center of consciousness. In essence, it is the conscious mind—one's identity from a conscious perspective. It is particularly important to the person whose unconscious self is not yet fully developed. As the unconscious self begins to develop, the importance of the conscious ego diminishes.

Beneath the conscious ego is the personal unconscious. This level involves material that has been removed from the consciousness of the person. This information may leave consciousness through forgetting or repression. Because the personal unconscious is close to the surface, which is consciousness, items in it may be recalled at a later date. The personal unconscious is similar to Freud's notion of the preconscious. Material within the personal unconscious is grouped into clusters called "complexes." Each complex contains a person's thoughts, feelings, perceptions, and memories concerning particular concepts. For example, the mother complex contains all personal and ancestral experiences with the concept of mother. These experiences can be both good and bad.

The deepest level of the psyche is called the "collective unconscious." This level contains the memory traces that have been passed down to all humankind as a function of evolutionary development. It includes tendencies to behave in specific ways, such as living in groups or using spoken language. Although individuals have their own unique personal unconscious, all people share the same collective unconscious. The key structures within the collective unconscious that determine how people behave and respond to their environment are labeled "archetypes." Each archetype enables people to express their unique status as human beings.

ARCHETYPES

Archetypes are divided into major and minor archetypes. The major archetypes include the persona, animus, anima, shadow, and self. The persona is the public personality, which the individual displays to be accepted by society. The individual's goal is to balance the needs of the persona with the desire to express his or her true self. In contrast to the persona, the shadow represents the dark side of the psyche. It includes thoughts and feelings that people typically do not express because they are not social. These cognitions can be held back on either a conscious or an unconscious level. The anima represents the feminine aspects of men, while the animus represents the masculine aspects of women. These archetypes have come about as a function of centuries of interactions between men and women. They have the potential to improve communication and understanding between the sexes. Finally, the most important psychic structure in Jung's theory is the self. It is the archetype that provides the whole psyche with a sense of unity and stability. The major goal of people's lives is to optimize the development of the self.

PSYCHIC STRUCTURES AND PERSONALITIES

In an effort to optimize the development of the self, people develop their own psychological type. Each type (Jung conceived of eight types) consists of a combination of a person's basic attitude and basic function. Jung's two attitudes are extroversion and introversion. These terms follow societal stereotypes, with the extrovert being outgoing and confident and the introvert being hesitant and reflective. These attitudes are combined with four basic functions, or ways of relating to the world. These functions are thinking, feeling, sensing, and intuiting, which are consistent with a general societal view of these terms. Jung used the possible combination of the attitudes and functions to form the eight possible psychological types. Each person is thought to have dominance within one of the available types.

In addition to providing key psychic structures, Jung provides personality dynamics. He claimed that each person is endowed with psychic or libidinal energy. Unlike Freud, however, Jung did not view this energy as strictly sexual. Rather, he perceived it as life-process energy encompassing all aspects of the psyche. According to Jung, this energy operates according to two principles of energy flow: equivalence and entropy. The principle of equivalence states that an increase in energy within one aspect of the psyche must be accompanied by a decrease in another area. For example, if psychic energy is increasing in the unconscious self, it must decrease elsewhere, such as in the conscious ego. The principle of entropy states that when psychic energy is unbalanced, it will seek a state of equilibrium. For example, it would not be desirable to have the majority of one's psychic energy located in the conscious ego. The energy needs of the other levels of consciousness must also be met.

Jung's psychic structures, along with his views on the dynamics of personality, have provided psychologists with a wealth of information to consider, many complexities to address, and numerous possible ways to apply his ideas to human development and personality assessment.

REALIZATION OF SELF

Jung made significant contributions to knowledge of areas such as human development and personality assessment. In terms of human development, Jung emphasized that personality development occurs throughout the life of the person. This was critical in that Freud's theory, the dominant theory at that time, emphasized the first five years of life in examining personality development. The overall goal of the person in Jung's approach to development is the realization of the self, which is a long and difficult process. Unlike Freud, Jung was particularly interested in development during the adulthood years. He emphasized the changes that occur beginning at the age of thirty-five or forty. He believed that this was often a time of crisis in the life of the person. This notion of a midlife crisis (which Jung experienced himself) has continued to be the source of significant theoretical and empirical claims.

Jung believed that the concept of a crisis during middle age was necessary and beneficial. Often, a person has achieved a certain level of material success and needs to find new meaning in life. This meaning can be realized by shifting from the material and physical concerns of youth to a more spiritual and philosophical view of life. The person seeks gradually to abandon the emphasis on the conscious ego that is dominant in youth. A greater balance between the unconscious and conscious is pursued. If this is successfully achieved, the person can reach a state of positive psychological health that Jung labels "individuation." Perhaps the key to the midlife years in Jung's theory is that these are the years in which the person is attempting to discover the true meaning of life. Finally, Jung stated that religion can play an important role in life during midlife and old age. During midlife, a sense of spirituality rather than materialism is important in personality development; looking at the possibility of life after death can be positive for the older adult.

ASSESSMENT TECHNIQUES

Jung made use of several interesting assessment techniques in addressing the problems of his patients. Like Freud, Jung was an advocate of the case study method. He believed that much could be learned through an in-depth analysis of the problems of his patients. In his cases, Jung made extensive use of dream analysis. Jung maintained that dreams serve many purposes. They can be used to address and resolve current conflicts or to facilitate the development of the self. Dreams can therefore be oriented toward the future. While Freud focused his analysis on individual dreams, Jung would examine a group of dreams to uncover the problems of the patient. This examination of multiple dreams was viewed by Jung as a superior approach to gaining access to the deeper meanings of dreams, which could often be found in the collective unconscious.

Another important assessment device used by Jung that continues to have applications today is the word-association test. In this test, a person responds to a stimulus word with whatever comes to mind. Jung originally worked with a group of one hundred stimulus words and would focus on issues such as the response word given by the patient, the length of time it took the patient to respond, the provision of multiple responses, the repetition of the stimulus word, and the absence of a response. These and other factors could be used to establish the existence of an underlying neurosis as well as specific conflicts and complexes.

SPLIT WITH FREUD

The development of Jung's analytical psychology can be traced to the development of his relationship with Freud and the subsequent split that occurred between the two theorists. In 1906, Jung published a book that concerned the psychoanalytic treatment of schizophrenia. He sent a copy of this book to Freud, who was thoroughly impressed by Jung's work. Jung became one of the strongest Freudian advocates from 1907 to 1912. During this time he collaborated with Freud and was viewed by many within psychoanalytic circles as the heir apparent to Freud. Jung had in fact been elected president of the prestigious International Psychoanalytic Association. In 1913 and 1914, however, he abandoned Freud and Freud's psychoanalytic theory. Three basic problems led to this split. The first was Freud's emphasis on sexuality. Jung believed that while sexual instincts did exist, they should not be emphasized at the expense of other relevant aspects of the psyche. Second, Jung believed that Freud overemphasized abnormality. He maintained that Freud appeared to have little to say about the normal aspects of human nature. Finally, unlike Freud, Jung wished to emphasize the biology of the species rather than the biology of the individual.

The split between Freud and Jung was important for practical as well as theoretical reasons. Jung was rejected for a period of time by other analytically oriented thinkers because of his split with Freud. In addition, the break with Freud led Jung to experience a mental crisis that lasted for several years. This combination of factors eventually led Jung to conclude that he must develop his own view of the psyche, along with appropriate treatment techniques.

Although the challenges encountered by Jung in his life were difficult to overcome, they clearly played a major role in his ability to develop the most complex theory of personality ever formulated. His key concepts and psychic structures, including the collective unconscious, personal unconscious, archetypes, self, and personality typology, continue to be among the most interesting theoretical contributions in the history of personality psychology.

BIBLIOGRAPHY

Brome, Vincent. *Jung: Man and Myth.* New York: Atheneum, 1981. Print.

Bulkeley, Kelly, and Clodagh Weldon, eds. *Teaching Jung.* New York: Oxford UP, 2011. Print.

Hannah, Barbara. *Jung: His Life and Work.* New York: Putnam, 1976. Print.

Huskinson, Lucy, ed. *Dreaming the Myth Onwards: New Directions in Jungian Therapy and Thought.* New York: Routledge, 2008. Print.

Jung, Carl Gustav. *Memories, Dreams, Reflections.* Trans. Richard and Clara Winston. Ed. Aniela Jaffé. Rev. ed. New York: Vintage, 1989. Print.

Jung, Carl Gustav. *Introduction to Jungian Psychology: Notes of the Seminar on Analytical Psychology Given in 1925.* Rev. ed. Ed. Sonu Shamdasani. Princeton: Princeton UP, 2012. Print.

Jung, Carl Gustav. *Psychological Types.* Trans. Richard and Clara Winston. New York: Harcourt Brace, 1923. Print.

McGuire, William, ed. *The Freud/Jung Letters.* Princeton: Princeton UP, 1974. Print.

Milton, Jane, Caroline Polmear, and Julia Fabricius. *A Short Introduction to Psychoanalysis.* 2nd ed. Thousand Oaks: Sage, 2011. Print.

Noll, Richard. *The Jung Cult: Origins of a Charismatic Movement.* New York: Free, 1997. Print.

Shamdasani, Sonu. *Cult Fictions: C. G. Jung and the Founding of Analytical Psychology.* New York: Routledge, 1998. Print.

Smythe, William E., and Angelina Baydala. "The Hermeneutic Background of C. G. Jung." *Journal of Analytical Psychology* 51.1 (2012): 57–75. Print.Tacey, David, ed. The Jung Reader. New York: Routledge, 2012. Print.

Young-Eisendrath, Polly, and Terence Dawson, eds. *The Cambridge Companion to Jung.* 2nd ed. New York: Cambridge UP, 2008. Print.

Lawrence A. Fehr

See Also: Abnormality: Psychological models; Analytical psychotherapy; Archetypes and the collective unconcious; Dreams; Jung, Carl; Jungian psychology; Midlife crises; Personality theory; Psychoanalytic psychology; Self.

Analytical psychotherapy

Type of psychology: Psychotherapy

Analytical psychotherapy is associated with the theory and techniques of Carl Jung. Similar to other psychodynamic therapies, it stresses the importance of discovering unconscious material. Unique to this approach is the emphasis on reconciling opposite personality traits that are hidden in the personal unconscious and collective unconscious.

Key Concepts

- Collective unconcious
- Compensatory function
- Confession
- Education
- Elucidation
- Method of active imagination
- Method of amplification
- Personal unconcious
- Transference
- Transformation

INTRODUCTION

Analytical psychotherapy is an approach to psychological treatment pioneered by Carl Jung, a Swiss psychoanalyst. A follower of Sigmund Freud, Jung was trained in the psychoanalytic approach, with its emphasis on the dark, inaccessible material contained in the unconscious mind. Freud was fond of Jung and believed that he was to be the heir to the legacy he had begun. Jung began to disagree with certain aspects of Freud's theory, however, and he and Freud bitterly parted ways in 1914.

Jung's concept of the structure of personality, on which he based his ideas of psychotherapy, was influenced by Freud and the psychoanalytic tradition, but he added his own personal and mystical interpretations to its concepts. Jung believed that the personality consists of the ego, which is one's conscious mind. It contains the thoughts, feelings, and perceptions of which one is normally aware. Jung also proposed a personal unconscious that contains events and emotions of which people remain unaware because of their anxiety-provoking nature. Memories of traumatic childhood events and conflicts may reside in the personal unconscious. Jung's unique contribution to personality theory is the idea of a collective unconscious. This consists of memories and emotions that are shared by all humanity. Jung believed that certain events and feelings are universal and exert a similar effect on all individuals. An example would be his universal symbol of a shadow, or the evil, primitive nature that resides within everyone. Jung believed that although people are aware of the workings of the conscious ego, it is the unavailable material contained in the personal unconscious and collective unconscious that has the greatest influence on people's behavior.

Jung's analytical psychotherapy was a pioneering approach during the very early era of psychological treatment. He conformed to the beliefs of other psychodynamic therapists, such as Freud and Alfred Adler, in the importance of discovering unconscious material. The psychoanalysts would be followed by the behavioral school's emphasis on environmental events and the cognitive school's focus on thoughts and perceptions. Psychoanalysis brought a prominence to psychology it had not known previously.

PERSONALITY AND THE UNCONSCIOUS MIND

Jung believed that emotional problems originate from a one-sided development of personality. He believed that this is a natural process and that people must constantly seek a balance of their traits. An example might be a person who becomes overly logical and rational in her behavior and decision making while ignoring her emotional and spontaneous side. Jung believed this one-sided development eventually would lead to emotional difficulty and that one must access the complementary personality forces that reside in the unconscious. Even psychotherapists must be aware that along with their desire to help others, they have complementary darker desires that are destructive to others. Jung believed that emotional problems are a signal that people are becoming unbalanced in their personality and that this should motivate them to develop more neutral traits.

The process of analytical psychotherapy, as in most psychodynamic approaches, is to make patients conscious or aware of the material in their unconscious mind. Jung believed that if the conscious mind were overly logical and rational, the unconscious mind, to balance it, would be filled with equally illogical and emotional material. To access this material, Jung advocated a free and equal exchange of ideas and information between the analyst and the patient. Jung did not focus on specific techniques as did Freud, but he did believe that the unconscious material would become evident in the context of a strong, trusting therapeutic relationship. Although the patient and analyst have equal status, the analyst serves as a model of an individual who has faced her or his unconscious demons.

STAGES OF ANALYTIC PSYCHOTHERAPY

Analytic psychotherapy proceeds in four stages. The first stage is that of confession. Jung believed that it is necessary for patients to tell of their conflicts and that this is usually accompanied by an emotional release. Jung did not believe that confession is sufficient to provide a cure for one's ills, however, nor did he believe (unlike Freud) that an intellectual understanding of one's difficulties is adequate. Patients must find a more neutral ground in terms of personality functioning, and this can be accomplished only by facing their unconscious material.

The second stage of psychotherapy is called elucidation, and it involves becoming aware of one's unconscious transferences. Transference is a process in which patients transfer emotions about someone else in their lives onto the therapist; patients will behave toward the therapist as they would toward that other person. It is similar to meeting someone who reminds one of a past relationship; for no apparent reason, one might begin to act toward the new person the same way one did to the previous person. Jung believed that these transferences to the analyst give a clue about unconscious material. A gentle, passive patient might evidence hostile transferences to the therapist, thus giving evidence of considerable rage that is being contained in the unconscious.

The third stage of analytic psychotherapy consists of education. Patients are instructed about the dangers of unequal personality development and are supported in their attempts to change. The overly logical business executive may be encouraged to go on a spontaneous vacation with his family with few plans and no fixed destinations. The shy student may be cajoled into joining a debate on emotional campus issues. Jung believed in the value of experiencing the messages of one's unconscious.

The final stage of psychotherapy, and one that is not always necessary, is that of transformation. This goes beyond the superficial encouragements of the previous stages and attempts to get patients to delve deeply into the unconscious and thereby understand who they are. This process of understanding and reconciling one's opposites takes considerable courage and exploration into one's personal and cultural past. It is a quest for identity and purpose in life that requires diligent work between the analyst and patient; the result is superior wisdom and a transcendent calm when coping with life's struggles.

ANALYTIC TECHNIQUES

Jung developed several techniques aimed at uncovering material hidden in the unconscious. Like Freud, Jung believed that the content of dreams is indicative of unconscious attitudes. He believed that dreams have a compensatory function; that is, they are reflections of the side of personality that is not displayed during one's conscious, everyday state. The sophisticated librarian may have dreams of being an exotic dancer, according to Jung, as a way of expressing the ignored aspects of personality.

Jung gives an example of the compensatory aspects of dreams when describing the recollections of a dutiful son. The son dreamed that he and his father were leaving home and his father was driving a new automobile. The father began to drive in an erratic fashion. He swerved the car all over the road until he finally succeeded in crashing the car and damaging it very badly. The son was frightened, then became angry and chastised his father for his behavior. Rather than respond, however, his father began to laugh until it became apparent that he was very intoxicated, a condition the son had not previously noticed. Jung interpreted the dream in the context of the son's relationship with his father. The son overly idealized the father while refusing to recognize apparent faults. The dream represented the son's latent anger at his father and his attempt to reduce him in status. Jung indicated to the young man that the dream was a cue from his unconscious that he should evaluate his relationship with his father with a more balanced outlook.

AMPLIFICATION METHOD

Jung employed the method of amplification for interpreting dreams. This technique involved focusing repeatedly on the contents of the dream and giving multiple associations to them. Jung believed that the dream often is basically what it appears to be. This differs dramatically from Freudian interpretation, which requires the patient to associate dream elements with childhood conflicts.

The amplification method can be applied to a dream reported by a graduate student in clinical psychology. While preparing to defend his dissertation, the final and most anxiety-provoking aspect of receiving the doctorate, the student had a dream about his oral defense. Before presenting the project to his dissertation committee that was to evaluate its worth (and seemingly his own), the student dreamed that he was in the bathroom gathering his resources. He noticed he was wearing a three-piece brown suit; however, none of the pieces matched. They were different shades of brown. Fortunately, the pieces were reversible, so the student attempted to change them so they would all be the same shade. After repeated attempts, he was unable to get all three pieces of the suit to be the same shade of brown. He finally gave up in despair and did not appear for his defense. With a little knowledge about the student, an analytical therapist would have an easy time with the meaning of this dream. This was obviously a stressful time in the young man's life, and the dream reflected his denied anxiety. In addition, the student did not like brown suits; one that does not match is even more hideous. It is apparent that he was unhappy and, despite his best attempts to portray confidence, the budding clinician was afraid that he was going to "look stupid." Jung would have encouraged him to face these fears of failure that were hidden in his unconscious.

ACTIVE IMAGINATION

A final application of analytical psychotherapy stems from Jung's method of active imagination. Jung believed that unconscious messages could come not only from dreams but also from one's artistic productions. He encouraged his patients to produce spontaneous, artistic material. Some patients sketched, while others painted, wrote poetry, or sang songs. He was interested in the symbols that were given during these periods, and he asked his clients to comment on them. Jung believed that considerable material in the unconscious could be discovered during these encounters. He also talked with his patients about the universal meanings of these symbols (as in his idea of the collective unconscious), and they would attempt to relate this material to their own cultural pasts.

Many modern therapies, such as art, music, and dance therapy, draw heavily from this idea that one can become aware of unconscious and emotional material through association involving one's artistic productions. These therapists believe, as did Jung, that patients are less defensive during these times of spontaneous work and, therefore, are more likely to discover unconscious material.

CONTRIBUTIONS TO PSYCHOLOGY

Analytical psychotherapy is not considered a mainstream approach to psychotherapy, but it does have a small group of devoted followers. Some of Jung's techniques have been adapted into other, more common approaches. Many therapists agree with Jung's de-emphasis on specific techniques in favor of a focus on the establishment of a supportive therapy relationship. Jung moved away from the stereotypical analyst's couch in favor of face-to-face communication between doctor and patient. Many psychotherapists endorse Jung's belief that the analyst and patient should have relatively equal status and input. Jung also reduced the frequency of meeting with his patients from daily (as Freud recommended) to weekly, which is the norm today.

Jung's analytical approach changed the focus of psychotherapy from symptom relief to self-discovery. He was interested not only in patients with major problems but also in those who were dissatisfied with their mundane existence. These people were usually bright, articulate, and occupationally successful.

Jung's most lasting contributions probably have been his insights into the polarity of personality traits. The Myers-Briggs Type Indicator, based on Jungian personality descriptions, is one of the most widely used personality tests in business and industry. Jung also believed that personality changes throughout one's life, and he encouraged a continual evaluation of oneself. The idea of a midlife crisis, a period when people reevaluate their personal and occupational goals, is a product of Jung's theory. He believed that individuals should continually strive to achieve a balance in their personality and behavior.

BIBLIOGRAPHY

Bishop, Paul, ed. *Jung in Contexts: A Reader*. New York: Routledge, 2000. Print.

Hall, Calvin S., and Vernon J. Nordby. *A Primer of Jungian Psychology.* New York: New American Library, 1973. Print.

Hergenhahn, B. R., and Matthew Olsen. *An Introduction to Theories of Personality.* 11th ed. Upper Saddle River: Pearson/Prentice Hall, 2011. Print.

Jones, Raya A. Jung, *Psychology, Postmodernity.* New York: Routledge, 2007. Print.

Jones, Raya A., ed. *Jung and the Question of Science*. New York: Routledge, 2014. Print.

Jung, Carl. *Man and His Symbols*. 1961. Reprint. New York: Laureleaf, 1997. Print.

Magnavita, Jeffrey J. *Theories of Personality: Contemporary Approaches to the Science of Personality.* New York: Wiley, 2002. Print.

Mathers, Dale. *An Introduction to Meaning and Purpose in Analytical Psychology.* Philadelphia: Taylor, 2001. Print.

Roesler, Christian. "Evidence for the Effectiveness of Jungian Psychotherapy: A Review of Empirical Studies." *Behavioral Sciences* 3.4 (2013): 562–75. Print.

Samuels, Andrew. *Jung and the Post-Jungians.* New York: Routledge, 1986. Print.

Stevens, Anthony. *Jung: A Very Short Introduction.* New York: Oxford UP, 2001. Print.

Brett L. Beck

See Also: Abnormality: Psychological models; Analytical psychology: Carl Jung; Archetypes and the collective unconcious; Dreams; Midlife crises; Music, dance and theater therapy; Myers-Briggs Type Indicator (MBTI); Personality theory; Psychoanalytic psychology.

Anger

Type of psychology: Emotion; Personality; Psychotherapy; Stress

Anger, a feeling of great displeasure and hostility toward others, has received modern research attention since the 1930s. The emotion is due to mental and physical processes related to perceived attacks on beliefs, values, and expectations, as well as to psychiatric conditions such as paranoia. Anger responds to psychological counseling and medication.

Key Concepts

- Depression
- Endocrine system
- Fight-or-flight response
- Parasympathetic nervous system
- Rage

INTRODUCTION

The modern definition of anger is a feeling of great hostility, displeasure, or exasperation toward other persons. The experience of anger is perceived as being beyond any conscious reason, because emotions are reflexive, involuntary experiences rather than purposeful acts. To be angry is not a conscious choice. It happens when an experience causes a change in biological and mental states. Anger is caused by both mental and physical stimuli. Its mental components are thoughts, beliefs, expectations, and values. Anger's physical components are changed biostatus, such as increased heart rate and blood pressure. These stimuli will differ in extent from person to person.

Anger occurs in all people. Psychologically, two things must occur to cause anger: people must form a belief that others have committed misdeeds that have wronged them, and they must assign blame to others, who are targeted for retribution. Anger is therefore a reaction to the actions of others and a judgment of the cause of those actions. To become angry, one must see an action of another person as intentional mistreatment. Whether this is true is irrelevant; the perception of mistreatment causes the anger response. The causes and expressions of anger vary with age and gender. Most frequently, anger is based on feeling unable to right wrongs committed against one, perceived violation of one's principles or values (such as honesty), physical or verbal attacks on one's self-esteem, and actions preventing the attainment of goals that are perceived to be correct.

A great many situations can cause anger. Some are created by psychological disorders, while others are more normal but may become excessively severe. Anger in the case of psychological disorders includes the anger of paranoids and of some people experiencing depression. The more usual instances of anger include anger at a spouse, anger at an employer, anger at a friend, and anger due to a situation caused by a stranger (such as road rage and aggression). Manifestations of anger will range from rage responses to anger suppression. Rage leads to screaming at others, striking them, and destroying property. Suppressed anger can lead to depression. Rage and depression should be treated professionally.

THE BIOLOGY OF ANGER

Biologically, human anger is a response of the nervous system to stresses, demands, threats, and pressures. When people are faced with a threat to survival, their nervous systems quickly, automatically meet it by raising body defenses in a fight-or-flight mechanism. The fight-or-flight response, identified by Harvard physiologist Walter Bradford Cannon in the 1930s, occurs whether life events require greatly changed lifestyle or are minor irritants. The nervous system does not await a conscious interpretation of an event, but simply reacts via the sympathetic nervous system, which is designed for immediate defense responses. The system trigger is the release of the hormone epinephrine (adrenaline), made by the adrenal glands located atop each kidney. Epinephrine causes dilation of the pupils, elevated heartbeat rate, increased blood pressure, rapid breathing, release of sugar into the blood by the liver, and movement of blood into the skeletal muscles.

These responses lead to arousal and readiness to fight or flee. Pupil dilation increases the ability to see danger and differentiate it from normal events. Increased heartbeat drives blood through the cardiovascular system more rapidly than usual. This hastens hormone and nutrient passage through the body, engendering swift signaling by hormones and bettering the readiness of skeletal muscles to be used in a fight or flight. The rerouting of blood and the increased heartbeat result in increased blood pressure, which, over the long term, endangers the body. However, if experienced infrequently and over a short time period, it is not dangerous.

Elevated blood sugar levels and rapid breathing are also related to anger. Elevated blood sugar content, circulating rapidly to all the tissues, provides the energy needed for skeletal muscles to engender the fight-or-flight response mechanism and better allows the brain to coordinate these actions. The increase in the breathing rate is essential to the use of the energy in the blood sugar, because sugar is converted to energy most effectively through respiration, a process that requires a large amount of oxygen. Respiration results in the production of carbon dioxide, water, and energy—the latter consumed by the fight-or-flight response.

It is crucial to find ways to handle or defuse anger, because, over the long term, mismanaged anger can lead to many disease conditions. These include heart disease, ulcers and other gastrointestinal disorders, frequent headaches, and susceptibility to microbial infection. The basis for such problems is the changed levels of hormones, other than epinephrine, caused by the experience of anger. Most often cited are the increased levels of testosterone in men and corticosteroids in both genders. Long-term elevation of these hormones increases occurrence of atherosclerosis (coronary artery disease). Excessive amounts of body corticosteroids (such as cortisol) depress the action of the immune system, damaging the body's first line of defense against infectious diseases.

Problems related to epinephrine and its close relative norepinephrine are related to the fight-or-flight response's ability to elevate heartbeat rates, raise blood pressure, release liver sugar into the blood, and enhance blood entry into skeletal muscle. When mismanaged or untreated anger causes these responses to occur too often, the liver is unable to remove blood cholesterol; this adds to the buildup of fat deposits in the heart and blood vessels (atherosclerosis). Elevated blood pressure results in a heart that overworks itself, becoming larger and less efficient.

DIAGNOSING ANGER

Almost everyone is angry at times, regardless of gender or age. Some individuals are subject to such frequent rage that they seek—or are sent to—a physician or psychotherapist for treatment. However, many individuals do not recognize their anger and blame reactions caused by it on job dissatisfaction, unsatisfactory marriages, dislike of minorities, and other life problems. Often, such anger will remain unnoticed until they visit a counselor or psychotherapist for help in such matters and it is suggested that they need to treat their anger with psychotherapy or medication.

There are many schools of thought on diagnosing and treating anger. Although the tools used for treatment differ, diagnosing, measuring, and evaluating anger are most often accomplished by administering assessment forms crucial to devising treatment. Diagnosis of severe anger is often occasioned when an enraged or depressed patient is admitted to a hospital emergency room or psychiatric ward and queries by physicians lead to psychiatric evaluation. More often, an angry individual seeks counseling for reasons ranging from marital or work-related problems to tiredness and general mental malaise. Psychotherapeutic consultation will then lead to diagnosis of anger. Some patients visit psychotherapists or counselors because they themselves recognize that they are angry too often or excessively belligerent.

ANGER TREATMENT OPTIONS

Anger associated with depression, extreme rage and belligerence, and the passive-aggressive state may be treated with tranquilizers, hormones, and antidepressants. In such individuals, medication is often followed by combined psychotherapy and medication as an inpatient in a hospital ward. More often, it is accomplished by means of medication and periodic outpatient visits to a psychotherapist or counselor.

There are many different schools of thought concerning anger treatment for people who are not overly belligerent, severely depressed, or in other states in which they will severely harm themselves or other persons. Some therapists recommend leaving the site of an anger outbreak until calmed down. Others suggest psychotherapy that identifies the basis for the anger (such as events in childhood) and gives curative insights. Still other psychotherapists, such as Albert Ellis and R. Chip Tafrate, propose techniques such as rational emotive therapy and similar methods that can often be applied by self-treatment. The suggestion that patients let out their anger to feel better and minimize aggressive tendencies remains highly debated. Psychologists have not reached a consensus regarding that and other treatments, largely because of the many and varied causes of anger.

THE HISTORY OF ANGER TREATMENT

Human anger has been reported since the beginning of written record keeping. For example, the emotion was discussed by the ancient Greek physician Hippocrates, and practitioners through the Middle Ages used herbs and bleeding to handle the emotion by bringing down the patient's blood pressure and "choler." Until the twentieth century, members of the poorer classes who were encumbered with extremes of rage and other anger manifestations such as paranoia were chained in madhouses. In the twentieth century, development of modern psychoactive drugs and psychotherapy engendered treatment of afflicted individuals as described in the American Psychiatric Association's *Diagnostic and Statistical Manual of Mental Disorders* (DSM).

Cannon's work in the 1930s on the fight-or-flight response mechanism was essential to the conceptualization of appropriate treatment for anger. Hans Selye, in the 1970s and 1980s, proposed that Cannon's fight-or-flight response mechanism was part of a general adaptation syndrome (GAS) used to handle all stresses a person encountered, from head colds to unexpected violence and anger. General adaptation syndrome was proposed to be nonspecific in humans, so the same basic reactions were deemed to occur due to good or bad news and regardless of the emotion currently being felt, whether fear, excitement, pleasure, or anger. The difference in the result, according to Selye, was not in the biology of the emotion but in the mind-set that accompanied it.

From the late twentieth century on, uncontrollable physical anger against one's spouse, acquaintances, and others has been treated by combinations of tranquilizers, hormones, antidepressants, psychotherapy, and hospitalization, when needed. Much milder anger is treated by psychotherapeutic methods conceptualized and used by psychiatrists and psychologists who often term themselves "angerologists."

BIBLIOGRAPHY

"Anger Management." *Mayo Clinic.* Mayo Foundation for Medical Education and Research, 23 June 2011. Web. 24 Feb. 2014.

Cannon, Walter B. "The Stresses and Strains of Homeostasis." *American Journal of the Medical Sciences* 189 (1935): 1–14. Print.

Cavell, Timothy A., and Kenya T. Malcolm, eds. *Anger, Aggression, and Interventions for Interpersonal Violence.* Mahwah: Erlbaum, 2007. Print.

"Controlling Anger before It Controls You." *American Psychological Association.* Amer. Psychological Assn., 2014. Web. 24 Feb. 2014.

DiGiuseppe, Raymond, and Raymond Chip Tafrate. *Understanding Anger Disorders.* New York: Oxford UP, 2010. Print.

Ellis, Albert. *How to Control Your Anger before It Controls You.* New York: Kensington, 1998. Print.

Gentry, W. Doyle. *Anger-Free: Ten Basic Steps to Managing Your Anger.* New York: Morrow, 1999. Print.

Kassinove, Howard, ed. *Anger Disorders: Definition, Diagnosis, and Treatment.* Washington, DC: Taylor, 1995. Print.

Potter-Efron, Ron. *Handbook of Anger Management: Individual, Couple, Family, and Group Approaches.* New York: Routledge, 2011. Digital file.

Robbins, Paul R. *Anger, Aggression, and Violence: An Interdisciplinary Approach.* Jefferson: McFarland, 2000. Print.

Weisinger, Hendrie. *Anger at Work.* New York: Morrow, 1995. Print.

Worth, Joseph. "Effect of Anger on Families." AAMFT. *American Association for Marriage and Family Therapy,* 2013. Web. 24 Feb. 2014.

Derived from: "Anger." *Psychology and Mental Health.* Salem Press. 2009.

Sanford S. Singer

SEE ALSO: Aggression; Aggression: Reduction and control; Air rage; Bipolar disorder; Conduct disorder; Domestic violence; Elder abuse; Ellis, Albert; Emotions; Impulse control disorders; Inhibitory and excitatory imulses; Hormones and behavior; Jealousy; Mood disorders; Road rage; Stress: Behavioral and psychological responses; Stress-related diseases; Violence and sexuality in the media; Violence by children and teenagers.

Anger management

Type of psychology: Clinical, Social

Social science and criminal justice researchers report that more than 80% of all non-war related violence stems from learned behavior. Because we learn aggressive behavior by observation, imitation, and reinforcement, it is theoretically possible to unlearn aggressive behaviors, and, thus, reduce or prevent them. Anger often follows a cascade of events, beginning with a perception that one has been unjustly wronged. Insolent language, offensive gestures, and posturing can lead to threats. Maltreatment then escalates and eventually individual or collective homicides are possible. Though a critically important emotion to experience, uncontrolled anger perpetuates a reciprocal cycle wherein violence is responded to with more violence. Uncontrolled anger is socially contagious and a contaminant of public welfare. Unmanaged anger respects no boundaries, borders, occupations, ages, cultures, religious beliefs, or socioeconomic levels.Controlled violence and managed anger can be marshaled for both individual and societal good.

Key Concepts

- Violence
- Aggressive behavior
- Observation and imitation
- Behavioral and cognitive treatment
- Collective efficacy

INTRODUCTION

Anger is a strong, negative psychobiological state that may result in aggression. Aggressive behavior is the application of anger for the purpose of harming others. When unchecked, it may result in failed relationships at home and at work, the creation of identifiable enemies, the possible instigation of psychological, physical, and sexual abuse, child and elder maltreatment or homicide or suicide. The experience of uncontrolled anger promotes one's perception that his or her use of violence is legitimate and justified. It also promotes victimization and gives the individual a false sense of control when he or she is actually out of control.

Aggressive behaviors can be learned from a variety of sources: direct reinforcement, imitation of social or cultural models (anti-heroes and antagonists as portrayed in movies and video games), and any variety of psychosocial factors such as low self-esteem, poor parental acceptance, inefficient and inadequate parental discipline, unmediated physical punishment, or academic failure.

SEQUENCES OF ANGER

Researchers have identified three anger sequences which have a taxonomy of triggers: 1) anger itself, experienced as an emotional state like annoyance, 2) hostility which can be expressed by attitudes and arguments, and 3) aggression which can be experienced as rage and behaviorally involve motoric behavior. Anger appears to arise from nowhere, though actually it is rarely random. Typically, anger requires one or more triggers. Examples include 1) frustration or disappointment stemming from unfulfilled expectations, 2) perceived injustice, and 3) experiences of verbal or physical harm. Even daily issues which commonly arise at home, school, or work can give rise to an unmanaged anger sequence. Furthermore, any of these triggers can be exacerbated by the presence of a wide range of situational factors like fatigue, the influence of substances, gang membership, or possession of or access to firearms and other weapons.

ASSESSMENT AND DIAGNOSIS

The diagnosis of anger is unlike that of diagnosing any other related mood or anxiety disorder. Certain personality disorders (e.g., antisocial personality disorder) are prone to include episodes of uncontrolled anger and aggression. More than verbal reporting or psychometric tests, the occurrence of unchecked aggressive behaviors like pinching, shouting, verbal and physical threats, intimidation, repeated sarcasm, hostile humor, hitting, throwing objects, and overt physical assault provide the necessary evidence to diagnose and identify anger in need of management. Often, in addition to the history of observed hostility, psychologists and allied behavioral health specialists will use one of a range of available questionnaires to more specifically assess the risk of repeated future violence. The Novaco Anger Scale, for example, contains 60 items to complete within a 15-minute timeframe. Yet, it still yields scores on five measures: cognitive, arousal, behavioral, anger, and regulation. The Provocation Inventory contains 25 items to complete within a 10-minute timeframe and also yields information on five domains: disrespectful treatment, unfairness, frustration, annoying traits of others, and irritations. Samples of other tests used in evaluating anger control are the Rathus Assertive Scale, a 30-item schedule that assesses assertive behavior and the widely used

State-Train Anger Expression Inventory. Now in its second edition, the inventory contains 57 items, takes about 15 minutes to complete, and measures state anger, trait anger, anger expression-out, anger expression-in, anger control-out, and anger control-in.

DEALING WITH ANGER

Programs such as the American Psychological Association's ACT Against Violence provide the general public with guides for self-management of anger like "What to do When You Are Angry," "Think before Acting," "Calm Down," and perhaps the most helpful of all, "RETHINK," which instructs the reader to Recognize what makes him or her angry, Empathize with others' feelings, Think positive things about the situation, Hear what the other person has to say, Notice what happens to his or her body, and Keep attention on the present situation.

EMOTIONAL ANGER CONTROL

The physiology of anger manifests itself in muscle tension, excessive breathing, and cognitive distortions. Inhibiting these unpleasant manifestations can be facilitated by diaphragmatic breathing rather than thoracic breathing, progressively relaxing muscles, praying, attaining a state of mindfulness, and listening to music.

COGNITIVE ANGER CONTROL

It is typical for anger to affect thinking, judgment, and rationality. Common cognitive distortions are overestimation, underestimation, misattributions, polarized thinking, overgeneralizations, inflammatory thinking, catastrophizing, and expressions of demanding and commanding.

Anger researcher Raymond Novaco developed a method for maintaining intellectual control over emotional anger. He suggested 1) preparing for the provocation with self-talk like "I can deal with this; I will not take it personally; 2) managing the impact during confrontation with phrasing like "I will not let this aggravate me; I don't have to prove anything to anyone, and I have total control of myself;" 3) monitoring feelings and thoughts throughout the confrontation, thinking ideas like "I feel tension in my muscles. Breathe deeply," and "I am right to be upset, but I am going to control myself." He additionally offers advice for both when the outcome of the confrontation is resolution ("Forget it. You tried your best so don't take it personally" and "Laugh, if possible.") and when the confrontation is not resolved ("I managed myself well during this provocation, and I achieved my goal without getting annoyed.)

Role playing is also a useful treatment to teach anger control. Research has shown that adolescents who learned to self-assess and role play accurately have improved their ability to negotiate conflict constructively and apply it to other real life, non-school setting situations.

Behavioral analysis is another mechanism for tracking the ebbs and flows of an individual's anger episodes. The patient notes the immediate source of his or her disturbance, what might have preceded it, the day of the week, time of day, and location. In this way, clinicians hope to spot patterns that will contribute to better understanding of what causes the anger and methods of mitigation and eventual prevention.

PREVENTING UNCONTROLLED ANGER

The two leading professional organizations of psychologists and pediatricians, the American Psychological Association and the American Academy of Pediatrics, published a series of commonsense but evidence-based recommendations to help parents manage their own uncontrolled anger in reaction to disciplining their children. These recommendations are summarized as follows:

- Avoid hitting your child. Model appropriate, safe, problem-solving responses that do not include hurting others. Hittingchildren communicates the idea that it is acceptable to hit others to solve disagreements or relieve one's anger.
- Non-physical methods (e.g., time outs, depriving privileges) are more effective long term in promoting positive behavioral changes.
- Verbally instruct children that violence is not a solution to problems and unchecked demonstration of anger produces worsening effects.
- Be consistent, fair, and reasonable about establishing rules and consequences for not observing them.

FORGIVENESS INTERVENTIONS

Forgiveness interventions replace blame, bitterness, and harbored resentment by consciously attempting to forgive the offense, assuming that the others' intentions were good though the outcome may have been otherwise. When people genuinely forgive rather than simply say the words "I forgive you," high emotional arousal states evolve into calmer, more serene states, and the individuals experience an integrated sense of wellness.

From a sense of calmness , attitudes reorient toward solving conflicts and disputes in a fair manner. To forgive does not mean to accept or forget an unjust situation; it does mean that one adopts a focus that ultimately reduces the frequency, duration, and intensity of resentment and need for vengeance.

CONCLUSION

Every day, we encounter bizarre and extreme acts of serial killings, assassinations, and genocidal wars in what we read and watch. Excluding wars and natural disasters, more people are likely to be the targets of unmanaged anger than perpetrators of violence are. But, for the perpetrators, research shows that violence is not fortuitous, uncontrollable, or foreordained. In the same way that we as a people face challenges like illness, addiction, and injustice, violence as the end product of unmanaged anger can be thwarted, mitigated, and, if not eliminated, better controlled. Most violence is a learned response and it can be unlearned in most cases.

BIBLIOGRAPHY

www.apa.org/helpcenter/warning-signs.aspx

Warning signs of youth violence including reasons, prevention, coping strategies,, risks, and violence against oneself.

www.apa.org/topics/anger/control.aspx

Control anger before it controls you: what it is and how to take command.

American Psychological and American Academy of Pediatrics. (1995). *Raising Children to Resist Violence.*

Description on how to use empathy and tenderness with young children.

Bandura, A. (1997). *Self-efficacy: The Exercise of Control.* New York, NY: Freeman. An extensive book about self-efficacy in health, athletic, organizational, and collective functioning.

Feindler, E. (1995). *An Ideal Treatment Package for Children and Adolescents With Anger Disorders.* In Kassinove, H. (Eds.) Anger disorders: Definition, diagnosis and treatment (173-194).

New York, NY: Taylor and Francis. Intended for parents and caregivers raising children with significant anger issues.

Jacobson, E. (1938). *Progressive Relaxation.* Chicago, IL: University of Chicago Press.

Describes the process of progressive muscle relaxation reducing more than 100 exercises to five major areas: face, shoulders, thorax, back, and legs.

Kort, F. (2007). *Manual de Emociones.* Caracas, Venezuela: Alfa. Only available in Spanish, this book provides user-friendly information on assertiveness training and collective efficacy, depression and passive behaviors, violence and anger behaviors, positive psychology, and creativity.

Novaco, R. (1979). *The Cognitive Regulation of Anger and Stress.* In P. Kendall & C. Hollon (Eds), Cognitive-behavioral interventions: Theory, research and procedures (241-285). New York, NY: Academic Press. Pioneer behaviorist Raymond Novaco discusses his theories, presents supporting research, and shows how cognition can regulate intense anger and the harmful effects of stress.

Novaco, R. (1994). *Novaco Anger Scale and Provocation Inventory (NASPI).* Chicago, IL: MacArthur Foundation in Mental Health and Law. Here Novaco focuses on the most useful internal phrases to prevent anger reactions.

Tomes, H. (2005). *The ACT Program: Giving Psychology Away.* APA Public Interest ,36(4).

A worldwide program for raising safe kids helps parents, caregivers, and professionals. It discusses angry children, discipline, parenting, and positive behaviors. Useful for the prevention of violence in the home and community. See also www.actagainstviolence.org.

Zimbardo, P. (2007). *The Lucifer Effect: Understanding How Good People Turn Evil.* New York, NY: Random House. It is easy for nice people to turn evil; on the other hand it is not difficult to become a hero in social challenges. Philip Zimbardo, pioneer social psychologist, discusses conversions in what he terms "the inhumanities and heroism."

Felicitas Kort

See Also: Emotional regulation; Control; Psychotherapy; Aggressive behavior.

Animal experimentation

Type of psychology: Psychological methodologies

Psychologists study animals and their behavior, sometimes with the goal of understanding the animal itself and sometimes with the goal of learning more about humans. Because there are many biological and psychological similarities between humans and other animals, the use of animal models can be extremely valuable, although it is sometimes controversial.

Key Concepts

- Analogy
- Applied research
- Basic research
- Biopsychology
- Ethology
- Homology
- Institutional Animal Care and Use Committees
- Invasive procedures
- Learning theory
- Situational similarity

INTRODUCTION

Before the general acceptance of Charles Darwin's theory of evolution in the late nineteenth century, in much of the Western world, animals were considered to be soulless machines with no thoughts or emotions. Humans, on the other hand, were assumed to be qualitatively different from other animals because of their abilities to speak, reason, and exercise free will. Therefore, it was thought that nothing could be learned about the mind by studying animals.

After Darwin, however, people began to recognize that although each species is unique, the chain of life is continuous, and species have similarities as well as differences. Because animal brains and human brains are made of the same kinds of cells and have similar structures and connections, it was reasoned, the mental processes of animals must be similar to the mental processes of humans. This new insight led to the introduction of animals as psychological research subjects around 1900. Since then, animal experimentation has yielded much new knowledge about the brain and the mind, especially in the fields of learning, memory, motivation, and sensation.

Psychologists who study animals can be roughly categorized into three groups: biopsychologists (psychobiologists), learning theorists, and ethologists and sociobiologists. Biopsychologists, or physiological psychologists, study the genetic, neural, and hormonal controls of behavior, for example, eating behavior, sleep, sexual behavior, perception, emotion, memory, and the effects of drugs. Learning theorists study the learned and environmental controls of behavior, for example, stress, stimulus-response patterns, motivation, and the effects of reward and punishment. Ethologists and sociobiologists concentrate on animal behavior in nature, for example, predator-prey interactions, mating and parenting, migration, communication, aggression, and territoriality.

REASONS FOR USING ANIMAL SUBJECTS

Psychologists study animals for a variety of reasons. Sometimes they study the behavior of a particular animal to solve a specific problem. They may study dogs, for example, to learn how best to train them as police dogs; chickens to learn how to prevent them from fighting one another in coops; and wildlife to learn how to regulate populations in parks, refuges, or urban areas. These are all examples of what is called applied research.

Most psychologists, though, are more interested in human behavior but study animals for practical reasons. A developmental psychologist, for example, may study an animal that has a much shorter life span than humans do so that each study takes a much shorter time and more studies can be done. Animals may also be studied when an experiment requires strict controls; researchers can control the food, housing, and even social environment of laboratory animals but cannot control such variables in the lives of human subjects. Experimenters can even control the genetics of animals by breeding them in the laboratory; rats and mice have been bred for so many generations that researchers can special order from hundreds of strains and breeds and can even obtain animals that are basically genetically identical to one another.

Another reason psychologists sometimes study animals is that there are fewer ethical considerations than in research with human subjects. Physiological psychologists and neuropsychologists, in particular, may use invasive procedures (such as brain surgery, hormone manipulation, or drug administration) that would be unethical to perform on humans. Without animal experimentation, much of this research simply could not be conducted. Comparable research on human victims of accident or disease would have less scientific validity and would raise additional ethical concerns.

A number of factors make animal research applicable for the study of human psychology. The first factor is homology. Animals that are closely related to humans are likely to have similar physiology and behavior, because they share the same genetic blueprint. Monkeys and chimpanzees are the animals most closely related to humans and thus are homologically most similar. Monkeys and chimpanzees make the best subjects for psychological studies of complex behaviors and emotions. However, they are expensive and difficult to keep, and there are serious ethical considerations when using them, so they are not used when another animal would be equally suitable.

The second factor is analogy. Animals that have a lifestyle similar to that of humans are likely to have some of the same behaviors. Rats, for example, are social animals, as are humans; cats are not. Rats also show similarity to humans in their eating behavior (which is one reason rats commonly live around human habitation and garbage dumps); thus, they can be a good model for studies of hunger, food preference, and obesity. Rats, however, do not have a similar stress response to that of humans; for studies of exercise and stress, the pig is a better animal to study.

The third factor is situational similarity. Some animals, particularly dogs, cats, domesticated rabbits, and some domesticated birds, adapt easily to experimental situations such as living in a cage and being handled by humans. Wild animals, even if reared by humans from infancy, may not behave normally in experimental situations. The behavior of a chimpanzee that has been kept alone in a cage, for example, may tell something about the behavior of a human kept in solitary confinement, but it will not necessarily be relevant to understanding the behavior of most people in typical situations.

By far the most common laboratory animal used in psychology is *Rattus norvegicus*, the Norway rat. Originally, the choice of the rat was something of a historical accident. Because the rat has been studied so thoroughly, it is often the animal of choice so that comparisons can be made from study to study. Fortunately, the rat shares many features analogous with humans. Other animals frequently used in psychological research include pigeons, mice, hamsters, gerbils, cats, monkeys, and chimpanzees.

SCIENTIFIC VALUE

One of the most important topics for which psychologists use animal experimentation is the study of interactive effects of genes and the environment on the development of the brain and subsequent behavior. These studies can be done only if animals are used as subjects, because they require subjects with a relatively short lifespan that develop quickly, they may involve invasive procedures to measure cell and brain activity, or they may require the manipulation of major social and environmental variables in the life of the subject.

In the 1920s, Edward C. Tolman and Robert Tryon began a study of the inheritance of intelligence using rats. They trained rats to run a complex maze and then, over many generations, bred the fastest learners with one another and the slowest learners with one another. From the beginning, offspring of the bright rats were substantially faster than offspring of the dull rats. After only seven generations, there was no overlap between the two sets, showing that intelligence is at least partly genetic and can be bred into or out of animals just as size, coat color, or milk yield can be.

Subsequent work with selectively bred rats, however, found that high-performing rats would outperform the slower rats only when tested on the original maze used with their parents and grandparents; if given a different task to measure their intelligence, the bright rats were in some cases no brighter than the dull rats. These studies were the first to suggest that intelligence may not be a single attribute that one either has much or little of; there may instead be many kinds of intelligence.

Over the years researchers have developed selectively bred rats as models of a variety of interesting human characteristics. Of particular value are animal models of human psychopathology. For example, genetic lines of rats have been developed that serve as models for susceptibility to depression, anxiety, alcoholism, and attention-deficit hyperactivity disorder (ADHD). These models are important not only in understanding genetic, environmental, and physiological factors associated with these disorders, but also in serving as early tests for possible drug treatments for them. Indeed, the area of behavioral pharmacology, where drug effects on behavior are studied in animal models, is an important and growing area of research.

BRAIN STUDIES

Another series of experiments that illustrate the role of animal models in the study of brain and behavior is that developed by David Hubel and Torsten Wiesel, who studied visual perception (mostly using cats). Hubel and Wiesel were able to study the activity of individual cells in the living brain. By inserting a microelectrode into a brain cell of an immobilized animal and flashing visual stimuli in the animal's visual field, they could record when the cell responded to a stimulus and when it did not.

Over the years, scientists have used this method to map the activities of cells in several layers of the visual cortex, the part of the brain that processes visual information. They have also studied the development of cells and the cell connections, showing how early experience can have a permanent effect on the development of the visual cortex. Subsequent research has demonstrated that the environment has major effects on the development of other areas of the brain as well. The phrase "use it or lose it" has some accuracy when it comes to development and maintenance of brain connections and mental abilities.

HARLOW'S EXPERIMENTS

Perhaps the most famous psychological experiments on animals were those done by Harry Harlow in the 1950s. Harlow was studying rhesus monkeys and breeding them in his own laboratory. Initially, he would separate infant monkeys from their mothers. Later, he discovered that, in spite of receiving adequate medical care and nutrition, these infants exhibited severe behavioral symptoms: They would sit in a corner and rock, mutilate themselves, and scream in fright at the approach of an experimenter, a mechanical toy, or another monkey. As adolescents, they were antisocial. As adults, they were psychologically ill-equipped to deal with social interactions: Male monkeys were sexually aggressive, and female monkeys appeared to have no emotional attachment to their own babies. Harlow decided to study this phenomenon (labeled "maternal deprivation syndrome") because he thought it might help to explain the stunted growth, low life expectancy, and behavioral symptoms of institutionalized infants which had been documented earlier by René Spitz.

Results of the Harlow experiments profoundly changed the way psychologists think about love, parenting, and mental health. Harlow and his colleagues found that the so-called mothering instinct is not very instinctive at all but rather is learned through social interactions during infancy and adolescence. They also found that an infant's attachment to its mother is based not on its dependency on food but rather on its need for "contact comfort." Babies raised with both a mechanical "mother" that provided milk and a soft, cloth "mother" that gave no milk preferred the cloth mother for clinging and comfort in times of stress.

Through these experiments, psychologists came to learn how important social stimulation is, even for infants, and how profoundly the lack of such stimulation can affect mental health development. These findings played an important role in the development of staffing and activity requirements for foundling homes, foster care, day care, and institutions for the aged, physically and mentally disabled, and mentally ill. They have also influenced social policies that promote parent education and early intervention for children at risk.

LIMITATIONS AND ETHICAL CONCERNS

However, there are drawbacks to using animals as experimental subjects. Most important are the clear biological and psychological differences between humans and nonhuman animals; results from a study using nonhuman animals simply may not apply to humans. In addition, animal subjects cannot communicate directly with researchers; they are unable to express their feelings, motivations, thoughts, and reasons for their behavior. If a psychologist must use an animal instead of a human subject for ethical or practical reasons, the scientist will want to choose an animal that is similar to humans in the particular behavior being studied.

For the same reasons that animals are useful in studying psychological processes, however, people have questioned the moral justification for such use. Because it is now realized that vertebrate animals can feel physical pain and that many of them have thoughts and emotions as well, animal experimentation has become politically controversial.

Psychologists generally support the use of animals in research. The American Psychological Association (APA) identifies animal research as an important contributor to psychological knowledge. The majority of individual psychologists would tend to agree. In 1996, S. Plous surveyed nearly four thousand psychologists and found that fully 80 percent either approved of or strongly approved of the use of animals in psychological research. Nearly 70 percent believed that animal research was necessary for progress in the field of psychology. However, support dropped dramatically for invasive procedures involving pain or death. Undergraduate students majoring in psychology produced largely similar findings. Support was less strong among newer rather than more established psychologists and was also less strong in women than in men.

Some psychologists would like to see animal experimentation in psychology discontinued altogether. In 1981, psychologists formed an animal rights organization called Psychologists for the Ethical Treatment of Animals (PsyETA), which was later renamed the Society and Animals Forum. It is highly critical of the use of animals as subjects in psychological research and has strongly advocated improving the well-being of those animals that are used through publication (with the American Society for the Prevention of Cruelty to Animals) of the *Journal of*

Applied Animal Welfare Science. The organization is also a strong advocate for the developing field of human-animal studies, in which the relationship between humans and animals is explored. Companion animals (pets) can have a significant impact on psychological and physical health, and they can be used as a therapeutic tool with, for example, elderly people in nursing homes and emotionally disturbed youth. In this field of study, animals themselves are not the subjects of the experiment; rather, it is the relationship between humans and animals that is the topic of interest.

REGULATIONS

In response to such concerns regarding the use of animals in experiments, the US Congress amended the Animal Welfare Act in 1985 so that it would cover laboratory animals as well as pets. (Rats, mice, birds, and farm animals are specifically excluded.) Although these regulations do not state specifically what experimental procedures may or may not be performed on laboratory animals, they do set standards for humane housing, feeding, and transportation. Later amendments were added in 1991 in an effort to protect the psychological well-being of nonhuman primates.

In addition, the Animal Welfare Act requires that all research on warm-blooded animals (except those specifically excluded) be approved by a committee before it can be carried out. Each committee (known as Institutional Animal Care and Use Committees, or IACUCs) is composed of at least five members and must include an animal researcher; a veterinarian; someone with an area of expertise in a nonresearch area, such as a teacher, lawyer, or member of the clergy; and someone who is unaffiliated with the institution where the experimentation is being done and who can speak for the local community. In this way, those scientists who do animal experiments must justify the appropriateness of their use of animals as research subjects.

The APA has its own set of ethical guidelines for psychologists conducting experiments with animals. The APA guidelines are intended for use in addition to all pertinent local, state, and federal laws, including the Animal Welfare Act. In addition to being a bit more explicit in describing experimental procedures that require special justification, the APA guidelines require psychologists to have their experiments reviewed by local IACUCs and do not explicitly exclude any animals. About 95 percent of the animals used in psychology are rodents and birds (typically rats, mice, and pigeons), which are not governed by the Animal Welfare Act. It seems likely that federal regulations will change to include these animals at some point, and according to surveys, the majority of psychologists believe that they should be. Finally, psychologists are encouraged to improve the living environments of their animals and consider nonanimal alternatives for their experiments whenever possible.

Alternatives to animal experimentation are becoming more widespread as technology progresses. Computer modeling and bioassays (tests using biological materials such as cell cultures) cannot replace animal experimentation in the field of psychology, however, because computers and cell cultures will never exhibit all the properties of mind that psychologists want to study. At the same time, the use of animals as psychological research subjects will never end the need for study of human subjects. Although other animals may age, mate, fight, and learn much as humans do, they will never speak, compose symphonies, or run for office. Animal experimentation will thus always have an important, though limited, role in psychological research.

BIBLIOGRAPHY

American Psychological Association. *Committee on Animal Research and Ethics*. http://www.apa.org/science/animal2.html.

Cuthill, I. C. "Ethical Regulation and Animal Science: Why Animal Behavior Is Not So Special." *Animal Behaviour* 72 (2007): 15–22. Print.

Fox, Michael Allen. *The Case for Animal Experimentation*. Berkeley: U of California P, 1986. Print.

Gross, Charles G., and H. Philip Zeigler, eds. *Readings in Physiological Psychology: Motivation*. New York: Harper, 1969. Print.

Miller, Neal E. "The Value of Behavioral Research on Animals." *American Psychologist* 40 (April, 1985): 423–40. Print.

National Academy of Sciences and the Institute of Medicine. Committee on the Use of Animals in Research. *Science, Medicine, and Animals*. Washington, DC: National Academy, 1991. Print.

National Research Council. *Guide for the Care and Use of Laboratory Animals*. Washington, DC: National Academy, 1996. Print.

Rose, Anne C. "Animal Tales: Observations of the Emotions in American Experimental Psychology, 1890–1940." *Journal of the History of the Behavioral Sciences* 48.4 (2012): 301–17. Print.

Saucier, D. A., and M. E. Cain. "The Foundations of Attitudes about Animal Research." *Ethics & Behavior* 16 (2006): 117–33. Print.

Society and Animals Forum (formerly PsyETA). http://www.psyeta.org.

Vicedo, Marga. "The Evolution of Harry Harlow: From the Nature to the Nurture of Love." *History of Psychiatry* 21.2 (2010): 190–205. Print.

Linda Mealey; updated by Linda R. Tennison

See Also: Behaviorism; Conditioning; Emotions; Ethology; Experimental psychology; Hunder; Imprinting; Instinct theory; Memory: Animal research; Pavlovian conditioning; Reinforcement; Sexual behavior patterns; Skinner, B. F.; Visual system.

Anorexia nervosa and bulimia nervosa

Type of psychology: Psychopathology

Anorexia and bulimia nervosa are disorders characterized by a distorted body image, an intense fear of becoming obese, and a desperate attempt to lose weight. These disorders most frequently occur in female adolescents, and they present serious health risks.

Key Concepts

- Behavioral therapy
- Binge eating
- Binge eating disorder (BED)
- Cognitive behavior therapy
- Distorted body image
- Neurotransmitters
- Psychoanalytic therapy
- Purging
- Weight phobia

INTRODUCTION

Anorexia nervosa and bulimia nervosa are two types of eating disorders. They are illnesses with a biological basis modified by emotional and cultural factors. Anorexia literally means a severe loss of appetite, while nervosa means nervousness. Actually, the word anorexia is somewhat of a misnomer, given that most people with anorexia nervosa have not lost their appetites.

HISTORY OF THE DISORDERS

Anorexia is a disorder that can be traced as far back as the twelfth century, when it was associated with religion—saints refused food to get closer to God. The disorder was specifically named as a diagnosis in 1874, when Sir William Gull published an article giving the disorder its present name.

The binge/purge behavior of bulimia has been around for centuries, and bulimia nervosa was identified as a disorder in the 1930s but was thought to be a form of anorexia. Bulimia nervosa was not named as a disorder separate from anorexia until the late 1970s, when both disorders began receiving media attention with stories of girls and women refusing to eat and dying from the behavior. Probably the most famous case at that time was that of Karen Carpenter, a singer who died at age thirty-two of heart failure caused by anorexia. There is evidence to suggest that the incidence of both disorders in the United States has increased since the 1970s. The increased emphasis on thinness within American society is a likely explanation for the increase in eating disorders.

SYMPTOMS

The disorder of anorexia nervosa consists of three prominent symptoms, according to the fifth edition of the American Psychiatric Association's *Diagnostic and Statistical Manual of Mental Disorders* (DSM-5). The first symptom is an abnormally low weight for one's age, height, and physical condition due to significant restriction of energy intake. Because many people with anorexia nervosa (known as anorectics or anorexics) are secretive about their eating behaviors and cover their weight loss with clothing, they are not diagnosed until they have already lost significant amounts of weight. The second symptom of anorexia nervosa can take the form either of an intense fear of gaining weight or being fat or of behavior that prevents weight gain. This second symptom has been labeled weight phobia by some researchers because of the anorectic's anxiety toward food and the desperate attempts the person makes to avoid food. The third major symptom of the syndrome is distorted body image. Distorted body image, which sometimes takes the form of body dysmorphic disorder, involves the anorectic seeing herself or himself as obese when in reality she or he is extremely underweight. Because of this, during treatment, anorectics are not allowed to know their weight. Premenopausal women with anorexia nervosa also often experience the absence of at least three menstrual cycles in a condition known as amenorrhea, which is caused by being severely undernourished. The lack of nutrients affects the hypothalamic, pituitary, gonadal axis, causing the lack of hormones that result in amenorrhea.

Bulimia nervosa refers to the recurring cycle of binge eating, a short period of excessive overeating, followed by purging or other compensatory behaviors as drastic efforts to lose the weight gained by binge eating. For the bulimic, binging has two components: eating large amounts in a limited amount of time and feeling a lack of control while eating. Purging may be accomplished through several means, including vomiting (done either by gagging oneself or through the consumption of certain drugs) and the use of laxatives, diuretics, or enemas; other inappropriate compensatory behaviors include fasting or strict dieting and excessive exercising.

To be diagnosed with bulimia, according to the DSM-5, a person must engage in the cycle of binge eating and compensatory behaviors at least once per week, on average, for three months. It is likely that the number of bulimics reported would be higher without this strict criterion. However, bulimia should not be confused with binge eating disorder, which, according to the DSM-5, is characterized by binge eating that is not followed by inappropriate compensatory behaviors such as purging.

HEALTH PROBLEMS

Numerous health problems may occur as a result of anorexia or bulimia. The health problems of anorectics include an abnormally low heart rate and low blood pressure as well as irregular heart functioning, often resulting in heart failure. Fatigue is common, and bone thinning (osteopenia) may lead to osteoporotic fractures if left untreated. Dehydration can lead to kidney failure, and lack of body fat combined with the change in hormones makes it difficult to regulate body temperature. Anorectics may develop lanugo hair over their bodies, including the face, to help with temperature regulation. The death rate for anorexia nervosa is one of the highest for any mental health condition, and generally, the longer the condition lasts, the higher the death rate.

Most of the health complications of bulimia are related to the purging behaviors. Electrolyte imbalances, particularly potassium reduction, can occur from all purging behaviors and can lead to irregular heartbeats and possibly heart failure and death. Vomiting leads to the erosion of tooth enamel and a variety of disorders affecting digestive organs. A significantly lower number of people are thought to die from bulimia as compared with anorexia. Those with binge eating disorder exhibit the same health consequences as anyone with obesity, so heart disease and type 2 diabetes are common.

When compared with obesity, which in some cases can be the result of an eating disorder, anorexia and bulimia are rare. According to a 2012 report by the Centers for Disease Control and Prevention, approximately 35.7 percent of American adults and 16.9 percent of American children are obese. In contrast, an estimated 0.6 percent of American adults will have anorexia during their life, according to 2007 statistics compiled by the National Institute of Mental Health. The incidence of anorexia among adolescents, especially female adolescents, however, is significantly higher than in the general population. Bulimia is likewise estimated to occur in 0.6 percent of American adults, and again, the incidence of bulimia among adolescents is estimated to be significantly higher. A subpopulation in which the incidence of eating disorders is higher is athletes. The type of eating disorder seems to correlate with the sport. In individual sports, in which lower weight is an advantage or looks are a factor, anorexia is more common, and in team sports, bulimia is more common. Male and female athletes show similar rates of eating disorders because the disorders are related to the sport and athletic performance.

CAUSES AND EXPLANATIONS

The proposed causes of anorexia and bulimia can be grouped into four categories: biological, sociocultural, familial, and psychological. The notion of biological causes of anorexia and bulimia involves the idea that anorectics and bulimics have specific brain or biochemical disturbances that lead to their inability to maintain a normal weight or eating pattern. One biological explanation researched for the occurrence of anorexia and bulimia is the existence of an abnormal amount of certain brain neurotransmitters, especially norepinephrine and serotonin. Neurotransmitters are chemical messengers within the brain that transmit nerve impulses between nerve cells.

In contrast to biological explanations, sociocultural causes are factors that are thought to exist within a society that lead certain individuals to develop anorexia or bulimia. Joan Brumberg, a historian of anorexia, has outlined the sociocultural forces of the late nineteenth and twentieth centuries that many believe promoted the increased incidence of eating disorders among women. These societal forces included an emphasis on weight reduction and aesthetic self-control and the treatment of women as sexual objects. The most prominent of these

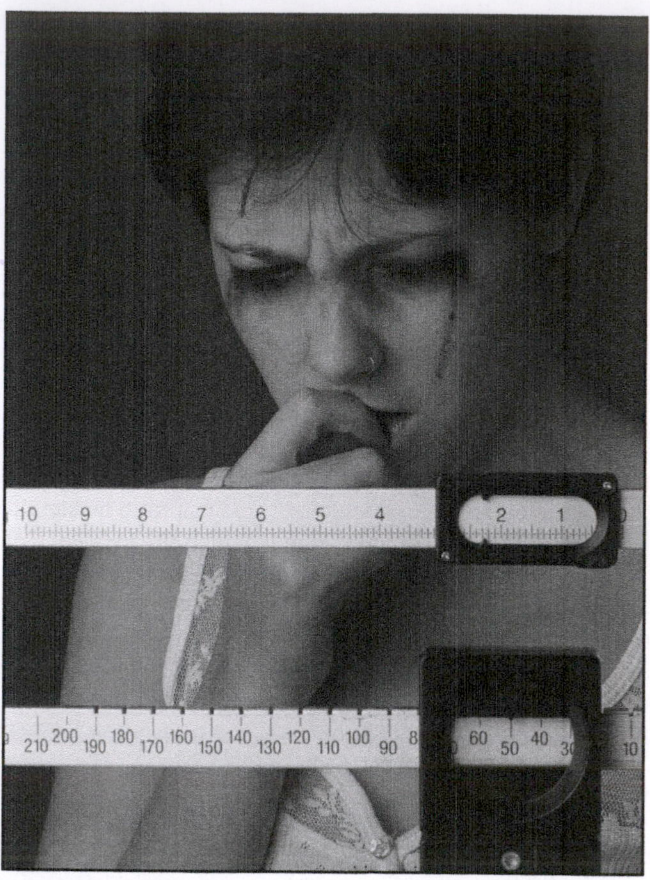

Photo: iStock

suggested cultural factors is the heightened importance placed on being thin.

Some researchers believe that particular family types cause certain of their members to develop anorexia and bulimia. For example, family investigators believe that a family whose members are emotionally too close to one another may lead one or more family members to strive for independence by refusing to eat, according to Salvador Minuchin, Bernice Rosman, and Lester Baker. Other researchers believe that families whose members are controlling and express an excessive amount of hostility toward one another promote the occurrence of bulimia. Some research also shows genetic tendencies; that is, if a parent had an eating disorder, it is more likely that one or more of his or her children will also be diagnosed with one, even if the parent is no longer exhibiting symptoms.

The most prominent of the suggested psychological causes for anorexia and bulimia are those expressed by researchers who take psychoanalytic or cognitive behavioral perspectives. For example, cognitive behavioral theorists emphasize the role of distorted beliefs in the development and continuation of anorexia and bulimia. These distorted beliefs include that the person is attractive only if she or he weighs a certain number of pounds, usually a number well below normal weight, or that consuming certain types of foods (such as carbohydrate-rich foods) will automatically make a person fat.

TREATMENTS

Numerous treatments have been used for individuals who have anorexia or bulimia, but they can be broadly grouped into the categories of medical and psychological therapies. If symptoms are life threatening, these disorders are treated in a hospital, and if they are more manageable, these disorders can be treated on an outpatient basis.

Before the 1960s, medical therapies for anorexia included such radical approaches as lobotomies and electroconvulsive therapy (ECT). The first goal for the treatment of anorexia is to ensure the person's physical health, which involves restoring the person to a healthy weight. Reaching this goal may require hospitalization. Although a controversial treatment, various types of tube feeding continue to be used when a patient's malnutrition from anorexia poses an imminent risk of death. Tube feeding can be accomplished either intravenously or by inserting a tube via a patient's nasal cavity into the patient's stomach.

Once a person's physical condition is stable, treatment usually involves individual psychotherapy and family therapy, during which parents help their children learn to eat again and maintain healthful eating habits on their own. Behavioral therapy also has been effective for helping anorectics return to healthful eating habits. Supportive group therapy may follow, and self-help groups within communities may provide ongoing support. There are a number of in-patient treatment facilities that specialize in anorexia throughout the United States. The most effective treatment no matter the location is team treatment addressing all three areas of concern. A physician treats the medical conditions and potentially the mental aspects if drugs are required, a counselor manages the behavioral aspect, and a dietician manages the dietary component.

When treating bulimia, unless malnutrition is severe, any substance abuse problems that may be present at the time the eating disorder is diagnosed are usually treated first. The next goal of treatment is to reduce or eliminate the person's binge eating and purging behavior. Behavioral therapy has proven effective in achieving this goal. Psychotherapy has proven effective in helping prevent the eating disorder from recurring and in addressing issues that led to the disorder. Studies have also found that fluoxetine (Prozac), an antidepressant, may help people who do not respond to psychotherapy. Some bulimics also exhibit obsessive-compulsive disorder (OCD), and drugs appropriate for OCD also help reduce the bulimic behaviors. As with anorexia, family therapy is also recommended.

The family treatment of anorectics involves the therapist seeking to change the interactions among family members that serve to maintain the self-starvation of the patient. In attempting to change family interactions, the family therapist might address the parents' overprotectiveness or the way family members manipulate one another's behavior. For bulimics, the family therapist would seek to lower the amount of family conflict or to redirect conflict between the parents away from the bulimic.

Another frequently employed method of treatment for bulimia is group therapy. Group treatment initially involves educating bulimics about their disorder, including its negative health consequences. The group experience provides members with the opportunity to share with fellow bulimics regarding their eating problems and to find support from one another in overcoming bulimia. In addition, the therapist or therapists initiate discussions regarding healthful eating and exercise habits as well as specific ways to end the cycle.

A final issue involved in surveying the different interventions for anorexia and bulimia is the effectiveness of these treatments. A meta-analysis of one hundred studies of anorectics in 1988 found only small differences between the various types of treatment in the amount of weight gained during therapy, although behavioral treatments appeared to work faster. A negative impact of changes in health insurance coverage for anorectics has been shorter treatment times and poorer outcomes. Definitive research shows that the closer anorectics are to their ideal weight on discharge, the less likely they are to be readmitted, even if that requires a longer treatment initially. Managed care generally allows a certain amount of time or certain number of treatment sessions rather than basing coverage on return to normal weight.

Less research has been conducted investigating the effectiveness of different therapies for bulimia. No single therapy for bulimia, however, whether medical or psychological, has shown clear superiority in its effectiveness as compared with other interventions. More important was when treatment began. Patients with bulimia nervosa demonstrated a better recovery rate if they received treatment early in their illness.

PREVENTION AND REMAINING QUESTIONS

Research has begun to focus on the prevention of eating disorders. Catherine Shisslak and colleagues have suggested that preventive efforts should be targeted at female adolescents, given that they are at increased risk for developing an eating disorder. One of the most important ideas that has come out of research on eating disorders is that outcomes are much better when treatment begins early. Research also suggests that if the disordered eating behaviors are caught when they begin and before they have reached diagnostic criteria, development of the eating disorder may be prevented. These preventive efforts should focus on issues such as the physical, emotional, and social changes that occur in maturation. Also, information regarding diet and exercise should be provided, and the connection between emotions and eating should be discussed, as should ways to resist the pressure to conform to peers' and societal expectations regarding appearance.

With evidence of the increasing prevalence of anorexia and bulimia and binge eating disorder, it is important to learn more regarding the causes and effective treatment methods of these disorders. Some of the questions that remain to be definitively answered are why certain groups have a greater likelihood of developing anorexia and bulimia (notably, white female adolescents), whether the underlying causes of anorexia are different from those of bulimia, and whether a more effective treatment can be developed for those with anorexia or bulimia.

BIBLIOGRAPHY

American College of Sports Medicine. "The Female Athlete Triad." *Medicine &; Science in Sports &; Exercise* 39.10 (2007): 1867–82. Print.

Arnold, Carrie. *Decoding Anorexia: How Breakthroughs in Science Offer Hope for Eating Disorders.* New York: Routledge, 2013. Print.

Bruch, Hilde. *The Golden Cage: The Enigma of Anorexia Nervosa.* Cambridge: Harvard UP, 2001. Print.

Brumberg, Joan J. *Fasting Girls: The History of Anorexia Nervosa.* Rev. ed. New York: Vintage, 2000. Print.

Centers for Disease Control and Prevention. "Overweight and Obesity." *Centers for Disease Control and Prevention.* CDC, 16 Aug. 2013. Web. 17 Feb. 2014.

Chambers, Natalie, ed. *Binge Eating: Psychological Factors, Symptoms, and Treatment.* New York: Nova Science, 2009. Print.

Dawson, Dee. *Anorexia and Bulimia: A Parent's Guide to Recognising Eating Disorders and Taking Control.* New York: Random, 2012. Print.

Fairburn, Christoper G., and Kelly D. Brownell. *Eating Disorders and Obesity: A Comprehensive Handbook.* New York: Guilford, 2005. Print.

Gordon, Richard. *Eating Disorders: Anatomy of a Social Epidemic.* 2nd ed. New York: Blackwell, 2000. Print.

Minuchin, Salvador, Bernice L. Rosman, and Lester Baker. *Psychosomatic Families: Anorexia Nervosa in Context.* Cambridge: Harvard UP, 1978. Print.

National Eating Disorders Association. http://www.nationaleatingdisorders.org/.

Natl. Inst. of Mental Health. "Statistics: Eating Disorders." Natl. Inst. of Mental Health. *US Dept. of Health and Human Services*, 2007. Web. 17 Feb. 2014.

Ogden, Jane. *The Psychology of Eating: From Healthy to Disordered Behavior.* Malden: Wiley, 2010. Print.

Sacker, Ira M., and Marc A. Zimmerman. *Dying to Be Thin: Understanding and Defeating Anorexia Nervosa and Bulimia.* New York: Warner, 2001. Print.

Walsh, Timothy B. "Fluoxetine for Bulimia Nervosa Following Poor Response to Psychotherapy." *American Journal of Psychiatry* 157 (2000): 1332–34. Print.

R. Christopher Qualls; updated by Wendy E. S. Repovich

SEE ALSO: Abnormality: Psychological models; Body dysmorphic disorder; Cognitive behavior therapy; Depression; Eating disorders; Feminist psychotherapy; Hunger; Impulse control disorders; Obesity.

Antianxiety medications

TYPE OF PSYCHOLOGY: Biological bases of behavior; Psychopathology; Stress

A wide variety of medications are used to treat anxiety disorders. The medications most commonly used are either antidepressants or anxiolytics.

KEY CONCEPTS

- Amydala
- Antidepressants
- Anxiolytics
- Azapirones
- Benzodiazepines
- Generalized anxiety disorder (GAD)
- Post-traumatic stress disorder (PTSD)

INTRODUCTION

More people develop anxiety disorders than any other mental health problem. In part, this is because there are many types of anxiety disorders, including generalized anxiety disorder (GAD), panic disorders, social anxiety, and post-traumatic stress disorder (PTSD). Individuals with anxiety disorders can be treated with psychotherapy, medication, or a combination of the two. When medications are used, they tend to be either antidepressants or anxiolytics. Antidepressants are used to treat anxiety disorders as well as depression, because both of these disorders often exhibit a lack of neurotransmitters in the cells within the brain. It has been shown that when people exhibit anxiety, there is increased activity within the amygdala (part of the limbic system). Increased presence of neurotransmitters has been correlated with decreased activity in the amygdala and decreased anxiety. Both selective serotonin reuptake inhibitors (SSRIs) and serotonin-norepinephrine reuptake inhibitors (SNRIs) have been used to treat depression and certain anxiety disorders. SSRIs, such as paroxetine (Paxil), fluoxetine (Prozac), and escitalopram (Lexapro), increase the amount of serotonin in the cells of the brain by inhibiting (preventing) their reuptake. SNRIs, including venlafaxine (Effexor) and duloxetine (Cymbalta), inhibit the reuptake of both norepinephrine (noradrenaline) and serotonin. Increasing the amounts of both of these neurotransmitters improves transmission of impulses along the neuron, thereby improving affect and decreasing anxiety.

ANXIOLYTICS

Antianxiety medications is the term for a category of medications that are commonly used to treat generalized anxiety disorders and panic disorders. These drugs are sometimes referred to as minor tranquilizers, but this is somewhat of a misnomer as the mechanism of action for these medications is not really understood. However, it is felt that the effect of most anxiolytics is tied into the functioning of gamma-aminobutyric acid (GABA). GABA is an inhibitory neurotransmitter that renders brain cells in the area of the amygdala less likely to respond to excitatory neurotransmitters, making individuals less likely to suffer from anxiety reactions.

Benzodiazepines are the most common type of anxiolytics. Diazepam (Valium), alprazolam (Xanax), and lorazepam (Ativan) are the most commonly used benzodiazepines in the United States. Benzodiazepines are typically used to treat anxiety for only short periods of time. They are often used as the first means of treatment for severe anxiety reactions. Individuals are not likely to remain on these medications for a long period of time because of severe side effects (including oversedation), dependence, and problems with withdrawal.

Other anxiolytics include azapirones and barbiturates. Azapirones, such as buspirone (BuSpar), appear to work by increasing the activity of serotonin in the brain. They work relatively slowly, taking two to four weeks to have an effect. Their chemical composition is dramatically different from that of most of the other drugs used to treat anxiety. They act more slowly, have fewer side effects, and are better tolerated. There are almost no reported cases of dependence or oversedation from azapirones. Barbiturates, including secobarbital (Seconal) and pentobarbital (Nembutal), were commonly used to treat anxiety in the past. Although their mechanism of action in treating anxiety is still unknown, it is believed that they also work on GABA reactors in the brain. They are generally considered to be sedative-hypnotics and as such have many adverse effects and great risk of dependence and withdrawal reactions. Therefore, with the advent of the newer anxiolytics, barbiturates have become much less commonly used in the treatment of anxiety disorders.

As with most categories of medication, there are some over-the-counter and natural remedies that have been used to treat anxiety. The nutritional supplement most commonly used to treat anxiety is GABA. Although this amino acid is produced naturally in the brain, if people have poor nutritional habits, they may not be ingesting adequate precursors for this inhibitory neurotransmitter. In such individuals, this nutritional supplement has been found to lessen symptoms of depression and decrease anxiety.

If a person has developed an anxiety disorder, many different types of treatment are available. Which treatment is chosen should always depend on characteristics of the individual as well as the type and severity of the anxiety disorder.

BIBLIOGRAPHY

Bongiorno, Peter. *Holistic Solutions for Anxiety & Depression: Combining Natural Remedies with Conventional Care*. New York: Norton, 2014. Print.

Charney, D. S., S. B. Nemeroff, and S. Braun. *The Peace of Mind Prescription: An Authoritative Guide to Finding the Most Effective Treatment for Anxiety and Depression*. Boston: Houghton Mifflin, 2004. Print.

Colman, I., et al. "Psychiatric Outcomes Ten Years After Treatment with Antidepressants or Anxiolytics." *British Journal of Psychiatry* 193 (2008): 327–31. Print.

National Institute of Mental Health. "Medications." Bethesda: Author, 2002. Print.

Newman, M. G., and W. B. Stiles. "Therapeutic Factors in Treating Anxiety Disorders." *Journal of Clinical Psychology* 62 (2006): 649–59. Print.

Pillay, N. S., and D. J. Stein. "Emerging Anxiolytics." *Expert Opinion on Emerging Drugs* 12 (2007): 541–54. Print.

Swartz, Karen L. *Depression and Anxiety: Your Annual Guide to Prevention, Diagnosis, and Treatment*. Baltimore: Johns Hopkins Medicine, 2013. Print. Tone, Andrea. The Age of Anxiety: A History of America's Turbulent Affair with Tranquilizers. New York: Basic Books, 2011. Print.

Robin Kamienny Montvilo

See Also: Agoraphobia and panic disorders; Antidepressant medications; Anxiety disorders; Depression; Drug therapies; Fear; Generalized anxiety disorder; Panic attacks; Phobias; Post-traumatic stress disorder; Psychopharmacology.

Antidepressant medications

Type of psychology: Biological bases of behavior; Psychopathology; Stress

Patients with depression were routinely treated with psychotherapy until the 1950s, when the first antidepressants were developed. Many medications have been developed to treat depression, with varying degrees of effectiveness and various side effects.

Key Concepts

- Atypical antidepressants
- Fluoxetine (Prozac)
- Imipramine
- Iproniazid
- Monoamine oxidase inhibitors (MAOIs)
- Selective seretonin reuptake inhibitors (SSRIs)
- St. John's Wort
- Tricyclics

INTRODUCTION

In the early 1950s, psychotherapy was being used to treat people with major depression, but researchers were looking for more effective means of treatment, including pharmaceuticals. The first antidepressant, iproniazid, was discovered accidentally while it was being used to treat tuberculosis. This monoamine oxidase inhibitor (MAOI) was found to improve the mood of the patients it was used to treat, and this suggested that depression could be treated through pharmacological means. When this first antidepressant was found to cause damage to the liver, it was replaced by imipramine, the first tricyclic antidepressant. Although imipramine was effective in treating nearly two-thirds of the cases of major depression, it was accompanied by a number of side effects, including sleepiness, palpitations, dry mouth, and constipation.

SECOND-GENERATION ANTIDEPRESSANTS

Over the next quarter century, there were many attempts to synthesize antidepressants that were not fraught prowith side effects. It became apparent that both MAOIs and tricyclics affected multiple neurotransmitters and thus had numerous side effects. Therefore, researchers directed their attention to the development of a medication that would affect a single neurotransmitter only. In 1971, the first antidepressant medication to block the uptake of only one neurotransmitter was released in the form of fluoxetine (Prozac). This medication, still widely used, was the first selective serotonin reuptake inhibitor (SSRI). Since the 1970s, the second-generation antidepressants Prozac, paroxetine (Paxil), and sertraline (Zoloft) have been the most commonly used antidepressants.

ADDITIONAL ANTIDEPRESSANTS

The pharmaceutical industry has improved technology to the point where drug makers are capable of producing antidepressant medications that act on more than one neurotransmitter without causing large numbers of side effects. This category of drugs is commonly referred to as the dual reuptake inhibitors. The most common of these dual reuptake inhibitors are the serotonin-norepinephrine reuptake inhibitors (SNRIs). SNRIs include venlafaxine (Effexor) and duloxetine (Cymbalta). These SNRIs increase the levels of both serotonin and norepinephrine (noradrenaline) in the brain by inhibiting the reabsorption of these neurotransmitters by brain cells. Although the mode of action by which these dual reuptake inhibitors function is uncertain, it is believed that the increased levels of serotonin and norepinephrine in the brain enhance the transmission of nerve impulses, thereby improving and elevating affect. These and other modern antidepressants fall into the category of atypical antidepressants. Medications that are considered atypical antidepressants do not easily fit in any other category of drugs while inhibiting the uptake of several neurotransmitters within the brain. Another commonly used drug in this category is buproprion (Wellbutrin). These medications are typically taken orally and in pill form.

NATURAL ANTIDEPRESSANTS

There are dozens of over-the-counter remedies and supplements that are marketed as antidepressants. For many of these substances, there is little, if any evidence of their safeness or effectiveness. One herbal supplement, St. John's wort, is quite commonly used to counter depression and has been shown to be highly effective in some studies. This herbal remedy comes from a plant with yellow flowers. Derivatives of this plant were first used medicinally in ancient Greece. Although St. John's wort was initially used to treat pain or for sedation, it has come to be used mainly as an over-the-counter antidepressant. Studies are ongoing to determine if St. John's wort really has antidepressant effects or if people are merely responding to their own expectations (creating a placebo effect).

BIBLIOGRAPHY

Baumel, S. *Natural Antidepressants: Tried and True Remedies from Nature's Pharmacy*. New York: McGraw-Hill, 1998. Print.

Breggin, Peter R. *The Anti-Depressant Fact Book: What Your Doctor Won't Tell You About Prozac, Zoloft, Paxil, Celexa, and Luvox*. Cambridge: Perseus, 2001. Print.

Glenmullen, J. *The Antidepressant Solution: A Step-by-Step Guide to Safely Overcoming Antidepressant Withdrawal, Dependence, and "Addiction."* New York: Simon & Schuster, 2006. Print.

Hansen, R. A., et al. "Efficacy and Safety of Second-Generation Antidepressants in the Treatment of Major Depressive Disorder." *Annals of Internal Medicine* 143 (2005): 415–26. Print.

Kee, Joyce LeFever, Evelyn R. Hayes, and Linda E, McCuistion. *Pharmacology: A Patient-Centered Nursing Process Approach*. 8th ed. St. Louis: Elsevier, 2014. Print.

Kirsch, Irving. *The Emperor's New Drugs: Exploding the Antidepressant Myth.* New York: Basic, 2011. Print.

Hart, Carl L., and Charles Ksir. *Drugs, Society, and Human Behavior.* New York: McGraw-Hill, 2011. Print.

Muir, Alice Jane. *Overcoming Depression*. New York: McGraw-Hill, 2013. Print.

Sharp, Katherine. *Coming of Age on Zoloft: How Antidepressants Cheered Us Up, Let Us Down, and Changed Who We Are.* New York: Harper Perennial, 2012. Print.

Robin Kamienny Montvilo

See Also: Antianxiety medications; Anxiety disorders; Bipolar disorder; Depression; Drug therapies; Psychotherapy: Effectiveness; Psychopharmacology.

Antipsychotic medications

Type of psychology: Biological bases of behavior; Psychopathology; Stress

Antipsychotics are medications used to treat people who are out of touch with reality. The first antipsychotics were developed in the 1950s, and numerous, more effective types followed.

Key Concepts

- Atypical antipsychotics
- Benzisoxidilgroup
- Chlorpromazine
- Clozapine
- Debenzapine derivatives
- Neuroleptics
- Phenothiazines
- Phenylbutylpiperadines
- Psychosis
- Typical antipsychotics

INTRODUCTION

Antipsychotic medications were first used to treat people who were out of touch with reality (psychotic) in the 1950s with the development of chlorpromazine (Thorazine). Originally developed for surgical patients, chlorpromazine was used on patients with psychiatric problems because of its calming effects. Its antipsychotic effect went well beyond calming, as it affected the nervous system, especially the anticholinergic, antidopaminergic, and antihistamine receptors. Chlorpromazine became the model for the class of drugs known as phenothiazines, the early antipsychotics. These and the other early antipsychotics (first-generation antipsychotic agents) are known as typical antipsychotics, or major tranquilizers. At the time that these drugs were developed, people who were deemed psychotic had traditionally been treated with brain surgery (lobotomies), so medications provided a great advance in treatment modalities.

A second class of typical antipsychotics is the phenylbutylpiperadines. This category of drugs includes haloperidol (Haldol), which was first developed in the late 1950s but not approved for use in the United States until 1988. Haloperidol is routinely used to treat delirium and acute psychotic states. It is also used to treat Tourette syndrome. Because of the effect of these drugs on the central nervous system, antipsychotic agents are also referred to as neuroleptics. These drugs can cause a decrease in delusions, hallucinations, confusion, and agitation in psychiatric patients and may normalize their motor activity. Such medications have been widely used to treat disorders such as schizophrenia and bipolar disorder.

In many patients, however, treatment with first-generation antipsychotics has been stopped because of adverse side effects. One set of common side effects is extrapyramidal reactions, including low blood pressure, impotence, lethargy, and tardive dyskinesia (movement disorders involving involuntary, purposeless movements, typically of the face, legs, or torso).

SECOND-GENERATION ANTIPSYCHOTICS

To avoid the adverse side effects of the typical antipsychotic agents, medications known as second-generation, or atypical, antipsychotics were developed. The first of these atypical antipsychotics, clozapine (Clozaril), was developed in 1970 (although not approved for use until 1989) and was used for treatment of schizophrenia. This medication, a debenzapine derivative, was found to have a potentially deadly side effect, agranulocytosis (a decrease in the white blood cells circulating in the bloodstream), and was voluntarily withdrawn from the market. In 1989, after further testing, it was approved for use by the Food and Drug Administration for individuals with treatment-resistant schizophrenia.

Another category of second-generation antipsychotics includes the benzisoxidil group, typified by resperidone (Risperdal). This drug is often used to treat bipolar disorder. Each of the atypical antipsychotics also causes side effects, but in general, these drugs are better tolerated than the first-generation antipsychotics.

USE OF THESE DRUGS

Typically, when deciding which medication to prescribe, a physician will take into account an individual's symptoms, age, weight, and personal, family, and medication history. Research has shown that most antipsychotic drugs actually alter the brain's structure. In some cases, these structural changes are a direct result of the treatment, while in other cases, they are side effects of the medication. Researchers hope that some of these structural changes in the brain may lead to a better understanding of how these antipsychotic drugs work.

BIBLIOGRAPHY

Burns, M. J. "The Pharmacology and Toxicology of Atypical Antipsychotic Agents." *Clinical Toxicology* 39 (2001): 1–14. Print.

Diamond, R. J., P. L. Scheifler, R. Ross, and P. J. Weiden. *Breakthroughs in Antipsychotic Medications: A Guide for Consumers, Families, and Clinicians.* New York: Norton, 1999. Print.

Essock, S. M., et al. "Effectiveness of Switching Antipsychotic Medications." *American Journal of Psychiatry* 163 (2006): 2090–95. Print.

MedlinePlus. "Psychotic Disorders." *MedlinePlus.* US Natl. Lib. of Medicine, 20 Jan. 2014. Web. 17 Feb. 2014.

Natl. Inst. of Mental Health. "Mental Health Medicines." *Natl. Inst. of Mental Health.* US Dept. of Health and Human Services, 2012. Web. 17 Feb. 2014.

Rothschild, Anthony J., ed. *The Evidence-Based Guide to Antipsychotic Medications.* Arlington: American Psychiatric, 2010. Print.

Schmetzer, A. "Primer for Prescription Medications: The Antipsychotic Medicines—Atypical." *Annals of the American Psychotherapy Association* 5.5 (2002): 26–27. Print.

Stahl, S. M., M. M. Grady, and N. Munter. *Antipsychotics and Mood Stabilizers: Stahl's Essential Psychopharmacology.* New York: Cambridge UP, 2008. Print.

Robin Kamienny Montvilo

See Also: Abnormality: Biomedical models; Borderline personality disorder; Drug therapies; Lobotomy; Psychopharmacology; Psychotic disorders; Schizophrenia: Background, types, and symptoms; Schizophrena:Theoretical explanations.

Antisocial personality disorder

Type of psychology: Psychopathology

Antisocial personality disorder is characterized by a pattern of behaviors and thinking that demonstrates callous disregard for the welfare of others, conventional systems of rules, and authority figures. Although extensively researched, it is a controversial diagnostic category because it takes into account criminal behavior. Crime is socially defined, not always prosecuted in a culture-fair manner, and not always a component of antisocial personality disorder.

Key Concepts

- Arousal modification
- Conduct disorder
- Dyssocial psychopathy
- Neurotic psychopathy
- Oppositional defiant disorder
- Personality disorder
- Psychopathic personality
- Somatization disorder
- Successful psychopathy

INTRODUCTION

By personality disorder, psychologists mean a disorder in which an individual's style of dealing with the world, relationship with self, problem solving, and management of emotions are inflexible to situations. As a result, the individual creates a maladaptive pattern of behavior and thinking that produces considerable impairment and distress. In the case of antisocial personality, these traits are thought to be manifested in criminal and otherwise irresponsible behaviors, which create problems for the individual and, more important, for society—hence the term "antisocial."

Individuals of all ages with an antisocial personality often have a childhood history of conduct disorder or oppositional defiant disorder. Conduct disorder is a pattern of behavior in which both the rights of others and age-appropriate social norms or rules are repeatedly violated. Oppositional defiant disorder is characterized by a pattern of hostile behavior toward authority figures in which the child is deliberately defiant, negative, hostile, annoying, and possibly vindictive, beyond what might be expected in children. Noteworthy antisocial behaviors include theft, school truancy, fire setting, vandalism, physical cruelty toward animals and people, financial irresponsibility, repeated lying, reckless driving, sexual promiscuity, and poor parenting. Not surprising, a large percentage of incarcerated criminals fulfill the criteria for antisocial personality disorder.

SYMPTOMS AND PREVALENCE

Many of the symptoms of antisocial personality were identified by the sociologist Lee Robins in her influential work *Deviant Children Grown Up* (1966). Robins found that between 20 and 30 percent of children with conduct disorder develop antisocial personality in adulthood. There is also evidence that a subset of children with hyperactivity (attention-deficit hyperactivity disorder) develop antisocial personality in adulthood. Nevertheless, because many of these same children have conduct disorder, it may be conduct disorder, rather than hyperactivity, that is the major determinant of antisocial personality.

In addition to the behaviors mentioned above, persons with antisocial personality disorder have a number of other psychological and interpersonal difficulties. For example, they have high rates of alcohol and drug abuse, divorce, sexually transmitted diseases, out-of-wedlock pregnancies, and depression. In addition, individuals with this disorder are more likely than those in the general population to die prematurely from violent crimes and accidents. Antisocial personality is also associated with criminal recidivism: Individuals with this disorder who are released from prison are at high risk for subsequent incarceration.

In the United States, about 3 percent of men and 1 percent of women have antisocial personalities. The reason for this sex difference is unknown. Some researchers have speculated that men and women may express antisocial tendencies in different ways. For instance, men may commit crimes more likely to be visible and prosecuted than women. Others have speculated that women who are predisposed to antisocial personality may be likely to develop somatization disorder, a condition characterized by multiple physical complaints lacking any demonstrated medical basis. Indeed, somatization disorder is found among many of the female relatives of antisocial personalities. Thus, somatization disorder may be an alternative manifestation of antisocial personality that is found primarily among women, although considerably more research will be needed to corroborate this hypothesis. Finally, antisocial personality is also associated with low social class, although the causes of this relationship are unknown and controversial. For instance, it may be that individuals in lower social classes are more likely to be prosecuted for criminal behavior than those in upper classes and therefore more likely to get labeled as antisocial.

THE ANTISOCIAL LIFE

What happens to antisocial personalities over time? There is evidence that many such individuals "burn out" in middle age: Their antisocial behaviors decrease in frequency and severity in later adulthood. The reasons for this burnout phenomenon are unclear, but it may be a consequence of the decline in activity level and energy seen in most individuals with age. It is also important to consider that participation in dangerous activities such as crime and risk taking may cause many individuals with antisocial personality disorder to die at young ages.

Little is known about the treatment of antisocial personality except that no clearly effective treatment has been found. A number of therapies have been attempted, including psychoanalysis, behavior therapy, group therapy, and medication, but there is little evidence that any of them have been especially successful. As the symptoms of antisocial personality begin early in life and are easily identifiable, it may be prevention, rather than treatment, that holds the greatest promise for reducing the prevalence of this disorder.

Many individuals with antisocial personality disorder possess a constellation of personality traits known as the psychopathic personality. In his classic book *The Mask of Sanity* (1941), psychiatrist Hervey Cleckley provided a detailed description of this syndrome. According to Cleckley, psychopathic personalities (or, as they are sometimes called, psychopaths) tend to be superficially charming individuals who are relatively free of anxiety and seem possessed of excellent reason. Nevertheless, they also tend to be guiltless, callous, dishonest, and self-centered persons who rarely learn from their mistakes or take responsibility for their behavior.

Some psychologists believe that psychopathic personality is a more valid category than antisocial personality. According to these researchers, many antisocial personalities lack the traits characteristic of psychopathic personality and instead exhibit antisocial behavior for a variety of other reasons. For example, some antisocial personalities may fall into a category known as dyssocial psychopathy, a syndrome in which antisocial behavior results from allegiance to a culturally deviant subgroup. Many gang delinquents or members of organized crime could probably be classified in this group. The behavior of still other antisocial personalities may result from neurotic psychopathy, a syndrome in which antisocial behavior is a consequence of internal psychological conflict and turmoil. Many neurotic psychopaths are probably socially anxious individuals who inhibit their anger for long periods of time and then erupt intermittently but violently.

Conversely, some critics of the antisocial personality diagnosis have argued that many psychopaths do not fulfill the criteria for antisocial personality. Indeed, some psychopaths may function highly in society and would thus not be detected by the antisocial personality criteria in many cases. Cathy Spatz Widom has found that many persons who possess the traits described by Cleckley can be found outside prisons and, in some cases, have socially valued occupations (for example, corporate executive). Further study of these "successful" psychopaths may shed light on factors that allow individuals at risk for antisocial personality to avoid legal and interpersonal problems. As a result, the diagnostic system used to identify this personality disorder has changed in recent years to bring in more of what Cleckley identified as problematic.

RESEARCH INTO CAUSES

One of the most active areas of research on antisocial personality concerns possible causes of the disorder. Psychologist David Lykken, for example, has theorized that the behavior of many antisocial personalities, particularly those who are psychopaths, can be traced to fearlessness.

Lykken has found that, compared with other individuals with antisocial behavior and with "normals," psychopaths tend to exhibit less sweating of the palms prior to hearing a buzzer that has been repeatedly paired with a painful electric shock. Robert Hare has similarly shown that psychopaths tend to show relatively little palmar sweating during the countdown period prior to a painful electric shock or jarring blast of white noise. Because palmar sweating is often indicative of fear or arousal, the findings of Lykken and Hare can be interpreted to mean that psychopaths are not frightened or aroused by signals of impending punishment. This, in turn, might explain why many psychopaths engage in repeated antisocial behavior: The warning signs that would deter most people from performing such acts have little impact on the psychopath.

The average child or adult is prevented from committing antisocial acts largely by signals that punishment or danger is imminent: a parent or teacher saying "No" as a child reaches for a forbidden piece of candy, the watchful eye of a museum guard as one passes by a valuable painting, or a light turning yellow as one approaches a busy intersection. If such signals arouse little or no fear in a person, however, his or her threshold for committing antisocial acts will be lowered.

Lykken also constructed a "mental maze" task, in which subjects were required to learn a complex series of lever presses. On each trial, some errors were punished with painful shock, whereas others were not. Lykken found that, compared with other subjects, psychopaths did not make more errors overall, indicating that they can learn certain tasks as well as other individuals. Nevertheless, Lykken found that psychopaths made more punished errors than other individuals, suggesting that they have difficulty learning from punishment. Again, this finding is consistent with the fearlessness hypothesis, because the capacity to benefit from punishment largely depends on the capacity to become frightened of this punishment. Moreover, this finding has important implications; the psychopath's failure to learn from punishment in the laboratory may be a useful model for the antisocial personality's recidivism in the real world.

AROUSAL LEVELS

An alternative hypothesis for the behavior of antisocial personalities is that these individuals have unusually low levels of arousal. According to the Yerkes-Dodson law, moderate levels of arousal are optimal for performance and psychological functioning. Thus, as Herbert Quay and other psychologists have argued, many of the thrill-seeking and dangerous behaviors of antisocial personalities may represent attempts to bring their arousal to higher and thus more optimal levels. George Skrzypek has found that psychopathic delinquents, compared with other delinquents, have a greater preference for complex and novel stimuli. This is consistent with Quay's hypothesis, because such stimuli would be expected to increase arousal. Skrzypek also found that after both groups were placed in sensory isolation, psychopaths' preference for complex and novel stimuli increased more compared with nonpsychopaths.

One implication of these findings is that at least some antisocial personalities might benefit from treatments that boost their arousal levels. For example, antisocial personalities could be encouraged to find occupations (for example, combat soldier) or avocations (for example, skydiving) that might provide outlets for their risk-taking tendencies. Similarly, some researchers have explored the possibility that some antisocial personalities might be helped by stimulant medication. Stanley Schachter and Bibb Latané found that when psychopaths were asked to perform Lykken's mental-maze task while taking adrenaline, a stimulant drug, they were as successful as were nonpsychopaths at learning to avoid punishment. Nevertheless, as these "arousal modification" approaches have not been adequately researched, their potential as treatments for antisocial personality remains speculative.

There is considerable evidence that antisocial personality is influenced by genetic factors. Identical twins (who share all their genes) with antisocial personality are much more likely than are fraternal twins(who share only half their genes on average) to have co-twins with the disorder. Nevertheless, many of the co-twins of identical twins with antisocial personality do not have the disorder, which indicates that environmental

Environment factors play an important role in the development of antisocial personality. In addition, adopted children whose natural parents had antisocial personality are more likely to develop the disorder than are adopted children whose natural parents did not. Again, this is consistent with a genetic influence on antisocial personality.

Nevertheless, several important questions concerning the genetics of antisocial personality remain. First, it is not known what factors are being genetically transmitted. Second, it is not known whether this genetic influence applies to all, or only some, individuals with antisocial personality. For example, this genetic influence might only play a role in individuals with psychopathic personality. Third, it is not known how environmental factors combine or interact with genetic factors to produce antisocial personality. These three questions are likely to occupy researchers for a number of years to come.

CHANGING LABELS

Although the term "antisocial personality" did not enjoy widespread currency until the latter half of the twentieth century, individuals with chronic antisocial symptoms have been described by a variety of labels over the years. In 1809, Philippe Pinel discussed a syndrome called *manie sans délire*, or mania without delusion. Individuals with this syndrome, according to Pinel, are driven by strong instinctual forces but maintain good contact with reality. In 1835, James Pritchard coined the term "moral insanity" to refer to a condition characterized by severe deficits in ethical behavior.

In 1891, German psychiatrist August Koch referred to a group of conditions called "psychopathic inferiorities." In doing so, Koch broadened the concept of the disorder to include a diverse spectrum of abnormalities, not all of which were characterized by moral depravity. Koch's tradition was followed by the great German classifier Kurt Schneider, who in 1923 described a wide variety of psychopathic personalities, each of which was considered to be an exaggeration of a normal personality style. Thus, the German conceptualization was generally more inclusive than that of Morel and Pritchard, and it viewed psychopathic personality as a set of conditions that created problems for the individual, society, or both.

It was authors such as Cleckley and Benjamin Karpman who were largely responsible for shaping contemporary notions of psychopathic personality. These authors emphasized personality traits as the key features of the disorder, and they deemphasized antisocial and criminal behaviors. This view was reflected in the second edition of the American Psychiatric Association's *Diagnostic and Statistical Manual of Mental Disorders* (DSM-II) in 1968, which focused on personality traits such as guiltlessness and selfishness as the primary criteria for the disorder.

This personality-based approach, however, came under attack in the 1970s and 1980s for its subjectivity. After all, what one diagnostician might view as a pathological absence of guilt might be viewed by another as a healthy absence of self-criticism. Thus, in 1980, the third edition of the *Diagnostic and Statistical Manual of Mental Disorders* (DSM-III) introduced "antisocial personality disorder," a new diagnosis in which explicit references to personality traits were all but expunged. Instead, the emphasis in DSM-III (as well as in its 1987 revision, DSM-III-R) was on easily agreed-on transgressions against society. The advantage of this new approach was its objectivity: Clinicians could easily agree on whether an individual had committed a robbery or driven while intoxicated. However, the fourth edition, DSM-IV (1994), and its text revision, DSM-IV-TR (2000), brought psychopathic personality traits back into the list of diagnostic considerations to allow for the diagnosis of individuals without extensive criminal behavior, but who were, nonetheless, threats to the well-being of others and likely to be causing themselves unnecessary impairment or distress.

The newest edition of the DSM, the DSM-5 (2013) lists antisocial personality disorder in two separate chapters: First, because of the disorder's close association with Conduct Disorder, it's diagnosis and treatment are discussed in two fifth edition chapters: "Disruptive, Impulse-Control, and Conduct Disorders" and "Personality Disorders."

BIBLIOGRAPHY

Black, Donald W., and C. Lindon Larson. *Bad Boys, Bad Men: Confronting Antisocial Personality Disorder.* New York: Oxford University Press, 2000. Print.

Clarke, Rebecca M. *Antisocial Behavior: Causes, Correlations, and Treatments.* New York: Nova Science, 2011. Print.

Cleckley, Hervey. *The Mask of Sanity*. 5th ed. Augusta, Ga.: Emily S. Cleckley, 1988. Print.

Fisher, Gary L. "Antisocial Personality Disorder (ASPD)." *Understanding Why Addicts Are Not All Alike: Recognizing the Types and How Their Differences Affect Intervention and Treatment.* Santa Barbara: Praeger, 2011. 51–78. Print.

Hare, Robert D. *Psychopathy: Theory and Research.* New York: John Wiley & Sons, 1970. Print.

Hare, Robert D. *Without Conscience: The Disturbing World of the Psychopaths Among Us.* New York: Guilford Press, 1999. Print.

Hare, Robert D., and Daisy Schalling, eds. *Psychopathic Behaviour: Approaches to Research*. New York: John Wiley & Sons, 1978. Print.

Hervé, Hugues, and John C. Yuille, eds. *The Psychopath: Theory, Research, and Practice.* Mahwah, N.J.: Lawrence Erlbaum, 2007. Print.

Kantor, Martin. *The Psychopathy of Everyday Life: How Antisocial Personality Disorder Affects All of Us.* Westport, Conn.: Praeger, 2006. Print.

Lykken, David T. *The Antisocial Personalities.* Hillsdale, N.J.: Lawrence Erlbaum, 1995. Print.

Reid, William H., John Ingram Walker, and Darwin Dorr, eds. *Unmasking the Psychopath: Antisocial Personality and Related Syndromes.* New York: W. W. Norton, 1986. Print.

Robins, Lee. *Deviant Children Grown Up.* Baltimore: Williams & Wilkins, 1966. Print.

Rubitel, Alla, and David Reiss. *Containment in the Community: Supportive Frameworks for Thinking About Antisocial Behavior and Mental Health.* London: Karnac, 2011. Print.

Scott O. Lilienfield; updated by Nancy A. Piotrowski

See Also: Addictive personality and behaviors; Alcohol dependence and abuse; Attention-deficit hyperactivity disorder; Borderline personality disorder; Conduct disorder; Histronic personality disorder; Impulse control disorders; Juvenile delinquency; Narcissistic personality disorder; Psychopathology; Sociopaths; Substance use disorders.

Anxiety disorders

Type of psychology: Psychopathology

Anxiety is a central concept in many different schools of psychology, and there are many widely varying theories concerning it; theories of anxiety often have spawned approaches to treating anxiety disorders.

Key Concepts

- Ego
- Libido
- Operant conditioning
- Pavlovian conditioning
- Phobia
- Prepardness
- Repression
- Three-systems approach
- Two-factor theory
- Vicarious transmission

INTRODUCTION

The concept of anxiety is one of the most often used and loosely defined concepts in psychology. It can be used to describe a temporary state ("You seem anxious today") or an enduring personality trait ("He is an anxious person"). It is used to assign cause ("He stumbled over the words in his speech because he was anxious") and to describe an effect ("Having to give a speech sure makes me anxious"). It is seen as the result of discrete objects or situations such as snakes or heights or as evolving from basic existential problems such as the trauma of birth or the fear of death. All major theories in psychology in some way confront anxiety.

Because of the preeminence of anxiety in the field of psychology, there are many different theories about the nature and origin of anxiety disorders. Anxiety disorders include generalized anxiety disorder, social anxiety disorder, panic disorder, obsessive-compulsive disorder, post-traumatic stress disorder, and specific phobias. The two most important and influential viewpoints on anxiety are the Freudian and the behavioral viewpoints.

Although these theories attempt to explain many anxiety disorders, an examination of how they apply to phobias presents a good indication of how they work. A specific phobia can be defined as an anxiety disorder involving an intense fear of a particular thing (such as horses) or situation (such as heights).

FREUDIAN APPROACH

Sigmund Freud, who said that understanding anxiety "would be bound to throw a flood of light on our whole mental existence," had two theories of anxiety, an early one in 1917 and a later one in 1926. In the early theory, libido (mental energy, often equated with sexual drive) builds up until it is discharged by some pleasurable activity. Sometimes the energy cannot be discharged, for example, when the sexual object is not attainable or is morally unacceptable. This undischarged energy is anxiety, and it remains even when its original, unacceptable object is repressed or eliminated from conscious awareness. This anxiety may attach itself to an otherwise harmless object, resulting in a phobia. This theory is best illustrated in one of Freud's most famous cases, that of "Little Hans," a five-year-old who developed a phobia of horses. Freud believed that Hans had a sexual desire for his mother and wanted his father dead so that he could have his mother to himself. This desire for his mother and hatred of his father were unacceptable impulses and so were repressed from consciousness, resulting in anxiety. This anxiety attached itself to horses, Freud thought, because the black blinders and muzzle of the horse symbolized his father's glasses and mustache.

In Freud's first theory, repression causes anxiety. In psychoanalytic theory, repression is a defense mechanism that keeps unacceptable thoughts and impulses from becoming conscious. In the later theory, the relationship between them has changed: anxiety causes repression. In this theory, anxiety acts as a signal to the ego (in Freud's theory, the rational, conscious part of the mind) that a forbidden impulse (such as Little Hans's desire for his mother) is trying to force its way into consciousness. This signal alerts the ego to try to repress the unwanted impulse. If the ego cannot successfully repress the forbidden impulse, it may try to transfer the forbidden impulse to an irrelevant object (horses, in Little Hans's case). This object can arouse all the emotions associated with the forbidden impulse, including the signal anxiety. In this way, it becomes a phobic object.

TWO-FACTOR THEORY

One influential behavioral approach to anxiety is O. Hobart Mowrer's two-factor theory. It uses the principles of Pavlovian learning—in which two stimuli are presented one after the other, and the response to the first changes because of the response automatically elicited by the second stimulus—and operant conditioning—learning in which a behavior increases or decreases depending on whether the behavior is followed by reward or punishment—to explain fear and phobic avoidance, respectively. Fear is acquired through Pavlovian conditioning when a neutral object or situation is paired with something painful or punishing. For example, having an automobile accident can result in a fear of driving. At this point, operant learning principles take over to explain phobic avoidance. In operant learning, any action that leads to a reward is likely to be repeated. The person who is anxious about driving might avoid driving. Because this avoidance is rewarded by reduced anxiety, the person is more likely to avoid driving in the future. Continued avoidance makes it harder to get back behind the wheel again.

Many problems were found with two-factor theory, and many modifications have been made to it. Two problems will be discussed here to illustrate these changes. First, the theory predicts that people will be likely to fear things that are most often associated with pain. There are very few people in modern society, however, who are phobic of electrical sockets and end tables, even though almost everyone has received a shock from the former and stubbed a toe on the latter. On the other hand, many people are afraid of snakes and spiders, even if they have never been bitten by one. This has been explained through the concept of preparedness: Evolutionary history has prepared people to learn that some things—such as reptiles, insects, heights, darkness, and closed spaces—are dangerous. These things are "easy" to learn to fear, and they account for a large proportion of phobias. On the other hand, people's evolutionary ancestors had no experience with electric sockets or guns, so people are not prepared to become phobic of these objects even though they cause much more pain in modern society than do snakes or spiders.

Two-factor theory states that for something to cause fear, it must be paired with a painful or punishing experience. Yet people sometimes become phobic of objects or situations with which they have never had a bad experience. Indeed, many people who have never seen a live snake are afraid of snakes. Thus, there must be other ways in which fear is acquired. One of these is vicarious transmission: seeing someone act afraid of something can lead to acquiring that fear. For example, whether an infant becomes afraid of being in a high place depends on whether its mother is smiling or has an expression of fear on her face. In an ingenious set of experiments, Susan Mineka and her colleagues showed that vicarious transmission of fear is influenced by preparedness. She showed that rhesus monkeys that watched a videotape of other monkeys acting afraid of a snake became afraid of snakes themselves. Monkeys that watched other monkeys act afraid of rabbits, however, did not become afraid of rabbits because they were not evolutionarily prepared to fear rabbits. Human beings also can acquire fear by being told that something is dangerous. Children can learn to avoid running in front of oncoming cars by being told not to do this by their parents; luckily, they do not have to be hit by a car or watch someone get hit to acquire this information.

TREATING ANXIETY

All theories of anxiety disorders attempt to explain and organize what is known about fear and anxiety. Some of the theories, including the ones described here, also have been applied in developing treatments for anxiety disorders. As might be expected, clinical psychologists with very different ideas about the cause of anxiety will recommend very different treatments to eliminate it.

In the case of Little Hans, Freud thought that his anxiety about horses was caused by repressed sexual impulses toward his mother and hatred of his father. From this, it follows that these repressed impulses would need to be brought out into the open and resolved before his anxiety about horses would diminish. This was the basic goal of the psychoanalytic therapy Freud recommended for Hans.

On the other hand, if Little Hans's parents had taken him to behavioral therapy, the therapist would have assumed that the child's fear stemmed from a fright he suffered in the presence of a horse. In fact, Freud stated that the phobia began when Hans saw a horse fall while pulling a bus. Further, the therapist would assume that now Hans was rewarded for avoiding horses by anxiety reduction and by getting extra attention from his parents. Treatment would involve having the boy gradually think about, look at, and even pet horses, and it would include being rewarded for approaching (rather than avoiding) horses.

Presented with these vastly different theories and treatments, the question arises: which is right? The theoretical issues are still debated, but it is clear that treatments based on a behavioral model of anxiety have been much more successful in reducing fear than have treatments based on the theories of Freud or his followers.

COGNITIVE THEORIES

Cognitive theories of anxiety also illustrate how theory is applied to develop a treatment. There are many different cognitive models of anxiety, but all are similar in that they assume that there is a cognitive cause of the fear state. This cognitive step is sometimes called an "irrational belief." A cognitive theorist might explain Little Hans's fear in the following way: Hans is afraid of horses because he has some irrational belief that horses are dangerous. The specific belief might be "The horse will bite me," or "The horse might get spooked and run into me," or even "Horses have germs, and if I go near one, I'll catch its germs and get sick." The theory assumes that anxiety will stop when the irrational belief is eliminated. Thus, a cognitive therapist would first carefully question Hans to find out the specific irrational belief causing his fear. Once that is determined, the therapist would use persuasion, logical reasoning, and evidence to try to change the belief. (Little Hans was used here only to continue with the same example. A therapist probably would not try to reason with a five-year-old, and a different treatment would be used. Cognitive therapies are more commonly used with adults.)

PHYSIOLOGICAL THEORIES

Physiological theories of anxiety are increasing in importance. As with behavioral, psychodynamic, and cognitive theories, there are many physiological theories. They differ with respect to the brain areas, pathways, or chemicals implicated in anxiety. It is likely that many physiological theories contain an element of truth. Anxiety is a complex state, involving multiple interacting parts of the nervous system, and it will take much additional research to develop a complete model of the brain's role in anxiety.

One physiological variable that has been integrated into many theories of anxiety is the panic attack. This is a sudden and usually short-lived attack that includes trouble with breathing, heart palpitations, dizziness, sweating, and fear of dying or going crazy. These attacks appear purely physiological at first in that they seem to come "out of the blue"; however, psychological factors determine whether they progress into a full-blown disorder. People can become anxious about having panic attacks, and this added anxiety leads to more attacks, producing panic disorder. Some people become afraid of having an attack in a place where they will be unable to cope or receive help. These people may progressively avoid more and more places. This is known as agoraphobia, which at its worst can result in people who are afraid to leave their homes.

The development of physiological theories also illustrates an important point in the relationship between theory and therapy. Thus far, it has been stressed that theories of anxiety help determine treatment. This relationship also works in reverse: success or failure of treatments adds information used in theory development. This is most clear in physiological theories. For example, the physiological mechanisms of different types of anxiety-reducing tranquilizers have been investigated to provide clues as to how the brain is involved in anxiety.

IMPACT ON FIELD OF PSYCHOLOGY

Just as most theories in psychology have a view of anxiety, anxiety is an important concept in many areas of psychology. Obviously, anxiety is very important in the fields of psychopathology and psychotherapy. It also has been very important in learning theory; experiments with conditioned fear have advanced knowledge about Pavlovian and operant conditioning. Anxiety is also an important trait in theories of personality, and it figures in theories of motivation. It might be said that anxiety is everywhere in psychology.

Theoretical developments in anxiety have been incorporated into other areas of psychology. For example, in the early 1960s, Peter Lang described fear and anxiety as being composed of three systems—that is, there are three systems in which fear is expressed: verbal (saying "I'm anxious"), behavioral (avoiding or running away from a feared object), and physiological (experiencing an increase in heart rate or sweating). An important point in understanding the three systems of fear is that the systems do not always run along parallel tracks. A person may speak of being anxious about the condition of the world environment without any physiological arousal. Alternatively, a boy's heart might pound at the sight of a snake in the woods, but he reports no fear and does not run away in the presence of his friends. Describing fear in a three-systems framework presents an important challenge to any theory of anxiety. An adequate theory must explain why the three systems sometimes give the same information and sometimes do not. The three-systems approach not only has been very influential in anxiety theory and research, but also has been applied to many other areas of psychology, such as studying emotion, stress, and pain. This approach is an important concept in behavioral formulations of anxiety, stating that anxiety has behavioral, physiological, and verbal components and that they do not necessarily provide the same information.

Another major challenge for theories of anxiety is to begin to integrate different positions. The present theories are not all mutually exclusive. The fact that a behavioral theory of anxiety has some validity does not mean that cognitive approaches are wrong. Also, psychological theories need to be integrated with physiological theories that describe brain activity during anxiety. Although theory and research in anxiety has a long and fruitful history, there is much work to be done, and many important developments lie ahead.

BIBLIOGRAPHY

Antony, Martin M., Susan M. Orsillo, and Lizabeth Roemer, eds. *Practitioner's Guide to Empirically Based Measures of Anxiety.* New York: Kluwer Academic, 2002. Print.

"Anxiety Disorders." *Psychiatry.org.* Amer. Psychiatric Assn., 2014. Web. 25 Feb. 2014.

Barlow, David H. *Anxiety and Its Disorders: The Nature and Treatment of Anxiety and Panic.* 2nd ed. New York: Guilford, 2004. Print.

Freud, Sigmund. "Analysis of a Phobia in a Five-Year-Old Boy." *The Standard Edition of the Complete Psychological Works of Sigmund Freud.* Ed. James Strachey. Vol. 10. London: Hogarth, 1955. Print.

Freud, Sigmund. "Inhibition, Symptoms, and Anxiety." *The Standard Edition of the Complete Psychological Works of Sigmund Freud.* Ed. James Strachey. Vol. 20. London: Hogarth, 1959. Print.

Hall, Kirsty. *The Stuff of Dreams: Fantasy, Anxiety, and Psychoanalysis.* London: Karnac, 2007. Print.

Kase, Larina, and Deborah Roth Ledley. *Anxiety Disorders.* Hoboken: Wiley, 2007. Print.

Marks, Isaac Meyer. *Living with Fear: Understanding and Coping with Anxiety.* 2nd ed. New York: McGraw-Hill, 2001. Print.

Scholten, Amy. "Anxiety Disorders." *Health Library.* EBSCO Information Services, 26 Sept. 2012. Web. 25 Feb. 2014.

Stahl, Stephen M., and Bret A. Moore, eds. *Anxiety Disorders: A Guide for Integrating Psychopharmacology and Psychotherapy.* New York: Routledge, 2013. Print.

Stein, Dan J., Eric Hollander, and Barbara Rothbaum. *Textbook of Anxiety Disorders.* 2nd ed. Washington, DC: American Psychiatric, 2009. Print.

Storch, Eric A., and Dean McKay, eds. *Handbook of Treating Variants and Complications in Anxiety Disorders.* London: Springer, 2013. Print.

Tuma, A. Hussain, and Jack D. Maser, eds. *Anxiety and the Anxiety Disorders.* New York: Erlbaum, 1985. Print.

Wolpe, Joseph, and Stanley Rachman. "Psychoanalytic 'Evidence': A Critique Based on Freud's Little Hans." *Journal of Nervous and Mental Disease* 131.2 (1960): 135–48. Print.

Scott R. Vrana

See Also: Abnormality: Psychological models; Agoraphobia and panic disorders; Antianxiety medications; Aversion therapy; Cognitive therapy; Conditioning; Fear; Generalized anxiety disorder; Implosion; Multiple personality; Observational learning and modeling therapy; Obsessive-compulsive disorder; Panic attacks; Pavlovian conditioning; Phobias; Systematic desensizitation.

Aphasias

Type of psychology: Language

Aphasias include a variety of conditions in which a partial or total loss of the ability to understand or produce language-based material occurs; the deficits can be in speech, reading, or writing. Knowledge of aphasias can aid in the localization of brain injuries. An understanding of aphasias is also important because they cause communication problems that require treatment.

Key Concepts

- Cerebral vascular disorders
- Equipotentiality
- Expressive (Broca's) aphasia
- Global or mixed aphasia
- Neuropsychology
- Paraphasia
- Primary progressive aphasia
- Receptive (Wenicke's) aphasia

INTRODUCTION

Nearly all definitions of aphasia agree on the following four points: aphasia refers to a condition in which a person suffers a loss in the ability to understand or produce language-based material; the deficits can be in speech, reading, or writing; the impairment is assumed to be caused by cerebral rather than peripheral impairments; and aphasias represent a devastation of a previously manifested ability rather than a developmental failure.

A fifth point, included or implied in most descriptions of aphasias, is that they occur as a result of structural damage or disease processes that directly affect the brain—an organic etiology. This view is taken because functional mental disorders, such as major depression, that produce aphasic-like symptoms are best understood in the context of the psychological and environmental events that produce them, while aphasias are best comprehended in relationship to the physical injuries and structural changes that cause them to manifest. Furthermore, interventions that would be effective for the treatment of aphasias would have little or no relevance for the amelioration of aphasic-like symptoms that result from functional causes.

Aphasia is most commonly associated with damage to the left hemisphere of the brain, which is where most people's language abilities are localized; damage to the right side of the brain seldom results in any noticeable effect on language skills. The fact that left-handed people sometimes show speech impairments following injury to the right side of the brain has often been taken as evidence that they are right-brain dominant in regard to language, but research has failed to support this contention. Most left-handed people show bilateral or left-hemisphere dominance for language, with no more than 15 percent showing primary control of speech via the right hemisphere.

Anyone can acquire aphasia, but most people who have this disorder are in their middle to late years. Men and women are equally affected, and there are no apparent ethnic differences in the prevalence of aphasia. Vascular disorders, particularly strokes, are the most frequent cause of aphasia; other conditions likely to lead to aphasia include traumatic head injuries, brain tumors, infections, toxins, and dementia. In 2011, the National Aphasia Association estimated that approximately one million people in the United States had been diagnosed with aphasia, with over one hundred thousand new cases diagnosed each year.

MAJOR FORMS

Aphasias can be divided into three general categories: expressive aphasias, receptive aphasias, and mixed or global aphasias. Most persons with aphasia show a mixture of expressive and receptive symptoms.

Expressive aphasia is often referred to as Broca's aphasia, motor aphasia, nonfluent aphasia, executive aphasia, or verbal aphasia. It describes a condition in which language comprehension remains intact but speech, and quite often the ability to write, is impaired. People who suffer from expressive aphasia understand what is being asked of them, and their ability to read is unaffected, but they have difficulty communicating their understanding. Expressive aphasia can be considered to subsume subfluent aphasia, anarthric aphasia, expressive dysprosody, kinetic (efferent) motor aphasia, speech apraxia, subcortical motor aphasia (pure word dumbness), transcortical motor aphasia (dynamic aphasia), conduction (central) aphasia, anomic (amnestic or nominal) aphasia, and agraphia, or the inability to write.

Verbal fluency, the capacity to produce uninterrupted phrases and sentences, is typically adversely affected in expressive aphasias. As a result of word-finding difficulties, speech may become halting and labored. For example, a person with Broca's aphasia may say "Walk dog" instead of "I will take the dog for a walk." The same sentence could also mean "You take the dog for a walk" or "The dog walked out of the yard," depending on the circumstances. When expressive aphasia is extreme, the affected person may be totally unable to speak (aphonia) or may only be able to speak in so distorted a way that he or she becomes incomprehensible. Still, as is the case with all other forms of aphasia, the abilities to sing and swear are generally preserved.

Paraphasias are a common form of expressive aphasia. Paraphasia differs from articulation problems, which are also quite prominent. When people with expressive aphasia have difficulties with articulation, they have trouble making recognizable speech sounds; paraphasia, on the other hand, refers to a condition in which articulation is intact but unintended syllables, words, or phrases are inserted. For example, one patient, in referring to his wife, always said "my dog."

Telegraphic speech, in which speech is reduced to its most elemental aspects, is frequently encountered in expressive aphasia. In telegraphic speech, the meaning is often clear, but communications are reduced to the bare minimum and consist of simple noun-verb phrases.

Receptive aphasia is often referred to as Wernicke's aphasia, sensory aphasia, fluent aphasia, or agnosia. Receptive aphasia can be considered to subsume semantic aphasia, jargon aphasia, visual aphasia (pure word blindness), transcortical sensory aphasia (isolation syndrome), syntactical aphasia, and alexia. In receptive aphasia, speech is generally fluent, with few, if any, articulatory problems; however, deficits in language comprehension are always present.

Although fluent, the speech of a person with receptive aphasia is seldom normal. People who have receptive aphasia may insert nonwords, or neologisms, into their communications, and in severe cases their communications may contain nothing but jargon speech. For example, one patient, when asked what he had for breakfast, responded, "Eating and food. Got no more heavy come to there. No come good, very good, in morning."

Unlike people who have expressive aphasia, who generally show great distress regarding their disorder, people with receptive aphasia may appear oblivious to their disorder. They may produce lengthy nonsensical utterances and then look at the listener as if confused by the listener's lack of comprehension.

Global aphasia describes a condition in which there is a mixture of receptive and expressive deficits. Global aphasia is typically associated with less focalized brain injury. Although comprehension is generally less impaired than production in global aphasia, this disorder does not fit neatly into either the expressive or the receptive category. The prognosis is generally much poorer for persons with global aphasia than for those with purely receptive or expressive deficits.

DIAGNOSING

Determining the nature and extent of an aphasia in an affected individual helps identify disease processes that may be affecting cerebral functioning, assists in the localization of brain injuries, and provides information that should be considered in making post-discharge placements. In addition, a thorough understanding of the nature and extent of symptoms in individual cases is extremely important, as aphasias cause significant communication deficits that require treatment.

There are a variety of conditions that can lead to aphasic-like symptoms: functional mental disorders, peripheral nervous system damage, peripheral motor impairments, congenital disorders, degenerative disease processes of the brain, cerebral vascular injury, central nervous system toxins, epilepsy, migraines, brain tumors, central nervous system infections, and cerebral trauma. Being able to discriminate between true aphasias caused by cerebral complications and aphasic-like symptoms brought on by other causes is necessary in order to provide the most effective treatment. For example, depression, Parkinson's disease, and certain focal lesions can all cause a person to appear emotionally unreactive (flat affect) and speak in a manner that lacks expressive intensity and intonation (dysprosody). The treatments of choice for these disorders are substantially different, and some interventions that would be recommended for one disorder would be contraindicated for another. Similarly, knowing that cerebral hemorrhage is most often associated with global aphasia and diffuse tissue damage, whereas cerebral embolisms typically damage areas served by the left middle cerebral artery and result in more specific aphasias, can significantly affect patient monitoring, treatment, and prognosis.

The interrelationships between aphasias and localized brain injuries have important ramifications. Among other implications, knowing the neural basis for language production and processing can facilitate the identification of the best candidate sites for surgical intervention and provide clues regarding whether a disease process has been arrested or continues to spread. For example, an aphasia that begins with clear articulation and no identifiable deficits in language production would be consistent with conduction aphasia, and it might be assumed that damage to the arcuate fasciculus had occurred. If, over time, the person began to manifest increasing difficulty with speech comprehension but articulation continued to appear intact, it could be inferred that damage was spreading downward and affecting a broader region of the temporal lobe. Such information would have important ramifications for treatment and prognosis.

Given the importance of language and the ability to communicate in everyday life, the nature and the extent of a patient's aphasia must be taken into account when making post-discharge plans. If the person's deficits are purely expressive in nature, he or she is more likely to be able to manage his or her daily affairs, while a person with receptive aphasia may have to be referred to a more restrictive environment. Not being able to understand the communications of others can compromise safety and judgment, and a person with receptive aphasia should be carefully assessed to ascertain the degree to which he or she is competent to manage his or her affairs.

TREATING APHASIAS

Aphasias cause significant communication problems that require treatment and amelioration. Although there is no doubt that many patients experience spontaneous recovery from aphasia, research shows that treatment can speed up the process. Furthermore, the earlier treatment is initiated, the more profound its effects.

Under most circumstances, therapy for aphasia is just one element of a more comprehensive treatment process. Aphasia seldom occurs in isolation, and, depending on the type of damage, one is likely to see paresis, memory deficits, apraxias, agnosias, and various difficulties related to information processing occurring in conjunction with the aphasia. As a result, the person with aphasia is likely to be treated by an interdisciplinary team, typically consisting of one or more physicians, nurses, nursing support personnel, physical therapists, occupational therapists, speech therapists, a rehabilitation psychologist or neuropsychologist, a clinical psychologist, and one or more social workers. Each team member is expected to have an area of expertise and specialization, but the team approach requires that team members work together and support each discipline's treatment goals.

Common treatments for aphasia include systematic stimulation, behavioral teaching programs, deblocking, and compensation therapy. Systematic stimulation involves the use of everyday objects and situations to stimulate language production and facilitate language comprehension. Behavioral teaching programs are similar to systematic stimulation but are more organized, are designed more precisely to take into account known structural damage, and frequently employ behavior modification techniques. Deblocking, a less frequently used therapy, consists of stimulating intact language functions as a vehicle for encouraging rehabilitation of damaged processes. Compensation therapy includes teaching the person alternative communication strategies and how to use intact abilities to circumvent the functional limitations caused by aphasia.

Computers may also be used in aphasia treatment. One approach incorporates software that enables a computer to understand spoken language. Another approach uses a "processing prosthesis" that allows aphasic persons to construct computer-generated spoken sentences and store them for future use. Researchers exploring computer-based methods believe that these new methods will play complementary roles with existing aphasia therapies such as systematic stimulation.

One treatment option being explored is the possibility of using medication to prevent or reduce the severity of aphasia following a stroke. Strategies include the administration of drugs to restore compromised levels of neurotransmitters, to minimize the extent of cell loss in the brain, or to restore blood flow to regions of the brain that have become ischemic following a stroke.

STUDY OF APHASIAS

The study of aphasias dates thousands of years. An Egyptian papyrus dated between 3000 and 2500 BCE provides a case example of language deficits following traumatic head injury. The Greeks variously subscribed to hypotheses that mental processes were located in the brain or the heart, and it was not until the time of second-century Roman physician Galen that the brain hypothesis gained full sway. Galen based his arguments on dissection and clinical experience; he had spent five years as a physician to the gladiators of the Roman circus, where he was exposed to multiple cases of traumatic head injury.

Over the next fourteen hundred years, little progress was made in terms of cerebral anatomy or physiology. With the anatomical observations of Andreas Vesalius and the philosophical speculations of René Descartes in the sixteenth century, however, the stage was set for a new understanding of cerebral functioning. In the early nineteenth century, phrenology, which postulated that specific areas of the brain controlled particular intellectual and psychological processes, became influential. Although it was subsequently discredited, phrenology provided the foundation for the localizationist position in neuropsychology.

Paul Broca can be credited with raising the study of cerebral localization of speech to a scientific level. Broca's first case study was a patient nicknamed "Tan," whose receptive abilities were apparently intact but whose expressive skills had been reduced to uttering the word "tan" and a few colorful oaths. According to Broca, Tan was shown in an autopsy to have a lesion of the left anterior lobe of his brain, which caused his speech problems. The syndrome subsequently became known as Broca's aphasia, and the posterior third of the left third frontal convolution of the left hemisphere of the brain was named Broca's area.

Carl Wernicke was the next person to make major contributions to the understanding of cerebral organization and language functioning. Wernicke proposed a sequential processing model in which several areas of the brain affected language development, production, and expression. Following his work, the left first temporal gyrus was named Wernicke's area, and the particular type of receptive aphasia that results from damage to this area became known as Wernicke's aphasia.

Over the ensuing years, arguments raged over whether the localizationist position was tenable. As a general rule, researchers supporting equipotentiality (sensory input may be localized, but perception involves the whole brain) held sway. By the 1950s, however, interactionist theory had gained the ascendancy. Interactionist theory holds that basic functions are localized, but there is redundancy in regard to function. Therefore, damage to a specific area of the brain may or may not cause a deficit in higher-order behaviors, since the damaged functions may be assumed by redundant or parallel backup components.

Recent years have seen notable advances in the understanding and treatment of aphasias. Psychometric instruments founded on modern principles of test construction have become available, and experimental techniques that take into account known aspects of cerebral functioning have been developed. Furthermore, advances in brain imaging, such as positron emission tomography (PET), computed tomography (CT), and magnetic resonance imaging (MRI), have done much to aid in understanding cortical function and the effects of injury as they relate to the development of aphasias. Functional magnetic imaging (fMRI) identifies areas in the brain that are used during activities such as speaking. This imaging technique may enable the field to address previously unanswerable questions, including what role the right hemisphere plays in recovery from aphasia, how individual differences in brain organization for language contribute to recovery from aphasia, and how rehabilitation for aphasia alters brain organization for language.

BIBLIOGRAPHY

Ball, Martin J., and Jack S. Damico, eds. *Clinical Aphasiology: Future Directions.* New York: Psychology, 2007. Print.

Benson, D. Frank, and Alfredo Ardila. *Aphasia: A Clinical Perspective.* New York: Oxford UP, 1996. Print.

Broida, Helen. *Coping with Stroke: Communication Breakdown of Brain Injured Adults.* San Diego: College-Hill, 1979. Print.

Brubaker, Susan Howell. *Sourcebook for Aphasia: A Guide to Family Activities and Community Resources.* Detroit: Wayne State UP, 1982. Print.

Collins, Michael. *Diagnosis and Treatment of Global Aphasia.* San Diego: College-Hill, 1986. Print.

Davis, G. Albyn. *Aphasia and Related Cognitive-Communicative Disorders.* Boston: Pearson, 2013. Print

Davis, G. Albyn. *Aphasiology: Disorders and Clinical Practice.* 2nd ed. Boston: Pearson, 2007. Print.

Ewing, Susan Adair, and Beth Pfalzgraf. *Pathways: Moving beyond Stroke and Aphasia.* Detroit: Wayne State UP, 1990. Print.

Fitch, James L. *Clinical Applications of Microcomputers in Communication Disorders.* Orlando: Academic, 1986. Print.

Murdoch, B. E. *Acquired Speech and Language Disorders: A Neuroanatomical and Functional Neurological Approach.* London: Chapman, 1990. Print.

Papathanasiou, Ilias, Patrick Coppens, and Constantin Potagas. *Aphasia and Related Neurogenic Communication Disorders.* Burlington: Jones, 2013. Print.

Simmons-Mackie, Nina, Julia M. King, and David R. Beukelman, eds. *Supporting Communication for Adults with Acute and Chronic Aphasia.* Baltimore: Brookes, 2013. Print.

Taylor, Martha, ed. *Acquired Aphasia.* 3rd ed. San Diego: Academic, 1998. Print.

Bruce E. Bailey; updated by Allyson Washburn

See Also: Alzheimer's disease; Dementia; Dsylexia; Grammar and speech; Language; Neuropsychology; Parkinson's disease; Speech disorders; Speech perception.

Archetypes and the collective unconscious

Type of psychology: Consciousness; Memory

Swiss psychologist Carl Jung, the founder of analytical psychology, proposed the theory of archetypes—universal human images, such as the Mother, Child, Trickster, and Wise Old Man, that reside in the unconscious—and the existence of a collective unconscious whose contents are shared by all human beings.

Key Concepts

- Anima and animus
- Archetypes
- Collective unconcious
- Ego-identity
- Individualization
- Mandalas
- Mother complex
- Personal unconcious
- Rebirth
- Transcendent function

INTRODUCTION

Analytical psychology, founded by Swiss psychologist Carl Jung, is based on the idea that the key to psychological adjustment and growth lies in making unconscious material conscious through hypnosis, active imagination (free association and guided imagery), and dream interpretation. For Jung, such psychological maturation is defined as individuation, "the process by which a person becomes a psychological 'individual,' that is, a separate, indivisible unity or 'whole.'" For the developing individual, this involves the emergence of ego from a pre-egoic state of being. Children, for example, develop a growing sense of themselves as separate from their mothers as they move from childhood into adulthood. Erik H. Erikson, in *Identity and the Life Cycle* (1959), refers to this as the achievement of ego-identity. It represents the "comprehensive gains which the individual, at the end of adolescence, must have derived from all of his preadult experiences in order to be ready for the task of adulthood." According to Jung, however, ego-identity is not a final stage in the individuation process but simply a step along the way. Full adult maturity implies a movement beyond ego-identity toward awareness of the collective, undivided nature of being and people's unity with all things. Achievement of psychological maturity, or individuation, requires an integration of both conscious and unconscious energy.

DREAMS

Jung believed that dreams provide a window into the individual's unconscious and thus are central to the process of individuation. According to Jung, there are, however, two types of dreams, personal and archetypal dreams, just are there are two types of unconscious, the personal and the collective unconscious. The personal dream arises from the personal unconscious, which consists of repressed personal memories and experiences, including the Shadow (which represents everything that the individual refuses to acknowledge about himself or herself, specifically negative character traits or tendencies).

The archetypal dream, by contrast, arises from the collective unconscious, which is made up of archaic or "primordial" types, "universal images that have existed since the remotest times" and that are shared by all. Thus, although the personal unconscious is specific to the individual and involves a personal inventory of material that may have been forgotten (memories of birth, for example) or repressed from consciousness (child abuse, for example), the collective unconscious represents a vast reservoir of elemental configurations or archetypes that are outside space and time (the Rebirth archetype, for example). The collective unconscious, in other words, is inherited. It is, as Jung explains, identical and present in all individuals and represents "a common psychic substrate of a suprapersonal nature." Jung's support for the existence of the collective unconscious is based, in part, on his assertion that the realm of consciousness does not account for the totality of the psyche, a claim supported through many years of clinical observations of patients' dreams and visions, particularly those of schizophrenics. Thus, achieving individuation through the "therapeutic method of complex psychology," according to Jung, requires rendering conscious the energy of both the personal and collective unconscious, to reconcile the conflict between conscious and unconscious content. Jung refers to this union of opposites as the "transcendent function."

ARCHETYPES

Unconscious energy is made manifest through archetypes, the "language" of the collective unconsciousness, or the way in which unconscious material is articulated. Archetypes not only represent unconscious content rendered into consciousness, as prototypes or patterns of instinctual behavior, but also exist outside space and time and thus speak to the universal nature of human experience. The Mother archetype, for example, is a preexistent form that is above and yet subsumes individual experiences of one's own mother. Archetypes may emerge in picture form (such as the universal mandala symbol, a squared circle) or in mythic narratives (such as a story of rebirth). Whether as pictures or stories, however, archetypes emerge during states of reduced intensity of consciousness, such as daydreams, visions, dreams, or delirium. In these states, according to Jung, "the check put upon unconscious contents by the concentration of the conscious mind ceases, so that the hitherto unconscious material streams, as through from opened side-sluices, into the field of consciousness." They can also emerge during strong emotional states brought on by, for example, intense anger, love, hate, confusion, or pain. Archetypes are spontaneous products of the psyche that seem to have a life of their own; as such, they can be neither permanently suppressed nor ordered to emerge. They are, as Jung says, in potentia, waiting to be revealed. Some examples of archetypes include the Child, the Hero, the Old Man, the Mother, and the Trickster.

IMPORTANT FUNCTIONS

Jung claims that it is dangerous to suppress or ignore the collective unconscious, particularly in important matters, because he believes that the individual's fate is predominantly determined by the unconscious. In extreme cases, suppression of the unconscious results in neurosis, a nervous disorder characterized by intense emotional instability. Indeed, Jung claims that "when an individual or social group deviates too far from their instinctual foundations, they then experience the full impact of unconscious forces." It is as if, as Jung explains, the unconscious "were trying to restore the lost balance." Although Jung asserts that archetypes are manifestations of instinctual behavior, such as the child's need to suck or the innate attraction to warmth and light over cold and darkness, he also asserts that they may speak to people's spiritual nature, and thus may be manifestations of the divine. He writes of archetypes, for example, that they "are meant to attract, to convince, to fascinate, and to overpower. They are created out of the primal stuff of revelation and reflect the ever-unique experience of divinity." Jung goes so far as to assert that "our concern with the unconscious has become a vital question for us—a question of spiritual being and non being."

Whether divine or instinctual, Jung makes a compelling argument for cultures' need to continually explore the archetypes of the unconsciousness. Indeed, he even claims that the practice of psychology (by which he means analytical psychology) would be "superfluous in an age and a culture that possessed symbols." Cultures, particularly Western cultures, according to Jung, have experienced a "growing impoverishment of symbols." Despite the universal qualities of the unconscious, Jung explains that archetypes must constantly be reborn and reinterpreted for every generation or they will die. Jung, in fact, argues that the primary role of art is to "dream the myth outward," to continually find new interpretations of the archetypes of the collective unconscious to live the fully human life.

Archetypes and archetypal stories, then, are continually produced and reproduced in all cultures in all ages. Manifest in dreams and delirium as well as in art (most notably in myths and fairy tales), they articulate human experiences, offer resources for psychological maturation, and provide a guide for living the fully human life. What, then, are some of these archetypes? How have they evolved? To what urgencies do they speak?

THE ANIMA AND MOTHER ARCHETYPES

According to Jung, hidden inside of the unconscious of every man is a "feminine personality"; likewise, hidden in the unconsciousness of every woman is a "masculine personality." Jung labels these the anima and animus, respectively. The anima-animus concept is best illustrated in the Chinese yin-yang symbol, where yang, representing "the light, war, dry, masculine principle" contains within it "the seed of yin (the dark, cold, moist, feminine principle)." Jung supports such an idea with biology, explaining that although a majority of male or female genes determines an individual's sex, the minority of genes belonging to the other sex do not simply disappear once the sex has been determined in the developing fetus. The idea of the anima and animus is also reflected in "syzygies" or dually gendered deities, such as god the father and god the mother, and in god's human counterparts, the "godmother" and "godfather," and in the child's own mother and father. Jung links the anima personality, in particular, with its "historical" archetypes of the sister, wife, mother, and daughter, with particular attention paid to the Mother archetype. or the image of the mother-goddess or Great Mother, is an archetype that spans the world's religions and cultures. In psychological practice, it is often associated with fertility, fruition, a garden, a cave, or a plowed field. It is connected with birth, the uterus, or any round cavernous place and, by extension, rebirth, or magical transformation and healing. These are positive connotations, but the archetype also has negative ones, as in the witch, the devouring dragon, the grave, deep water, or any suffocating or annihilating energy. Thus, the mother archetype represents both the nurturing-protecting mother, as in the Roman Catholic image of the Virgin Mary, and the punishing-devouring mother, as in Medea of classical Greek mythology. Sometimes she represents both the loving and the devouring mother, as in the dual-natured Indian goddess Kali.

In clinical practice, the Mother archetype is manifest in what Jung refers to as the mother-complex, which also has both positive and negatives aspects. For the daughter, the mother-complex can either unduly stimulate or inhibit her feminine instinct. The exaggeration of the feminine instinct, particularly the maternal instinct, is represented in the daughter whose only goal is childbirth, who views her husband primarily as an instrument of procreation, and who is self-defined as "living for others" while unable to make any true or meaningful sacrifices for others. A second manifestation of the mother-complex, according to Jung, is the daughter with an overdeveloped eros, or sexual instinct. In this case, the maternal instinct, potentially wiped out, is instead replaced with an overdeveloped sex drive, often leading to an unconscious incestuous relationship with the father driven by jealousy of the mother. By contrast, a third type of identification with the mother involves a complete paralysis of the daughter's feminine will, such that "everything which reminds her of motherhood, responsibility, personal relationships, and erotic demands arouses feelings of inferiority and compels her to run away—to her mother, naturally, who lives to perfection everything that seems unattainable to her daughter." Finally, the daughter who resists or rejects the mother and everything she represents exemplifies the extreme negative mother complex.

The Mother archetype in a man's psychology is entirely different in character from that of a woman. Jung claims that while the mother-complex exemplifies the daughter's own gendered conscious life, for the son, it typifies the alien, unknown, or yet-to-be-experienced, since it exists only as unconscious imagery. The mother-complex for sons, in other words, is connected with the man's sexual counterpart, the anima. Jung's discussion of the mother-complex in sons is some of his most controversial work, primarily because he argues that it produces homosexuality, Don Juanism, or impotence. In the case of homosexuality or impotence, he argues that the man's heterosexuality is unconsciously tied to his mother, and thus is dormant. By contrast, in Don Juanism, which is marked by an overly developed sexual instinct, the "unconscious seeks his mother in every woman he meets." Jung supports the idea of the strong influence of the mother on the son's sexuality by explaining she is the first female with whom the man comes in contact. The man becomes increasingly aware of her femininity and responds to it instinctually or unconsciously.

THE CHILD AND REBIRTH ARCHETYPES

Another significant archetype of the collective unconscious, according to Jung, is the Rebirth archetype.Stories and images of rebirth, or about being twice born, abound in all cultures across time. Underlying all rebirth stories, according to Jung, is "dual descent," the idea of both human and divine parents. For example, just as Jesus Christ is twice born, from his mother Mary and by his baptism by John the Baptist in the river Jordan, he also has a dual descent from a heavenly father and an earthly mother. Rebirth, then, is about acknowledging and experiencing the divine through the corporeal. Jung explains that there are five forms in which the rebirth archetype manifests itself and there are two central ways to experience it. The five forms are reincarnation (the continuity of a personality, accessible to memory, that is successively reborn in various human bodies), metempsychosis (the transmigration of souls into successive bodies, possibly without the continuity of personality or memory, as in karma, or soul debt), resurrection (the re-establishing of human existence after death, usually in a resurrected body rather than a corporeal one), participation in the process of transformation (an indirect rebirth through involvement in a ritual of transformation, such as taking part in the Catholic Mass), and rebirth (rebirth within an individual's life span involving a renewal or transformation of personality). The two central ways of experiencing rebirth are through ritual, as in the aforementioned Catholic Mass, or through immediate experience, as in a divine revelation or a significant insight gained through hypnosis or dream therapy.

The Rebirth archetype may manifest itself in numerous ways, such as the diminution of personality, or "soul loss"; the enlargement of personality, through, for example, a divine revelation; a change in internal structure, a transformation brought about, for example, by possession, whether possession by the persona (the public self), the Shadow (the dark self), the anima or animus (the opposite-sex self), or even the "ancestral soul"; identification with a group, such that the individual identity is subsumed or transformed into that of the group (for example, mob psychology); identification with a cult hero, as in the Christian idea of rebirth and salvation through Jesus Christ; technical transformation, achieved through certain meditative practices such as yoga; and finally natural transformation, whereby the individual undergoes the death of the old personality and the birth of a new or greater personality (individuation). This last manifestation of rebirth, individuation, is the most important from the perspective of analytical psychology.

The Child archetype represents the potential for such a rebirth, since the child, according to Jung, is an individuation archetype. It signifies the preconscious (the childhood aspect of the collective psyche) and the past, while also representing future possibilities. The child, in other words, represents the idea of an "a priori existence of potential wholeness" while also anticipating future developments for the individual and the culture. In Jung's words, it "paves the way for future change of personality," and, in the largest sense, is a "symbol which unites opposites," as a "mediator, a bringer of healing, that is, one who makes whole." Analytical psychology, and the work of Jung, is primarily responsible for drawing attention to this and other archetypes of the collective unconscious and their role in the process of psychological maturity, or individuation.

BIBLIOGRAPHY

Alister, Ian, and Christopher Hauke. *Contemporary Jungian Analysis: Post-Jungian Perspectives from the Society of Analytical Psychology.* Hoboken, NJ: Taylor, 2013. Print.

Goertzel, Ben. "World Wide Brain: Self-Organizing Internet Intelligence as the Actualization of the Collective Unconscious." *Psychology and the Internet: Intrapersonal, Interpersonal, and Transpersonal Implications.* Ed. Jayne Gackenbach. 2d ed. Boston: Elsevier, 2007. Print.

Jung, Carl. *The Archetypes and the Collective Unconscious.* Trans. R. F. C. Hull. 2d ed. Princeton, NJ: Princeton UP, 1981. Print.

Jung, Carl. *The Essential Jung.* Ed. Anthony Storr. Princeton: Princeton UP, 1983. Print.

Jung, Carl. *The Practice of Psychotherapy.* Translated by R. F. C. Hull. 2d ed. Princeton: Princeton UP, 1966. Print.

Jung, Carl. *The Structure and Dynamics of the Psyche.* Trans. R. F. C. Hull. 2d ed. Princeton: Princeton UP, 1970. Print.

Jung, Carl. *Symbols of Transformation.* Trans. R. F. C. Hull. 2d ed. Princeton: Princeton UP, 1977. Print.

Odajnyk, V Walter. *Archetype and Character: Power, Eros, Spirit, and Matter Personality Types.* New York: Palgrave, 2012. Print.

Papadopoulos, Renos K. *The Handbook of Jungian Psychology: Theory, Practice, and Applications.* Hoboken, NJ: Taylor, 2012. Digital file.

Stevens, Anthony. *Archetype: A Natural History of the Self.* Hoboken, NJ: Taylor, 2013. Digital file.

Stevens, Anthony. *Jung: A Very Short Introduction.* New York: Oxford UP, 2001. Print.

Walker, Steven F. *Jung and the Jungians on Myth: An Introduction*. New York: Routledge, 2002. Print.

Susan Mackey-Kallis

See Also: Analytical psychology: Carl Jung; Dreams; Introverts and extroverts; Jung, Carl; Personality theory; Self.

Archival data

Type of psychology: Psychological methodologies

Archival data, or information already on record, offer several advantages to resourceful researchers: saving of time, access to large quantities of information, and avoidance of some ethical issues, to list a few. At the same time, use of such data carries with it several risks, the worst of which is potential inaccuracy..

Key Concepts

- Experimentation
- Observation
- Reliability
- Self-report measures
- Validity

INTRODUCTION

A major part of any research enterprise is the gathering of data—the information from which conclusions will be drawn and judgments made. This gathering can be accomplished in many ways, each with its advantages and drawbacks. Often, by using a combination of methods, a skilled researcher can let the strengths of one method compensate for the weaknesses of another. Which method, or combination of methods, is most appropriate depends on several factors. If research is intended to be only descriptive, the scientist may find observation adequate; if the research is intended to establish cause-and-effect relationships clearly, experimentation is all but essential.

The methods mentioned—observation and experimentation—actively involve the scientist in the gathering of data to be used. This involvement allows considerable control over possible sources of error, but it also limits what can be accomplished. For example, a scientist cannot step back into the past, cannot observe (or experiment with) more than a fairly small number of subjects during most research, and cannot avoid the possibility that the subjects' knowledge that they are involved in research will distort the answers most people give or the behaviors they display. When they can be located and used, archival data eliminate many of these problems for descriptive research and may, because they extend across time, give hints of cause-and-effect relationships typically revealed only by experimentation.

The term "archival data" may first suggest only information shelved in public archives, such as courthouse records. Indeed, such a location may hold much useful information, but it is only one of dozens of possibilities. Similarly, "data" may first suggest only collections of numbers; here again, however, many other possibilities exist. For example, Aurelius Augustinus, better known as Saint Augustine, wrote his autobiography, *Confessiones* (397–400; *Confessions*, 1620), well aware that its contents would fascinate his own and later generations. It seems likely that he also realized that he was presenting more than information about himself to his readers. Personal documents may also be used by contemporary researchers in ways unlikely to have been anticipated by their source. Comparing many autobiographies written over the centuries, a developmental psychologist might today examine how earlier generations behaved during the period now known as adolescence. A career counselor might examine how people who changed their original occupations in midlife managed to do so.

With worldwide distribution of printed material, films, and electronic media, mass communications have been able to serve well as archival data pertaining to hundreds of topics. One problem, however, may be the presence of so much information that a sampling procedure must be devised to decide what to use. A caution regarding the use of mass media as sources can also apply to personal documents and statistical data. Researchers who want to extract data from, for example, United States newspaper reports of 1945 must consider the reliability of what they find. If they plan to use the reports as indicators of national public opinion, they must select several newspapers published across the nation. A single newspaper might serve to suggest what its own editor and readers believed, but dozens might be required to suggest national beliefs, and even dozens might not provide what researchers originally sought. If different papers carried very different accounts of an event, or divergent editorials regarding it, researchers might have to focus on differences rather than unanimity of belief.

In his *Confessions*, Saint Augustine discussed the possibilities that writers might not know something about themselves or might state something they know to be untrue. This validity issue also applies to the electronic media and, like differences of opinion across several newspapers, must be dealt with by consulting several independent sources, if they can be located.

Statistical data—measurements or observations converted to numerical form—can be the most immediately useful, yet possibly the most dangerous, archival data for a researcher to use. Most typically in psychological research, information is converted to numbers, the numbers are processed in some manner, and conclusions are drawn. When researchers gather data themselves, they know where the numbers came from, whether they should be considered approximations or precise indicators, and a host of other facts essential to their interpretation. When researchers process archival data—information gathered by others for their own purposes—such information essential to understanding their interpretation is often unknown and must be sought as part of the research.

For example, a psychologist seeking information about the education levels of employees in a company might find it directly available on application blanks on file. If those blanks recorded the applicants' stated education levels, however, and there was no evidence that those statements had been verified as a condition of hiring, it would be risky to consider them highly accurate data. Most archival data need to be verified in some manner; how fully this is done should depend on the degree of certainty needed in the research.

USES AND DRAWBACKS

The use of archival data in the classic work *Le Suicide* (1897; *Suicide*, 1951) by sociologist Émile Durkheim illustrates how much a master researcher can learn from already available material. Hypothesizing that social factors are key bases for suicide, he first gathered years of suicide records from European countries where they were available and then examined these statistics in the light of additional archival data to evaluate several alternative hypotheses.

Noting that suicide rates increased from January to June, then fell off, he considered the possibility that suicide is influenced by temperature. Finding, again from records, that suicides did not vary directly with temperature increases and decreases, he was drawn back to his favored hypothesis that social factors were of key importance. To elaborate on such factors, he considered religion, family, and political atmosphere, again through archival data.

The advantages that Durkheim gained over limiting himself to data personally gathered were enormous. For example, had he personally interviewed families and friends of suicide victims, far fewer cases would have been available to him, probably ones restricted to a fairly limited geographic area. He also would have been limited by time factors: It seems unlikely that interviewing years after the event would have been possible for most of the cases. Unavoidably, he ran risks in accepting available records as accurate, but he judiciously chose records likely to have been carefully assembled and unlikely to have contained willful distortions. As the world has changed remarkably since Durkheim's day, so have the opportunities to apply archival data to research questions. Part of the change results from there now being more numerous and more varied archives; additionally, there are almost incredible new methods of searching them.

For Durkheim, information that existed in print or in still photographs, or could be told to him from someone's memory, was all that was available. For modern researchers, those possibilities remain, and the addition of new, mainly electronic, media since the beginning of the twentieth century has dramatically changed both the form and the amount of archival data in existence. Silent motion pictures, phonograph records, radio (with transcription discs), sound motion pictures, audio recording wire and then tape, television (with video recording tape), and computer storage have increased available information almost immeasurably. They have also created the possibilities for finding obscure fragments of data not before available.

Researchers studying attitudes leading to war, for example, have for centuries been able to work with written sources—documents, books, and newspapers. From the early 1900s on, social psychologists could add to those archival sources newsreel footage of political leaders' participation in war-related events as well as a few phonograph records of their speeches. From the late 1920s on, they could add transcriptions (disc recordings) of radio broadcasts and sound motion-picture coverage. From the late 1940s on, they could add films, then television broadcasts and videotapes of them.

Beginning in the mid-1980s, a new sort of archive emerged, one that allows enormous amounts of information to be saved, distributed worldwide, and searched electronically for desired information. Computer storage of data has created a change in the handling of information comparable to the change sparked by the invention of the printing press. Pulling information from storage media ranging from magnetic tape to CD-ROM (compact disc read-only memory) storage to Internet databases, researchers can gain access to libraries of information—from indexes to research literature to archival data—and can sort through it with speed and accuracy never before known.

For example, a researcher with a personal computer and an Internet connection can search the entire works of William Shakespeare, encyclopedias, atlases, Bartlett's *Familiar Quotations*, world almanacs, and more, in a fashion that can be considered a modern version of looking for a needle in a haystack. The old phrase suggests looking for something that exists but is so hidden that chances of finding it are nil. Computer searching is the equivalent of searching the haystack with a powerful metal detector and electromagnet to pull the needle from the depths of the stack.

Studying attitudes toward old age, for example, a scientist could direct searches for many key words and phrases (old age, elderly, retiree, senile, respected, and so on), some only very remotely related to the topic. The speed and accuracy of digital technology make feasible needle-in-haystack searches that were impractical to consider by earlier methods. A world atlas might contain very few age-related references, but with a search at lightning speed possible, the one or two references to retirement might be worth seeking.

ASSESSING RESOURCES

Although scientific psychology has always taught its students how to generate data through their own research, in no way has it denied them the right to use data already available if the data meet their needs. Like other data, archival data must meet reasonable standards of reliability and validity, standards not always easy to assess when several sources, perhaps over an extended span of time, have generated the data.

Researchers who use other researchers' data probably have the fewest worries. Since the 1920s, published research standards have been uniform enough that modern readers can clearly understand what was done to produce data and from that understanding can judge their quality. Researchers who work from personal documents have a more difficult task in determining data quality. What the writers stated might be distorted for a variety of reasons, ranging from intentional deception to an incomplete comprehension of the subject matter. If the new researcher is working to assess the personality of an author, for example, checking the internal consistency of the document may be a useful, if not definitive, way of evaluating data quality. If the new researcher is studying some historical event, comparing the diary of one observer with those of others could help validate data obtained.

Researchers who work from mass media, which may carry carelessly assembled or intentionally slanted information, or those who work from public records that might, a century or more ago, have ignored minority populations—or even those who work from an online database that contains only works written in the English language—have special problems of data accuracy, and each must devise ways of discovering and working around them.

As compensation for the special problems that archival data present, they possess an advantage that all but eliminates worry about invasion of privacy, often a major issue in the area of research ethics. By their very definition, archival data are already public, and rarely does new analysis by researchers produce sensitive conclusions. In the rare case where it does, the researcher can simply decide not to report a particular conclusion, and no one has been hurt. By contrast, in certain experimental research, when subjects reveal something that they prefer had remained unknown (perhaps that they would cheat to succeed at some task), the ethical harm is already done if the subjects realize that the experimenter knows of their failing. Not publishing the results cannot remove their discomfort.

BIBLIOGRAPHY

Comer, Jonathan S., and Philip C. Kendall, eds. *The Oxford Handbook of Research Strategies for Clinical Psychology.* New York: Oxford UP, 2013. Print.

Elder, Glen H., Eliza K. Pavalko, and Elizabeth C. Clipp. *Working with Archival Data: Studying Lives.* Newbury Park: Sage, 1992. Print.

Freud, Sigmund, and William C. Bullitt. *Thomas Woodrow Wilson, Twenty-Eighth President of the United States: A Psychological Study.* New Brunswick: Transaction, 1999. Print,

Iversen, Gudmund R. *Contextual Analysis.* Newbury Park: Sage, 1998. Print.

Langer, Walter Charles. *The Mind of Adolf Hitler.* New York: Basic, 1972. Print.

McBride, Dawn M. *The Process of Research in Psychology.* 2nd ed. Thousand Oaks: Sage, 2013. Print.

Schweigert, Wendy A. *Research Methods in Psychology: A Handbook.* 3rd ed. Long Grove: Waveland, 2012. Print.

Selltiz, Claire, Marie Johoda, Morton Deutsch, and S. Cook. *Research Methods in Social Relations*. New York: Holt, 1976. Print.

Harry A. Tiemann, Jr.

See Also: Case study methodologies; Complex experimental designs; Developmental methodologies; Experimentation: Ethics and participant rights; Field experimentation; Observational methods; Qualitative researchl Research ethics; Scientific methods.

Artificial intelligence

Date: 1956 forward

Type of psychology: Biological bases of behavior; Cognition; Consciousness; Intelligence and intelligence testing; Language; Learning; Memory; Sensation and perception

Artificial intelligence is a conceptual framework for how a system can be implemented to process information and behave in a manner considered intelligent. Artificial intelligence, from the perspective of cognitive psychology, provides a means for developing and testing computer models of human cognitive processes. This approach is useful in terms of theory development and modification.

Key Concepts

- Chinese room
- Connectionism
- Expert systems
- Intelligent tutoring systems
- Physical symbol system hypothesis
- Strong AI
- Subsumption architecture
- Traditional AI (pure AI)
- Turing test
- Weak AI

INTRODUCTION

Ideas proposed in cybernetics, developments in psychology in terms of studying internal mental processes, and the development of the computer were important precursors for the area of artificial intelligence (AI). Cybernetics, a term coined by Norbert Wiener in 1948, is a field of study interested in the issue of feedback for artificial and natural systems. The main idea is that a system could modify its behavior based on feedback generated by the system or from the environment. Information, and in particular feedback, is necessary for a system to make intelligent decisions. During the 1940s and 1950s, the dominant school in American psychology was behaviorism. The focus of research was on topics in which the behaviors were observable and measurable. During this time, researchers such as George Miller were devising experiments that continued to study behavior but also provided some indication of internal mental processes. This cognitive revolution in the United States led to research programs interested in issues such as decision making, language development, consciousness, and memory, issues relevant to the development of an intelligent machine. The main tool for implementing AI, the computer, was an important development that came out of World War II.

The culmination of many of these events was a conference held at Dartmouth College in 1956, which explored the idea of developing computer programs that behaved in an intelligent manner. This conference is often viewed as the beginning of the area of artificial intelligence. Some of the researchers involved in the conference included John McCarthy, Marvin Minsky, Allen Newell, and Herbert Simon. Before this conference, Newell, Simon, and Shaw's Logic Theorist was the only AI program. Subsequent projects focused on the development of programs in the domain of game playing. Games of strategy, such as checkers and chess, were selected because they seem to require intelligence. The development of programs capable of "playing" these games supported the idea that AI is possible.

Cognitive science, an interdisciplinary approach to the study of the mind, was influenced by many of the same factors that had an impact on the field of AI. Some of the traditional disciplines that contribute to cognitive science are AI, cognitive psychology, linguistics, neuroscience, and philosophy. Each discipline brings its own set of questions and techniques to the shared goal of understanding intelligence and the mind.

TRADITIONAL AI VERSUS COMPUTER SIMULATIONS

"Artificial intelligence" is a general term that includes a number of different approaches to developing intelligent machines. Two different philosophical approaches to the development of intelligent systems are traditional AI and computer simulations. This term can also refer to the development of hardware (equipment) or software (programs) for an AI project. The goal remains the same for traditional AI and computer simulations: the development of a system capable of performing a particular task that, if done by a human, would be considered intelligent.

The goal of traditional AI (sometimes called pure AI) is to develop systems to accomplish various tasks intelligently and efficiently. This approach makes no claims or assumptions about the manner in which humans process and perform a task, nor does it try to model human cognitive processes. A traditional AI project is unrestricted by the limitations of human information processing. One example of a traditional AI program would be earlier versions of Deep Blue, the chess program of International Business Machines (IBM). The ability of this program to successfully "play" chess depended on its ability to compute a larger number of possible board positions based on the current positions and then select the best move. This computational approach, while effective, lacks strategy and the ability to learn from previous games. A modified version of Deep Blue in 1997 eventually won a match against Gary Kasparov, the reigning chess champion at that time. In addition to the tradition AI approach, this particular version incorporated strategic advice from Joel Benjamin, a former US chess champion.

The goal of computer simulations is to develop programs that take into consideration the constraints of how humans perform various cognitive tasks and incorporate these constraints into a program (for example, the amount of information that humans can think about at any given time is limited). This approach can take into account how human information processing is affected by a number of mechanisms such as processing, storing, and retrieving information. Computer simulations vary in the extent to which the program models processes that can range from a single process to a model of the mind.

THEORETICAL ISSUES

A number of important theoretical issues influence the assumptions made in developing intelligent systems. Stan Franklin, in his book *Artificial Minds* (1995), presents these issues in what he labels the three debates for AI: Can computing machines be intelligent? Does the connectionist approach offer something that the symbolic approach does not? and Are internal representations necessary?

Thinking Machines. The issue of whether computing machines can be intelligent is typically presented as "Can computers think in the sense that humans do?" There are two positions regarding this question: weak AI and strong AI. Weak AI suggests that the utility of artificial intelligence is to aid in exploring human cognition through the development of computer models. This approach aids in testing the feasibility and completeness of the theory from a computational standpoint. Weak AI is considered by many experts in the field as a viable approach. Strong AI takes the stance that it is possible to develop a machine that can manipulate symbols to accomplish many of the tasks that humans can accomplish. Some would ascribe thought or intelligence to such a machine because of its capacity for symbol manipulation. Alan Turing proposed a test, the imitation game, later called the Turing test, as a possible criterion for determining if strong AI has been accomplished. Strong AI also has opponents stating that it is not possible for a program to be intelligent or to think. John Searle, a philosopher, presents an argument against the possibility of strong AI.

Turing proposes a potential test of intelligence as a criterion for determining whether a computer program is intelligent. The imitation game is a parlor game consisting of three people: an examiner, one man, and one woman. The examiner can ask the man or woman questions on any topic. Responses from the man and woman are read. The man's task is to convince the examiner that he is the woman. The woman's job is to convince the examiner that she is the woman. Turing then proposes replacing either the man or woman with a computer. The examiner's task, then, is to decide which one is human and which one is the computer. This version of the imitation game is called the Turing test. The program (computer) passes the test if the examiner cannot determine which responses are from the computer and which ones are from the human. The Turing test, then, serves as a potential criterion for determining if a program is intelligent. Philosopher Daniel Dennett, in his book *Brainchildren: Essays on Designing Minds* (1998), discusses the appropriateness and power of the Turing test. The Loebner Prize competition, an annual contest, uses a modified version of the Turing test to evaluate real AI programs.

Searle, for his part, proposed a thought experiment he called the Chinese room. This thought experiment provides an argument against the notion that computers can be intelligent. Searle suggests a room from which information can be fed both in and out. The information coming into the room is in Chinese. Inside the room is a person who does not understand Chinese, but this person does have access to a set of instructions that will allow the person to change one symbol to another. Searle argues that this person, while truly capable of manipulating the various symbols, has no understanding of the questions or responses. The person lacks true understanding even though, over time, the person may become proficient in this task. The end results look intelligent even though the symbols carry no meaning for the person manipulating them. Searle then argues that the same is true for computers. A computer will not be capable of intelligence since the symbols carry no meaning for the computer, and yet the output will look intelligent.

Connectionism Versus Symbolism. The second debate deals with the approaches to the cognitive architecture, the built-in constraints that specify the capabilities, components, and structures involved in cognition. The classic approach, or symbol system hypothesis, and the connectionist approach are both different cognitive architectures. Cognitive architecture can be thought of in terms of hardware of a computer; it can run a number of different programs but by its nature places constraints on how things are conducted. The questions here is, does the contribution of connectionism differ from that of traditional AI?

The physical symbol system hypothesis is a class of systems that suggests the use of symbols or internal representations, mental events, that stand for or represent items or events in the environment. These internal representations can be manipulated, used in computations, and transformed. Traditionally, this approach consists of serial processing (implementing one command at a time) of symbols. Two examples of this approach are John R. Anderson's adaptive control of thought theory of memory (ACT;) model (1983) and Allen Newell's *Soar* (1989). Both models are examples of architectures of cognition in which the goal is to account for all cognition.

The connectionist architecture is a class of systems that differ from the symbolic in that this model is modeled loosely on the brain and involves parallel processing, the ability to carry out a number of processes simultaneously. Other terms that have been used for this approach include parallel distributed processing (PDP), artificial neural networks (ANN), and the subsymbolic approach. The general makeup of a connectionist system is a network of nodes typically organized into various levels that loosely resemble neurons in the brain. These nodes have connections with other nodes. Like neurons in the brain, the nodes can have an excitatory or inhibitory effect on other nodes in the system. This is determined by the strength of the connection (commonly called the weight). Information then resides in these connections, not at the nodes, resulting in the information being distributed across the network. Learning in the system can take place during a training session in which adjustments are made to the weight during the training phase. An advantage that the connectionist approach has over the symbolic approach is the ability to retrieve partial information. This graceful degradation is the result of the information being distributed across the network. The system is still able to retrieve (partial) information even when part of the system does not work. This tends to be an issue for symbolic systems.

Internal Representation. Rodney Brooks, working at the Massachusetts Institute of Technology (MIT), proposed in 1986 a different approach to traditional AI, a system that relies on a central intelligence responsible for cognition. Brooks's approach, a subsumption architecture, relies on the interaction between perception and actuation systems as the basis for intelligence. The subsumption architecture starts with a level of basic behaviors (modules) and builds on this level with additional levels. Each new level can subsume the functions of lower levels and suppress the output for those modules. If a higher level is unable to respond or is delayed, then a lower level, which continues to function, can produce a result. The resulting action may not always be the most "intelligent," but the system is capable of doing something. For Brooks, intelligent behavior emerges from the combination of these simple behaviors. Furthermore, intelligence (or cognition) is in the eye of the beholder. Cog, one of Brooks's robot projects, is based on the subsumption architecture. Cog's movements and processing of visual information are not preprogrammed into the system. Experience with the environment plays an important role. Kismet, another project at MIT, is designed to show various emotional states in response to social interaction with others.

APPROACHES TO MODELING INTELLIGENCE

Intelligent tutoring systems (ITSs) are systems in which individual instruction can be tailored to the needs of a particular student. This is different from computer-aided instruction (CAI), in which everyone receives the same lessons. Key components typical of ITSs are the expert knowledge base (or teacher), the student model, instructional goals, and the interface. The student model contains the knowledge that the student has mastered as well as the areas in which he or she may have conceptual errors. Instruction can then be tailored to help elucidate the concepts with which the student is having difficulty.

An expert system attempts to capture an individual's expertise, and the program should then perform like an expert in that particular area. An expert system consists of two components: a knowledge base and an inference engine. The inference engine is the program of the expert system. It relies on the knowledge base, which "captures the knowledge" of an expert. Developing this component of the expert system is often time-consuming. Typically, the knowledge from the expert is represented in if-then statements (also called condition-action rules). If a particular condition is met, this leads to execution of the action part of the statement. Testing of the system often leads to repeating the knowledge-acquisition phase and modification of the condition-action rules. An example of an expert system is MYCIN, which diagnoses bacterial infections based on lab results. The performance of MYCIN was compared with that of physicians as well as with that of interns. MYCIN's performance was comparable to that of a physician.

Case-based reasoning systems use previous cases to analyze a new case. This type of reasoning is similar to law, in which a current situation is interpreted by use of previous types of problems. Case-based reasoning is designed around the so-called four R's: Retrieve relevant cases to the case at hand, reuse a previous case where applicable, revise strategy if no previous case is appropriate, and retain the new solution, allowing for the use of the case in the future.

Other approaches to modeling intelligence have included trying to model the intelligence of animals. Alife is an approach that involves the development of a computer simulation of the important features necessary for intelligent behavior. The animats approach constructs robots based on animal models. The idea here is to implement intelligence on a smaller scale rather than trying to model all of human intelligence. This approach may be invaluable in terms of developing systems that are shared in common with animals.

BIBLIOGRAPHY

Bechtel, William, and George Graham, eds. *A Companion to Cognitive Science*. Malden: Blackwell, 1998. Print.

Clark, Andy, and Josefa Toribio, eds. *Cognitive Architectures in Artificial Intelligence*. New York: Garland, 1998. Print.

Cristianini, Nello. "On the Current Paradigm in Artificial Intelligence." *AI Communications* 27.1 (2014): 37–43. Print.

Dennett, Daniel C. *Brainchildren: Essays on Designing Minds*. Cambridge: MIT P, 1998. Print.

Franklin, Stan. *Artificial Minds*. Cambridge.: MIT P, 1995. Print.

Gardner, Howard. *The Mind's New Science: A History of the Cognitive Revolution*. New York: Basic, 1998. Print.

Johnston, John. *The Allure of Machinic Life: Cybernetics, Artificial Life, and the New AI*. Cambridge: MIT P, 2008.

Muggleton, Stephen. "Alan Turing and the Development of Artificial Intelligence." *AI Communications* 27.1 (2014): 3–10. Print.

Vardi, Moshe Y. "Artificial Intelligence: Past and Future." *Communications of the ACM* 55.1 (2012): 5. Print.

Von Foerster, Heinz. *Understanding Understanding: Essays on Cybernetics and Cognition*. New York: Springer, 2003. Print.

Michael S. Bendele

See Also: Brain structure; Computer models of cognition; Concept formation; Conciousness; Decision making; Grammar and speech; Hypothesis development and testing; Intelligence; Learning; Memory; Memory: Empirical studies; Memory storage; Pattern recognition; Problem-solving stages; Problem-solving strategies; Rule-governed behavior.

Asperger syndrome

Type of Psychology: Clinical; Counseling; Developmental; Educational; Family; Neuropsychology; School

Asperger syndrome is a mild form of autistic spectrum disorder characterized by deficiencies in social and communication skills. It is differentiated from other autism spectrum disorders by normal early development and the absence of a language delay. Individuals with Asperger syndrome have obsessive interests in narrow subjects to the exclusion of everything else. This makes people with Asperger syndrome relationally awkward and emotionally stunted, but their ability to intensely focus on one thing makes them adept at certain tasks that others would find tedious and uninteresting.

Key Concepts

- Autism spectrum disorder
- Repetitive behaviors.
- Echolalia

- Interventions
- Alexithymia
- Pervasive developmental disorders

INTRODUCTION

Asperger syndrome (AS) is an autistic spectrum disorder (ASD) characterized by deficits in social interaction and communication, fixated interests, and repetitive, stereotypical behaviors. AS differs from other ASDs in that language skills and cognitive development tend to be relatively normal. AS is one of the five pervasive developmental disorders (PDDs) recognized by mental health professionals; the other four are childhood disintegrative disorder, Rett syndrome, pervasive developmental disorder (not otherwise specified), and autism.

The incidence and prevalence of AS vary substantially from one study to another, ranging from 0.03 to 4.84 per 1,000 people. Males are 1.6 to 4 times more likely to have AS than females.

The lack of standardization of diagnostic instruments for AS causes the majority of AS cases to be identified later in life when a patient experiences relational problems that result from the extremely literal and logical thought processes symptomatic of AS. Diagnosing AS and understanding these features can help close family members and friends adequately deal with them, and adult interventions that consist of training the AS individual in the right ways to communicate and deal with other people can enrich the lives of the AS patients and all those who interact with them. Without a proper diagnosis and intervention, AS individuals go from one failed relationship to another which can cause deep disappointment, depression, social withdrawal and isolation, and increased suicide risk.

Because of the tendency for AS individuals to have almost obsessive interests and their ability to focus on problems or subjects for long periods of time, AS has been dubbed the "geek syndrome" on the Internet. This characteristic of AS individuals makes them ably suited for tasks that most people would find impossible. This can make AS individuals some of the most creative and productive members of society, as illustrated by several famous people with AS that include Nobel Prize-winning economist Vernon Smith, electropop rocker Gary Numan, and Satoshi Tajiri, creator of Pokémon.

HISTORY

Eva Sucharewa, a Russian neuroscientist, was the first person to formally describe the symptoms of AS in a 1926 paper. In 1944, the Austrian pediatrician Hans Asperger published similar clinical descriptions of the condition that would later bear his name. Asperger based his diagnosis on detailed observations of four boys from his medical practice in Vienna. All four boys began to speak at approximately the same time as other children, but they had difficulty using pronouns correctly, and the content of their speech was abnormal and pedantic and consisted of lengthy discussions on their favorite subjects. They often repeated a word or phrase over and over again in a stereotypical fashion. Asperger also noted that these boys displayed impaired two-way social interaction, a complete disregard for the demands of their environment, repetitive and stereotyped play, and isolated areas of interests. At school, the boys routinely talked back to and sassed their teachers, hit and verbally abused other children, and lashed out and knocked objects over. They seemed to have no regard for the feelings of others or the consequences of their actions. Asperger called their condition "autistic psychopathy." Furthermore, those with this condition were capable of creative and original innovation in their chosen fields and showed excellent, logical abstract thinking. Because of their ability to talk at length and in great detail about their favorite subject, Asperger referred to these boys as "little professors." Unfortunately, because Asperger published in German and during wartime, his work was not widely read.

The German psychiatrist Gerhard Bosch first used the term "Asperger's syndrome" in a 1962 monograph. The British physician Lorna Wing popularized this term in the English-speaking medical community in her influential and widely-read 1981 publication of a series of case studies of children who showed similar symptoms. Wing considered AS part of the "autistic continuum" and thought that AS could be a mild variant of autism in intelligent children. The third edition and revised third edition of the *Diagnostic and Statistical Manual of Mental Disorders* (DSM-III) adopted Wing's views of AS but did not provide any specific definition or diagnostic criteria for it. The first systematic studies of AS appeared in the late 1980s and the diagnostic criteria for Asperger's syndrome were outlined 1989. At this time, Asperger's original work became more widely available in English when Uta Frith, an early autism researcher, translated his original paper in 1991. AS became a distinct diagnosis in 1992, when it was included in the 10th edition of the World Health Organization's diagnostic manual, *International Classification of Diseases* (ICD-10), and in 1994, when it was added to the fourth edition of the DSM.

In May 2013, the publication of the fifth edition of the DSM subsumed AS into the overarching category of ASD and designated AS as a mild form of ASD. This reclassification was based on work from several psychiatric research groups that failed to find significant differences between AS and high-functioning autism (HFA). However, more recent analyses of AS and HFA have demarcated distinct clinical and neurological features between these two conditions, and some mental health professionals think that future DSM editions will distinguish AS from HFA.

SIGNS AND SYMPTOMS

AS is a "wide spectrum" disorder which means that the characteristics of those diagnosed with AS vary substantially from person to person. There are, however, particular features commonly observed in the majority of AS patients.

Obsessive interests. Many children with AS become experts on a single object or topic, often to the exclusion of other topics. These compulsive interests can range from household objects such as vacuum cleaners and lawn mowers to model cars, trains, or computers, and they will usually collect, list, and number their objects of interest. The acquisition of large amounts of information on their topic of interest motivates AS children to incessantly talk about it, but their conversations with other people will consist of a collection of facts without any useful synthesis of those facts. Their desire to speak only of their singular interest makes conversation with them difficult.

Distinctive speech patterns. AS individuals often speak in a monotone voice, devoid of rhythm and with a limited range of intonation. Children with AS often lack the capacity to properly modulate the volume of their voices and must be routinely reminded to speak softly. AS children can possess large vocabularies for their age, and the pedantic content and sometimes formal nature of their speech can cause them to sound much older than they actually are.

Routines. People with AS tend to rigidly adhere to various rules, rituals, and methodical routines, and disruptions of these routines can generate anxiety or even anger. An AS child, for example, might take the same route to school every day and wear particular outfits for specific days of the week. They also may engage in repetitive behaviors including finger flapping or twisting or whole body movements and can occasionally include self-injury. Echolalia, the routine repetition of a word or phrase, is sometimes observed. AS children also show obsessions with objects and how they are arranged (e.g., they may spend hours lining up toy cars or trains).

Diminished social and communication skills. AS individuals have trouble reading social cues and tend to give inappropriate social and emotional responses. They have difficulty interpreting gestures, vocal inflections and changes in tone, and facial expressions. AS individuals also show alexithymia which is difficulty describing or even identifying emotions. They lack social skills that most people take for granted. For example, AS individuals often fail to detect when the listener has lost interest in their monologues. They also do not easily understand irony, jokes, or sarcasm, and they tend to not understand the figurative use of language. AS individuals may not understand basic rules of social engagement such as the appropriate topics for conversation or the proper distance to stand next to someone. Because of their inability to master the rules of social interaction, AS individuals may come off across as insensitive or uncaring. Additionally, because of their tendency to talk about their singular interest, AS individuals often spend a good deal of time alone. Social isolation can cause them to become withdrawn and inured to any desire for companionship or depressed and anxious.

Motor and sensory difficulties. Though not a required sign of AS, many AS children display poor physical coordination, and they typically show delayed mastery of physical skills such as riding a bicycle or tying their shoes. Their gait is sometimes bouncy and odd. They may also have poor handwriting. AS children are often sensitive to loud noises and unfamiliar textures. Particular foods are often eschewed because of the way they feel in their mouths.

CAUSE

The precise cause of AS is presently unknown. Inheritance studies have firmly established that AS and ASD run in families. Several twin studies in which the AS rates of identical twins who were separated at birth and adopted by different families were compared with nonidentical twins subjected to the same conditions have confirmed a significant genetic contribution to the development of AS. However, the precise genes responsible for the onset of AS have not been definitively identified, and it is likely that AS is due to more than one gene. The candidate genes that have been identified encode enzymes that help synthesize neurotransmitters and neurotransmitter receptors, nerve cell adhesion molecules and migration factors, proteins involved in gene expression (transcription factors), cell signaling molecules, and several others. Nevertheless, the role these genes play in the development of AS remains unclear.

In a few cases, exposure of the fetus to particular chemicals during the first eight weeks after conception has been linked to AS. Other environmental factors might also contribute to the cause of AS. Brain scans of AS patients, while revealing abnormalities in particular AS patients, have not established that such structural defects are common to most AS patients.

DIAGNOSIS

No standardized diagnostic tests exist for AS. There are several screening instruments in use such as the Autism Diagnostic Interview-Revised which consists of a semi-structured parent interview and the Autism Diagnostic Observation Schedule which includes a conversation and play-based interview with the child. Unfortunately, the absence of standardization of AS screening instruments may cause children to receive disparate diagnoses from different physicians.

Typically, the child first receives an initial diagnosis during his or her routine check-up by the family doctor. This is followed by a more extensive series of tests by a medical team that consists of psychologists, neurologists, psychiatrists, speech therapists, and others who specialize in diagnosing AS children. The team usually assesses the child's verbal and non-verbal communication skills, speech patterns, ability to carry on a conversation and the content of their conversations, motor coordination, and cognitive abilities. Interviews with the parents to determine the developmental history of the child are also used to confirm the diagnosis.

THERAPIES

There is no cure for AS, but several available interventions can help AS children and adults manage their condition and live more fulfilling lives. Applied behavior analysis teaches AS children social skills to help them more successfully interact with other people. Cognitive behavior therapy gives AS children the skills they need to manage stress and temper tantrumsand mediate their obsessive interests and repetitive routines to live more balanced lives. Occupational therapy can help AS children overcome their clumsiness and improve their coordination. Social communication intervention is a speech therapy program designed for AS children to help them learn how to master the back-and-forth nature of normal conversation.

In some cases medications can ameliorate the symptoms of AS. Such medications include the antipsychotic medicine risperidone (Risperdal) which can reduce irritability, aggression, repetitive behavior, and depression in AS children. Likewise stimulants such as methylphenidate (Ritalin, Concerta, Metadate) and clonidine (Catapres) can reduce the hyperactivity that afflicts high-functioning AS children. Another group of drugs called the selective serotonin reuptake inhibitors (SSRIs) can effectively reduce the repetitive interests and behaviors in adults with AS but is not indicated for children or adolescents.

AS CULTURE

Because of the Internet, AS individuals have formed their own communities and refer to themselves as "aspies." Internet sites such as the Wrong Planet site provide ways for AS individuals to connect with each other.

AS individuals have lobbied to change the perception of AS from a neurological disease that needs to be treated or cured to a difference that has its advantages. Some have even argued that AS should be removed from the DSM. However, it is the judgment of most mental health professionals that even though AS individuals can make positive contributions to society, their emotional difficulties that result from lack of empathy makes it useful to include AS in the DSM.

BIBLIOGRAPHY

Attwood, T. (2008). *The complete guide of Asperger's syndrome.* London, UK: Jessica Kingsley. A very readable and useful compendium of case studies, research summaries, and personal anecdotes by a clinical psychologist who specializes in AS.

Cook O'Toole, J. (2012). *The Asperkid's (secret) book of social rules: The handbook of not-so-obvious social guidelines for tweens and teens with Asperger syndrome*. London, UK: Jessica Kingsley. A self-help book for young people with AS by a mother with AS.

Emlet, M. R. (2011). *Asperger syndrome.* Greensboro, NC: New Growth Press. An informative, sensitive book on AS by a Christian counselor who is also a physician and writes for pastors and lay workers who want to know more about AS children and adults.

Smith Myles, B., & Southwick, J. (2005). *Asperger syndrome and difficult moments: Practicalsolutions for tantrums, rage and meltdowns*. Shawnee Mission, KS: Autism Asperger Publishing Company. Practical advice for parents of AS children by a recognized AS expert.Welton, J. (2003).

Can I tell you about Asperger syndrome?: A guide for friends and family. London, UK: Jessica Kingsley. For children between ages 7-15 on how to successfully deal with family members or friends who have AS.

Michael A. Buratovich

See Also: Autism spectrum disorders; Communication disorders; Pervasive developmental disorders; Social interaction.

Asian Americans/Pacific Islanders and mental health

Type of psychology: Multicultural psychology; Psychotherapy; Stress

The number of Asian Americans and Pacific Islanders in the American population is growing rapidly. Although research on the utilization of mental health services by this group has been inconsistent, evidence suggests that individuals from Asian cultures tend to underutilize formal mental health services. It is not clear, however, whether this is primarily due to discriminatory mental health practices and culturally unaware mental health practitioners or to cultural values that inhibit self-referral.

Key Concepts

- Acculturation
- Asian Americans
- Ethnic subgroups
- Immigrants
- Pacific Islanders

INTRODUCTION

Asian Americans/Pacific Islanders constitute the fastest-growing ethnic category in the United States according to the US Census Bureau (2010). Between the 2000 and 2010, the population of US residents of Asian descent grew 46 percent between the 2000 and 2010 census, while the population of Native Hawaiians and other Pacific Islanders grew 40 percent. As of the first decade of the twenty-first century, the majority of every Asian American subgroup, except for Japanese Americans, was foreign born. The acculturation process—the acquisition of values, norms, language, and behavior when an Asian American and Pacific Islander immigrant moves from one culture to another—can place the individual at risk for serious illness or depression. Studies of immigrants in the United States suggest that the acculturation process places the immigrant at risk for a lifetime of psychiatric disorders. Whether illness occurs is influenced by a number of factors, including the degree to which reality matches the immigrant's expectations.

THE ASIAN AMERICAN COMMUNITY

Although Asian Americans are all placed in the same ethnic category, they are a very heterogeneous group, representing from thirty to fifty different cultural subgroups, depending on whether Pacific Islanders are included. Subgroups include East Asians such as the Chinese, Koreans, and the Japanese; Southeast Asians such as the Vietnamese, Laotians, Cambodians, Thais, Malaysians, Indonesians, the Burmese, Hmongs, and Filipinos; and South Asians such as people from India, Bangladesh, Bhutan, the Maldives, Nepal, Pakistan, and Sri Lanka. Pacific Islanders include the indigenous peoples of Hawaii, Samoa, and Guam.

Much of the literature regarding the psychology of Asian Americans/Pacific Islanders is based on the Chinese and Japanese subgroups and therefore does not necessarily apply to the other subgroups, particularly the Pacific Islanders, whose cultural traditions are markedly different from those of Asian Americans.

The stereotypical image of Asian Americans is of a well-educated and financially successful group of people. In fact, the US Census Bureau reported in 2011 that the median income of Asian American families exceeds that of American families as a whole by more than $16,500; in 2010, 52.4 percent of all Asian/Pacific Islanders, versus 29 percent of US residents overall, hold at least a bachelor's degree. However, despite the group's higher median income, poverty was slightly more prevalent among the Asian/Pacific Islander community at 12.5 percent than among whites at 12.3 percent, according to data from the US Census Bureau's report, Income, Poverty, and Health Insurance Coverage in the United States: 2009. A 2004 study found that 53 percent of Hmongs, 41 percent of Cambodians, and 33 percent of Laotians had household incomes of less than fifteen thousand dollars, compared with 22 percent of non-Hispanic whites. Also, while the Asian American/Pacific Islander group exhibits a high level of educational achievement, it contains large undereducated populations. Fewer than 14 percent of Cambodians, Laotians, and Hmongs twenty-five years and older have a bachelor's degree.

UNDERUTILIZATION OF MENTAL HEALTH SERVICES

The successful image of Asian Americans is at odds with the growing recognition that this population needs more mental health services than it receives. The underutilization of such services may be due to a number of factors, including discriminatory mental health practices, the shame and disgrace associated with having mental or emotional problems in many Asian cultures, language barriers, and lack of insurance. In addition, many Asians place a high value on handling problems within the family, as opposed to relying on outside resources, especially in a culture that is not their own. Asian Americans have demonstrated a pattern of prematurely terminating psychotherapy.

In recent years, research has been conducted to explore how differences in birthplace (overseas or in the United States), age, social status, and immigration status may affect the prevalence of mental health disorders, as well as the likelihood of seeking professional help. The National Latino and Asian American Study, concluded in 2003, found that mental illness rates are lower among Asian Americans than whites, but Asian Americans are less likely to seek treatment for their problems. However, the study also found that although Vietnamese Americans are diagnosed with mental illness at rates similar to those of other Asian American groups, they were found to be much more likely to seek help, possibly because many of them had experienced war-related trauma in their country of origin. Asian Americans who were born in the United States or immigrated at an early age were found to have higher rates of mental illness than Asian Americans as a whole, perhaps because they were more exposed to American culture and thus experienced more conflict in everyday life.

Mental health centers typically do not reach out to any ethnic population, including Asian Americans/Pacific Islanders, unless they employ professionals from that ethnicity. However, some mental health centers and professionals are taking a holistic approach to mental health for Asian Americans by combining primary and mental health care. This approach is effective for Asian immigrants, who often assume that their illness has a physical rather than mental cause. They therefore typically consult a physician instead of a mental health professional with conditions caused or worsened by mental or emotional problems. The holistic approach is also effective for integrating Western and Eastern philosophies and finding a way to make dealing with mental illness more acceptable for Asians.

THE NATURE OF THE PROBLEMS

Often the mental health problems of Asian Americans are directly related to the immigrant experience. Learning to deal with the values, norms, language, and behaviors of another culture often adds to the stress levels of immigrants and later generations of their families who identify with the ethnic subgroup and want to maintain its traditions. Common stressors for Asian Americans/Pacific Islanders include intergenerational conflict, the process of developing cultural identities, immigration status, and racism.

Stress, depression, and suicide have been identified as mental health problems within the Asian American community. Asian immigrants may become depressed when they are unable to obtain professional employment equivalent to the highly respected positions they held in their home country because of language difficulties or differences in accreditation. According to data compiled by the Asian Counseling and Referral Service (ACRS), 40 percent of Southeast Asian refugees have depression and significant anxiety. Many older Cambodian and Vietnamese refugees experience post-traumatic stress disorder. According to the ACRS, female Asian Americans have the highest suicide rates among female Americans ages fifteen to twenty-four. Additionally, Asian women aged sixty-five or older are ten times more likely to commit suicide than are their white counterparts. A 2004 study found significant emotional problems among Pacific Islanders. Higher rates of depression and attempted suicide were found among native Hawaiian adolescents than their non-Hawaiian counterparts.

THE ROLE OF CULTURAL VALUES

People vary in the degree that they experience cultural stress and in the degree to which they reveal its direct relationship to the problem they are experiencing. Mental health personnel who are culturally competent will be sensitive to the increased possibility for this type of stress to be experienced by Asian Americans/Pacific Islanders.

Mental health professionals treating Asian Americans will find it useful to know their traditional cultural values and how they differ from Western values. At the same time, they must remember that great variation exists within and between groups. In addition, the degree to which Asian Americans adhere to traditional cultural values will vary, influenced by factors such as their place of birth (overseas or the United States) and their family upbringing (traditional or unconventional).

An examination of one subgroup, the East Asians, reveals both differences of the group as a whole from Western culture and variations within the subgroup. East Asian cultures, some of the oldest continuously existing cultures in the world, have significantly different values from Western cultures. For example, the prominent East Asian philosophical approaches to life are Confucianism, Daoism, and Buddhism rather than Judaism and Christianity. The family and the family network are valued above the individual. Although Western families value the autonomy of their members, families that adhere to the Confucian tradition are more likely to support the establishment of a hierarchy among their members. Under the Confucian tradition, an individual must adhere to a code of conduct that reflects the beliefs of the family and kinship network to which the individual belongs, rather than one that reflects the individual's beliefs.

Just as important are the differences among East Asian cultures. Individuals from Western cultures often assume there is little difference among Chinese, Japanese, and Koreans. In reality, there are many differences, the most obvious of which is language.

A group of Asian American mental health practitioners identified cultural values or traits that they believed played a role in mental health settings. Listed in declining order of importance, they were feelings of shame and guilt, respect for others based on role and status, reserved interpersonal styles of behavior, the stigma of mental illness, the restraint of self-expression, a group orientation, the high value placed on achievement, a sense of duty and obligation, and role expectations.

Although mental health professionals must be mindful of Asian cultural influences, they also must be careful not to automatically assign Asian values and traits to Asian American individuals.

BIBLIOGRAPHY

Kline, Michael V., and Robert M. Huff. *Health Promotion in Multicultural Populations: A Handbook for Practitioners and Students*. 3d ed. Thousand Oaks: Sage, 2015. Print.

Lee, Wanda M. L., et al. *Introduction to Multicultural Counseling for Helping Professionals*. 3d ed. New York: Routledge, 2013. Print.

McAuliffe, Garrett, et al., eds. *Culturally Alert Counseling*. 2d ed. Thousand Oaks: Sage, 2013. Print.

McGoldrick, M., et al., eds. *Ethnicity and Family Therapy*. 3d ed. New York: Guilford, 2005. Print.

Shea, Munyi, and Christine J. Yeh. "Asian American Students' Cultural Values, Stigma, and Relational Self-Construal: Correlates of Attitudes Toward Professional Help Seeking." *Journal of Mental Health Counseling* 30.2 (2008): 157–172. Print.

Suzuki, L. A., et al. *Handbook of Multicultural Assessment: Clinical, Psychological, and Educational Applications*. 3d ed. San Francisco: Jossey-Bass, 2008. Print.

Uba, L. *Asian Americans: Personality Patterns, Identity, and Mental Health*. 1994. New York: Guilford, 2003. Print.

US Census Bureau. "The 2012 Statistical Abstract." *US Census Bureau*. 28 May 2014. Web. 28 May 2014.

US Census Bureau. "Profile America Facts for Features: Asian/Pacific American Heritage Month: May 2013." *US Census Bureau News*. US Census Bureau's Public Information Office, 27 Mar. 2013. Digital file.

Voget, D. L., et al. "Perceived Public Stigma and the Willingness to Seek Counseling: The Mediating Roles of Self-Stigma and Attitudes Toward Counseling." *Journal of Counseling Psychology* 54 (2007): 40–50. Print.

Lillian J. Breckenridge

See Also: Anxiety disorders; Cross-cultural psychology; Cultural competence; Culture and diagnosis; Culture-bound syndromes; Depression; Help-seeking; Identity crises; Multicultural psychology; Suicide.

Assessment

Type of psychology: Psychological methodologies

Assessment is a general term for a broad range of processes for testing, measuring, and evaluating performance. Standardized, alternative, and self-assessment methods are used for the purposes of replacement, diagnosis of performance, and provision of formative and summative evaluation. The quality of an assessment depends on its validity and reliability.

Key Concepts

- Alternative assessment
- Diagnostic assessment
- Formative assessment
- Placement assessment

- Self-assessment
- Standard assessment
- Summative assessment
- Validity and reliability of assessment

INTRODUCTION

Every person has experienced some type of assessment. Those who have had public education in the United States are familiar with the SAT Reasoning Test and the Iowa Test of Basic Skills (ITBS) administered in schools. Those whose native language is not English and have pursued education in the United States particularly know about the Test of English as Foreign Language (TOEFL). Those who have applied to graduate schools are familiar with the Graduate Record Examination (GRE) or the Graduate Management Admission Test (GMAT). Assessment is used quite often, for different purposes, in daily life.

Assessment is a general term for a broad range of processes that includes testing, measuring, and evaluation. Testing is simply a particular part of assessment, usually a set of questions that participants must answer in a fixed time period and under certain conditions.

Measuring is a process that assigns numbers to assessment results, such as the number of correct or incorrect answers to a project or performance. A rubric rating scale is usually created to record quantitative or qualitative data.

Evaluation is a process of assessment that emphasizes a value or a judgment to match with the correlated objectives of a project, an instruction, or a performance to see how well the project or performance is done.

STANDARD, ALTERNATIVE, AND SELF-ASSESSMENT

There are different types of assessment, using specific tests, measurements, and ways of evaluation, and they are used for different purposes. Generally, the assessment can be classified as standardized assessment, alternative assessment, or self-assessment.

Standardized assessment adopts standardized tests to measure and evaluate a performance. Standardized tests are always developed by a major test publisher for a large population and administered under the same conditions and time limits to all participants. The SAT Reasoning Test is a typical example. Standard assessment is carried out to see how the results are norm-referenced for interpretation, that is, to compare an individual's performance with the performance of his or her peers. For example, a person's SAT score can be ranked in percentile compared with others of the same age or grade. If a person's percentile rank is 84, that means that 84 percent of all of the scores are lower than this individual's score.

According to educator James H. McMillan, in the 2007 edition of *Classroom Assessment: Principles and Practice for Effective Instruction*, alternative assessment and self-assessment are weighted more toward assessment of the process than assessment of a product or a performance. Individually created tests, portfolios, exhibitions, journals, and other forms of assessment are commonly used. Alternative assessment is intended to engage an individual in the process of learning and thinking and in demonstrating during a performance. For example, a teacher who adopts a performance-based assessment will observe and make a judgment about the student's demonstration of a skill or a competency in creating a product, constructing a response, or making a presentation. Self-assessment is a part of the learning process aimed at seeing where one is and how one is doing. Instead of relying on feedback from others, the person is expected to self-assess: to think about and change what he or she is doing while doing it. Self-assessment is also a reflective practice to bring past events to a conscious level and to devise appropriate ways to think, feel, and behave in the future, through techniques such as an annual review portfolio or a self-checklist.

OTHER ASSESSMENTS

According to educator Donald Orlich in 2006's *Teaching Strategies*, assessment can also be classified by the use of tests: placement assessment, diagnostic assessment, formative assessment, and summative assessment. Either standardized tests or self-made tests can be adopted in the process of these assessments.

Placement assessment determines whether an individual has the required knowledge and skills to begin a new position. In education, placement-assessment instruments are those pretests to see whether a student can be accepted or placed into a certain grade for instruction. Spontaneous, informal observations and interviews are also usually adopted in the placement assessment.

Diagnostic assessment tends to identify an individual's strengths and weaknesses. For example, the Kaufman Assessment Battery for Children (K-ABC) and Woodcock-Johnson Psychoeducational Battery-Revised (WJ-R) are two specific diagnostic assessment instruments. K-ABC is used to diagnose the learning potential and learning styles of children between 2.5 and 12.5

years old. WJ-R is used to assess the intellectual and academic development of individuals from preschool to adulthood.

Formative assessment monitors a person's learning or working progress to provide feedback to enrich knowledge and skills. It is believed that formative assessments and feedback can play an important role in supporting a performance. The portfolio is one of the commonly adopted formative-assessment instruments in education today. The data that are collected as part of the process of evaluating students' learning progress are used to help teachers provide feedback to students, make changes in teaching strategies, and inform parents of specific needs from family for students' success.

Summative assessment assesses final results, achievements, or projects for decision making. It occurs at the conclusion of instruction, such as at the end of a teaching unit or of an academic year. Instead of establishing students' proficiency in knowledge and skills, it provides an overview of achievement across the knowledge base and skills. Term papers, chapter achievement tests, final exams, and research projects are often adopted for a summative assessment in schools.

VALIDITY AND RELIABILITY

The quality of an assessment depends on its validity and its reliability. Validity refers to the appropriateness of the inferences, uses, and consequences that result from the assessment. It is the degree to which a test measures what it is supposed to measure. A specific test may be valid for a particular purpose and for a particular group. Therefore, the question is not whether a test is valid or invalid, but rather what it is valid for and for which group. However, it is important that a test is valid to measure or evaluate a typical situation or typical group of students. In the 2004 edition of *Assessment*, John Salvia and James E. Ysseldyke classify validity as content validity, criterion-related validity, or construct validity. Content validity is the degree to which a test's items actually represent the contents to be measured. Test items cannot measure each or every content area, but it is expected that the test items will adequately sample the content area. If a test does not measure what students are supposed to learn, the test score will not reflect a student's achievement. Criterion-related validity is the degree to which an individual's performance can be estimated on the assessment procedure being validated. Concurrent criterion-related validity and predictive criterion-related validity are commonly described. Concurrent criterion-related validity refers to how accurately a test score is related to the scores on another test administered or to some other valid criterion available at the same time. Predictive criterion-related validity refers to how accurately a test score can predict how well an individual will do in the future. Thus, since the validity of a test is related to a criterion, the criterion itself, either for the test or for its prediction for the future, must be valid.

Construct validity is the degree to which a test measures an intended theoretical construct or characteristic. The construct is "invented" to explain behavior; it cannot be seen, but its effect can be observed. For example, it is hypothesized that there is something called intelligence that is related to learning achievement; therefore, the higher the intelligence one has, the better the learning achievement one will make. A test is developed to measure how much intelligence an individual has. If the individual's test score and learning achievement were high, it would be evidence to support the construct validity of the test. However, if the higher score on the test did not indicate a higher learning achievement, it would not necessarily mean that the test did not measure learning achievement; the hypotheses related to the learning achievement of a high-intelligence individual might be incorrect.

Reliability refers to the dependability, trustworthiness, or consistency of the test results. It is the degree to which a test consistently measures whatever it measures. If a test is not reliable, then the results of the test will be expected to be different every time the test is administered.

There are three types of reliability: internal-consistency reliability, test-retest reliability, and inter-scorer reliability. When an individual is given a test with two similar but different groups of questions, the results from the two parts should be the same. It means the two groups of tests are internal-consistency reliable. The results from one part of the test items can be generalized to the other group of test items. If a test is administered at two different times, such as in a test and retest procedure, the results of the tests administered at different times should be quite stable. That means the results of a test and a retest are highly correlated. In this case, one test result can be generalized to the same test administered at a different time, for example, a week later. Inter-scorer reliability indicates that when two or more different scorers score a test, the results judged by different scorers are almost the same and highly correlated. With high inter-scorer reliability, one individual scorer's judgment can be generalized to different scorers.

An interesting relationship exists between validity and reliability. A valid assessment is always reliable, because when an assessment measures what it is supposed to measure, it will be reliable every time the assessment is administered. However, a reliable assessment is not necessarily valid, since an assessment may consistently measure the wrong thing.

BIBLIOGRAPHY

Bates, John A., and Brian A. Lanza. "Conducting Psychology Student Research via the Mechanical Turk Crowdsourcing Service." *North American Journal of Psychology* 15.2 (2013): 385–94. Print.

Maroemau, C. "Self-Assessment at Work: Outcomes of Adult Learners' Reflections on Practice." *Research Methods 01/02*. Ed. Mary Renck Jalongo, Gail Gerlach, and Wenfan Yan. Guilford: McGraw-Hill, 2001. Print.

McMillan, James H. *Classroom Assessment: Principles and Practice for Effective Instruction*. 2d ed. Boston: Pearson/Allyn & Bacon, 2007. Print.

Orlich, D., R. Harder, and R. Callahan. *Teaching Strategies*. Boston: Houghton, 2006. Print.

Ruiz-Primo, M. A., S. E. Schultz, and M. Li. "Comparison of the Reliability and Validity of Scores from Two Concept-Mapping Techniques." *Journal of Research in Science Teaching* 38.2 (2001): 260–78. Print.

Salvia, J., and J. E. Ysseldyke. *Assessment*. 7th ed. Boston: Houghton, 2004. Print.

Schmitt, Neal. "Research in Consulting Psychology Journal: Practice and Research: Reactions and Suggestions." *Consulting Psychology Journal: Practice & Research* 65.4 (2013): 278–83. Print.

Zeliff, N. D. "Alternative Assessment." *National Business Education Yearbook* (2000): 91–102. Print.

Ronghua Ouyang

SEE ALSO: Ability tests; Career and personnel testing; Career Occupational Preference System (COPS); College entrance examinations; Creativity: Assessment; General Aptitude Test Battery (GATB); Human resource training and development; Intelligence tests; Interest inventories; Kuder Occupational Interest Survey (KOIS); Peabody Individual Achievement Test (PIAT); Race and intelligence; Scientific methods; Stanford-Binet test; Strong Interest Iventory (SII); Survey research: Questionaires and interviews; Testing: Historical perspectives; Wechsler Intelligence Scale for Children Third Edition (WISC-III).

Assessment of the Hispanic community

TYPE OF PSYCHOLOGY: Assessment; Cross-cultural psychology; Psychopathology

A growing proportion of the population is Hispanic. Thus, appropriate assessment approaches are urgently needed in order to accurately and validly work with this community. Assessment of the Hispanic community attends to professional guidelines as well as scientific advancements in the field. Particular attention to bilingual influences in normative and atypical development as well as in the creation and selection of measures is needed.

KEY CONCEPTS

- Communicative proficiency
- Cognitive academic language proficiency
- Translation
- Multilingual assessment

INTRODUCTION

According to the 2010 census, Hispanics constituted 16% (or 50.5 million) of the nation's population. In a decade this ethnic group grew 43% and they accounted for over half the growth of the country's total population. As of 2013, Hispanics represented the largest ethnic minority in the country, and it is expected that by the year 2060, 128.8 million Latinos (or 31% of the nation's total population) will be living in the United States. When examining Hispanics by country of origin several trends are evident. For example, Mexicans had the largest population increase over the course of this century's first decade and were the largest Hispanic group in the United States. Puerto Ricans constituted the second largest group followed by Cubans. In total, these three groups represent approximately three quarters of the total Hispanic community. Additionally, census data suggests that 75% of Hispanics reside in eight states: California, Texas, Florida, New York, Illinois, Arizona, New Jersey, and Colorado.

In 2012, the average income for Hispanics was $39,005 (the country's was $51, 324), and more than a quarter of them experienced poverty. Recent household demographic information estimates that over 70% of Latinos speak Spanish at home. Further, Hispanic married couples are more likely to have children compared to the nation's average household. At present, 1 out of 4 children in the United States is Hispanic, and by 2050 it will be 1 in 3. Therefore, these children will be an important part of our future workforce. Unfortunately, more than 60% of Latino children live in low-income families, making them more likely to live in crowded houses and neighborhoods with high crime rates and less likely to access quality health and education services. Studies have also found that they are at greater risk for obesity and mental health difficulties, including depression and suicidal ideation among adolescent girls. Therefore, greater investment in education and health programs could prove invaluable for the Hispanic community. For example, investment in early childhood programs promoting strong foundations for school readiness have been evidenced to be beneficial, particularly for young Hispanic families.

Several protective factors within the Hispanic community are noteworthy. For example, a strong value is placed on close familial ties. Most children live with both parents and report frequent shared family meals. Extended family members are also valued and represent a strong social support system, particularly during times of distress. Furthermore, Hispanic children show strong socio-emotional skills when entering kindergarten and the number of adolescents who drop from high school, smoke, or drink has been steadily decreasing.

PROFESSIONAL GUIDELINES FOR ASSESSING HISPANICS

According to the American Psychological Association's Ethical Principles of Psychologists and Code of Conduct, the work of psychologists is driven by the principles of beneficence and non-maleficence, fidelity and responsibility, integrity, justice, and respect for people's rights and dignity. This means that psychologists strive to benefit their clients, promote trusting relationships, and are responsible and transparent in their work. Additionally, they recognize that every individual deserves equal quality of services. In this vein, psychologists strive to protect the right to privacy and confidentiality and consider cultural and socio-demographic factors to avoid prejudice. When conducting psychological assessments with their clients (including Hispanics), psychologists should demonstrate competency in the administration, scoring, and interpretation of measures. Importantly, they use validated measures for the community. If this is not possible, psychologists document and acknowledge the strengths and weaknesses of findings.

The Guidelines on Multicultural Education, Training, Research, Practice, and Organizational Change for Psychologists, developed by the American Psychological Association, also encourage psychologists to understand and consider cultural factors when providing services to ethnic minorities, including Hispanics. For instance, acculturation, education, cultural values, beliefs around

Photo: iStock

therapy and testing, and preferred language should be taken into account in assessment. They make sure whether the constructs being measured present similarily or differently amongst cultural groups. For example, studies show that somatic symptoms related to anxiety are more commonly endorsed in Hispanics compared to other ethnic groups. Therefore, culturally competent professionals would consider assessing these symptoms when suspecting that a Hispanic client might suffer from an anxiety disorder. Psychologists strive to communicate test results using language that can be understood, while avoiding discriminatory practices. If psychologists do not feel comfortable assessing a particular ethnic group, they make appropriate referrals.

The Council of National Psychological Associations for the Advancement of Ethnic Minority Interest has also written specific guidelines when working with ethnic minorities. The National Latina/o Psychological Association is part of this group. In the Guidelines for Research in Ethnic Minority Groups, they highlight significant variability within the Hispanic community at the level of language proficiency, country of origin, education attainment, socio-economic status, and acculturation, amongst other variables. These aspects must be considered when administering a psychological measure. For example, the guidelines note that with paper and pencil tasks, reading proficiency needs to be taken into account while with verbal tasks, psychologists should be mindful that English proficiency does not reflect Spanish abilities (both at the oral and written levels). In sum, heterogeneity in the Latino community should not be ignored when administering and interpreting results. Rather, psychologists should be attentive to differences that exist within the Hispanic community. In an achieving such goals, it is recommended that psychologists working with Hispanics seek training to become culturally competent.

DIAGNOSTIC AND ASSESSMENT RECOMMENDATIONS FOR HISPANICS

In addition to the professional guidelines, the assessment of Hispanics should stem from empirically based knowledge and scientific advancements in the field. The cumulative body of this work underlies the following six recommendations:

1) Ask all clients about their racial and ethnic heritage as well as the languages they speak. Clinicians should not assume that a client is Hispanic by skin color, comportment, name, English fluency, or pronunciation. There is tremendous variability within the Hispanic community across all of these dimensions. Misidentification of racial/ethnic heritage and language abilities can lead to incorrect case conceptualizations, along with misestimating neurocognitive abilities. For example, in the case of accents, a client may be fully fluent in two languages and not have an accent in either one. This is particularly the case for individuals who migrated early in life as they are less likely to have accents than those who migrated as adults.

2) Consider the length of residence in the United States when assessing linguistic and learning abilities. Different trajectories exist for the development of language and academic skills over time. Namely, individuals (including children) develop communicative proficiency at a quick pace. Within one to three years of immigrating to a country, individuals acquire receptive and expressive skills and can engage in substantive conversations in their second language. However, it takes five to seven years to fully develop the deeper linguistic skills needed to engage in extensive reading and writing (termed Cognitive Academic Language Proficiency). The timeframe for bilingual development is essentially similar to monolingual development where children learn to speak well around the ages of 2-3 years and then read and write between 5-7 years. Thus, assessment approaches and interpretations of results are improved if these elements are taken into consideration with the immigrant Hispanic community.

3) Assess in the client's multiple languages, to the extent possible. Immigrant Hispanics may have knowledge and abilities within and across their languages. Thus, assessments in only one language may underestimate the abilities of bilingual Hispanics. This is the case even if the client speaks English fluently. Assessments conducted solely in English yield an understanding of present English abilities, rather than complete abilities. Only by assessing in both languages can the full skills of immigrant Hispanics be identified, particularly in the language domain. This is pertinent for a variety of clinical diagnoses, including autism, among others.

4) Both verbal and non-verbal measures are administered to bilingual clients, if consistent with the referral question. Given the influence of bilingualism on language tasks, some psychologists may erroneously consider only administering non-verbal measures to their bilingual clients in an effort to be culturally fair. However, just as

English-speaking monolinguals vary in their non-verbal abilities, so do monolinguals. Thus, it is not a suggested approach to obtaining an estimate of overall functioning. Further, completely forgoing language assessments may cause the clinician to miss the presence of a language disorder or other disorder with a linguistic feature.

5) Measures are continually being developed and standardized in Spanish. Thus, psychologists do not need to rely on informal translations of the English measures that they have on hand. Such translations can inadvertently cause a misestimation of the immigrant Hispanics' abilities and/or symptoms. Each item and item order on a published measure has been precisely examined and validated through empirical studies. Consider the word "ball" as an example. Easy to verbalize, it can often be an early item on a developmental screener for young English-speaking children. In comparison, "pelota" is more difficult with its three syllables. Therefore, a developmental screener in Spanish may have such a word listed later. If psychologists informally translated English versions to Spanish without scientific examination of the items and ordering, they can inadvertently bias assessments with the immigrant Hispanic community.

6) The development and standardization of Spanish measures are considered. There are a number of Spanish measures that have been carefully developed with a translation/Spanish team, psychometric analysis and potential reordering of items, large standardization sample, and consideration of cultural and linguistic variations. Complete statistical analyses are needed on the Spanish versions, rather than assumptions that the Spanish and English versions of a measure are equivalent. Indeed, special analytic techniques are used to examine such equivalencies. An additional feature to consider in the assessment of the Hispanic community is how measures incorporate dialectical variations among Hispanic subgroups. For example, some words (like "cake" or "straw") vary substantially across Latin America and the Caribbean.

BIBLIOGRAPHY

American Psychological Association. (2010). *Ethical principles of psychologists and code of conduct.* Washington, DC: APA. Ethical principles and guidelines driving the work of psychologists are outlined in this document.

American Psychological Association. (2003). "Guidelines on multicultural education, training, research, practice, and organizational change for psychologists." *American Psychologist*, 58, 377–402. Multicultural guidelines in different domains of psychology, including assessment are specified in this document.

Barrueco, S., López, M., Ong, C.A., & Lozano, P. (2012). *Assessing young children within and across two languages.* Baltimore, MD: Paul H. Brookes. This book examines and compares the linguistic, cultural, and psychometric strengths and weaknesses of measures available in English and Spanish for young children.

Council of National Psychological Associations for the Advancement of Ethnic Minority Interest. (2000). *Guidelines for research in ethnic minority groups.* Washington, DC: APA. Specific guidelines on research with ethnic minorities are provided.

Cummins, J. (1979). "Linguistic interdependence and the educational development of bilingual children." *Review of Educational Research,* 49(2), 222–251. A foundational article in the field about the development of language across distinct dimensions (e.g., CALP).

Murphey, D.A.; Guzman, L.; & Torres, A. (2014). *America's Hispanic children: Gaining ground, looking forward.* Bethesda, MD: Child Trends. This report provides an overview of recent Hispanic child trends in the areas of family, education, and health.

Paradis, J., Genesee, F., & Crago, M.B. (2011). *Dual language development and disorders.* Baltimore, MD: Paul H. Brookes. This book summarizes the typical and atypical development of children's language in the context of bilingualism.

United States Census Bureau (2011). The

Hispanic population: 2010. Retrieved from: http://www.census.gov/prod/cen2010/briefs/c2010br-04.pdf. This census brief presents an overview of socio-demographic characteristics of the Hispanic community from 2010 census data.

Sandra Barrueco

SEE ALSO: Cross-cultural differences; Diversity; Ethnocentrism; Multicultural counseling; Multiculturalism; Multicultural psychology.

Assimilative family therapy model

TYPE OF PSYCHOLOGY: Clinical; Consulting; Counseling; Family; Psychopathology

This approach to family therapy focuses on clients' developing understanding of the origins of their dilemmas as stemming from patterns that were developed and modeled

within their family of origin. With this perspective of families as high dynamic systems, clients take responsibility for their behaviors, thoughts, and feelings and in doing so take an important step toward healing. The family therapist integrates interventions and concepts from other therapies (cognitive behavioral, psychodynamic, communications) within clients' unique system perspectives enabling effective change to occur.

Key Concepts

- Modern family dilemmas
- Assimilative family therapy model
- Integration
- Bowen family systems therapy
- Context
- Dilemmas

INTRODUCTION

The modern family presents many new challenges for mental and behavioral health providers because new family structures require a reformulation of strategies and interventions that differ from those employed when working with "traditional families." Traditional models of family therapy no longer adequately address the dilemmas brought to consultation rooms. A treatment model sensitive to the many unique contexts presented by the modern family is needed. A new model, the assimilative family therapy model, is an attempt to meet this need by shaping the inclusion of necessary interventions to address the specific dilemmas of a client or family. This therapy addresses the many dilemmas that are faced throughout the life cycle: differentiation of the individual, parenting and couple relationship issues, midlife issues, and caring for the elderly.

What is the assimilative family therapy model? It is an integrative, as opposed to eclectic, approach. An eclectic eater goes to a buffet and chooses several items, combining different food items at times while at other times eating one food by itself. An integrationist goes to the buffet, selects ingredients, and combines them together to create a new dish (Goldfried & Norcross, 2005). Thus, the integrationist evaluates a client's dilemmas and combines approaches, concepts, and other variables to create the most effective treatment to enable clients to heal.

The assimilative approach falls within the field of integration (Messer, 1992). In an assimilative approach, the therapist chooses a home theory that becomes the focal therapy of the approach. Then the therapist integrates other concepts and interventions from other theories to meet the goals of the home theory and goals set by the therapist and client(s). In the assimilative family therapy model (AFT), the home theory is a systems theory. Family therapists consider clients' dilemmas from a systems point of view. They focus on the patterns of interaction of the family of origin and extended family. They also evaluate families' physical and psychological vulnerabilities, how members connect to each other and negotiate conflict,) and those patterns of behavior that get transmitted from generation to generation. For example, say Bobby is a child who suffers from anxiety. His paternal family members also struggle with anxiety. Is this a pattern that has been transmitted to Bobby through genetics or is it learned by repeating his father's behaviors? The family therapist looks at an individual's or family's dilemmas by systematically considering where the behaviors and adjustments occurred in past generations.

In AFT, family therapists rely on the Bowen family systems therapy model as the home theory. They then integrate other concepts and interventions from other therapies such as psychodynamic, cognitive behavioral, communications, and other systems therapies to better meet the needs and goals of the clients. The goals of the Bowen approach are to reduce anxiety, lower emotional reactivity, and increase differentiation among all family members.

Lowering emotional reactivity is an important goal for individuals to be able to problem solve and think rationally when one is being emotionally challenged by a situation, event, feeling, or person. In the process of learning to control reactions to situations, family members also learn how to state their positions in a respectful manner even when emotions are charged or there is pressure from another to change a position. By working this way, clients' anxiety levels are lowered, enabling them to think, act, and feel in a modulated manner. In Bobby's case, the AFT therapist realizes that Bobby needs to separate his behaviors from those of his anxious father. The therapist will also incorporate mindfulness strategies and relaxation exercises to help Bobby differentiate himself from his father's behaviors and adjustments.

The individual or family context is another important concept that informs AFT therapists' work with clients. Our context sets the stage for how we view the world we live in, how we interact, and what we value. Context includes age, sex, sexual orientation, religion, spirituality, ethnicity, culture, socioeconomic level, level of attachment, and level of resilience and optimism. These contexts all contribute to clients' adjustment to life's circumstances. The more therapists understand clients' contexts, the more helpful they are in enabling them to affect change in behaviors, thinking, and actions. Because Bobby's parents come from a strict German family where children "should be seen and not heard," his level of attachment to his parents is avoidant. He does not feel safe expressing his feelings which further increases his anxiety. The family's more stoical outlook works against their ability to enjoy the positive parts of their lives which also contributes to Bobby's anxiety. If Bobby's attachment to his parents were close and warm, even though he has a genetic propensity for anxiety, he might not become symptomatic due to feeling supported. As a result, he would be more resilient and less apt to become anxious. Therefore, as therapists integrate clients' context with the theory, they begin to conceptualize the best way to help clients change their thinking, feelings, and behaviors to solve the presented dilemmas.

The assimilative family therapy model is useful in treating individuals suffering from anxiety and depression and for child and adolescent centered issues where adjustment to school, friends, or family relationships is compromised. AFT may also be effective with couple dilemmas and midlife and end of life issues and, in fact, dilemmas throughout the life cycle. The best way to understand how to use AFT is to apply it with different populations.

Many couples that come to treatment are anxious, angry, and frightened that their marriage may end, but they cannot mobilize their emotions, thoughts, and actions to do something constructive to start saving the relationship. Others enter therapy, and they desperately work at saving their relationships and are committed to each other and the process. In AFT, it is essential to help couples realize that their behaviors are most likely a repeat of their parent or family patterns in some capacity. Many clients state that they want a relationship different from their parents, but they repeat behaviors without being aware that they are doing so. The next step is enabling couples to take responsibility for their individual behaviors. With therapists' help, they jointly decide what needs to be changed within each individual and in their manner of interacting between each other. Social scientist John Gottman, who is known in family therapy circles for his work on marital stability and relational analysis, has rightly stressed the need to communicate in a more respectful manner with lowered emotional reactivity and anxiety. The couple is encouraged to develop a more differentiated stance on what each needs and wants as individuals and as a couple unit (or dyad). Once this process begins, and not until it begins, can the couple learn to create a more intimate and satisfying relationship.

Meet Kayla and Joe who have been married for six years. Kayla identified with her very strong and angry mother and was repeating these patterns when dealing with her husband. Though Joe also came from a family where his mother was dominant, he consciously decided that he would never become like his dismissed and diminished dad. When Kayla expressed anger at Joe, Joe responded with so much anger that it would exacerbate Kayla's anger. Soon, they both would be shouting at each other until battle fatigue set in and they retreated. A cessation of hostilities was achieved, but Kayla and Joe never solved their issues. At some point, they would again begin this cycle and ignite anger. Once the AFT therapist could point out patterns, it was easier and safer for Kayla and Joe to accept responsibility for their own behavior and reactions to the other. Each understood how he or she was a catalyst for the other to become increasingly angry, because each was actually, though not consciously planning to do so, repeating patterns in their family of origin. For this couple, the AFT therapist also integrated mindfulness techniques developed by Professor Emeritus of Medicine, Jon Kabatt-Zinn, who founded Mindfulness-Based Stress Reduction (MBSR). These techniques enabled each to change the way he or she reacted tothe other by using role-play and other effective communication techniques (e.g., teaching them to listen, validate each other feelings by repeating them, and respond empathetically to the other) to help enable each one to feel heard and cared for. As a result, Kayla and Joe were able to change the way they viewed their own behaviors and create an identity that was different from their parents. The couple began to feel more connection and enjoyment with each other. When situations arose that ignited their mutual angers, they were able to modulate the way they interacted, avoid escalating the dilemmas, and resolve the issues presented.

A stressful time of life is midlife when caretaking responsibilities can become paramount to anything else. Many midlifers, particularly women, find themselves caring for elderly parents as well as being parents to adult children. Some midlifers become the caretakers for grandchildren as well. These midlifers are known in social science research as the "sandwich generation." The elderly population is increasing as individuals live longer and the need for informal caregiving (i.e., without pay or compensation) is growing. How the family interacted before the elderly became a pressure in the system will determine how the family is able to deal with the needs and desires of the elderly. The more connected the generations, the better they will be able to deal with the elderly member's needs and decline. Family caregivers have more mental health issues, with depression being the most common. The mortality rate of caregivers of elderly spouses (ages 66-96) is 63% higher than among non-caregivers in the same age bracket (*Family Caregiving Alliance*, 2006). The family history of elder care will likely be repeated from the previous generation with a new twist.

The therapist can help the adult children work through the mourning process of denial, bargaining, anger, depression, and acceptance. Feeling sad, helpless, and ashamed are normal feelings when interacting with our onetime strong parent who is losing his or her abilities. Adult children and elderly parents are both mourning in different ways, but both generations need to face their sadness and celebrate their function so they can establish new patterns to help the elderly and for the elderly to receive help in this difficult stage of life. In the final stage of a parent's life, the patterns that were developed over the course of a lifetime continue. Caregivers have the responsibility to change their positions within the family while working through feelings and dysfunctional individual and family patterns.

AFT also offers a practical approach to managing relationships between adult children and elderly parents. The therapy enables the caregiver and elder (if able and appropriate) to deal with feelings, identify dilemmas, and find solutions. Meet Selma, a midlife woman who has adult children and a 92-year-old mom. Selma's mom has been a widow for more than 40 years. Selma has been the backbone for her mom since her father's untimely death. Even though Grandma has been independent until the last five years, the strain of Selma's roles as an employee, wife, parent to adult married children, and caregiver of her elderly mom has taken a toll on Selma's health and sense of well-being in the form of heightened anxiety and inability to sleep. The therapist looked at the family patterns of how Selma with her siblings became the caretaker of her mom. It became obvious that this was a repeated pattern from Selma's mother's family of origin. However, today's longevity means this pattern will persist far longer and has overwhelmed Selma. The therapist was able to identify the family patterns and coach Selma to approach her siblings to ask for help in dealing with their mom. Rather than caring for her adult children, she was instructed to ask them to help with Grandma. Selma also hired some outside help within the monetary ability of Grandma's funds. Her husband, relatively absent in helping, was asked to step in. This was very difficult for Selma to learn to ask for help and let go of control as she began to take control of her own life. Along with family members, Selma needed to mourn the loss of her mother rather than avoid these feelings while caring for her. This enabled the family to be a support for Grandma who was also mourning the loss of her abilities and the eventual ending of her life. Being able to do this provided stability for the family and healthier individual functioning. By making the mourning process visible and identifiable, Selma could free her repressed anger, sadness, and energy to enable her to start caring for herself by communicating appropriately with family members, going to the doctor for check-ups, exercising, losing weight,going out with her husband, and enjoying her midlife years while at the same time continuing to balance her many responsibilities.

BIBLIOGRAPHY

Chisholm, J. F. (1999). "The Sandwich Generation." *Journal of Social Distress and the Homeless,* 8(3), 177-191. Reviews the literature on the sandwich generation and includes related theories and research as well as case vignettes.

Gottman, J., & Declaire, J. (1996). *The Heart of Parenting: Raising an Emotionally Intelligent Child.* New York, NY: Simon & Schuster. This book is an easy read for the lay-person as well as professional on parenting.

Gottman, J., & Declaire, J. (2001). *The Relationship Cure: A Five-Step Guide to Strengthening Your Marriage, Family, and Friendships.* New York, NY: Three River Press. A guide to improving family relationships, this book can be read by the general population as well as the professional.

Johnson, M. (2005). *Religion, Spirituality and Older People.* In M. Johnson (Ed.). Age & Aging. New York: Cambridge University Press. Covers a highly specific area of aging.

Kabat-Zinn, J. (2005). *Coming To Our Senses: Healing Ourselves and The World Through Mindfulness.* New York, NY: Hyperion Books. Addresses the healing aspects of mindfulness.

Messer, S. B. (1992). "A Critical Examination of Belief Structures in Integrative and Eclectic Psychotherapy." In J.C. Norcross and M.R. Goldfried (Eds.), *Handbook of Psychotherapy Integration* (130-168). New York, NY: Basic Books. Explains assimilative family therapy model as a treatment modality for the lay population.

Messer, S.B. (2001). "Assimilative Integration". *Journal of Psychotherapy Integration*, special edition, 11(1). Discusses the genesis and theoretical underpinnings of the field of assimilative integration.

Norcross, J.C. (2005). *A Primer on Psychotherapy Integration* (2nd ed.). New York: Oxford University Press. Directed toward therapists, this book is for those wanting to learn about the integrative therapy movement.

Pitta, P. (l995). "Adolescent-Centered Family Integrated Philosophy and Treatment". *Psychotherapy,* 3(1). Washington, DC: American Psychological Association. Includes information for those looking for help with adolescent struggles.

Pitta, P. (2003). *Parenting Your Elderly Parents*. (Video). Washington, DC: Washington, D.C.: American Psychological Association. Includes a therapy session-with a couple struggling with caretaking issues.

Pitta, P. (2005). "Integrative Healing Couple's Therapy: A Search for the Self and Each Other". In M. Harway (Ed.), *Handbook of Couples Therapy.* New York, NY: Wiley. A chapter written for the professionals and could be helpful for couples looking for a model of treatment for couple issues as well as understanding on how to resolve couple issues by looking at the contribution of both members of the couple.

Pitta. P. (2014). *Solving Modern Family Dilemmas: An Assimilative Therapy Model.* New York, NY: Routledge. Provides understanding of modern family dilemmas within a context of normalcy rather than pathology.

Patricia Pitta

SEE ALSO: Family; Family conflict; Family therapy; Intervention.

Assisted living

TYPE OF PSYCHOLOGY: Social psychology

Assisted living is one of many managed care alternatives that offer assistance in group surroundings to those who cannot live completely independently. It provides the level of care best suited to people's needs, with an emphasis on keeping them as active and independent as possible while attending to areas in which they need assistance.

KEY CONCEPTS

- Alzheimer's disease
- Board and care facilities
- Dementia
- Enhanced care
- Extensive contracts
- Hospice
- Long-term care
- Modified contracts
- Personal care
- Service plan

INTRODUCTION

Assisted living facilities provide assistance to people who require or desire some level of assistance in activities of daily living—eating, bathing, dressing, laundry, housekeeping, and assistance with medications—but do not require constant care, and are able to live somewhat independently. Residents in these facilities range from youths with independence-limiting disorders to the elderly.

Assisted living facilities differ from nursing homes or rest homes in that their residents are more independent and do not require around-the-clock care. Therefore, assisted living facilities typically provide emergency medical assistance for their residents twenty-four hours a day, but nursing homes have a substantial medical staff on duty at all times.

LEVELS OF ASSISTED LIVING

Upon reaching retirement age, some people are fully capable of living independently but prefer to reside in an assisted living facility because it will relieve them of the necessity of doing housekeeping, of shopping for food and preparing their own meals, and of attending to such matters as home repair and upkeep. Such people prefer assisted living facilities because they not only can reduce their responsibilities in the present but also, in most cases, can provide enhanced care as they age and require increased personal care and attention.

Assisted living facilities are not the same as board and care facilities in which residents are generally housed in multiple occupancy bedrooms with shared bathrooms. Most assisted living facilities offer self-contained apartments or cottages, usually with rudimentary kitchen facilities. They range from one-room studios, to three-bedroom suites. Most attempt to appear residential rather than institutional. Weekly housekeeping is generally included in the assessed fees, as are such services as the frequent changing of bed linens, exercise facilities, directed social events, and transportation to medical and shopping facilities. Extra charges are generally levied for such services as doing personal laundry and supervising the administration of required medications.

Meals, included in the assessed fees, are generally served in a communal dining room but can, in most cases, be served on a temporary basis in the units of people who are unable to come to the dining room. Dining rooms are important in assisted living facilities because of the social interaction that occurs among people who eat together.

Many assisted living communities can provide more intense attention if a resident's health declines to the point that independence is compromised. Even in such situations, however, residents are encouraged to help each other with such routine matters as dressing and bathing. Assuming some responsibility for fellow residents adds to the independence of both the giver and recipient of such assistance. People whose health makes it necessary for them to receive more intensive nursing care usually vacate the apartment in which they have been living and enter the associated facility that provides enhanced care on a long-term basis. This facility may be likened to a hospice, which is a facility for the terminally ill, although a hospice is generally available to people who are thought to have less than six months to live, whereas an enhanced care unit attached to an assisted living facility may admit people who are frail but whose life expectancy could be several years.

COST OF ASSISTED LIVING

Assisted living facilities generally cost 20 to 30 percent less than a nursing home. Those residing in assisted living facilities often enter such facilities when they are relatively healthy and may remain in them for a decade or more. Such facilities offer graduated levels of care as those living in them begin to need more intensive care than they initially required.

Some facilities offer extensive contracts that provide unlimited long-term nursing care as needed. Such contracts, however, are initially more costly than modified contracts that guarantee only specific amounts of long-term nursing care. As residents need increasing levels of care, the monthly assessments of those holding extensive contracts will be unchanged; however, the monthly assessments of those with modified contracts will increase after a specified amount of long-term nursing care is exceeded.

In most cases, the cost of living in assisted living facilities is the responsibility of the residents, although some may have private insurance policies to cover their expenses if they require long-term nursing care. Those who exhaust their financial resources usually qualify for long-term care reimbursement under Medicaid, but to qualify, they must be approaching utter destitution.

DEMAND FOR ASSISTED CARE

During the first half of the twentieth century, the population of the United States doubled, and by the beginning

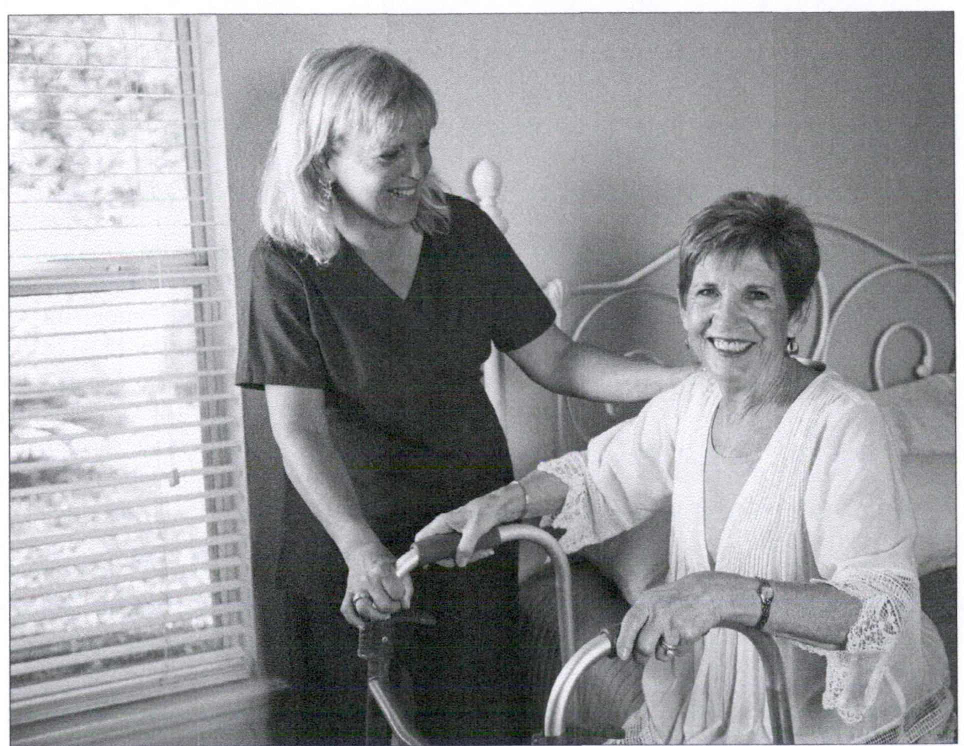

Photo: iStock

of the twenty-first century, it had doubled again. Part of this dramatic increase was the result of higher birthrates, but the greater portion resulted from a significant rise in the elderly population. According to the US Bureau of the Census, the number of people aged eighty-five or older about doubled between 1990 and 2009, and it is anticipated to more than double between 2010 and 2040. People are not only living longer, but they also are remaining active well into their seventies or eighties, sometimes continuing to work either full time or part time during these advanced years.

As the Social Security system becomes increasingly strained for funds, the age to which people will be forced to work to qualify for full benefits will gradually increase, possibly to between seventy and seventy-four years. Diseases that earlier resulted in fatalities are increasingly instead becoming chronic conditions because of advanced medications and procedures. Such advances in medical care and increased control of chronic diseases have made working to an advanced age a realistic expectation.

DEALING WITH DEMENTIA

A major problem among the aging is dementia, often the result of Alzheimer's disease. People suffering from this disorder may become increasingly forgetful and often appear to be confused. Because people usually slip into dementia gradually, the condition may go untreated for longer than is desirable.

In assisted living apartments or cottages that have kitchen facilities, a considerable fire danger is posed by those who are forgetful. They forget that food is cooking on stovetops, causing fire alarms to sound. This sort of problem often suggests that it is time for a resident to vacate the assisted living facility and move into a facility in which closer supervision is offered.

Although Alzheimer's patients gradually lose their ability to live independently, their overall physical condition may be quite good. They require special care and monitoring on a regular basis. Many continuing care retirement communities offer such care and also involve those suffering from Alzheimer's disease in as much social interaction as they are capable of pursuing.

NEED FOR SERVICE PLANS

To ensure that there is no misunderstanding about the responsibilities of an assisted care facility, people entering them, in collaboration with the administrators of such facilities, usually are signatories to a written document or contract that clearly states what will and will not be provided. Such service plans are subject to modification as conditions, particularly the health of residents, warrant. Such documents should indicate the period of time covered and provide for updates at specific intervals and for changes to be made if the physical condition of a resident changes significantly.

Documents of this sort are designed to protect both the facility and the resident. The resident should be represented both by concerned parties—family members or trusted friends—and by an attorney who represents the resident's interests. Such an attorney may be an active participant in drawing up this document that specifies the provisions of the service plan.

BIBLIOGRAPHY

Administration on Aging. *A Profile of Older Americans*. Washington: Department of Health and Human Services, 2002. Print.

Ball, Mary M., et al. *Communities of Care: Assisted Living for African American Elders*. Baltimore: Johns Hopkins UP, 2005. Print.

Baltes, Margaret. "Aging Well and Institutional Living: A Paradox?" *Aging and Quality of Life: Charting New Territories in Behavioral Science Research*. Ed. Ronald P. Abeles, Helen G. Gift, Marcia G. Ory, and Donna M. Cox. New York: Springer, 1994. Print.

Citro, J., and S. Hermanson. *Assisted Living in the United States*. Washington: American Assoc. of Retired Persons, Public Policy Institute, 1999. Print.

Hoban, Sandra. "Assisted Living 2013: On the Upswing." *Long-Term Living: For the Continuing Care Professional* 62.3 (2013): 28–30. Print.

Kozar-Westman, Maryalice, Meredith Troutman-Jordan, and Mary A. Nies. "Successful Aging Among Assisted Living Community Older Adults." *Jour. of Nursing Scholarship* 45.3 (2013): 238–46. Print.

Matthews, Joseph L. *Choose the Right Long-Term Care: Home Care, Assisted Living, and Nursing Homes*. 4th ed. Berkeley: Nolo, 2002. Print.

National Center for Assisted Living. *Facts and Trends: The Assisted Living Source Book*. Washington: American Health Care Association, 2001. Print.

Plys, Evan J., and Nancy G. Bliwise. "Family Involvement and Well-Being in Assisted Living." *Seniors Housing & Care Jour.* 21.1 (2013): 21–35. Print.

Schwarz, Benyamin, and Ruth Brent, eds. *Aging, Autonomy, and Architecture: Advances in Assisted Living*. Baltimore: Johns Hopkins UP, 1999. Print.

R. Baird Shuman

See Also: Ageism; Aging: Cognitive changes; Aging: Physical changes; Aging: Theories; Alzheimer's disease; Death and dying; Dementia; Elder abuse; Elders' mental health; Health maintenance organizations; Hospice; Law and psychology; Retirement

Attachment and bonding in infancy and childhood

Type of psychology: Developmental psychology

Bonding and attachment are two theoretical constructs that psychologists have used to describe and explain the intense emotional tie that develops between a caregiver and child. Research has helped psychologists explain the development of several common social behaviors in infancy and use individual differences in infant behavior to predict aspects of later development.

Key Concepts
- Approach behaviors
- Attachment behaviors
- Avoidance
- Felt security
- Resistance
- Separation protest
- Signaling behaviors
- Strange situation
- Stranger anxiety

INTRODUCTION

Bonding refers to the development of an emotional tie of the mother to the infant. This biologically based process is believed to occur in mothers shortly after the birth of an infant, when the mother's intense emotional response is triggered by contact with her newborn. The existence of such a bond is then evidenced in the mother's behavior. Attachment, on the other hand, refers to a relationship between the caregiver and infant that develops over the infant's first year of life; the quality of the attachment is apparent in the behavior of the infant.

Evidence for the biologically based bonding process remains limited. According to Karl Heinz Brisch, neurobiological research suggests that mirror neurons play a role in a mother's sensitivity, that is, her empathic capability and responsiveness to the infant's needs, and that maternal sensitivity is heritable. Oxytocin, a hormone released during pregnancy and after birth, is thought to be not only responsible for regulating labor and lactation but also for promoting the maternal bonding process. The concept of attachment, in contrast to bonding, has more empirical support. Thus, the remainder of this discussion will focus on the development of the attachment relationship.

The work of British psychiatrist John Bowlby played an important role in the acceptance and understanding of the notion of mother-infant attachment. Bowlby argued that the behaviors of infants are not random and that some of the behaviors exhibited most commonly by infants actually serve a single goal. Specifically, he argued that the behaviors of crying, babbling, smiling, clinging, nonnutritional sucking, and following all play an important role in bringing infants into close contact with the caregiver. He believed that, for infants, seeking and maintaining proximity to their caregivers are essential for survival because infants depend on the caregiver for food, shelter, and protection. Thus, infants' behavior is organized and goal-directed. Infants neither understand this goal nor learn this behavior but rather are born with a biological predisposition to engage in certain behaviors that aid in maintaining proximity to the caregiver. With further development, infants become more aware of the goal, and therefore their behaviors become more intentional.

The emotional state of infants is also believed to play an important role in attempts to seek and maintain proximity to the caregiver. That is, infants' behavior depends on their sense of emotional security. For example, as long as children are in the immediate presence of the attachment figure, or within easy reach, they feel secure and may then attend to important developmental tasks such as exploration of the environment, using the mother as a secure base from which to explore. On the threat of loss of the attachment figure, however, infants may lose that sense of security and may exhibit attachment behaviors designed to increase the proximity of the attachment figure. Thus, infants' attempts to seek or maintain proximity to the caregiver are determined by how secure they feel with the caregiver in a specific environment.

The attachment relationship and infants' sense of security develop over the period of infancy. Bowlby has described four phases in the development of attachment to the caregiver. In phase 1, newborns show limited discrimination among people and therefore exhibit no preferential or differential behaviors, thus behaving in a friendly manner toward all people. In phase 2, eight- to twelve-week-old infants show the ability to discriminate the caregiver from others but exhibit no preferential behavior toward the caregiver. In phase 3, which generally appears at approximately seven or eight months of age, infants clearly discriminate the caregiver from other people and begin to show preferential treatment toward the caregiver. For example, infants begin to follow their departing mother, greet her on her return, and use her as a base from which to explore an unfamiliar environment. Furthermore, during phase 3, infants begin to treat strangers with caution and may withdraw from them. In phase 4, children maintain a goal-directed partnership with the caregiver, a more complex relationship in which children are acquiring some insight into the caregiver's own feelings and motives, and thus interact with the caregiver as a partner. This final phase is apparent in most children by preschool.

PATTERNS OF INFANT-MOTHER ATTACHMENT

During the second half of the first year of life (after about eight months of age), infants begin to show very clear attempts at exploration when their mothers are present. In fact, research reported by Mary Ainsworth in the mid-1970s suggests that once infants are able to crawl, they do not always remain close to their mother. Instead, they begin to move away from their mother, more carefully exploring objects and people. From time to time children return to her, as if to check her whereabouts or to check in with her. If their mother moves away, however, or if the infants are frightened by some event, they will either approach their mother or will signal to bring her closer. For example, infants often fuss, cry, and cling to their caregiver at the first sign of their caregiver's possible departure, a response known as "separation protest." At about the same time, infants begin to express stranger anxiety or stranger wariness by fussing and crying when an unfamiliar person enters the room or approaches. Ainsworth designed a special laboratory technique, known as the "strange situation," that allows direct observation of the interactions between the behaviors associated with exploration, attachment, separation protest, and stranger anxiety. This situation places an infant in an unfamiliar setting with a stranger, both in the presence and in the absence of the child's mother. The procedure consists of a series of three-minute episodes (the process lasts a total of about twenty minutes) in which the child is exposed to an unfamiliar playroom containing a set of age-appropriate toys. During the initial episodes, the mother remains in the playroom with the infant. Mother and infant are then joined in the playroom by a female stranger, who first talks to the mother, then approaches the child. Next, the mother leaves the room, and the infant and stranger are left alone together. The mother then returns and the stranger leaves, so that the infant is reunited with the mother. Following this episode, the infant is left alone in the room, then joined by the stranger; finally, the mother again returns and the stranger leaves.

This strange situation, therefore, exposes a child to three potentially upsetting experiences: separation from the caregiver, contact with a stranger, and unfamiliar surroundings. The episodes are arranged in such a way that they present a series of stressful experiences to the infant and thus present an opportunity to observe not only the infant's immediate response to a stranger and to separation from the mother, but also the child's ability to derive comfort from the mother and to use her as a secure base for exploration.

Ainsworth has reported that, while there are many similarities in infant responses to this strange situation, there are also important individual differences. In her initial study of twelve-month-old infants and their mothers, Ainsworth reported three distinct patterns of responding to the events of the strange situation, and the validity of these behavior patterns has been demonstrated by much additional research.

A majority of the infants exhibited active exploration of the new environment and the available toys when their mothers were present. Some of these infants showed distress during the first separation from their mother, and by the second separation, the majority of these infants expressed distress. On reunion with their mother, they actively sought contact with her and were easily comforted by her, showing considerable signs of positive emotion but very few, if any, signs of negative emotion. Furthermore, these infants frequently returned to play and exploration after a period of contact with their mother. In general, then, these infants used their mothers as a secure base from which to explore the novel environment, exhibited appropriate attachment behaviors following her departure, and were easily comforted by the mother on her return. Ainsworth suggested that this pattern of behavior reflects a secure attachment relationship.

A second group of infants showed a very different pattern of behavior. This minority group showed no evidence of distress during separation. They did sometimes show distress when left alone in the playroom but were easily comforted by the returning stranger. Furthermore, this group actually avoided or ignored their mothers when they returned. In essence, the mothers were treated very much as were the strangers. These infants showed virtually no signs of separation protest or stranger anxiety and exhibited very few attachment behaviors. Ainsworth suggested that this pattern of behavior reflects an insecure-avoidant attachment relationship.

Finally, a third group of children were extremely distressed on separation, but, despite their obvious separation and stranger anxiety, resisted comfort from their mothers. Their behavior suggested an angry ambivalence—they objected to being left alone, but they refused to be consoled when reunited with their mothers. This group of infants often exhibited distress on first entering the unfamiliar room with their mothers, and they rarely left the mother's side to explore the toys or the environment, either before or after separation, suggesting a lack of a sense of security. Ainsworth suggested that this behavior pattern reflects an insecure, resistant, or ambivalent attachment relationship.

It is important to note that Ainsworth's research was done in the United States in the 1970s. Follow-up work has demonstrated that various sociocultural factors can influence the patterns of attachment behavior seen in the strange situation. For instance, studies done in Germany in the 1980s revealed that as many as 60 percent of babies in that culture were classified as insecure-avoidant because of their lack of distress at separation from their mothers in the strange situation test. In contrast, studies of attachment carried out in Japan in the 1980s and 1990s indicate that up to 40 percent of Japanese infants are classified as insecure-ambivalent in the strange situation due to their tendency to cling to their mothers throughout the procedure. These differing cross-cultural patterns imply that the wider sociocultural context influences how mothers and infants interact: German mothers expect their infants to be relatively self-sufficient and confident, even during short separations such as those characteristic of the strange situation procedure. Japanese mothers, on the other hand, expect their infants to be upset when they are out of close proximity and in daily practice are unlikely to leave their infants alone even for short periods. These cross-cultural variations in patterns of attachment highlight the importance of considering mother-infant attachment in context.

Several follow-up studies were conducted by E. Hesse, M. Main, C. C. George, J. Solomon, K. Lyons-Ruth, and others in the 1990s using the strange situation. Their findings showed that a number of children could not be categorized as secure, insecure-avoidant, or insecure-ambivalent. Those children instead exhibited contradictory or partial responses to the experimental conditions and, often, repetitive behaviors or movements. This attachment type has been termed "insecure-disorganized" or "insecure-disoriented," and further research by M. L. Rutter and T. G. O'Connor in the late 1990s and early 2000s indicates a correlation between disorganized attachment and attention-deficit hyperactivity disorder (ADHD) in school-aged children.

The development of these distinct patterns of attachment is believed to be the result of the history of interaction between the caregiver and infant. Specifically, attachment theory suggests that responsive and consistent ("sensitive") caregiving results in a secure mother-infant attachment, unresponsive caregiving results in an avoidant attachment, and inconsistent caregiving results in a resistant/ambivalent attachment. The avoidant mother has been described as cold and disliking physical contact with the infant, who responds by acting aloof and avoiding social interaction. The resistant mother, however, has been described as unpredictable, sometimes responding but sometimes not, and the infant often responds with anger and ambivalence. Risk factors for disorganized attachment appear to include unresolved parental trauma, preterm birth, early abuse or neglect, infant health conditions, and genetic variation in dopamine regulation

As the infant matures, the specific behaviors that indicate the existence of the attachment relationship may change. The research evidence strongly suggests, however, that such individual differences in the quality of the mother-infant attachment relationship are predictive of later behavior. For example, infants who exhibit secure attachment patterns at one year of age have been found to be more cooperative with adults, to show greater enthusiasm for learning, to be more independent, and to be more popular with their peers during the preschool years. Thus, the quality of the mother-infant attachment relationship may have long-range effects. This does not mean that the child's future is determined solely by the quality of the attachment relationship. The evidence indicates that certain negative consequences of an insecure attachment relationship may be overcome by changes in the nature of the child's important relationships.

ATTACHMENT IN NONHUMAN PRIMATES

The existence of a mother-infant attachment relationship has been recognized for many years. For most of those years, however, psychologists explained the development of this attachment by way of traditional learning theory. That is, behaviorists argued that the infant-mother attachment develops because mothers are associated with the powerful, reinforcing event of being fed. In this way, the mother becomes a conditioned reinforcer. This reinforcement theory of attachment, however, came into question as a result of the work of Harry and Margaret Harlow in the early 1960s. Harlows' work was not with human infants but with infant rhesus monkeys. They removed newborn monkeys from their mothers at birth and raised them in the laboratory with two types of artificial or surrogate mothers. One surrogate mother was made of terrycloth and could provide "contact comfort." The other surrogate mother was made of wire. A feeding bottle was attached to one of the substitute mothers for each of the monkeys. Half of the monkeys were fed by the wire mother; the other half were fed by the cloth mother. This allowed the Harlows to compare the importance of feeding with the importance of contact comfort for the monkeys.

To elicit attachment behaviors, the Harlows introduced some frightening stimulus, such as a strange toy, into the cages of the young monkeys. They expected that if feeding were the key to attachment, then the frightened monkeys should run to the surrogate mother that fed them. This was not the case, however: all the young monkeys ran to their cloth mothers and clung to them, even if they were not fed by them. Only the cloth mothers were able to provide security for the frightened monkeys. The Harlows concluded that a simple reinforcement explanation of attachment was inaccurate and that the contact comfort, not the food, provided by a mother plays a critical role in the development of attachment.

This research provided the impetus for the development of Bowlby's ethological account of attachment. Since that time, research by Ainsworth and Alan Sroufe, as well as many others, has provided important information for the continuing development of understanding of the complex relationship between caregivers and infants.

BIBLIOGRAPHY

Ainsworth, Mary D. Salter, et al. *Patterns of Attachment: A Psychological Study of the Strange Situation.* 1978. New York: Psychology, 2014. Print.

Bowlby, John. *Attachment and Loss.* 2nd ed. New York: Basic, 1999. Print.

Brisch, Karl Heinz. "Attachment Theory and Its Basic Concepts." *Treating Attachment Disorders: From Theory to Therapy.* New York: Guilford, 2012. 7–71. Print.

Cassidy, Jude, and Phillip R. Shaver, eds. *Handbook of Attachment: Theory, Research, and Clinical Applications.* 2nd ed. New York: Guilford, 2008. Print.

Crittenden, Patricia McKinsey, and Angelika Hartl Claussen, eds. *The Organization of Attachment Relationships: Maturation, Culture, and Context.* 2000. New York: Cambridge UP, 2003. Print.

Hirsch, Larissa. "Bonding with Your Baby." *KidsHealth.org.* Nemours Foundation, Jan. 2012. Web.19 Feb. 2014.

Posada, Germán, and Garene Kaloustian. "Attachment in Infancy." *Wiley-Blackwell Handbook of Infant Development.* Malden: Wiley-Blackwell, 2010. 483–509. Print.

Oppenheim, David, and Douglas F. Goldsmith, eds. *Attachment Theory in Clinical Work with Children: Bridging the Gap between Research and Practice.* New York: Guilford, 2007. Print.

Rubin, Kenneth H., Wonjung Oh, Melissa Menzer, and Katie Ellison. "Dyadic Relationships from a Cross-Cultural Perspective: Parent–Child Relationships and Friendships." *Socioemotional Development in Cultural Context.* Ed. Xinyin Chen and Kenneth H. Rubin. New York: Guilford, 2011. 208–38. Print.

Loretta A. Reiser-Danner; updated by Virginia Slaughter

See Also: Affliliation and friendship; Birth: Effects on physical development; Birth order and personality; Child abuse; Children's mental health; Development; Father-child relationships; Gender identity formation; Imprinting; Mother-child relationship; Parenting styles; Reactive attachment disorder; Reflexes in newborns; Separation anxiety.

Attention

Type of psychology: Consciousness

Humans are not able to be fully conscious of everything around them simultaneously. Attention refers to a person's selection of only some of a number of things of which a person could be conscious. Studies have provided information on what things enter consciousness and how a person selects those things.

Key Concepts

- Bottom-up
- Early selection
- Feature integration theory

- Illusory conjuction
- Late selection
- Shadowing
- Top-down

INTRODUCTION

Attention usually refers to concentration on a particular aspect of the external environment, although it is possible to attend to one's own thoughts and other internal states. The flavor of the typical use of the term is captured in a statement by nineteenth-century German physiologist Hermann von Helmholtz, who noted that an observer who is steadily gazing at a fixation mark can, at the same time, concentrate attention on any given part of the visual field. The point in space to which one is directing one's eyes and the point to which one is attending thus are not necessarily the same, and one does not have to move the eyes to shift visual attention.

Attention has been of interest for a long time. Helmholtz wrote about attention in an 1850 book on physiological optics. William James, a pioneer in the study of psychology, devoted much space to attention in his book *The Principles of Psychology* (1890), noting that it can be either involuntary and effortless or voluntary and effortful. According to James, attention allows people to perceive, conceive, distinguish, and remember better than they otherwise could. Edward Titchener, in his *Lectures on the Elementary Psychology of Feeling and Attention* (1908), reinforced this point by stating that attention determines what people are conscious of as well as the clarity of their conscious experience.

Other leading figures from the early history of psychology, such as Wilhelm Wundt, agreed with James that the issue of attention was of great importance. Titchener regarded the prominence of the topic as one of the major achievements of experimental psychology. Interest was maintained through the period following World War I; Karl Dallenbach noted in the late 1920s that more studies had been reported on attention in the preceding three years than in any comparable period in history. After World War II, the study of attention received an even greater boost with the increasing concern over human-machine interactions, especially in the military.

Attention can be drawn automatically (involuntarily and effortlessly) by certain characteristics of stimuli in the environment. These include abrupt brightness changes or vivid colors at particular locations; both intensity and clarity are important. Auditory attention is automatically drawn by changes in pitch or location. Such automatic attentional capture is often termed "bottom-up" or "data-driven." A person readily attends to familiar stimuli, although these more often invoke voluntary and effortful processing, which is "top-down" or "internally driven." A person can voluntarily attend to any aspect of the environment he or she chooses.

ATTENTION SELECTION

How does a person select the things to which to attend? This question leads to a consideration of "early" (before meaning is analyzed) versus "late" selection. In 1958, Donald Broadbent championed the view that selection is made early through a process analogous to filtering incoming information according to its sensory properties. After a brief glimpse, a person can report the identity of items in the environment accurately if a cue indicating which items to report refers to their spatial location, but that person is much less accurate if the cue refers to semantic properties—for example, if it asks for only the letters from a display of several letters and digits intermixed.

Other researchers, such as J. Anthony Deutsch and Diana Deutsch, have argued that people unconsciously analyze all incoming information for its meaning, although selection cannot be made on this basis as easily as on a sensory basis. Support for this process, termed late selection, can be seen in tasks such as naming the ink colors of printed letters. J. Ridley Stroop found that if a word that is the name of a color is printed in ink that is a different color from the one it names—for example, the word "blue" written in red ink—it takes much longer to name the ink color than if the combination of letters is meaningless, such as a row of red Xs. People cannot avoid reading the word, no matter how hard they try. Thus, word meaning appears to be activated automatically, and a person cannot selectively attend to the color. Nevertheless, if the color to be named appears as a patch, separated in space from the inconsistent color word, color naming is not slowed. Selection of what to attend to thus can be made easily on the basis of location, color, or brightness but not on the basis of meaning.

VISUAL, SENSORY, AND SPATIAL ATTENTION

Attention is necessary because people do not have the capacity to be conscious of all aspects of their environment at once. Questions arise concerning the extent to which people can be conscious of more than one aspect simultaneously and of what aspects they can be simultaneously conscious. Because what is to be attended to can so easily be selected on the basis of its location, these questions often have been posed in relation to whether people can attend to nonadjacent areas simultaneously.

It is important first to point out that the observations of Helmholtz, James, and Titchener have been verified in sensitive laboratory experiments. Subjects gazing at the center of a computer screen were first given information about the spatial location on the screen of a target that would later appear away from fixation. The correct location usually was indicated, but sometimes an incorrect location was indicated. In comparison with instances when no location information was shown, detection of the target was aided by valid information but harmed by invalid information. If the target did not appear in the indicated location, however, detection was better when it appeared near the indicated location than when it appeared farther away. The edges of the attended area are thus vaguely rather than sharply defined. Yet can attention be split between nonadjacent locations? Most research has shown that this is not possible; people cannot attend to two separate areas simultaneously, although a few studies have indicated that they can attend to ring-like areas with attention devoted to the ring but not the surrounding area or the center.

In contrast to splitting visual attention between two separate locations, dividing attention between two different senses is possible. People can, for example, listen (attend) to a conversation while watching (attending to) the road when driving. Nevertheless, unless one of the tasks is very easy or highly practiced, performance still suffers in comparison to when attention is dedicated to one sense.

Directing attention on the basis of spatial location appears to be very important. Ulric Neisser described the visual determination of what is present as occurring rapidly in two stages. The first he called "preattentive" because it involves only a rough global analysis of information in the entire visual field, before attention is directed to any one location. People can detect simple visual features such as color, brightness, and the direction in which a straight line points on the basis of preattentive analysis. More precise determination of combinations of these simple features requires what is called focal attention, in which attention is focused on particular spatial locations containing the preattentively detected simple features. For example, seeing that a line in a particular orientation is of a certain color requires focal attention. Without it, a person could tell that the color is present somewhere, and that a line of that orientation is present somewhere, but not that the line is of that color. Focal attention is required to combine simple features. This process has been termed feature integration theory, and focused attention is described as the metaphorical glue that binds separate features into a unitary object.

Feature integration theory has received experimental confirmation in the work of Anne Treisman and her colleagues. They found that when focal attention is diverted or cannot be applied because of an interfering task, simple features are often matched incorrectly to produce what they termed "illusory conjunctions." For example, when a red horizontal line and a green vertical one are shown, in the absence of focal attention, a subject is likely to be conscious of the horizontal line as green and the vertical line as red.

USE OF SCHEMATA

A person can direct attention on bases other than a spatial one. That is, even overlapping shapes can be selectively attended. Neisser has described a study in which a basketball game and a hand-slapping game were shown simultaneously in outline form in the same location on a television screen. Observers could attend to only one game and were largely unaware of events occurring in the unattended game, but they were just as able to indicate each occurrence of some event in the game being attended, such as a throw of the ball from one player to another, as they were when that game was shown alone. The inability to divide attention between two games is due to expectations inherent in the way people understand and mentally represent each game. These mental representations are called schemata. Through them, attention has its effects as an alerting and sustaining process whereby receptivity to certain information can be maintained over the short or long term.

One additional phenomenon involves what Colin Cherry referred to as the "cocktail party phenomenon." The setting is a cocktail party or any gathering where people are engaged simultaneously in different conversations. A person can listen selectively to one conversation and apparently not be conscious of others. Auditory attention therefore seems fully focused on only one conversation. However, the listener might hear his or her name mentioned in any one of a number of other conversations and immediately shift attention to it. How can people attend fully to one source of information, yet simultaneously be sensitive to important information from other sources? Can their attention be focused and yet divided among a number of possible sources of information at the same time? The answer lies in the fact that stimuli outside the focus of attention are sometimes processed to the level of meaning, especially if they correspond to active and important schemata such as one's name.

PRACTICAL USES OF RESEARCH

Understanding how attention operates makes it possible to design environments that enable people to better attend to important characteristics. For example, hunters often are cautioned to wear a piece of clothing colored "blaze orange." A bright color is a simple feature that draws attention automatically. Another hunter's attention will be drawn to the blaze orange, and focusing attention on the color will allow it to be conjoined with other simple features, such as shape. The second hunter thus will almost immediately be conscious of the hunter wearing the blaze orange as a hunter and will be unlikely to misperceive this hunter as game (in addition, the color of game is never blaze orange). The same principle is applied when emergency vehicles such as fire trucks are painted bright red or yellow.

Principles stemming from basic research on attention have been applied in the development of what is known as head-up displays (HUDs) in aircraft such as helicopters. Typically, a pilot faces a windscreen through which the environment can be seen, with a cluster of instruments designating altitude, speed, and so on nearby. With this configuration, the pilot must look away from the windscreen and at the instruments to check them. As helicopters are capable of traveling at high speeds and often are flown close to the earth and to objects into which they might crash, it is important that looking away from the windscreen be minimized. In a HUD, the data from the instruments is projected onto the windscreen so that the pilot can see the information without having to divert his or her eyes from the windscreen.

Can the pilot attend to the instruments and the environment outside the windscreen simultaneously? They spatially overlap and thus are visible at the same time, yet studies of attention indicate that the pilot cannot attend to them both at once. The experiment described by Neisser in which two games were superimposed on a screen is relevant here. An observer could attend to one game or the other but not to both at the same time. This does not mean that HUDs are without value. Attention can be directed from the instruments to the environment or vice versa without the pilot moving his or her head or eyes, and either type of physical movement is much more time consuming than a relatively rapid shift of attention.

SHADOWING

One popular laboratory task is to have listeners "shadow" material presented to them. In shadowing, the listener hears a series of words spoken at a normal conversational rate and tries to repeat aloud each word as it is heard. The task is difficult, and subjects must devote considerable attention to the shadowing. Often a listener is asked to shadow material played with a tape recorder to one ear while different material is played by another tape recorder to the other ear (earphones are used). Certain characteristics of the material not being shadowed can be varied. After the task, the listener can be asked a number of questions regarding what he or she was conscious of in the unshadowed message.

Consistent with Cherry's cocktail party phenomenon, listeners are conscious of the presence of the unshadowed message and of whether there is an abrupt change of pitch (as in a change of voice from a man's to a woman's, or the introduction of a whistle). These global physical characteristics of the unshadowed message can be determined preattentively. Listeners are not conscious, however, of the contents or the language of the unshadowed message, of whether the language changed during the message, or even of whether speech or nonsense sounds were presented, unless a change of pitch occurred. Many variations of this experiment have been performed, and all have produced the same results: consciousness of the unshadowed material is limited to information that could be detected preattentively. There is no consciousness of the meaning of the unshadowed message, except that listeners sometimes are conscious of their own name if it appears, as a result of powerful schemata for something as important as one's own name. The results are exactly what would be expected from what has been shown to be true of attention thus far and from the original description of the cocktail party problem.

EMERGENCE OF ATTENTION THEORIES

The first complete theory of attention was not proposed until 1958, when Broadbent introduced his concept of attention as a filter that admitted only certain information, selected on the basis of sensory characteristics, into the limited-capacity system. This marked the continuation of interest in attention by researchers in England, beginning with Cherry in 1953. In 1963, J. Anthony and Diana Deutsch proposed that all incoming information is analyzed to the level of meaning.

Many of the fundamental issues in attention have been recast somewhat in an information-processing mode, beginning in the late 1960s. For example, attention is described in terms of "selection," "resources," "features," "input," and so on. Whereas the emphasis had previously been on hearing, visual attention began to receive more emphasis. Many of the findings were like those on hearing, although factors such as color and brightness were considered.

Attention remains central to the study of consciousness and cognitive psychology. As Michael Posner noted in 1975, "Attention is not a single concept, but the name of a complex field of study." Accordingly, questions about early versus late selection, automatic processing, and other issues in the control of attention have not yet been fully answered.

BIBLIOGRAPHY

Gazzaniga, Michael S. *The Cognitive Neurosciences.* Cambridge: MIT P, 2004. Print.

Gopher, Daniel, and Asher Koriat, eds. *Attention and Performance XVII.* Cambridge: MIT P, 1999. Print.

Humphreys, Glyn, John Duncan, and Anne Treisman, eds. *Attention, Space, and Action: Studies in Cognitive Neuroscience.* New York: Oxford UP, 2003. Print.

Johnston, William A., and Veronica J. Dark. "Selective Attention." *Annual Review of Psychology* 37 (1986): 43–75. Print.

Lehmann, Alexandre, and Marc Schönwiesner. "Selective Attention Modulates Human Auditory Brainstem Responses: Relative Contributions of Frequency and Spatial Cues." *PLOS ONE* 9.1 (2014): 1–10. Web. 18 Feb. 2014.

McColeman, Caitlyn M., et al. "Learning-Induced Changes in Attentional Allocation during Categorization: A Sizable Catalog of Attention Change As Measured by Eye Movements." *PLOS ONE* 9.1 (2014): 1–22. Web. 18 Feb. 2014.

West, Greg L., Jay Pratt, and Mary A. Peterson. "Attention Is Biased to Near Surfaces." *Psychonomic Bulletin & Review* 20.6 (2013): 1213–20. Print.

Garvin Chastain

SEE ALSO: Attention-deficit hyperactivity disorder; Automaticity; Cognitive psychology; Conciousness; James, William; Memory: Sensory; Pattern recognition; Vision: Color.

Attention-deficit hyperactivity disorder (ADHD)

TYPE OF PSYCHOLOGY: Psychopathology

Attention-deficit hyperactivity disorder is one of the most common disorders of childhood and adolescence, and it can also be one of the most disturbing and debilitating disorders that a child or adolescent can experience. Research into this disorder has identified its primary causes; however, it remains a difficult disorder to treat effectively.

KEY CONCEPTS

- Hyperactivity
- Impulsivity
- Inattention
- Overactivity
- Treatment

INTRODUCTION

Attention-deficit hyperactivity disorder (ADHD) is one of the most extensively studied behavior disorders that begin in childhood. Thousands of journal articles, chapters, and books have been published on the disorder. There are a number of reasons this disorder is of such interest to researchers and clinicians. The two primary reasons are that ADHD is a relatively common disorder of childhood (it is regarded as a childhood disorder although it can persist into adulthood) and that there are numerous problems associated with ADHD, including lower levels of intellectual and academic performance and higher levels of aggressive and defiant behavior.

In national and international studies of childhood emotional and behavioral disorders, ADHD has been found to be relatively common among children. Although prevalence estimates range from 1 to 20 percent, most researchers agree that between 3 and 7 percent of children could be diagnosed as having ADHD. The fifth edition of the *Diagnostic and Statistical Manual of Mental Disorders: DSM-5*, published by the American Psychiatric Association in 2013, describes the diagnostic criteria for ADHD. To receive the diagnosis of ADHD according to DSM-5, a child must show abnormally high levels of inattention, hyperactivity-impulsivity, or both when compared with peers of the same age. The DSM-5 lists two sets of behavioral symptoms characteristic of ADHD. The first list contains nine symptoms of inattention such as "often has difficulty sustaining attention in tasks or play activities," while the second list contains nine symptoms of hyperactivity-impulsivity such as "often talks excessively" and "often has difficulty awaiting turn." To be diagnosed with ADHD, a child must exhibit at least six symptoms from at least one of the lists. Although many of these behaviors are quite common for most children at some point in their lives, the important point to consider in the diagnosis of ADHD is that these behaviors must be in excess of the levels of behaviors most frequently exhibited for children of that age and that the behaviors must cause functional impairment in at least two settings (for instance, at home and at school). Additionally, it is expected that "several inattentive or hyperactive-impulsive symptoms were present prior to age twelve."

Boys tend to outnumber girls in the diagnosis of ADHD, with the male-to-female ratio estimated at 2:1 to 9:1, depending on the source. ADHD boys tend to be more aggressive and antisocial than ADHD girls, while girls are more likely to display inattentive symptoms.

ASSOCIATED PROBLEMS

There are a number of additional problems associated with ADHD, including the greater likelihood of ADHD boys exhibiting aggressive and antisocial behavior. Although some ADHD children do not show any associated problems, many ADHD children show deficits in both intellectual and behavioral functioning. For example, a number of studies have found that ADHD children score an average of seven to fifteen points below normal children on standardized intelligence tests. It may be, however, that this poorer performance reflects poor test-taking skills or inattention during the test rather than actual impairment in intellectual functioning. Additionally, ADHD children tend to have difficulty with academic performance and scholastic achievement. It is assumed that this poor academic performance is a result of inattention and impulsiveness in the classroom. When ADHD children are given medication to control their inattention and impulsiveness, their academic productivity has been shown to improve.

ADHD children have also been shown to have a high number of associated emotional and behavioral difficulties. As mentioned before, ADHD boys tend to show higher levels of aggressive and antisocial behavior than ADHD girls and normal children. Additionally, it is estimated that up to 50 percent of ADHD children have at least one other disorder, and the DSM-5 now allows ADHD to be included in a comorbid diagnosis with autism spectrum disorder. Many of these problems are related to depression and anxiety. Many ADHD children also have severe problems with temper tantrums, stubbornness, and defiant behavior. It is also estimated that up to 50 percent of ADHD children have impaired social relations; that is, they do not get along with other children. In general, there are many problems associated with ADHD, and this may be part of the reason that researchers have been so intrigued by this disorder.

Researchers must understand a disorder before they can attempt to treat it. There are a variety of theories on the etiology of ADHD, but most researchers have come to believe that there are multiple factors that influence its development. It appears that many children may have a biological predisposition toward ADHD; in other words, they may have a greater likelihood of developing ADHD as a result of genetic factors. This predisposition is exacerbated by a variety of factors, such as complications during pregnancy, neurological disease, exposure to toxins, family adversity, and inconsistent parental discipline. Although a very popular belief is that food additives or sugar can cause ADHD, there has been almost no scientific support for these claims. Because so many factors have been found to be associated with the development of ADHD, it is not surprising that numerous treatments have been developed for the amelioration of ADHD symptoms. Although numerous treatment methods have been developed and studied, ADHD remains a difficult disorder to treat effectively.

DRUG THERAPIES

Treatments of ADHD can be broken down into roughly two categories: medication and behavior or cognitive behavior therapy with the individual ADHD child, parents, or teachers. It should be noted that traditional psychotherapy and play therapy have not been found to be effective in the treatment of ADHD. Stimulant medications have been used in the treatment of ADHD since 1937. The most commonly prescribed stimulant medications are methylphenidate (Ritalin and Concerta), pemoline (Cylert), and dextroamphetamine (Dexedrine). As of 2014, the Federal Drug Administration (FDA) had approved three nonstimulant medications to treat ADHD. Strattera was the first nonstimulant drug approved and is prescribed to both children and adults. Intuniv and Kapvay are approved for children ages six through seventeen. Behavioral improvements caused by medications include better impulse control and improved attending behavior. Overall, approximately 75 percent of ADHD children on stimulant and nonstimulant medication show behavioral improvement, and 25 percent show either no improvement or decreased behavioral functioning. The findings related to academic performance are mixed. It appears that these medications can help the ADHD child with school productivity and accuracy but not with overall academic achievement. In addition, although ADHD children tend to show improvement while they are on a stimulant or a nonstimulant medication, there are rarely any long-term benefits to their use and can, in general, can be seen as only a short-term management tool.

Antidepressant medications such as imipramine and fluoxetine (Prozac) have also been used with ADHD children. These medications are sometimes used when stimulant medication is not appropriate (for example, if the child has motor or vocal tics). Antidepressant medications, however, like stimulant and nonstimulant medications, appear to provide only short-term improvement in ADHD symptoms. Overall, the use or nonuse of medications in the treatment of ADHD should be carefully evaluated by a qualified physician (such as a psychiatrist). If the child is started on medication for ADHD, the safety and appropriateness of the medication must be monitored continually throughout its use.

BEHAVIOR THERAPIES

Behavioral and cognitive behavior therapy has been used with ADHD children, their parents, and their teachers. Most of these techniques attempt to provide the child with a consistent environment in which on-task behavior is rewarded (for example, the teacher praises the child for raising his or her hand and not shouting out an answer) and in which off-task behavior is either ignored or punished (for example, the parent has the child sit alone in a chair near an empty wall, a "time-out chair," after the child impulsively throws a book across the room). In addition, cognitive behavior therapies try to teach ADHD children to internalize their own self-control by learning to "stop and think" before they act.

One example of a cognitive behavior therapy, which was developed by Philip Kendall and Lauren Braswell, is intended to teach the child to learn five "steps" that can be applied to academic tasks as well as social interactions. The five problem-solving steps that children are to repeat to themselves each time they encounter a new situation are the following: Ask "What am I supposed to do?" and then ask, "What are my choices?" Concentrate and focus in; make a choice and ask, "How did I do?" (If I did well, I can congratulate myself, and if I did poorly, I can try to go more slowly the next time.) In each therapy session, the child is given twenty plastic chips at the beginning of the session. The child loses a chip each time he or she does not use one of the steps, goes too fast, or gives an incorrect answer. At the end of the session, the child can use the chips to purchase a small prize; chips can also be stored in a "bank" to purchase an even larger prize in the following sessions. This treatment approach combines the use of cognitive strategies (the child learns self-instructional steps) and behavioral techniques (the child loses a desired object, a chip, for impulsive behavior).

Overall, behavioral and cognitive behavior therapies have been found to be relatively effective in the settings in which they are used and at the time they are being instituted. Like the effects of medication, however, the effects of behavioral and cognitive behavior therapies tend not to be long lasting. There is some evidence to suggest that the combination of medication and behavior therapy can increase the effectiveness of treatment. In the long run, however, no treatment of ADHD has been found to be truly effective, and in a majority of cases, the disorder persists into adulthood.

HISTORY AND CHANGING DIAGNOSTIC CRITERIA

Children who might be diagnosed as having ADHD have been written about and discussed in scientific publications since the mid-1800s. A focus on ADHD began in the United States after an encephalitis epidemic in 1917. Because the damage to the central nervous system caused by the disease led to poor attention, impulsivity, and overactivity in children who survived, researchers began to look for signs of brain injury in other children who had similar behavioral profiles. By the 1950s, researchers began to refer to this disorder as "minimal brain damage," which was then changed to "minimal brain dysfunction" (MBD). By the 1960s, however, the use of the term MBD was severely criticized because of its overinclusiveness and nonspecificity. Researchers began to use terms that more specifically characterized children's problems, such as "hyperkinesis" and "hyperactivity."

The *Diagnostic and Statistical Manual of Mental Disorders* (DSM), first published by the American Psychiatric Association in 1952, is the primary diagnostic manual used in the United States. In 1968, the second edition, called DSM-II, presented the diagnosis of "hyperkinetic reaction of childhood" to characterize children who were overactive and restless. By 1980, when the third edition (DSM-III) was published, researchers had begun to focus on the deficits of attention in these children, so two diagnostic categories were established: "attention-deficit disorder with hyperactivity (ADD with H)" and "attention-deficit disorder without hyperactivity (ADD without H)." After the publication of DSM-III, many researchers argued that there were no empirical data to support the existence of the ADD without H diagnosis. In other words, it was difficult to find any children who were inattentive and impulsive but who were not hyperactive. For this reason, in 1987, when the revised DSM-III-R was published, the only diagnostic category for these children was "attention-deficit hyperactivity disorder (ADHD)."

With the publication of the fourth version of the manual, the DSM-IV, in 1994, three distinct diagnostic categories for ADHD were identified: ADHD predominantly hyperactive-impulsive type, ADHD predominantly inattentive type, and ADHD combined type. The type of ADHD diagnosed depends on the number and types of behavioral symptoms a child exhibits. Six of nine symptoms from the hyperactivity-impulsivity list but fewer than six symptoms from the inattention list lead to a diagnosis of ADHD predominantly hyperactive-impulsive type. Six of nine symptoms the inattention list but fewer than six symptoms from the hyperactivity-impulsivity list lead to a diagnosis of ADHD predominantly inattentive type. A child who exhibits six of nine behavioral symptoms simultaneously from both lists receives a diagnosis of ADHD combined type.

The eighteen criteria used in the DSM-IV to diagnose ADHD were carried over to the DSM-5, which was published and released in 2013. The wording criterion for onset of ADHD has been changed, however, from "some" of the inattentive or hyperactive "symptoms that caused impairment were present before age seven years" in the DSM-IV to "several" inattentive or hyperactive "symptoms were present prior to age twelve" in the DSM-5. The DSM-5 also added a reduced symptom threshold for adults with a minimum of five symptoms (as opposed to the six required for children) for both the inattention and the hyperactivity/impulsivity aspects of the disorder.

Although the diagnostic definition and specific terminology of ADHD will undoubtedly continue to change throughout the years, the interest in and commitment to this disorder will most likely persist. Children and adults with ADHD, as well as the people around them, have difficult lives to lead. The research community is committed to finding better explanations of the etiology and treatment of this common disorder.

BIBLIOGRAPHY

Alexander-Roberts, Colleen. *The ADHD Parenting Handbook: Practical Advice for Parents from Parents.* Dallas: Taylor Trade, 1994. Print.

Barkley, Russell A. *Attention-Deficit Hyperactivity Disorder: A Handbook for Diagnosis and Treatment.* 3d ed. New York: Guilford Press, 2005. Print.

Goldstein, Sam, and Joy Jansen. "The Neuropsychology of ADHD." *In The Neuropsychology Handbook,* edited by Arthur MacNeill Horton, Jr., and Danny Wedding. 3d ed. New York: Springer, 2007.Print.

Hallowell, Edward M., and John J. Ratey. *Driven to Distraction: Recognizing and Coping with Attention Deficit Disorder.* New York: Random House, 2011. Print.

Kendall, Philip C., and Lauren Braswell. *Cognitive-Behavioral Therapy for Impulsive Children.* 2d ed. New York: Guilford Press, 1993.Print.

Parker, Charles E. *New ADHD Medication Rules: Brain Science and Common Sense.* 2nd ed. New York: Köehler Books, 2013. Print.

Ramsay, Russell J. *Cognitive-Behavioral Therapy for Adult ADHD: An Integrative Psychosocial and Medical Approach.* 2nd ed. New York: Routledge, 2015. Print.

Wender, Paul H. *ADHD: Attention-Deficit Hyperactivity Disorder in Children and Adults.* New York: Oxford University Press, 2000. Print.

Vicky Phares; updated by Virginia Slaughter

See Also: Abnormality: Biomedical models; Antidepressant medications; Attention; Behavioral therapy; Childhood disorders; Children's mental health; Cognitive behavior therapy; Conduct disorder; Drug therapies; Gender differences; Psychopharmacology; Teenagers' mental health.

Attitude-behavior consistency

Type of psychology: Social psychology

Research on attitude-behavior consistency examines the extent to which self-reported attitudes predict and guide behavior. It has outlined the conditions under which attitudes can and cannot be expected to be consistent with behavior and has provided an understanding of the process by which attitudes may influence behavior.

Key Concepts

- Attitude

- Attitude accessibility
- High self-monitors
- Low self-monitors
- Subjective norm

INTRODUCTION

Why does John go to see films often? Why will Sue not eat broccoli? Why does Mark read mystery novels? Why does Mary usually wear green? Most people would answer these questions by referring to the attitudes of the person in question. An attitude is defined as a positive or negative evaluation of a person, place, or thing. John goes to films because he likes them; Sue will not eat broccoli because she does not care for broccoli; Mark reads mystery novels because he enjoys them; and Mary wears green because it is her favorite color.

Social psychologists have found that most people routinely explain behavior in terms of underlying attitudes. People tend to believe that attitudes influence and are predictive of most behaviors. Despite these intuitive notions, however, research has suggested that attitudes in general are actually very limited predictors of behavior. There is generally not a high degree of consistency between people's attitudes and their behaviors; in fact, the extent to which attitudes predict and are consistent with behavior appears to depend on a number of variables, including what type of behavior is to be predicted, how the attitude was formed, what kind of personality the person has, and how easily the attitude can be recalled.

Imagine that a researcher wanted to predict whether people regularly attend religious services. He or she might reasonably ask them about their attitudes toward organized religion, expecting that those with more favorable attitudes would be more likely to attend services regularly than those with less favorable attitudes. If the researcher did this, however, he or she would not be likely to find much correspondence at all between attitudes and behaviors.

The reason for this is that the researcher would be asking about a very general attitude and very specific behavior. For attitudes to predict behavior, both must be measured at the same level of specificity. If the researcher wants to predict a specific behavior, he or she needs to ask about an attitude specific to that behavior. In this example, rather than asking about general attitudes toward religion, the researcher should ask about attitudes toward attending religious services, which would be much more predictive of behavior. Attitudes that best predict behavior are attitudes about that specific behavior.

Sometimes, however, even specific attitudes will not correspond to specific behaviors. Icek Ajzen and Martin Fishbein's theory of reasoned action proposes that attitudes toward a behavior are only one influence on behavior, and a second factor to consider is the subjective norm, which refers to individuals' beliefs about what important others (for example, parents, teachers, or peers) think they should do. For some behaviors, the subjective norm is more important than attitude in predicting behavior. Even though someone might have a positive attitude toward attending religious services, he or she still might not go because of a belief that important others do not think that he or she should go.

FACTORS IN PREDICTING BEHAVIOR

Even in the case of behaviors that are primarily influenced by attitude, there are other factors that determine the extent of that influence. One such factor is how the attitude was formed, which generally is in one of two ways. Attitudes may be based on direct, personal experience with the object or person in question; a person may dislike religious services because he or she attended a few and had a number of unpleasant experiences. Alternatively, attitudes may be based on indirect, secondhand experiences; a person may dislike services because of what he or she has read and heard about them. In general, attitudes based on direct experience are much more predictive of behavior than are attitudes based on indirect experience.

A second factor is the type of person someone is. According to psychologist Mark Snyder, when deciding how to behave in a social situation, some people look to the environment and try to be the type of person called for by the situation; they are known as high self-monitors. If the situation calls for a quiet, introverted person, they will be quiet and introverted. If the situation calls for a loud, extroverted person, they will be loud and extroverted. In contrast, low self-monitors look inside themselves and ask, "How do I feel right now?" They base their behavior on their feelings regardless of what is called for in the situation. If they feel like being introverted, they will be introverted; if they feel like being extroverted, they will be extroverted. As might be expected, low self-monitors display a higher degree of attitude-behavior consistency than do high self-monitors.

A third, and perhaps most important, factor is the ease with which an attitude can be recalled from memory, known as the degree of attitude accessibility. Simply put, the more accessible the attitude, the more likely it is that the attitude will predict behavior. Attitudes based on direct experience tend to be more accessible than attitudes based on indirect experience, and low self-monitors tend to have more accessible attitudes than do high self-monitors. In general, any factor that increases attitude accessibility increases the extent to which that attitude will guide future behavior.

IMPACT ON POLITICS

One arena in which attitude-behavior consistency is an important concern is politics. Millions of dollars are spent on advertising during a political campaign in an effort to influence attitudes, in the hope that attitudes will then influence behavior. This raises the question of whether this money is well spent—that is, whether attitudes toward political candidates predict voting behavior.

To investigate this question, psychologists Russell Fazio and Carol Williams examined the relations between attitudes toward the two major-party candidates in the 1984 United States presidential election, Ronald Reagan and Walter Mondale, and various behaviors, such as perceptions of the televised presidential debates and voting. They assessed individuals' attitudes toward the candidates in June and July of the election year. The presidential debates were held in October, the election in November. As it turned out, overall, attitudes were indeed very predictive of behaviors. Attitudes toward the candidates predicted reactions to the presidential debates, with Reagan supporters believing he was more impressive than Mondale and Mondale supporters believing the opposite. Attitudes also generally predicted voting behavior very well: those supporting Reagan tended to vote for him, and those supporting Mondale tended to vote for Mondale. Although it is impressive that attitudes assessed in the summer months predicted behaviors three and four months later, so far the results may not be very surprising.

Fazio and Williams did not only examine the relations between attitudes and behaviors, however. When they assessed individuals' attitudes during the summer months, they also measured the accessibility of those attitudes—that is, how easily the subjects could call the attitudes to mind. To do this, they asked participants in their study to agree or disagree with different tape-recorded statements (for example, "A good president for the next four years would be Ronald Reagan") as quickly as possible by pressing one of five buttons on a computer; the buttons represented "strongly agree," "agree," "neutral," "disagree," and "strongly disagree." The computer then recorded how long it took the participants to respond after they heard the statements. Fazio and Williams reasoned that the more quickly people could respond, the more accessible their attitudes were.

Based on the results, Fazio and Williams classified some people as having highly accessible attitudes and others as having less accessible attitudes. When they then reexamined reactions to the presidential debates and voting behavior, they found that attitude-behavior consistency was much higher for those with highly accessible attitudes than for those with less accessible attitudes. That is, those with highly accessible attitudes were much more likely to act in a way consistent with their attitudes than were those with less accessible attitudes. For example, not everyone who agreed in June or July that Reagan would be a good president for the next four years voted for him in November. Those for whom this attitude could easily be brought to mind were much more likely to act on it and vote for Reagan than were those who had the same attitude but could not bring it to mind as quickly. It appears that, for attitudes to guide behavior successfully, they must be easily retrieved from memory.

FREQUENCY OF ATTITUDE EXPRESSION

Two of the factors that influence the ease with which attitudes can be recalled have already been discussed: how the attitude was formed and whether one is a high or low self-monitor. An additional factor seems to be the number of times the attitude is expressed. In one study, students watched a videotape of five different puzzles and then expressed their interest in each of the puzzles. Some students were asked to express their attitudes once, while others were asked to express them three different times, on three different forms. When they were later asked to rate the puzzles along different dimensions as quickly as they could on a computer, just as in the voting study discussed above, those who had initially expressed their attitudes three times had quicker reaction times than those who had initially expressed their attitudes once, suggesting that repeated attitude expression makes attitudes more accessible. In a follow-up study, after students had seen the videotape of the puzzles and had expressed their attitudes toward them either one or three times, the researchers allowed the students actually to play with the puzzles. Attitudes toward the puzzles predicted playing behavior much better for those who had initially expressed their attitudes three times than for those who had initially expressed their attitudes once. The more often an attitude is expressed, the more accessible it becomes and the more likely it is to influence behavior.

EVOLUTION OF ATTITUDE-BEHAVIOR THEORIES

The extent to which attitudes predict and influence behavior is at the heart of social psychology. At its inception, social psychology was defined as the study of attitudes, and although the importance of attitudes has waxed and waned as the field has matured, most social psychologists would still consider them to be a central concept.

In this context, one can imagine the shock that the social psychological community felt when, in 1969, A. W. Wicker published a review of numerous studies examining the relations between attitudes and behaviors that concluded that attitudes generally bear little relation to overt behavior and do not predict behavior well at all. At about the same time, a personality psychologist named Walter Mischel was making similar conclusions about personality traits, noting that in the research he reviewed, there did not seem to be much relationship between people's personality traits and their behavior.

The reaction to Wicker's review was mixed. Some called for social psychology to abandon attitudes as a focal point of research, arguing that, since the goal of any field of psychology is to predict behavior, if attitudes could not predict behavior, it would be foolish to spend more time and effort studying them. Others took a more optimistic approach to addressing what became known as the attitude-behavior problem; while Wicker's review concluded that, on average, attitudes do not seem to predict behavior, in some of the studies he reviewed, attitudes did predict behavior quite well. The question for these researchers, then, was not whether attitudes predict behavior—because in some cases, they clearly do—but rather when and under what circumstances. As a result, in the 1970s and 1980s, considerable research was directed at identifying those factors that seemed to increase or decrease the degree of attitude-behavior consistency. It was these efforts that shed light on the role of direct experience and self-monitoring.

BIBLIOGRAPHY

Ajzen, Icek, and Martin Fishbein. *Understanding Attitudes and Predicting Social Behavior*. Englewood Cliffs: Prentice, 1997. Print.

Elen, Maarten, et al. "The Influence of Mood on Attitude-Behavior Consistency." *Journal of Business Research* 66.7 (2013): 917–23. Print.

Fazio, Russell H. "How Do Attitudes Guide Behavior?" *Handbook of Motivation and Cognition: Foundations of Social Behavior.* Ed. Richard M. Sorrentino and E. Tory Higgins. Vol. 1. New York: Guilford, 1986. 204–43. Print.

Fazio, Russell H., and Mark P. Zanna. "Direct Experience and Attitude-Behavior Consistency." *Advances in Experimental Social Psychology.* Vol. 14. Ed. Leonard Berkowitz. New York: Academic, 1981. Print.

Manning, Mark. "When We Do What We See: The Moderating Role of Social Motivation on the Relation between Subjective Norms and Behavior in the Theory of Planned Behavior." *Basic and Applied Social Psychology* 33.4 (2011): 351–64. Print.

Moraes, Caroline, Marylyn Carrigan, and Isabelle Szmigin. "The Coherence of Inconsistencies: Attitude-Behaviour Gaps and New Consumption Communities." *Journal of Marketing Management* 28.1/2 (2012): 103–28. Print.

Terry, Deborah J., and Michael A. Hogg, eds. *Attitudes, Behavior, and Social Context: The Role of Norms and Group Membership*. Mahwah: Erlbaum, 2000. Print.

van der Pligt, Joop, et al. "The Importance of Being Selective: Weighing the Role of Attribute Importance in Attitudinal Judgment." *Advances in Experimental Social Psychology.* Vol. 32. Ed. Mark P. Zanna. San Diego: Academic, 2000. Print.

Van Kerckhove, Anneleen, Iris Vermeir, and Maggie Geuens. "Combined Influence of Selective Focus and Decision Involvement on Attitude-Behavior Consistency in a Context of Memory-Based Decision Making." *Psychology and Marketing* 28.6 (2011): 539–60. Print.

Zanna, Mark P., E. Tory Higgins, and C. Peter Herman, eds. *Consistency in Social Behavior: The Ontario Symposium*. Vol. 2. Hillsdale: Erlbaum, 1982. Print.

Kenneth D. DeBono

See Also: Attitude formation and change; Bystander intervention; Casual attribution; Cognitive dissonance; Crowd behavior; Groups; Media exposure and mental health; Personality theory; Self-perception theory; Violence and sexuality in the media; Violence: Psychological causes and effects.

Attitude formation and change

Type of psychology: Social psychology

Research has suggested many theories of attitude change; these theories have led to the development of numerous persuasion tactics and principles that find use in a variety of settings, including mass media, consumer sales, and organizational negotiations.

Key Concepts

- Attitude
- Central and peripheral routes
- Cognitive dissonance theory
- Cognitive response theory
- Dual-mode processing model
- Functional theories
- Learning theory of persuasion
- Persuasion
- Self-perception theory
- Social influence
- Social judgement theory

INTRODUCTION

An attitude is a person's positive or negative evaluation of an object or thought; examples include "I support gun control," "I dislike brand X," and "I love the person next door." Much research finds that attitudes can influence a broad range of cognitive processes, such as social inference, reasoning, perception, and interpretation, and can thereby influence behavior. In general, people favor, approach, praise, and cherish those things they like and disfavor, avoid, blame, and harm those things they dislike. Given that attitudes can have pervasive effects on social behavior, it is important to understand how they are formed and changed.

Attitudes can be formed directly through observation of one's own behavior or through experience with the attitude object. They may also be formed by exposure to social influences such as parents, peers, the mass media, schools, religious organizations, and important reference groups. William McGuire notes that attitudes are one of the most extensively studied topics in social psychology. Much of this research has centered on the question, Who says what to whom, with what effects?

For example, research has varied the source (the "who") of a message and found that people tend to be most persuaded by credible, trustworthy, attractive, and similar communicators. Research on message characteristics (the "what") has shown that appeals to fear increase persuasion if accompanied by specific recommendations for how to avoid the fear; that there is a tendency for arguments presented first to have more impact, especially if there is a delay between hearing the arguments and making an evaluation; and that messages that present only one side of an issue are most effective when the recipient lacks the skills or motivation to process the information. In general, research has shown that an audience (the "whom") is less persuaded if the message is wildly discrepant from their original beliefs; such research also finds that an audience is less persuaded if they have been forewarned about the persuasion attempt and take steps to prepare a counterargument. The effects of social influence are usually described in terms of compliance (attitude change, often short-lived, as a result of wanting to obtain rewards or avoid punishment), identification (change as a result of seeking to be similar to or distinguished from the source of a message), and internalization (change as a result of accepting a position on the basis of its merits).

EARLY RESEARCH

The learning model, perhaps social psychology's first theory of persuasion, is based on the research of Carl Hovland and his colleagues at Yale University in the 1950s. According to this model, a message is persuasive when it rewards the recipient at each of the following stages of psychological processing of a message: attention, comprehension, message learning, and yielding. For example, a highly credible source is persuasive because people find it rewarding to attend to and comprehend what he or she says and then to act on it.

One problem with the learning model of persuasion is that subsequent research in the 1960s found that persuasion could occur even if the message was only minimally comprehended and the message's content was forgotten or never learned. To account for these results, the cognitive response approach posited that the key determinant of persuasion was not message learning but the thoughts running through a person's head as that individual received a communication. Effective communications are ones that direct and channel thoughts so that the target thinks in a manner agreeable to the communicator's point of view.

Later research reversed the causal sequence of the learning model from one of "attitudes cause behavior" to "behavior causes attitudes." Two theories that use this counterintuitive approach are cognitive dissonance theory and self-perception theory. According to consistency theories such as cognitive dissonance theory, people attempt to rationalize their behavior and to avoid a state of dissonance, or simultaneously holding two contradictory cognitions (ideas, beliefs, or opinions). Persuasion occurs as a result of resolving this dissonance. For example, fraternity and sorority pledges often must perform embarrassing behavior to gain admission to the organization. The thoughts "I just ate a plate of grasshoppers as an initiation rite" and "It is stupid to eat grasshoppers" are dissonant with a positive view of the self. One way to reduce this dissonance is to reevaluate the fraternity or sorority more positively: "I ate those grasshoppers because I wanted to join a great club."

Self-perception theory states that attitudes are based on observing one's own behavior and then attributing the behavior to underlying beliefs. For example, suppose a man is at a dinner party and is served brown bread, which he then eats. When asked if he likes brown bread, he observes his eating behavior and concludes that he does (unless there is some other plausible reason, such as coercion or politeness). Although dissonance theories serve to explain attitude change when existing attitudes conflict with a person's current behavior, self-perception theory proposes that when there is no better available explanation for a person's behavior, observing what the person does is the best indication of his or her attitudes.

Social judgment theory attempts to explain how attitude formation and change occur within a single social context. Attitude change can occur when the context for making judgments is changed. For example, in one study, men rated photographs of women as much less attractive after viewing the 1970s television show Charlie's Angels. In other words, the very attractive female stars of Charlie's Angels provided a highly positive context in which to rate the photographs and thus made women of average attractiveness appear much less attractive.

DUAL-MODE PROCESSING MODELS

In an effort to synthesize the vast amount of persuasion research, psychologists proposed a dual-mode processing approach to attitude formation and change. Dual-mode processing models emphasize two factors that influence the success of a persuasion attempt: the recipient's motivation and the recipient's ability to process an argument.

Richard Petty and John Cacioppo have suggested that there are two routes to persuasion. In the peripheral route, recipients give little thought to a message, perhaps because they have little motivation to think about it or lack the necessary skills. Persuasion via this route is based less on the arguments made and more on simple persuasion cues or heuristics such as the credibility of the source and the number of other people who agree with the message. Cognitive dissonance, self-perception, and social judgment theory models of attitude change often emphasize peripheral routes, as anxiety reduction, the lack of alternative explanations, and contextual cues are the important determinants of persuasion, rather than careful analysis of the message.

In the central route, where people are motivated and able to process the message, recipients carefully scrutinize the communication, and persuasion is determined by the quality and cogency of the arguments. The central route is emphasized in cognitive response theories of persuasion. Although cognitive responses can vary on a number of dimensions, two of the most important ones are evaluation and elaboration. Most cognitive responses to a message are either positive evaluations (support arguments) or negative evaluations (counterarguments) of the message's conclusion. Studies have shown that disrupting these cognitive responses and decreasing the recipient's ability to process the argument using a mild distraction, such as background noises or difficult-to-read print, results in more persuasion when the recipient's natural tendency would be to make arguments against the message and less persuasion when the recipient normally would have supported the message. Elaboration refers to how much thought a recipient gives to a message. Recipients who are highly motivated to analyze an argument are likely to give it more thought.

Dual-process models of attitude change have led researchers to examine when and why recipients are motivated to process a message carefully. Three such motivations have been suggested: to make sense of themselves and their world, to protect or defend existing self-perceptions or worldviews, and to maintain or enhance their social status. When the message corresponds to an individual's immediate motivations, persuasion attempts are more effective. For example, individuals who are more image conscious and motivated to enhance their social status are more likely to be persuaded by arguments that emphasize the social consequences of a behavior, while messages that emphasize the personal benefits of a behavior are more effective with those who are more internally guided.

Functional theories of attitude change incorporate these motivational goals. Functional theories posit that attitude formation and change are made when such change would function to serve a recipient's needs. For example, consider someone who is prejudiced against an ethnic group. This negative attitude helps the person interpret, often incorrectly, social reality ("Members of this ethnic group can do no good and often are the cause of problems") and maintain a positive view of self ("I am better than they are"), and it may also enhance the person's social status ("I am a member of a superior social group"). Advertisers make use of functional theories when they market products to appeal to self-images; in such cases, a product is used in order to obtain a desired image, such as appearing to be sophisticated, macho, or a modern woman.

HISTORY OF PERSUASION RESEARCH

In an article published in 1935, Gordon Allport declared that attitude is social psychology's "most indispensable construct." Research on attitudes began in the 1920s in the United States as a response to changing social conditions. The period was marked by the rise of new mass media such as radio and mass-circulated magazines, the development of large-scale consumer markets, and the changing nature of political activity. Such developments required that citizens' attitudes and opinions regarding a variety of issues be measured and tracked. Academic researchers responded by developing techniques of attitude scaling and measurement and by laying the foundation for survey methodology. The first empirical research on attitudes sought to address questions such as "How are movies changing Americans' attitudes and values?" and "Has modern life changed traditional cultural attitudes?"

World War II changed the focus of attitude research from measurement to understanding attitude change and persuasion. Many of the post–World War II attitude researchers had either fled Nazi Germany or worked for the Allies in an attempt to defuse Nazi propaganda and bolster their fellow citizens' attitudes toward the war effort. After the war, in the 1950s, many researchers attempted to explain the propaganda and attitude-change tactics used during the war and later increasingly employed in the mass media. This research resulted in the development of learning, functional, social judgment, and cognitive consistency theories of persuasion.

PRACTICAL APPLICATIONS

Research and theorizing on attitude change have led to the development of numerous tactics and principles of persuasion. These principles are useful for interpreting persuasion effects, such as those that occur in mass media and interpersonal or organizational settings, and for directing persuasion attempts. Three of the more popular tactics will be discussed here.

One of the simplest and most surefire ways to ensure positive cognitive responses is to induce the target to argue for the message conclusion, a tactic known as self-generated persuasion. For example, in one study during World War II, women were asked to "help" a researcher by coming up with reasons that other women should serve organ and intestinal meats (brains, kidneys, and so on) to their families as part of the war effort. These women were eleven times as likely to serve such meats as those who were merely lectured to do so. In another study, some consumers were asked to imagine the benefits of subscribing to cable television, while others were simply informed about those benefits. Those who imagined subscribing were two and a half times as likely to subscribe as those who were merely told why they should.

The foot-in-the-door technique makes use of cognitive dissonance theory. In this tactic, the communicator secures compliance with a large request by first putting his or her "foot in the door" by asking for a small favor that almost everyone will typically do. For example, in one study, residents were asked to place in their yards a large, ugly sign that read "Drive Carefully." Few residents complied unless they had been "softened up" the week before by an experimenter who got them to sign a petition favoring safe driving. For those residents, putting the ugly sign in the yard helped avoid cognitive dissonance: "Last week I supported safe driving. This week I will be a hypocrite if I do not put this ugly sign in my yard."

Another effective tactic is to add a decoy, or a worthless item that no one would normally want, to a person's set of choices. For example, a real-estate agent may show customers overpriced, run-down homes, or a car dealer may place an old clunker of a used car on his or her lot. Consistent with social judgment theory, such decoys create a context for judging the other "real" alternatives and make them appear more attractive. An unsuspecting consumer is then more likely to select and buy these more attractive items.

Attitude research since the 1960s has sought to test and develop the major theories of attitude change, to refine the principles of persuasion, and to apply these principles to an ever-expanding list of targets. For example, research on the relationship between attitude change and memory of a communication led to the development of a cognitive response analysis of persuasion in the late

1960s. Many of the compliance techniques described by Robert Cialdini and by Anthony Pratkanis and Elliot Aronson were first elaborated in this period. As knowledge of persuasion improves, the principles of persuasion are increasingly applied to solve social problems. Prosocial goals to which theories of persuasion have been applied include decreasing energy consumption and increasing waste recycling, slowing the spread of acquired immunodeficiency syndrome (AIDS) by changing attitudes toward safe-sex practices, lowering the automobile death toll by increasing seat-belt use, improving health by promoting practices such as good dental hygiene and regular medical checkups, improving worker morale and worker relationships, and reducing intergroup prejudice.

BIBLIOGRAPHY

Allport, Gordon W. "Attitudes." *Handbook of Social Psychology.* Ed. Carl Allanmore Murchison. Worcester: Clark UP, 1935. 798–844. Print.

Chen, Frances S., et al. "In the Eye of the Beholder: Eye Contact Increases Resistance to Persuasion." *Psychological Science* 24.11 (2013): 2254–61. Print.

Cialdini, Robert B. *Influence: Science and Practice*. 5th ed. Boston: Pearson, 2009. Print.

Crano, William D., and Radmila Prislin, eds. *Attitudes and Attitude Change.* New York: Psychology, 2008. Print.

Eagly, Alice H., and Shelly Chaiken. *The Psychology of Attitudes*. Fort Worth: Harcourt, 1993. Print.

Jay Frye, G. D., Charles G. Lord, and Sara E. Brady. "Attitude Change following Imagined Positive Actions toward a Social Group: Do Memories Change Attitudes, or Attitudes Change Memories?" *Social Cognition* 30.3 (2012): 307–22. Print.

Perloff, R. M. *The Dynamics of Persuasion*. New York: Erlbaum, 2008. Print.

Petty, Richard E., and John T. Cacioppo. *Attitudes and Persuasion: Classic and Contemporary Approaches.* Boulder: Westview, 1996. Print.

Petty, Richard E., and Duane T. Wegener. "Attitude Change: Multiple Roles for Persuasion Variables." *Handbook of Social Psychology*. Ed. Daniel T. Gilbert, Susan T. Fiske, and Gardner Lindzey. 4th ed. Vol. 1. New York: McGraw, 1998. 323–90. Print.

Pratkanis, Anthony R., and Elliot Aronson. *Age of Propaganda: The Everyday Use and Abuse of Persuasion*. Rev. ed. New York: Freeman, 2001. Print.

Pratkanis, Anthony R., Steven J. Breckler, and Anthony G. Greenwald, eds. *Attitude Structure and Function.* Hillsdale: Erlbaum, 1989. Print.

Rudman, Laurie A., Meghan C. McLean, and Martin Bunzl. "When Truth Is Personally Inconvenient, Attitudes Change: The Impact of Extreme Weather on Implicit Support for Green Politicians and Explicit Climate-Change Beliefs." *Psychological Science* 24.11 (2013): 2290–96. Print.

Seo, Kiwon, James Price Dillard, and Fuyuan Shen. "The Effects of Message Framing and Visual Image on Persuasion." *Communication Quarterly* 61.5 (2013): 564–83. Print.

Zimbardo, Philip G., and Michael R. Leippe. *The Psychology of Attitude Change and Social Influence.* Philadelphia: Temple UP, 1991. Print.

Anthony R. Pratkanis and Marlene E. Turner; updated by Michelle Murphy

See Also: Advertising; Allport, Gordon; Attitude-behavior consistency; Cognitive dissonance; Consumer psychology; Decision making; Media exposure and mental health; Media psychology; Self-perception theory; Survey research: Questionaires and interviews.

Attraction theories

Type of psychology: Social psychology

Theories of interpersonal attraction attempt to specify the conditions that lead people to like, and in some cases love, each other. Attraction is a two-way process, involving not only the person who is attracted but also the attractor.

Key Concepts

- Equity theory
- Matching phenomenon
- Mere exposure
- Physical attractiveness stereotype
- Proximity
- Reciprocity
- Reinforcement model
- Social exchange theory

INTRODUCTION

Relationships are central to human social existence. Personal accounts by people who have been forced to endure long periods of isolation serve as reminders of people's dependence on others, and research suggests that close relationships are the most vital ingredient in a happy and meaningful life. In short, questions dealing with attraction are among the most fundamental in social psychology.

The major theories addressing interpersonal attraction have a common theme: reinforcement. The principle of reinforcement is one of the most basic notions in all of psychology. Put simply, it states that behaviors that are followed by desirable consequences, often in the form of rewards, tend to be repeated. Applied to interpersonal relations, this principle suggests that when one person finds something rewarding in an interaction with another person (or if that person anticipates some reward in a relationship that has not yet been established), then the person should desire further interaction with that other individual. In behavioral terms, this is what is meant by the term "interpersonal attraction," which emerges in everyday language in such terms as "liking" or, in the case of deep romantic involvement, "loving." Appropriately, these theories, based on the notion that individuals are drawn to relationships that are rewarding and avoid those that are not, are known as reinforcement or reward models

The first and most basic theory of this type was proposed in the early 1970s by Donn Byrne and Gerald Clore. Known as the reinforcement-affect model of attraction ("affect" meaning "feeling" or "emotion"), this theory proposes that people will be attracted not only to other people who reward them but also to those people with whom they associate rewards. In other words, a person can learn to like others through their connections to experiences that are positive for that individual. It is important to recognize that a major implication here is that it is possible to like someone not so much for him- or herself but rather as a consequence of that person's merely being part of a rewarding situation; positive feelings toward the experience itself get transferred to that other person. It also follows that a person associated with something unpleasant will tend to be disliked. This is called indirect reinforcement.

For example, in one experiment done during the summer, people who evaluated new acquaintances in a cool and comfortable room liked them better than when in a hot and uncomfortable room. In another study, subjects rating photographs of strangers gave more favorable evaluations when in a nicely furnished room than when they were in a dirty room with shabby furniture. These findings provide some insight into why married couples may find that their relationship benefits from a weekend trip away from the children or a romantic dinner at a favorite restaurant; the pleasant event enhances their feelings for each other.

There are other models of interpersonal attraction that involve the notion of reward but consider the degree to which rewards are offset by the costs associated with a relationship. Social exchange theory suggests that people tend to evaluate social situations. In the context of a relationship, a person will compare the costs and benefits of beginning or continuing that relationship. Imagine, for example, that Karen is considering a date with Dave, who is kind, attractive, and financially stable but fifteen years older. Karen may decide that this relationship is not worth pursuing because of the disapproval of her mother and father, who believe strongly that their daughter should be dating a man her own age. Karen's decision will be influenced by how much she values the approval of her parents and by whether she has other dating options available.

A third model of attraction, equity theory, extends social exchange theory. This approach suggests that it is essential to take into account how both parties involved in a relationship assess the costs and benefits. When each person believes that his or her own ratio of costs to benefits is fair (equitable), then attraction between the two tends to be promoted. On the other hand, a relationship may be placed in jeopardy if one person thinks that the time, effort, and other resources being invested are justified but the other person does not.

Considering the rewards involved in the process of interpersonal attraction provides a useful model, but one that is rather general. To understand attraction fully, one must look more specifically at what people find rewarding in relationships. Social psychological research has established some definite principles governing attraction that can be applied nicely within the reward framework.

FACTORS OF ATTRACTION

The first determinant of attraction, reciprocity, is probably fairly obvious, since it most directly reflects the reinforcement process. Reciprocity is a powerful force; people tend to like others who like them back. There are few things more rewarding than genuine affection, support, concern, and other indicators that one is liked by another person.

The second principle, proximity, suggests that simple physical closeness tends to promote attraction. Research has confirmed what many people probably already know:

people are most likely to become friends (or romantic partners) with others with whom they have worked, grown up, or gone to school. Other studies have shown that people living in dormitories or apartments tend to become friends with the neighbors who live closest to them. Simply being around people gives an individual a chance to interact with them, which in turn provides the opportunity to learn who is capable of providing the rewards sought in a relationship.

There is, however, yet another force at work, a very basic psychological process known as the mere exposure effect. Research has demonstrated consistently that repeated exposure to something new tends to increase one's liking for it, and examples of the process are quite common in everyday life. It is not uncommon, for example, for a person to buy a new compact disc by a favorite musical artist without actually having heard the new material, only to be disappointed on listening to it. The listener soon discovers, however, that the album "grows" on him or her and finds that he or she likes it quite a bit after hearing it a few times. Such occurrences probably involve the mere exposure phenomenon. In short, familiarity breeds liking, and physical closeness makes it possible for that familiarity to develop.

BEAUTY AND ROMANCE

Generally speaking, the same factors that promote the development of friendships also foster romantic attraction. The third principle of attraction, physical attractiveness, is somewhat of an exception, however, since it is more powerful in the romantic context.

In a classic study published by Elaine Walster and her associates in 1966, first-year men and women at the University of Minnesota were randomly paired for dates to a dance. Prior to the date, these students had provided considerable information about themselves, some of it through personality tests. During the evening, each person individually completed a questionnaire that focused primarily on how much the person liked his or her date, and the participants were contacted for follow-up six months later. Despite the opportunity to discover complex facts about attraction, such as what kinds of personality traits link up within a couple to promote it, the only important factor in this study was physical appearance. For both sexes, the better-looking the partner, the more the person liked his or her date, the stronger was the desire to date the person again, and the more likely the individual was to do so during the next six months.

The potent effect of physical attractiveness in this study sparked much interest in this variable on the part of researchers over the next decade or so. The earliest studies determined rather quickly that both men and women, given the opportunity to select a date from a group of several members of the opposite sex representing a range of attractiveness levels, almost invariably would select the most attractive one. Dating in real life, however, is seldom without the chance that the person asking another out might be turned down. When later experiments began building the possibility of rejection into their procedures, an interesting effect emerged, one that has been termed the matching phenomenon: people tend to select romantic partners whose degree of attractiveness is very similar to their own.

Other research revealed that physically attractive people are often judged favorably on qualities other than their appearance. Even when nothing is known besides what the person looks like, the physically attractive individual is thought to be happier, more intelligent, and more successful than someone who is less attractive. This finding is referred to as the physical attractiveness stereotype, and it has implications that extend the role of appearance well beyond the matter of dating. Studies have shown, for example, that work (such as a writing sample) will be assessed more favorably when produced by an attractive person than when produced by someone less attractive, and that a cute child who misbehaves will be treated more leniently than a homely one. What is beautiful is also good, so to speak. Finally, physical attractiveness fits well with the reward model: it is pleasant and reinforcing both to look at an attractive person and to be seen with him or her, particularly if that person is one's date.

The last principle of attraction, similarity, is the most important one in long-term relationships, regardless of whether they are friendships or romances. An extremely large body of research has demonstrated consistently that the more similar two people are, especially attitudinally, the more they will like each other. It turns out that the adage "opposites attract" is simply false. (Note that the matching phenomenon also reflects similarity.) A friend or spouse who holds attitudes similar to one's own will provide rewards by confirming that one's own feelings and beliefs are correct; it is indeed reinforcing when someone else agrees.

EVOLUTIONARY THEORIES OF ATTRACTION

Evolutionary psychologists have provided an important new way to look at why individuals are attracted to others. Borrowing from the basic theorizing of the English biologist Charles Darwin, psychologists are paying increasing attention to the information provided by both physical and social features of living creatures. Everyone is influenced by what people look like, in that they form impressions of others before they even hear them speak. People often use the appearance and behavior of others to make a variety of judgments about them; these judgments are made quickly and unconsciously and are fairly resistant to change. What sort of impressions are formed? What aspects of a person are focused on? Evolutionary psychology has some answers to these questions.

Specifically, evolutionary psychologists suggest that the attractiveness of a person's body serves as a valuable and subtle indicator of social behavior, social relationship potential, fitness, quality, reproductive value, and health. Evolutionary psychologists place heavy emphasis on clearly observable features of human bodies and do not focus as much on internal, unobservable aspects of personality, such as kindness or trustworthiness. There is a growing body of research that supports these ideas. For example, significant relationships were found between attractiveness and measures of mental health, social anxiety, and popularity, so the idea behind evolutionary theory does seem to be relevant.

Much of the work studying how body characteristics relate to attractiveness has focused on a single factor, such as the face, although many features of the body can influence attractiveness. Faces are often the first part of a person that is observed, and the face is almost always clearly visible (except in certain cultures). Social psychologists have shown that people often make quick judgments about others based on their faces, and more than 80 percent of studies on judging attractiveness have focused on the face alone. The sex, age, culture, and past experiences of the perceiver; specific facial features, such as large lips for women and strong jaws for men; body and facial symmetry; and specific body ratios, such as the waist-to-hip ratio (the number attained by dividing the waist measurement by the circumference of the hips), all influence judgments of attractiveness. Consistent with this idea are findings that some standards of attractiveness are consistent across time and cultures. For example, people who have symmetrical faces—those with eyes and ears of equal size and equal distances from the center line of the face—are preferred over people who do not.

FEMALE SHAPELINESS

Another example of a body characteristic that is tied to attractiveness from an evolutionary perspective is women's waist-to-hip ratio. Around the world, men prefer women with lower waist-to-hip ratios (between 0.7 and 0.8). Evolutionary psychology research emphasizes the importance of waist-to-hip ratios as a major force in social perception and attraction because shape is a visible sign of the location of fat stores, which consequently signals reproductive potential and health. Low waist-to-hip ratios do indeed directly map onto higher fertility, lower stress levels, and resistance to major diseases. For example, women with waist-to-hip ratios of 0.8 are almost 10 percent more likely to get pregnant than women with waist-to-hip ratios around 0.9.

Although not as much research has focused on female breasts as a signaler of reproductive fitness, a variety of studies suggest that it is also an important factor, although the evidence is mixed. Some studies support the commonly held stereotype that men prefer larger breasts, although others seem to show no such preference, and some have shown that small and medium breasts are preferred. Much of this work has focused either on the bust or on waist-to-hip ratios, not both together. The appeal of breast size should depend on overall body fat, waist, and hips, and both bust size and waist-to-hip ratio should interact to influence ratings of attractiveness. In support of this idea, research now suggests women with lower waist-to-hip ratios and larger breasts are the ones considered most attractive. Unfortunately, methodological restrictions and poor stimulus materials limit the generalizability of most previous work using waist-to-hip ratios and other bodily features. For example, many studies used line drawings or verbal descriptions of figures instead of pictures of real people. Research continues on ways to provide clearer tests of evolutionary psychology theories of attraction.

The most consistently documented finding on the evolutionary basis of attraction relates to gender differences in human mate choice. Consistent with Darwin's ideas that humans are naturally programmed to behave in ways to ensure that their genes will be passed on to future generations, thus ensuring survival, evidence indicates that men tend to prefer young, healthy-looking mates, as these characteristics are associated with the delivery of healthy babies. An examination of the content of more than eight hundred personal advertisements found that men stressed attractiveness and youth in mates more than did women, a finding supported by marriage statistics. Women have been shown to place more emphasis on a prospective mate's social and financial status, because these traits are often related to being able to take good care of children. The fact that women in Western societies are achieving higher economic positions, however, would suggest that this pattern of preferences may change in time.

HISTORICAL DEVELOPMENT

Although it would seem to be of obvious importance, physical appearance as a determinant of romantic attraction was simply neglected by researchers until the mid-1960s. Perhaps researchers mistakenly assumed the widespread existence of an old ideal that one should judge someone on the basis of the person's intrinsic worth, not on the basis of a superficial characteristic. Nevertheless, when the Minnesota study discussed earlier showed the effect of physical attractiveness to be so strong as to eliminate or at least obscure any other factors related to attraction in the context of dating, social psychologists took notice. In any science, surprising or otherwise remarkable findings tend to stimulate additional research, and such a pattern definitely describes the course of events in this area of inquiry.

By around 1980, social psychology had achieved a rather solid understanding of the determinants of attraction to strangers, and the field began turning more of its attention to the nature of continuing relationships. Social psychologist Zick Rubin had first proposed a theory of love in 1970, and research in that area flourished in the 1980s as investigators examined such topics as the components of love, different types of love, the nature of love in different kinds of relationships, and the characteristics of interaction in successful long-term relationships. Still other lines of research explored how people end relationships or attempt to repair those that are in trouble.

People view relationships with family, friends, and lovers as central to their happiness, a research finding that is totally consistent with common experience. A quick look at the content of motion pictures, television programs, songs, novels, and poetry, where relationships, particularly romantic ones, are so commonly a theme, provides evidence for that point. Yet nearly half of all marriages end in divorce, and the lack of love in the relationship is usually a precipitating factor. Whatever social psychology can teach people about what determines and maintains attraction can help improve the human condition.

BIBLIOGRAPHY

Berscheid, Ellen, and Harry T. Reis. "Attraction and Close Relationships." *The Handbook of Social Psychology*. Ed. Daniel T. Gilbert, Susan T. Fiske, and Gardner Lindzey. 4th ed. Vol. 2. Boston: McGraw, 1998. 193–281. Print.

Berscheid, Ellen, and Elaine Walster. *Interpersonal Attraction*. 2nd ed. Reading: Addison, 1978. Print.

Berscheid, Ellen, and Elaine Walster. "Physical Attractiveness." *Advances in Experimental Social Psychology.* Vol. 7. Ed. Leonard Berkowitz. New York: Academic, 1974. 157–215. Print.

Buss, David M. *Evolutionary Psychology: The New Science of the Mind*. 3rd ed. Boston: Pearson, 2008. Print.

Duck, Steve. *Relating to Others.* 2nd ed. Philadelphia: Open UP, 1999. Print.

Hatfield, Elaine, and Susan Sprecher. *Mirror, Mirror: The Importance of Looks in Everyday Life*. Albany: State U of New York P, 1986. Print.

Langlois, Judith H., et al. "Maxims or Myths of Beauty? A Meta-Analytic and Theoretical Review." *Psychological Bulletin* 126.3 (2000): 390–423. Print.

Menadier, Veronica Hernández. "How Personality and Physical Attraction Lead to Possible Dating: A Reflection." *Journal of Multidisciplinary Research* 4.2 (2012): 111–19. Print.

Myers, David G. *Social Psychology.* 11th ed. New York: McGraw, 2013. Print.

Prokop, P., and Peter Fedor. "Physical Attractiveness Influences Reproductive Success of Modern Men." *Journal of Ethology* 29.3 (2011): 453–58. Print.

Quist, Michelle C., et al. "Integrating Social Knowledge and Physical Cues When Judging the Attractiveness of Potential Mates." *Journal of Experimental Social Psychology* 48.3 (2012): 770–73. Print.

Steve A. Nida; updated by Regan A. R. Gurung

SEE ALSO: Affililation and friendship; Affililiation motive; Love; Prejudice reduction; Self-presentation; Social perception.

Attributional biases

Type of psychology: Social psychology

Attributions of the causes of one's own behavior and the behavior of others play an important role in self-perception and the perception of others. Attributional biases are systematic errors that distort perceptions and attributions; studying them provides insight into stereotyping, the blaming of victims, faulty decision making, conflict, and depression.

Key Concepts

- Actor-observer bias
- Attribution
- Defensive attribution
- Depression
- Expectancy comfirmation bias
- Fundamental attribution error
- Generalization fallacy
- Self-serving bias
- Stereotype

INTRODUCTION

For human behavior to make sense, it must be perceived accurately and its causes must be understood. Theories that describe ways in which people make judgments about these causes are called attribution theories. Attribution can be defined as the process by which one gathers information and interprets it to determine the cause of an event or behavior.

Most attribution theories propose models that describe how people collect information and how attributions are formed from that information. Many specific attributions are possible, but generally they can be grouped into two categories: personal and situational. In a situational attribution, the behavior is attributed to external forces or circumstances; for example, someone who trips may attribute the incident to a slippery floor rather than to his or her clumsiness. In a personal attribution, an internal cause, such as the person's personality, or an internal force, such as ability or effort, is seen as being the cause of the behavior. For example, if David observes Lois making a donation to charity, he may attribute her behavior to her generous personality rather than to some external circumstance. Attribution theories predict and explain the circumstances under which a personal or a situational attribution will be made.

FUNDAMENTAL ATTRIBUTION ERROR

Attribution theories provide logical models of how people gather and use information to form attributions, but people do not always seem to follow a logical process. Researchers have discovered that people frequently fall prey to attributional biases. These systematic errors teach much about human social cognition.

One attributional bias is so pervasive that it has earned the right to be called the fundamental attribution error. Social psychologist Lee Ross discovered that people tend to overestimate the role of personal, internal factors and underestimate the influence of situational factors, thus making unwarranted personal attributions. In an experiment, subjects were given essays supporting a particular position on an issue (in favor of abortion, for example). Despite the fact that the subjects were told that the authors had no choice but to take the stated positions, the subjects rated the authors' attitudes as being in agreement with their essays.

Two explanations have been proposed for the fundamental attribution error. In 1958, Fritz Heider proposed that people are more aware of persons than situations because persons are the obvious, attention-getting figures, whereas situations are the more easily ignored background. Daniel Gilbert proposed in 1989 that, contrary to what most attribution models propose, people do not initially use information to decide between personal and situational attributions; instead, they initially assume a personal attribution and then revise that attribution to include situational forces only if information that is inconsistent with a personal attribution forces them to do so. Supporting this hypothesis, he has found that if he keeps subjects too busy to use incoming information to revise their attributions, they are more likely to make personal attributions than are subjects who are allowed time to think about the information they are given.

ATTRIBUTIONAL BIASES

The fundamental attribution error is related to the actor-observer bias. Research has shown that the fundamental attribution error pattern is often reversed when people are attributing their own actions; actors tend to overestimate situational factors and underestimate personal ones. This bias leads to situations in which people attribute their own actions to circumstances and others' often-identical actions to personal factors: "I am late because of traffic, but you are late because you do not care about being punctual." This bias has been demonstrated in numerous studies; in one, researchers examined letters to "Ann Landers" and "Dear Abby" and found that the letter writers were more likely to attribute their own actions to situational factors and others' behavior than to personal factors.

Perceivers are often motivated to make a particular attribution. One motivation that may affect attribution is the desire to be correct, which may lead the person making the attribution to interpret ambiguous information as being supportive of an initial expectation or attribution. This bias often takes the form of "seeing" a trait that one associates with another trait. For example, if Glenda has attributed Jennie's astute decisions to her intelligence, she may also assume that Jennie is exceptionally outgoing, not because she has actually observed that trait, but because Glenda associates being intelligent with being outgoing. This expectancy confirmation bias is robust; unless the target person behaves in a way that is inconsistent with the assumption, the perceiver is unlikely to test the assumption.

One well-documented motivated attributional bias is the self-serving bias in attributing success and failure. When people succeed, they tend to attribute that success to personal, internal factors, such as ability and effort; however, when they fail, they are likely to attribute the failure to situational, external factors, such as being assigned a difficult task or having bad luck. As its name implies, the self-serving bias is thought to be motivated by a desire to preserve or enhance self-esteem by taking credit for success and denying one's role in failure.

Another motivated bias is the tendency for observers to blame victims for their situations. This is called defensive attribution, because it has been found to be more likely to occur when the observer is similar to the victim than when the observer is dissimilar, and when the victim's harm is severe rather than mild. Kelly Shaver, the social psychologist who first discussed this bias, believes that it is motivated by fear. If observers blame the victims rather than their situations, the observers can also believe that they themselves are unlikely to be harmed. This is related to what Melvin Lerner calls the belief in a just world. People are motivated to believe that there is justice in the world and that people get what they deserve. This is comforting, because it leads to the conclusion that if one is good, one will get good outcomes; however, the belief in a just world also leads one to assume that victims deserve their outcomes.

Finally, people may fall prey to a group of biases that are collectively called the generalization fallacy. This fallacy is seen when people overgeneralize information from individual cases and personal experience and ignore more reliable information. One example of this bias is the common belief that air travel is more dangerous than auto travel, when in fact the opposite is true. Because accidents involving airplanes are given greater attention than those involving automobiles, they are more vivid and therefore more memorable than the dangers associated with automobiles. As Heider suggested, vivid figures may be more salient than dull, statistical background information.

RELATIONSHIP TO CONFLICT

Because accurate attributions help perceivers negotiate complex social environments, attributional biases can interfere with that process. Therefore, it is not surprising that examples of attributional bias are found in situations in which there is conflict. One situation in which the fundamental attribution error and the actor-observer bias are often involved is arguments. If both parties believe that their own behavior is caused by circumstances but the other person's behavior is caused by his or her personality, they are likely to experience conflict. This can even be seen between nations; for example, each nation may attribute the other's cache of weapons to an aggressive personality but its own to necessity.

Another area of conflict that may involve attributional bias is stereotyping. Because stereotyping involves assuming the presence of certain traits based on membership in some group, the expectancy confirmation bias has been used as a model for stereotyping. Further, if people act on stereotypes in ways that encourage the targets to behave in certain ways, they may behaviorally confirm the stereotype. For example, if a perceiver believes that all dark-haired men are hostile, he or she may act in ways that prompt hostility from them, thereby confirming the stereotype. Defensive attribution and the belief in a just world may also play a part in stereotyping. In general, stereotypes of minority or less powerful groups are negative. The belief in a just world may lead people to reason that the targets of their stereotypes deserve their poorer outcomes because they have these negative traits. Defensive attributions may add to this by motivating perceivers to overestimate differences between themselves and the target group out of fear that if they are similar, they may receive similar outcomes.

ROLE IN DECISION MAKING AND DEPRESSION

Researchers who investigate the generalization fallacy are often concerned that falling victim to it may lead to poor decisions. In one study, subjects who were given both reliable statistical information from a large group of car owners and the testimonial of one person tended to weigh the testimonial more heavily than the statistical information. Logically, a testimonial based on one car owned by one person is poorer data than information based on many cars owned by many people. Overreliance on vivid but unreliable data can lead to poor decisions.

Some psychologists believe that the absence of an attributional bias may be involved in depression. People who are depressed do not show the usual self-serving bias in attributing their successes and failures; severely depressed people can even show a reversal of the usual pattern, attributing failure to internal causes (such as lack of ability) and success to external factors (such as luck). In working with these patients, psychotherapists may help them learn to attribute their outcomes in ways that enhance their self-esteem.

EVOLUTION OF COGNITION STUDY

In the late nineteenth century, psychology was defined as the science of the mind, and human cognition was at the forefront of early psychologists' interests. Wilhelm Wundt and his followers relied on introspection for their data; they observed their own cognitive processes and reported on them. Hermann Ebbinghaus taught himself lists of words and tested his knowledge after varying time periods to investigate human memory. Beginning in 1913, however, this early cognitive research was largely ignored in the United States, as John B. Watson redefined psychology as the science of behavior. The main proposition of behaviorism, as this school of psychology is known, is that psychology should use scientific methods of observation and data collection. Behaviorists argue that since cognitive processes are not observable and behaviors are, behaviors are the only proper subject for psychological study. Behaviorism ruled psychology almost exclusively until approximately 1960; although it is still an important force in psychology, it is no longer the dominant force it once was.

As behaviorism's influence has lessened, cognition has become once again a topic of interest to psychologists. Behaviorism left its mark on cognition in the form of more rigorous experimental methods; introspection has been replaced by objective data collection using groups of subjects. As research methods in cognitive psychology continue to become more sophisticated, theories that might have been untestable in earlier years have become the subject of research. One indication of the strength of cognition in the academic world as a whole is that many universities have introduced interdisciplinary departments of cognitive science in which psychologists, neuroscientists, philosophers, linguists, and experts in artificial intelligence study different aspects of cognition.

Attribution played a significant part in the cognitive revolution; Heider's *The Psychology of Interpersonal Relations* (1958) was an important early work in social cognition. Attribution is one of the most researched topics in social psychology; in fact, some would argue that it is one of the most influential concepts in the field, especially since it has been found to be useful in applied areas such as health psychology, cognitive psychology, and clinical psychology as well as social psychology. One of the characteristics of the cognitive revolution is an interest in such topics as ambiguity, uncertainty, and the effects of emotion on cognition. This emphasis provides an interesting context for the study of attributional bias and opens new avenues of inquiry for theorists and researchers. Because of this and the applied areas that have adopted and adapted attributional bias, it has become an area of interest in its own right as well as being important for the refinement of attribution theories.

BIBLIOGRAPHY

Carless, Sally, and Ruth Waterworth. "The Importance of Ability and Effort in Recruiters' Hirability Decisions: An Empirical Examination of Attribution Theory." *Australian Psychologist* 47.4 (2012): 232–37. Print.

Fischhoff, Baruch, and Ruth Beyth-Marom. "Hypothesis Evaluation from a Bayesian Perspective." *Psychological Review* 90.3 (1983): 239–60. Print.

Försterling, Friedrich. *Attribution: An Introduction to Theories, Research, and Applications.* Philadelphia: Psychology, 2001. Print.

Gonzalo, Désirée, et al. "How Disorder-Specific Are Depressive Attributions? A Comparison of Individuals with Depression, Post-Traumatic Stress Disorder and Healthy Controls." *Cognitive Therapy and Research* 36.6 (2012): 731–39. Print.

Harvey, J. H., and G. Weary. "Current Issues in Attribution Theory and Research." *Annual Review of Psychology* 35 (1984): 427–59. Print.

Hayes, Brett, and Beryl Hesketh. "Attribution Theory, Judgmental Biases, and Cognitive Behavior Modification: Prospects and Problems." *Cognitive Therapy and Research* 13.3 (1989): 211–30. Print.

Kassin, Saul, Steven Fein, and Hazel Rose Markus. "Perceiving Persons." *Social Psychology.* 9th ed. Belmont:

Wadsworth, 2014. 102–49. Print.

Ross, M., and G. J. O. Fletcher. "Attribution and Social Perception." *The Handbook of Social Psychology.* Ed. Gardner Lindzey and Elliot Aronson. 3rd ed. Vol. 2. New York: Random, 1985. 73–122. Print.

Schneider, D. J. "Social Cognition." *Annual Review of Psychology* 42 (1991): 527–61. Print.

Seidel, Eva-Maria, et al. "Neural Correlates of Depressive Realism: An fMRI Study on Causal Attribution in Depression." *Journal of Affective Disorders* 138.3 (2012): 268–76. Print.

Strömwall, Leif A., Helen Alfredsson, and Sara Landström. "Rape Victim and Perpetrator Blame and the Just World Hypothesis: The Influence of Victim Gender and Age." *Journal of Sexual Aggression* 19.2 (2013): 207–17. Print.

Brynda Holton

SEE ALSO: Casual attribution; Cognitive dissonance; Decision making; Depression; Ebbinghaus, Hermann; Emotions: Motivation; Motivation: Intrinsic and extrinsic; Self-perception theory; Social perception.

Autism

TYPE OF PSYCHOLOGY: Psychopathology

Autism, a poorly understood, nonschizophrenic psychosocial problem, includes great social unresponsiveness, speech and language impairment, ritualistic play activity, and resistance to change. Research on the causes of autism suggests multiple risk factors. A wide variety of treatments are available, and they can be tailored to suit the needs of individual children and their families.

KEY CONCEPTS:

- Affective
- Cognitive
- Dopamine
- Eholalia
- Electroencephalogram (EEG)
- Epileptic seizure
- Norepinephrine
- Schizophrenia
- Secretin
- Serotonin

INTRODUCTION

The modern term "autism" was originated by Leo Kanner in the 1940's. In "Autistic Disturbances of Affective Contact" (1943), he described a group of autistic children; he viewed them as much more similar to one another than to schizophrenics, with whom they generally had been associated. Until that time, the classical definition for autism (still seen in some dictionaries) was "a form of childhood schizophrenia characterized by acting out and withdrawal from reality." Kanner believed that these children represented an entirely different clinical psychiatric disorder. He noted four main symptoms associated with the disorder: social withdrawal or "extreme autistic aloneness"; either muteness or failure to use spoken language "to convey meaning to others"; an "obsessive desire for maintenance of sameness"; and preoccupation with highly repetitive play habits, producing "severe limitation of spontaneous activity." Kanner also noted that autism, unlike other types of childhood psychoses, began in or near infancy and had both cognitive and affective components.

Over the years, several attempts have been made to establish precise diagnostic criteria for autism. The criteria that are given in the current edition of the American Psychiatric Association's *Diagnostic and Statistical Manual of Mental Disorders: DSM-IV-TR*(rev. 4th ed., 2000), are onset prior to thirty-six months of age; pervasive lack of responsiveness to other people; gross deficits in language development and, if speech is present, peculiar patterns (such as delayed echolalia and pronoun reversals); bizarre reaction to environmental aspects (resistance to change); and the absence of any symptoms of schizophrenia. These criteria are largely a restatement of Kanner's viewpoint.

In the first decade of the twenty-first century, the prevalence of autism has been estimated at around 1 in 150 children. Study of the sex distribution shows that it is approximately three to four times as common in male as in female children. The causes of autism have not been conclusively determined, although the possibilities are wide-ranging and said to be rooted in both biology and environment. One of the most controversial proposals in the 1990's was that the mumps, measles, and rubella (MMR) vaccination that is given at approximately eighteen months of age caused at least some forms of autism because the timing of the vaccine often corresponds with the earliest detected symptoms of autism. However, researchers in the United States and Europe have determined that this vaccine does not cause autism. This is based on the fact that vaccination rates held steady throughout the 1990's at almost 97 percent of children, yet the rate of autism diagnosis increased sevenfold during the same time period.

Research on physiological causes of autism indicate a genetic component: Siblings of autistic children are fifty times more likely to be diagnosed with autism than children who do not have an autistic brother or sister. Other potential physiological causes include abnormal neurochemistry, low birth weight, and brain abnormalities such as reduction of tissue in the cerebellum and enlarged ventricles in the cerebrum.

Largely because of Kanner's original sample (now known to have been atypical), many people believe that autistic children come from relatively wealthy, professional families. Subsequent studies have indicated that this is not so. Rather, autistic children come from families within a wide socioeconomic range, and more than 75 percent of them score in the moderately intellectually disabled range on intelligence tests before, or in the absence of, effective treatment.

The behavior that characterizes autism strongly suggests that the disorder is related to other types of neurologic dysfunction. Identified neurological correlations include soft neurologic signs (such as poor coordination), seizure disorders, abnormal electroencephalograms, and unusual sleep patterns. This emphasis on neurologic (or organic) explanations for autism is relatively new; autism was previously thought to be an entirely emotional disorder.

The difficulties that autistic children show in social relationships are exhibited in many ways. Most apparent is a child's failure to form social bonds. Autistic children are typically less "cuddly" and affectionate than children without autism, though they do show attachment toward their parents and prefer them to strangers. In their peer groups, however, children with autism rarely initiate interactions with other children, preferring to play alone and often showing avoidance or aggression when other children try to join in. Autistic children tend to avoid direct eye contact and often look through or past other people. Unlike nonautistic children, older autistic children rarely indulge in any cooperative play activities or strike up close friendships with peers.

Another characteristic is disordered communication. Early nonverbal communication such as gaze following and pointing to share information is delayed or fails to emerge. Sometimes speech does not develop at all. When speech development does occur, it is very slow and may even disappear again. A prominent speech pathology in autism is either immediate or delayed repetition of something heard (such as a television commercial) not in a meaningful way but as a simple parroting back; these phenomena are called immediate and delayed echolalia, respectively. Another characteristic is lack of true language comprehension, shown by the fact that an autistic child's ability to follow instructions often depends on situational cues. For example, such a child may understand the request to come and eat dinner only when a parent is eating or sitting at the dinner table.

Behavior denoting resistance to change is often best exemplified by rigid and repetitive play patterns, the interruption of which results in tantrums and even self-injury. Some autistic children also develop very ritualistic preoccupations with an object or a schedule. For example, they may become extremely distressed with events as minor as the rearrangement of furniture in a particular room at home.

TREATMENT

Autistic children can be very frustrating to both parents and siblings, disrupting their lives greatly. Often, having a child diagnosed with autism causes grief and guilt feelings in parents. According to Mary Van Bourgondien, Gary Mesibov, and Geraldine Dawson, this can be ameliorated by psychodynamic, biological, or behavioral techniques. These authors point out that all psychodynamic therapy views autism as an emotional problem, recommending extensive psychotherapy for the individual with autism and the rest of the family. In contrast, biological methodology applies psychoactive drugs and vitamins. Finally, behavioral therapy uses the axioms of experimental psychology, along with special education techniques that teach and reinforce appropriate behavior.

Psychodynamic approaches are based on the formation of interpersonal relationships between the child and others. One example is holding therapy, which involves the mother holding the child for long periods of time so that a supposedly damaged bond between the two can be mended. The intervention technique called Floortime, in which the therapist or parent joins the child in his or her activities and follows the child's lead in play, is a more active method of establishing a bond with a child.

Biological methods of treatment attempt to influence how the brain receives and processes information. Sensory integration is favored by occupational therapists who take the perspective that the nervous system of the autistic child is attempting to regain homeostasis, causing him or her to behave oddly. The approach involves trying to meet the child's sensory needs through a "sensory diet" of activities throughout the day, such as close physical contact, balance exercises, and moving to music. Drug therapies include antiseizure medications, tranquilizers, stimulants, antidepressants, and antianxiety medications that have varying results. One of the most controversial drug therapies is the injection of the hormone secretin, which reportedly causes remarkable improvements in the symptoms of some children but no change in others. Dietary interventions include megadoses of vitamins and minerals that could have very harmful side effects and are not reliably beneficial. Some parents cut out food additives or coloring, or follow a gluten-free and casein-free regimen that eliminates all milk and wheat products from their autistic child's diet. Only anecdotal evidence exists of the effectiveness of these and other special diets.

The last category of therapies is behavioral or skill-based techniques. The Treatment and Education of Autistic and Related Communication Handicapped Children (TEACCH) Treatment and Education of Autistic and Related Communication Handicapped Children program emphasizes modifying the environment to improve the adaptive functioning of individuals given their unique characteristics and teaching others to accommodate autistic children at their particular level of functioning. In contrast, applied behavior analysis programs, such as those advocated by Norwegian psychologist Ivar Lovaas, involve manipulating the environment only for the initial purpose of shaping an individual's skills toward more normal functioning, with the eventual goal of mainstreaming the child with his or her typically developing peers in the regular education setting, an outcome that is estimated to be more likely for children whose treatment begins by two or three years of age.

All these varying therapeutic techniques have their supporters, but no single intervention is recognized to work for all children with autism. In general, the most

DSM-IV-TR CRITERIA FOR AUTISM

Autistic Disorder (DSM code 299.00)
Six or more criteria from three lists

1) Qualitative impairment in social interaction, manifested by at least two of the following:
- marked impairment in use of multiple nonverbal behaviors (eye-to-eye gaze, facial expression, body postures, gestures)
- failure to develop peer relationships appropriate to developmental level
- lack of spontaneous seeking to share enjoyment, interests, or achievements with others
- lack of social or emotional reciprocity

2) Qualitative impairments in communication, manifested by at least one of the following:
- delay in, or total lack of, development of spoken language, not accompanied by attempts to compensate through alternative modes of communication such as gesture or mime
- in individuals with adequate speech, marked impairment in ability to initiate or sustain conversation
- stereotyped and repetitive use of language or idiosyncratic language
- lack of varied, spontaneous make-believe play or social imitative play appropriate to developmental level

3) Restricted, repetitive, and stereotyped patterns of behavior, interests, and activities, manifested by at least one of the following:
- preoccupation with one or more stereotyped and restricted patterns of interest abnormal in either intensity or focus
- apparently inflexible adherence to specific, nonfunctional routines or rituals
- stereotyped and repetitive motor mannerisms (hand or finger flapping, complex whole-body movements)
- persistent preoccupation with parts of objects

Delays or abnormal functioning in at least one of the following areas, with onset prior to age three:
- social interaction
- language as used in social communication
- symbolic or imaginative play

Symptoms not better explained by Rett Disorder or Childhood Disintegrative Disorder effective treatment involves a mixed program tailored to the individual child.

CHANGING PERCEPTIONS

As defined by Kanner in the 1940's, autistic children were at first perceived to be victims of an affective disorder brought on by their emotionally cold, very intellectual, and compulsive parents (so-called refrigerator mothers). The personality traits of these parents, it was theorized, encouraged such children to withdraw from social contact with them and then with all other people.

In the years that have followed, additional data, as well as conceptual changes in medicine and psychology, have led to the belief that autism, which may actually be a constellation of disorders that exhibit similar symptoms, has a biological basis that may reside in subtle brain and hormone abnormalities. Increasingly since the beginning of the twenty-first century, scientists and practitioners have begun to refer to autism spectrum disorders (ASD) to capture the fact that children as well as adults with autism vary widely in terms of the severity of their symptoms, their strengths and weaknesses, and their responses to different treatments.

BIBLIOGRAPHY

Baron-Cohen, Simon. *Autism and Asperger Syndrome (The Facts)*. New York: Oxford University Press, 2008. This volume by one of the world's experts on autism and related disorders provides a broad overview of the indicators and diagnosis of autism, its biological bases, and various treatments.

Frith, Uta. *Autism: A Very Short Introduction*. New York: Oxford University Press, 2008. This brief volume outlines the research on the brain bases of autism and integrates the results with modern theories of the disorder.

Grandin, Temple. *Thinking in Pictures: My Life with Autism*. London: Vintage Press, 2006. A firsthand account of what it is like to be a high-functioning person with autism. Grandin overcame early difficulties with communication and social relationships to become a successful animal scientist, professor, and expert on her own disorder, autism.

Greenspan, Stanley I., and Serena Wieder. *Engaging Autism: Using the Floortime Approach to Help Children Relate, Communicate, and Think*. Cambridge, Mass.: Da Capo Lifelong Books, 2006. This book first describes autism, highlighting the positive as well as the negative elements of autistic behavior, then describes the Floortime approach to intervention and therapy and reviews the research on its effectiveness.

Maurice, Catherine, Gina Green, and Stephen C. Luce, eds. *Behavioral Intervention for Young Children with Autism: A Manual for Parents and Professionals*. Austin, Tex.: Pro-Ed, 1996. With the mother of two children who were diagnosed with autism and successfully treated with behavior therapy among its editors, the book provides clear guidance for parents embarking on a search for effective treatment methods for their children. Included is information on the effectiveness of various treatments, funding behavior therapy, working with educators and other professionals, and what is involved in behavior therapy.

Sanford S. Singer; updated by Virginia Slaughter

See Also: Abnormality: Biomedical models; Abnormality: Psychological models; Antianxiety medications; Asperger syndrome; Attention; Behavior therapy; Childhood disorders; Children's mental health; Genetics and mental health; Language; Nutrition and mental health; Schizophrenia: Background, types, and symptoms; Schizophrenia: Theoretical explanations; Stimulant medications; Teenagers' mental health.

Autism spectrum disorder

Type of psychology: Biological bases of human behavior; Clinical; Counseling; Health; Neuropsychological; Rehabilitation; School

Autism spectrum disorder (ASD) is a neurodevelopmental disorder which negatively impacts many important areas of human development and functioning. The most common symptom of ASD is significant impairment in the ability to initiate and maintain appropriate, reciprocal, social interaction. Problems with verbal and nonverbal communication skills are sometimes accompanied by unusual and intense interests in a highly restrictive range of topics, a rigid need to adhere to an intensely routine schedule, and sometimes unusual movements such as rocking and arm flapping. Difficulty with sensory processing is common. Some people with ASD may have unusual and highly developed abilities in a very specific skill or area of interest. ASD is sometimes accompanied by intellectual impairment.

KEY CONCEPTS
- Pervasive developmental disorders
- Sensory abnormalities
- Savant syndromes
- Applied behavioral analysis
- Social interaction

INTRODUCTION

The first known written use of the word autism was about 100 years ago when the Swiss psychiatrist Eugene Bleuler used the term to describe a subcategory of symptoms of schizophrenia. The origin of the term autism comes from the Greek word autos meaning self. In the 1940s, Leo Kanner used the term to describe children he was studying who seemed to demonstrate a cluster of similar symptoms. Concurrently, Hans Asperger identified a group of children who seemed to manifest significant difficulty with social skills and interaction yet possessed uncommonly highly developed knowledge and skill in a very specific and often unusual area.

Some psychoanalytically oriented professionals, including Bruno Bettleheim and others, postulated that autism was the result of emotional rejection by the child's mother that resulted in the child turning inward and detaching from the outside world. In 1964 Bernard Rimland vehemently disagreed with this theory and published his seminal work entitled *Infantile Autism: The Symptoms and Its Implications for a Neural Theory of Behavior*.

Modern thinking posits that autism is a neurobiological disorder and completely unrelated to maternal neglect. Unfortunately, blaming parents for causing autism created more pain and anguish for families. This blame was both erroneous and pernicious.

PRESENTATION

Autism is a complex disorder which presents with a host of symptoms. Some children with autism suffer from severe impairment in almost all areas of functioning while others experience only minimal difficulties and are able to live productive and fulfilling lives. Previously, the less severe form of autism was called Asperger's syndrome. However, in the fifth edition of the *Diagnostic and Statistical Manual of Mental Disorders* (DSM-5), the term autistic spectrum disorder covers the full range of the disorder from severe to mild and the term Asperger's syndrome is no longer used.

The most common difficulty experienced by children and adults who fall on the autistic spectrum involves initiating and maintaining appropriate social interaction. Many people with autism appear to have little or no interest in relating to other people, often preferring to engage in isolated sensory behaviors such as gazing at shapes or colors. Objects that rotate are often particularly interesting to some people with autism. Making and maintaining eye contact can pose a real challenge.

Sensory abnormalities are also common in children and adults with autism. Certain sounds or colors that do not disturb most people can be perceived as intensely noxious and result in a kind of neurological overflow. Sometimes this can develop into tantrums and an intense need to self-sooth which frequently includes rocking, arm flapping, and other behaviors. Light touch is another sensation that many people with autism find intolerable. This is known as tactile defensiveness. Interestingly, much stronger touch such as tight squeezing can often be quite soothing. Psychologist Temple Grandin, a high functioning individual with autism, has described how she designed and utilized a squeeze machine that would calm and sooth her.

Difficulty with both receptive and expressive language and especially emotive language is very common in people with autism. While most children learn language naturally from their environment, children with autism often do not and require much more specific and intense assistance.

Focus, controlling distractibility, and maintaining attention, all necessary prerequisites for learning, are often very challenging. Many people with autism do not automatically understand what to focus on. When someone is speaking to them they may be focusing on a button on the person's shirt, the way his shoe lace may be hanging or other irrelevant stimuli. They may be intensely distracted or overwhelmed by too much stimuli. Processing a group discussion where several different people speak and respond almost simultaneously may be more than some people with autism can understand or tolerate. Recent research has demonstrated that babies as young as six months, who were later diagnosed with autism, demonstrated very different patterns of eye gaze and focus than their peers who never received the diagnosis. Essentially, the at risk babies tended to gaze and focus on extraneous and irrelevant stimuli when an adult tried to interact with them while the other babies tended to intensely gaze at the adult's face and particularly their eyes. At some point in the not too distant future it may be possible to diagnose autism at a very early age and to offer interventions while the nascent brain is most amenable to modification.

ETIOLOGY

The exact cause of autism spectrum disorder is not known. What is known however is that contrary to some pop culture theories, ASD is not caused by vaccines. This erroneous belief started after a very small study was published in the British medical journal *Lancet*. The data from that study was proven to be fraudulent and the author lost his medical license. For many years numerous studies were conducted and none found any connection between childhood vaccinations and the development of autism spectrum disorder.

Although the exact causes of autism are not known, ongoing research points to many factors that may increase the probability of developing autism. One of the most important factors to consider when investigating the etiology of autism is genetics. Autism runs in families and is approximately four times more frequent in males. The concordance rate (the likelihood that one person will have the same diagnosis as another) for identical twins, who of course share all their genes and the intrauterine environment, is approximately 77%. The rate for fraternal twins who share 50% of their genes and the intrauterine environment is around 30%. Finally, the rate for siblings, who share 50% of their genes but do not share the intrauterine environment, is less than 20%. Researchers estimate that anywhere between 200 to 400 genes may be involved in the development of autism.

Another factor that increases the chance of autism is advanced paternal age. Older fathers tend to sire babies with autism at a rate higher than younger fathers. Maternal exposure to valproate acid, a medication used to control seizures, also increases the risk of autism. Additionally, prenatal exposure to infectious agents and certain particulate pollutants increase the chances of autism.

At the present time autism is estimated to occur in approximately one out of 88 births. Once considered to be a rare disorder, autism is now extremely common. One reason for the huge increase in children diagnosed with autism may be that as legislation passed mandating more services for people with autism, parents and professionals alike become much more sensitized to the syndrome and its symptoms and diagnosed the disorder much more frequently. Additionally, over the last two decades, the definition and diagnostic criteria of autism broadened to include a wider range of behaviors and hence more people qualified for the diagnosis. Unknown factors may have also contributed to the increasing number of children diagnosed with autism in recent years.

TREATMENT

Considerable advances in the treatment of autism have been made. Many therapies including occupational, physical, and speech/language therapy have helped children and adults with autism live fuller and more productive lives. Occupational therapy can assist with sensory issues and neurological overflow. Physical therapy helps with motor strength and coordination while speech/language therapy addresses the whole range of communication issues which are intimately related to social interaction and the ability to form interpersonal relationships.

Recently, two medications, risperidone and aripiprazole, have been approved by the FDA to treat the agitation sometimes seen in persons with autism. Other medications are frequently used "off label" to treat the depression, anxiety, and difficulty concentrating sometimes associated with autism.

The most effective psychosocial treatment for autism is known to be applied behavioral analysis (ABA). This is an intense and scientifically oriented way of teaching people with autism. It takes its techniques directly from learning theory, specifically operant or instrumental conditioning. This theory posits that behavior is largely influenced and controlled by its consequences. Very clearly defined behaviors are elicited and reinforced. Data is constantly collected and techniques are modified as needed. In this manner, over time, complex patterns are learned. Much of the work of ABA is conducted on a one to one basis called discreet trials. A great deal of research supports the efficacy of this approach. However, it is both expensive and labor intensive.

Other psychosocial treatments involve direct social skills training, modeling, and educational interventions. While much remains to be learned, great advances for children and adults with autism spectrum disorder are forthcoming. Future advances will likely include very early diagnosis, more intense use of technology, and possibly direct neurological approaches. Hopefully, science will continue to find increasingly effective ways of assisting people with autism to live full, happy, and productive lives.

BIBLIOGRAPHY

Autism Society. Autism-society.org A website for individuals with autism and their friends and families. Offers current information, facts and statistics, and information regarding relevant legislation and fundraising.

Autism Speaks. Autismspeaks.org This is the website for what is probably the largest advocacy group for children and adults with autism. It is full of information, lists events and fundraising activities, and reviews current research. Extremely informative for families and professionals alike.

Fisher, W. W., Piazza, C. C., & Roane, H. S. (2011.) *Handbook of Applied Behavioral Analysis.* New York, NY: Guildford Press. The authors present a detailed overview of ABA.

Rimland, B. (2014). *Infantile Autism: The Syndrome and Its Implications for a Neural Theory of Behavior* (2nd ed.). New York, NY: Jessica Kingsley Publishing. This is the 50th anniversary edition of Dr. Rimland's text on autism which revolutionized thinking about the disorder.

Sicile-Kira, C. (2014). *Autism Spectrum Disorder: The Complete Guide to Understanding Autism.* New York, NY: Penguin Books. This book offers an easily understandable guide for the interested person regarding many aspects of autism.

Williams, D. (1992). *Nobody Nowhere.* New York, NY: Doubleday.

Williams, D. (1994). *Somebody Somewhere.* New York, NY: Times Books. These two books offer a first person view of the inner world of a young autistic woman as she improves and struggles to understand the world around her.

Molly E. Sweetland and John D. Sweetland

See Also: Asperger syndrome; Pervasive developmental disorder not otherwise specified (PDD-NOS)

Automaticity

Type of psychology: Consciousness

Automaticity refers to the ability to perform certain types of mental and motor skills with very little attention. Such skills become automatic when they are highly practiced under consistent conditions. The development of automaticity can improve human performance in many ways, but it can also lead to errors in responding when conditions change rapidly.

Key Concepts

- Automatic process
- Consistent mapping
- Controlled process
- Dual-task methodology
- Reaction time
- Varied mapping

INTRODUCTION

Psychologists have found it useful to classify many aspects of human mental and motor performance as either "automatic" or "controlled." Automatic processes are those that are carried out with ease, often requiring little or no attention. They can usually also be performed simultaneously with other tasks. Controlled processes, on the other hand, are more difficult and typically require a person's full attention. Because they require so much attention, it is difficult to do anything else at the same time. Research on automaticity has outlined the conditions under which each type of processing can develop, as well as the conditions under which each works best.

To illustrate automaticity and its development, consider the task of driving an automobile. Driving really involves many tasks, such as steering, looking out for traffic and pedestrians, obeying traffic lights and signs, changing speed, starting and stopping as traffic changes, and perhaps even discussing directions with a passenger. When first learning to drive, most people have difficulty doing all these things at once. When they see a stop sign, for example, they may have to decide consciously and deliberately which pedal to push to stop the car. For novice drivers, holding a conversation while driving is also difficult; if they pay attention to their driving, they will not hear what their passenger says, but if they listen and respond to their passenger, they may be endangering themselves and others. After some experience, however, the same person may be able to stop at a stop sign, check for oncoming traffic, and then proceed safely, all while holding up his or her end of a conversation.

What has changed to make reacting to a stop sign so much easier? Psychologists describe this phenomenon by saying that for a novice driver, the act of stopping at a stop sign is controlled, but through practice, it becomes automatic. Another activity in which this change occurs is reading, which is initially very difficult. With practice, however, a skilled reader no longer has to think about reading as a deliberate act. Instead, when the reader points his or her eyes at a printed page, he or she recognizes the words automatically.

ROLE OF MAPPING

Walter Schneider and Richard Shiffrin have done extensive research on how and under what conditions a process changes from controlled to automatic. The shift is a gradual one; to put it another way, automaticity is a matter of degree. From the examples above, it is clear that practice is a key ingredient in automaticity. Schneider and Shiffrin's research has highlighted the relevance of both the type and the degree of practice. They have described two kinds of practice: practice with consistent mapping, which promotes automaticity; and practice with varied mapping, which does not. The term "mapping" here refers to the relationship between stimulus and response, specifically which response is mapped onto each stimulus. Varied mapping refers to a situation in which a stimulus should sometimes be responded to and sometimes be ignored.

To return to the driving example, the difference between consistent and varied mapping can be illustrated by the difference between a stop sign and a yield sign. A stop sign involves consistent mapping, because the only response one should ever make to a stop sign is to stop; the sign never calls for any other response. Such is the hallmark of consistent mapping: there is only ever one response to make to a certain stimulus, and the stimulus never appears under circumstances in which it should be ignored, so that particular response is always (consistently) mapped to that particular stimulus. As a result of always stopping at stop signs, the response becomes automatic and can be executed without a pause in a conversation between the driver and a passenger. A yield sign, on the other hand, involves varied mapping, as its presence calls on the driver to make a decision in response to current conditions. If no traffic is coming, the yield sign means that the driver should continue without stopping; if there is other traffic coming, however, it means that the driver should stop.

To promote automatic processing, large amounts of practice with consistent mapping are needed. The mental or physical act thus practiced becomes automatic: easy to perform, even in conjunction with other activities, but very difficult to change, in part because it calls so little attention to itself. Automaticity has costs as well as benefits. One such cost is the large amount of practice required to develop automaticity. The inflexibility of automatic processes can also lead to inappropriate responses if the situation changes. As an example, imagine the difficulties faced by drivers in Sweden in the 1960s, when the nation switched from driving on the left side of the road to driving on the right. Drivers setting off to work on the morning after the change might well have found themselves driving on the (now) wrong side of the road. This is an extreme example, but any time that flexibility of response is required, controlled processes, though somewhat slower, may be better. Where flexibility is not a problem and quick response is needed, automaticity should be encouraged.

DUAL-TASK METHODOLOGY

Much of the research conducted on the development of automaticity has involved a letter-search task, in which a subject is seated before a computer monitor and told to look for a letter (or several different letters). The subject starts the task and begins seeing a series of letters on the screen. Whenever one of the items the subject is looking for appears, he or she must press a key on the computer keyboard. Usually subjects do many such trials, divided into two types. In some trials, they always search for the same letters, such as P and C; this is consistent mapping, because the stimulus and the expected response are always the same. In another series of trials, however, the letters they are searching for change every few trials. This is varied mapping. Note that if the letters P and C were used for the consistently mapped condition, they never appear as distractors (nontargets) in the varied mapping condition. The only time the subject sees them is when they are targets.

To test for the development of automaticity, a common approach is to employ a dual-task methodology. After considerable training at the task described above, typically twenty to thirty hours, a second task is added that the subject must perform at the same time. One task that has often been used is a category-search task, in which the subject is shown words as well as letters and must decide whether each word fits into a certain category (for example, "pieces of furniture") while continuing to search for the letters. The typical finding is that subjects who are searching for the consistently mapped letters (P and C, in this example) will show little change in their reaction time, that is, the time between seeing the letter and responding to it. They will continue to make rapid, accurate responses to the letter-search task while also doing well at the category-search task. On the other hand, subjects who practiced the letter-search task with different letters, and thus experienced varied mapping, will suddenly become slower and less accurate, and they will do poorly in the category-search task as well. Just as the novice driver has to think about what to do when approaching a stop sign and will pause in a conversation, so the subject searching for varied targets will find sharing two tasks difficult.

One interesting example of the degree to which a task may become automatic was given by the concert pianist Charles Rosen. When practicing for a performance of a piano concerto that he knew well, he found that he became bored, so he began to read light novels while practicing. Reading is a relatively automatic task, which he could apparently combine easily with the (at least partially) automatic task of playing a well-practiced piece of music.

ROLE OF DRILLING

Upon examining many skills, it becomes evident that at least some aspects of most, if not all, of them are (and probably must be) automatic. Driving consists of many component skills—some automatic, such as steering and braking at stop signs, and some controlled, such as choosing at which corner to turn. The same is true in other areas as well. One reason for drills during sports practices is to increase automaticity so that responses are quick and reliable. In baseball, a base runner who had to stop to plan how to slide into base would have a short career. In education, a teacher must be able to recall the multiplication tables quickly and accurately to use them easily at each step in multiplying two three-digit numbers.

One practical issue raised by research on automaticity is the degree to which drilling is necessary in educational practice. At one time, educational practice relied heavily on large amounts of drilling. More recently, drilling has been seen as boring and irrelevant to education, promoting memorization rather than understanding. The truth is that drilling, or repetitive practice, is absolutely essential to gaining many of the fundamental skills necessary for deeper and more nuanced learning. Without enough drilling in algebra, for example, students find that their first course in calculus is mostly spent trying to figure out the algebra of the equations, with an accompanying reduction in understanding of the new material. Further research will provide more information about the optimum amount of drilling: enough so that the skill being practiced can be easily integrated into more complex tasks, but not so much that students are discouraged through boredom.

EVOLUTION OF AUTOMATICITY STUDY

In *The Principles of Psychology* (1890), William James, who was a principal founder of American psychology, described the fact that some mental acts are so easy that one hardly notices them, while others require careful thought and attention. It is exactly this distinction that finds modern expression in the distinction between automatic and controlled processes. It was not until the 1970s that experimental psychologists, including Schneider and Shiffrin, developed ways to study automatic processes and especially the acquisition of these processes.

The development of cognitive psychology, beginning in the 1950s, has shown the benefit to psychology of studying complex psychological processes by trying to identify and study their various components. By focusing on one part of the overall task at a time, more adequate experimental control can be gained and each component skill can more easily be studied. By knowing the conditions under which automaticity develops and using approaches such as dual-task methodology to help measure it, those parts of a complex task that are best performed automatically can be isolated. That isolation can lead to improvements in learning, because aspects of a complex skill that can be performed automatically can be subject to drilling. It also can help improve understanding of complex mental processes, such as reading, which can lead to the discovery of ways to help new learners understand what is required for mastery.

CONTRIBUTION TO ATTENTION STUDIES

The study of automaticity has added to the general study of phenomena of attention. Fully automatic processes, such as well-trained letter searches in a Schneider and Shiffrin experiment or braking at a stop sign, seem to require almost no attention at all. A popular view of attention is the "resource" approach, suggested by Daniel Kahneman, which treats attention as a limited resource that can be assigned fairly flexibly. When a task to which one is paying attention is fairly easy (that is, uses few attentional resources), it can often be performed at the same time as another task. If a task requires considerable attentional resources, however, one is unable to perform another task at the same time. For example, driving in a thunderstorm or on icy roads makes conversation difficult for the driver, who will probably not even respond if a passenger tries to start a conversation. In this case, the driver must attend and respond in a controlled manner to many aspects of driving that are usually automatic.

Thus, the concepts of automatic and controlled processes fit well with one of the major approaches to the study of attention.

BIBLIOGRAPHY

Bargh, John A., et al. "Automaticity in Social-Cognitive Processes." *Trends in Cognitive Sciences* 16.12 (2012): 593–605. Print.

Charlton, Samuel G., and Nicola J. Starkey. "Driving on Familiar Roads: Automaticity and Inattention Blindness." *Transportation Research: Part F* 19 (2013): 121–33. Print.

D'Angelo, Maria C., et al. "Implementing Flexibility in Automaticity: Evidence from Context-Specific Implicit Sequence Learning." *Consciousness and Cognition* 22.1 (2013): 64–81. Print.

Kahneman, Daniel. *Attention and Effort*. Englewood Cliffs: Prentice, 1973. Print.

Schneider, Walter. "Training High-Performance Skills: Fallacies and Guidelines." *Human Factors* 27.3 (1985): 285–300. Print.

Smyth, Mary M., et al. *Cognition in Action*. 2nd ed. Hillsdale: Erlbaum, 1994. Print.

Solso, Robert L. *Cognitive Psychology.* 8th ed. Boston: Pearson, 2008. Print.

Teachman, Bethany A., et al. "Automaticity in Anxiety Disorders and Major Depressive Disorder." *Clinical Psychology Review* 32.6 (2012): 575–603. Print.

Wickens, Christopher D., et al. *Engineering Psychology and Human Performance*. 4th ed. Boston: Pearson, 2013. Print.

Wyer, Robert S., ed. *The Automaticity of Everyday Life.* Mahwah: Erlbaum, 1997. Print.

James D. St. James

SEE ALSO: Attention: Cognitive maps; Conciousness; James, William; Pattern recognition; Reflexes; Reflexes in newborns.

Aversion therapy

TYPE OF PSYCHOLOGY: Learning

Aversion therapy aims at replacing undesirable learned behavior with desirable behavior by associating the targeted behavior with something unpleasant.

KEY CONCEPTS

- Classical conditioning
- Desensitization
- Flooding
- Garcia effect
- Response
- Stimulus

INTRODUCTION

version therapy, or the use of stimuli to change unwanted behavior, derives from the experiments of Nobel Prize–winning Russian physiologist Ivan Petrovich Pavlov in the early 1900s, wherein dogs exhibited a learned response by first salivating in the presence of the attendant who regularly fed them and later salivating at the sound of the bell that rang to announce the attendant bringing their food. Classical conditioning, as illustrated by Pavlov, involves an unconditioned response (salivating) to an unconditioned stimulus (food), accompanied by an emotional reaction of pleasure. Exposed to a neutral stimulus (bell) that sounded immediately before the food was served, the dogs, in time, exhibited a conditioned response (salivating) to the sound of the bell rather than the serving of the food, resulting in the neutral stimuli becoming the conditioned stimuli (bell) and eliciting a conditioned response (salivation).

In 1920, another early practitioner of behaviorism, John B. Watson, demonstrated classical conditioning in the case of Little Albert, a child who was fond of playing with rabbits. When Albert made contact with a rabbit, Watson produced a loud clash behind Albert's head, frightening the boy, who came to associate the sound with the rabbit. Eventually, he became terrified of animals.

Classical conditioning, through which one develops an aversion to food thought to have caused illness, was explored by John Garcia in an experiment involving irradiated rats that avoided sweetened water because they associated it with nausea. The Garcia effect differed from Pavlov's behavioral finding in that although Pavlov's stimulus required repeated applications, Garcia found taste aversion occurred after only one stimulus.

Taste aversion was first used in the 1930s as a cure for alcohol addiction. Individuals were given emetics (substances that induce vomiting) before they drank alcohol, eventually leading to their associating alcohol with nausea. In later years, persons participating in aversive therapy for alcohol addiction have been hospitalized to undergo an extended process of conditioning, and other programs advocate the use of electric shock rather than emetics. Classic conditioning techniques are also used as curatives for overeating, smoking, and substance abuse.

OTHER BEHAVIORS

Aversion therapy figured prominently during the 1950s and 1960's in efforts to "treat" homosexuality. Believing homosexuality to be a mental illness, those trying to "cure" homosexuality frequently required homosexuals to look at "inappropriate" images of sexuality while emetics were being administered, with the aim of conditioning the individuals to associate homosexual acts with nausea. Later, electric shocks replaced the emetics. Similarly, transvestites were made to stand barefoot in an electrified area, where they continued to receive electric shocks until they removed all vestiges of gender-inappropriate clothing. "Treatment" for exhibitionism worked in the reverse; exhibitionists were shocked until they stopped exposing themselves. Aside from being inhumane, aversion therapy for sexual deviance did not produce the desired results. In fact, many homosexuals became asexual and some became suicidal. The use of aversion therapy on homosexuals declined after the rise of the gay rights movement in 1969, although its decline is attributed not as much to the movement as to the American Psychiatric Association's removal in 1973 of homosexuality from the list of mental illnesses. This change suggested that homosexuality is not an illness and therefore not something to be cured, but something that develops over an individual's lifetime and involves little if any choice.

Individuals with strong gambling urges frequently undergo aversion therapy wherein small electric shock devices are strapped to their wrists and used to shock them whenever they view gambling paraphernalia, such as betting forms or written material that appeals to their interest in gambling.

Intense fears or phobias are treated by a process known as systematic desensitization, developed by South African psychiatrist Joseph Wolpe, in which the individual systematically moves from the least-feared situation or object to the most-feared. Using relaxation techniques, the individual with the phobia undergoes a gradual process, coping with successively more frightening situations or objects, until the fear is gone.

Initially designed to help children lose their fear of animals, the desensitization process has also been used to help children and adults cope with fears such as an intense aversion to spiders. Over a period of time, people progress from seeing spiders at a distance, to coping with being in the same room with them, to touching them, and finally to allowing them to crawl up their arm and onto their faces. Each step reduces the fear by proving that what the person feared the most does not happen. This process has worked well in overcoming a fear of flying. Individuals gradually, in a relaxed manner, progress from paralyzing fright to flying without fear, and in some instances to flying their own planes. Occasionally, in an attempt to eliminate a fear of heights, individuals are subjected to flooding; instead of undergoing a gradual process, individuals are immediately taken to a high location to bring home the fact that nothing bad has really happened to them.

BIBLIOGRAPHY

Antony, Mark, and Mark Watling. *Overcoming Medical Phobias: How to Conquer Fear of Blood, Needles, Doctors, and Dentists*. Oakland: New Harbinger, 2006. Print.

Dodes, Lance M. *The Heart of Addiction: A New Approach to Understanding and Managing Alcoholism and Other Addictive Behaviors*. New York: Harper, 2002. Print.

Fritz, Julia, and Gesine Dreisbach. "Conflicts as Aversive Signals: Conflict Priming Increases Negative Judgments for Neutral Stimuli." *Cognitive, Affective, & Behavioral Neuroscience* 13.2 (2013): 311–317. Print.

Jenk, S. P. K. *Behaviour Therapy: Techniques, Research, and Application*. London: Sage, 2008. Print.

McCown, William G., and William A. Howatt. *Treating Gambling Problems*. New York: Wiley, 2007. Print.

Rice, Deanna K., and Patty Kohler. "Aversive Intervention: Research and Reflection." *Education* 132.4 (2012): 764–770. Print.

Saunders, Barbara R. Ivan Pavlov: *Exploring the Mysteries of Behavior*. Berkeley Heights: Enslow, 2006. Print. .

Volman, Susan F., et al. "New Insights into the Specificity and Plasticity of Reward and Aversion Encoding in the Mesolimbic System." *Journal of Neuroscience* 33.45 (2013): 17569–17576. Print.

Mary Hurd

See Also: Alcohol dependence and abuse; Behavior therapy; Conditioning; Fear; Homosexuality; Learning; Little Albert study; Pavlov, Ivan Petrovitch; Pavlovian conditioning; Phobias; Sexual variants and paraphilias; Shock therapy; Taste aversion; Transvestism; Watson, John B.

Avoidant personality disorder

Date: 1981 forward

Type of psychology: Psychopathology

Persons with avoidant personality disorder show a pattern of excessive sensitivity to being rejected. This fear of rejection from other people leads to a pattern of withdrawing from social situations and avoiding interactions with people. While fearing rejection, the person with avoidant personality disorder wants to have friendships and be socially active.

Key Concepts

- Agoraphobia
- Inferiority complex
- Personality disorder
- Schizoid personality
- Social phobia

INTRODUCTION

Avoidant personality disorder is one of the psychiatric disorders described in the American Psychiatric Association's *Diagnostic and Statistical Manual of Mental Disorders: DSM-V* (5th ed., 2013) and is included in the category of personality disorders. Personality disorders are problems in personality development that begin in childhood and continue to cause problems for a person throughout adulthood. Personality is a combination of a person's behavioral tendencies and inner feelings. Development of personality begins in childhood, and once formed, personality remains essentially stable throughout adulthood. Persons with personality disorders develop certain feelings about themselves and behaviors toward other people that can cause problems in their everyday functioning.

The individual with avoidant personality disorder fears rejection from other people and avoids social situations. Although uneasy in social situations, the person with avoidant personality disorder desires or wishes for companionship and social interaction. Avoidant personality disorder is often described as an inferiority complex, which means that the person feels a lack of competence in social skills and is highly self-critical. The inferiority complex produces a wide variety of negative feelings about the self that inhibit confidence in social situations. Avoidant personality was first formally included among psychiatric disorders in 1981.

WHO AND WHY

Avoidant personality disorder is considered to be a fairly common condition. The National Institute of Mental Health (NIMH) cited a 2007 report stating that the condition affects 5.2 percent of the US adult population . According to the same report, sex and race were not shown to be associated with personality disorders, including avoidant personality disorder.

In attempts to identify the possible causes of avoidant personality, researchers have focused on innate or inborn characteristics exhibited by an infant and early childhood experiences. Infants have been found to display different types of temperaments, including one that is inhibited. Considered to be innate or inherited, the inhibited temperament is characterized by a timid orientation to the external world. Whenever an inhibited infant encounters new situations, the infant's response is subdued and fearful. This early inhibited temperament has been found to be consistent throughout infancy and early childhood before developing into a pattern of shyness whenever around people.

In addition to the innate temperament, persons with avoidant personality often have experienced some negative events in their infancy and early childhood. As they go through childhood, these children are often punished or shamed in a manner that promotes their fears of being humiliated. Apparently persons who develop avoidant personality disorder did not receive parental affection and were subjected to rejecting behavior from their parents.

The combination of an inhibited temperament in infancy and rejecting behavior on the part of parents appears to produce an individual with low self-esteem and fears of being publicly humiliated. These feelings solidify into an avoidant personality or inferiority complex that then prevents a person from engaging in satisfying social interactions despite the desire to do so.

DIAGNOSIS

The person with an avoidant personality disorder exhibits high levels of anxiety in any social situation. The person appears tense and vulnerable to criticism whenever being asked to engage in social exchange. The formal diagnosis of avoidant personality disorder requires that the person demonstrate a continuing social inhibition, feel inadequate, show hypersensitivity to being evaluated, avoid situations that involve interpersonal contact, be very restrained in expressing feelings, have a preoccupation with being criticized, be fearful of being embarrassed, and view the self as socially inept. Hypersensitivity toward any signs of being rejected by other people is a prominent characteristic of the disorder.

Avoidant personality disorder is often confused with three other psychiatric diagnoses: schizoid personality, social phobia, and agoraphobia. The schizoid personality also shows a pattern of avoiding social situations, but the key difference is the presence of indifference toward and disinterest in social situations. This is unlike the person with avoidant personality, who has a desire for social interactions. Social phobia is diagnosed among persons who are fearful of performance situations such as speaking in public. However, outside the performance situation, the person has comfortable social interactions, unlike the person with avoidant personality.

Agoraphobia is the condition in which a person may avoid crowds or social situations because of fears of having a panic attack, which is not true of persons with avoidant personality.

TREATMENT OPTIONS

The typical treatment for persons with avoidant personality is a combination of psychotherapy and medications. Psychotherapy is used to help the patient overcome fears of rejection and humiliation in social situations. The therapy focuses on methods to cope with these fears and helps to guide the patient toward engaging in an increasing number of social activities. Assertiveness training or group therapy is often a part of the psychotherapy process. Both provide the patient with opportunities to learn effective ways to interact with other people without the fear of rejection. Psychoactive medications that alleviate anxiety are usually prescribed for the patient. With anxiety controlled, the patient is able to enter into social situations. Patients with avoidant personality disorder often experience depression because of their isolation from other people. In cases in which depression is present, an antidepressant medication is added to the treatment regimen.

BIBLIOGRAPHY

DePanfillis, C., et al. "Parental Bonding and Personality Disorders: The Mediating Role of Alexithymia." *Journal of Personality Disorders* 22 (2008): 496–508.

Dobbert, Duane L. *Understanding Personality Disorders: An Introduction.* Westport: Praeger, 2007. Print.

Kantor, Martin. *Distancing: Avoidant Personality Disorder.* Rev. ed. Westport: Praeger, 2003. Print.

Kienast, T., et al. "Psychotherapy of Personality Disorders and Concomitant Substance Abuse." *Current Opinions in Psychiatry* 21 (2008): 619–624. Print.

Miller, J., et al. "Scoring the DSM-IV Personality Disorders Using the Five-Factor Model: Development and Validation of Normative Scores for North American, French, and Dutch-Flemish Samples." *Journal of Personality Disorders* 22 (2008): 433–450. Print.

National Institute of Mental Health. "The Numbers Count: Mental Disorders in America." *National Institute of Mental Health.* National Institutes of Health, n.d. Web. 19 Feb. 2014.

Rogge, Timothy. "Avoidant Personality Disorder." *MedlinePlus.* MedlinePlus, 3 Feb. 2014. Web. 19 Feb. 2014.

Sellborn, Martin. "Personality Disorders in the DSM-5 and Beyond." *Gavel.* APA Division 18: Psychologists in Public Service, July 2013. Web. 19 Feb. 2014.

Frank J. Provost

See Also: Agoraphobia and panic disorders; Antianxiety medications; Anxiety disorders; Depression; Fear; Generalized anxiety disorder; Introverts and extroverts; Personality disorders; Phobias; Schizoid personality disorder; Self-esteem; Shyness.

B

Bad-Boy appeal

TYPE OF PSYCHOLOGY: Clinical; Community; Psychopathology; Social

A collision between lust and enduring love, "bad-boy appeal" has been exploited by countless movies, advertising campaigns, and romance novels. The motion-picture industry (James Dean and Marlon Brando) and rock musicians (Elvis Presley's pelvic thrusts) have long capitalized on the appeal of rebellion. Research indicates, however, that in real life, fidelity often wins the battle with lust over the long term. Usually such behavior is private and not a matter for psychological therapy. No official diagnosis exists for bad-boy appeal, and no credible estimate exists for the number of people subject to it.

KEY CONCEPTS

- Narcissism
- Bad-girl appeal
- Male competition for female sexual partners
- Bad-boy appeal declines with age and experience.

INTRODUCTION

Students of Darwinist evolution point out that bad-boy appeal may have roots in Paleolithic male competition for female sexual partners. Why are bad boys seen as a good choice (at least in the short term) by so many women? Nando Pelusi writes in *Psychology Today* (2009) that "evolutionary psychologists define 'good genes' for men as high-testosterone-fueled masculinity, symmetry, height, and, believe it or not, parasite resistance. Men who are blessed with these qualities tend to be confident and dominant, and able to get away with roguish behavior." In an earlier time, the fighting skills, risk-taking, and drive of the "bad boy" may have provided a survival advantage, although such men may also have been more prone to injury or death in fights and accidents.

Pelusi also writes, "Women intuitively get attracted to brave acts of altruism more than to altruism per se," said Daniel Kruger, principal author of a study on "dads and cads." "A distinction between long-term and short-term relationships is important for understanding women's partner choices." A love of boldness helps women find strong males as mates. Secretly they harbor the fantasy of turning their genetically gifted cads into loving dads who stick around long term, long enough to help raise the kids. Think Warren Beatty and Keith Richards; fairy tales sometimes come true.

LOVE, LUST, AND MURDER

In the same article, Pelusi states, "Rock stars, the dudes with the smoldering eyes at the bar, the strong, silent types. The template can morph, but the assessment is the same—the guy's got genes that make women weak in the knees, and the power and confidence that signal them. So the answer may be that the scoundrel gets the girl—but not for long. His roguish behavior wins out: either he moves on, hawking his testosterone-rich genetic wares on the romantic market, or she gets exasperated with his impulsiveness and pulls away...Bad boys will always be with us because they have good genes to spare." The bad boy becomes truly psychopathic when he abuses a sense of lust and trust to turn the people he engages – women, usually – into victims. This goes beyond the play rebellion of the movie theater and rock concert into sexual abuse and even murder. Witness the Green River Killer, or Ted Bundy, for example, the "boy next door," once an assistant to some of Washington state's best-known politicians during the 1970s, who lured his many targets into murder. Between these two poles, a spectrum of men uses lustiness and a roguish nature to play with women's emotions to dominate and eventually erode relationships.

The bad boy sets up a conflict between love and lust. Enduring love seeks a long-term relationship, while short-term lust wants to take a chance on the fantasy of Mr. Tall, Dark, and Handsome. Lusty best-selling books – Harlequin romances, for example – sell in the millions. "The male protagonists are invariably studs on steeds who morph into devoted dads by novel's end. That is, the women get the best of both worlds," writes Pelusi (2009). The fantasy world of the novel stokes the hope that the rough edge of the bad boy exists side-by side with tempting, redeeming innocence. A good girl more often than not gets into such a relationship after hearing of a bad boy's heartrending childhood laced with drugs and sexual abuse at the hands of relatives. A Christian sense of redemption often runs through such narratives. The bad boy has a way of telling his story to many potential bed partners, in quick succession, and then casting himself as a victim when relationships crumble.

A yearning for lust early in life creates an opening for the bad boy who, in the real world, may or may not develop into a loving, long-term family man who possesses a steady job and willingness to father children and create a life-long relationship. Many women, however, must survive a rocky breakup with a bad boy (perhaps more than one) before finding that one true love with whom to steer through life.

One observer (O'Malley, 2012) comments that some "Nice Guys" (also known as "White Knights") complain that some women do not appreciate "nice" men," at least not at first. They seem to prefer a taste of risk, as "the 'bad boy' seems to win women's hearts and loins." This is not new, argues O'Malley. Lord Byron, for example, was widely known as a "rake" who was famously "mad, bad and dangerous to know." Even at the risk of narcissistic, drug-abusing, and often self-destructive behavior, even if they cannot handle money, hold their liquor, or keep their dating to one woman at a time, bad boys seem more "alpha," and therefore more seductive than more steady, reliable men, at least in youth, when hormones rule emotions.

THE ROLE OF NARCISSISM

Dominant bad boys (and bad girls) manipulate others by means of narcissism, an ongoing narrative in which everyone in such a person's ambit is assigned a bit part in his or her script. With dominance comes a sense of manipulation that allows the individual to direct others' lives as well as "reckless thrill-seeking, selfishness, lack of remorse and affect and a certain level of superficial charm." (O'Malley, 2012).

Nicholas Holtzman and Michael Strube, both working at Washington University in St. Louis, examined 111 college students (64% of whom were female) who were dressed in as close to an identical manner as possible (in grey, monotonic sweatshirts, without makeup, with differences in hairstyles subdued). They were then photographed as control subjects and asked to rate themselves on a personality scale regarding narcissism, manipulation, and so forth. Acquaintances of the subjects also were asked to rate them on so-called "dark triad personality types." Subjects who did not know the 111 students were asked to view photographs of the control group (in their usual garb and then in the neutral uniform) and asked to rate them for physical attractiveness. To a significant degree, those who were shown "dressed up" scored higher on attractiveness. Pictured in the drab "uniform," their advantage largely disappeared. Or, to quote an old (and entirely unscientific) aphorism: "The clothes make the man" (or woman).

"In other words," writes Daisy Grewal in *Scientific American* (2012), "People with dark personality traits are not seen as more physically attractive than others when you take away their freedom to wear their own clothes and makeup. People with dark personalities seem to be better at making themselves physically appealing, a take on the old aphorism that 'you can't tell a book by its cover.'" The findings reinforce previous research showing that narcissists are more appealing to than others "literally at first sight." Other studies, conducted in 2012 by Stefan Schmukle of Westfalische Wilhelms-University as well as Mitja Back and Boris Egloff of Johannes Gutenberg-University (Mainz and Muenster universities) came to similar conclusions.

A set of reactions and assumptions known as "the halo effect" indicates that many give people whom they perceive as physically attractive credit for being smarter and kinder as well, though the traits may or may not reflect this perception. However the effect tends to wear off over time. "Since the hallmark of these personality traits is interpersonal exploitation, it is only a matter of time before those closest to them get wise to their ways and start to avoid them," writes Grewal (2012). Many people are also wary of forming long-term relationships with "dark personality traits" after an initial flash of attraction.

In a 2012 article, Harris O'Malley summed up the phenomenon best: "The dark triad personality types are pre-disposed to short-term goals;...they focus on immediate goals (How do I get her in bed?) and less on long-term ones (How do I get her to go out with me again?)... They're prone to stealing partners from others and are more likely to have substance-abuse issues and [have] a correlation with excessive aggression towards others, bullying behavior and racist attitudes. Thus, a person who may have seemed attractive in the short term ends up being dismissed as repulsive as experience renders its judgment. According to O'Malley, "What can seem charmingly rakish at 20 quickly becomes boorish at 30 and just embarrassing at 40.".

BAD-GIRL APPEAL

In today's world, might we also have 'bad-girl appeal," a la Thelma and Louise, tempting innocent young men? Could we also have same-sex couples tempted by the same appeal? Screenwriters, novelists, and advertising agencies seem not to have yet caught this drift. Do we not now live in a world in which female "players" are not only possible, but likely? As if to welcome the new era of equal-opportunity badness, Amazon.com marketed a silver-studded, black leather "Bad Girl Purse" in time for Christmas in 2014.

In fact, in a Google search (November, 2014) "bad-girl appeal" outhit "bad-boy appeal"155,000 to 104,000, with major contributions from the likes of Miley Cyrus. Daily Mail even posted a list of "Top 10 Celebrity Bad Girls" (Modern Men, 2011). Angelina Jolie tops this list:

1. Angelina Jolie
2. Megan Fox
3. Charlotte Church
4. Sienna Miller
5. Lily Allen
6. Christina Aguilera
7. Lindsey Lohan
8. Britney Spears
9. Paris Hilton
10. Nicole Richie

As evidence of bad girl appeal, some mention the "Queen Bee at the top of the high-school pecking order, the most popular girl in school, enforcing her will through manipulation and cruelty" (O'Malley, 2012). Emma Meade writes (2009) that horror fiction, long "a masculine genre, saturated with submissive, weak females" depicting women dying violent deaths at the hands of a stronger male has recently cultivated "female characters repossess[ing] their power and authority, equaling the strength and cunning of their male counterparts," citing the example of Buffy the Vampire Slayer "with the central heroine having greater physical prowess than anyone else, male or female, in the world."

BIBLIOGRAPHY

Horzepa, H. R. (2013, April 27). "The Appeal of the Bad Boy and How Women Get Sucked In". *Huffington Post*. Practical advice for the bad-boy smitten.

Grewal, D. (2012). "Psychology Uncovers Sex Appeal of Dark Personalities: Why Are Narcissists More Physically Attractive?". *Scientific American*. A summary of research on the role of physical attraction in bad-boy appeal.

Meade, E.(2009). *The Bad Boy Appeal: Female Sexuality and Development in The Young Adult Horror Fiction of L.J. Smith*. Saarbrucken, Germany: VDM Verlag. A case study in the rise of bad-girl appeal.

Author. (2011, March 25). "Modern Men Prefer Powerful Women (But Also 'Bad Girls' Like Angelina Jolie)". *Daily Mail*. Bad-girl appeal, sexuality, and celebrities.

O'Malley, H. (2012, December 3). "The Appeal of 'Bad Boys'". Retrieved from Paging Dr. Nerdlove website: http://www.doctornerdlove.com/2012/12/appeal-bad-boys/

Pelusi, N. (2009). "Neanderthink: The Appeal of The Bad Boy." *Psychology Today*, A down-to-earth primer on the subject.

Bruce E. Johansen

See Also: Antisocial behavior; Defiance; Desire; Resistance; Sexuality.

Bandura, Albert

Born: December 4, 1925
Identity: Canadian-born professor and psychological scientist
Birthplace: Mundare, Alberta, Canada
Type of psychology: Cognition; Motivation; Social psychology

Bandura became internationally recognized for his study of how beliefs are formed and how they influence behavior and motivation.

Albert Bandura attended rural elementary and high schools staffed by resourceful and encouraging teachers, and he attended college at the University of British Columbia, where he earned his bachelor's degree in psychology in 1949. Intrigued by the work of Kenneth Spence, he went to the University of Iowa to pursue his graduate degrees in psychology, studying under Arthur Benton. He received an MA in 1951 and a year later earned a Ph.D., focusing his attention on learning theory. Following graduation, he took a postdoctoral position in Kansas at the Wichita Guidance Center.

In 1953, Bandura began teaching at Stanford University in Northern California, becoming a full professor in 1964 and serving as chair of the psychology department in 1976 and 1977. He was named David

Starr Jordan Professor of Social Sciences in Psychology. Throughout his teaching career, he wrote many books; his most notable contributions are *Aggression: Social Learning Analysis* (1973), *Social Learning Theory* (1977), *Social Foundations of Thought and Action: A Social Cognitive Theory* (1985), and *Self-Efficacy: The Exercise of Control* (1997). He was the recipient of numerous honorary degrees, president of the American Psychological Association and Western Psychological Association, and honorary president of the Canadian Psychological Association.

Bandura's work on social cognitive theory is at the core of his prominence. In this theory, cognition plays a central role in the regulation of and motivation for behavior. Its key concepts include vicarious learning, symbolic thought, outcome expectancies, self-efficacy, self-reflection, and self-regulation. His arguments suggest that learning comes from more than trial and error. His emphasis on the importance of cognition as a motivational force to behavior was a major step forward for psychological theory and practice.

BIBLIOGRAPHY

Bandura, Albert, et al. "Impact of Family Efficacy Beliefs on Quality of Family Functioning and Satisfaction with Family Life." *Applied Psychology: An International Review* 60.3 (2011): 421–48. Print.

Evans, Richard I. *Albert Bandura, the Man and His Ideas—A Dialogue*. Westport: Praeger, 1989. Print.

Ferrari, Michel, David K. Robinson, and Anton Yasnitsky. "Wundt, Vygotsky, and Bandura: A Cultural-Historical Science of Consciousness in Three Acts." *History of the Human Sciences* 23.3 (2010): 95–118. Print.

Maddux, James E. *Self-Efficacy, Adaptation, and Adjustment: Theory, Research, and Application*. New York: Plenum, 1995. Print.

Miller, Neal E., and John Dollard. *Social Learning and Imitation*. 1941. Reprint. Westport: Greenwood, 1979. Print.

Nancy A. Piotrowski

See Also: Aggression; Aggression: Reduction and control; Anger; Child abuse; Codependency; Depression; Domestic violence; Elder abuse; Fear; Feminist psychotherapy; Law and psychology; Learned helplessness; Post-traumatic stress disorder; Rape and sexual assault; Sexual variants and paraphilias; Support groups; Violence and sexuality in the media; Women's mental health.

Battered woman syndrome

Date: 1970s forward

Type of psychology: Psychotherapy; Social psychology

Battered person syndrome, which affects many more women than men and is also called battered woman syndrome, describes the common emotional, interpersonal, and behavioral patterns that develop in individuals who are abused by their intimate partners and has been argued to be a subcategory of post-traumatic stress disorder (PTSD). It is usually treated through empowering psychotherapy and community resources. When an individual kills an abuser, the syndrome has been invoked as part of legal self-defense arguments.

INTRODUCTION

As the women's movement raised social awareness of domestic violence in the 1970s, Lenore Walker, an American psychologist, began interviewing women who had been physically, sexually, and emotionally abused by their husbands and boyfriends. Contrary to the notion that battered women are masochistic, her interviewees abhorred the abuse and wished to be safe. Walker formulated the concept of battered woman syndrome, also called battered person syndrome, to describe a constellation of reactions to domestic violence, especially traumatic responses, lowered self-esteem, and learned helplessness.

DIAGNOSTIC FEATURES

Walker and others argue that battered woman syndrome is a subtype of post-traumatic stress disorder (PTSD), in that it stems from an unusually dangerous, life-threatening stressor rather than personality, and that it involves traumatic stress symptoms, including cognitive intrusions (such as flashbacks), avoidant or depressive behaviors (such as emotional numbness), and arousal or anxiety symptoms (such as hypervigilance). American psychologist Angela Browne describes further correspondence between battered woman syndrome and PTSD, including recurrent recollections of some abusive events, memory loss for others, psychological or social detachment, and constricted or explosive emotions. Complex PTSD, as formulated by American psychiatrist Judith Herman, further recognizes the multifaceted pattern of personality, relationship, and identity changes in the survivor.

The low energy and decreased self-care that come with depression, and associated coping mechanisms such as substance use, may impede a woman's ability to seek safety. Walker's research participants often developed learned helplessness when efforts to avoid abuse led to increased violence. However, American psychologist Edward Gondolf and others have found that battered women are more resourceful and persistent in their self-protection and help-seeking than Walker's sample suggested.

Walker's cycle of violence consists of a tension-building stage, an acute battering stage, and a loving contrition stage. The battered woman often becomes acutely aware of the warning signs of the first stage that signal imminent danger in the second stage. Canadian psychologists Donald Dutton and Susan Painter have found that while this cycle is not universal, the intermittence of battering often leads to traumatic bonding, in which the woman finds love, self-esteem, and even protection from the same person who alternately abuses and woos her.

INCIDENCE, PREVALENCE, AND RISK FACTORS

A task force of the American Psychological Association estimated in 1994 that four million women in the United States are victims of domestic violence each year, and one in three women will be assaulted by a partner sometime in their lives. Research in the 1990s found that between 31 percent and 89 percent of battered women meet the criteria for PTSD. The National Center for Injury Prevention and Control's 2010 National Intimate Partner and Sexual Violence Survey (2011) found that 25 percent of women and about 14 percent of men have been severely physically assaulted by an intimate partner; 81 percent of women and 35 percent of men who were violently assaulted by an intimate partner, raped, or stalked reported being severely affected by post-traumatic stress disorder symptoms, injuries, or other impacts. Few individual predictors for becoming a victim of or being vulnerable to battered person syndrome have been confirmed. Among those suggested are witnessing or experiencing violence in one's family of origin, leaving home at an early age, and holding traditional, nonegalitarian gender roles.

TREATMENT

Psychological treatments are usually most effective when integrated with community services that aim to eliminate the economic, legal, and social obstacles to women's safety by offering temporary shelter, support groups, and financial, job, and legal assistance. Partner violence often comes to light in the context of couples therapy, and then only with appropriate assessment questions. Because of the power differential and coercion present when a partner is violent, batterer treatment should precede consideration of couples therapy.

Therapy for the survivor usually begins with danger assessment and safety planning, exploration of the abuse history, and screening for PTSD and other psychological reactions. In the American Psychiatric Association's (APA) *Diagnostic and Statistical Manual of Mental Disorders* (5th ed.; DSM-5), PTSD is included in a new chapter on trauma- or stress-related disorders. It is vital that therapy empower the client to make her own decisions, to avoid re-creating the powerlessness felt under the abuser's control. The therapist helps the woman recognize her strengths while providing an empathic, nonjudgmental space for her to tell her story and evaluate the patterns of abuse. Individual or group treatment may be recommended, and symptom management techniques or medication may be introduced. When the woman feels safer, treatment may move into a healing stage in which emotions, self-blame, body issues, childhood abuse, and power and intimacy issues are more fully addressed.

ROLE OF BATTERED WOMAN SYNDROME IN COURT

In cases in which a battered woman kills her abuser, battered woman syndrome has become admissible in many courts as part of the defense of provocation or self-defense. Expert testimony is used to combat misconceptions and provide information about battering, so that the jury can interpret the woman's perception that defensive action was necessary, much as in other self-defense arguments. The admissibility of expert testimony about battered woman syndrome has been challenged on the grounds that the experience and the symptom patterns of battered woman syndrome are not universal or adequately researched. However, evidence regarding battered woman syndrome has been admitted in the majority of cases in which it has been introduced in the United States.

BIBLIOGRAPHY

American Psychiatric Association. *Diagnostic and Statistical Manual of Mental Disorders*. 5th ed. Washington, DC: APA, 2013. Print.

Blowers, Anita Neuberger, and Beth Bjerregaard. "The Admissibility of Expert Testimony on the Battered Woman Syndrome in Homicide Cases." *Journal of Psychiatry and Law* 22.4 (1994): 527–560. Print.

Dutton, Donald G., and Susan Painter. "The Battered Woman Syndrome: Effects of Severity and Intermittency of Abuse." *American Journal of Orthopsychiatry* 63. 4 (1993): 614–622. Print.

Finley, Laura L., ed. *Encyclopedia of Domestic Violence and Abuse*. [N.p.]: ABC-CLIO, 2013. Digital file.

Herman, Judith. *Trauma and Recovery.* New York: Basic, 2003. Print.

National Center for Injury Prevention and Control, Div. of Violence Prevention. *NISVS: An Overview of 2010 Summary Report Findings*. Centers for Disease Control and Prevention, 2011. Digital file.

Russell, Brenda L. *Battered Woman Syndrome as a Legal Defense: History, Effectiveness and Implications*. Jefferson: McFarland, 2010. Digital file.

Russell, Brenda, Laurie Ragatz, and Shane Kraus. "Expert Testimony of the Battered Person Syndrome, Defendant Gender, and Sexual Orientation in a Case of Duress: Evaluating Legal Decisions." *Journal of Family Violence* 27.7 (2012): 659–670. Print.

Walker, Lenore E. *Abused Women and Survivor Therapy.* Washington, D.C.: American Psychological Association, 1996. Print.

Walker, Lenore E. *The Battered Woman Syndrome*. 3d ed. New York: Springer, 2009. Print.

Mary L. Wandrei

See Also: Aggression; Aggression: Reduction and control; Anger; Child abuse; Codependency; Depression; Domestic violence; Elder abuse; Fear; Feminist psychotherapy; Law and psychology; Learned helplessness; Post-traumatic stress disorder; Rape and sexual assault; Sexual variants and paraphilias; Support groups; Violence and sexuality in the media; Women's mental health.

Beck, Aaron T.

Born: July 18, 1921
Identity: American psychiatrist
Birthplace: Providence, Rhode Island
Type of psychology: Cognition; Psychological methodologies; Psychopathology

Beck developed a cognitive therapy for depression and several tests to assess depression.

From the time that he was a child, Aaron T. Beck had a keen interest in psychiatry. His parents encouraged his learning and interest in science. While attending Brown University, he served as an associate editor of the Brown Daily Herald and earned many honors and awards for his writing and oratorical skills.

After graduating magna cum laude from Brown in 1942, Beck entered Yale Medical School, eventually serving a residency in pathology at the Rhode Island Hospital. Although still interested in psychiatry, Beck became attracted to neurology and served a residency at the Cushing Veterans Administration Hospital in Framingham, Massachusetts. During this residency, he became interested in psychoanalysis and cognition, and he earned a doctorate in psychiatry from Yale University in 1946. He gained substantial experience in conducting long-term psychotherapy while serving for two years as a fellow at the Austin Riggs Center in Stockbridge, Massachusetts. During the Korean War, Beck served as the assistant chief of neuropsychiatry at the Valley Forge General Hospital.

In 1954, Beck joined the department of psychiatry at the University of Pennsylvania and graduated from the Philadelphia Psychoanalytic Institute in 1956. Initially, he explored the psychoanalytic theories of depression, but, finding no confirmation of these theories, he developed the cognitive therapy approach, including several well-known tests to assess depression, such as the Beck Depression Inventory and the Scale for Suicide Ideation. In 1959, he began to investigate the psychopathology of depression, suicide, anxiety disorders, panic disorders, alcoholism, and drug abuse. He also researched personality disorders and cognitive therapy for these disorders.

Beck served on many review panels for the National Institute of Mental Health and on the editorial boards of several journals, and he lectured throughout the world. He served as a consultant for psychiatric hospitals and managed-care organizations, and he set up inpatient and outpatient programs organized according to the cognitive therapy model. A prolific writer, Beck published hundreds of articles and many books, including *Depression: Clinical, Experimental, and Theoretical Aspects* (1967), *Cognitive Therapy and the Emotional Disorders* (1979), *Cognitive Therapy and Depression* (1980, coauthor), *Cognitive Therapy of Personality Disorders* (1990), and

Prisoners of Hate: the Cognitive Basis of Anger, Hostility, and Violence (1999).

BIBLIOGRAPHY

Beck, Aaron T. Foreword. *Cognitive Behavior Therapy: Basics and Beyond.* 2nd ed. By Judith S. Beck. New York: Guildford, 2011. Print.

Chadwick, Paul D., Max J. Birchwood, and Peter Trower. *Cognitive Therapy for Delusions, Voices, and Paranoia.* New York: Wiley, 1996. Print.

Dattilio, Frank M., and Arthur M. Freeman, eds. *Cognitive-Behavioral Strategies in Crisis Intervention.* 3rd ed. New York: Guilford, 2008. Print.

Ingram, Rick E., Jeanne Miranda, and Zindel V. Segal. *Cognitive Vulnerability to Depression.* New York: Guilford, 1998. Print.

Miller, Michael C. "Dr. Aaron T. Beck's Enduring Impact on Mental Health." *Harvard Mental Health Letter* 28.4 (2011): 8.

Alvin K. Benson

See Also: Beck Depression Inventory (BDI); Children's Depression Inventory (CDI); Children's mental health; Cognitive behavior therapy; Cognitive psychology; Cognitive therapy; Depression; Personality rating scales; Suicide; Teenage suicide; Teenagers' mental health.

Beck depression inventory (BDI)

Date: 1972 forward

Type of psychology: Cognition; Emotion; Motivation; Psychopathology; Psychotherapy

The Beck Depression Inventory is a self-rating scale for screening depression that measures the severity of depression. It can be used to assess progress as treatment for depression proceeds.

Key Concepts

- Depression
- Depression screening
- Depressive disorders
- Mental health
- Suicide

INTRODUCTION

The Beck Depression Inventory (BDI) is an assessment used to measure the presence and severity of depression. It was developed in 1972 by psychiatrist Aaron T. Beck, who earned his PhD in psychiatry from Yale University in 1946. He became interested in psychoanalysis and cognition during his residency in neurology. Beck was the assistant chief of neuropsychology at Valley Forge General Hospital during the Korean War. He graduated from the Philadelphia Psychoanalytic Institute in 1956 and began research to validate psychoanalytic theories. However, his research did not support his hypotheses, so he began to develop cognitive therapy for depression. He developed several depression screening tests, including the Beck Depression Inventory.

THE NATURE OF DEPRESSION

Depression is a mental state characterized by extreme feelings of sadness, dejection, and lack of self-esteem. Depression affects men and women, young and old, of all races and socioeconomic statuses. According to statistics from the Substance Abuse and Mental Health Services Administration (SAMHSA) combined data from the 2008 to 2012 National Surveys on Drug Use and Health, approximately 15.2 million adults in the United States experience a major depressive episode (MDE) each year. Of the respondents surveyed from 2008 to 2012, 38.3 percent of adults who had an MDE within the past year did not talk to a professional about it. Of those who did seek professional help, 48 percent talked to a health professional such as a general practitioner or family doctor, while 10.7 percent talked to a health professional and an alternative service professional, and 2.9 percent talked to an alternative service professional only. In 2012, the World Health Organization reported that more than 350 million people of all ages experienced depression, with 1 million suicide deaths reported annually. In 2001, the World Health Organization (WHO) asserted that by the year 2020, depression would be the second greatest cause of premature death in the world.

Depression is a common and costly mental health problem, seen frequently in primary-care settings. Between 5 and 13 percent of those seen in a physician's office have a major depressive disorder. Depression is more prevalent in the young, female, single, divorced, separated, and seriously ill and those with a history of depression.

The National Institute of Mental Health reports that in 2002 the annual total direct and indirect costs of serious mental illness, including depression, were about \$317 billion; in July 2013 the *New York Times* estimated that these annual costs approached \$500 billion. According to a study published in May 2010 by the *Journal of General Internal Medicine*, 25 percent of people in the United States with major depression are not diagnosed with the condition, and fewer than 50 percent receive treatment for it. Therefore, it has been proposed that routine depression screening may be instrumental in early identification and improved treatment of depressive disorders. Side effects from medications, medical conditions such as infection, endocrine disorders, vitamin deficiencies, and alcohol or drug abuse can cause symptoms of depression. The possibility of physical causes of depressive symptoms can be ruled out through a physical examination, medical history, and blood tests. If a physical cause for depression is excluded, a psychological evaluation, called a depression screening, should be performed. This screening includes a history of when symptoms started, the length of time they have been present, the severity of symptoms, whether such symptoms have been experienced previously, the methods of treatment, and whether any family members have had a depressive disorder and, if so, what methods were used to treat them.

The *Diagnostic and Statistical Manual of Mental Disorders: DSM-5* (5th ed., 2013) is the standard for diagnosing depression. DSM-5 criteria for a major depressive episode, require a depressed mood or loss of interest or pleasure, in addition to five or more of the following symptoms during a single two-week period that are a change from previous functioning: lack of energy, thoughts of death or suicide, sleep disturbances, changes in appetite, feelings of guilt and worthlessness, poor concentration, and difficulty making decisions. Depression screening questionnaires assist in predicting an individual's risk of depression.

SELF-RATING WITH THE BDI

The BDI is a self-rating scale that measures the severity of depression and can be used to assess the progress of treatment. It consists of twenty-one items and is designed for multiple administrations. Modified, shorter forms of the BDI have been designed to allow primary care providers to screen for depression. Each symptom of depression is scored on a scale of 0 for minimal to 3 for severe. Questions address sadness, hopelessness, past failure, guilt, punishment, self-dislike, self-blame, suicidal thoughts, crying, agitation, loss of interest in activities, indecisiveness, worthlessness, loss of energy, insomnia, irritability, decreased appetite, diminished concentration, fatigue, and lack of interest in sex. A score less than 15 indicates mild depression, scores from 15 to 30 indicate moderate depression, and a score greater than 30 indicates severe depression.

BIBLIOGRAPHY

American Medical Association, ed. *Essential Guide to Depression*. New York: Pocket, 2000. Print.

American Psychiatric Association. *Diagnostic and Statistical Manual of Mental Disorders*. 5th ed. Washington, DC: APA, 2013. Print.

American Psychological Association. "Beck Depression Inventory (BDI)." *American Psychological Association*. American Psychological Association, 2014. Web. 25 Feb. 2014.

Greden, J. "Treatment of Recurrent Depression." *In Review of Psychiatry*. Ed. J. Oldham and M. Riba. Vol. 20. Washington, DC: American Psychiatric P, 2001. Print.

Greist, J., and J. Jefferson. *Depression and Its Treatment*. 2d ed. New York: Warner, 1994. Print.

Moyer, Christine S. "Depression Often Undiagnosed, As Symptoms Vary among Patients." *American Medical News*. American Medical Association, 8 June 2010. Web. 25 Feb. 2014.

National Institute of Mental Health. "Major Depressive Order among Adults." *National Institute of Mental Health*. National Institutes of Health, n.d. Web. 25 Feb. 2014.

Rampel, Catherine. "The Half-Trillion-Dollar Depression." *New York Times*. New York Times, 2 July 2013. Web. 25 Feb. 2014.

Scholten, Amy. "Depression." *Health Library*. Health Library, 30 Sept. 2013. Web. 25 Feb. 2014.

Substance Abuse and Mental Health Services Administration. "More than One Third of Adults with Major Depressive Episode Did Not Talk to a Professional." *NSDUH Report* 20 Feb. 2014. Digital file.

World Health Organization. "Depression: Fact Sheet No. 369." *World Health Organization Media Centre*. WHO, Oct. 2012. Web. 25 Feb. 2014.

Sharon Wallace Stark

See Also: California Psychological Inventory (CPI); Children's Depression Inventory (CDI); Clinical interviewing, testing, and observation; Depression; Diagnosis; Minnesota Multiphasic Personality Inventory (MMPI); Personality interviewing strategies; Personality: Psychophysiological measures; Personality rating scales; State-Trait Anxiety Inventory (STAI); Thematic Apperception Test (TAT).

Bed-wetting

Type of psychology: Psychopathology

Bed-wetting, technically known as nocturnal enuresis, is a disorder characterized by the frequent failure to maintain urinary control by a certain age. It most frequently occurs in young children, although it may continue through adulthood.

Key Concepts

- Arginine Vasopression
- Diurnal enuresis
- Functional bladder capacity
- Functional enuresis
- Nocturnal enuresis
- Organic enuresis
- Primary type
- Secondary type
- Urine alarm

INTRODUCTION

Enuresis is a disorder characterized by an individual's repeated inability to maintain urinary control after having reached a chronological or developmental age of five years. Although enuresis may continue into adulthood, it most frequently occurs in young children. According to the American Academy of Pediatrics in 2013, 20 percent of five-year-olds, 10 percent of seven-year-olds, and five percent of ten-year-olds may still wet the bed. Of these, only approximately 2 to 3 percent will still have problems with bed-wetting as adults. Bed-wetting affects twice as many boys as girls, according to Matthew Hoffman, MD, for WebMd in 2008. It should be noted that bed-wetting by children under five years of age and occasional bed-wetting by older children are common and usually not cause for concern.

Enuresis is a disorder that has probably existed since the beginning of humankind. In spite of the fact that since the 1960s considerable scientific research has been conducted examining enuresis, many misconceptions continue to exist. For example, many believe that children's bed-wetting is a result of laziness and not wanting to take the time to use the bathroom. This is not the case; most enuretic children desperately want to stop their bed-wetting.

Another misconception is that children will "outgrow" their bed-wetting. In fact, the yearly spontaneous remission rate for enuretic children, a measure of how many children stop wetting their beds without treatment during a year's time, is only about 15 percent according to the National Kidney and Urologic Diseases Information Clearinghouse in 2012. On average, it takes more than three years for enuretic children to stop wetting the bed on their own. During this time, the enuretic child may develop poor self-esteem and feelings of failure and isolation.

Misconceptions also continue regarding the effectiveness of different treatments for enuresis. For example, many parents believe that the bed-wetting will cease if they sufficiently shame or punish their child. This is not an effective approach; it exerts a negative influence on a child's self-concept and may actually worsen the problem. A more humane but also ineffective treatment technique is the restriction of fluids given to the child prior to bedtime. The bladder will continue to empty even when fluids are withheld for long periods of time.

One of the reasons for these continued fallacies is the secrecy that often accompanies the disorder. Because of embarrassment, the parents of enuretic children are often unwilling to ask others, including professionals, for assistance in dealing with an enuretic child. When the parents of an enuretic child do seek guidance, they are often given advice that is ineffective in treating the problem. For this reason, better efforts are needed to educate parents and professionals who work with enuretics. The basic message that should be delivered to parents is that enuresis is a treatable problem and that they should not be reluctant to take their child to a qualified professional for evaluation and treatment.

TYPES AND SUBTYPES

Because there are different types of enuresis, several distinctions should be made in discussing the disorder. The first distinction involves the cause of the disorder. If enuresis is the result of physical causes, such as a urinary tract infection or diabetes, it is referred to as organic enuresis. Although estimates vary, a low percentage of enuretic cases overall are thought to be the result of physical causes. According to the *Merck Manual* (2012), about 30 percent of nocturnal enuresis cases are caused by organic disorders. The majority of the cases of enuresis are referred to as functional enuresis because no physical cause can be identified. Even though most cases are functional, a medical examination always should be conducted before treatment to make certain that the enuresis is not the result of a physical problem.

Another important distinction to make in discussing enuresis involves the time at which it occurs. Nocturnal enuresis, or bed-wetting, refers to lack of urinary control when an individual is sleeping. Diurnal enuresis refers to lack of urinary control during an individual's waking hours. Nocturnal enuresis occurs much more frequently than diurnal enuresis; the *Merck Manual* (2012) reports that by age five, more than 90 percent of children have achieved daytime continence, while nighttime bed-wetting affects 30 percent of four-year-olds 10 percent of seven-year-olds, three percent of twelve-year-olds, and 1 percent of eighteen-year-olds. A combined type consisting of both nocturnal and diurnal enuresis is rare. Diurnal enuresis is more often the result of physiological causes, such as urinary tract infections.

A final useful distinction is that between primary and secondary enuresis. Primary enuretics are individuals who have never demonstrated bladder control. Secondary enuretics are individuals who, after a substantial period of urinary control (at least six months), become enuretic again. A large percentage of all nocturnal enuretics have never gained proper urinary control. Although professional differences of opinion exist, most researchers believe that the causes of primary and secondary enuresis are usually the same and that children with both types respond equally well to treatment. To avoid possible confusion, the remainder of this entry will focus on the most common type of enuresis in children: functional primary nocturnal enuresis.

POSSIBLE CAUSES

Over the years, numerous explanations have been given for the occurrence of nocturnal enuresis. These explanations can be grouped into three areas: emotional, biological, or learning. An emotional explanation for the occurrence of enuresis involves the idea that the enuretic is suffering from an emotional disorder that causes him or her to lose urinary control. Examples of these proposed emotional disturbances include anxiety disorders, poor impulse control, and passive-aggressive tendencies. Recent research indicates, however, that few enuretic children have emotional problems that cause their enuresis. In fact, among enuretic individuals who do have an emotional disturbance, it may be that their enuresis actually causes their emotional problems. In this regard, it is widely accepted that the occurrence of enuresis lowers children's self-esteem and increases family conflict.

Biological factors are a second suggested cause of enuresis. Included in these factors are genetic components, sleep disorders, small functional bladder capacity, maturational lag, and a deficiency of antidiuretic hormone. The evidence for a possible genetic component arises from research that suggests a strong link between parental enuresis and enuresis in offspring. Von Gontard, Schaumburg, Hollmann, et al. reported in the *Journal of Urology* (2001) that if one parent was enuretic as a child, 44 percent of his or her offspring were diagnosed as enuretic. When both parents had a history of enuresis, 77 percent of their offspring were enuretic as well. If neither parent was enuretic as a child, only 15 percent of their children were diagnosed with enuresis.

The relationship between sleep and enuresis is unclear. Early studies provided mixed results on the relationship between arousability and enuresis. A study by S. S. Gellis published in *Pediatric Notes* (1994) found that enuretic children awoke during only 8.5 percent of arousal attempts, whereas nonenuretic children awoke during 39.6 percent of arousal attempts. These differences in arousability may indicate that enuretic children sleep more deeply than nonenuretic children, a conclusion with which many parents of enuretic children would agree. Enuresis is not more likely to occur during one stage of sleep than another and rarely occurs during rapid eye movement (REM), or dream, sleep. If dreams do occur that involve urination, it is more likely that the dream was caused by urinating as opposed to the urinating being a product of the dream.

Functional bladder capacity (FBC) refers to the voiding capacity of the bladder. True bladder capacity (TBC) refers to the physical structure of the bladder. Research consistently suggests that the functional bladder capacity of enuretic children is less than that of their nonenuretic siblings and peers. Although their true bladder capacities are about the same, enuretic children urinate more frequently and produce less urinary volume than their nonenuretic siblings and peers.

There is strong evidence that delays in maturation may be related to enuresis. For instance, an inverse relationship exists between birth weight and enuresis; as birth weight decreases, the likelihood of developing enuresis increases. Children with lower developmental scores at one and three years of age are also more likely to develop enuresis than children with higher developmental scores. The fact that enuresis occurs more frequently in boys than in girls also points to delays in maturation being related to enuresis because boys tend to develop more slowly than girls.

Arginine vasopressin is an antidiuretic hormone produced by the pituitary gland. The theory behind an antidiuretic hormone as a cause for enuresis is that insufficient amounts are produced during the day, which leads to increased urine production at night. Although a small body of research has shown that a subset of enuretic children do not exhibit normal daytime secretion of antidiuretic hormone, there is no physiological reason that the lack of antidiuretic hormone would prevent a child from awakening with the sensation of a full bladder.

The final explanation for enuresis is that the child has failed to acquire the skills necessary to maintain continence at night. These skills include attending to the sensation of a full bladder while asleep and either contracting the pelvic floor muscles to prevent the flow of urine or awakening to void in the toilet. The most effective treatments for enuresis are based on this etiology.

TREATMENT

Early treatments for enuresis, dating back some three thousand years, included such things as giving the child juniper berries, cypress, and beer, or having the child consume ground hedgehog. Currently, drug and behavioral therapies are the two treatments that have been used and studied to the greatest extent.

One of the most common treatments for enuresis is drug therapy. Historically, imipramine, an antidepressant, has been the drug of choice. Imipramine helps to reduce enuretic episodes in 85 percent of cases within the first two weeks, although the exact mechanism is unclear. Despite this initial success, only about 10 to 50 percent of enuretic children stop wetting completely while on imipramine, according to the National Kidney Foundation (2013). More important, there is a high relapse rate when the drug is discontinued according to *American Family Physician* (2003). Significant side effects are associated with the use of imipramine, including sleep disturbance, lethargy, and gastrointestinal distress.

More recently, the drug of choice for treating enuresis has been desmopressin acetate (DDAVP) a synthetic version of the antidiuretic hormone arginine vasopressin, that is administered intranasally. It reduces enuretic episodes by concentrating urine, which results in decreased urine output from the kidneys to the bladder. Despite immediate effects of desmopressin, only about 25 percent of children achieve short-term complete dryness and with relapse rates of 80 to 100 percent after discontinuing the drug, according to C. Carolyn Thiedke for *American Family Physician* (2003). The major advantage of desmopressin over imipramine is that is has fewer side effects.

The most effective treatment for enuresis is the urine alarm. The alarm is attached to the child's underwear and is activated when moisture comes in contact with the sensors. When the alarm is activated, the child awakens, which momentarily halts the flow of urine and allows him or her the opportunity to get out of bed and void in the toilet. After voiding, children check their underwear, pajamas, and bedsheets for wetness. If there is any need for any of these elements to be changed, the child does so before returning to bed. If underwear is changed, the sensors are reattached. During the initial stages of treatment, parents may need to assist their child with awakening until he or she becomes conditioned to the sound of the alarm. It is also not unusual for a child to void completely before awakening to the sound of the alarm during the first weeks of treatment. The amount voided before awakening should decrease as treatment progresses. Use of the urine alarm alone has been shown to result in a 75 percent success rate, with a 41 percent relapse rate, according to Thiedke (2003).

When the urine alarm is used, some type of positive reinforcement system is also utilized. Positive reinforcement programs will not cure enuresis, but they help to promote motivation and compliance with treatment. One example of an often-used positive reinforcement program is the dot-to-dot or grab-bag system. In this system, the child identifies a mutually agreed on prize with his or her parents, who then draw a picture of the prize with dots circling the picture. Every third or fourth dot is larger than the others. For each night the child remains dry, two dots are connected. When a large dot is reached, the child obtains access to a grab bag containing small prizes such as gum, coins, games with a parent, or special privileges. The big prize is earned when the child completely connects the dots that encircle its picture.

The success rate of the urine alarm can be further increased and the relapse rate decreased when ancillary components are used with the alarm. Some of these components include retention control training (sometimes called "hold it and wait"), Kegel exercises (sometimes called "stop and go"), and responsibility training. In retention control training, which is designed to increase functional bladder capacity, the child drinks extra fluids and is instructed to delay urination for as long as possible. Kegel exercises involve initiating and terminating the flow of urine at least once per day. Kegels strengthen the pelvic floor muscles that terminate urination.

Responsibility training involves removing diapers or pull-ups at night and assigning age-appropriate duties associated with the urinary accidents.

BIBLIOGRAPHY

Azrin, Nathan H., and Victoria A. Besalel. *A Parent's Guide to Bedwetting Control.* New York: Pocket, 1981. Print.

Azrin, Nathan H., and Richard M. Foxx. *Toilet Training in Less than a Day.* New York: Pocket Books, 2000. Print.

Bauer, Stuart, and Stephen Koff. "What I Need to Know about My Child's Bedwetting." *National Kidney and Urologic Diseases Information Clearinghouse.* NIDDK, 26 June 2012. Web. 19 Feb. 2014.

Friman, Patrick C., and Kevin M. Jones. "Elimination Disorders in Children." *Handbook of Child Behavior Therapy.* Ed. T. Steuart Watson and Frank M. Gresham. New York: Plenum, 1998. Print. .

Hoffman, Matthew. "Bedwetting: What Causes It?" 2008. *WebMd.* WebMd, 25 Feb. 2012. Web. 19 Feb. 2014.

Houts, Arthur C., and Hillel Abramson. "Assessment and Treatment for Functional Childhood Enuresis and Encopresis: Toward a Partnership Between Health Psychologists and Physicians." *Child and Adolescent Disorders.* Ed. Sam B. Morgan and Theresa M. Okwumabua. Hillsdale: Erlbaum, 1990. Print.

MedlinePlus. "Bedwetting." *MedlinePlus.* MedlinePlus, 4 Jan. 2014. Web. 19 Feb. 2014.

Nemours. "Bedwetting." *KidsHealth.* Nemours Foundation, 1995–2014. Web. 19 Feb. 2014.

Mills, Joyce C., and Richard J. Crowley. *Sammy the Elephant and Mr. Camel.* New York: Magination, 1988. Print.

Ondersma, Steven J., and C. Eugene Walker. "Elimination Disorders." *Handbook of Child Psychopathology.* Ed. Thomas H. Ollendick and Michel Hersen. 3d ed. New York: Plenum, 1998. Print.

Thiedke, C. Carolyn. "Nocturnal Enuresis." *American Family Physician* 67.7 (2003): 1499–1506. Print.

Wood, Debra. "Bed-wetting." Health Library. Health Library, 30 Sept. 2013. Web. 19 Feb. 2014.

R. Christopher Qualls; updated by T. Steuart Watson

See Also: Behavior therapy; Childhood disorders; Children's mental health; Conditioning; Development; Psychotherapy: Children; Self-esteem; Sensation and perception; Sleep.

Behavior therapy

Type of psychology: Learning; Psychotherapy

Behavior therapy consists of a wide array of therapeutic techniques that directly change abnormal behaviors by modifying the conditions that maintain them. Behavior therapy is further distinguished by four defining themes: scientific, action-oriented, present-focused, and learning emphasis.

Key Concepts

- Behavior modification
- Behavioral assessment
- Behavioral medicine
- Behaviorism
- Cognitive behavioral therapy
- Maintaining conditions
- Target behavior

INTRODUCTION

Behavior therapy is a major field of psychotherapy comprised of a wide array of therapeutic techniques (or specific behavior therapies) that directly change problem behaviors by altering the conditions that presently maintain them. At the core of behavior therapy are four defining themes.

First and foremost, behavior therapy is scientific in its commitment to precision and empirical validation. Behaviors to be changed, goals for therapy, and procedures used to assess and change the problem behaviors are defined precisely. The validity or effectiveness of assessment and therapy procedures is evaluated through controlled studies that can be independently replicated by other researchers.

Second, behavior therapy is action-oriented, in that clients engage in specific behaviors to alleviate their problems rather than just talk about them (as in traditional, verbal psychotherapies). Generally, there is a collaboration between the therapist and the client throughout therapy, and sometimes key people in a client's life (such as a parent or a spouse) are recruited to assist in the treatment. With the guidance of the behavior therapist, clients may actively plan, implement, and evaluate their therapy in their home environments.

Third, the focus of therapy is in the present, rather than in the past. The reason is simple: Clients' problems always occur in the present, and only present conditions can directly affect present behaviors. Although clients' problems may have begun at some time in the past, past conditions no longer exist; if they still are in effect, they are present conditions.

Fourth, learning is a major element in behavior therapy. Clients' problems frequently develop and are maintained by learning, and principles of learning, such as reinforcement, often are used in behavior therapy.

In addition to these defining themes, behavior therapies have four common characteristics. First, although standard treatment procedures are used, they always are individualized for each client's unique problems and circumstances. Second, therapy often proceeds in an incremental, stepwise progression, such as beginning with easier or less threatening elements of a problem. Third, treatment plans are likely to consist of more than one therapy to increase their effectiveness and efficiency. Fourth, in general, behavior therapies result in therapeutic changes in relatively brief time frames, especially compared to many "long-term" psychotherapies.

THE BEHAVIORAL MODEL

A simple but comprehensive theoretical model of human behavior underlies behavior therapy. It assumes that people are best understood in terms of their behaviors, both overt (actions others can directly observe) and covert (private behaviors, including thoughts and emotions). This perspective directly contrasts with the way in which people typically are viewed—namely, in terms of their personality traits. The behavioral model deals with specific behaviors, such as "working on a project until it is completed," rather than an assumed trait of "conscientiousness."

According to the behavioral model, the maintaining conditions, or causes of a client's problem behaviors, are found in their present antecedents and consequences. Antecedents, which occur before a behavior is performed, set the stage for and cue a person to engage in the behavior. Consequences, which occur after a behavior is performed, determine the likelihood that the individual will perform the behavior again. The chances are greater that the person will engage in the behavior again if the consequences are positive or favorable than if they are negative or unfavorable.

For a male college student who frequently gets drunk, the antecedents might include being at places where alcohol is readily available, observing others drinking, and feeling anxious or socially inhibited. The consequences might be reduced anxiety, being able to converse easily with women, and feeling like "one of the guys." To deal with this problem behavior, therapy would change one or more of the maintaining conditions, such as reducing the client's anxiety (which changes a maintaining antecedent) and teaching him social interaction skills (which changes a maintaining consequence).

THE PROCESS OF BEHAVIOR THERAPY

Behavior therapy proceeds in a series of seven interrelated steps. First, the client's presenting problems are clarified and, if there are multiple problems, prioritized. Second, the client and therapist establish the goals for therapy. Third, the problem is defined as a target behavior, a narrow, discrete aspect of the problem that can be unambiguously stated, can be measured, and is appropriate for the problem and the client. Behavior therapy generally involves treating just one or two target behaviors at a time; if several target behaviors are appropriate, each is dealt with successively rather than at the same time. Fourth, the current maintaining conditions of the target behavior are identified. Fifth, a treatment plan consisting of specific, individualized therapy procedures is specified to change the maintaining conditions of the target behavior, which, in turn, will change the target behavior and the client's presenting problem. Sixth, the treatment plan is implemented. Seventh, after the treatment plan has had time to have an effect, its success is evaluated. The evaluation is based on a comparison of the client's functioning before and after treatment. This is possible because measurement of the target behavior begins before treatment to provide a pretreatment baseline and continues throughout the treatment.

The success of behavior therapy is evaluated in terms of three criteria: The changes that occur in therapy must transfer to the client's everyday life, make a meaningful impact on the client's problem, and endure after the treatment ends.

BEHAVIORAL ASSESSMENT

Behavioral assessment procedures are an integral component of behavior therapy. They are used to gather information for identifying the maintaining conditions of target behaviors and measure the effectiveness of treatment. Like behavior therapy, behavioral assessment is individualized for each client; has a narrow focus (in contrast to broad, personality assessment); and focuses on assessing current (rather than past) conditions. Also like behavior therapy, there are many different behavioral assessment procedures, and more than one assessment procedure generally is employed. This practice results in a comprehensive assessment of the client's problems. It also provides corroborative evidence from assessment procedures that tap different modes of behavior (overt actions, thoughts, emotions, and physiological responses) gathered through different methods. A brief description of eight methods of behavioral assessment follows.

Behavioral Interviews. Behavioral interviews are the most widely used assessment procedure because of their efficiency in gathering data. The behavior therapist asks "what," "where," "when," and "how" questions rather than "why" questions. The former questions yield specific, known information, whereas questions that ask "why" typically involve speculation. Moreover, from a behavioral perspective, the important issue of why a problem behavior is occurring (that is, what is causing it) is answered by the types of questions asked in a behavioral interview because the causes of behaviors are found in the current maintaining conditions that are tapped by those questions. For example, "where" and "when" questions concern the antecedent conditions under which the behavior is performed.

Inventories. Direct self-report inventories are short questionnaires specifically related to the type of problem experienced by the client. They are efficient means of assessment, requiring little time for clients to complete and no therapist time. Hundreds of direct self-report inventories have been developed and standardized for particular problems, including depression, anxiety, sexual dysfunctions, eating disorders, and marital discord. Because they are standardized instruments, they provide information that may not be specific to a particular client. Accordingly, direct self-report inventories primarily are used for initial screening and to provide leads that can be followed by individualized assessment procedures.

Self-Recording. Self-recording (or self-monitoring) involves clients' observing and keeping a record of their own overt and covert behaviors. A major advantage of self-recording is that the client is the observer and thus always is present. This is especially useful for recording behaviors that occur in private settings. Additionally, self-recording can assess a client's thoughts and emotions directly.

Checklists and Rating Scales. Interviews, inventories, and self-recording are based on clients' self-reports, which can result in a variety of unintentional and intentional errors and biases. Thus, there are behavioral assessment procedures that employ other people to assess clients' behaviors. The simplest of these are behavioral checklists and rating scales. Similar in format to self-report inventories, these paper-and-pencil measures are completed by someone who knows the client well, such as a parent, a teacher, or a spouse. Checklists consist of a list of behaviors related to the client's problem, and the observer merely indicates which of them the client engages in or are problematic for the client. With rating scales, the observer evaluates each behavior on a scale, such as rating how frequently or intensely the client performs a behavior. Standard behavioral checklists and rating scales have been developed for different problems, as with direct self-report inventories.

Naturalistic Observation. Systematic naturalistic observation may be the optimal method for gathering information about clients' overt behaviors. One or more trained individuals observe and record predetermined behaviors as clients engage in the behaviors in their natural environments. For example, a child who has difficulty interacting appropriately with other children in play situations might be observed during recess to assess aspects of the child's peer interactions. Valid naturalistic observation requires agreement among observers (interobserver reliability) and that the observers remain as unobtrusive as possible so that they do not interfere with the client's behaving naturally.

Simulated Observation. Naturalistic observation may require a large investment in time for observers, especially when clients perform a target behavior infrequently and observers must wait a long time to observe the client engaging in it. A more efficient, though potentially less valid way to collect data about clients' overt actions is through simulated observation. Observations are made in contrived conditions that closely resemble the natural setting in which the client engages in the target behavior. The observations themselves are made in the same way as with systematic naturalistic observation. For example, the assessment of attention-deficit hyperactivity disorder might involve simulated observation of various predefined categories of on- and off-task behaviors as a child engages in schoolwork in a room that looks like a classroom. The simulated conditions are expected to elicit the target behavior, which means that observations are likely to be completed more quickly than with naturalistic observation. However, the key to valid simulated observation is that clients perform in the simulated conditions similarly to the way in which they perform in their natural environments.

Role-Playing. Role-playing is a form of simulated observation that is most frequently employed to assess clients' difficulties dealing with interpersonal situations.

Clients are told to imagine that they are in a problematic situation and to act "as if" they were actually in it. The therapist plays the role of the other person(s) involved. For instance, a man who has difficulty expressing his concerns and needs to his supervisor would be asked to role-play talking to his supervisor about an important issue, with the therapist responding as the man's supervisor might. The specific ways in which the man talks and interacts with his "supervisor," including the content of what he says as well as his tone, body language, and presentation, can provide important data about the maintaining conditions of the man's difficulties in dealing with his supervisor.

Physiological Measures. With some problems, such as anxiety, physiological reactions are key components and may even be target behaviors. Physiological measures range from the simple and inexpensive, such as clients' taking their own pulse, to complex electroencephalography (EEG) recordings of brain activity that require elaborate and expensive equipment. Portable physiological recording devices that clients can use in their everyday lives are becoming increasingly available, affordable, and reliable.

TYPES OF BEHAVIOR THERAPY

Behavior therapies can be classified into four categories. One category, often referred to as behavior modification, primarily changes the consequences of behaviors. Reinforcement and punishment are employed to increase desirable behaviors and to decrease undesirable behaviors, respectively. For example, token economies employ token reinforcers (such as points or poker chips) that are earned for adaptive behaviors and can be exchanged for desirable goods and access to activities. Contingency contracts set up a written agreement detailing the target behaviors that the client is expected to perform and the consequences for performance and nonperformance. The responsibilities of the therapeutic agents (such as the therapist or parents) are spelled out, and all participants in the treatment plan sign the contract.

A second category of behavior therapies consists of exposure therapies for alleviating fear and anxiety-related disorders. In exposure therapies, clients confront previously threatening situations or engage in threatening behaviors without incurring negative consequences, which has the result of reducing or eliminating the fear or anxiety. The exposure can occur in a variety of ways. Joseph Wolpe, a South African psychiatrist, developed the first exposure therapy, systematic desensitization. Clients briefly and repeatedly imagine anxiety-evoking scenes while relaxed (which counteracts muscle tension associated with anxiety). The exposure begins with scenes that elicit little anxiety, and progressively more anxiety-evoking scenes are presented gradually. In contrast, in vivo flooding involves exposure to the actual anxiety-evoking stimuli for a prolonged period without any response that competes with the anxiety.

A third category consists of modeling therapies, in which clients observe other people engaging in adaptive behaviors that they need to learn or perform. Modeling therapies are used to teach clients adaptive skills (such as assertive behaviors) and to reduce debilitating fears and anxiety.

The fourth category, which represents the most widely practiced type of behavior therapy, is cognitive behavioral therapy. A wide array of techniques is used to directly and indirectly change maladaptive cognitions (thoughts, beliefs, or expectations) associated with psychiatric disorders. Cognitive restructuring changes maladaptive cognitions directly, such as when a client who views life crises as threats comes to view crises as opportunities. Stress inoculation training provides clients with coping skills to handle stressors in their lives, which indirectly changes their perceptions of what is stressful.

Clients in behavior therapy are treated individually and in groups. The latter includes behavioral couples therapy and family therapy. Beyond the treatment of psychiatric disorders, behavior therapy principles and procedures have been harnessed for other practical ends. Prominent among these has been their widespread use in behavioral medicine, the interdisciplinary field devoted to the assessment, treatment, and prevention of physical disease. Behavioral procedures sometimes are employed to treat medical disorders less intrusively and less expensively than physical medical treatments, such as medication, and without negative side effects. Behavioral therapy is used to increase patients' adherence to medical treatments, such as engaging in physical exercises and maintaining a prescribed diet; to help patients cope with debilitating medical tests and treatments, such as chemotherapy; and to prevent physical disease by increasing healthful behaviors, such as eating low-fat foods, and decreasing unhealthful behaviors, such as unprotected sexual activity. Other applications of behavior therapy principles and procedures beyond therapy have included classroom management, child rearing, coping with problems of aging, enhancing athletic performance, and solving community-related problems, such as safety and ecology.

HISTORICAL ROOTS OF BEHAVIOR THERAPY

The inspiration for behavior therapy came from behaviorism, the school of psychology that emphasized the influence of the environment on observable behaviors, and the experimental work on learning in the early nineteenth century by Russian physiologist Ivan Petrovich Pavlov and in the twentieth century by American psychologists Edward Thorndike and John B. Watson. The modern practice of behavior therapy began simultaneously in South Africa, Great Britain, and North America in the 1950s. It developed, in part, as a reaction and alternative to psychoanalysis, the predominant psychotherapy at the time.

In South Africa, Wolpe, arguably the founder of behavior therapy, was disenchanted with psychoanalysis, and he developed treatments based on Pavlovian conditioning, such as systematic desensitization. Similar reactions to psychoanalysis and experimentation with learning approaches to therapy occurred in Great Britain. In the United States, Ogden Lindsley and Nathan Azrin, students of Harvard operant-conditioning researcher B. F. Skinner, began to apply principles of operant conditioning to the treatment of severe psychiatric disorders, as did Teodoro Ayllon in Canada. These early applications were met by skepticism, criticism, and resistance from the established mental health community, which was still firmly ensconced in psychoanalysis.

In the 1960s, as empirical evidence supporting behavioral treatment methods mounted, behavior therapy began to be accepted. Also in this period, the idea of dealing with cognitions began to take root. Independently, psychiatrist Aaron T. Beck and psychologist Albert Ellis developed the first cognitive behavioral therapies—cognitive therapy and rational emotive therapy, respectively. The advent of cognitive behavioral therapies, which broadened the domain of the field, increased acceptance of behavior therapy in general. Professional journals devoted exclusively to behavior therapy, including Behaviour Research and Therapy, Journal of Applied Behavior Analysis, and Behavior Therapy, commenced publication. The Association for Advancement of Behavior Therapy, the major professional organization in the field, was established. Behavior therapy was on its way to becoming the prominent field of psychotherapy that it is today.

BIBLIOGRAPHY

Antony, Martin M., Lizabeth Roemer, and the American Psychological Association. *Theories of Psychotherapy Series: Behavior Therapy*. Washington: American Psychological Assoc., 2011. Print.

Burns, David D. *Feeling Good: The New Mood Therapy.* Rev. ed. New York: Morrow, 2002. Print.

Dobson, Kenneth S., ed. *Handbook of Cognitive-Behavioral Therapies*. 2d ed. New York: Guilford, 2000. Print.

Kazdin, Alan E. *Behavior Modification in Applied Settings*. 6th ed. Long Grove: Waveland, 2008. Print.

Kazdin, Alan E. *History of Behavior Modification: Experimental Foundations of Contemporary Research*. Baltimore: University Park P, 1978. Print.

Lenz, A. Stephen, Rebecca Taylor, Molly Fleming, and Nina Serman. "Effectiveness of Dialectical Behavior Therapy for Treating Eating Disorders." *Jour. of Counseling & Development* 92.1 (2014): 26–35. Print.

Spiegler, Michael D., and David C. Guevremont. *Contemporary Behavior Therapy.* 5th ed. Pacific Grove: Brooks, 2009. Print.

Ullmann, Leonard P., and Leonard Krasner, eds. *Case Studies in Behavior Modification*. New York: Holt, 1965. Print.

Williams, Chris, and Allan House. "Cognitive Behavior Therapy for Health Anxiety." *Lancet* 383.9913 (2014): 190–91. Print.

Wolpe, Joseph. *The Practice of Behavior Therapy.* 4th ed. Boston: Allyn, 2008. Print.

Michael D. Spiegler

See Also: Agoraphobia and panic disorders; Aversion therapy; Beck, Aaron T.; Behavioral family therapy; Behaviorism; Cognitive behavior therapy; Conditioning; Couples therapy; Depression; Ellis, Albert; Fear; Habituation and sensitization; Implosion; Learned helplessness; Learning; Observational methods; Operant conditioning therapies; Pavlovian conditioning; Phobias; Punishment; Reinforcement; Self-disclosure; Skinner, B. F.; Systematic desensitization; Watson, John B.

Behavioral addiction

TYPE OF PSYCHOLOGY: Addiction; Clinical; Counseling; Psychopathology

While ancient history tells of compulsive behaviors involving activities like sex or gambling, the term behavioral addiction has only recently come into use. Behavioral addiction refers to a persistent, compulsive dependence on a behavior. Addictions are chronic conditions that affect the brain's reward and motivational systems. In the case of behavioral addictions, the reward is the result of experience rather than related to a chemical substance. When a behavior produces a potential reward in spite of threatened negative consequences and it is frequently repeated, it has likely become a behavioral addiction. In 2013, a form of behavioral addiction was included in the DSM-5 although it is in a category denoted as in need of additional research.

KEY CONCEPTS

- Addiction
- Compulsive behavior
- Habit
- Impulsivity
- Compulsivity
- Process addiction
- Psychological dependency

INTRODUCTION

The terms behavioral addiction and process addiction are often used interchangeably. The criteria for behavioral addiction were published in the *American Journal of Preventive Psychiatry & Neurology* in 1989. A behavioral or process addiction is said to exist when a person repeatedly engages in a behavior to a significantly greater extent than they had intended. When such an addiction exists, the behavior occurs repeatedly in spite of the person's attempts to control it. A person with a behavioral addiction tends to be preoccupied with the behavior and spends enormous amounts of time in activities dedicated to the behavior. This will often interfere with the ability to perform other activities and fulfill obligations. The addictive behavior tends to persist in spite of the fact that it may have adverse effects on life and may cause social, financial, psychological, or physical problems for the person involved. The individual will often find that he or she must spend increasing amounts of time devoted to the behavior in order to receive the desired effect. In the 25 years since these criteria were established, many different types of behavioral addictions have been researched. At this time only gambling addiction has been recognized as a behavioral addiction in the fifth edition of the *Diagnostic and Statistical Manual of Mental Disorders* (DSM-5).. As research of these process addictions continues, the category of behavioral addictions will continue to grow.

TYPES OF BEHAVIORAL ADDICTION

While the field of behavioral addiction still is in the midst of much ongoing research, many types of activities have been tentatively categorized as behavioral addictions. If an individual engages in an activity or behavior to such a great extent that it tends to not leave time for other activities or relationships, that behavior is considered to be a behavioral addiction. In most cases, these behaviors adversely affect the individual and cause social, financial, psychological, or physical problems for the individual. Generally behavioral addiction involves behavior that is repeated persistently while seeking reward in spite of the fact that those rewards often do not materialize.

The only form of behavioral addiction recognized in the DSM-5 is gambling addiction though many addiction researchers consider there to be a wide range of problematic, addictive behaviors that warrant clinical treatment. These other behaviors are also persistently repeated by individuals to their detriment and to the exclusion of other activities and social interactions. These behaviors generally fit the criteria for behavioral addiction established in 1989 and are currently being researched as types of behavioral addiction. Examples of such behavior that involve technology include television watching, video game playing, and/or using the computer/Internet. As is evident from these examples, a behavioral addiction can be active like playing video games or passive like watching television.

Moreover, addictive behavior may include various types of physical exercise. Exercise addiction, for example, may be seen in someone who spends an increasing number of hours at the gym or running or bicycling increasingly longer distances, leaving little time for other activities. People with exercise addictions often also demonstrate some type of eating disorder. Another common behavioral addiction is sex addiction that again may involve being an active participant (including exhibitionism or voyeurism) or an observer. Such an observer may have a pornography addiction in which case he spends excessive amounts of time and money collecting pornographic pictures or magazines or accessing pornography on the Internet. Another commonly investigated form of behavioral addiction is a shopping addiction (compulsive buying disorder). A person who is a compulsive shopper will spend money repeatedly and unnecessarily on virtually anything. Making purchases provides these individuals with pleasure so they tend to do it repeatedly, often spending money that they do not have or should be devoting to other aspects of life. Finally, a person who is commonly dubbed a workaholic may actually have a work addiction. People who have a work addiction are unable to stop themselves from engaging in work to the extent that it interferes with the rest of their lives. Such behavior often starts out as a desire to succeed or get ahead and is often found in people who are viewed as perfectionists. While these are the behaviors that are routinely considered to turn into addictive behaviors, any activity or behavior that seemingly takes over one's life can become a behavioral addiction.

BIOLOGICAL BASIS OF BEHAVIORAL ADDICTION

While substance use disorders or substance addictions have been recognized for much longer than behavioral addictions have, all addictions seem to have the underlying common denominator of reward seeking. The human brain seems to respond to rewards as equivalent whether they occur in response to a chemical substance or as a result of a particular behavior. It is felt that behavioral addiction can affect the release of neurotransmitters in the brain and that these neurotransmitters will then affect the brain as directly as chemical substances that are ingested by the individual. This may then help explain why individuals with behavioral addictions actually exhibit cravings and develop a tolerance requiring them to engage in ever increasing amounts of that behavior in order to feel the same effect. Neurotransmitters that are involved in addiction are most likely to include serotonin, dopamine, and noradrenalin. Studies done with functional magnetic resonance imaging (MRI) indicate that the same areas of the brain seem to be involved in both chemical addiction and behavioral addiction. The ventral tegmental area, ventral striatum, and amygdala seem to play parts in both types of addiction. It has also been found that families whose members exhibit substance addictions often also exhibit behavioral addictions. Research is currently ongoing to investigate whether there may be a genetic link to any or all types of addiction.

DIAGNOSIS AND TREATMENT OF BEHAVIORAL ADDICTION

There are currently a large number of scales and inventories available to help diagnose those forms of behavioral addiction that are not recognized in DSM-5. There currently are recognized scales available to help diagnose addictions to work, exercise, video game playing, Internet use, compulsive buying, problem gambling, sex, and binge eating. In 2010, the Behavioral Addiction Scale was developed as a means to screen for behavioral addiction in general, rather than trying to screen for each individually.

While gambling addiction is the only behavioral addiction recognized in the DSM-5, many of the above mentioned behaviors that are being researched as forms of behavioral addiction respond to the same treatments as substance use disorders. These treatments range from self-help groups to behavior modification and cognitive behavioral therapies. Medications have also been used to treat various forms of behavioral addiction. Some of these medications are again the same drugs that have been used in treating chemical addictions. Potential for relapse is also something that all forms of addiction share. Relapse prevention and harm reduction models are commonly used with all forms of addiction.

SIMILARITIES BETWEEN SUBSTANCE ADDICTIONS AND BEHAVIORAL ADDICTION

Much of the current evidence indicates that there are many similarities between substance use disorders and behavioral addiction. These similarities exist in terms of the onset and progression of the condition up to and including family history, the biological functioning of the brain and systems of neurotransmitters involved, types of symptoms displayed, existence of cravings, development of a tolerance, and types of treatment that appear effective in dealing with these disorders. The main distinguishing factor between substance addiction and behavioral addiction is that the various forms of behavioral addiction involve only a psychological need while substance addiction involves both a physical and psychological need. In spite of the fact that many forms of behavioral addiction are not yet officially recognized as such, it is believed that the category of behavioral addiction is much broader than currently recognized and in most ways is equivalent to substance addiction.

BIBLIOGRAPHY

Alavi, S. S., Ferdosi, M., Jannatifard, F., Eslami, M., Alaghemandan, H., & Setare, M. (2012). "Behavioral Addiction Versus Substance Addiction: Correspondence of Psychiatric and Psychological Views". *International Journal of Preventive Medicine,* 3(4), 290-294. This article, based on a great deal of archival research, discusses similarities between substance use disorders and behavioral addiction. It also identifies measures that can be used to prevent the onset of behavioral addiction.

Demetrovics, Z., & Griffiths, M.D. (2012). "Behavioral Addictions: Past, Present and Future". *Journal of Behavioral Addiction,* 1(1), 1-2. This brief article focuses on the field of behavioral addiction and its history over the past few decades. It introduces a journal that will focus on various types of behavioral addiction.

Grant, J. E., Potenza, M. N., Weinstein, A., & Gorelick, D. A. (2011). "Introduction to Behavioral Addictions". *American Journal of Drug and Alcohol Abuse,* 36(5), 233-241. This landmark article highlights the concept of behavioral addiction by pointing out ways in which they are similar to substance use and other addictive disorders. It acknowledges that gambling addiction is the only currently recognized behavioral addiction but sets the stage for the recognition of other such behavioral addictions.

Rosenberg, K. P., & Feder, L. C. (2014). *Behavioral Addictions: Criteria, Evidence, and Treatment.* Salt Lake City, UT: Academic Press. This textbook focuses on the concept of behavioral addiction, describing various types that are thought to exist and making a case for their inclusion in the DSM-5. It goes on to discuss symptoms and potential treatment for each type of behavioral addiction.

Shaw, B. S., Ritvo, P., & Irvine, J. (2005). *Addiction and Recovery for Dummies.* Hoboken, NJ: Wiley. This is a straightforward, easy read dealing with both substance use disorders and behavioral addiction. It can help people understand the various types of addictions (whether involving substances or behavior), the nature of these addictions, and various ways of treating them.

Robin Kamienny Montvilo

See Also: Addiction; Behavior; Emotional regulation; Response inhibition; Self control.

Behavioral assessment

Type of psychology: Learning; Personality

Behavioral assessment uses reports by the person or others of observable behavior rather than making inferences from more subjective sources.

Key Concepts

- Consequent variable
- Discriminative stimulus
- Organismic variable
- Response variable
- Triple-response system

INTRODUCTION

Behavioral assessment arose from behavioral research, which offered explanations of human behavior that differed from traditional theories. For example, early behaviorists believed that a person's behavior was the appropriate focus for understanding the person, while other psychologists believed that behavior was only a symbolic representation of an unconscious conflict. Rating scales were developed by psychologists interested in behavioral assessment and in determining the intensity of a behavior experienced by a person.

Traditional assessment approaches describe a person as having a particular trait or characteristic. For example, a person might be described as having an authority conflict or an anxious personality. In contrast, behavioral assessment describes the person's behavior in specific situations. For example, the behavioral assessment might say, "When the person is given an order by a superior, the person argues and makes sarcastic remarks." The behavioral assessment would go on to describe the consequences of arguing and talking back, which could be anything from the superior withdrawing the order to the superior punishing the person who argued.

Contemporary behavioral assessment is concerned with both internal and external events. Marvin Goldfried describes a model of behavioral assessment that includes a systematic analysis of internal and external events. Four classes of variables are assessed in this model: stimulus antecedents, organismic variables, response variables, and consequent variables. Stimulus antecedents refer to the environmental events that precede the occurrence of the target behavior. Sometimes called discriminative stimuli, they may be either external or internal. An example of an external event that serves as a stimulus antecedent is drinking a cup of coffee, which may serve as a discriminative stimulus for lighting a cigarette. An internal event that might serve as a prompt for an emotional response is thinking about taking a test, which may result in a feeling of anxiety. Both internal and external stimulus antecedents can produce behaviors that are experienced as either external (observable) or internal (unobservable).

This model of behavioral assessment includes a thorough description of organismic variables. These variables include anything that is personally relevant and could influence the response to the stimulus antecedents. Both acute and chronic medical conditions that may affect the perception of or response to the discriminative stimuli are noted. The influence of the person's genetic makeup is assessed when it seems relevant to the target behavior. Finally, the person's learning history is considered to be important in understanding the response to the antecedent stimuli. Organismic variables serve as mediators or filters between the stimulus antecedents and the responses.

Response variables are the person's behaviors in response to the stimulus antecedents and filtered through the organismic variables. The response variables are considered to be part of the triple-response system.

The triple-response system requires the assessment of behavior in each of three domains: motor, physiological, and cognitive-emotional. Motor behavior refers to the observable actions of the person. Examples of motor behavior include lighting a cigarette, leaving a room, and throwing a temper tantrum. Physiological responses are unobservable behaviors that can be made observable by using specialized instruments. Heart rate is an unobservable physiological response until an instrument detects and displays it. Cognitive and emotional responses are also unobservable events. The behavioral assessment of these responses requires the person to report his or her own thoughts and feelings in the presence of the stimulus antecedents.

The triple-response system is important from the perspectives of both assessment and treatment. Although behaviorists have historically focused on motor behavior, it is well known that people experience physiological changes and cognitive-emotional changes concurrently with the motor behavior in the presence of the stimulus antecedents. As behavioral assessment has become more sophisticated, it has become apparent that the relative importance of the components of the triple-response system varies in different people. Thus, treatment may focus on cognition in one person because it is the most important behavior and on physiological responses in another.

The final component of this model of behavioral assessment requires a consideration of consequent variables, which are the events that follow a response. These variables are important in determining whether the response will be continued or discontinued. The consequences of a response also determine the strength of the response. Any consequence that leads to a reward for the person is positive reinforcement and will strengthen the response it follows. Rewards may include getting something one wants (for example, studying results in a good grade on a test) or ending something that is unpleasant (for example, leaving a situation results in reduced anxiety). Consequences that do not reward or reinforce the person lead to a weakening of the behavior.

The goal of behavioral assessment is to describe fully the problem behavior and the events that surround it. Although earlier approaches tried to limit the assessment to one or two behaviors identified as problems, more recent approaches apply the assessment methodology to clusters of behaviors that may form syndromes or diagnostic categories.

A variety of observational methods are used to gather the information that constitutes a behavioral assessment. Naturalistic observation is used to observe the person's behavior in the settings most germane to the behaviors of interest, such as home, school, work, or a hospital. In self-monitoring, the person observes and records each instance of the behavior of interest. Researchers use role-playing and controlled observations to study the behaviors of interest while maintaining more control over the environment than is possible with naturalistic observation. Rating scales are also used to determine the intensity of the behavior under study.

USES AND INTERPRETATIONS

Behavioral assessment has many uses in psychology. There are three major ways of interpreting the data obtained from these assessment procedures. Client-referenced interpretation compares two different performances of the same task by the same person. The simplest example is a comparison of pretreatment and posttreatment performance to see if the person improved after the intervention. There is no consideration of how other people perform the task. Criterion-referenced interpretation compares the person's performance to a previously established level of acceptable performance.

Finally, norm-referenced interpretations compare an individual's performance to normative data; thus, it is possible to learn how a person compares to all others for whom norms are available. The comparison could be with everyone who has completed the task or taken the test in the normative sample or with specific age or ethnic groups, genders, or occupational groups. Norm-referenced interpretations can be used to compare an individual to any group for which norms are available. It is up to the psychologist to ensure that the normative group used for comparison is one that is appropriate for the person being evaluated.

Behavioral assessment has been used in industrial and organizational settings. A 1990 study by Robert P. Bush and others described a procedure for developing a scale to assess the performance of people working in retail sales. Another 1990 study, by Richard Reilly and others, described the use of a behavioral assessment procedure within the context of an assessment center. Assessment centers are established by businesses to simulate the tasks associated with different positions. It is assumed that superior performance in the assessment center will translate into superior performance on the job. Reilly and others demonstrated that by incorporating behavioral assessment procedures—namely, checklists—into the assessment center procedures, the validity of the assessment center results was improved.

The clinical use of behavioral assessment procedures is quite extensive and includes both children and adults. Thomas Ollendick and Greta Francis have reviewed the use of behavioral assessment techniques in the assessment and treatment of children with phobias. These authors provide examples of how to obtain information about fears and phobias from children by asking them questions in both direct and indirect ways. A variety of rating scales are reviewed, including the Fear Survey Schedule for Children and the Children's Manifest Anxiety Scale. The Fear Survey Schedule for Children consists of eighty items pertaining to childhood fears, which the child rates on a scale ranging from "none" to "a lot." Normative data are available for children between the ages of seven and sixteen years. It is possible to obtain information about fear of failure, fear of the unknown, fear of danger and death, and so on. The Children's Manifest Anxiety Scale measures the extent of anxiety that the child feels. This scale assesses the child's anxiety in the domains of physiological responsiveness, worry/oversensitivity, and concentration and is appropriate for children between the ages of six and eighteen years.

Other scales for children, reviewed by Larry D. Evans and Sharon Bradley-Johnson, assess adaptive behavior. Adaptive behavior is the degree to which a child is able to cope effectively with the environment based on his or her age. Deficits in adaptive behavior are an important part of the definition of intellectual disability. These authors review several measures of adaptive behavior that were completed by teachers, caregivers, and psychologists. Comparisons are made to existing scales assessing adaptive behavior. Rating scales are used to measure various behaviors in adolescents and children. In addition to the behaviors mentioned above, there are rating scales for attention and distractibility, autism, and various psychiatric syndromes.

Randall Morrison describes a variety of rating scales that assess adult psychopathology. They include scales of schizophrenic symptoms that are completed by a psychologist who interviews and observes the person suspected of having schizophrenia. A scale of global adjustment is also reviewed by Morrison. This 100-point rating scale, which focuses on the extent to which the person has coped effectively with environmental events during the past year, is useful with a wide variety of psychiatric patients. According to Morrison, it has some value in predicting how well a person will cope after treatment, as well as in assessing the effectiveness of the treatment.

There are many rating scales for children, adolescents, and adults. They assess a wide range of behaviors and vary in the degree to which they have been constructed with attention to the standards for test development and the compilation of appropriate norms.

THE DEVELOPMENT OF BEHAVIORAL ASSESSMENT

The history of psychological assessment is replete with examples of attempts to measure people's characteristics and traits, which are defined as underlying psychological processes that are pervasive aspects of personality. In fact, for many psychologists, characteristics and traits define the personality. Traditional approaches to psychotherapy try to identify the traits to develop a therapeutic strategy that will reveal the unconscious conflicts.

Unlike traditional approaches to psychological assessment and psychotherapy, behavioral assessment arose from the need of behavior therapists to describe more completely the events surrounding the problem behavior. The history of behavior therapy is one of defining a target behavior and designing a program to change the behavior. As behavior therapy developed and became more sophisticated, it became apparent that more information was needed to identify the antecedent stimuli, the organismic filters that were operating, which aspect of the triple-response system was relevant, and what the consequences of the target behavior were. In response to that need, behavioral assessment was developed. Initially, behavioral assessment was rather straightforward and did not bother much with the procedures of psychological test construction, since the process itself was one of observing behavior rather than making inferences about behavior from test responses. As behavioral assessment has matured, it has become more concerned with meeting the standards of test construction applied to other assessment methods and has become more sophisticated and complex.

Behavioral assessment is used to measure clusters of behaviors and syndromes rather than merely isolated problem behaviors. More attention is paid to the extent to which standards of validity and reliability are met. Psychologists are putting behavioral assessment to the test of demonstrating its worth as an assessment procedure; to justify its use, it must add something to the understanding of the person being assessed. The challenge is being met, and behavioral assessment continues to provide valuable information about the person being assessed. Information obtained is useful in determining the extent to which certain behaviors are problems. Other information is used in determining the personality of the individual, with all the attendant traits and characteristics.

BIBLIOGRAPHY

Barrios, Billy A. "On the Changing Nature of Behavioral Assessment." *Behavioral Assessment: A Practical Handbook*. Ed. Alan S. Bellack and Michel Hersen. 3rd ed. New York: Pergamon, 1988. 3–41. Print.

Bunker, L. N., Subhash Meena, and Laxmi Prajapat. "Behavioral Assessment of Mentally Challenged Children." *SIS Journal of Projective Psychology and Mental Health* 20.2 (2013): 137–40. Print.

Bush, Robert P., et al. "Developing a Behavior-Based Scale to Assess Retail Salesperson Performance." *Journal of Retailing* 66.1 (1990): 119–36. Print.

Evans, Larry D., and Sharon Bradley-Johnson. "A Review of Recently Developed Measures of Adaptive Behavior." *Psychology in the Schools* 25.3 (1988): 276–87. Print.

Goldfried, Marvin R. "Behavioral Assessment: An Overview." *International Handbook of Behavior Modification and Therapy*. Ed. Alan S. Bellack, Michel Hersen, and Alan E. Kazdin. New York: Plenum, 1982. 81–107. Print.

Haynes, Stephen N. "The Changing Nature of Behavioral Assessment." *Behavioral Assessment: A Practical Handbook*. Ed. Alan S. Bellack and Michel Hersen. 4th ed. Boston: Allyn, 1998. 1–21. Print.

Haynes, Stephen N., William H. O'Brien, and Joseph Keawe'aimoku Kaholokula. *Behavioral Assessment and Case Formulation*. Hoboken: Wiley, 2011. Print.

Kanfer, Frederick H., and W. Robert Nay. "Behavioral Assessment." *Contemporary Behavior Therapy: Conceptual and Empirical Foundations*. Ed. G. Terence Wilson and Cyril M. Franks. New York: Guilford, 1982. 367–402. Print.

Ollendick, Thomas H., and Greta Francis. "Behavioral Assessment and Treatment of Childhood Phobias." *Behavior Modification* 12.2 (1988): 165–204. Print.

Reilly, Richard R., Sarah Henry, and James W. Smither. "An Examination of the Effects of Using Behavior Checklists on the Construct Validity of Assessment Center Dimensions." *Personnel Psychology* 43.1 (1990): 71–84. Print.

Richard, David C. S., and Steven K. Huprich, eds. *Clinical Psychology: Assessment, Treatment, and Research*. London: Academic, 2008. Print.

Thompson, Elizabeth, et al. "Identifying Youth at Risk for Psychosis Using the Behavior Assessment System for Children, Second Edition." *Schizophrenia Research* 151.1–3 (2013): 238–44. Print.

Trull, Timothy J., and E. Jerry Phares. *Clinical Psychology*. 6th ed. Belmont: Wadsworth, 2001. Print.

Whitcomb, Sara A., and Kenneth W. Merrell. *Behavioral, Social, and Emotional Assessment of Children and Adolescents*. 4th ed. New York: Routledge, 2013. Print.

James T. Trent

SEE ALSO: Assessment; Behavior therapy; Behaviorism; Clinical interviewing, testing, and observation; Cognitive behavior therapy; Emotions; Observational methods; Personality: Psychophysiological measures; Personality rating scales.

Behavioral economics

Type of psychology: Biological bases of behavior; Cognition; Organizational; Social

Behavioral economics is a specialty area in the discipline of economics that relies on psychological investigative methods and psychological concepts to understand and ultimately predict people's economic behavior. Behavioral economics differs from traditional economics in that it does not assume the primacy of rationality and logic and does not predominantly rely on mathematical and statistical models to explain observed economic behaviors. In contrast, behavioral economics examines emotional motives for economic choices.

Key Concepts

- *Homo economicus*
- Bounded rationality
- Expected utility theory
- Neuroeconomics

INTRODUCTION

Behavioral economics seems like a recent hybrid, as it melds abstract, mathematically oriented economic theory with field-based, experimentally oriented motivation psychology; however, the relationship between the two was identified in the 1940's, though it found little academic support at that time.

Classical and neoclassical economics investigate how people allocate resources, using mathematical language and methods. Economic theory is constructed with mathematical tools, statistical modeling, and theorems, and it has traditionally assumed that people weigh costs against benefits, and maximize profits and value for their own benefit. The traditional, mainstream model that economists have used in developing theory is based on the concept of the economic man, or homo economicus. The economic man was assumed to make economic and financial decisions based on logic. If aware of all the pertinent facts, the economic man would take the actions that led to the most profitable outcome. The economic man was assumed to be self-aware, self-disciplined, analytical, self-centered, and able to delay gratification for a greater gain or good. The reasoning of such a person is in this way "unbounded."

Traditional economics has a great deal of theoretical robustness. Intellectually, deductive economic theories and models make sense. They work on paper and in statistical software. Academics in general and economists in particular believed the theories were solid, and if the theories failed to explain observed behavior, the problem was assumed to lie in people's not having enough pertinent data on which to base their decisions. The underlying mathematics and the theories conceptually made sense. However, the economic theories often failed to predict actual behavior. People, companies, or countries did not operate the way the theories said they would. What was so clear conceptually was rarely seen practically.

By the 1950's, economist Herbert Simon of Carnegie Mellon University had begun to advocate an economic theory that included the observation that rationality accounts for only part of the human mind, that rationality was in fact "bounded." He reasoned that rationality, logic, and mathematics are important but have inherent limitations in their ability to explain people's behavior and choices. Rational thought by itself does not account for how people make economic, or any other, decisions. Individual cognition includes emotion, feelings, memory, intuition, and undisciplined needs, passions, and drives. The concept of bounded rationality was unpopular when Simon introduced it to professional economists in the 1940's, but it has become widely accepted.

In 1976, preeminent economist Adam Smith began to describe another factor present in economic activities, altruism, in which people care for the interests of others even at a cost to themselves. The "head" in theoretical economics was beginning to find the "heart" of psychological insight into human motivation and behavior. Behavioral economics studies not how people should act, but how they really behave.

IMPACT ON ECONOMIC THEORY

Economics produced a series of theories that were intended to explain and predict economic behavior. Theories and concepts such as equilibrium, exponential discounting, expected utility (EU), and social utility were proposed to explain various types of commercial and trade behaviors. However, observed economic behaviors often have not been adequately explained or predicted by classical theories, forcing revisions of these theories that include social psychological, behavioral, and motivation psychology concepts. For example, in classical expected utility theory, people weigh possible outcomes by how likely they judge those outcomes to be. A man will loan his tools to a neighbor whom he believes can use them safely, will return them in a timely manner, and has the potential to loan him something of an approximately equivalent value. A fundamental, but flawed, assumption made by expected utility theory is that people consider such exchanges linearly—they do not. People make economic decisions not from the vantage of absolute net gains or losses, but gains or losses from a self-referred point.

Research shows that people mentally categorize sources and types of money differently even if the amounts are the same. Most school teachers who have the option to be paid their full annual salary over the ten-month school year or over the twelve-month calendar year choose the second option, even though the first option provides an economic advantage in the form of an investment opportunity. The ten-month option creates an opportunity to invest the portion that would be allocated to the eleventh and twelfth months, increasing the total amount of pay received. Yet few teachers take the ten-month option. Most teachers experience psychological tension and anxiety in the two months when they do not receive a paycheck (despite their having already been paid the money for the two months) and feel insecure about their fiscal self-discipline and budgeting practices. For the overwhelming majority, the ten-month option feels riskier.

How options are perceived has a lot to do with framing, the context in which an item, idea, statement, product, or other stimulus is presented. The classic example of framing involves presenting a glass of water that is filled to half of its capacity to a person. When the glass is presented as "half full," the recipient will be more likely to believe that he or she is gaining something, a half glass of water. The emotional experience will probably be positive. When the glass is presented as "half empty," the recipient will be more likely to believe that he or she is being short-changed. The recipient has not gained a half glass of water but is being cheated or deprived of the second half of the glass of water, the portion that is empty. The emotional experience in this case is probably negative, although the amount of water is identical in both cases.

Behavioral economics provides a psychological dimension of human decision making. It amplifies expected utility theory by blending it with prospect theory, which acknowledges that people adapt to their recent experiences and consider possibilities in nonlinear ways. Gains and losses are experienced psychologically, not rationally. Research in the social psychology of loss aversion shows that losses are experienced twice as negatively as gains are positively experienced, even when the absolute amounts are nearly identical. People also overvalue investing in low-probability events such as experiencing catastrophic home damage or buying a winning lottery ticket. Most are willing to secure the guaranteed loss of purchasing homeowner's insurance or paying for a lottery ticket even though most will never experience the benefit of the purchase. Prospect theory explains the existence of an inner weighing of probabilities that is emotionally, nonlinearly driven. Expected utility theory on its own cannot easily explain these common behaviors.

APPLIED BEHAVIORAL ECONOMICS

Real world, observed economic activities are not the result of careful cognitive calculation and reasoning. Choice is not always economically purposeful. For example, economists and policy makers promote the importance of long-term investing for retirement, which most people would agree is a good thing. However, people are more likely to save for retirement if they are automatically enrolled in a plan than if they have to take deliberate steps to save money. Even the way the investment form is designed has an impact on whether employees choose to invest. Complicated, cluttered forms are generally not read in their entirety, and the boxes they frequently contain often remain unchecked.

Harvard professor of economics Sendhil Mullainathan conducted an illuminating study of how conditions at the moment of decision making are more influential than the objectively derived numbers associated with economic activity. He worked with a South African bank that had a mission of improving the general economic conditions of the country. The bank sought to accomplish this by making loans more readily available. Under Mullainathan's guidance, the bank marketed the loans while simultaneously investigating whether other, unrelated variables would affect customers' decisions to apply for a loan. The bank targeted previous borrowers, 70,000 in all, and informed the recipients that they had automatically qualified for a new loan. The bank randomized multiple versions of the letter. Some customers received a desirable low rate and others an undesirable high rate. All letters contained a photograph of a bank employee, with those depicted of various races and both genders. Some letters featured complex tables intended to illustrate how the loan would operate; others had simple tables. Some letters contained deadlines, and some offered to enroll customers in a lottery to win a free cell phone if they came into the local branch just to talk about getting a loan. Because Mullainathan randomized the sending of the letters, he was able to correlate which factors, in addition to the interest rate, influenced customers' loan application behavior. Using a photograph of a woman rather than a man was as likely to generate an application as offering a rate that was lower by 5 percentage points. The level of complexity of the tables, the chance of getting into the cell phone lottery, and the presence of a deadline all influenced customers' behavior as much as the interest rates did.

Though his study is fascinating and informative, it is not well known outside the world of professional and academic economists. Still, it illustrates the critical, sometimes determinative role that psychological factors play in making important economic decisions. To a classical economist, Mullainathan's work in South Africa had one singular variable of worth, the interest rate. A classical economist would argue that if the bank wants to increase its loan business, it should lower the interest rate offered. To a behavioral economist, Mullainathan's work demonstrates that a comfortable social climate, the intelligibility of the letter and subsequent forms, and a chance to get something (the cell phone) for nothing are of equal importance to getting people to borrow money.

A BIOLOGICAL BASIS

Neuroeconomics is a growing, though controversial, branch of behavioral economics that uses the premise that people never fully escape their biology. It uses imaging technologies such as magnetic resonance imaging (MRI) to map and understand the brain cell's (neuronal) pathways and brain blood flow that are activated as people feel motivation to do or not do something. It studies the parts of the brain responsible for emotion and intuition, the limbic and paralimbic systems. It compares and contrasts how these areas are activated with the activation of the reasoning-analytical parts of the brain, the frontal and parietal areas, when people are asked to make decisions about delaying gratification. It is the interaction of the limbic and reasoning centers that provide the basis for how people make decisions.

FUTURE

Economists widely accept the premise that financial decisions and economic activities come out of a complex array of motivations, most having little to do with what makes purely rational economic sense. Applying behavioral economic principles in developing policies and initiatives is essential if they are to achieve their ends. People use reason but are not exclusively rational. Behavioral economics has proven to be as important as classical economics in understanding and predicting human economic activity and decision making.

BIBLIOGRAPHY

Ariely, Dan. *Predictably Irrational: The Hidden Forces That Shape Our Decisions.* New York: HarperCollins, 2008. Behavioral economist at Duke University and the Massachusetts Institute of Technology presents a discussion of how people fundamentally behave more irrationally than rationally. He argues that expectations, mores, emotions, and other "invisible" factors affect human decision making in ways that render it illogical. Uses everyday examples as well as findings from economic research.

Cox, Donald. "Good News! Behavioral Economics Is Not Going Away Anytime Soon." *Journal of Product & Brand Management* 14, no. 6 (2005): 375-378. A Boston College economist argues in this special issue of this journal that behavioral economics is similar to marketing as it draws on multiple disciplines to research consumer behavior.

Lambert, Craig. "The Marketplace of Perceptions." *Harvard Magazine* 108, no. 4 (March/April, 2006): 50-95. Deputy editor Craig presents a clear, lucid, and well-written introduction to the role behavioral economics plays in explaining the range of illogical and often self-defeating behaviors in which people engage. Includes a summary of Mullainathan's research in South Africa.

Mancio, Lisa. "Insidious Consumption: Surprising Factors That Influence What We Eat and How Much." *Amber Waves* 5, no. 3 (June, 2007): 10-15. Presents the limits of standard economic tools and the need to use findings from behavioral economics to understand and develop coherent, practical policy for combating the prevalence of obesity and diet-related diseases.

Mir, On, et al. "Psychology, Behavioral Economics, and Public Policy." *Marketing Letters* 16, nos. 3/4 (2005): 443-454. The authors, all academic economists, argue for the incorporation of behavioral science in governmental policy making. Cites successful examples of research that has informed policy. Warns researchers to present findings in language accessible to nonscientist policy makers.

Thaler, Richard H. *The Winner's Curse: Paradoxes and Anomalies of Economic Life.* Princeton, N.J.: Princeton University Press, 1994. One of the founders of behavioral economics, University of Chicago professor of economics Thaler describes the shortcomings of classic economic theory. His work is solidly researched and complete with mathematics for those so inclined.

Thaler, Richard H., and Cass R. Sunstein. *Nudge: Improving Decisions About Health, Wealth, and Happiness.* Chicago: University of Chicago Press, 2008. Calling their approach "libertarian paternalism," these University of Chicago economists argue for the application of behavioral economics in planning government and industry policies. They suggest that people would be better off if systems were put in place that nudged them in the "right" direction. As much a political work as a psychological one.

Paul Moglia

SEE ALSO: Behavior; Consequences; Cost analysis; Decision making.

Behavioral family therapy

TYPE OF PSYCHOLOGY: Psychotherapy

Behavioral family therapy is a type of psychotherapy that applies the principles of learning theory to the treatment of family problems. It is most frequently used to treat parent-child problems, with the parents being taught to apply behavioral techniques to correct their children's misbehavior.

KEY CONCEPTS

- Circular Causality
- Classical conditioning
- Contingency management
- Learning theory
- Linear view of causality
- Operant conditioning
- Positive reinforcement
- Response cost

INTRODUCTION

Behavioral family therapy is a type of psychotherapy used to treat families in which one or more members are exhibiting behavior problems. Behavioral therapy was employed originally in the treatment of individual disorders such as phobias (irrational fears). Behavioral family therapy represents an extension of the use of behavioral techniques from the treatment of individual problems to the treatment of family problems. The most common problems treated by behavioral family therapy are parent-child conflicts; however, the principles of this type of therapy have been used to treat other familial difficulties, including marital and sexual problems.

ROLE OF LEARNING THEORY

The principles of learning theory underlie the theory and practice of behavioral family therapy. Learning theory was developed through laboratory experimentation largely begun by Ivan Petrovich Pavlov nd Edward L. Thorndike during the early 1900s. Pavlov was a Russian physiologist interested in the digestive processes of dogs. In the process of his experimentation, he discovered several properties regarding the production of behavior that have become embodied in the theory of classical conditioning. Pavlov observed that his dogs began to salivate when he entered their pens because they associated his presence (new behavior) with their being fed (previously reinforced old behavior). From this observation and additional experimentation, Pavlov concluded that a new behavior that is regularly paired with an old behavior acquires the same rewarding or punishing qualities of the old behavior. New actions become conditioned to produce the same responses as the previously reinforced or punished actions.

Another component of learning theory was discovered by Thorndike, an American psychologist. Thorndike observed that actions followed closely by rewards were more likely to recur than those not followed by rewards. Similarly, he observed that actions followed closely by punishment were less likely to recur. Thorndike explained these observations on the basis of the law of effect. The law of effect holds that behavior closely followed by a response will be more or less likely to recur depending on whether the response is reinforcing (rewarding) or punishing.

Building on the observations of Thorndike, American behaviorist B. F. Skinner developed the theory of operant conditioning in the 1930s. Operant conditioning is the process by which behavior is made to occur at a faster rate when a specific behavior is followed by positive reinforcement—the rewarding consequences that follow a behavior, which increase the rate at which the behavior will recur. An example that Skinner used in demonstrating operant conditioning involved placing a rat in a box with different levers. When the rat accidentally pushed a predesignated lever, it was given a food pellet. As predicted by operant conditioning, the rat subsequently increased its pushing of the lever that provided it with food.

Gerald Patterson and Richard Stuart, beginning in the late 1960s, were among the first clinicians to apply behavioral techniques, previously used with individuals, to the treatment of family problems. Although Patterson worked primarily with parent-child problems, Stuart extended behavioral family therapy to the treatment of marital problems.

Given the increasing prevalence of family problems, as seen by the rise in the number of divorces and cases of child abuse, the advent of behavioral family therapy has been welcomed by many therapists who treat families. The findings of a 1984 study by William Quinn and Bernard Davidson revealed the increasing use of this therapy, with more than half of all family therapists reporting the use of behavioral techniques in their family therapy.

CONDITIONING AND DESENSITIZATION

The principles of classical and operant conditioning serve to form the foundation of learning theory. Although initially derived from animal experiments, learning theory also was applied to humans. Psychologists who advocated learning theory began to demonstrate that all behavior, whether socially appropriate or inappropriate, occurs because it is either classically or operantly conditioned. John B. Watson, an American psychologist of the early twentieth century, illustrated this relationship by producing a fear of rats in an infant known as Little Albert by repeatedly making a loud noise when a rat was presented to Albert. After a number of pairings of the loud noise with the rat, Albert began to show fear when the rat was presented.

In addition to demonstrating how inappropriate behavior was caused, behavioral psychologists began to show how learning theory could be used to treat people with psychological disorders. Joseph Wolpe, a pioneer in the use of behavioral treatment during the 1950s, showed how phobias could be alleviated by using learning principles in a procedure termed systematic desensitization. Systematic desensitization involves three basic steps: teaching the phobic individual how to relax; having the client create a list of images of the feared object (for example, snakes), from least to most feared; and repeatedly exposing the client to the feared object in graduated degrees, from least to most feared images, while the individual is in a relaxed state. This procedure has been shown to be very effective in the treatment of phobias.

Behavioral family therapy makes the same assumptions regarding the causes of both individual and family problems. For example, in a fictional case, the Williams family came to treatment because their seven-year-old son, John, refused to sleep in his own bed at night. In attempting to explain John's behavior, a behaviorally oriented psychologist would seek to find out what positive reinforcement John was receiving in response to his refusal to stay in his own bed. It may be that when John was younger his parents allowed him to sleep with them, thus reinforcing his behavior by giving him the attention he desired. Now that John is seven, however, his parents believe that he needs to sleep in his own bed, but John continues to want to sleep with his parents because he has been reinforced by being allowed to sleep with them for many years. This case provides a clinical example of operant conditioning in that John's behavior, because it was repeatedly followed by positive reinforcement, was resistant to change.

TREATMENT PROCESS

Behavioral family therapy is a treatment approach that includes the following four steps: problem assessment, family (parent) education, specific treatment design, and treatment goal evaluation. It begins with a thorough assessment of the presenting family problem. This assessment process involves gathering the following information from the family: what circumstances immediately precede the problem behavior; how family members react to the exhibition of the client's problem behavior; how frequently the misbehavior occurs; and how intense the misbehavior is. Behavioral family therapy differs from individual behavior therapy in that all family members are typically involved in the assessment process. As a part of the assessment process, the behavioral family therapist often observes the way in which the family handles the presenting problem. This observation is conducted to obtain firsthand information regarding ways the family may be unknowingly reinforcing the problem or otherwise poorly handling the client's misbehavior.

Following the assessment, the behavioral family therapist, with input from family members, establishes treatment goals. These treatment goals should be operationalized; that is, they should be specifically stated so that they may be easily observed and measured. In the example of John, the boy who refused to sleep in his own bed, an operationalized treatment goal would be as follows: "John will be able to sleep from 9:00 p.m. to 6:00

a.m. in his own bed without interrupting his parents during the night."

APPLYING LEARNING THEORY PRINCIPLES

Once treatment goals have been operationalized, the next stage involves designing an intervention to correct the behavioral problem. The treatment procedure follows from the basic learning principles previously discussed. In cases involving parent-child problems, the behavioral family therapist educates the parents in learning theory principles as they apply to the treatment of behavioral problems. Three basic learning principles are explained to the child's parents. First, positive reinforcement should be withdrawn from the unwanted behavior. For example, a parent who meets the demands of a screaming preschooler who throws a temper tantrum in the checkout line of the grocery store because he or she wants a piece of candy is unwittingly reinforcing the child's screaming behavior. Time-out is one procedure used to remove the undesired reinforcement from a child's misbehavior. Using time-out involves making a child sit in a corner or other nonreinforcing place for a specified period of time (typically, one minute for each year of the child's age).

Second, appropriate behavior that is incompatible with the undesired behavior should be positively reinforced. In the case of the screaming preschooler, this would involve rewarding him or her for acting correctly. An appropriate reinforcer in this case would be giving the child the choice of a candy bar if the child were quiet and cooperative during grocery shopping, behavior inconsistent with a temper tantrum. For positive reinforcement to have its maximum benefit, before the specific activity (for example, grocery shopping) the child should be informed about what is expected and what reward will be received for fulfilling these responsibilities. This process is called contingency management because the promised reward is made contingent on the child's acting in a prescribed manner. In addition, the positive reinforcement should be given as close to the completion of the appropriate behavior as possible.

Third, aversive consequences should be applied when the problem behavior recurs. When the child engages in the misbehavior, he or she should consistently experience negative costs. In this regard, response cost is a useful technique because it involves taking something away or making the child do something unrewarding as a way of making misbehavior have a cost. For example, the preschooler who has a temper tantrum in the checkout line may have a favorite dessert, which he or she had previously selected while in the store, taken away as the cost for throwing a temper tantrum. As with positive reinforcement, response cost should be applied as quickly as possible following the misbehavior in order for it to produce its maximum effect.

DESIGNING TREATMENT INTERVENTION

Once parents receive instruction regarding the principles of behavior therapy, they are actively involved in the process of designing a specific intervention to address their child's behavior problems. The behavioral family therapist relates to the parents as cotherapists with the hope that this approach will increase the parents' involvement in the treatment process. In relating to Mr. and Mrs. Williams as cotherapists, for example, the behavioral family therapist would have the couple design a treatment intervention to correct John's misbehavior. Following the previously described principles, the couple might arrive at the following approach: They would refuse to give in to John's demands to sleep with them; John would receive a token for each night he slept in his own bed (after earning a certain number of tokens, he could exchange them for toys); and John would be required to go to bed fifteen minutes earlier the following night for each time he asked to sleep with his parents.

Once the intervention has been implemented, the therapist, together with the parents, monitors the results of the treatment. This monitoring process involves assessing the degree to which the established treatment goals are being met. For example, in the case of the Williams family, the treatment goal was to reduce the number of times that John attempted to get into bed with his parents. Therapy progress, therefore, would be measured by counting the number of times that John attempted to get into bed with his parents. Careful assessment of an intervention's results is essential to determine whether the intervention is accomplishing its goal.

DETRACTIONS

In spite of its popularity, this type of therapy has not been without its critics. For example, behavioral family therapists' explanations regarding the causes of family problems differ from those given by the advocates of other family therapies. One major difference is that behavioral family therapists are accused of taking a linear (as compared to a circular) view of causality. From a linear perspective, misbehavior occurs because A causes B and B causes C. Those who endorse a circular view of causality, however, assert that this simplistic perspective is inadequate in explaining why misbehavior occurs. Taking a circular perspective involves identifying multiple factors that may be operating at the same time to determine the reason for a particular misbehavior. For example, from a linear view of causality, John's misbehavior is seen as the result of being reinforced for sleeping with his parents. According to a circular perspective, however, John's behavior may be the result of many factors, all possibly occurring together, such as his parents' marital problems or his genetic predisposition toward insecurity.

INTEGRATION WITH OTHER THERAPIES

Partially in response to this criticism, attempts have been made to integrate behavioral family therapy with other types of family therapy. Another major purpose of integrative efforts is to address the resistance often encountered from families during treatment. Therapeutic resistance is a family's continued attempt to handle the presenting problem in a maladaptive manner in spite of having learned better ways. In the past, behavioral family therapists gave limited attention to dealing with family resistance; however, behavioral family therapy has attempted to improve its ability to handle resistance by incorporating some of the techniques used by other types of family therapy.

In conclusion, numerous research studies have demonstrated that behavioral family therapy is an effective treatment of family problems. One of the major strengths of this type of therapy is its willingness to assess objectively its effectiveness in treating family problems. Because of its emphasis on experimentation, behavioral family therapy continues to adapt by modifying its techniques to address the problems of the modern family.

BIBLIOGRAPHY

Atwood, Joan, ed. *Family Therapy: A Systemic Behavioral Approach*. Chicago: Nelson, 1999. Print.

Clark, Lynn. *The Time-Out Solution*. Chicago: Contemporary, 1989. Print.

Falloon, Ian R. H., ed. *Handbook of Behavioral Family Therapy*. New York: Guilford, 1988. Print.

Gladding, Samuel T. *Family Therapy: History, Theory, and Practice*. Boston: Prentice, 2011. Print.

Goldenberg, Herbert, and Irene Goldenberg. *Family Therapy: An Overview*. 7th ed. Belmont: Brooks, 2008. Print.

Gordon, Thomas. *Parent Effectiveness Training: The Proven Program for Raising Responsible Children*. Rev. ed. New York: Three Rivers, 2000. Print.

Nichols, Michael P. "Cognitive-Behavioral Family Therapy." *Family Therapy: Concepts and Methods*. Ed. Michael P. Nichols and Richard C. Schwartz. 8th ed. Boston: Allyn, 2008. Print.

Podell, Jennifer, and Philip Kendall. "Mothers and Fathers in Family Cognitive-Behavioral Therapy for Anxious Youth." *Jour. of Child & Family Studies* 20.2 (2011): 182–95. Print.

Rasheed, Janice M., Mikal N. Rasheed, and James A. Marley. *Family Therapy: Models and Techniques*. Los Angeles: SAGE, 2011. Print.

Robin, Arthur L., and Sharon L. Foster. *Negotiating Parent-Adolescent Conflict: A Behavioral Family Systems Approach*. New York: Guilford, 2003. Print.

R. Christopher Qualls

See Also: Behavior therapy; Cognitive behavior therapy; Conditioning; Family life: Adult issues; Family life: Children's issues; Family systems theory; Group therapy; Misbehavior; Operant conditioning therapies; Pavlovian conditioning; Phobias; Psychotherapy: Children; Punishment; Reinforcement; Skinner, B. F.; Strategic family therapy; Systematic desensitization; Thorndike, Edward L.

Behaviorism

Date: 1912 forward
Type of psychology: Learning

Behaviorism uses the methods of natural science to search for lawful relationships between behavior and the observable social and physical environment. The focus on observable and measurable behavior-environment relationships distinguishes behaviorism from other psychological perspectives that rely on unobservable and hypothetical explanations, such as the mind, the ego, the self, and consciousness.

Key Concepts
- Classical conditioning
- Operant behavior
- Operant conditioning
- Punisher
- Reflex
- Reinforcer
- Stimulus control

INTRODUCTION

Behaviorism was founded in 1912 by the American psychologist John Broadus Watson. Watson's position was formed as a reaction to the then-current focus of psychology on consciousness and the method of research known as introspection, which he considered to be highly subjective. Using the research of the Nobel Prize–winning Russian physiologist Ivan Petrovich Pavlov, Watson argued that psychology could become a natural science only by truly adopting the methods of science. What he meant was that psychology must have an empirical, objective subject matter and that the events to be investigated as possible causes of behavior must also be described objectively and verified empirically through experimental research. This latter point meant that introspection would have to be abandoned, for it was unscientific. Watson presented the goals of psychology as the prediction and control of behavior rather than as the understanding of the mind and the consciousness.

Watson's behaviorism was an extension of Pavlov's discovery of the conditioning of stimulus-response reflexive relationships. The term "reflex" refers to the connection between some environmental event, or stimulus, and the response that it elicits. The response is involuntary and relatively simple, and no prior learning is necessary for the response to occur when the stimulus is presented. Pavlov had already demonstrated experimentally how previously neutral parts of the environment could become effective in stimulating or eliciting an animal's salivation response. By repeatedly pairing a bell with food powder, which elicited salivation, and then presenting the bell alone, Pavlov showed that the bell by itself could then elicit salivation. This process, alternately termed classical, Pavlovian, or respondent conditioning, in turn offered Watson an explanation for behavior that relied on observable elements, thus eliminating the need to use unobservable and hypothetical mental explanations.

Watson's significant contribution resulted from his attempt to show how Pavlov's discovery of the conditioning process with animals could also explain the behavior of human beings. Watson assumed that human behavior and the behavior of animals were both governed by the same laws of nature. Given this assumption, the objective methods of study that were appropriate for the scientific study of nonhuman animals were therefore appropriate for the study of human beings as well. Watson demonstrated the application of these methods in the famous but ethically controversial case study of Little Albert, in which Watson and his graduate student, Rosalie Rayner, showed how human emotional responses could be conditioned to previously neutral environmental stimuli. They began their study by showing that Albert, who was eleven months old at the time, initially approached and smiled when he was shown a live rat. At a time when the rat was not present, Watson struck a metal bar with a hammer. Albert then flinched and began to cry. Next, the rat and the loud, unexpected sound were presented together on seven occasions. On these occasions, Albert reacted to the sound of the hammer striking the metal bar by withdrawing from the rat, moving away from the sound, whimpering, and then crying. Finally, the rat alone was shown to Albert. Now, when only the rat was placed before Albert, he would instantly move away from the rat, whimper, and then cry. Watson and Rayner had demonstrated through the process of classical conditioning that the once-neutral object, the rat, would now elicit a strong emotional response.

Watson attempted to present an objective, behavioristic account of the full range of human behavior in *Behaviorism* (1924), written for a popular audience. In it, he proposed that the stimulus-response reflex was the essential building block of all human behaviors. A collection of separate elemental reflexive responses, unlearned and as yet unconditioned, could become integrated into a complex habit through the regular presentation of the appropriate stimuli in the physical and social environment by parents, siblings, teachers, and others. The result would be, in Watson's words, "habits, such as tennis, fencing, shoe-making, mother-reactions, religious reactions, and the like." The process by which these habits were formed was presumably the conditioning process discovered by Pavlov. In addition, Watson attempted to show that the conditioning of neutral environmental stimuli to existing reflexive responses could also account for thinking and the personality.

B. F. SKINNER AND RADICAL BEHAVIORISM

A different form of behaviorism came from the work of the American psychologist B. F. Skinner. Skinner, too, focused his research on behavior and searched for lawful relationships between behavior and environment. Skinner's thinking began with an acceptance of Watson's stimulus-response approach, but he ultimately took behaviorism in a fundamentally different direction. The first presentation of Skinner's approach was in *The Behavior of Organisms* (1938). In this book, Skinner described the methods and results of systematic research that demonstrated the key points of what was later to become known as radical behaviorism:

- Stimulus-response relationships, or reflexes, include only a narrow range of behavior.
- Classical, or Pavlovian, conditioning could not account for the development of new behavior or the complexity of human behavior.
- Behavior does show lawful relationships with the environment.
- The consequences immediately following a behavior determine the future strength of that behavior.
- New behavior can be acquired by the process of shaping (from existing behavior, elemental forms can be strengthened by consequences that follow the step-by-step approximations until the new behavior is present).
- Once acquired, behavior is maintained by a particular arrangement of environmental consequences.
- Certain events are present when a behavior is strengthened.
- Often, one of those antecedent events is by design especially correlated with the behavior and the consequence that makes that behavior stronger in the future.
- At a later time, the presence of that antecedent event by itself will make the behavior more likely to occur.

Skinner named the process used to investigate these behavior-environment relationships operant conditioning. Skinner called the behavior in this process operant behavior because it operates or acts on the environment, thus producing consequences or changes in that environment. Consequences in turn affect the behavior for the future. Skinner was able to detect the relationship between present consequences and future behavior by observing and measuring the behavior of interest over long periods of time, a method he used initially with rats and later with pigeons. The behavior was observed both at the time that the attendant consequences occurred and continuously subsequent to the consequences.

Skinner observed two effects of consequences on the future strength of behavior. Some consequences reinforced the behavior, thus strengthening it, while other consequences punished the behavior, thus weakening it. It is important to note that for Skinner and his followers, the consequences of behavior that serve as reinforcers or punishers are defined only in terms of their effects on the future strength of a behavior. Events or things in themselves are not reinforcers or punishers. For example, a harsh command to a learner in the classroom ("Sit down and get to work!") is assumed by many teachers to "punish" wandering around the room and inattentiveness to seatwork. Yet in countless instances the teacher's consequence serves only to strengthen or maintain the learner's wandering and inattentiveness. In this case, the teacher's remarks function as a reinforcer irrespective of what the teacher believes.

Skinner also showed that once a behavior has been acquired and was maintained, the occurrence of the behavior can be made more or less probable by the presentation or removal of events that precede the behavior. These antecedent events—for example, the ringing of a telephone—have been reliably present when one picks up the telephone and says "Hello." On the other hand, if one picks up the telephone and says "Hello" when the telephone has not rung, the voice of another person responding to the greeting is extremely unlikely. The term for this process is stimulus control, defined as the effect that events preceding a behavior can have on the likelihood of that behavior occurring. Stimulus control comes about because of the presence of particular events when a behavior is reinforced.

THE CAUSES OF BEHAVIOR

For Skinner, the causes of behavior lie in humans' genetic endowment and the environment in which they live. The specific ways in which the environment causes behavior can be seen in the experimentally derived principles noted previously.

Skinner's approach differs sharply from most psychological theories, which put the causes of behavior inside the person. Skinner believed that these internal causes were not scientific explanations but rather behaviors themselves in need of explanation, or else explanations taken from disciplines other than psychology.

Skinner regarded the "mind" as an unscientific explanation because of its status as an inference from the behavior that it was supposed to explain. While psychological theory has, since the 1970s, redefined the mind in two broad ways, Skinner noted that the redefining did not solve the problems posed by the requirements of science. In one definition, mental processes became cognitive processes, a metaphor based on computer operations; humans are said to "process" information by " encoding, decoding, storing, and retrieving" it. However, all these hypothesized activities remain inferences from the behavior that they are said to explain. There is no independent observation of these hypothetical activities.

In the other definition, the mind was translated to mean the brain, which can be studied scientifically. Thus, the physiology of the brain is thought to explain behavior. Neither Skinner nor other radical behaviorists deny the role of the brain in a complete understanding of behavior. However, psychology and brain physiology look for the causes of behavior at different levels of observation. Psychology is viewed as a separate discipline with its own methods of scientific investigation leading to the discovery of distinct psychological explanations for behavior. In addition, research results suggest that rather than brain physiology explaining behavior, changes in both behavior and the brain appear to result from changes in the environment. Changes in behavior are correlated with changes in the brain, but changes at both levels appear to be the result of the environment.

Thoughts and feelings are also considered to be causes of behavior. One thinks about talking with a friend and then goes to the telephone and dials the number. These two people talk together on the telephone regularly because they feel affection for each other. Yet the "thinking" or "feeling" referred to as causes for the actions involved in dialing the telephone and talking with each other are themselves viewed as responses in need of explanation. What gave rise to thinking in early development, and what now makes thoughts of this particular friend so strong? How have feelings of affection become associated with this friend? From the radical behaviorist perspective, both the thoughts and the feeling are explained by the principles of operant or classical conditioning.

RADICAL BEHAVIORISM AND COMPLEX HUMAN BEHAVIOR

Some of the facts of human experience include talking, thinking, seeing, problem solving, conceptualizing, and creating new ideas and things. A common point of view holds that behaviorism either rejects or neglects these aspects of human experience. However, a fuller reading of Skinner's works reveals that he offered a serious examination of these topics and demonstrated that behavioral principles could account for their presence in the repertoire of human behavior.

For example, Skinner's examination of verbal behavior resulted in his book *Verbal Behavior* (1957), in which he showed that behavioral principles are capable of explaining the acquisition and continuation of behaviors such as talking, reading, and thinking. Basic processes such as imitation, reinforcement, shaping, and stimulus control are all shown to have likely roles in the various aspects of verbal behavior.

Behaviorism's analysis of verbal behavior is directly related to the more complex forms of human behavior often referred to as higher mental processes. For example, radical behaviorism views thinking as an activity derived from talking out loud. Parents and teachers encourage children to talk to themselves, initially by encouraging whispering, then moving the lips as in speaking but without making sounds. What results, then, is talking privately, "in our own heads." In a similar fashion, a parent asks a child to "think before you act" and a teacher asks learners to "think through" the solution to a problem in mathematics or ethics. The social environment thus encourages people to think, often shows them how to do so, and then reinforces the behavior when the overt results of their thinking are praised or given high scores.

More complex behavior-environment relationships, such as those found in concept formation, have also been analyzed in terms of the principles of behaviorism. The term "concept" is defined as a characteristic that is common to a number of objects that are otherwise different from one another. People are said to have concepts in their heads that produce the behaviors they observe. A radical behavioral analysis, however, views concepts as the appropriate response to the common characteristic. The appropriate response has been reinforced only when it occurs in the presence of the specific characteristic. For example, a child is said to understand the concept of "red" when the child reliably says "red" in response to the question "What color are these objects?" in the presence of a red hat, red fire truck, red tomato, and red crayon.

APPLICATIONS OF THE PRINCIPLES OF BEHAVIORISM

The behaviorism of Watson has resulted in applications in psychology and many other disciplines, most notably in the form of the psychological treatment known as systematic desensitization, created by South African psychiatrist Joseph Wolpe. Systematic desensitization was designed to reverse the outcome of the classical conditioning process, in which extremely intense negative emotional responses such as fear or anxiety are elicited by everyday aspects of the environment. Such an outcome is referred to as a phobia. The treatment first requires training in relaxation. The second component of treatment takes a person through a hierarchy of steps, beginning with a setting very distant from the feared stimulus and ending with the problem setting. At each step, the individual is asked to signal when he or she experiences fear or anxiety and then is instructed to relax. Movement through the hierarchy is repeated until the person can experience each step, including the one that includes the feared stimulus, and report feeling relaxed at every step. This treatment has been employed both in the clinic and in real-life settings. Systematic desensitization has been shown to be an effective intervention for fears associated with dental treatment and flying, for example, as well as the intense anxiety that accompanies social phobia and panic disorder.

Another application of Skinner's behavioral principles is the field of applied behavioral analysis, which was introduced first in educational settings. Applications in education have occurred at every level, from preschool to university classrooms. Equally important has been repeated successful application to learners with autism, severe and profound delays in behavioral development, and attention-deficit disorder, both with and without hyperactive behavior.

Applications of behavioral principles have been shown to be effective across behaviors, settings, individuals, and teachers. They have also been shown to be effective in reducing behaviors that pose a threat to public health, including smoking, overeating, essential hypertension, and domestic violence. Finally, behavioral principles have found application in the arena of public safety. For example, researchers using techniques based on Skinner's science of behavior have increased seat-belt usage by automobile drivers.

BIBLIOGRAPHY

Alberto, Paul A., and Anne C. Troutman. *Applied Behavior Analysis for Teachers*. 9th ed. Boston: Pearson, 2013. Print.

Baum, William J. *Understanding Behaviorism: Behavior, Culture, and Evolution*. 2nd ed. Malden: Blackwell, 2005. Print.

Johnson, Kent R., and T. V. Joe Layng. "Breaking the Structuralist Barrier: Literacy and Numeracy with Fluency." *American Psychologist* 47.11 (1992): 1475–90. Print.

Ledoux, Stephen F. "Behaviorism at 100." *American Scientist* Jan.–Feb. 2012: 60–65. Print.

Moore, Jay. "Three Views of Behaviorism." *Psychological Record* 63.3 (2013): 681–91. Print.

Nye, Robert D. *The Legacy of B. F. Skinner: Concepts and Perspectives, Controversies and Misunderstandings*. Pacific Grove: Brooks, 1992. Print.

Pierce, W. David, and Carl D. Cheney. *Behavior Analysis and Learning*. 5th ed. New York: Psychology, 2013. Print.

Skinner, B. F. *About Behaviorism*. 1974. London: Penguin, 1993. Print.

Skinner, B. F. *Walden Two*. 1948. Indianapolis: Hackett, 2005. Print.

Staddon, John. *The New Behaviorism*. 2nd ed. New York: Psychology, 2014. Print.

Watson, John B. *Behaviorism*. Rev. ed. Chicago: U of Chicago P, 1930. Print.

Derived from: "Behaviorism." *Psychology and Mental Health*. Salem Press. 2009.

Robert Jensen

See Also: Aversion therapy; Behavior therapy; Conditioning; Environmental psychology; Habituation and sensitization; Implosion; Learned helplessness; Learning; Operant conditioning therapies; Pavlovian conditioning; Phobias; Punishment; Radical behaviorism: B. F. Skinner; Reflexes; Reinforcement; Skinner, B. F.; Systematic desensitization; Thought: Study and measurement; Watson, John B.

Bilingualism

Type of psychology: Cognition; Language; Learning

Bilingualism refers to the ability to communicate effectively in more than one language. The study of bilingualism involves linguistics, psycholinguistics, and sociolinguistics.

Key Concepts

- Code switching
- Communicative competence
- Compound bilingualism
- Coordinate bilingualism
- Critical period
- Sequential bilingualism
- Simultaneous bilingualism
- Subordinate bilingualism

INTRODUCTION

Bilingualism is generally defined as the state of knowing two languages. This term is now commonly extended to include multilingualism, the state of knowing three or more languages. Bilingualism has long been of interest to psychologists because it raises interesting questions about the nature of linguistic knowledge and the nature of learning. In addition, because language is intimately tied to culture and one's sense of group identification, bilingual people may have a more complex and multifaceted sense of self and group identity than monolinguals.

TO KNOW A LANGUAGE

Knowing a language requires, at a minimum, knowledge of vocabulary (words, how they are pronounced, and the concepts to which they refer) and grammar (the rules for combining words into well-formed sentences). Conventionally, knowing a language also means understanding how to read and write it and how to use it (for example, when to use formal or informal language, proper forms of address, and so forth). This last type of knowledge is often called "communicative competence."

Knowledge of one's native language usually involves all these components. However, knowledge of a second or third language may be limited: for example, a bilingual person may be better at reading and writing in the second language than at listening and speaking, know only a specific vocabulary (such as that related to work), speak with a heavy accent, or produce ungrammatical sentences.

TYPES OF BILINGUALISM

Bilingualism is considered to be coordinate, compound, or subordinate. In coordinate bilingualism, a person has parallel but separate systems for each language. This type of bilingualism is most common among people who grew up in two-language households and acquired both languages from infancy. In compound bilingualism, the person does not completely separate the two languages. Typically, the person has a unified concept for physical objects or abstract ideas that is expressed by two different words. Subordinate bilingualism arises when the second language is learned after childhood and sometimes in formal settings: in this case, the person is clearly less proficient in the second language than in the first. Also relevant to this discussion is the notion of language dominance. A bilingual person's native language is usually the dominant one, but there are exceptions. For example, immigrant children who speak their native language at home may be more eloquent and literate in the ambient language, their second language.

Another common distinction is between simultaneous bilingualism, in which two languages are acquired at the same time in early childhood, and sequential bilingualism, in which the second language is learned later in life. Simultaneous bilingual people, sometimes called "early bilinguals," are typically fully proficient in both languages. However, it is also typical for one language to become more dominant than the other, based on the amount of use. Sequential, or late, bilinguals are likely to exhibit characteristics of nonnative speakers (such as foreign accents or errors in sentence construction), which has led to the idea that the age of language acquisition has an effect on the ability to learn language. The critical period hypothesis proposes that there is a critical developmental period for the acquisition of language, after which native proficiency may never be achieved.

APPROACHES TO THE STUDY OF BILINGUALISM

Bilingualism is a complex, multifaceted area of study that can be approached from many perspectives, including linguistic and psycholinguistic, social, and pedagogical.

Linguistic and Psycholinguistic. In 1957, linguist Noam Chomsky proposed that human beings are endowed with an innate capacity to acquire language: all they need is exposure to language, and the acquisition device figures out the grammar. It has been a matter of some debate whether bilinguals, especially sequential bilinguals, are able to acquire their second language in the same fashion as their first or whether they require the use of general learning strategies, such as rote memorization, and the explicit learning of grammar.

It is clear that on the way to becoming bilingual, second-language learners, unlike native speakers, develop an interlanguage. Certain aspects of this interlanguage may be due to transfer of some aspect of a first language to a second: for example, second-language words may be pronounced with a foreign accent or inflections may be omitted. Other aspects may reflect a universal developmental sequence that learners of a first or second language go through. At a given point in time, a second-language learner develops a stable grammar, or set of rules, for the interlanguage.

Psycholinguistic approaches to bilingualism acknowledge a distinction between knowing a second language (as demonstrated in paper-and-pencil tests) and being able to use that knowledge under time constraints. As speakers and listeners, human beings are time bound: by some estimates, the average speaking rate is 180 words per minute, or 3 words per second. Listeners, of course, must be able to process spoken language efficiently or risk lagging behind and missing some portion of the spoken message. Reading rates, interestingly enough, are typically even faster, with proficient readers reading at a rate of 4 words per second. Hence, one focus of psycholinguistic research on bilingualism has been on the extent to which second-language learners are able to accurately extract the meaning conveyed by spoken or written language and whether they do so in the same time frame as native-language users do.

Research on the production of a second language focuses less on timing. Of course, speaking is also time constrained: listeners have trouble attending to very slow speech. However, speakers are certainly able to impose their own internal constraints on the language they produce, pausing, for example, in the face of word-retrieval difficulty. This is even truer of written production—writers may pause indefinitely—and this is one reason that this area has received relatively less attention. Issues of interest include how speakers manage to keep one language suppressed while speaking the other and the degree to which they can shut off the language that is not in use. Many bilinguals who interact regularly with other bilinguals do not do this; rather they routinely switch between languages (this is called "code switching"), sometimes several times per sentence.

Sociolinguistic. These approaches to the study of bilingualism emphasize communicative competence—knowledge of the implicit rules governing interactions with others in the same speech community. These rules include which topics are suitable in given situations, which speech styles are appropriate for different people, and even when to speak or be silent. If they lack communicative competence, even bilinguals with near-native linguistic competence will stand out as nonnative or be received uneasily by monolinguals in a given speech community. For example, American English speakers expect a response of "Fine," "Great," or even "Hey" to the question "How are you?" which is functionally a greeting rather than a question. Nonnative speakers may not know this.

Bilinguals' varying degrees of communicative competence in their multiple speech communities can complicate their sense of identity and their sense of belonging to a specific community. This, combined with other factors, such as the relative social status of their languages, may increase or decrease the likelihood that they will desire (or be able) to belong to a certain speech community. Communicative competence can even vary across different situations, such as interactions with elders versus those with peers. Some bilinguals may report feeling that they do not completely belong in any given community or feeling uncomfortable using their native language because of the limited contextual rules they know for it. Others, however, report appreciating the larger social access they have because of their ability to communicate in more than one language.

Pedagogical. The pedagogical approach examines two major populations of interest: the students who are nonnative speakers of the community language (second-language learners) and the students who are native speakers of the community language and are learning another language (foreign-language learners). In general, these two types of learners acquire a target language under vastly different circumstances.

Many second-language learners are immigrants who are immersed in the new language and must gain communicative and academic competence quickly. In some cases, a student's native language is not used at all to teach the new language. This is particularly true of school-aged students because in the United States, they are most likely to be subject to state laws regarding bilingual education. These laws determine whether and how long nonnative English speakers may receive instruction or support in their native or heritage language within American public schools. Many states do not allow any instruction in a student's native language, and students are simply expected to acquire the language, along with communicative competence to interact in the new language in the new culture.

Foreign-language learners must gain some communicative competence in the relatively short amount of time they spend in the classroom. Foreign-language teaching methods vary depending on the context and the learners' goals. Large classes and minimal instructor support generally require the grammar-translation method, as it includes little writing, speaking, or interaction, and instead focuses on grammar learning. Given the readily available teaching materials developed for this method, lesson preparation may be relatively less time consuming. This method is also commonly used for those who want to learn to read in a language for research purposes but do not plan to write or otherwise communicate in the language. If listening and speaking skills are the focus, then the audiolingual method may be employed. This involves listening to, repeating, and memorizing dialogues, giving a learner practice with vocabulary, word order, and pronunciation. Most basic language programs in American universities favor the communicative language teaching approach, which counts communicative competence as the ultimate learning goal, even if some grammatical accuracy is sacrificed. This is ideal for those who plan to travel, study, or work abroad for a limited amount of time, but who do not need to be highly proficient in the language. Those who need higher proficiency for work, study, or assimilation purposes typically move on to content-based learning, where a given field is studied in the foreign language (for example, business in German or literature in Russian).

Foreign-language students who wish to become highly fluent generally need a period of time in an immersion situation, living and interacting with speakers of the target language. Not only does this provide a context for the development of communicative competence, it provides a way for learners to achieve real fluency in the language through sheer practice.

BIBLIOGRAPHY

Birdsong, David, ed. *Second Language Acquisition and the Critical Period Hypothesis.* Mahwah: Erlbaum, 1999. Print.

De Bot, Kees, Wander Lowie, and Marjolyn Verspoor. *Second Language Acquisition: An Advanced Resource Book.* New York: Routledge, 2005. Print.

Grosjean, François, and Ping Li. *The Psycholinguistics of Bilingualism.* Malden: Wiley-Blackwell, 2012. Print.

Kroll, Judith F., and Annette M. B. De Groot, eds. *Handbook of Bilingualism: Psycholinguistic Approaches.* Oxford: Oxford UP, 2009. Print.

Nicol, Janet, ed. *One Mind, Two Languages: Bilingual Language Processing.* Malden: Blackwell, 2001. Print.

Rosé, Carlos D. "Bilingual Families." *KidsHealth.org.* Nemours Foundation, Aug. 2011. Web. 18 Feb. 2014.

Sanz, Cristina, ed. *Mind and Context in Adult Second Language Acquisition.* Washington, DC: Georgetown UP, 2005. Print.

Saville-Troike, Muriel. *Introducing Second Language Acquisition.* 2nd ed. Cambridge: Cambridge UP, 2012. Print.

Spada, Nina, and Patsy M. Lightbown. *How Languages Are Learned.* 4th ed. Oxford: Oxford UP, 2013. Print.

Karen Barto-Sisamount and Janet Nicol

See Also: Bilingualism and learning disabilities; Cognitive psychology; Cross-cultural psychology; Cultural competence; Identity crises; Language; Learning; Multicultural psychology.

Bilingualism and learning disabilities

Date: 1920s forward

Type of psychology: Intelligence and intelligence testing; Language; Learning

The practice of placing bilingual students (those whose second language is English) into special education classes has a controversial history. Originally, it was considered a simple act of discrimination; however, as time passed, it became clear that unintentional bias, based on cultural and linguistic misunderstandings, led to placing many bilingual students into special education programs.

Key Concepts

- Culturally and linguistically diverse children
- Educational testing
- English language learners
- Learning disabilities
- Sign bilingualism
- Special education

INTRODUCTION

The issues of bilingualism and disability intersect in the limitations inherent in testing culturally and linguistically diverse children, many of whom are English language learners, so as to prevent their linguistic problems from being incorrectly interpreted as learning disabilities, and in the recent movement toward sign bilingualism, which will enable hearing-impaired children to become more fully integrated into both the deaf and hearing worlds.

ENGLISH LANGUAGE LEARNERS

Educators have become increasingly aware of the difficulties faced by culturally and linguistically diverse children, many of whom are either recent immigrants or are raised by first-generation American parents who speak little or no English. Bilingualism has also been found to cause speech delays in some children and stuttering in others. Because many are either bilingual or still learning English when they enter a school system, their scores on placement testing can also be misinterpreted, either unintentionally or as a product of testing bias, thus resulting in their being inappropriately placed in special education classes. Early problems of this nature were often a result of discriminatory practices in testing, so in the 1950s, Robert Eels developed tests that he felt lacked cultural bias and were thus free of the traditional weaknesses associated with intelligence tests, but psychometricians questioned his efforts.

By the 1960s, federal courts had become involved in the testing of minority children for special education placement, and an attempt was made to determine whether cultural and linguistic differences did indeed make tests biased. In the 1970s, Jane Mercer developed the System of Multicultural Pluralistic Assessment (SOMPA), which had as its basis the idea that diverse tests from various assessment models could negate the effect that different cultural experiences in a test taker's background had on scoring, but it was unsuccessful in garnering support. Like Eels's testing, SOMPA did not address linguistic differences nor did it provide for any controls for bilingualism.

The literature chronicles the main reasons that English language learners are sometimes mistakenly thought to be students with learning disabilities and therefore placed into special education. The most obvious culprit is inadequately trained school personnel. If testers and assessment handlers are not trained to use multiple variables, their assessment instruments are limited and therefore flawed. Researchers in the field also cite problems in the referral process, wherein educators discount or are unaware of the impact on learning of cultural and linguistic variables. Inconsistencies in the interpretation of assessment results are also problematic, because many of the behaviors associated with the problems of English language learners are similar to those used as markers for learning disabilities. To complicate matters, assessing whether an English language learner has a true learning disability could lead to a student's being kept out of special education when the child actually should be placed in the program. In short, assessment of English language learners may not be accurate because the primary problem is the number of variables at play (for example, environment issues, such as poor instruction and poverty, which can adversely affect student learning).

The best method of differentiating between language differences and learning disabilities involves gathering and integrating data from multiple sources (such as the student, parents, caretakers, service providers, and therapists) and multiple contexts (informal settings and formal settings), while using multiple methods (formal, informal, and alternative assessment procedures). One of the key reforms initiated by the Education for All Handicapped Children Act of 1975 and continued through the 2004 reauthorization of the Individuals with Disabilities Education Act is nondiscriminatory assessment. Federal specifications require that tests be selected and administered so as not to be racially, culturally, or sexually discriminatory. However, one 2006 study by Richard A. Figueroa and Patricia Newsome found that school psychologists typically continue to include an intelligence test, a standardized achievement test, and a test of perceptual or memory processing, and that bias among school psychologists continues to result in some English language learners being mistaken for children with learning disabilities.

SIGN BILINGUALISM

As far as bilingualism and the hearing impaired are concerned, the central issue is that sign languages used in different countries (such as American Sign Language, Auslan, and British Sign Language), despite their similarities, have distinct features. The concept of sign bilingualism, or "bimodal bilingualism," a term that began to be used in the 1990s, involves overcoming deafness as a learning disability by incorporating both the sign language of the hearing-impaired community and the spoken and written languages of the hearing community. As researcher Miranda Pickersgill argued, this enables deaf students to become "bilingual," or to be able to participate fully in both the deaf and hearing communities. Actual bilingual hearing-impaired children typically are first taught the language of the ethnic community (which would naturally be their first language) and then later are taught English (as a second language), perhaps beginning at school. The problem is that these students then become deaf English language learners, and their problems in learning English could be misinterpreted as cognitive learning disabilities. Some services and schools that use a total communication philosophy most likely adopt sign bilingualism as a teaching approach for educating deaf students. A sign bilingual approach may also involve the systematic use of both British Sign Language and American Sign Language. Overall, the desired outcome of sign bilingualism is a lifelong learning outcome—that all children attain levels of competence and proficiency that will be sufficient for them in both their student and adult lives.

BIBLIOGRAPHY

Bursztyn, *Alberto M. Praeger* Handbook of Special Education. Westport: Greenwood, 2007. Print.

Figueroa, Richard A., and Patricia Newsome. "The Diagnosis of Learning Disabilities in English Learners:

Is It Nondiscriminatory?" *Journal of Learning Disabilities* 39.3 (2006): 206–14. Print.

Grosjean, Francois. "Sign Language and Bilingualism." Psychology Today. Sussex, 27 Mar. 2011. Web. 18 Feb. 2014.

Kohnert, Kathryn. *Language Disorders in Bilingual Children and Adults*. 2nd ed. San Diego: Plural, 2013. Print.

Langdon, Henriette W. *Assessment and Intervention for Communication Disorders in Culturally and Linguistically Diverse Populations*. Clifton Park: Thomson Delmar Learning, 2008. Print.

Pickersgill, Miranda. "Bilingualism: Current Policy and Practice." *Issues in Deaf Education. Ed. Susan Gregory,* et al. London: Fulton, 1998. Print.

Shenker, Rosalee. "Stuttering and the Bilingual Child." *Stuttering Foundation*. Stuttering Foundation of America, 2014. Web. 18 Feb. 2014.

Anthony J. Fonseca

See Also: Assessment; Bilingualism; Cross-cultural psychology; Cultural competence; Language; Learning; Learning disorders; Multicultural psychology.

Binet, Alfred

Born: July 11, 1857
Died: October 18, 1911
Identity: French developmental psychologist
Birthplace: Nice, France
Place of death: Paris, France
Type of psychology: Intelligence and intelligence testing

Binet developed the first valid test of intellectual ability.

Alfred Binet is renowned for his contributions in the field of intelligence testing even though he had no formal education in psychology. After studying law and medicine, Binet gravitated to the discipline when he began reading psychological articles at Bibliothèque Nationale in Paris. He worked for six years at Salpêtrière Hospital and published papers on a variety of topics such as consciousness and hypnosis. However, he left Salpêtrière in near disgrace after his reports that magnetism could produce physical effects on hypnotized patients were shown to be the result of suggestion.

In the absence of a professional position, Binet spent nearly a year intensively studying his two young daughters. He published papers highlighting age-related performance differences between the girls. These observations, very similar to the later ones made by Jean Piaget, laid the foundation for Binet's notions concerning intelligence assessment.

In 1903, the French Ministry of Public Instruction (FMPI) appointed Binet to a committee that was charged with the task of developing a method to distinguish children ready for first-grade instruction from their subnormal age mates, who needed special classes. Working with his assistant Théodore Simon, Binet developed a series of tasks that could be used to assess a child's intellectual development. Binet reasoned that the age at which a child can perform a task could be used as a measure of intelligence. For example, a four-year-old child who was unable to do things typically accomplished by three-year-olds was demonstrating subnormal intellectual development. The 1905, the Binet-Simon Scale incorporated thirty tasks or tests arranged in increasing order of difficulty.

Binet tested dozens of children to establish age norms for his tests. A task that could be performed by most children of a given age but not by those a year younger was placed at the older age level. In 1908, Binet published a longer, revised scale arranging tests from age three to thirteen years based on his data collection. Binet's scale proved useful for the FMPI and was well received in other countries.

Other psychologists later introduced the concepts of mental age and intelligence quotient (IQ). Mental age was determined by test performance. For example, a child correctly answering all of the age-four items and missing all of the age-five items would have a mental age of 4.0 years. IQ was computed by dividing the mental age by chronological age and multiplying this ratio by one hundred.

Binet's unexpected death from a stroke in 1911 meant that he did not live to see intellectual prowess quantified in this way.

BIBLIOGRAPHY

Fancher, Raymond E. "Alfred Binet, General Psychologist." *Portraits of Pioneers in Psychology*. Ed. Gregory A. Kimble and Michael Wertheimer. Washington, DC: American Psychological Association, 1998. Print.

Hothersall, David. *History of Psychology*. 4th ed. New York: McGraw-Hill, 2004. Print.

Nicolas, Serge, et al. "Sick? Or Slow? On the Origins of Intelligence as a Psychological Object." *Intelligence* 41.5 (2013): 699–711. Print.

Wolf, Theta H. *Alfred Binet*. Chicago: U of Chicago P, 1973. Print.

Charles H. Evans

See Also: Assessment; Cognitive development: Jean Piaget; Intelligence; Intelligence Quotient (IQ); Intelligence tests; Piaget, Jean; Race and intelligence; Stanford-Binet test.

Biofeedback and relaxation

Type of psychology: Stress

Responses to stress by the body have traditionally been thought to be made up of involuntary reactions that are beyond the control of the individual. Some of these responses become maladaptive and may now be brought under control by using various relaxation techniques and biofeedback.

Key Concepts

- Autogenic phrases
- Cheating
- Classical conditioning
- Electroencephalography (EEG)
- Electromyography (EMG)
- Galvanic skin response (GSR)
- Instrumental conditioning
- Progressive muscle relaxation

INTRODUCTION

From the day that people are born, and even before, they are subjected to a variety of stressors from the environment around them. Each one of these exacts a certain toll on their bodies. Some stressors seem to affect individuals differently, while others seem to have a universal effect; in any case, both the mind and the body must mobilize to deal effectively with these factors. The individual is usually able to handle these problems by using various coping strategies to help alleviate the stress. The problem arises when too many stressors are present at one time or when these stressors last too long. Individuals must adapt or change their coping strategies to return to a normal equilibrium. A coping strategy is a process that takes effort and is learned; the individual must acquire this coping skill as one acquires any skill. It must be practiced.

If the stressors are not dealt with adequately, fatigue and illness may result. In the most serious circumstances, the organism can die. Hans Selye reported on what he termed the "general adaptation syndrome (GAS)." As stressors affect an organism, a series of neurological and biological responses occur to protect the body. If these responses are prolonged and go unchecked, however, the body will begin to break itself down. In the first phase, the alarm phase, the body mobilizes itself. The adrenal glands enlarge and release epinephrine (adrenaline) and steroids to cope. After a while, the body adapts and seems to be normal; this is the resistance stage. In fact, the body is not normal. It is very vulnerable to further stress, and, if subjected to additional stressors, it will enter the third stage, exhaustion. The organism can then become extremely sick or die.

DEVELOPMENT OF COPING STRATEGIES

It becomes essential for the individual to adopt a successful coping strategy to avert this progression of events. Two such techniques will be discussed here. Biofeedback is a procedure whereby the individual is given information about how a variety of body responses react in various circumstances. The individual is generally unaware of these reactions, but biofeedback technology allows the individual to monitor them and eventually bring them under control. Autonomic, visceral responses to stress have traditionally been thought to be involuntary and automatic. Biofeedback is a technique aimed at gaining control over these reactions. Voluntary responses can affect these visceral responses, and this fact complicates the ultimate effectiveness of biofeedback.

Neal E. Miller was one of the early pioneers in the field. His work has been applied to the control of a wide variety of stress-related problems through the use of biofeedback. The control of what have been termed "psychosomatic problems" has been accomplished using Miller's assumptions. Individuals have learned to control blood pressure, heart rate, muscle spasms, headaches, and myriad other ailments through biofeedback techniques.

Miller believed that these responses to stress can be changed through the use of operant, or instrumental, conditioning and reinforcement. "Operant conditioning" refers to learning that occurs from reinforcing a response and is traditionally thought to be successful with voluntary responses mediated by the skeletal nervous system. When a machine makes this information available to a person, the responses can be reinforced (or they can reinforce themselves) when a therapeutic change occurs. The same principle is at work when an experimental rat learns to press a bar for food.

Another coping strategy that can be used to deal with stressors is the adoption of one of a variety of relaxation procedures. As odd as it may sound to some, people must learn to relax in many situations, and this takes practice. Relaxation techniques are often used in conjunction with biofeedback, which sometimes makes it difficult to determine which of the two procedures is responsible for the changes that occur and to what degree they are acting in relationship to each other.

There are several relaxation techniques, and different techniques are successful for different individuals. One of the most widely used techniques is progressive muscle relaxation, proposed by Edmund Jacobson. The individual is instructed to tense a particular muscle group and hold it for several seconds, paying attention to the feelings associated with this state. Then the individual is told to relax the muscle group and is asked to concentrate on the different feelings while the muscle is relaxed. The major muscle groups of the body are put through this procedure. Ultimately, the individual is able to reproduce the relaxed sensations when feeling tense.

Rhythmic breathing techniques are also used for relaxation to combat stress. The person learns to inhale through the nose to a specified count and exhale through the mouth to another specified count. The breathing should be with the diaphragm as much as possible, as opposed to the chest. Meditation, another relaxation technique that often incorporates rhythmic breathing, may require that the person either visualize an object or repeat a word or phrase with each breath. This action prevents the person's mind from wandering to the anxiety-provoking stimuli.

BIOFEEDBACK EXPERIMENTS

One of the experiments that pioneered the use of biofeedback in a clinical setting was conducted by Miller using white rats. Miller wanted to demonstrate that the animal was able to learn to increase the blood flow to one ear by dilating the capillaries in the ear. He needed to ensure that the animal was not using a skeletal response ("cheating") to influence this response. For example, a human can accomplish this task by covering the ear with the palm of the hand for a period of time. Miller asked whether this could be done without a skeletal response. He administered the drug curare to the rat to incapacitate the skeletal nervous system and kept the animal alive by using an artificial respirator. He attached a sensitive thermometer, which was able to detect slight changes in temperature caused by differential blood flow, to the animal's ear. When a slight increase in temperature was detected, the message was sent to a computer, which delivered an electrical reinforcement to the brain of the subject. This represents the same mechanism that establishes the bar-pressing response in a white rat: operant conditioning. The experiment was successful.

One of the first applications of this experiment to humans came when a woman who had suffered paralysis in an automobile accident was unable even to remain in a sitting position without her blood pressure dropping to dangerous levels. Miller and his staff assembled a biofeedback device that allowed the woman to determine the nature of her blood pressure from moment to moment. No external reinforcement (such as food) was necessary in this case; knowing that the response was therapeutic was reinforcement enough. The woman was able to learn how to raise and lower her blood pressure at will through the use of the biofeedback device. By learning to control her blood pressure (and eventually wean herself off the biofeedback machine), she was able to become more productive and do some tasks on her own.

BIOFEEDBACK APPLICATIONS

The concept of biofeedback, then, can be generalized to learning to control any of the visceral responses to accomplish a healthier state. As society's stressors increase, many of the visceral responses can cause clinical problems. Among the most common are headache symptoms, muscular (tension) and vascular (migraine). By using electromyography (EMG) biofeedback, a person can monitor the muscle tension in the forehead and learn to decrease the tension by obtaining constant auditory feedback. By the same token, thermal biofeedback machines can monitor blood flow to the cranial arteries and can teach a person how to reduce the volume of blood to this area and redirect it to the periphery of the body. This change may help other problems associated with migraines, such as Raynaud disease, in which the extremities are cold because of lack of blood flow.

The galvanic skin response is one of the most common responses used to measure the degree of anxiety and stress. In fact, it is one of the measures in a lie detector, which assumes that when one lies, anxiety increases automatically. The galvanic skin response can be brought under control using biofeedback methods. For example, if a pregnant woman is anxious about the upcoming birth, she can receive constant feedback from a galvanic skin response biofeedback apparatus and learn to lower the galvanic skin response by attending to the machine. As she learns to accomplish this, she can apply these skills on her own and eventually use them during the birth process.

Yet another application of biofeedback in coping with stress has been the use of the technique in controlling brain waves through electroencephalography (EEG) biofeedback. EEG measures the electrical output of the brain, which may be brought under voluntary control by biofeedback and relaxation. It is thought that the brain's alpha wave (eight to thirteen cycles per second) represents the resting brain. By having a machine monitor the amount of alpha activity from moment to moment through electrodes on the scalp, a person can learn to increase alpha production and thereby reduce stress.

Another common biofeedback technique is heart rate variability biofeedback, which helps the person to reduce high blood pressure and improve lung function. Evidence suggests that biofeedback may also be beneficial in managing gastrointestinal conditions such as irritable bowel syndrome and chronic pain.

USE OF RELAXATION TECHNIQUES

Prior to and during biofeedback training, various relaxation techniques are employed to help with the procedure. This arrangement actually leads to an academic problem: which technique is working and to what degree? The use of Jacobson's progressive muscle relaxation with asthmatic children and adults helped to reduce the frequency and severity of the incidents. One of the common problems that arises from increased stress is insomnia; the use of Jacobson's technique has proved useful in combating this problem in several documented cases. Autogenic phrases—phrases used by the therapist to help the client while relaxing and performing biofeedback (for example, "Your hands feel heavy and warm")—are often employed with biofeedback as well. For muscular disorders, phrases such as "My leg is heavy" can be used. For cardiac problems, a common phrase is "My heartbeat is calm and regular."

Meditation has been shown to produce an increase in alpha-wave activity, as has biofeedback. Practitioners of yoga focus on a phrase or word (mantra) and exclude everything else. The nervous system shows evidence of reduced stress and arousal. A variety of businesses have used meditation programs for their employees and have realized improved health and raised productivity.

IMPLICATIONS FOR THE FIELD OF PSYCHOLOGY

The ability to achieve voluntary control over autonomic nervous system responses to help cope with stressors is a valuable skill. The area of biofeedback has important implications for both the theoretical and clinical sides of the field of psychology. First, it is traditionally thought that classical conditioning deals with the "involuntary" nervous system responses, while instrumental conditioning mediates the "voluntary" skeletal responses. "Classical conditioning" refers to learning that occurs by contiguously pairing two stimuli, whereby the second stimulus comes to yield a response similar to the first; it is traditionally thought to be successful with involuntary responses mediated by the autonomic nervous system. Because biofeedback deals with visceral autonomic nervous system reactions and is basically a form of instrumental conditioning, this traditional dichotomy must be brought into question. Biofeedback, a phenomenon of the second half of the twentieth century, remains a relatively new field. Biofeedback techniques ultimately aim toward bringing unconscious, previously uncontrolled body responses into conscious awareness to control them therapeutically. It is a wonderful example of the interaction of the mind and body and the complicated dilemma of how and when they interact.

Biofeedback therapy invariably uses other therapies, such as relaxation and meditation, in the clinical setting. This situation naturally raises the questions of whether and to what degree biofeedback, relaxation, meditation, and their interactions are responsible for changes in the condition of the client. Many experiments are being conducted to determine the answers to these questions, and the results have been equivocal. It is also important to know what type of feedback, what type of feedback schedule, and what additional therapies are indicated for various problems.

The control of stress-related disorders without drugs or surgery is obviously a desirable goal, and biofeedback, relaxation, and meditation seem to hold some promise in this field for certain types of cases. The applications seem extensive. Hypertension, insomnia, sexual dysfunction, cardiac arrhythmias, asthma, and gastrointestinal disorders are but a few of the problems that have been addressed so far, with varying degrees of success. The degree of success of biofeedback and relaxation as coping strategies for dealing with stress is not yet clear. The results so far, however, are promising and are spawning much research.

BIBLIOGRAPHY

"Biofeedback." *Health Library.* EBSCO Information Services, 22 Aug. 2013. Web. 20 Feb. 2014.

"Biofeedback: Using Your Mind to Improve Your Health." *Mayo Clinic.* Mayo Foundation for Medical Education and Research, 2014. Web. 20 Feb. 2014.

Fehmi, Les, and Jim Robbins. *The Open-Focus Brain: Harnessing the Power of Attention to Heal Mind and Body.* Boston: Trumpeter, 2007. Print.

Lazarus, Judith. *Stress Relief and Relaxation Techniques.* Boston: McGraw-Hill, 2000. Print.

"Relaxation Techniques for Health: An Introduction." *National Center for Complementary and Alternative Medicine.* National Institutes of Health, US Dept. of Health & Human Services, Feb. 2013. Web. 20 Feb. 2014.

Robbins, Jim. *A Symphony in the Brain: The Evolution of the New Brain Wave Biofeedback.* Rev. ed. New York: Grove, 2008. Print.

Schwartz, Mark, and Frank Andrasik. *Biofeedback: A Practitioner's Guide.* 3rd ed. New York: Guilford, 2005. Print.

Jonathan Kahane

SEE ALSO: Adrenal gland; Cognitive behavior therapy; Coping: Strategies; Emotions; Endocrine system; General adaptation syndrome; Meditation and relaxation; Operant conditioning therapies; Pain management; Psychosomatic disorders; Reinforcement; Selye, Hans; Stress: Physiological responses; Stress-related diseases.

Bipolar disorder

TYPE OF PSYCHOLOGY: Biological bases of behavior; Psychopathology; Psychotherapy

Bipolar disorder is a serious mental illness that is characterized by depressive and manic episodes. Advanced neurobiological research and assessment techniques have shown this disorder to have biochemical origins and a genetic element. Research indicates that stress may play a role in the precipitating recurrence of episodes. The main treatment interventions include lithium, mood-stabilizing anticonvulsants, antipsychotics, and psychotherapy.

KEY CONCEPTS

- Diathesis-stress model
- Lithium carbinate
- Mania
- Melatonin
- Neurotransmitter
- Psychotic symptoms
- Seasonal affective disorder

INTRODUCTION

Although mood fluctuations are a normal part of life, individuals with bipolar disorder experience extreme mood changes. Bipolar disorder, or bipolar affective disorder (also called manic-depressive disorder), has been identified as a major psychiatric disorder characterized by dramatic mood and behavior changes. These changes, ranging from episodes of high euphoric moods to deep depression, with accompanying behavioral and personality changes, are devastating to those with the disorder and perplexing to the loved ones of those affected. The National Institute for Mental Health (NIMH) reported that approximately 2.5 percent of the US population over the age of eighteen suffers from bipolar disorder. The disorder is divided fairly equally between men and women.

Clinical psychiatry has been effective in providing biochemical intervention in the form of mood stabilizers such as lithium carbonate or valproate, which both stimulate the release of the neurotransmitter glutamate in order to stabilize or modulate the ups and downs of this illness. Lithium treatment is most effective when treating individuals with pure mania, which is characterized by periods of euphoria and depression. Mood-stabilizing anticonvulsant medications, such as oxcarbazepine (Trileptal), carbamazepine (Tegretol), and lamotrigine (Lamictal) are often used to treat bipolar. Atypical antipsychotic medications, antidepressants, electrocovulsive therapy (ECT), and nonmedical therapies such as sleep management and psychotherapy are increasingly utilized to treat individuals with bipolar disorder. Psychotherapy is seen by most practitioners as a necessary adjunct to medication.

SYMPTOMS

In the manic phase of a bipolar episode, individuals may experience inappropriately good moods, or "highs," or may become extremely irritable. During a manic phase, they may overcommit to work projects and meetings, social activities, and family responsibilities in the belief that they can accomplish anything; this is known as manic grandiosity. At times, psychotic symptoms such as delusions, severe paranoia, and hallucinations may accompany a manic episode. These symptoms may lead to a misdiagnosis of other psychotic disorders such as schizophrenia. Although it may be difficult to arrive at a differential diagnosis between schizophrenia and bipolar disorder when a person is acutely psychotic, a long-term view of the individual's overall symptoms and functioning can distinguish between the two disorders.

The initial episode of bipolar disorder is typically one of mania or elation, although in some people, a depressive episode may signal the beginning of the disorder. Episodes of bipolar disorder can recur rapidly—within hours or days—or may have a much slower recurrence rate, even of years. The duration of each episode, whether it is depression or mania, varies among individuals but normally remains fairly consistent for each individual.

TYPES

According to the fifth edition of the *Diagnostic and Statistical Manual of Mental Disorders* (DSM-5, 2013), which is the diagnostic manual of the American Psychiatric Association, there are several types of bipolar disorder. Bipolar disorder specifiers are categorized according to the extent of severity; the types of the symptoms; the changes in activity, energy, and mood; and the duration of the symptoms.

Bipolar I disorder is characterized by alternating periods of mania and depression. At times, severe bipolar disorder may be accompanied by psychotic symptoms such as delusions and hallucinations. For this reason, bipolar I disorder is also considered a psychotic disorder. The prevalence of bipolar I disorder is divided fairly equally between men and women. However, women report more episodes of depression than men and are more likely to be diagnosed with bipolar II disorder.

Bipolar II disorder is characterized by alternating episodes of a milder form of mania (known as hypomania) and depression. In bipolar II disorder, although there is an observable change in mood and functioning, the hypomanic episode causes less severe impairment than that seen in mania. It is very rare for an individual's diagnosis to change from bipolar II disorder to bipolar I disorder.

CYCLOTHYMIA

Cyclothymic disorder is a form of bipolar disorder in which hypomania alternates with a low-level, chronic depressive state. Seasonal affective disorder (SAD) is characterized by alternating mood episodes that vary according to seasonal patterns; the mood changes are thought to be related to changes in the amount of sunlight and accompanying effects on an individual's circadian rhythm and levels of the hormone melatonin.

In the northern hemisphere, the typical pattern is associated with manic symptoms in the spring and summer and depression in the fall and winter. Manic episodes often have a shorter duration than the depressive episodes. Bipolar disorder must be differentiated from depressive disorders, which include major depression (unipolar depression) and dysthymia, a milder but chronic form of depression.

COMORBIDITY

Clinical comorbidity is the existence of two or more disorders in the same individual. in In 2011, the Archives of General Psychiatry (now JAMA Psychiatry) reported on a World Mental Health survey conducted by researchers from Harvard University. The survey found that 75 percent of participants with bipolar spectrum disorder also met the criteria for at least one other psychiatric disorder, with anxiety disorder as the most prevalent co-occurring condition. Less than half of those with bipolar disorder reported receiving mental health treatment for the condition. Other frequently occurring comorbid disorders are attention-deficit hyperactivity disorder (ADHD), personality disorders, and substance use disorder.

CAUSES

The causes of bipolar disorder are not fully understood. However, family, twin, and adoption studies indicate that genetic factors play a major role. The Depression and Bipolar Support Alliance reports that approximately two-thirds of individuals with bipolar have at least one close relative with the disorder. In fact, it is not uncommon to see families in which several generations are affected by bipolar disorder. Serotonin, norepinephrine, and dopamine, brain chemicals known as neurotransmitters that regulate mood, arousal, and energy, respectively, are thought to be altered in bipolar disorder.

One theory is that bipolar disorder is associated with dysregulation in brain regions that are implicated in emotion such as the amygdala and basal ganglia. This theory is supported by functional brain imaging studies that indicate that during cognitive or emotional tasks, people with bipolar I disorder show different patterns of activity in the amygdala. In terms of structural brain imaging, people with bipolar disorder also display differences in the volume of activity in certain regions such as the amygdala and basal ganglia.

A diathesis-stress model has been proposed for some psychosomatic disorders such as hypertension. This model has also been applied to bipolar disorder. In a diathesis-stress model, there is a susceptibility (the diathesis) for the disorder. An individual who has a diathesis is at risk for the disorder but may not show signs of the disorder unless there is sufficient stress. In this model, a genetic, structural, or biochemical predisposition toward the disorder (the bipolar diathesis) may lie dormant until stress triggers the emergence of the illness. The stress may be psychosocial, biological, neurochemical, or a combination of these factors.

A diathesis-stress model can also account for some of the recurrent episodes of mania in bipolar disorder. Investigators suggest that positive life events, such as the birth of a baby or a job promotion, as well as negative life events, such as divorce or the loss of a job, may trigger the onset of episodes in individuals with bipolar disorder. Stressful life events and the social rhythm disruptions that they cause can have adverse effects on a person's circadian rhythms. Circadian rhythms are normal biologic rhythms that govern such functions as sleeping and waking, body temperature, and oxygen consumption. Circadian rhythms affect hormonal levels and have significant effects on both emotional and physical well-being. For those reasons, many clinicians encourage individuals with bipolar disorder to work toward maintaining consistency in their social rhythms.

Investigators have compared the course of bipolar disorder to kindling, a process in which epileptic seizures increase the likelihood of further seizures. According to the kindling hypothesis, triggered mood episodes may leave the individual's brain in a sustained sensitized state that makes the person more vulnerable to further episodes. After a while, external factors are less necessary for a mood episode to be triggered. Episode sensitization may also account for rapid-cycling states, in which the individual shifts from depression to mania over the course of a few hours or days. Some individuals are diagnosed with a subtype of bipolar disorder known as rapid cycling bipolar disorder, which is defined as four or more episodes per year. Rapid cycling is characterized by poorer outcome.

IMPACT

The burden of bipolar disorder is considerable. In addition to experiencing functional impairment during illness episodes, many people with bipolar disorder experience ongoing functional impairment between episodes. In 2002, the World Health Organization (WHO) reported that bipolar disorder was responsible for more adjusted life-years than any form of cancer or such major neurologic diseases as Alzheimer's and epilepsy. It was estimated that bipolar disorder was the sixth leading cause of disability worldwide among adults between the ages of fifteen and forty-four. Bipolar disorder is associated with the highest rate of suicide out of all of the psychiatric disorders. According to Kay Redfield Jamison, one of the foremost experts on bipolar disorder, approximately 50 percent of people with bipolar disorder attempt suicide at least once during their lives. In one large-scale study, when asked to rate their perception of their well-being in terms of their culture, values, and how they live in relation to their goals, standards, and expectations (that is, their quality of life), individuals with bipolar disorder rated their quality of life lower than members of the general population did. Indeed, study findings suggest that quality-of-life ratings are poorer in bipolar disorder than they are in anxiety disorders and in depression but are better than compared with quality-of-life ratings in schizophrenia.

Organizations such as the National Alliance on Mental Illness (NAMI) and support groups such as the Depressive and Bipolar Support Alliance (DBSA) have provided a way for people with bipolar disorder to share their pain as well as to triumph over the illness. Many people have found comfort in knowing that others have suffered from the mood shifts, and they can draw strength from one another. Family members and friends can be the strongest supporters and advocates for those who have bipolar disorder or other psychiatric illnesses. Many patients have credited their families' constant, uncritical support in addition to competent effective treatment including medications and psychotherapy, with helping them cope with the devastating effects of the illness. As many as 15 percent of those with bipolar disorder commit suicide; this reality makes early intervention, relapse prevention, and treatment of the disorder necessary to prevent such a tragic outcome.

TREATMENT APPROACHES

Medications have been developed to aid in correcting the biochemical imbalances thought to be part of bipolar disorder. Lithium carbonate is effective for the majority of individuals who take it. Many brilliant and successful people have reportedly suffered from bipolar disorder and have been able to function successfully with competent and responsible treatment. Some people who have taken lithium for bipolar disorder, however, have complained that it robs them of their energy and creativity. They say that they actually miss the energy associated with manic phases of the illness. This perceived loss, some of it realistic, can be a factor in relapse associated with lithium noncompliance.

Other medications have been developed to help those individuals who are considered lithium nonresponders or who find the side effects of lithium intolerable. Anticonvulsant medications, such as divalproex sodium (Depakote), carbamazepine (Tegretol), and lamotrigine (Lamictal), which have been found to have mood-stabilizing effects, are often prescribed to individuals with bipolar disorder. During the depressive phase of the disorder, electroconvulsive therapy (ECT) and lamotrigine (Lamictal) have also been administered to help restore the individual's mood to a normal level. Phototherapy is particularly useful for individuals who have Seasonal Affective Disorder (SAD). Atypical antipsychotic medications such as risperidone (Risperdal), olanzapine (Zyprexa), and quetiapine (Seroquel) have also been prescribed to individuals with bipolar I disorder for the treatment of mania.

Cognitive behavior therapy is a form of therapy that addresses an individual's beliefs, assumptions, and behaviors to improve that person's emotional responses and health. Interpersonal social rhythms therapy encourages individuals to achieve and maintain stable routines, emphasizing the link between regular routines and moods, whereas the interpersonal component of the therapy focuses on the interpersonal issues that arise in individuals' lives. Psychotherapy, especially cognitive behavior therapy or interpersonal social rhythm therapy, is viewed by most practitioners as a necessary adjunct to medication. Indeed, psychotherapy has been found to assist individuals with bipolar disorder in maintaining medication compliance.

Local mental health associations are able to recommend psychiatric treatment by board-certified psychiatrists and licensed psychologists who specialize in the treatment of mood disorders. Often, temporary hospitalization is necessary for complete diagnostic assessment, initial mood stabilization and intensive treatment, medication adjustment, or monitoring of an individual who feels suicidal.

BIBLIOGRAPHY

Correa, R., et al. "Is Unrecognized Bipolar Disorder a Frequent Contributor to Apparent Treatment Resistant Depression?" *Journal of Affective Disorders* 127 (2012): 10–18. Print.

Deckersbach, Thilo, et al. *Mindfulness-Based Cognitive Therapy for Bipolar Disorder.* New York: Guilford, 2014. Print.

Goodwin, Frederick K., and Kay R. Jamison. *Manic Depressive Illness.* 2d ed. New York: Oxford University Press, 2007. Print.

Jamison, Kay R. *An Unquiet Mind.* New York: Knopf, 1995. Print.

Miklowitz, David J. *The Bipolar Disorder Survival Guide: What You and Your Family Need to Know.* New York, N.Y.: Guilford, 2002. Print.

Miklowitz, David J., and Sheri E. Johnson. "The Psychopathology and Treatment of Bipolar Disorder." *Annual Review of Clinical Psychology* 2 (2006): 199–235. Print.

Merikangas, Kathleen, et al. "Prevalence and Correlates of Bipolar Spectrum Disorder in the World Mental Health Survey Initiative." *Archives of General Psychiatry* 68.3 (2011): 241–51. Print.

Post, RM, and P. Kalivas. "Bipolar Disorder and Substance Misuse: Pathological and Therapeutic Implications of their Comorbidity and Cross-Sensitisation." *British Journal of Psychiatry* 202 (2013): 172–76. Print.

Yatham, Lakshmi N., and Vivek Kusumakar, eds. 2nd ed. New York: Brunner-Routledge, 2009. Print.

Diane C. Gooding and Karen Wolford; updated by Diane C. Gooding

See Also: Abnormality: Biomedical models; Alcohol dependence and abuse; Antianxiety medications; Antidepressant medications; Anxiety disorders; Attention-deficit hyperactivity disorder; Beck Depression Inventory (BDI); Borderline personality disorder; Children's Depression Inventory (CDI); Comorbidity; Conduct disorder; Depression; Drug therapies; Generalized anxiety disorder; Genetics and mental health; Histronic personality disorder; Hysteria; Mental illness: Historical concepts; Mood stabilizer medications; Personality disorders; Psychotic disorders; Schizophrenia: Backgrounds, types and symptoms; Schizophrenia: Theoretical explanations; Seasonal affective disorder; Suicide; Synaptic transmission.

Biracial heritage and mental health

Type of psychology: Multicultural psychology; Psychopathology; Psychotherapy

The study of the mental health of biracial and multiracial people has been dominated by the view that mixed-race people will have severe identity and other mental health issues because of their ancestry. Additionally, society has tended to classify mixed-race people as members of a sin-

gle race, often based on their dominant physical characteristics. As a result, little empirical study has been made of the mental health issues and needs of mixed-race people.

Key Concepts
- Biracial
- Identity
- Mestizo
- Mulatto
- Multiracial
- One-drop rule

INTRODUCTION

In 2000, the US Census Bureau allowed respondents to check more than one racial or ethnic category for the first time in history. Previous censuses forced respondents to choose from distinct racial or ethnic categories such as black or African American, white or Caucasian, American Indian or Alaskan Native, Asian or Pacific Islander, and Hispanic. The 2000 census had fifteen check boxes for racial or ethnic categories and three write-in areas to enable respondents to clarify their ancestry. Additionally, it expanded traditional racial categories to include more distinct subgroups. These changes were significant because they marked the first time biracial and multiracial individuals were able to identify as such and not as a member of a single race on the census forms. Approximately seven million people (2.4 percent of the overall population) identified themselves as biracial or multiracial in the 2000 census; in the 2010 census, approximately nine million people (2.9 percent of the overall population) identified themselves as being of two or more races. Biracial and multiracial individuals are among the fastest-growing segments of the US population.

Biracial individuals are those who claim any two racial groups (not limited to black and white) as part of their heritage; multiracial individuals are those who claim more than two. Historically, the United States has viewed race dichotomously by characterizing people as either blacks or whites. Race was defined by the "one-drop rule," which states that a person with any black ancestry (one drop of black blood) is part of the black race. The one-drop rule, developed during the slavery era, reflected society's significant bias for individuals of European ancestry over individuals of color and a desire to maintain racial purity. The dominating (and erroneous) belief for much of US history was that racial mixing threatened white racial, moral, social, and intellectual superiority because it diluted white blood with inferior blood from lesser races. In the 1660s, the United States began enacting laws preventing the mixing of races (miscegenation) and stipulating a person's race by how much African ancestry the individual possessed. Many states had laws prohibiting interracial marriage until a 1967 US Supreme Court ruling overturned these statutes. Other Jim Crow laws mandated segregation in areas such as voting, housing, and schools. Thus, the cost of having any black ancestry was extremely high.

Historically, the term "mulatto" was used to describe an individual with black and white ancestry, particularly a person with one white and one black parent. Mulatto was an official US Census category until 1930, but this term has come to be regarded as offensive and outdated. The term "mestizo" was used to refer to individuals of mixed European (often Spanish) and American Indian ancestry, and the term "half-breed" described an individual whose parents were of different races, usually white and American Indian. The terms "biracial" and "multiracial" are more inclusive, describing individuals with varied racial ancestry. Those individuals who identify with multiple racial or ethnic backgrounds are said to have a biracial or multiracial identity.

MENTAL HEALTH

Early models of mental health often assumed that because a person was biracial or multiracial, that individual would become mentally ill. The "tragic mulatto" stereotype portrayed biracial individuals as self-hating, depressed, sexually perverse, and chronically suicidal. The core of the mulatto's despair was that the individual could never live fully as a white person despite having white ancestry. This stereotype dominated fictional literature and societal views through the early 1980s. Biracial and mixed-race individuals were automatically assumed to have deeply ingrained psychological issues. Because of these negative stereotypes and biases, little scientific study of the mental health of biracial and multiracial individuals has been conducted.

Historically, biracial and multiracial individuals have been excluded from full membership in monoracial communities. This exclusion causes feelings of isolation and a sense of not belonging to or being accepted by any racial or ethnic group. This negativity results in struggles with issues of self-identification and self-esteem. It has been demonstrated that biracial and multiracial individuals face unique social and psychological stressors related to being multiracial. One of these stressors is having to continually answer the question "What are you?" Sometimes, these individuals have been ostracized by members of their extended families because they are of mixed race. Monoracial individuals of color can often have their social and self-esteem needs met within their own racial group, even if they run into discrimination and prejudice in the greater society. This kind of support network is usually not available to multiracial individuals. Additionally, because society continues to dichotomize race into discrete categories, multiracial individuals tend to feel as if they have to defend their multiracial ancestry and psychological well-being. This can be especially difficult for multiracial children and adolescents.

Modern society continues to label individuals based on their perceived racial background, as suggested by their physical characteristics. As a result, many biracial individuals feel forced to choose a racial identity based on their physical appearance. For example, a biracial person with an Asian and a white parent may feel pressure to identify as Asian American because he or she has Asian features. This "forced choice" identification was especially common before the US Census Bureau expanded the choice of racial categories in its surveys. Increasingly, biracial and multiracial individuals are self-identifying as such, in ways that make clear their specific multiracial ancestry. Society has become more accepting of individuals who identify as biracial or multiracial. The recognition of biracial and multiracial people as distinct from other racial groups has helped the social and psychological adjustment of biracial and multiracial individuals.

It is difficult to assess the prevalence of psychological disorders among multiracial individuals because very little empirical study of mental health issues within this group has been conducted. However, there is some evidence to suggest that multiracial individuals are at a slightly higher risk for depression, anxiety, and substance abuse disorders than their monoracial counterparts.

BIBLIOGRAPHY

Kaeser, Gigi. *Of Many Colors: Portraits of Multiracial Families.* Amherst: U of Massachusetts P, 1997. Print.

Jones, Nicholas A., and Jungmiwha Bullock. *The Two or More Races Population: 2010.* Washington, DC: US Census Bureau, 2012. Digital file.

Reddy, Maureen, ed. *Everyday Acts Against Racism: Raising Children in a Multiracial World.* Seattle: Seal, 1996. Print.

Rockquemore, Kerry Ann, and Tracey A. Laszloffy. *Raising Biracial Children: From Theory to Practice.* New York: Altimira, 2005. Print.

Root, Maria. *The Multiracial Experience: Racial Borders as the New Frontier.* Thousand Oaks: Sage, 1996. Print.

Root, Maria, and Matt Kelley. *Multiracial Child Resource Book: Living Complex Identities.* Seattle: MAVIN, 2003. Print.

Smith, Christopher L. "Biracial Americans' Experience with Identity, Gender Roles, and Anxiety." *Journal of Human Behavior in the Social Environment* 24.4 (2014): 513–28. Print.

Townsend, Sarah S., et al. "Being Mixed: Who Claims a Biracial Identity?" *Cultural Diversity and Ethnic Minority Psychology* 18.1 (2012): 91–96. Print.

Zack, Naomi. *American Mixed Race: The Culture of Microdiversity.* Lanham: Rowman, 1995. Print.

Katherine M. Helm

See Also: African Americans and mental health; Asian Americans/Pacific Islanders and mental health; Latinos and mental health; Native Americans/Alaskan Natives and mental health; Prejudice; Prejudice reduction; Race and intelligence; Racism.

Birth

Effects on physical development

Type of psychology: Biological bases of behavior; Developmental psychology

Birth represents a baby's transition from intrauterine existence to life outside the mother's womb. Although most births progress smoothly, some involve complications that can have an adverse impact on the physical and neurological development of the baby.

Key Concepts

- Afterbirth
- Anoxia
- Breech position
- Cervix
- Cesarean section
- Immature birth
- Labor
- Midwife
- Miscarriage

- Oxytocics
- Premature birth

INTRODUCTION

Birth represents the culmination of an involved journey from a single-celled fertilized egg to a newborn baby. Normal, uncomplicated childbirth does not have any significant physical impact on the development of the baby. Neurological or physical abnormalities following a smooth delivery are most likely attributable to disruptions during prenatal development. Prenatal disruptions may be chromosomal, environmental, or some combination of the two and are studied in the field of teratology. Although the second and third trimesters of pregnancy are important, the first trimester of prenatal development is often considered most sensitive to disruptions. Disturbances during prenatal development can produce fetal death or severe abnormalities, such as deformed or missing limbs, cerebral palsy, or intellectual disabilities, as well as more subtle complications such as mood disorders or learning disabilities that may not manifest until later stages of development.

Most pregnancies in industrialized countries progress smoothly. When a mother experiences birth complications, however, the baby is at increased risk for adverse physical and neurological outcomes. Some of the more serious birth complications include anoxia, premature delivery, low birth weight, and contact with maternal genital herpes lesions at birth. In developing countries, babies may be at greater risk for physical or neurological damage due to a lack of medical facilities or trained medical personnel. As a result, birth complications can lead to fetal, and sometimes maternal, death; physical abnormalities such as paralysis or cerebral palsy; or neurological abnormalities such as intellectual disability or schizophrenia.

STAGES OF LABOR

"Labor" is the term used to describe the process of the birth of the baby. Labor has three stages and begins when the cervix dilates. The cervix is the opening in the women's vagina through which the baby passes. A common misconception is that labor begins with the onset of uterine contractions, but these are often present several hours before dilation. The duration of labor depends on a number of factors, the most important being the mother's previous birth experience. On average, first-time mothers experience longer labors (eight to fourteen hours) than mothers who have given birth previously (three to eight hours).

The first stage of labor is the longest and most uncomfortable for the mother. It officially begins when the uterine contractions occur within fifteen-minute intervals and ends when the cervix is fully dilated so that the fetus can pass through. The second stage of labor represents the actual delivery of the baby. In vaginal childbirth (as opposed to cesarean section), the baby is pushed out through the expanding cervix, and average delivery time ranges from thirty to forty minutes. The third stage of labor takes about ten minutes and involves expulsion of the afterbirth, which comprises the placenta and other membranes. A physician will typically examine the afterbirth to ensure that all of it has been expelled. If not, the physician may scrape the uterus to remove the remaining portions and prevent infection.

The birth process is thought to be stressful on the baby but also adaptive. The contractions of the uterus during labor help push the baby out but may also restrict the oxygen supply to the fetus. This decrease of oxygen, called anoxia, can cause brain damage or fetal death if it persists beyond four minutes. In response to contractions during labor and the subsequent oxygen restriction, the fetus secretes hormones that increase blood flow to the brain and ensure that the baby will breathe on its own when it finally enters the extrauterine environment.

CHILDBIRTH POSITIONS AND SETTINGS

There are considerable cultural variations in the childbirth process. For some cultures, childbirth is a communal occasion, while for others, it takes place in isolation. In most non-Western societies, childbirth takes place in a vertical position, such as squatting or sitting; in Western societies the mother is often placed on her back or side.

In the United States before the 1800s, the birth of a child took place at home, where the expectant mother was surrounded by family, relatives, and friends. In contrast, a modern setting is most likely to be a hospital. A majority of the births in the United States (98.8 percent in 2010) occur in a hospital setting. This percentage is lower in some European countries, where home births attended by midwives are more common.

Childbirth in a hospital setting is thought to have both advantages and disadvantages. The hospital setting is perceived to be less comfortable, less likely to allow extensive mother-baby contact at birth, and more likely to perform unnecessary medical interventions for issues that could be resolved without the risk of surgery. However, this setting is the most appropriate for older mothers and mothers who are likely to experience birth complications. Freestanding birth centers are thought to be more flexible, less likely to use unnecessary medical procedures, and more likely to encourage early contact between parents and the baby. Some developmental psychologists argue that the first twelve hours following birth are a critical period in the bonding experience between mother and baby. Without such initial contact, some developmental psychologists argue that the baby's development will be suboptimal. The research in this area is inconclusive.

Home births are more frequent in Europe and developing countries than in North America. Advantages include a familiar environment and a setting that is in a position to promote parent-infant contact. Advocates of this setting indicate that the benefits of early attachment to the caregiver and the comfort level of the mother during the birth process outweigh any possible risks of being away from a hospital setting in the event of an emergency. If complications occur, however, the mother and baby must be transported to the hospital, jeopardizing the physical health of the baby by delaying what could be critical intervention.

In 2010, a midwife attended approximately 8 percent of US births in any of the described settings. A midwife is an individual experienced in the process of childbirth who assists with the delivery of the baby and provides emotional as well as educational support to the expectant mother. Midwives are common in many countries around the world, assisting pregnant women not only through birth but also through all stages of pregnancy.

METHODS OF DELIVERY

There are three types of delivery: natural, medicated, and cesarean. Natural childbirth avoids medication and requires education of the expectant mother to reduce fear and anxiety during childbirth, which are thought to increase the duration of labor and, as a result, the possibility of fetal complications. Prepared childbirth (the Lamaze method) was developed by French obstetrician Ferdinand Lamaze and is a type of natural childbirth. It includes not only education about childbirth but also training in special breathing techniques to control pushing in the final stages of labor. Other natural childbirth techniques, such as the Bradley method, have been developed, but these are usually variations of the Lamaze method.

Medicated childbirth uses a nonsurgical approach to expedite the delivery of the baby and to decrease the mother's pain. Expectant mothers are commonly given oxytocics, synthetic hormones that expedite the birth process by stimulating uterine contractions. The American Academy of Pediatrics recommends the least possible use of medication such as tranquilizers or pain medications due to potential adverse impact on the newborn baby. Although it is difficult to predict the precise effects of medication on the fetus, it is customary to use minimal medicinal therapy. A general anesthetic such as Demerol is sometimes given to relieve the mother's muscle tension and anxiety. This medication passes through the placenta and can lead to detrimental changes in the fetus, such as decreases in heart rate, muscle tone, breathing, and general attentiveness. One commonly used alternative is an epidural block, which has fewer side effects on the fetus than intravenous or oral medications. An epidural block entails the insertion of a needle into the spinal canal of the mother and the introduction of local anesthesia to numb the woman's body from the waist down. A cesarean section commonly involves epidural analgesia so that the expectant mother can remain alert to greet her newborn baby.

A cesarean delivery is a surgical birth. The physician makes an incision in the mother's abdomen and surgically removes the baby from her uterus. The indications for a cesarean section include previous cesarean births, abnormal labor, the presentation of the baby in breech position (buttocks first), and infant distress due to oxygen deprivation. In addition, a cesarean section might be necessary if there is serious maternal illness such as diabetes, premature separation of the placenta from the uterus (placenta abruptio), or maternal infection with genital herpes. Cesarean births require extra recovery time for the mother. Babies tend to be less alert and have greater breathing difficulties following cesarean delivery. However, there does not appear to be any significant lasting deleterious impact with cesarean delivery.

BABY'S PHYSICAL APPEARANCE

At the time of birth, the baby is covered with protective grease called the vernix caeosa. This covering serves to protect the baby's skin during birth. At birth the baby appears bluish in color (from oxygen deprivation) and may have a misshapen head, a flattened nose, and bruises. These characteristics are related to passage through the birth canal. The head is large compared to the rest of the body, and it has spaces between the skull bones (fontanelles) that allow it to contort slightly to fit through the birth canal. The fontanelles will close shortly after birth.

There are times during natural childbirth when a physician uses forceps or a vacuum extractor to deliver the baby. Forceps are a tonglike device used to pull the baby out of the mother's birth canal. A vacuum extractor is a suction device that attaches to the baby's head and pulls the baby out through the birth canal. Both forceps and vacuum extraction can contribute to transient bruises and misshapen features at birth.

ASSESSMENT OF THE BABY

There are two widely used methods of assessing the baby's physical and neurological status following birth. The Apgar test assesses the baby's vital functions within sixty seconds of birth and again five minutes after birth by looking at heart rate, respiratory effort, reflex irritability, muscle tone, and color. A low score suggests possible physical or neurological abnormalities. A more thorough assessment may be conducted using the Brazelton Neonatal Behavior Assessment Scale (NBAS), which is administered a few days after birth. Areas assessed by the NBAS include reflex and respiratory responses and the infant's capacity to respond to stimuli in an interactive process. For the NBAS, the baby is manipulated from sleep to wakefulness to crying and then back down to a quiet state. The baby's coping and adaptive strategies are thus examined, and the baby's physical and central nervous system functioning can be assessed.

BIRTH COMPLICATIONS

Although most births progress smoothly, some involve complications that can have a profound impact on the physical and neurological development of the baby. Premature birth is a significant risk factor for physical and neurological abnormalities. A baby's physical status may be classified along two dimensions: birth weight and the length of time spent in the mother's womb. A normal birth usually occurs between thirty-seven and forty-two weeks of pregnancy, and the baby averages 7.5 pounds. A fetus that is born prior to the twentieth week of pregnancy or weighs less than 1 pound will die. This type of birth is called a miscarriage. A fetus delivered between the twentieth and twenty-eighth week of pregnancy and weighing between 1 and 2 pounds is called immature. With the advancement of medical practices, it is possible for babies that are born as early as four months prematurely and weighing only 1.5 pounds to survive. A baby born between the twenty-ninth and thirty-sixth week of pregnancy and weighing between 2 and 5.5 pounds is termed premature. Both immature and premature births predispose a baby to a variety of adverse outcomes, ranging from death to severe physical and mental disabilities.

Low birth weight is another complication that predisposes a baby to adverse physical and neurological outcomes. Complications of low-birth-weight babies include greater incidences of intellectual disability, cerebral palsy, and general intellectual and gross motor delay. Babies weighing less than two pounds at birth are at risk for the most severe outcomes should they survive beyond infancy. Research indicates that nearly a quarter of these children experience intellectual disabilities, vision problems, and hearing difficulties. Babies weighing less than three pounds at birth continue to have a smaller physical stature and a significantly higher incidence of various illnesses throughout childhood. There is a clear relationship between premature birth, low birth weight, and adverse physical and neurological outcomes. A baby delivered prematurely is commonly a low-birth-weight baby. Both of these complications increase the baby's risk for fetal death, physical abnormalities such as paralysis or cerebral palsy, and neurological abnormalities such as intellectual disability or schizophrenia.

Anoxia is another birth complication that is cause for particular concern. A cesarean section is performed when the fetus is at risk for prolonged oxygen deprivation. Newly born babies can tolerate oxygen deprivation for as long as four minutes, after which it can cause severe brain damage. There are several causes of anoxia. In many cases, the condition may occur as a result of constriction of the umbilical cord. This is common in a breech birth, in which the baby's buttocks present for delivery rather than the baby's head. A second cause of anoxia is premature separation of the placenta from the uterus, which interrupts the supply of oxygen to the fetus. Sedation given to the mother during childbirth is another risk factor for anoxia. Sedation crosses the placenta and interferes with the baby's impetus to breathe. Anoxia may also occur as a result of airway obstruction from mucus inhaled during the birth process. This problem is typically alleviated through suctioning of the newborn's airway at birth.

BIBLIOGRAPHY

Berk, Laura E. *Infants, Children, and Adolescents.* 7th ed. Boston: Allyn, 2012. Print.

Johnson, Robert V. *Mayo Clinic Complete Book of Pregnancy and Baby's First Year.* New York: Morrow,

1994. Print.
Kail, Robert V., and John C. Cavanaugh. *Human Development: A Life-Span View.* 6th ed. Belmont: Wadsworth, 2013. Print.
Lansky, Vicki. *Complete Pregnancy and Baby Book.* Lincolnwood: Publications Intl., 1996. Print.
Lefrançois, Guy R. *The Lifespan.* 6th ed. Belmont: Wadsworth, 1999. Print.
Moore, Keith L., T. V. N. Persaud, and Mark G. Torchia. *Before We Are Born: Essentials of Embryology and Birth Defects.* 8th ed. Philadelphia: Saunders, 2013. Print.
Moore, Keith L., T. V. N. Persaud, and Mark G. Torchia. *The Developing Human: Clinically Oriented Embryology.* 9th ed. Philadelphia: Saunders, 2013. Print.
Santrock, John W. *Life-Span Development.* 14th ed. New York: McGraw, 2013. Print.
Sydsjö, Gunilla. "Long-Term Consequences of Non-Optimal Birth Characteristics." *Supp. to American Journal of Reproductive Immunology* 66.1 (2011): 81–87. Web. 20 Feb. 2014.
Van Hus, Janeline W. P., et al. "Comparing Two Motor Assessment Tools to Evaluate Neurobehavioral Intervention Effects in Infants with Very Low Birth Weight at 1 Year." *Physical Therapy* 93.11 (2013): 1475–83. Print.

Stefan C. Dombrowski

See Also: Attachment and bonding in infacy and childhood; Birth order and personality; Childhood disorders; Children's mental health; Development; Developmental disabilities; Family life: Children's issues'; Father-child relationship; Learning; Mother-child relationship; Parenting styles; Physical development: Environment versus genetics; Piaget, Jean; Reflexes in newborns.

Birth order and personality

Type of psychology: Developmental psychology

Although there is debate over the effects of birth order on personality, with some researchers claiming there is no effect, studies have found subtle differences between firstborn and later-born children; the order of children's births has also been found to influence how the parents treat them.

Key Concepts
- Anxiety
- Creativity
- Scientific method
- Self-image

INTRODUCTION

A child's order of birth into a family may influence how the parents treat the child. This treatment, in turn, can produce personality differences. Most research has focused on comparing the firstborn child with later-born children. Thus, most of what is known about birth order has to do with ways in which firstborns and later-borns are different.

Parents tend to be overly anxious with regard to their first child. The birth of their first child is a major event in their lives, and it can be somewhat threatening. They have never been parents before, and they do not know what to do in many instances. Thus, many parents tend to be overly restrictive with their first child, having many fears of the terrible things that may happen if they do not monitor and care for their child constantly. This anxiety can influence the personality of the child. Firstborns often grow up to be more anxious than later-born children. By the time parents have a second, third, or fourth child, they are more comfortable caring for children and know that they do not have to be overly concerned with protecting their child from every imaginable harm. Thus, they relax and allow the later-born children more freedom.

It should be made clear that this does not mean that every firstborn child is more anxious than every later-born child. It only means that there is a tendency, greater than could be expected by chance, for firstborns to be more anxious than later-borns. There will be many exceptions and instances where a firstborn is not anxious or where a later-born is.

ACHIEVEMENT AND RISK TAKING

When the firstborn child is growing up and until the birth of a sibling, the child has the parents all to himself or herself. This situation probably accounts for another personality difference of firstborns relative to later-borns: Firstborns tend to score higher on such measures of intelligence as intelligence (IQ) tests. When the later-born children come along, the parents will probably spend less time with them than they did with the first child; the later-born child will have as models the other children in the family. The first child had adults as models and thus may acquire a more adultlike interest in things—and therefore score higher on intellectual measures. This effect may account, in part, for the fact that firstborns achieve at a greater rate than later-borns. For example, there are more famous firstborn scientists (for their proportion in the population) than would be expected by chance.

Another difference in personality is found with the kinds of risks firstborns or later-borns will take. Firstborns will take risks if they believe that they can handle the situation safely but will be less likely to engage in behavior that exposes them to potential injury. Thus, firstborns are less likely than later-borns to be college football players. On the other hand, firstborns are overrepresented among astronauts and aquanauts. They would seem to be potentially dangerous occupations, but firstborns probably believe that they can avoid harm via good training and high-quality skills. Thus, the issue may be perceived harm: Firstborns may believe that they can avoid harm as astronauts or aquanauts, while it is extremely difficult to avoid injury in sports.

CREATIVE DIFFERENCES

Although differences in creativity have been found between firstborns and later-borns, it is important to also consider gender differences. By looking at both birth order and gender, creativity results become clear. Firstborn males tend to score higher on creativity measures than do later-born males. Creativity can be defined as the combination of originality and usefulness, and there are tests developed to measure it. When testing women, however, the results are the opposite: Later-born women score higher on creativity than firstborn women. This finding could be explained by the ways in which parents treat their firstborn child as well as how parents treat their female children. The firstborn female child has two disadvantages. Not only are the parents anxious and restrictive because she is a firstborn, but the parents are also likely to restrict female children more so than they do their male children. Thus, the female firstborn would be the most restricted of all the birth order and sex groupings. Other researchers have found that the female firstborn tends to grow up with traditional values, which some researchers believe tend to restrict creativity.

APPLICATIONS OF BIRTH ORDER RESEARCH

Knowledge of the effects of birth order often promotes greater self-understanding in those people who are most affected. For example, a male firstborn seeing his friends try out for the football team may have a dilemma. He knows that he does not wish to join them, but he feels pressured by the choices of his peers. His self-image makes him feel inadequate because he is not like his friends. If he knew the research findings concerning firstborns, however, he would realize that he might be quite courageous and risk taking in other pursuits but probably will not be when there is clear-cut physical danger. His personality was established long ago, as he grew up the firstborn child in his family. Thus, he would see the causes of his personality and be more self-accepting.

When people are anxious, they tend to talk. This talking may be an attempt to relieve their anxiety. This fact and the findings about birth order could be used in group situations to foster effective discussion. Thus, a teacher or a group therapist could make sure that the group was composed of a combination of firstborns and later-borns. The anxious firstborns will be likely to speak up, and discussion will be facilitated. If the group were all firstborns, there might be too many people talking at once, while if the group were all later-borns, there might be too little discussion. Thus, a mixture of firstborns and later-borns may produce the best group discussion.

Another application might be in changing people from their typical tendencies. Thus, if it is known that female firstborns tend not to be as creative because of a predilection toward traditional beliefs, one could educate the female firstborns about different ways of thinking. Education could focus on challenging some of the traditional beliefs by offering alternative, more questioning attitudes for the female firstborn to consider. This approach might increase the chances that the female firstborn would come up with creative solutions and ideas.

Birth order and gender difference findings can also serve as a basis for making interventions to help people in all the different birth order and gender combinations. The major recipient of help might be the female firstborn, since she has probably received an overly restrictive upbringing. Teachers or therapists, if aware of the tendency of some female firstborns to be inhibited in their challenging of society's conventional beliefs, might help these individuals to think more critically. Male later-borns may also, to a lesser extent, be inclined toward this inhibited thinking, if generalizations from the research are correct. They, too, could benefit from training or assistance in greater critical thinking that challenges the conventional beliefs they have learned. It should be emphasized that conventional beliefs are not necessarily wrong; one should, however, learn to think for oneself and not accept everything one is told automatically.

Although firstborn men and later-born women perform the best on creativity measures, they are by no means immune to society's conventions, which in some cases lead to an inhibition of creativity. Firstborn men seem to have a high need for social approval, which at times may inhibit creativity and lead to conformity. When this conformity is undesirable or restricts creativity, it needs to be overcome. Later-born women, although scoring more creatively than firstborn women, still have the burden of being female in a society that places many inhibitions on women. Everyone can use help to think more critically, to challenge what they have been taught, and in this way to increase the likelihood of creative thinking and of production of creative products.

EVOLUTION OF RESEARCH

Alfred Adler was an Austrian psychoanalyst who was a follower of Sigmund Freud. Adler, like several of Freud's early followers, believed that Freud neglected the social context of his research, and Adler broke away to establish his own school of psychology, which he called individual psychology. Among the many concepts that formed the basis of Adler's approach was his belief that birth order is worthy of study. He speculated in detail about how the ordinal position of the child affected the child's personality.

For many years, research psychologists did not study birth order to any extent. One reason is that birth order is an actuarial variable, like age, gender, or social class, and psychologists did not view it as worthwhile to study. In 1959, however, Stanley Schachter published the book *The Psychology of Affiliation,* in which he showed that birth order is an important variable. Many other researchers started looking at birth order in their studies. Sometimes they had little understanding of what birth order should mean, but it was easy to ask subjects to list their birth order to see if any patterns became apparent. One problem was that the early researchers included only children (children with no siblings) as firstborns. It is now known that while these groups are sometimes similar, they are often different from one another. It is best to include children who have no siblings in a separate category. Unfortunately, there have been too few "only children" in the population for statistical testing. Thus, researchers often simply drop that group from their analysis. As a greater understanding of birth order has been gained, it has become possible to conduct research based on what is known rather than to treat birth order as simply one more variable.

BIBLIOGRAPHY

Adler, Alfred. *What Life Should Mean to You*. Edited by Alan Porter. New York: Putnam, 1980. Print.

Blair, Linda. *Birth Order: What Your Position in the Family Really Tells You about Your Character.* London: Piatkus, 2013. Print.

Blake, Judith. *Family Size and Achievement.* Berkeley: U of California P, 1989. Print.

Cheng, C-C. J., et al. "Effect Modification by Parental Education on the Associations of Birth Order and Gender with Learning Achievement in Adolescents." *Child: Care, Health, and Development* 39.6 (2013): 894–902. Print.

De Neve, Jan-Emmanuel, et al. "Born to Lead? A Twin Design and Genetic Association Study of Leadership Role Occupancy." *Leadership Quarterly* 24.1 (2013): 45–60. Print.

Eisenman, Russell. *From Crime to Creativity: Psychological and Social Factors in Deviance.* Dubuque: Kendall/Hunt, 1991. Print.

Leman, Kevin. *The Birth Order Book: Why You Are the Way You Are.* Grand Rapids: F. H. Revell, 2004. Print.

Leman, Kevin. *The Firstborn Advantage: Making Your Birth Order Work for You.* Grand Rapids: F. H. Revell, 2008. Print.

Schachter, Stanley. *The Psychology of Affiliation.* Stanford: Stanford UP, 1974. Print.

Sulloway, Frank. *Born to Rebel: Birth Order, Family Dynamics, and Creative Lives.* New York: Vintage, 1997. Print.

Wallace, Meri. *Birth Order Blues: How Parents Can Help Their Children Meet the Challenges of Birth Order.* New York: Owl, 1999. Print.

Russell Eisenmann

See Also: Achievement motivation; Adler, Alfred; Adolescence: Cognitive skills; Birth: Effects on physical development; Children's mental health; Creativity and intelligence; Development; Family life: Children's issues; Parenting styles; Sibling relationships; Teenagers' mental health.

Blau, Theodore H.

Born: March 3, 1928
Died: January 28, 2003
Identity: American clinical, police, and forensic psychologist
Birthplace: Huntington, West Virginia
Place of death: St. Petersburg, Florida
Type of psychology: Motivation; Social psychology

Blau was a clinical psychologist whose research and writings included police training and forensic psychology.

Theodore H. Blau was a clinical psychologist whose research was in police training and forensic psychology. He received his master's degree in psychology in 1949 and his doctorate in psychology in 1951 from Pennsylvania State University. His postdoctoral training from 1951 to 1952 was at US Veteran's Administration Hospital at Perry Point, Maryland. He was a follower of B. F. Skinner and Kenneth B. Clark. After moving to Tampa, Florida, in 1955, he developed a successful private clinical practice, specializing in child and cognitive psychology and behavior modification. Blau became prominent over the next thirty years in academic and clinical psychology. During the 1970s and 1980s, he taught psychology to undergraduate and graduate students at academic institutions, including the University of South Florida. In 1985, he began work in police psychology and lectured regularly at the Federal Bureau of Investigation (FBI) Academy in Quantico, Virginia, on the credibility of child witnesses. He was a chief inspector of the Manatee County Sheriff's Behavioral Science Unit for more than ten years and testified as a psychological expert for prosecutors at the District Attorney's Office of Santa Fe, New Mexico, and the US Attorney for the Eastern District of Tennessee. He wrote technical books in the field of forensic psychology, including *The Psychologist as Expert Witness* (1984).

Blau was elected president of the American Psychological Association in 1977, becoming the first independent clinical psychologist to be elected. Also that year, he was honored as alumni fellow by Pennsylvania State University. He was named an honorary life member of the New York Society of Clinical Psychologists and received the Distinguished Service Award of the Florida Psychological Association, the Distinguished Contribution Award of the Philadelphia Society of Clinical Psychologists, and the Distinguished Psychologist Award of the California State Psychological Association.

Blau was an expert on drug addiction. As a tobacco industry consultant, he repeatedly testified before the US Congress that tobacco smoking was a "habit not an addiction." In 1988, before the House Subcommittee on Health and the Environment, he maintained that "There is no substantial scientific evidence that smoking creates a physical dependence to nicotine" and criticized the surgeon general's report, *The Health Consequences of Smoking: Nicotine Addiction* (1988). Blau argued that tobacco smoking was a habit rather than an addiction because it did not cause intoxication and its withdrawal symptoms were no worse than those experienced by people who stopped using caffeine. He argued that smokers choose to smoke and that ceasing to smoke was also a matter of choice.

BIBLIOGRAPHY

Barclay, Alan, and Fred L. Alberts, Jr. "Theodore Hertzl Blau." *American Psychologist* 59.1 (2004): 41. Print.

Blau, Theodore H. *The Forensic Documentation Sourcebook: The Complete Paperwork Resource for Forensic Mental Health Practice*. New York: Wiley, 2004. Print.

Blau, Theodore H. *Psychotherapy Tradecraft: The Technique & Style of Doing Therapy.* Hoboken: Taylor, 2014. Digital file.

Krieshok, Thomas S. "Psychologists and Counselors in the Legal System: A Dialogue with Theodore Blau." 66.2 (1987): 69–72. Print.

Trotter, Robert J. "Psychologist with a Badge." *Psychology Today* 21.11 (1987): 26. Print.

Ursula Goldsmith

See Also: Children's mental health; Forensic psychology; Nicotine dependence; Substance use disorders.

Bobo doll experiment

Date: 1960s forward
Type of psychology: Cognition; Learning; Social psychology

This experiment looked at the role of imitation in social learning among children, in particular examining the premise that children can learn aggressive behavior and engage in aggressive actions toward other individuals as a consequence of observing other individuals engaged in aggressive behavior.

Key Concepts

- Aggression
- Attention
- Imitation
- Observational learning
- Reproduction
- Retention
- Social learning theory

INTRODUCTION

The Bobo doll experiment was conceptualized by Canadian psychologist Albert Bandura as a test of early social learning theory. The basic premise of this experiment was that imitation is one source of learning. The Bobo doll experiment was designed to investigate the role of observational learning in social behavior; specifically, the role of observation of

A Bobo doll is an inflatable weighted toy that is approximately the same size as a prepubescent child. During the original 1961 experiment, children aged three to six years old were assigned to one of eight experimental conditions plus a control group. Participants in the experimental conditions were exposed to either aggressive or nonaggressive models, were male or female, and observed either same-sex or opposite-sex models. Participants in the control group were not exposed to an adult model. The experimenter attempted to match groups on personality types. Subsequent to viewing the adult behavior (as per their experimental condition), the children were taken to a second room filled with entertaining toys. The children's play time was limited, with the goal of mild arousal of aggression. Then the children were taken to a third room filled with "aggressive" and "nonaggressive" toys that they could play with for twenty minutes, in the absence of the adult model. Eight measures of aggression were recorded, including physical aggression toward the Bobo doll, verbal aggression toward the doll, other forms of aggression demonstrated by the adult models, and forms of aggression not demonstrated by the adult models toward the Bobo doll.

RESULTS

Children exposed to aggressive models were more likely to behave in physically and verbally aggressive ways than children exposed to nonaggressive models or children not exposed to adult models. Children exposed to nonaggressive models exhibited the least frequent aggressive behaviors, even when compared with children who had not viewed an adult model. Male children tended to behave more aggressively than female children. Children were more influenced by same-sex models who were behaving aggressively than by opposite-sex models who were behaving aggressively, although relationships between sex of the model and sex of the participant in demonstrating aggression are complex. Sex of the model may influence imitation of aggression or nonaggression for reasons not examined directly in this research. The aggressive behaviors demonstrated by the children resembled the behaviors of the adult models, pointing to the role of imitation in social learning.

In 1963, Bandura reported that observing aggressive behavior displayed on video has less of an effect on children's behavior than observing live models. In this work, the role of imitation and reinforcement on children's behavior cannot be disentangled. In 1965, Bandura, studying the role of reinforcement in imitation, reported that children who viewed aggressive behavior being punished were less likely to exhibit the behavior than were children who viewed aggressive behavior being either rewarded or having no consequence. In 1977, Bandura suggested that there are four steps in the modeling process:

- Attention is related to the perceived prestigiousness of the perpetrator
- Retention of actions is necessary for those actions and their consequences to be remembered
- Imitation requires skill, which comes from reproduction of a behavior
- Reinforcement plays a role in imitation by enhancing motivation

SUMMARY

The original experiment can be criticized on two points. First, because the Bobo doll rights itself when hit, children may have viewed the doll as a target intended to be struck rather than as a bona fide object of aggression. Second, drawing a conclusion about a child's likelihood of striking an actual child or adult from the child's striking a doll is problematic.

With respect to social learning theory, behaviors such as aggression can be learned by observation and skill can be developed through repeated imitation even in the absence of reinforcement—whether of the model or the child. Bandura and his colleagues postulated that exhibiting aggression, over time, is related to diminishing inhibitions toward aggression. In later work, Bandura studied the role of viewing live versus videotaped aggression on behavior, and he studied the role of reinforcement in imitation. Social learning researchers are interested in whether the behavior exhibited in the Bobo doll experiment can be generalized to other life situations. Considerable attention on the part of researchers, educators, security and mental health professionals, and the general public has been directed toward discovering the causes of aggression in children and, specifically, the effects of viewing violence on children's behavior and on their behavior as adults.

BIBLIOGRAPHY

Association for Psychological Science. "Bandura and Bobo: How a Doll Revolutionized Social-Learning Theory." *Observations. Association for Psychological Science*, 2012. Web. 24 Feb. 2014.

Bandura, Albert. *Social Learning Theory.* 1977. Englewood Cliffs: Prentice, 2002. Print.

Bandura, Albert, D. Ross, and S. A. Ross. "Imitation of Film-Mediated Aggressive Models." *Journal of Abnormal and Social Psychology* 66 (1963): 3–11. Print.

Bandura, Albert, D. Ross, and S. A. Ross. "Transmission of Aggressions through Imitation of Aggressive Models." *Journal of Abnormal and Social Psychology* 63. 3 (1961): 575–582. Print.

Kosslyn, S. M., and R. S. Rosenberg. *Fundamentals of Psychology: The Brain, the Person, the World.* 2d ed. Boston: Pearson, 2005. Print.

Mayer, R. E. *Learning and Instruction.* 2d ed. Upper Saddle River: Pearson, 2008. Print.

Zimmerman, Barry J., and Dale H. Schunk, eds. *Educational Psychology: A Century of Contributions.* 2003. Mahwah: Erlbaum, 2010. Print.

Ronna F. Dillon and Amber D. Dillon

SEE ALSO: Aggression; Aggression: Reduction and control; Bandura, Albert; Children's mental health; Experimentation: Independent, dependent, and control variables; Family life: Children's issues; Juvenile delinquency; Learning; Reinforcement; Social learning: Albert Bandura.

Body dysmorphic disorder

TYPE OF PSYCHOLOGY: Psychopathology, Psychotherapy, Sensation and perception

A perceptual and cognitive disturbance in which people are preoccupied with one or more imagined bodily defects. Preoccupation occurs even though bodily appearance is objectively well within the range of normal. People with body dysmorphic disorder (BDD) find some aspect of their physical appearance loathsome. They commonly complain about minor flaws such as facial wrinkles, freckles, facial hair, baldness, or some other feature that is repugnant: shape of the chin, nose, eyebrow, for example. Treatment usually involves combinatory therapy: use of a selective serotonin reuptake inhibitor (SSRI) and cognitive behavioral therapy (CBT).

KEY CONCEPTS

- Cognitive behavioral therapy
- Dysmorphophobia
- Selective serotonin reuptake inhibitor (SSRI)

INTRODUCTION

Amusement park goers often enjoy viewing themselves in "carnival mirrors" which distort their bodies to make them seem hideously deformed: stretched tall and thin, squashed short and thick, or bulging in the midsection. Fans of this entertainment enjoy the images because they know them to be optical illusions. Though not as extreme, people who suffer from BDD perceive some aspect of their physical selves as grossly deformed and become preoccupied in attempting to improve, remove, or hide it. Believing the misperception is their reality promotes self-hatred, depression, social embarrassment and isolation. They are often confused that others are not repulsed.

Though the psychiatric and psychological communities did not formally recognize BDD until 1987, Italian psychiatrist, Enrico Morselli described it in some of his patients more than a century earlier. Patients reported feeling ugly or complained of having horrific physical defects even though others never noticed them. Morselli noted that these patients were depressed and miserable, often tormented by obsessions over the imagined deformity, and named this disorder dysmorphophobia. Today, body dysmorphic disorder (BDD) is understood as an involuntary preoccupation with an imagined, or actual but slight, defect in appearance. The anxiety and rumination about the defect causes enough psychological distress that it impairs social, educational, and occupational functioning even to the point of social isolation.

POSSIBLE CAUSES

While the causes of BDD are not entirely known, experts feel a combination of triggers is responsible. Like many mental disorders, brain chemicals responsible for how brain cells communicate with each other, neurotransmitters, seem to play a major role. Serotonin, a chemical linked to mood, is one that is of particular interest in developing BDD and treating it.

Additional evidence suggests one or more genetic factors may be at work, especially in persons with a family history of BDD. The specific genetic action remains unknown, however. The presence of BDD among family members though also supports the idea that family environmental factors, like the expectation of flawless appearance in a family of models, actors, athletes, the socially prominent, or public figures, may play a role though research suggests genetics is the more important player.

Environmental and cultural reinforcement may also play a large role. Over the years, society has become obsessed with achieving perfect physical appearance, and the obsession fuels a huge economy. Advertisements for makeup, hair products, cosmetic surgery, tanning salons, diet pills and plans all attest to the obsession with improved, and for some the obsession with perfect, appearance. The media constantly presents perfectly-sculpted superstars whom millions aspire to emulate but who cannot possibly duplicate stars' flawless physical appearance.

DIAGNOSING BDD

The American Psychiatric Association's *Diagnostic and Statistical Manual of Mental Disorders* (DSM-III-R) officially recognized BDD in 1987 as a variant of obsessive-compulsive disorder. In 1999, it refined its view, designating BDD as a discrete disorder in the DSM-IV-R. The primary symptom is an involuntary obsessive focus on a particular body part or feature that is normal or near-normal in appearance. Often, people with BDD are most concerned with some part of their face. Common flaws like acne, blemishes, scars, or wrinkles can be intensely scrutinized for hours. Frequent symptoms of BDD are incessant mirror-gazing or comparing one's features to others. People with BDD may also be obsessed with grooming such as plucking eyebrows, skin-picking, or shaving. Often, these activities cause significant skin damage which stresses afflicted persons even more, resulting in exhaustive efforts to camouflage the defect with makeup, clothes, or frequently plastic surgery. BDD should be suspected when behaviors of inspecting, treating, and/or camouflaging consume enough time and energy to interfere patients' work, school, finances or social life, or when grooming becomes ritualistic. People with BDD often appear generally anxious or worried. BDD differs from other body image disorders such as what occurs in anorexia nervosa. People with BDD are obsessed over a defect (slight or imagined) in a specific part of the body. People with anorexia nervosa have the perceptual distortion that their bodies are as a whole overweight; they misperceive skin plasticity as fat tissue.

BDD results from a complex combination of biological, psychological and environmental factors though their precise interactions are not fully understood. BDD does have striking similarities to obsessive compulsive disorder, and these similarities may help to explain why many of the same treatments for OCD are also effective for it. Because its symptoms are easily mistaken for OCD and other disorders like major depression, BDD is often misdiagnosed. Some studies suggest 1-2% of the world's population meet all diagnostic criteria for BDD, but others put this percentage much higher.

WHO SUFFERS

BDD occurs in men and women equally, typically developing when appearance begins to matter a lot: adolescence or early adulthood with average onset between 16 and 17. Older adults can develop obsessive concerns about the physical effects of normal aging and develop BDD. People with BDD seek cosmetic surgery and dermatological procedures much more often than other groups seeking elective surgical interventions. Because BDD symptoms overlap with OCD symptoms, and because people with BDD are often too ashamed of their "defective" feature, they often do not seek help and their BDD remains undiagnosed and untreated.

TREATMENT OPTIONS

The first-line treatment of BDD involves taking an SSRI and starting CBT counseling in conjunction. SSRI's are generally effective in treating other conditions whose symptoms are similar to those in BDD, like major depressive disorder and OCD, both conditions in which serotonin levels are low and both of which get better as serotonin levels increase—at least to a point. It would be dangerous to assume that the more serotonin one has, the happier and more care free he or she would be.

BDD often requires higher doses than those prescribed for depression and more similar to those prescribed for OCD. The SSRI's used typically include fluoxetine (80mg/day), sertraline (200 mg/day), paroxetine (40-60 mg/day), and citalopram (40-60 mg/day). Patients are typically treated at the maximum effective and tolerated dose for 12-16 weeks before any symptoms might improve. If successful, use of the medication should continue indefinitely as relapse after discontinuation is high though this is a decision that should only be reached between the provider and the patient. Sometimes, when the patient has tried a second or third SSRI without success, the psychiatrist might recommend a medicine from the group known as the "anti-psychotics" which like the antidepressants are effective for many other conditions than the category they are in, psychosis. Common antipsychotics used for BDD are olanzapine or risperidone.

The cognitive part of CBT involves identifying and rethinking patient's self-loathing and disparaging thoughts. Then, through repetitive exposure, systematic desensitization, and step-wise implementation of adaptive behavioral strategies, CBT attempts to systematically remove the harmful and maladaptive behaviors associated with patients' coping with BDD on their own. Though widely practiced, not all psychologists or other mental health providers are specifically trained in CBT. People with BDD should seek out from among those with training and experience, the providers they believe they will develop effective therapeutic rapport: professionals who will challenge patients to work hard and support them in non-judgmental ways as they strive to meet the challenge of defeating this emotionally painful and socially limiting condition.

BIBLIOGRAPHY

Claiborn, James and Cherry Pedrick, *The BDD Workbook: Overcoming Body Dysmorphic Disorder and End Body Image Obsessions.* Oakland, CA: New Harbinger, 2004. Solid, useful introduction to this widely under-recognized condition. Exercises are practical and while not requiring supervision, do not constitute professional clinical treatment on their own.

Mayo Clinic Staff, *Body dysmorphic disorder.* Clear, second-person and plain spoken overview of the condition, how it develops, how it can be diagnosed and effectively treated. Available on-line or in print. Rochester, MN: The Mayo Foundation for Medical Education and Research, 2009. www.mayoclinic.com/health/body-dysmorphic-disorder/DS00559.

Phillips, Katharine A. *The Broken Mirror: Understanding and Treating Body Dysmorphic Disorder.* New York, NY: Oxford, 1998. Perhaps the classic work on BDD written for the lay audience. This is a hopeful, helpful, and well-informed approach to understanding BDD's various manifestations and their treatment. Clinical vignettes are particularly illustrative and illuminating.

Wilhelm, Sabine. *Feeling Good about the Way You Look: A Program for Overcoming Body Image Problems.* New York, NY: Guildford, 2006. Directly focused on the person suffering with BDD, this is a cognitive behavioral approach for starting self-treatment and includes the author's thoughts about medication and focused psychotherapy. Is also helpful for those who have concerns that a friend or family member might have BDD.

Paul Moglia and Thomas G. Zimmerman

SEE ALSO: Anorexia nervosa; Anxiety; Appearance; Bulimia nervosa; Health; Self-esteem.

Borderline personality disorder

TYPE OF PSYCHOLOGY: Personality; Psychopathology

Borderline personality is characterized by a longstanding pattern of instability in mood and interpersonal relationships. It is the most prevalent personality disorder—modest estimations suggest 2 to 4 percent of the population is affected—and has been the focus of significant research.

KEY CONCEPTS

- Chronic instability
- Cognitive Behavior therapy
- Dialectic behavioral therapy
- Personality disorder
- Self-mutilation

INTRODUCTION

Borderline personality disorder (BPD) is a psychological condition characterized by oversensitivity, fear of abandonment, and chronic instability in mood and interpersonal relationships. BPD is classified in section III in the American Psychiatric Association's *Diagnostic and Statistical Manual of Mental Disorders: DSM-5* (2013), which implies that the disorder is the result of permanent traits (such as personality) and requires sustained treatment. The personality disorder did not appear until the manual's third edition in 1980. The term "borderline" was used to refer to people who, it was believed, displayed behaviors that fell on the borderline between neurosis and psychosis. Over the years, the term has come to refer to a collection of symptoms that constitute an unstable personality structure.

According to the DSM-5, BPD is characterized by a longstanding pattern of instability in mood and relationships. To be classified as having a borderline personality disorder, a patient must exhibit the following diagnostic criteria: impaired self-function (e.g., problem with self-image, chronic feelings of emptiness or worthlessness) or self-direction (e.g., unstable goals, aspirations, values, etc.), and diminished capacity for empathy or for intimacy (characterized by frequent, intense, unstable relationships with others; vacillating between devaluing and overidealizing significant people in his or her life; and efforts to avoid abandonment). People with BPD typically experience or exhibit frequent, extreme mood changes and disproportionate emotions; fears of rejection, separation, and paradoxically, excessive dependency; depressive feelings; suicidal thoughts and behavior; impulsivity and unnecessary risk taking; and hostility or irritability. BPD's characteristic intense fear of abandonment is commonly reflected in impulsive, damaging behavior, such as drug or alcohol abuse, promiscuity, binge eating, or overspending. Many people with BPD also engage in self-mutilating behaviors, such as self-inflicted cigarette burns or self-inflicted cutting or stabbing; although self-mutilation was formerly seen as inherent almost exclusively to those with BPD, the DSM-5 recognizes it as its own psychiatric problem independent of, albeit often coincidental with, BPD. People with BPD will often report that they self-mutilate because of these chronic feelings of emptiness in an effort to feel something. People with BPD frequently engage in conflict with others. Symptoms begin by early adulthood and tend to be persistent. According to a 2007 study, approximately 1.4 percent of the population is said to have BPD, although many researchers consider this estimation low because the disorder often goes undiagnosed or is misdiagnosed. In 2005 and 2006, Marsha M. Linehan et al. and M. C. Zanarini et al. published studies suggesting that 4 to 9 percent of those with BPD commit suicide, although as many as 80 percent of people with BPD exhibit suicidal behaviors.

CAUSES

A great deal of research has focused on the possible causes of BPD. Although legitimate causes are still the source of research, there are certain predetermined factors that make someone more susceptible to BPD. Often, mood disorders such as anxiety or depression coincide with BPD. The 2008 National Institute of Mental Health–funded National Comorbidity Survey Republican found that as many as 85 percent of those with BPD also meet the criteria for another mental illness, including disorders of anxiety, impulse control, substance abuse, or mood. Other personality disorders, such as antisocial personality disorder (APSD), histrionic personality disorder (HPD), and narcissistic personality disorder (NPD), are also associated with the disorder. People with BPD, in their stressful states, also can be classified as having paranoid schizophrenia. A 2011 literature review by Randy and Lori Sansone indicates that while women have historically been diagnosed with BPD more often than men have, this has often been the result of confusion with other, coexisting psychiatric conditions in men. The Sansones argue that the prevalence of BPD is in fact equal in both sexes. Research has not determined that race or education are predispositions for BPD. The diathesis-stress model examines how the effects of stress, combined with a diathesis, or genetic vulnerability to develop a psychological disorder, may instigate the development of BPD. The underlying personality traits of BPD, such as impulsivity and emotional instability, are inheritable. According to the diathesis-stress model, a person with these personality traits, combined with ineffective means of managing stress, may be at greater risk of developing BPD. Certain hereditary genes, such as those that lead to mood instability, could imply that the disorder is genetic. An irregular level of the neurotransmitter serotonin, which is linked to depression, has also been found in those with BPD. Other researchers have explored the role of the limbic system in people with BPD. The limbic system is the part of the brain associated with the regulation of emotional responses. Research indicates that people with BPD report a higher incidence of sexual abuse, separation from or early loss of a parental figure, verbal and emotional abuse, and family chaos during childhood.

TREATMENT

Treatment for BPD is a challenging issue. The "cure" requires extended treatment and involves a significant change in behavior for the patient. People who have personality disorders such as BPD lack the insight that the dysfunction of their personality is the source of impairment. Many with BPD, therefore, may never seek treatment. When a person with BPD does seek treatment, it is usually for a reason other than their BPD. There is a high risk that the BPD patient will end treatment prematurely because of their difficulties with relationships and emotional functioning. When a person with BPD does engage in psychotherapy, the individual can be a challenge to a therapist—those with BPD can exhibit elements of the disorder in treatment, such as fear of abandonment or neediness.

American psychologist Marsha M. Linehan developed a treatment program called "dialectical behavioral therapy," or DBT, to treat BPD patients. Dialectical behavioral therapy involves a combination of cognitive, behavioral, and Zen principles to develop a balance between acceptance and change. Dialectical behavioral therapy focuses on helping patients develop tools to solve problems, regulate their emotions, reframe suicidal or destructive behaviors, and become more mindful of themselves and others. Linehan's therapy emphasizes the importance of the patient-therapist relationship in establishing progress. Linehan's treatment model has gained widespread attention and has been implemented in treatment programs worldwide. Dialectical behavioral therapy can be used in both individual therapy and group therapy. Individual therapy using the dialectical behavioral therapy model focuses on six core areas: suicidal behaviors, behaviors that are counterproductive to the therapy process, behaviors that compromise the quality of life, the development of behavioral skills, post-traumatic stress behavior, and self-respecting behaviors. Individual therapy with the BPD patient can be very stressful. The therapist needs to set clear limits with the BPD patient and to be consistent in abiding by those limits, as these patients are characteristically manipulative and emotionally demanding.

Cognitive-behavioral therapies for BPD are grounded in the belief that these patients have distorted and self-defeating thinking patterns, or schemas, which include themes about abandonment, mistrust, low self-worth, and guilt. University of Pennsylvania psychiatrist Aaron T. Beck states that dichotomous thinking (black-and-white thinking) is an essential problem among borderline patients and results in the extreme emotional responses that they display.

Other types of psychotherapy used for BPD treatment include mentalization-based therapy, which helps patients sort out thoughts as their own or others' and improve impulse control; schema therapy, which focuses on recognizing and modifying patterns of thought and behavior; and transference-focused psychotherapy, a psychodynamic approach in which the evolving client-therapist relationship serves as a model for the patient's other relationships.

Psychopharmacological therapy involves a combination of therapy and medication in treating BPD. Certain antidepressant medications (selective serotonin reuptake inhibitors, or SSRIs) have been effective in alleviating some of the symptoms of depression in BPD. Antianxiety and antipsychotic drugs have also been used in treatment.

BIBLIOGRAPHY

A.D.A.M. Medical Encyclopedia. "Borderline Personality Disorder." *MedlinePlus.* US National Library of Medicine, 10 Nov. 2012. Web. 12 Feb. 2014.

American Psychiatric Association. *Diagnostic and Statistical Manual of Mental Disorders.* 5th ed. Washington, DC: American Psychiatric, 2013. Print.

Insel, Thomas. "What's in a Name? The Outlook for Borderline Personality Disorder." *National Institute of Mental Health.* National Institutes of Health, US Dept. of Health and Human Services, 19 Apr. 2010. Web. 24 Feb. 2014.

Kreisman, Jerold J., and Hal Straus. *I Hate You, Don't Leave Me: Understanding the Borderline Personality.* Rev. ed. New York: Penguin, 2010. Print.

Kreisman, Jerold J., and Hal Straus. *Sometimes I Act Crazy.* Hoboken: Wiley, 2006. Print.

Linehan, Marsha M. *Cognitive-Behavioral Treatment of Borderline Personality Disorder.* New York: Guilford, 1993. Print.

Livesley, W. John, Marsha L. Schroeder, Douglas N. Jackson, and Kerry L. Jang. "Categorical Distinctions in the Study of Personality Disorder—Implications for Classification." *Journal of Abnormal Psychology* 103.1 (1994): 6–17. Print.

Moskovitz, Richard. *Lost in the Mirror: An Inside Look at Borderline Personality Disorder.* 2nd ed. Dallas: Taylor Trade, 2001. Print.

Sarkis, Stephanie. "Borderline Personality Disorder: Big Changes in the DSM-5." *Psychology Today.* Sussex, 13 Dec. 2011. Web. 24 Feb. 2014.

Trull, Timothy J., J. David Useda, Kelly Conforti, and Bao-Tran Doan. "Borderline Personality Disorder Features in Nonclinical Young Adults: 2. Two Year Outcome." *Journal of Abnormal Psychology* 106.2 (1997): 307–14. Print.

Janine T. Ogden; updated by Jean Prokott

SEE ALSO: Anger; Antianxiety medications; Antidepressant medications; Beck, Aaron T.; Behavior therapy; Dialectical behavior therapy; Emotional expression; Emotions; Genetics and mental health; Histronic personality disorder; Mood disorders; Mood stabilizer medications; Narcissistic personality disorder; Personality disorders; Schizoid personality disorder; Stress: Theories; Suicide.

Brain damage

Type of psychology: Biological bases of behavior; Cognition; Consciousness; Emotion; Language; Memory; Personality; Psychopathology

Brain damage can be localized, when nerve-cell destruction is centered in a part of the brain, causing specific behavioral defects, or it may be diffuse, when the injury causes deterioration throughout the brain, leading to severe physical or mental impairments.

Key Concepts:
- Aphasia
- Cerebral cortex
- Equipotentiality
- Imaging techniques
- Localizationism
- Plasticity

INTRODUCTION

The brain, often called the final scientific frontier, has challenged investigators with its labyrinthine complexities, and much that is known about its structure and functioning has been acquired through the study of the damaged brains of animals and humans. The brain structure most commonly affected by brain lesions is the cerebral cortex. A brain lesion is nervous-tissue damage that impairs the normal functioning of neurons (nerve cells). The cerebral cortex is the outer layer of the cerebrum, the rounded and fissured structure with two symmetric hemispheres occupying most of the cranial cavity. Damage to the cerebral cortex has been related to dysfunctions of perception, memory, language, and thought. Located in the depths of the cerebrum is the limbic system, a connected set of structures that includes the hippocampus, hypothalamus, and amygdala. Damage to the amygdala has been related to emotional dysfunctions. The story of how scientists used brain damage to discover the connections between brain parts and bodily behavior has been called the most astonishing in the history of medicine.

HISTORY OF RESEARCH ON BRAIN DAMAGE

Two centuries of research on brain-damaged animals and humans helped establish how brain components divide the work of sensing, learning, remembering, and thinking. This research also led to a number of theories, from an extreme reductionist view in which every human behavior is rooted in a highly localized brain component (localizationism) to an extreme holistic view in which every human function is rooted in all parts of the brain (equipotentiality). A researcher whose work supported both views was the French physiologist Pierre Flourens, who decided to test localization by the surgical removal, or ablation, of parts of the brains of animals. He found that ablations of small sections did not cause any change in behavior, which controverted strict localizationism. Very large ablations did result in the impairment of functions. Thus Flourens's experiments in the 1820's could be used to support both localization (since the removal of a certain large section of the brain caused the animals to become blind) and unity (since the animal returned to normal behavior after partial ablations).

Another French researcher who was interested in localization was Paul Broca. For thirty years he studied a patient who, despite a healthy vocal apparatus, could not talk. Finally, in 1861, after the patient's death, Broca was able to examine the man's brain, and he discovered a lesion in a frontal convolution on the left side (a region now known as Broca's area). This phenomenon—loss of speech due to a brain lesion—came to be called aphasia. Broca's pinpointing of a certain brain function stimulated so many other researchers that aphasia became the disease par excellence for studying cerebral localization.

Further evidence supporting localization was found by two German investigators, Gustav Fritsch and Eduard Hitzig, who used the electrical stimulation of the cerebral cortex to discover the principle of contralateral representation, according to which the left hemisphere controls the right side of the body and vice versa. Their work had important neurophysiological implications. If specific cerebral areas controlled certain functions, then brain lesions could be localized by means of clinical observations.

The detailed brain mapping envisioned by localizationists encountered difficulties when scientists discovered that certain brain functions were not susceptible to localization. For example, in the twentieth century the American psychologist Karl Lashley conducted experiments on rats to study how brain lesions affected a rat's ability to solve mazes. Although he found that lesions retarded learning, he also discovered no relation between this dysfunction and the locus of the lesion. All parts of the relevant region of the rat's brain seemed to be equivalent (or equipotential) in storing information.

Because of ethical concerns, the ablation of the cerebral cortex in humans was not as common as the use of this procedure in animals, but in the late 1920's and through the 1930's, the Portuguese neurosurgeon António Egas Moniz developed prefrontal lobotomy, or leukotomy, in which he severed nerve tracts from the limbic system to a frontal lobe to mitigate the anxiety accompanying such conditions as schizophrenia. Though the anxiety of many patients lessened, serious side effects such as apathy, headaches, and memory difficulties also occurred.

In 1940, a neurosurgeon working in Rochester, New York, treated several patients suffering from epilepsy by severing the nerve fibers connecting the right and left hemispheres of their brains. These operations lessened the severity of their seizures, but the patients also experienced serious side effects. Other split-brain studies in the second half of the twentieth century showed that certain surgically brain-damaged patients, despite profound impairment of their conscious knowledge, preserved access to their nonconscious knowledge. A good example is the phenomenon of "blindsight," where patients deny that they see an object but can in some way sense its location and other attributes.

Research on brain-damaged animals and humans has advanced scientific understanding of the cerebral cortex. Most scientists accept that such functions as vision are related to such brain structures as the visual cortex. However, the goal of the localizationists, a highly detailed functional map of the brain, has not been fully achieved, nor will it, holists point out, because the functional units that have been discovered are also interconnected with the brain's information-processing system. Many scientists have abandoned extreme reductionist and holistic positions, believing instead that the truth lies between the extremes.

CAUSES

Brain damage can be caused directly or indirectly, suddenly or gradually. Direct causes include concussions, gunshot wounds, and surgical ablations. Cerebral tissue may be destroyed indirectly and gradually through tumors, viruses, syphilis, or epilepsy. One of the most common causes of brain injury is cerebral vascular accident, formerly called apoplexy and now commonly called stroke. More than two million Americans suffer strokes annually. A clot can cause a stroke by blocking blood flow to a part of the brain (an occlusive stroke) or by the rupture of a weakened blood vessel (a hemorrhagic stroke). The location of the damaged tissue is pivotal, because a large lesion in some areas of the cerebral cortex may have negligible consequences, whereas a little lesion in the limbic system may have such devastating consequences as uncontrollable, violent behavior. After stroke, the most common cause of brain damage is cancer. Among the elderly, several brain-damaging illnesses are widespread, most notably Alzheimer's disease.

Among the young, the most common causes of brain injury are accidents and assaults. During wartime, bullets and shrapnel become major causes of brain injuries. During peacetime, traumatic brain injury from motor-vehicle accidents is the leading cause of death and disability in the first four decades of life. For the United States in the early twenty-first century, statisticians conservatively estimate half a million new cases of brain injury annually. By a three-to-one ratio, men are at greater risk of brain injury than women, and the costs of all brain injuries are estimated at about 40 billion dollars per year.

EFFECTS

Because of the complex interconnectivity of various brain structures, the effects of brain damage on behavior have been difficult to quantify. Even in cases in which the lesion is circumscribed and the deficit in function is well defined, a precise link between a lesion and behavioral problem cannot be securely deduced, since lesions in one area may cause interference in other areas. Nevertheless, patients with brain lesions exhibit behavioral problems that can be attributed to damaged areas of the brain. For example, lesions in the left hemisphere often lead to problems in understanding and remembering verbal information, whereas lesions in the right hemisphere often lead to impairment of visual and other nonverbal abilities. A stroke in the right hemisphere often leaves patients with their left side paralyzed, and sometimes patients deny their paralysis, a phenomenon known as anosognosia.

Brain damage can have significant effects on consciousness. For example, damage to the brain stem frequently results in loss of consciousness. However, localizationists who once identified the frontal lobes of the cerebral cortex with intelligence had to retreat from this position when patients missing much of their frontal cortex tested normal for intelligence. These observations convinced holists of the plasticity of the cerebral cortex, which means that the cerebral cortex is not simply a permanent arrangement of neuronal circuits but a dynamic system that is constantly being changed and reorganized by experiences and feedback. On the other hand, reductionists point to "diseases of consciousness" in which specific lesions cause specific disorders. For example, patients with midbrain lesions can manifest retrograde amnesia (the inability to recall information acquired just before the brain damage) but not anterograde amnesia (the inability to form new permanent memories after the brain damage).

DIAGNOSING BRAIN DAMAGE

Because of the structural complexities of the brain, determining the nature and amount of functional impairment after brain damage is difficult. A neurologist may diagnose the nature and extent of brain damage by an astute interpretation of the symptoms (the subjective manifestations of disease)—for example, a patient's complaint about her difficulties in speaking—and signs (objective manifestations of disease)—for example, the physician's observation that a patient can no longer move her right arm. In the early days of medicine, diagnosis of brain damage was mainly through simple observations of patients in natural situations, but the need to make diagnoses more scientific led psychiatrists, as early as the late 1800's, to construct batteries of tests to discover the details of various impairments. For example, some patients, called conduction aphasics, were unable to repeat correctly a word or phrase that they had just heard. Development of objective tests was problematic, however, because of interconnectivities among symptoms. For example, patients who had a dysfunction in speech might or might not have a parallel dysfunction in hearing.

In the late nineteenth and early twentieth centuries, instruments were invented that aided physicians in diagnosing brain damage. In the late 1890's, X rays, discovered by Wilhelm Röntgen, were used to locate tumors and other brain lesions, and this technique was refined in 1918 when Walter Dandy invented pneumoencephalography. This technique involved replacing the fluid within certain brain cavities by such gases as oxygen or helium and then taking X-ray pictures of the brain. These pictures, called encephalograms, helped physicians to diagnose such localized lesions as tumors.

The diagnosis of brain-damaged patients was sharpened during the twentieth century's two world wars. Because of numerous head injuries, much material became available to scientists who were interested in the relationship between brain lesions and psychological disorders. Test batteries became highly sophisticated, and testers examined brain-damaged soldiers for such abilities as naming, repeating, and visual-image recognition. In this way, diagnosticians were able to understand more fully than before the many variations in aphasic disorders.

The person who devoted himself more than many others to the study of brain-damaged soldiers was Aleksandr Luria, a Russian neuropsychologist. He reported on a series of eight hundred cases of brain wounds sustained by soldiers during World War II. His evidence showed that such behavioral functions as perception, speech, or calculation are never lost in a patient with a circumscribed lesion. Furthermore, complex behavioral functions may be lost due to lesions in widely different areas of the brain. Luria's clinical data revealed to him how difficult precise diagnosis was because many specific brain structures are involved in even the simplest forms of mental activity.

After the war, diagnosis improved because of better test batteries and more sophisticated instruments. During the 1950's and 1960's, various psychological tests were developed that located brain lesions with a high degree of accuracy. Significant, too, was the development of advanced imaging techniques. Even before World War II, Hans Berger used the brain's electrical activity to invent the electroencephalograph, an apparatus that records electric potentials of the brain. The record of the variations in electric potential, the electroencephalogram (EEG), helped physicians diagnose disturbances within the brain. Neurological disorders such as epilepsy, brain tumors, and acute brain trauma produced distinctive features in EEGs. During the final decades of the twentieth century, several new imaging techniques became important tools in the neurological diagnosis of brain damage. Such techniques as magnetic resonance imaging (MRI), magnetic resonance angiography (MRA), computed tomography (CT) scanning, and positron emission tomography (PET) have allowed diagnosticians to picture in detail noninvasively various brain structures, thereby facilitating the correlation between cerebral lesions and patient symptoms. Computers have also been used to create models of the cerebral cortex, and although these models vastly oversimplify complex realities, they nevertheless help scientists to understand how, for example, the brain reorganizes itself after a stroke.

HISTORY OF TREATMENT

The history of the care of brain-damaged people is intimately connected with the history of theories about brain function. What physicians do about brain damage depends on what they think it is. Throughout the early history of medicine, physicians relied on the healing power of nature, and cases certainly existed of brain-damaged patients who experienced spontaneous recovery. With the development of modern knowledge about the cerebral cortex, physicians were able, with reasonable confidence, to ascribe various disabilities in brain-damaged patients to lesions in particular cortical areas. This theory created a problem in treating these patients. Because scientists believed that neurons could not be regenerated, how could a patient restore a function if the brain location responsible for that function was destroyed? When Broca, a champion of localization, proclaimed in 1865 that "one speaks with the left hemisphere," physicians countered with examples of children with atrophied left hemispheres who grew up to be normal, not aphasic. It gradually became clear that when one part of the brain is damaged, resulting in the loss of a specific function, another brain area may take over and make possible a partial or complete recovery of that function. In short, the capacity for various functions is initially widely distributed throughout the brain. This explains why young people often recover from strokes completely, whereas older people who sustain the same brain injury may never speak normally again.

Just as the carnage of two world wars provided ways of improving diagnoses of brain-damaged patients, so these same wars provided new ways of rehabilitation. For example, some physicians who believed that recovery of function was the outcome of compensatory changes in the structure of the brain emphasized that rehabilitation of brain-damaged soldiers should not be focused on remedying specific impairments but rather on creating an environment in which soldiers could use their intact capacities to successfully complete tasks.

During the decades following World War II, observations were made and experiments performed that suggested a critical period existed for recovery from brain damage, and it was therefore important to use certain drugs and rehabilitation techniques as early as possible during the recovery period. As more was learned about brain damage, an entire continuum of specialized brain-injury rehabilitation programs developed. They helped dramatically increase the quantity and quality of restored functions after brain damage.

TREATMENT OPTIONS

Since clinicians' approaches to treatment are inextricably tied to their philosophy of rehabilitation, different treatment options for brain-damaged patients exist. However, the goal of all these treatments is the same: to restore patients to the normal life they had before the injury. Some scholars distinguish between two types of treatment, restoration and compensation. Those who practice restoration, after brain damage believe that damaged brain functions can be regenerated, even enhanced, by techniques that help the brain to become "reorganized." Those who favor compensation, after brain damage hold that the task of the rehabilitator is to encourage a different part of the brain to take over from the damaged part. Other scholars see an even larger number of models of recovery, from traditional and paternalistic through educational and empowering to biomedical models based on a reductionist view of the brain. In general, these different models conceptualize disease and disability within the context of the provider-patient relationship.

Brain damage often results in the impairment of physical, cognitive, behavioral, emotional, sexual, occupational, and social skills, and rehabilitating these skills is a complex task. Few therapists have training or experience in all these areas. Therefore, rehabilitation involves the efforts of many specialists.

Treatment begins as soon as the brain-damaged patient comes into the care of professionals, for example, at the scene of an accident. Basic life support is an important part of this prehospital phase of treatment. By using hemorrhage control and other techniques, paramedics can make sure that a patient with a brain injury enters a trauma center with the best possible chances for recovery. These trauma centers are usually part of a network of facilities equipped with modern medical technologies and staffed by teams of specialists. Rehabilitation can begin as early as the patient's stay in the intensive-care unit. During this early phase of recovery, treatments include behavioral therapy as well as the use of such chemicals as nerve growth factors.

Treatment of the brain-injured patient is often long, and because the patient's problems change over time, so must the rehabilitation process. The places of treatment may be outpatient clinics, office buildings, group homes, or the patient's family setting. The family is particularly important, because studies have shown that the success of rehabilitation depends not only on professional treatment but also on the quality and amount of family support.

CONCLUSION

Because all that people experience, feel, and know depends on a healthy brain, damage to this crucial organ can have devastating consequences. The study and treatment of brain damage have deepened scientific knowledge of the mind-brain interaction. This knowledge has come from scientists who were materialists, holists, and interactionists (those who believe a dynamic relationship exists between cerebral structures and functions). As the sciences concerned with the brain have matured, traditional demarcations between specialties have blurred and a healthy cross-fertilization among disciplines has led to new insights that in turn have resulted in more effective treatment of brain-damaged individuals. Much still remains to be discovered about the brain, how it is structured, and how the brain-damaged can best be helped. The goal of a perfect understanding of the complexities of the human brain may be unattainable, as some critics contend, but everyone can certainly agree that a deep, detailed, and coherent knowledge of brain structures and functions will benefit all individuals, whether their brains are damaged or healthy.

BIBLIOGRAPHY

Cassidy, John W. *Mindstorms: The Complete Guide for Families Living with Traumatic Brain Injury.* Cambridge, Mass.: Da Capo Press, 2009. A look at dealing with brain injury from the families of those affected.

Churchland, Paul. *Neurophilosophy at Work.* New York: Cambridge University Press, 2007. Explores the unfolding impact of the several empirical sciences of the mind, especially cognitive neurobiology and computational neuroscience, on a variety of traditional issues central to the discipline of the philosophy.

Damasio, Antonio R. *Descartes' Error: Emotion, Reason, and the Human Brain.* 1994. New York: Penguin Books, 2005. Drawing on his experiences with brain-damaged patients, Damasio shows how the absence of emotion in some of these patients can destroy rationality. His thesis is that emotions provide a bridge between the body and its "survival-oriented regulations," on one hand, and consciousness, on the other.

Jallo, Jack, and Christopher M. Loftus, eds. *Neurotrauma and Critical Care of the Brain.* New York: Thieme, 2009. A collection of essays on brain damage and its treatment. Topics covered include brain trauma imaging, wartime penetrating injuries, rehabilitation, ethics, and legal issues.

Levin, Harvey S., and Jordan Grafman, eds. *Cerebral Reorganization of Function After Brain Damage.* New York: Oxford University Press, 2000. This book uses the insights of neuroscientists to illuminate ways of rehabilitating brain-injured patients. The expert contributors to this volume lead the reader through the background, significance, practical applications, and potential future of "neuroplasticity" as a tool in the treatment of neurological impairments.

Mackay, Linda E., Phyllis E. Chapman, and Anthony S. Morgan. *Maximizing Brain Injury Recovery: Integrating Critical Care and Early Rehabilitation.* Austin, Tex.: Pro-Ed, 2004. This textbook, written with the endorsement of the Brain Injury Association, is intended to supply helpful information for people coming to terms with brain injury. The authors' chief theme is the necessity of an interdisciplinary approach in treating brain-injured patients and in returning them to some degree of normalcy.

Robert J. Paradowski

SEE ALSO: Abnormality: Biomedical models; Alzheimer's disease; Animal experimentation; Aphasias; Dementia; Developmental disabilities; Forgetting and forgetfulness; Incompetency; Lobotomy; Memory: Animal research; Mental retardation; Motor development; Nervous system; Neuropsychology; Prenatal physical development; Shock therapy; Speech disorders; Split-brain studies; Synaptic transmission.

Brain lateralization

TYPE OF PSYCHOLOGY: Biological bases of human behavior; Cognition; Neuropsychology; Psychopathology

Brain lateralization refers to the anatomical asymmetry and the functional division of labor between the left and right cerebral hemispheres. Diverse research methods, including studies of split-brain subjects who have had connecting tissues between the hemispheres severed, have revealed that the hemispheres function differently. Most prominent among these differences are that the left hemisphere is usually dominant in language production and comprehension, whereas the right hemisphere is typically dominant in visuospatial processing. Degree of lateralization varies among individuals, however, and both hemispheres contribute to most thinking functions.

KEY CONCEPTS

- Broca's area
- Cerebral hemispheres

- Corpus callosum
- Cortical lobes
- Split-brain people

INTRODUCTION

In 1861, Paul Broca performed an autopsy on a man who had spent the last thirty years of his life in an asylum because he would not speak. Broca discovered a lesion in the posterior frontal lobe of the left, but not the right, hemisphere and concluded that this location was the speech area of the brain. Subsequent research confirmed his conclusion and the area was named after Broca. Broca's discovery was the first tangible evidence that a function of the brain was localized to one cerebral hemisphere. It would be nearly a century, however, before the extent of cerebral lateralization would be more fully explored with individuals known as split-brain people.

Ronald Myers and Roger Sperry had demonstrated in the 1950s that severing the corpus callosum, the large band of fibers that connects the cerebral hemispheres, and smaller hemispheric connecting bands known as commissures caused behavior changes in animals. However, similar operations performed on humans in the 1940s by William Van Wagenen in order to reduce epileptic seizures appeared to result in no discernible psychological changes in these split-brain patients. This seeming contradiction between the animal and human findings was resolved in the 1960s by Sperry and Michael Gazzaniga's research with split-brain people. Knowing that stimuli presented to the right visual field of each eye go to only the left hemisphere and that stimuli presented to the left visual field only go to the right hemisphere, they presented visual stimuli briefly to one visual field or the other. Because the corpus callosum and commissures were disconnected, the brief visual presentations were available to only one hemisphere. Just as the findings in animal research, they demonstrated that there were striking differences in the functions of the two hemispheres.

Other research methods have expanded upon Sperry and Gazzaniga's findings. The Wada test, in which one hemisphere is briefly anesthetized by an injection of amobarbital into the carotid artery that supplies the hemisphere, has been used to identify the functions of one hemisphere when the other is dormant. A less invasive approach is the dichotic listening task in which competing auditory information is presented to both hemispheres simultaneously. Because information presented to one ear reaches more to the contralateral hemisphere, dichotic listening tasks can reveal which hemisphere is more active in auditory processing. Additionally, a variety of brain imaging techniques can elucidate anatomical and functional differences between the two hemispheres.

ANATOMICAL LATERALIZATION

The right hemisphere typically protrudes more toward the front of the skull and is larger in the frontal lobe than the left hemisphere. Conversely, the left hemisphere typically bulges more toward the back and is larger in the temporal (particularly in areas associated with language) and parietal lobes than the right hemisphere. The Sylvian fissure, a deep groove between the temporal and frontal lobes, is normally more horizontal in orientation in the left hemisphere but has a prominent upward curl in the right hemisphere.

The muscles and senses of the body are controlled by the contralateral hemisphere. However, there are some differences in the degree of control. The left hemisphere is engaged more closely in the copying of motor movements than the right hemisphere. Conversely, damage to the right hemisphere parietal lobe is more likely than damage to the left hemisphere parietal lobe to lead to sensory neglect of the opposite side of the body. The senses of smell and taste are ipsilateral; sense organs on the right side of the body provide input to the right hemisphere and vice versa.

Lateralization is affected by handedness, sex, and experience. About 96% of those primarily right-handed are left hemisphere dominant for language; of those primarily left-handed, approximately 70% show the same pattern, 15% show the opposite pattern, and little to no lateralization is found in 15%. Males tend to have a greater right hemispheric cell development than females, particularly the right side of the corpus callosum, whereas females often have more extensive cell development in left hemisphere language areas. Overall, males and those more dominantly right-handed appear to have a higher degree of lateralization than females and those primarily left-handed or ambidextrous. Regarding experience, research has demonstrated that practicing music increases the size of the left, but not the right, planum temporale, a temporal lobe area crucial for language comprehension.

FUNCTIONAL LATERALIZATION

Language. The most prominent hemispheric difference for the majority of people is that most aspects of language expression and comprehension are primarily the domain of the left hemisphere. For example, Broca's area, which controls speaking, is usually located in only the left hemisphere. Likewise, grammatical ability is based heavily on the functioning of the left hemisphere. When people listen to different conversations in their right and left ears in dichotic listening tasks, they tend to favor listening with the right ear (especially for consonant sounds). The right ear providing more input to the left hemisphere demonstrates a larger role of the left hemisphere in language comprehension. Damage to the left hemisphere is much more likely than the right to disrupt linguistic abilities, including reading and writing.

Nevertheless, the right hemisphere contributes to language comprehension and expression in a number of ways. It is necessary for the comprehension of the emotional aspects of language, prosody (tone of speech), figures of speech, and the interpretation of non-language sounds. The non-verbal aspects of language, such as understanding gestures and facial expressions, usually involve the right hemisphere more than the left hemisphere. If a person has damage to the temporal lobe of the right hemisphere, he or she typically has problems understanding sarcasm and humor, detecting lies in others, and speaking in an inflected voice. Additionally, vocabulary is represented in both hemispheres, though more so in the left hemisphere.

Music. When people listen to music, they tend to favor the left ear. The left ear inputting more to the right hemisphere demonstrates a dominant role of the right hemisphere for music perception. Many aspects of music perception, such as melody, pitch, and intensity, depend more upon the right hemisphere. However, lyric recitation, keeping a rhythm, and musical ability in singing or playing an instrument are more dependent upon the left hemisphere.

Visuospatial Processing. The ability to draw, understand spatial layout, comprehend maps, give and follow directions, and think in abstract spatial ways depends on the right hemisphere. Research has also shown that the right hemisphere is better, overall, at facial recognition and enables one to follow the gazes of others. However, while the right hemisphere is more active in the perception of others' faces, the left hemisphere plays the dominant role in the recognition of one's own face. Studies with composite faces (half the face is yours; the other half is someone else's) shown briefly to each hemisphere has demonstrated that the right hemisphere interprets the composite face as someone else while the left hemisphere interprets the composite as the self. Other research suggests that the right hemisphere emphasizes processing same sex faces, whereas the left hemisphere focuses more on opposite sex faces. Additionally, the left hemisphere is more involved in voluntary facial expressions (e.g., "Smile for the camera!"); the right hemisphere plays the primary role in spontaneous facial expressions.

Perceptual Style. Researchers have presented a visual stimulus consisting of a large letter (e.g., "P") composed of small letters (e.g., "q") briefly to each hemisphere's visual field and then tested to determine what each hemisphere would interpret. For most people, the left hemisphere reports the small letters and the right hemisphere reports the big letter. From such research, it has been deduced that the left hemisphere focuses on details whereas the right emphasizes the big picture. In other words, the right hemisphere has a more holistic and global processing framework; the left has a more reductionistic and sequential processing approach.

Split-brain people cannot divide their attention efficiently (i.e., one hemisphere attending to one event; the other hemisphere attending to a different event). In other words, despite the disconnection between their hemispheres, they maintain a unitary focus toward perceiving the world. However, the left hemisphere is more involved in conscious decisions while the right hemisphere plays a greater role in automatically attending to events. In general, the right hemisphere plays a bigger role in attentional focus than the left hemisphere.

Cognitive Style. The left hemisphere usually plays the dominant role in major problem solving, such as solving mathematical problems, testing hypotheses, and determining the specific course of action in implementing personal plans. It is adept at slower, more deliberate reasoning and determining explanations. Michael Gazzaniga has called the left hemisphere the "interpreter" due to its role in making inferences, deriving interpretations, understanding the self, finding order, and forming beliefs. It appears that the left hemisphere plays a bigger role in self-consciousness.

In contrast, the right hemisphere tends to favor a fast, simplest possible approach toward solving problems. It makes quick judgments about others and is of crucial importance in understanding the motives and beliefs of others.

Feelings and Emotions. In the 1990s, Richard Davidson suggested that the left hemisphere is specialized for approach behaviors whereas the right hemisphere is designed for withdrawal actions. Introverts, who tend to shy away from social stimulation, have some areas in their right frontal lobe larger than the left frontal lobe; conversely, extraverts, who gravitate toward social events, show the opposite pattern. Anesthetizing the left hemisphere leaves most people feeling sad and socially withdrawn; anesthetizing the right hemisphere results in most people feeling happy and socially engaged. Overall, however, the right hemisphere plays a greater role in processing emotion, especially humor. When people look at composite faces where half the face is smiling and the other half is not, they typically interpret a happier face when the left half is smiling – the half of the visual field that goes to the right hemisphere.

CONCLUSION

The cerebral hemispheres are specialized for different functions; however, for most tasks both hemispheres are active contributors. Thus, the idea that people are either right-brained or left-brained is an overstatement of the facts and a dubious assertion. The functions of the two hemispheres are more complementary than oppositional, and this fosters a more efficient use of the brain's resources.

BIBLIOGRAPHY

Erdmann, E., & Stover, D. (1991). *Beyond a World Divided: Human Values in The Brain-Mind Science of Roger Sperry.* Boston, MA: Shambhala. The split brain research of Nobel Prize winning laureate Roger Sperry is discussed in the context of the "divided world" of science and religion.

Gazzaniga, M.S. (2005). "Forty-Five Years of Split Brain Research and Still Going Strong". *Nature Reviews Neuroscience,* 6, 653-659, doi:10.1038/nrn1723. One of the pioneers of split brain research discusses the original research done with Roger Sperry and Joseph Bogen and relates it to subsequent and future research on hemispheric specialization.

Gazzaniga, M.S. (2011). *Who's In Charge? Free Will and The Science of The Brain.* New York, NY: (Ecco) Harper Row. Gazzaniga argues against a deterministic view that reduces free will to mere physical properties and eliminates moral necessities by drawing on research with split-brain patients.

Gazzaniga, M.S., Ivry, R.B., & Mangun, G.R. (2014). *Cognitive Neuroscience: The Biology of The Mind* (4th ed.). New York, NY: Norton. Chapter four presents an excellent overview of the research on brain lateralization.

Springer, S.P., & Deutsch, G. (2001). *Left Brain, Right Brain: Perspectives From Cognitive Neuroscience* (5th ed.). New York, NY: Freeman and Company/Worth. Award-winning book provides a comprehensive summary of the research on hemispheric specialization and its implications for understanding thinking and behavior.

Paul J. Chara, Jr.

See Also: Brain; Functional specialization; Left hemisphere; Motor processes; Neuroscience; Right hemisphere.

Brain structure

Type of psychology: Biological bases of behavior

Different areas of the brain have specialized functions that control activities ranging from basic biological processes to complex psychological operations. Understanding the distinctive features of different neurological areas provides insight into why people and other animals act, feel, and think as they do.

Key Concepts

- Cerebral cortex
- Cerebral hemispheres
- Forebrain
- Hindbrain
- lobes
- Midbrain
- Neural tube
- Neurons

INTRODUCTION

About two weeks after conception, a fluid-filled cavity called the neural tube begins to form on the back of the human embryo. This neural tube will sink under the surface of the skin, and the two major structures of the central nervous system (CNS) will begin to differentiate. The top part of the tube will enlarge and become the brain; the bottom part will become the spinal cord. The cavity will persist through development and become the fluid-filled central canal of the spinal cord and the four ventricles of the brain. The ventricles and the central canal contain cerebrospinal fluid, a clear plasmalike fluid that supports and cushions the brain and also provides nutritive and eliminative functions for the CNS. At birth, the average human brain weighs approximately twelve ounces (350 grams), a quarter of the size of the average adult brain, which is about three pounds (1,200 to 1,400 grams). Development of the brain in the first year is rapid, with the brain doubling in weight in the first six months.

The development of different brain areas depends on intrinsic and extrinsic factors. Internally, chemicals called neurotrophins promote the survival of neurons, the basic cells of the nervous system that are specialized to communicate electrochemically with one another, and help determine where and when those neurons will form connections and become diverse neurological structures. Externally, diverse experiences enhance the survival of neurons and play a major role in the degree of development of different neurological areas. Research has demonstrated that the greater the exposure a child receives to a particular experience, the greater the development of the neurological area involved in processing that type of stimulation. Although this phenomenon occurs throughout the life span, the greatest impact of environmental stimulation in restructuring and reorganizing the brain occurs in the earliest years of life.

Experience can alter the shape of the brain, but its basic architecture is determined before birth. The brain consists of three major subdivisions: the hindbrain (rhombencephalon, or "parallelogram-brain"), the midbrain (mesencephalon, or "midbrain"), and the forebrain (prosencephalon, or "forward brain"). The hindbrain is further subdivided into the myelencephalon ("marrow-brain") and the metencephalon ("after-brain"), while the forebrain is divided into the diencephalon ("between-brain") and the telencephalon ("end-brain"). To visualize roughly the locations of these brain areas in a person, one can hold an arm out, bend the elbow ninety degrees, and make a fist. If the forearm is the spinal cord, where the wrist enlarges into the base of the hand corresponds to the hindbrain, with the metencephalon farther up than the myelencephalon. The palm of the hand, enclosed by the fingers, would be the midbrain. The fingers would be analogous to the forebrain, with the topmost surface parts of the fingers being the telencephalon.

One can take the analogy a step further. If a fist is made with the fingers of the other hand and placed next to the fist previously made, each fist would represent the two cerebral hemispheres of the forebrain, with the skin of the fingers representing the forebrain's cerebral cortex, the six layers of cells that cover the two hemispheres. Finally, the meninges cover the cortex like close-fitting gloves. The three layers of the meninges play a protective and nutritive role for the brain.

The more advanced the species, the greater the development of the forebrain, particularly the cortex. The emphasis here is placed on a neuroanatomical examination of the human brain, beginning with a look at the hindbrain and progressing to an investigation of the cerebral cortex. The terms "anterior" (toward the front) and "posterior" (toward the back) will be used frequently in describing the location of different brain structures. Additionally, the words "superior" (above) and "inferior" (below) will be used to describe vertical locations.

THE HINDBRAIN

As the spinal cord enters the skull, it enlarges into the bottommost structure of the brain, the medulla oblongata, often simply called the medulla. The medulla controls many of the most basic physiological functions necessary for survival, particularly breathing and the beating of the heart, as well as reflexes such as vomiting, coughing, sneezing, and salivating. It is sensitive to opiate and amphetamine drugs, and overdoses of these drugs can impair its normal functioning. Severe impairment can lead to a fatal shutdown of the respiratory and cardiovascular systems.

Just above the medulla lie the pons, parts of the reticular formation, the raphe system, and the locus coeruleus. All these structures play a role in arousal and sleep. The pons plays a major role in initiating rapid eye movement (REM) sleep. REM sleep is characterized by repeated horizontal eye movements, increased brain activity, and frequent dreaming. The reticular system, sometimes called the reticular activating system (RAS), stretches from the pons through the midbrain to projections into the cerebral cortex. Activation of the reticular system, by sensory stimulation or thinking, causes increases in arousal and alertness in diverse areas of the brain. For the brain to pay attention to something, there must be activation from the reticular formation. The raphe system, like the reticular system, can increase the brain's readiness to respond to stimuli. However, unlike the reticular formation, the raphe system can decrease alertness to stimulation, decrease sensitivity to pain, and initiate sleep. Raphe system activity is modulated somewhat by an adjacent structure called the locus coeruleus. Abnormal functioning of this structure has been linked with depression and anxiety.

The largest structure in the metencephalon is the cerebellum, which branches off from the base of the brain and occupies a considerable space in the back of the head. The cerebellum's primary function is the learning and control of coordinated perceptual-motor activities. Learning to walk, run, jump, throw a ball, ride a bike, or perform any other complex motor activity causes chemical changes to occur in the cerebellum that result in the construction of a sort of program for controlling the muscles involved in the particular motor skills. Activation of specific programs enables the performance of particular motor activities. The cerebellum is also involved in other types of learning and performance. Learning language, reading, shifting attention from auditory to visual stimuli, and timing, such as in music or the tapping of fingers, are just a few tasks for which normal cerebellar functioning is essential. Children diagnosed with learning disabilities often are found to have abnormalities in the cerebellum.

THE MIDBRAIN

The superior and posterior part of the midbrain is called the tectum. There are two enlargements on both sides of the tectum known as the colliculi. The superior colliculus controls visual reflexes such as tracking the flight of a ball, while the inferior colliculus controls auditory reflexes such as turning toward the sound of a buzzing insect. Above and between the colliculi lies the pineal gland, which contains melatonin, a hormone that greatly influences the sleep-wake cycle. Melatonin levels are high when it is dark and low when it is light. High levels of melatonin induce sleepiness, which is one reason that people sleep better when it is darker. Another structure near the colliculi is the periaqueductal gray (PAG) area of the ventricular system. Stimulation of the PAG helps to block the sensation of pain.

Beneath the tectum is the tegmentum, which includes some structures involved in movement. Red nucleus activity is high during twisting movements, especially of the hands and fingers. The substantia nigra smooths out movements and is influential in maintaining good posture. The characteristic limb trembling and posture difficulties of Parkinson's disease are attributable to neuronal damage in the substantia nigra.

THE FOREBRAIN

Right above the midbrain, in the center of the brain, lies the thalamus, which is the center of sensory processing. All incoming sensory information except for the sense of smell goes to the thalamus first before it is sent on to the cerebral cortex and other areas of the brain. Anterior to and slightly below the thalamus is the hypothalamus.

Hypothalamic activity is involved in numerous motivated behaviors such as eating, drinking, sexual activity, temperature regulation, and aggression, largely through its regulation of the pituitary gland, which is attached beneath the hypothalamus. The pituitary gland controls the release of hormones that circulate in the endocrine system.

Subcortical Structures. Numerous structures lie beneath the cerebral cortex in pairs, one in each hemisphere. Many of these structures are highly interconnected with one another and are therefore seen to be part of a system. Furthermore, most of the subcortical structures can be categorized as belonging to one of two major systems. Surrounding the thalamus is one system called the basal ganglia, which is most prominently involved in movements and muscle tone. The basal ganglia deteriorate in Parkinson's and Huntington's diseases, both disorders of motor activity. The three major structures of the basal ganglia are the caudate nucleus and putamen, which form the striatum, and the globus pallidus. The activities of the basal ganglia extend beyond motor control. The striatum, for instance, plays a significant role in the learning of habits as well as in obsessive-compulsive disorder, a disorder of excessive habits. In addition, disorders of memory, attention, and emotional expression (especially depression) frequently involve abnormal functioning of the basal ganglia.

The nucleus basalis, while not considered part of the basal ganglia, nevertheless is highly interconnected with those structures (and the hypothalamus) and receives direct input from them. Nucleus basalis activity is essential for attention and arousal.

The other major subcortical system is the limbic system, which was originally thought to be involved in motivated or emotional behaviors and little else. Later research, however, demonstrated that many of these structures are crucial for memory formation. The fact that people have heightened recall for emotionally significant events is likely a consequence of the limbic system's strong involvement in both memory and motivation or emotion.

Two limbic structures are essential for memory formation. The hippocampus plays the key role in making personal events and facts into long-term memories. For a person to remember information of this nature for more than thirty minutes, the hippocampus must be active. In people with Alzheimer's disease, deterioration of the hippocampus is accompanied by memory loss. Brain damage involving the hippocampus is manifested by amnesias, indecisiveness, and confusion. The hippocampus takes several years to develop fully. This is thought to be a major reason that adults tend to remember very little from their first five years of life, a phenomenon called infantile amnesia.

The second limbic structure that is essential for learning and memory is the amygdala, which provides the hippocampus with information about the emotional context of events. It is also crucial for emotional perception, particularly in determining how threatening events are. When a person feels threatened, his or her amygdala will become very active. Early experiences in life can fine-tune how sensitive a person's amygdala will be to potentially threatening events. A child raised in an abusive environment will likely develop an amygdala that is oversensitive, predisposing that person to interpret too many circumstances as threatening. Two additional limbic structures work with the amygdala in the perception and expression of threatening events, the septal nuclei and the cingulate gyrus. High activity in the former structure inclines one to interpret events as nonthreatening, while activity in the latter structure is linked to positive or negative emotional expressions such as worried, happy, or angry looks.

Other major structures of the limbic system include the olfactory bulbs and nuclei, the nucleus accumbens, and the mammillary bodies. The olfactory bulbs and nuclei are the primary structures for smell perception. Experiencing pleasure involves the nucleus accumbens, which is also often stimulated by anything that can become addictive. The mammillary bodies are involved in learning and memory.

Cortical Lobes. The most complex thinking abilities are primarily attributable to the thin layers that cover the two cerebral hemispheres, known as the cortex. It is this covering of the brain that makes for the greatest differences between the intellectual capabilities of humans and those of other animals. Both hemispheres are typically divided into four main lobes, the distinct cortical areas of specialized functioning. There are, however, many differences between people, not only in the relative size of different lobes but also in how much cerebral cortex is not directly attributable to any of the four lobes.

The occipital lobe is located at the back of the cerebral cortex. The most posterior tissue of this lobe is called the striate cortex, due to its distinctive striped appearance. The striate cortex is also called the primary visual cortex because it is where most visual information is eventually processed. Each of the layers of this cortical area is specialized to analyze different features of visual input. The synthesis of visual information and the interpretation of that result involve other lobes of the brain. The occipital lobe also plays the primary role in various aspects of spatial reasoning. Activities such as spatial orientation, map reading, or knowing what an object will look like if rotated a certain amount of degrees all depend on this lobe.

Looking down on the top of the brain, a deep groove called the central sulcus can be seen roughly in the middle of the brain. Between the central sulcus and the occipital lobe is the parietal lobe. The parietal lobe's predominant function is the processing of the bodily sensations: taste, touch, temperature, pain, and kinesthesia (feedback from muscles and joints). A parietal band of tissue called the postcentral gyrus that is adjacent to the central sulcus (posterior and runs parallel to it) contains the somatosensory cortex in which the surface of the body is represented upside down in a maplike fashion. Each location along this cortical area corresponds to sensations from a different body part. Furthermore, the left side of the body is represented on the right hemisphere and vice versa. Damage to the right parietal cortex usually leads to sensory neglect of the left side of the body—the person ignores sensory input from that side. However, damage to the left parietal cortex causes no or little sensory neglect of the right side of the body.

The parietal lobe is involved with some aspects of distance sensation. The posterior parietal lobe plays a role in the visual location of objects and the bringing together of different types of sensory information, such as coordinating sight and sound when a person looks at someone who just called his or her name. Some aspects of the learning of language also engage the operation of the parietal cortex.

On the sides of each hemisphere, next to the temples of the head, reside the temporal lobes. The lobes closest to the ears are the primary sites of the interpretation of sounds. This task is accomplished in the primary auditory cortex, which is tucked into a groove in each temporal lobe called the lateral sulcus. Low-frequency sounds are analyzed on the outer part of this sulcus; higher-pitched sounds are represented deeper inside this groove. Closely linked with auditory perception are two other major functions of the temporal lobe: language and music comprehension. Posterior areas, particularly Wernicke's area, play key roles in word understanding and retrieval. More medial areas are involved in different aspects of music perception, especially the planum temporale.

The temporal cortex is the primary site of two important visual functions. Recognition of visual objects is dependent on inferior temporal areas. These areas of the brain are very active during visual hallucinations.

One area in this location, the fusiform gyrus, is very active during the perception of faces and complex visual stimuli. A superior temporal area near the conjunction of the parietal and occipital lobes is essential for reading and writing.

The temporal lobe is in close proximity to, and shares strong connections with, the limbic system. Thus, it is not surprising that the temporal lobe plays a significant role in memory and emotions. Damage to the temporal cortex leads to major deficits in the ability to learn and in maintaining a normal emotional balance.

The largest cerebral lobe, comprising one-third of the cerebral cortex, is the frontal lobe. It is involved in the greatest variety of neurological functions. The frontal lobe consists of several anatomically distinct and functionally distinguishable areas that can be grouped into three main regions. Starting at the central sulcus, which divides the parietal and frontal lobes, and moving toward the anterior limits of the brain, one finds, in order, the precentral cortex, the premotor cortex, and the prefrontal cortex. Each of these areas is responsible for different types of activities.

In 1870, German physicians Gustav Fritsch and Eduard Hitzig were the first to stimulate the brain electrically. They found that stimulating different regions of the precentral cortex resulted in different parts of the body moving. Subsequent research identified a "motor map" that represents the body in a fashion similar to the adjacent and posteriorly located somatosensory map of the parietal lobe. The precentral cortex, therefore, can be considered the primary area for the execution of movements.

The premotor cortex is more responsible for planning the operations of the precentral cortex. In other words, the premotor cortex generates the plan to pick up a pencil, while the precentral cortex directs the arm to do so. Thinking about picking up the pencil but not actually doing so involves more activity in the premotor cortex than in the precentral cortex. An inferior premotor area essential for speaking was discovered in 1861 by Paul Broca and has since been named for him. Broca's area, usually found only in the left hemisphere, is responsible for coordinating the various operations necessary for the production of speech.

The prefrontal cortex is the part of the brain most responsible for a variety of complex thinking activities, foremost among them being decision making and abstract reasoning. Damage to the prefrontal cortex often leads to an impaired ability to make decisions, rendering the person lethargic and greatly lacking in spontaneous behavior. Numerous aspects of abstract reasoning, such as planning, organizing, keeping time, and thinking hypothetically, are also greatly disturbed by injuries to the prefrontal cortex.

Research with patients who have prefrontal disturbances has demonstrated the important role of this neurological area in personality and social behavior. Patients with posterior prefrontal damage exhibit many symptoms of depression, such as apathy, restlessness, irritability, lack of drive, and lack of ambition. Anterior abnormalities, particularly in an inferior prefrontal region called the orbitofrontal area, result in numerous symptoms of psychopathy, including lack of restraint, impulsiveness, egocentricity, lack of responsibility for one's actions, and indifference to others' opinions and rights.

The prefrontal cortex also contributes to the emotional value of decisions, smell perception, working memory (the current ability to use memory), and the capacity to concentrate or shift attention. Children correctly diagnosed with attention-deficit hyperactivity disorder (ADHD) often have prefrontal abnormalities.

Hemispheric Differences. The two cerebral hemispheres are connected by a large band of fibers called the corpus callosum and several small connections called commissures. In the early 1940s, American surgeon William van Wagenen, to stop epileptic seizures from crossing from one hemisphere to the other, performed the first procedure of cutting the two hundred million fibers of the corpus callosum. The results were mixed, however, and it was not until the 1960s that two other American surgeons, Joe Bogen and Philip Vogel, decided to try the operation again, this time also including some cutting of commissure fibers. The results reduced or stopped the seizures in most patients. However, extensive testing by American psychobiologist Roger Sperry and his colleagues demonstrated unique behavioral changes in the patients, called split-brain syndrome. Research with split-brain syndrome and less invasive imaging techniques of the brain, such as computed tomography (CT) and positron-emission tomography (PET) scans, has demonstrated many anatomical and functional differences between the left and right hemispheres.

The degree of differences between the two cerebral hemispheres varies greatly depending on a number of factors. Men develop greater lateralization—larger differences between the hemispheres—and develop the differences sooner. Those with a dominant right hand have greater lateralization than left- or mixed-handers.

Therefore, when there is talk of "left brain" versus "right brain," it is important to keep in mind that a greater degree of difference exists in right-handed men. A minority of people, usually left-handers, show little differences between the left and right hemispheres.

The right hemisphere tends to be larger and heavier than the left hemisphere, with the greatest difference in the frontal lobe. Conversely, several other neurological areas have been found to be larger in the left hemisphere, including the occipital lobe, the planum temporale, Wernicke's area, and the Sylvian fissure. One gender difference in hemispheric operation is that the left-hemisphere amygdala is more active in women and the right-hemisphere amygdala is more active in men.

The left-brain/right-brain functional dichotomy has been the subject of much popular literature. Although there are many differences in operation between the two hemispheres, it is important to realize that many of the differences are subtle, and in many regards both hemispheres are involved in a given psychological function, only to different degrees. The most striking difference between the two hemispheres is that the right hemisphere is responsible for sensory and motor functions of the left side of the body and the left hemisphere controls those same functions for the body's right side. This contralateral control is found to a lesser degree for hearing and, due to the optic chiasm, not at all for vision.

In the domain of sound and communication, the left hemisphere plays a greater role in speech production, language comprehension, phonetic and semantic analysis, visual word recognition, grammar, verbal learning, lyric recitation, musical performance, and rhythm keeping. A greater right-hemisphere contribution is found in interpreting nonlanguage sounds, reading Braille, using emotional tone in language, understanding humor and sarcasm, expressing and interpreting nonverbal communication (facial and bodily expressions), and perceiving music. Categorical decisions, the understanding of metaphors, and the figurative aspects of language involve both hemispheres.

Regarding other domains, the right hemisphere plays a greater role in mathematical operations, but the left hemisphere is essential for remembering numerical facts and the reading and writing of numbers. Visually, the right hemisphere contributes more to mental rotation, facial perception, figure-ground distinctions, map reading, and pattern perception. Detail perception draws more on left-hemisphere resources. The right hemisphere is linked more with negative emotions, such as fear, anger, pain, and sadness, while positive affect is associated more with the left hemisphere. There are exceptions to this, however; schizophrenia, anxiety, and panic attacks have been found to be related more to increases in left-hemisphere activity.

SUMMARY

It has been estimated that the adult human brain contains one hundred billion neurons forming more than thirteen trillion connections with one another. These connections are constantly changing, depending on the health of the brain and how much learning is taking place. In this dynamic system of different neurological areas concerned with diverse functions, the question arises of how a sense of wholeness and stability emerges. In other words, where is the "me" in the mind? While some areas of the brain, such as the frontal lobe, appear more closely linked with such intimate aspects of identity as planning and making choices, it is likely that no single structure or particular function can be equated with the self. It may take the activity of the whole brain to give a sense of wholeness to life. Moreover, the self is not to be found anyplace in the brain itself. Instead, it is what the brain does—its patterns of activity—that defines the self.

BIBLIOGRAPHY

Evans, Amanda, and Patricia Coccoma. *Trauma-Informed Care: How Neuroscience Influences Practice*. New York: Routledge, 2014. Print.

Getz, Glen E. *Applied Biological Psychology.* New York: Springer, 2014. Print.

Goldberg, Stephen. *Clinical Neuroanatomy* Made Ridiculously Simple. 4th ed. Miami: MedMaster, 2010. Print.

Hendleman, Walter J. *Atlas of Functional Neuroanatomy.* 2nd ed. Boca Raton: CRC, 2006. Print.

Kalat, James W. *Biological Psychology.* 11th ed. Belmont: Wadsworth, 2013. Print.

Ornstein, Robert. *The Right Mind: Making Sense of the Hemispheres.* San Diego: Harcourt, 1997. Print.

Ornstein, Robert, and Richard F. Thompson. *The Amazing Brain.* Boston: Houghton, 1984. Print.

Swaab, D. F. *We Are Our Brains: A Neurobiography of the Brain, from the Womb to Alzheimer's.* Trans. Jane Hedley-Prôle. New York: Random, 2014. Print.

Paul J. Chara, Jr.

See Also: Adrenal gland; Animal experimentation; Brain damage; Consciousness; Consciousness: Altered states;

Endocrine system; Endorphins; Gonads; Hormones and behavior; Memory; Memory: Empirical studies; Memory: Physiology; Nervous system; Neurons; Neuropsychology; Neurotransmitters; Pituitary gland; Psychobiology; Split-brain studies; Synaptic transmission; Thyroid gland, Visual system.

Breuer, Josef

BORN: January 15, 1842, in Vienna, Austria
DIED: June 20, 1925, in Vienna, Austria
IDENTITY: Austrian physiologist, physician, and pioneer of psychoanalysis
TYPE OF PSYCHOLOGY: Psychopathology; Psychotherapy

After making important physiological discoveries, Breuer, with Sigmund Freud, helped found psychoanalysis.

Josef Breuer was born in Vienna and spent his entire life there. His mother died when he was four, and his father, who educated him until he was eight, became his inspirational model. His formal schooling began at the Akademisches Gymnasium, and after his graduation in 1858, he entered the University of Vienna where, in 1859, he began his medical studies. After receiving a medical degree in 1867, he married Matilda Altmann, a union that produced five children.

Breuer achieved his first recognition through research in physiology. Working with the German physiologist Ewald Hering, Breuer discovered how a certain nerve regulated respiration (the Hering-Breuer reflex). He then studied, on his own, the inner ears of fish, reptiles, birds, and mammals, concluding, in 1873, that the inner ear's semicircular canals regulate the animal's balance. Though his successful physiological research assured him of a scientific career at the University of Vienna, he refused to become an Extraordinary Professor, deciding instead to devote himself to his successful medical practice, which included university professors and well-known politicians.

One of his patients serendipitously led to another of his great scientific discoveries. In 1880, Breuer began treating Anna O., a young woman whose symptoms included paralysis and an aversion to drinking water. Breuer, who interpreted her illness as hysteria, decided to use hypnosis to get at the emotional roots of her problems. When the emotional event behind the problem was made conscious and Anna O.'s repressed feelings were fully expressed, this catharsis cured her symptoms.

Reluctant to generalize from a single case, Breuer did not publish his observations, but in 1882 he told Sigmund Freud about them. Freud himself did not use this new therapeutic technique until 1889, and he and Breuer did not fully publish their results until 1895, with *Studienüber Hysterie* (*Studies in Hysteria,* 1950). Soon after this book appeared, their relationship ended, perhaps due to Freud's insistence that every hysteria had a sexual cause whereas Breuer believed that psychoses had other causes.

Breuer's later work centered on his medical practice. His skill as a diagnostician and his deep humaneness brought him numerous patients from all walks of life, some of whom (colleagues and the destitute) he treated for free. An exceptionally cultured man, he was a lover of art, music, and literature. He counted among his friends the composer Hugo Wolf, the writer and physician Arthur Schnitzler, and the philosopher and priest Franz Brentano. Even in his old age he kept abreast of new medical discoveries. According to his friends, he maintained his critical acumen and personal warmth until his death, which occurred in Vienna in 1925.

BIBLIOGRAPHY

Dimen, Muriel, and Adrienne Harris, eds. *Storms in Her Head: Freud and the Construction of Hysteria.* New York: Other Press, 2001. A series of articles reconsidering the impact of Breuer and Freud's Studies on Hysteria in the light of the later development of psychology.

Ellenberger, Henri. *The Discovery of the Unconscious: The History and Evolution of Dynamic Psychiatry.* Reprint. New York: Basic Books, 2006. By using unpublished information provided by Breuer's family, Ellenberger provides fresh interpretations of the Freud-Breuer relationship.

Jones, Ernest. *The Life and Work of Sigmund Freud.* New York: Basic Books, 1981. Though scholars have discovered faults of fact and interpretation in Jones's work, it still contains much useful information about the Breuer-Freud collaboration.

Sulloway, Frank J. Freud, *Biologist of the Mind: Beyond the Psychoanalytic Legend.* Cambridge, Mass.: Harvard University Press, 1992. This intellectual biography by a historian of science reassesses Freud's life and work, including Freud's relationship with Breuer.

Robert J. Paradowski

See Also: Freud, Sigmund; Freudian psychology; Hypnosis; Hysteria; Psychotherapy: Historical approaches.

Brief therapy

Type of psychology: Psychotherapy

Brief therapy is a time-limited treatment that encourages change in how a person behaves and thinks. This form of psychotherapy improves a person's coping skills and can improve self-esteem. Brief therapy is designed for those who are already functioning fairly well occupationally and have some positive relationships. The person needs a good motivation level for successful brief therapy.

Key Concepts

- Brief focal psychotherapy
- Forced choice questions
- Short-term psychotherapy
- Time-limited psychotherapy
- Trial interpretations

INTRODUCTION

Brief therapy is a form of psychotherapy that uses short-term treatment methods to help people handle current life problems and crises. The distinctive features of brief therapy include a time limit and a focus on specific problems and topics. During brief therapy, the therapist takes an active role in directing the participant to specific issues and limiting the exploration of other aspects of the person's life. This approach contrasts with traditional open-ended therapy, which seeks to explore numerous topics as they are uncovered during psychotherapy.

Although brief therapy is time limited, there is no consensus concerning the ideal number of therapy sessions for this form of treatment. It may last anywhere from a single session to twenty or more. Brief therapy is also known as time-limited psychotherapy or short-term psychotherapy. Consensus is also lacking regarding the type of person who benefits most from this form of therapy. Sometimes focusing on a particular problem may bring forth additional problems that cannot be addressed in the time-limited format.

Because of the time-limited nature of brief therapy, the costs associated with psychotherapy are less than with traditional forms. Brief therapy has become popular with managed-care organizations, as it helps to contain treatment costs.

HISTORICAL TRENDS

The foundations for brief therapy were laid by Franz Alexander and Thomas French in 1946, when they identified the critical elements for a time-limited form of psychotherapy. They suggested that new ways of thinking, acting, and feeling could be promoted in individuals through the establishment of a corrective emotional experience during treatment. If the individuals being treated were highly motivated and worked effectively with a therapist, they could achieve change in a short time.

In the 1950s, while working in London, David Malan developed brief focal psychotherapy as a time-limited treatment. In this type of therapy, the patient and therapist formulate a focus for the treatment and set a termination date before the therapy begins. The average number of sessions for this treatment is twenty meetings. To be selected for this therapy, a person must be able to think in feeling terms, have a high motivation level, and respond to the trial interpretations from the therapist. Trial interpretations are explanations provided by the therapist about why a person is behaving in a certain manner.

Also developed during the 1950s was short-term anxiety-provoking psychotherapy. Peter Sifneos identified individuals who could select a specific problem in their lives and had the motivation to solve the problem in therapy. For those persons, Sifneos confronted their problems using forced-choice questions, which do not permit a person to avoid problems or ideas that may be upsetting. The focus of this form of brief therapy is on anything related to the identified problem that provokes worry and anxiety.

James Mann developed time-limited psychotherapy in the 1970s while working at Boston University. Mann selected individuals who had an easily identifiable central conflict in their lives and limited treatment to only twelve sessions. The conflicts usually related to problems with maturation and psychological development. For example, a young man may be having difficulty moving away from his parents and be afraid of living alone. This conflict of independence versus dependence would become the central focus of the time-limited psychotherapy. The treatment would then focus on possible solutions to this conflict.

CURRENT ISSUES

One of the major similarities among all brief therapies is the importance of the therapist's behavior during the sessions. In brief therapy, the therapist is very active in the process of focusing on specific problems and confronting the patient to solve his or her problem. Because the therapist is very direct with the patient, there is a dynamic interaction between them that is designed to obtain solutions in the least amount of time. Modern brief therapy uses many cognitive and behavioral techniques to facilitate the changes sought from the person seeking treatment. Cognitive techniques focus on modifying how a person thinks about the surrounding environment. Behavioral techniques attempt to reinforce desired behaviors and remove actions that are causing problems in a person's life. Specific exercises are performed to solve problems and improve interpersonal skills. Research investigations of brief therapy have shown that it is effective for a specific range of mental-health problems, but controversy has emerged over its extensive use.

Brief therapy is frequently the treatment of choice for managed-care organizations, which often discourage long-term treatments. Outpatient psychotherapy is usually approved for six to eight sessions of brief therapy. Critics charge that the mental-health profession is being driven by economic considerations rather than the needs of its patients. The support that brief therapy receives from managed-care organizations has created a conflict with those providing psychotherapy that may take years to resolve.

BIBLIOGRAPHY

Engler, Jack, and Daniel Goleman. *The Consumer's Guide to Psychotherapy.* New York: Simon, 1992. Print.

Franklin, Cynthia, et al., eds. *Solution-Focused Brief Therapy: A Handbook of Evidence-Based Practice.* New York: Oxford UP, 2012. Print.

Horowitz, Mardi Jon. *Personality Styles and Brief Psychotherapy*. Northvale: Aronson, 2001. Print.

Lazarus, Arnold. *Brief but Comprehensive Psychotherapy.* New York: Springer, 2006. Print.

MacKenzie, K. Roy. "Principles of Brief Intensive Psychotherapy." *Psychiatric Annals* 21.7 (1991): 398–404. Print.

Piper, William E., and Anthony S. Joyce. "A Consideration of Factors Influencing the Utilization of Time-Limited, Short Term Group Therapy." *International Journal of Group Psychotherapy* 46.3 (1996): 311–28. Print.

Ratner, Harvey, Evan George, and Chris Iveson. *Solution Focused Brief Therapy: 100 Key Points and Techniques.* New York: Routledge, 2012. Print.

Strosahl, Kirk, Patricia Robinson, and Thomas Gustavsson. *Brief Interventions for Radical Change: Principles and Practice of Focused Acceptance and Commitment Therapy.* Oakland: New Harbinger, 2012. Print.

Frank J. Prerost

See Also: Behavior therapy; Behavioral family therapy; Cognitive behavior therapy; Cognitive therapy; Couples therapy; Drug therapies; Gestault therapy; Group therapy; Music dance and theater therapy; Observational learning and modeling therapy; Person-centered therapy; Play therapy; Psychotherapy: Children; Psychotherapy: Effectiveness; Psychotherapy: Goals and techniques; Psychotherapy: Historical approaches; Rational emotive therapy; Reality therapy; Shock therapy.

Bronfenbrenner, Urie

Born: April 29, 1917
Died: September 25, 2005
Identity: Russian-born American psychologist
Birthplace: Moscow, Russia
Place of death: Ithaca, New York
Type of psychology: Developmental psychology

Bronfenbrenner introduced the concept of an ecology of human development and co-founded the Head Start program for children from low-income families.

Urie Bronfenbrenner came to the United States at the age of six. He completed an undergraduate degree in psychology at Cornell University, a master's degree at Harvard University, and a PhD at the University of Michigan in 1942. After World War II, he accepted a faculty position with Cornell University, where he spent most of his professional career. At the time of his death, he was the Jacob Gould Schurman Professor Emeritus of Human Development and of Psychology at Cornell University.

Bronfenbrenner was chair to the White House Conference on Children in 1970. In 1996, he was the first recipient of the American Psychological Association's new award named in his honor, the Urie Bronfenbrenner Award for Lifetime Contribution to Developmental Psychology in the Service of Science and Society. The award recognized individuals whose lifetime careers contributed to the science of developmental psychology and its application to benefit society.

Bronfenbrenner introduced his views regarding ecological psychology in *The Ecology of Human Development* (1979), advocating the study of the behavior of children in their natural life space of family, school, peer group, and community. His model was an ecology of human development, but he later renamed it a bioecological theory, presenting behavior as the interaction of person and environment. His theory was that development is a process of social initiation. He identified four systems in his model, characterized by roles, norms, and expected behaviors. He later added a fifth system, the historical context, outlined in *The Ecology of Developmental Process* (1998), which resulted in his complex process-person-context-time model (PPCT).

His culminating work, *Making Human Beings Human* (2005), described possible applications of the bioecological model to programs and policies. His groundbreaking ecology of human development has called attention to the fact that humans do not develop in isolation, but in relation to family, community, and society.

BIBLIOGRAPHY

Bergen, Doris. *Human Development: Traditional and Contemporary Theories*. Upper Saddle River: Prentice Hall, 2008.

Brendtro, Larry K. "The Vision of Urie Bronfenbrenner: Adults Who Are Crazy About Kids." *Reclaiming Children and Youth: The Journal of Strength-Based Interventions* 15.3 (2006): 162–166.

Thelen, E., and L. B. Smith. *A Dynamic Systems Approach to the Development of Cognition and Action*. Boston: MIT P, 1994.

Derived from: "Bronfenbrenner, Urie." *Psychology and Mental Health*. Salem Press. 2009.

Lillian J. Breckenridge

See Also: Children's mental health; Cognitive psychology; Developmental psychology; Educational psychology; Learning.

Bruner, Jerome

Born: October 1, 1915
Identity: American developmental and educational psychologist
Birthplace: New York, New York
Type of psychology: Cognition

Bruner has contributed to the fields of cultural psychology and psychological anthropology. His constructivist theory forms the general framework for instruction based on the study of cognition.

Jerome Bruner was born in New York City in 1915 and completed his undergraduate degree at Duke University in 1937. He interrupted his educational plans to become involved with survey research during World War II. He then completed his PhD at Harvard University in 1947, staying on as a member of the Harvard faculty for the next twenty-seven years. He became a research professor of psychology at New York University, where he also became a senior research fellow in law. He has received honorary doctorates from numerous universities, including Yale University. He was the cofounder and director of the Center for Cognitive Studies while at Harvard. He is also recognized as one of the founders of the federally funded Head Start preschool program for children from low-income families. During the 1960s, he was instrumental in the creation of Man, A Course of Study (MACOS), an elementary school science curriculum based on anthropology that was funded by the National Science Foundation.

In 1987, the American Psychological Association identified Bruner as one of the outstanding contributors to the field of educational psychology since 1960. His major thesis is that learning is an active process in which learners construct new ideas or concepts based on their current knowledge. In The Process of Education (1960), Bruner introduced his basic concept that any student is capable of learning anything if properly taught. For this to be possible, the instructor must translate information to be learned into a format appropriate to the learner's current understanding. He envisioned a spiral curriculum that made it possible for the student to continually build on what had already been learned.

Bruner advocated a social-interactionist approach to language development as an alternative to the nativist theory. He theorized that parents and teachers play a role in constructing what he called a language acquisition support system (LASS).

Bruner's meaning-centered approach to psychology has focused on the role that culture plays in learning and cognition. His work on narrative inquiry places attention on the potential of stories to give meaning to people's lives.

BIBLIOGRAPHY

Bakhurst, David, and Stuart G. Shanker, eds. Jerome Bruner: *Language, Culture, Self.* Thousand Oaks: Sage, 2001. Print.

Bruner, Jerome. *In Search of Mind: Essays in Autobiography.* New York: Harper, 1983. Print.

Bruner, Jerome, and Helen Weinreich-Haste. *Making Sense: The Child's Construction of the World.* New York: Routledge, 2011. Print.

Olson, David. *Jerome Bruner: The Cognitive Revolution in Educational Theory.* 2007. New York: Continuum, 2011. Print.

Smidt, Sandra. *Introducing Bruner: A Guide for Practitioners and Students in Early Years Education.* Hoboken: Taylor, 2013. Digital file.

Takaya, Keiichi. *Jerome Bruner: Developing a Sense of the Possible.* New York: Springer, 2013. Digital file.

Lillian J. Breckenridge

SEE ALSO: Children's mental health; Cognitive psychology; Developmental psychology; Educational psychology; Learning.

Bullying

DATE: 1980s forward

TYPE OF PSYCHOLOGY: Developmental psychology; Social psychology

Bullying is an intentional, aggressive, recurring act involving a power imbalance between the individuals involved. Targets of bullying have higher rates of depression and anxiety, lower levels of self-esteem, and lower academic performance than their peers who are not bullied.

KEY CONCEPTS

- Anxiety
- Cyberbullying
- Depression
- Prevention
- Victimization

INTRODUCTION

Research professor of psychology Dan Olweus defined bullying as an intentional act of aggression that is designed to harm another person, is often repeated, and reflects a power imbalance between the individuals involved. Bullying can be either direct (as in hitting, kicking, pushing, teasing, verbal harassment, and obscene gestures) or indirect (as in spreading rumors, excluding others, and cyberbullying). Although most people equate bullying with physical attacks, in fact the most common type of bullying involves verbal taunts or threats.

Olweus began the systematic study of bullying in the 1970s in Norway and Sweden. In a survey of more than 150,000 children and youth, Olweus found that 15 percent of the respondents had experienced bullying—9 percent as victims, 7 percent as bullies, and 2 percent as both bully and victim. He later developed the Olweus Bullying Prevention Program in response the 1983 suicide of three bullying victims in Norway.

The first national study of bullying in the United States was conducted by researcher Tonja R. Nansel and colleagues in 1998, and the results were published in 2001. In a survey of more than 15,000 students in sixth though twelfth grades, the researchers found that 17 percent reported being victims of bullying, 19 percent reported perpetrating bullying, and 6 percent reported being both bully and victim.

With the advent of electronic communication, bullying has taken on a new form known as cyberbullying, or online social cruelty. Cyberbullying is defined as bullying that occurs via the Internet (e-mails, instant messages, chat rooms, online games, and so on) or text messages. Unlike traditional bullying, which is most likely to occur at school, cyberbullying can occur anywhere that children and youth have access to technology, leaving targets accessible to perpetrators at any time of the day or night.

CONSEQUENCES OF BULLYING

Children and youth who are bullied experience a number of adverse physical and psychological effects. Children who are bullied are more likely to be anxious and depressed and to have lower self-esteem than their peers who do not experience bullying. They are also more likely to have lower academic performance, as assessed by school grades and number of school absences. A survey of Dutch children by researcher Minne Fekkes, Frans I. M. Pijpers, and S. Pauline Verloove-Vanhorick found that, relative to children who are not bullied, children who are bullied have more frequent headaches and stomachaches. These consequences of bullying are most problematic for children and youth who are both bully and victim.

THE BULLY AND THE VICTIM

The typical bullying victim does not fit any specific profile. However, children who are bullied are more likely to be in elementary school than in middle or high school. Some research reports that boys are more likely than girls to be victimized. Other research suggests that boys and girls are equally likely to be victimized, albeit in different ways: boys are more likely than girls to be physically bullied, while girls are more likely to be bullied through indirect methods such as social exclusion and rumor spreading. Unlike boys, who tend to be bullied most often by other boys, girls are bullied by both girls and boys.

Children who are bullied are often quiet, sensitive children who may have low self-esteem. They tend to be social isolates who are more comfortable spending time with adults than with their peers. They also frequently experience anxiety and depression. It is often difficult to know whether these characteristics predispose an individual to be bullied or whether they are a consequence of the bullying that subsequently sets the child up for further victimization.

Just as there is no prototype for a victim of bullying, so too is there no single profile of an individual who bullies. However, children who bully are more often boys than girls and more likely to be in middle or high school. Children and youth who bully are often assertive and impulsive. They fail to follow rules and show little empathy toward others. Although children and youth who bully are often thought to have low self-esteem, in fact they tend to have higher self-esteem and to be less anxious and less depressed than their nonbullied peers. Indeed, psychology professor Jaana Juvonen and her colleagues found in 2003 that children who bully are often the most popular children in the class.

PREVENTION

The US Health Resources and Services Administration (HRSA) created a list of recommended practices regarding bullying prevention and intervention. Included among these is that bullying prevention efforts must involve changing the school climate and norms. The prevalence of bullying needs to be assessed, and parents, educators, and administrators must unite in their efforts to combat bullying. Staff should be trained to recognize and intervene in bullying situations, and school policies should be clear regarding the consequences for bullying. Bullying prevention needs to be an ongoing effort with repeated training sessions for staff and educational sessions for students and parents.

BIBLIOGRAPHY

Bazelon, Emily. *Sticks and Stones: Defeating the Culture of Bullying and Rediscovering the Power of Character and Empathy.* New York: Random, 2013. Print.

Englander, Elizabeth Kandel. *Bullying and Cyberbullying: What Every Educator Needs to Know.* Cambridge: Harvard UP, 2013. Print.

Fekkes, Minne, Frans I. M. Pijpers, and S. Pauline Verloove-Vanhorick. "Bullying Behavior and Associations with Psychosomatic Complaints and Depression in Victims." *Journal of Pediatrics* 144.1 (2004): 17–22. Print.

Hirsch, Lee, and Cynthia Lowen, eds. *Bully: An Action Plan for Teachers, Parents, and Communities to Combat the Bullying Crisis.* With Dina Santorelli. New York: Weinstein, 2012. Print.

Kowalski, Robin M., Susan P. Limber, and Patricia W. Agatston. *Cyber Bullying: Bullying in the Digital Age.* Malden: Blackwell, 2008. Print.

Nansel, Tonja R., et al. "Bullying Behavior among US Youth: Prevalence and Association with Psychosocial Adjustment." *Journal of the American Medical Association* 285.16 (2001): 2094–100. Print.

Olweus, Dan. *Bullying at School: What We Know and What We Can Do.* New York: Blackwell, 1993. Print.

Patchin, Justin W., and Sameer Hinduja, eds. *Cyberbullying Prevention and Response: Expert Perspectives.* New York: Routledge, 2012. Print

United States. *Dept. of Health and Human Services.* Stop Bullying.gov. US Dept. of Health and Human Services, n.d. Web. 27 Feb. 2014.

Robin M. Kowalski

See Also: Aggression; Aggression: Reduction and control; Children's mental health; Computer and Internet use and mental health; Self-esteem; Teenangers' mental health; Violence by children and teenagers; Violence: Psychological causes and effects.

Bystander intervention

Type of psychology: Social psychology

The study of the psychology of bystander intervention has led to an understanding of the processes that often prevent witnesses to an incident from offering needed assistance, even if an emergency is involved; such events may have tragic consequences, and knowledge of the dynamics of

these situations may sometimes keep them from occurring.

Key Concepts

- Audience inhibition
- Bystander effect
- Confederate
- Diffusion of responsibility
- Social influence

INTRODUCTION

In early 1964, Kitty Genovese was stabbed to death in front of her New York City apartment building as she returned from work around 3:30 a.m. The assault was particularly brutal, actually consisting of three separate attacks stretching over a period of more than half an hour. Perhaps most shocking about this tragedy, however, was a troubling fact that emerged in the police department's subsequent investigation: Thirty-eight of the woman's neighbors had witnessed the incident without intervening. No one had even called the police during the episode.

This case was only one of several similar occurrences that took place in the mid-1960s, attracting considerable attention and prompting much commentary. The remarks of newspaper columnists, magazine writers, and the like focused on such notions as "alienation," "apathy," "indifference," and "lack of concern for our fellow humans." Bibb Latané and John Darley, social psychologists who at the time were professors at universities in New York City, reasoned that ascribing such personality characteristics to bystanders who fail to help is not the key to understanding how onlookers can remain inactive while another individual is victimized. Rather, one must look to the situation itself to uncover the powerful social forces that inhibit helping.

Latané and Darley thus embarked on a program of research that culminated in their classic 1970 book *The Unresponsive Bystander: Why Doesn't He Help?* They began their analysis of the " bystander effect" by recognizing several good reasons that one should not necessarily expect bystanders to offer help in an emergency. For example, most people are not prepared to deal with emergencies, which tend to happen quickly and without warning. In addition, direct intervention may involve real physical danger, as in the Genovese incident. Finally, becoming involved in such situations may lead to court appearances or other legal consequences.

Latané and Darley also proposed a model describing a sequence of cognitive events that must occur before a bystander will offer assistance in an emergency. First, a bystander must notice the event. Second, he or she must interpret that event as an emergency. Third, the bystander must decide that it is his or her responsibility to do something. At this point, two steps in the process still remain: The bystander must decide exactly what to do, and then he or she must successfully implement that decision. It is important to recognize that a negative outcome at any of these steps in the decision-making process will prevent helping. In the light of this cognitive process and the other reasons that people fail to intervene in emergencies, it is perhaps surprising, Latané and Darley suggested, that bystanders ever help.

FACTORS THAT PREVENT ASSISTANCE

Remarkably (and ironically), one situational factor is primarily responsible for the social inhibition of helping: the presence of other people. Latané and Darley proposed three social psychological processes to explain precisely how the presence of others inhibits helping. Each operates within the decision-making framework described earlier, and all three appear to be necessary to account completely for the bystander effect.

The first of these processes is audience inhibition, which refers to people's general reluctance to do things in front of others. When people are aware that their behavior is on public display and are concerned about what other people think, they may be hesitant to offer help for fear of appearing incompetent. Furthermore, a bystander who decides to offer help will be embarrassed if it turns out that he or she has misinterpreted the situation when it is not really an emergency. For example, how might a person feel if he or she stepped out of the crowd to administer CPR to a man lying unconscious on the ground, only to roll him over and realize that he is merely intoxicated? Risks of this sort are greater when larger numbers of other people are present.

The second process, social influence, frequently contributes to the social inhibition of helping by leading bystanders to misinterpret the event. Emergencies are often ambiguous, and a person confronted with ambiguity will look to the behavior of other people for clues about how to behave. While the person is attempting to appraise the reactions of other people, he or she will probably attempt to remain calm. That person, then, is likely to see a group of others doing exactly the same: appearing calm and doing nothing while trying to figure out whether a true emergency is taking place. Each person will be fooled by the inaction of everyone else into thinking that the situation is less serious than it really is and that not intervening is the appropriate course of action. The ultimate result is a sort of group behavioral paralysis, and the victim goes without help.

The final process, the most powerful of the three, was probably the main force at work in the Genovese incident (social influence was probably not involved, since witnesses remained isolated from one another in their own apartments). This phenomenon, known as diffusion of responsibility, occurs when an individual knows that others are available to help. While a lone bystander at an emergency bears the total responsibility for helping, those in a group share the responsibility equally with the others present. Thus, the larger the number of other witnesses, the smaller is each individual's obligation to act. As a result, individuals in groups are likely to assume that someone else will intervene.

SOCIAL PSYCHOLOGICAL RESEARCH

Latané and Darley tested their ideas in a number of ingenious experiments, several of which are considered classic examples of social psychological research. In one of these, Columbia University students arrived individually at a laboratory to take part in a study that they believed would involve an interview. Each subject was sent to a waiting room to complete a preliminary questionnaire. Some of them found two other people already seated in the room, while others sat down alone.

Soon after the subject began working on the questionnaire, smoke began filling the room through a wall vent. The smoke could hardly be ignored; within four minutes the room contained enough smoke to interfere with vision and breathing. Latané and Darley were primarily interested in how frequently subjects simply got up and left the room to report the emergency. Most (75 percent) of the subjects who were waiting alone reported the smoke, but those in groups were far less likely to do so. Groups consisting of three naïve (never tested) subjects reported it only 38 percent of the time; when the subject waited (unknowingly) with two confederates who were instructed to do nothing, only 10 percent responded. In a social psychological experiment, a confederate is a person instructed to behave in a certain way.

Observations of the unresponsive subjects supported the researchers' notion that the social influence process in groups would inhibit helping by leading people to misinterpret the situation. Interviews with these participants revealed that they had produced a variety of explanations for the smoke: air conditioning vapor, steam, smog, and even "truth gas." In other words, lone subjects for the most part behaved responsibly, but those in groups were generally led by the inaction of others to conclude almost anything but the obvious—that a legitimate emergency was taking place. It is important to realize that social influence, as demonstrated in this experiment, is most potent when bystanders in groups do not communicate with one another; such was the case in this experiment, and such tends to be the case with analogous groups in real life. Simply talking to the others present can clarify what really is happening, thus eliminating the bystander effect.

DIFFUSION-OF-RESPONSIBILITY RESEARCH

A second classic study demonstrates the power of the diffusion-of-responsibility process. In this experiment, college students thought they were participating in a group discussion about the difficulties of adjusting to college. To reduce the discomfort that could be associated with discussing personal matters, each subject was ushered to a private cubicle from which he or she would communicate with other group members through an intercom system. In each case, however, there was only one actual subject; the other "group members" had been previously tape recorded. Thus, Latané and Darley were able to manipulate the size of the group as perceived by the subject.

Each "member" of the group talked for two minutes, with the actual subject speaking last. A second round then began, and the first "group member" to speak began suffering a frighteningly severe epileptic seizure, choking and pleading for help. Since the subject had no idea where the other "group members" were located, the only available course of helping action was to leave the cubicle and report the emergency to the person in charge.

On the basis of the diffusion-of-responsibility concept, Latané and Darley expected that the likelihood of helping would decrease as the perceived size of the group increased. When the subject was part of a two-person group (only the subject and the victim, thus making the subject the only person available to help), 85 percent of the participants reported the seizure. When the subject believed that he or she was in a group of three, 62 percent responded. Only 31 percent of those who thought they were in a six-person group offered help. Without question, the responsibility for acting in this emergency was perceived to be divided among everyone believed to be available to help.

The circumstances of this experiment correspond directly to those of the Genovese murder. Most important, the subjects in this study were not in a face-to-face group, just as the witnesses to the Genovese murder were isolated in their own apartments; consequently, social influence could not lead to a misinterpretation of the event (which was not ambiguous anyway). In short, simply knowing that others are available to respond acts as a powerful deterrent to helping. It is also significant that this experiment demonstrated that bystanders who fail to intervene are usually not the least bit apathetic or indifferent. Rather, the typical unresponsive subject showed clear signs of distress over the plight of the victim; nevertheless, the belief that others were present still tended to suppress intervention.

Diffusion of responsibility is a common social force and is not restricted to serious situations. Anyone who has failed to work as hard as possible on a group task, heard a doorbell go unanswered at a party, or experienced a telephone ringing seven or eight times even though the entire family is at home has probably fallen victim to the same process.

POWER OF SITUATIONAL FORCES

The work of Latané and Darley attracted much attention and acclaim. From a methodological standpoint, their experiments are still regarded as some of social psychology's most clever and intriguing. Their findings, however, were even more remarkable: Demonstrating consistently the social inhibition of helping, they destroyed the common belief in "safety in numbers." This research also provides a powerful illustration of one of the major lessons of social psychology—that situational forces affecting behavior can be overpowering, eliminating at least temporarily the influence of personality. The work of Latané and Darley showed convincingly that a person cannot rely on human nature, kindness, or any other dispositional quality if he or she should become the victim of an emergency.

This program of research also provided the impetus for much work on helping that has been conducted by other investigators. Various kinds of precipitating incidents were examined, as were differences between experiments conducted in laboratories and those performed in natural settings. Other studies investigated the effects of a wide range of different characteristics of the subjects, victims, and other bystanders involved. It was discovered, for example, that people are more likely to offer assistance when someone else has already modeled helping behavior and if the victim is particularly needy, deserving, or somehow similar to the helper; certain transitory mood states, such as happiness and guilt, were also found to increase helping.

Despite the large assortment of factors investigated, many of these other studies included a manipulation of the variable that had been the principal concern of Latané and Darley: group size. Two major articles published by Latané and his colleagues in 1981 reviewed nearly one hundred different instances of research comparing helping by individuals in groups with that by lone bystanders. They found in these studies, almost without exception, that people were less likely to help in groups than when they were alone, suggesting that the bystander effect is perhaps as consistent and predictable as any within the domain of social psychology.

Although incidents such as the murder of Genovese do not occur every day, it is important to recognize that scores of them have been reported over the years, and they continue to occur regularly. Unfortunately, the understanding provided by the research has not led to strategies for avoiding these tragedies. (Considering the ability of situational forces to override personality influences, one should not be too surprised by this.) There is, however, one bit of hope: At least one study has demonstrated that students who have learned about the bystander effect in a psychology class are more likely to intervene in an emergency than those who have not been exposed to that material.

BIBLIOGRAPHY

Abbate, Costanza Scaffidi, Stafano Ruggieri, and Stefano Boca. "The Effect of Prosocial Priming in the Presence of Bystanders." *Jour. of Social Psychology* 153.5 (2013): 619–22. Print.

Baron, Sally J. F. "Inaction Speaks Louder Than Words: The Problems of Passivity." *Business Horizons* 56.3 (2013): 301–11, Print.

Batson, C. D. "Prosocial Motivation: Is It Ever Truly Altruistic?" *Advances in Experimental Social Psychology.* Ed. Leonard Berkowitz. San Diego: Academic Press, 1987. Print.

Cialdini, Robert B. *Influence: Science and Practice*. 5th ed. Boston: Pearson Education, 2009. Print.

Fischer, Peter, and Tobias Greitemeyer. "The Positive Bystander Effect: Passive Bystanders Increase Helping in Situations With High Expected Negative

Consequences for the Helper." *Jour. of Social Psychology* 153.1 (2013): 1–5. Print.

Latané, Bibb, and John M. Darley. *The Unresponsive Bystander: Why Doesn't He Help?* New York: Appleton, 1970. Print.

Latané, Bibb, S. A. Nida, and D. W. Wilson. "The Effects of Group Size on Helping Behavior." *Altruism and Helping Behavior: Social, Personality, and Developmental Perspectives.* Ed. J. Phillipe Rushton and Richard M. Sorrentino. Hillsdale: Lawrence Erlbaum, 1981. Print.

Macaulay, Jaqueline, and Leonard Berkowitz, eds. *Altruism and Helping Behavior: Social Psychological Studies of Some Antecedents and Consequences.* New York: Academic Press, 1970. Print.

Rushton, J. Phillipe, and Richard M. Sorrentino, eds. *Altruism and Helping Behavior: Social, Personality, and Developmental Perspectives.* Hillsdale: Lawrence Erlbaum, 1981. Print.

Staub, Ervin. "Helping a Distressed Person: Social, Personality, and Stimulus Determinants." *Advances in Experimental Social Psychology.* Ed. Leonard Berkowitz. New York: Academic Press, 1987. Print.

Steve A. Nida

See Also: Altruism, cooperation and empathy; Attitude-behavior consistency; Cooperation, competition and negotiation; Crowd behavior; Group decision making; Groups; Helping; Inhibitory and excitatory impulses.

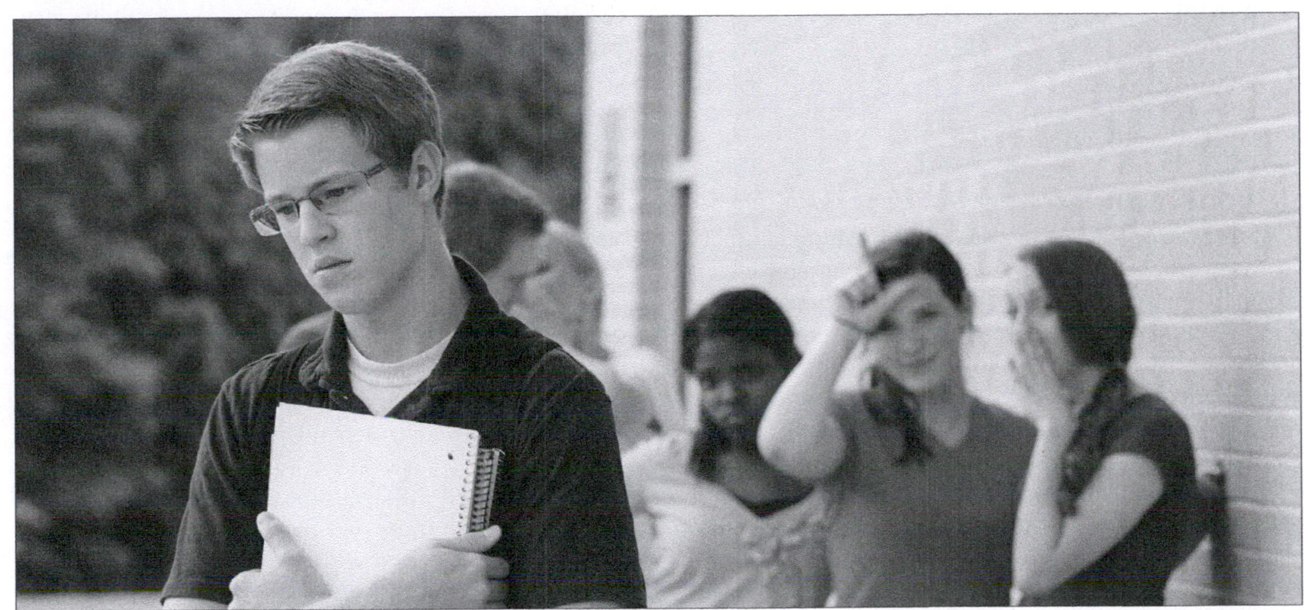

Photo: iStock

C

Caffeine and mental health

Type of psychology: Psychopathology; Psychotherapy

Caffeine is a mild stimulant drug found in common foods, beverages, and over-the-counter medications. While its use is generally nonproblematic and part of many people's daily routines, overuse or misuse can lead to physical and mental health problems.

Key Concepts

- Anxiety
- Bruxism
- Diuresis
- Insomnia
- Intoxication
- Psychopathology
- Stimulant
- Substance-induced disorders

INTRODUCTION

Caffeine is a legal drug that in its natural form has a bitter taste. Chemically, it is a xanthine-type drug, which is alkaloid in nature, meaning that it is nitrogen based. It is a mild diuretic, or substance that encourages urination, and a mild stimulant. Stimulants are a broad group of substances that can excite the body's central and peripheral nervous system and the cardiovascular system. Because of these properties, stimulants can have therapeutic and otherwise desirable effects. In fact, stimulants and their derivatives have been used to treat conditions such as drowsiness, narcolepsy, asthma, attention-deficit hyperactivity disorder (ADHD), autism, and obesity.

Caffeine is commonly found in coffee, tea, and other beverages, such as soft drinks and energy drinks. It is also present in chocolate, cocoa, over-the-counter medications for avoiding drowsiness, and even some headache remedies. The general effect of caffeine is mild relative to other stimulants; nonetheless, caffeine is considered a psychoactive substance. Its most basic effect is to trigger increased alertness; other, positive effects such as enhanced cognitive performance and increased selective attention remain the subject of debate. The most common form of administration of the drug is oral ingestion. Because caffeine products are mild stimulants, legal, and available worldwide, they are part of daily rituals in many countries. People gather to drink caffeinated beverages, enjoying them as part of social rituals. Therefore, as with other drugs, some psychosocial benefits are associated with caffeine.

DISORDERS RELATED TO CAFFEINE USE

As with any drug, pros and cons of usage exist; potential problems can occur if caffeine is not used properly. In fact, from a physical health perspective, regular overuse of caffeine can result in mild to serious gastrointestinal problems such as gastroesophageal reflex disease (GERD). Untreated, such conditions can result in ulcers and erosion of the esophageal tract. Problems such as GERD have been associated with cancer. Therefore, in terms of the link between caffeine and GERD, caffeine intake may be a controllable factor relevant to cancer prevention. Regular use of caffeine can also lead to tolerance, the need to use more of a drug to achieve a previous effect or the use of the same amount resulting in a lessened effect. Frequently when this happens, individuals may also be subject to caffeine withdrawal symptoms, such as headaches, if they stop using the drug. Such effects contrast markedly to the more severe withdrawal syndromes—confusion, depression, and fatigue—experienced by individuals dependent on stimulants such as amphetamine.

In addition to physical problems, caffeine is associated with at least three types of mental health problems in which it is a causative factor. These conditions are known as "caffeine-related disorders." One of these problems is caffeine intoxication, which is characterized by a pattern of symptoms: When individuals consume more than two or three cups of coffee, they may show symptoms such as a flushed face, physical agitation, muscle twitches, excitement, restlessness, nervousness, insomnia, diuresis, gastrointestinal problems, and a feeling of inexhaustibility. When an individual shows many of these symptoms, experiences distress or impairment, and the problems are not because of other problems, clinicians diagnose caffeine intoxication. Again, review of these symptoms underscores that caffeine is mild relative to other stimulants, such as amphetamines, which can cause paranoia, panic, psychosis, rapid pulse rates, hallucinations, aggression, violence, suicidal or homicidal tendencies, bruxism (teeth grinding), arrhythmias, heart damage, and even seizures.

A few other disorders are known as "caffeine-induced disorders," a subset of substance-induced disorders, which are problems caused by taking a drug. Caffeine-induced sleep disorder occurs when the use of caffeine significantly disturbs an individual's sleep. Caffeine-induced anxiety disorder occurs when caffeine use causes a person to experience distressing anxiety, a mood state characterized by extreme fear, worry, and uneasiness that may be cognitive, emotional, or physical. In a few case studies, extremely high doses of caffeine has reportedly induced psychosis, with the affected person exhibiting symptoms such as paranoid delusions and bizarre behavior. With caffeine-induced disorders, clinicians must rule out other causes, such as a primary sleep disorder, anxiety disorder, or other existing psychiatric condition. One method of doing this is to observe if the person continues to have symptoms after they have abstained from caffeine. If symptoms persist, a caffeine-related diagnosis is dismissed. If the symptoms do not persist, the problem is deemed related to the use of caffeine.

BIBLIOGRAPHY

Bourne, Edmund, and Lorna Garano. *Coping with Anxiety: Ten Simple Ways to Relieve Anxiety, Fear, and Worry.* Oakland: New Harbinger, 2003.

Chu, Yi-Fang. *Coffee: Emerging Health Effects and Disease Prevention.* Ames: Wiley-Blackwell, 2012. Print.

Epstein, Lawrence, and Steven Mardon. *The Harvard Medical School Guide to a Good Night's Sleep.* New York: McGraw-Hill, 2006.

Goiney, Christopher, Devin Gillaspie, and Clara Alvarez Villalba. "Addressing Caffeine-Induced Psychosis: A Clinical Perspective." *Addictive Disorders & Their Treatment* 11.3 (2012): 146–49. Print.

Hale, Jamie. "Caffeine's Effect on Your Thinking." PsychCentral.com. *Psych Central,* 15 Apr. 2012. Web. 24 Feb. 2014.

Inaba, Darryl S., and William E. Cohen. *Uppers, Downers, and All-Arounders: Physical and Mental Effects of Psychoactive Drugs.* 7th ed. Ashland: CNS, 2011. Print.

Kassel, Karen Schroeder. "Decreasing Your Caffeine Intake." *Health Library.* EBSCO Information Services, 2 June 2012. Web. 20 Feb. 2014.

Rosen, Winifred, and Andrew T. Weil. *From Chocolate to Morphine: Everything You Need to Know about Mind-Altering Drugs.* Rev ed. Boston: Houghton-Mifflin, 2004. Print.

Weinberg, Bennette Alan, and Bonnie K. Bealer. *The World of Caffeine: The Science and Culture of the World's Most Popular Drug.* New York: Routledge, 2002. Print.

Nancy A. Piotrowski

See Also: Addictive personality and behaviors; Alcohol dependence and abuse; Anxiety disorders; Insomnia; Mood disorders; Nicotine dependence; Sleep; Stimulant medications; Substance use disorders.

California psychological inventory (CPI)

Date: 1957 forward
Type of psychology: Personality

The California Psychological Inventory is a paper-and-pencil personality test used to assess normal people in terms of a wide range of personality characteristics. Although the test has been criticized for overlap among subscales and cultural bias, it is considered among the best validated and most useful of such tests.

Key Concepts

- Empirical criterion keying
- Externality-internality
- Folk concepts
- Norm favoring versus norm questioning
- Realization
- Structural scales

INTRODUCTION

The California Psychological Inventory (CPI) is a paper-and-pencil test designed for a comprehensive analysis of traits that describe a normal adult personality. The test itself consists of 462 statements about feelings and opinions, ethical and social attitudes, personal relationships, and characteristic behavior. The testee responds to each item as "true" or "false." Responses to these statements are analyzed, first of all, according to how well they fit twenty different patterns, each of which corresponds to a specified personality characteristic. The personality characteristics that are assessed include such everyday traits as sociability, dominance, independence, responsibility, self-control, tolerance, and achievement. The individual test-taker's scores on each scale are evaluated by how these scores compare with the range of scores established by a nationwide comparison group or norm group. Such comparisons also permit evaluating the test-taker on three structural scales that summarize patterns underlying the twenty primary scales at a more abstract and basic level: externality-internality (self-confident assertive extraversion versus introversion), norm-favoring versus norm-questioning (allegiance to the conventional social rules versus its lack), and the degree of one's "realization" of these tendencies, an index of self-fulfillment or satisfaction.

DEVELOPMENT

Harrison Gough, the author of the CPI, began assembling items relevant to the measurement of everyday personality characteristics in the late 1940s. It was 1957, however, before the completed eighteen scales of the CPI were published by Consulting Psychologist Press. In 1987, modest revisions in the scale were initiated. At this time, a few items were modified to reflect cultural changes, and two new primary scales, independence and empathy, were added to the original eighteen. The most important change, however, was the addition of the three summary, structural scales.

Two important principles governed the CPI's development. The first of these was Gough's interest in measuring "folk concepts," characteristics which in many cultures and over centuries made sense to ordinary people. This principle was in contrast to many existing tests that assessed concepts based on psychiatric diagnosis or academic personality theories or were abstracted from a mathematical procedure called factor analysis.

A second guiding principle was that of empirical criterion keying, which means that the validity of items on scales, as well as the scales themselves, should be established by actual research. In such research, items and scales are tested to assure that people who show evident differences in real-life functioning answer the item or the scale in the different ways one would expect. For example, the socialization scale was conceived to measure moral uprightness in the sense of observing society's rules and customs. One would expect that convicted felons would answer questions on this scale in ways different from Eagle Scouts, and felons would be expected to score much lower on this scale. Research verifying this difference supported the validity of the item and the scale. Hundreds of such predictions derived from the meaning of various CPI scales were tested. Only thereafter was the test considered valid.

EVALUATION

A major criticism of the CPI is that there is much overlap between highly similar scales. Dominance and capacity for status, for example, seem to involve only slightly nuanced measurements of almost the same thing. It has been argued, therefore, that the essential information could be gleaned from fewer, simpler scales. Gough answered this criticism by pointing out that everyday descriptions of others by ordinary folk also show this sort of overlap. He also pointed out that the structural scales, added in 1987, permit such simple, efficient description of a personality without depriving the test-taker of the refined and detailed analysis offered by assessing twenty primary traits.

It has also been charged that the CPI is often employed beyond the uses for which its validity has been established. Clinicians are prone to apply the test to abnormal populations for which validity data is incomplete. The test has also been frequently used for people from cultures outside the United States and for minorities within the United States. Although Gough selected his "folk concepts" for their apparent cross-cultural relevance, validity studies in minority and Third World subcultures have been neglected. Interpreting the test results of those from different cultural backgrounds must, therefore, be done with caution.

These admitted limitations could be addressed by adding more studies of minority or clinical populations to the already impressive research with this instrument. For more than half a century, the CPI has served such purposes as predicting vocational choice, academic success, and antisocial behavior. Few other personality tests have been as thoroughly validated. Its many scales permit a detailed description of a person in language that makes sense. Useful and much used, the CPI remains one of the best personality tests for normal populations.

BIBLIOGRAPHY

Anastasi, Anne, and Susan Urbina. *Psychological Testing.* 7th ed. Upper Saddle River: Prentice, 1997. Print.

Bolton, B. "Review of the California Psychological Inventory, Revised Edition." *Eleventh Mental Measurements Yearbook.* Ed. J. J. Framer and J.

C. Conly. Lincoln: Buros Institute of Mental Measurements, 1992. Print.

Gough, H. G. "The California Psychological Inventory." *Testing in Counseling Practice*. Ed. C. E. Walker and V. L. Campbell. Hillsdale.: Erlbaum, 1992. Print.

Gough, H. G., and P. Bradley. "Delinquent and Criminal Behavior as Assessed by the Revised California Psychological Inventory." *Journal of Clinical Psychology* 48 (1992): 298–308. Print.

Groth-Marnat, Gary. *Handbook of Psychological Assessment*. Rev. ed. New York: Wiley, 2009. Print.

Kulas, John T., Richard C. Thompson, and Michael G. Anderson. "California Psychological Inventory Dominance Scale Measurement Equivalence: General Population Normative and Indian, UK, and US Managerial Samples." *Educational & Psychological Measurement* 71.1 (2011): 245–57. Print.

Megargee, E. I. *The California Psychological Inventory Handbook*. San Francisco: Jossey, 1977. Print.

Melton, Gary B., et al. *Psychological Evaluations for the Courts: A Handbook for Mental Health Professionals and Lawyers*. 3d ed. New York: Guilford, 2007. Print.

Nestor, Paul, and Russell K. Schutt. *Research Methods in Psychology: Investigating Human Behavior*. Los Angeles: SAGE, 2012. Print.

Reynolds, Cecil R., and Ronald B. Livingston. *Mastering Modern Psychological Testing: Theory & Methods*. Boston: Pearson Education, 2012. Print.

Thomas E. DeWolfe

See Also: Beck Depression Inventory; Children's Depression Inventory; Children's mental health; Clinical interviewing, testing and observation; Depression; Diagnosis; Minnesota Multiphasic Personality Inventory; Personality: Psychophysiological measures; Personality interviewing strategies; Personality rating scales; State-Trait Anxiety Inventory; Thematic Apperception Test.

Cancer and mental health

Type of psychology: Emotion; Personality; Stress

A diagnosis of cancer is a mental challenge. In addition to their physical symptoms, cancer patients must deal with their fears, denial, anger, sadness, and depression. They may feel hopeless and powerless, and unless their mental health problems are severe, they usually must seek out support and assistance on their own. Cancer can, however, serve as the impetus for patients to make life changes and set priorities.

Key Concepts

- Acceptance
- Anger
- Bargaining
- Denial
- Depression
- Life stressor
- Massage
- Reflexology
- Reiki
- Support groups

INTRODUCTION

There is no single psychological response to cancer. Individuals respond in their own ways, based on their past experiences. Some common emotions include fear, denial, anger, sadness, depression, hopelessness, and powerlessness. For most people, the diagnosis of cancer causes fear of the unknown and fear of deformity, suffering, loss, and death. This is also a common reaction to other severe illnesses such as heart disease.

ADAPTING TO CANCER

Most people view the diagnosis of cancer as a loss. In this case, the loss would be of good health and a long life. In *On Death and Dying* (1969), psychologist Elisabeth Kübler-Ross set forth a theory of how people respond to the prospect of dying. Later scholars discovered that her stages of adaptation to the prospect of death—denial, bargaining, anger, depression and sadness, and acceptance—are similar to the stages of adaptation to change. Acceptance is the goal, but a person can go back and forth through these stages many times, and some people are unable to achieve acceptance. Cancer patients go through these stages in dealing with their disease. Some patients become stuck in one of these stages and are unable to progress any further. This is not necessarily a failure on their part, but rather a reflection of their personality and acquired coping skills. With a chronic illness such as cancer, acceptance is really only for the moment because of the ongoing changes in condition experienced by patients.

In many instances, cancer patients do not go beyond denial of their illness and its implications for their lives. Sometimes, family members feel that a person would be unable to cope with having cancer, so they do not reveal the true diagnosis to the patient. Other patients refuse to accept that they have cancer, and they continue to deny its impact the rest of their lives. Some people, despite developing a severe form of cancer, do not seek medical care until the cancer is advanced. Denial is a pathological response to cancer in that it robs the patient and the person's friends and family of the opportunity to express their love and to comfort one another.

Bargaining is a brief interim stage in which patients try to strike a bargain with their body, with some spiritual figure, or with life. Such a bargain might take the form of a promise to attend religious services for the rest of a patient's life if the cancer is cured or disappears. It is unusual for a person to become stuck in this stage. It usually becomes obvious that the cancer has not been cured, and the deal is fruitless.

Anger is another emotion that cancer patients often experience. They may be angry at their doctors, at their bodies, or at life. Although their anger is justified, it can drive away other people who might be of assistance. Some patients cannot let go of their anger, and it continues to simmer beneath the surface. However, retention of anger can lead to insomnia, heartburn, increased pain, and muscle tension.

Some people are able to let go of their anger, only to become stuck in depression and sadness. This can lead to feelings of hopelessness and an unwillingness to live their altered lives. Tremendous strides have been made in the treatment of cancer, and for many people it becomes a chronic illness. However, the treatments can have severe side effects and can be life altering. Some patients just give up on life and die before they might have. Certainly, coping with cancer treatments is difficult for most people.

The goal is acceptance of the disease and its treatments. This acceptance provides the cancer patient with a realistic view of the challenges of the disease and the willingness to undergo the treatments and deal with the side effects and limitations placed on their life. Often, the patients who learn to accept the disease do best with their cancer diagnosis and live the longest. Acceptance gives these patients the ability to learn about their illness and its treatments so that they can determine what is best for them. This can increase their feelings of power over their illness.

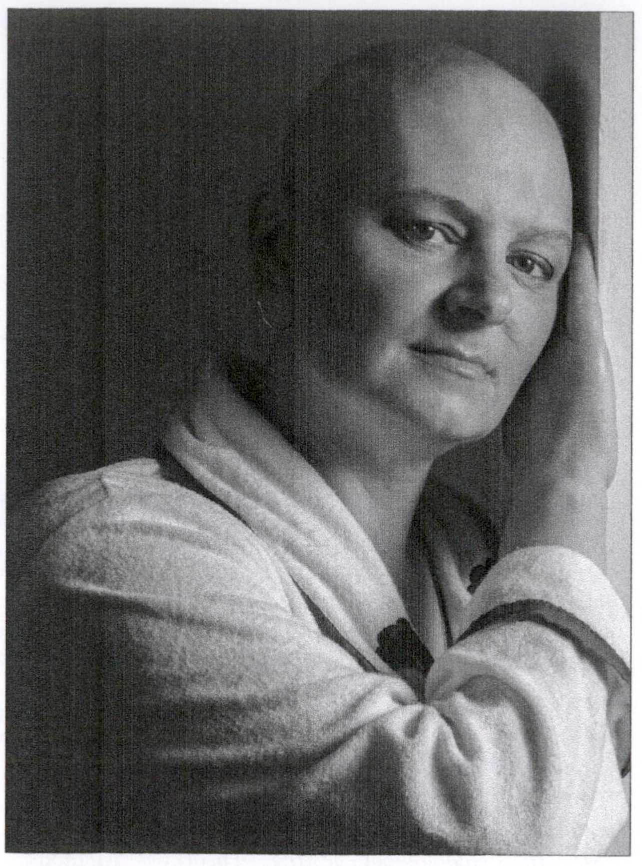

Photo: iStock

CHANGES IN LIFE VIEW

Dealing with a potentially life-threatening condition such as cancer causes people to review their lives and decide what is important to them. As a result, they may change jobs or retire, devote more time to their loved ones, or even leave a problem relationship. They may also find the strength to accomplish things that previously seemed impossible. Cancer survivors often state that they feel that their cancer was a gift in a way because it led them to appreciate their lives more and to make difficult but desired changes.

Living with cancer can increase people's courage as they learn to face their mortality and the uncertainty of their future life and to value their relationships. Studies involving breast and ovarian cancer survivors describe the redefinition of the patient's self. People often define themselves by their appearance or by a favorite body feature such as their hair or their figure. Cancer can force patients to redefine themselves, which is a very difficult task.

Another emotional issue faced by cancer patients is that many blame themselves for getting cancer. In the past, some experts theorized that people with certain personalities or who had particular reactions to stressful situations were more likely to develop cancer. However, it has been proved that this is not the case. People cannot prevent cancer by their mental efforts, nor can they cure it by imagining bodily defenses destroying it. However, leading a healthful lifestyle can lower people's risk of developing cancer, although it cannot prevent it entirely.

PEOPLE AFFECTED

Cancer affects people of all ages, not just adults. Children often cope well with cancer because they are better able to focus on the moment and not worry about the past or future. They do not judge their experiences but rather adapt to their lives as they are. Adolescents can find cancer particularly difficult to deal with because they want most to fit in with their peers. They do not want to be different and to stand out from the crowd, as a sick person does. Cancer most often attacks adults, who have choices as to how to deal with the changes in their health. Young adults tend to be angry because of the impact of cancer on their lives and feel that it is not fair that they have the disease. Older adults are more likely to be aware that they are at risk for conditions such as cancer and that they are not going to live forever. For the elderly, cancer can be more problematic. If they have been struggling with the changes of advanced age, cancer can be another sign that life is coming to an end. In fact, research has demonstrated that older people are more likely than younger people to commit suicide after a cancer diagnosis.

In addition to the cancer patient, the family of the patient suffers. Every day, family members are faced with a sick individual, who may not be able to contribute to family life as before. In some cases, it may be necessary to get outside care for the cancer patient, such as a home health aide or a nurse. Family members also must deal with the fear that the patient will die. Having a family member with cancer can be a heavy burden, and support for families of cancer patients can be hard to find.

TREATMENT OPTIONS

There is no formal treatment for mental health issues related to cancer. Patients who are receiving cancer treatments often have the support of the medical staff, but once patients have completed treatment, they are typically on their own in dealing with mental health issues. If patients have severe mental health issues, most likely their physicians will make sure that they get psychiatric care. However, patients with less severe mental problems must seek out support on their own. Many medical centers have support groups for patients with specific types of cancer. Support groups can vary in their effectiveness, although if a medical professional conducts the group, it is more likely to be helpful. A medical professional, such as a registered nurse, can draw generalizations from patient issues and assist patients in searching for solutions to their problems. Some patient-led support groups can become forums in which patients vent their frustrations and complain but accomplish nothing constructive.

When dealing with a cancer diagnosis, patients need to provide much of their own mental health care. After being diagnosed, patients should take the time to understand what they are facing and how they feel about it. Their feelings are normal, as are their fears. Instead of trying to be upbeat, patients should focus on confronting their feelings and, when possible, letting them go.

Often when people have a serious illness, their family members are able to express the love that they have for them by providing assistance and emotional support. There are many stories of how a cancer diagnosis strengthened a marriage or other family relationship. Most of the time, people forget that everyone will die and that there is no apparent schedule for this. A diagnosis of a life-threatening disease can force family members to realize that they could lose a loved one. As a result, they no longer take each other for granted, but rather begin to express their love every day.

Cancer patients may find it difficult to deal with the reactions of others. Some people may voice platitudes such as "It will all work out for the best." This type of statement is not particularly helpful to cancer patients, but it does reflect the difficulty that society has in dealing with serious illness and death. Other people may just ignore the fact that the patient has cancer. People have the tendency to try to insulate themselves from the reality that a friend or loved one has cancer. They find it hard to deal with a person's cancer because it forces them to confront their own fears.

Ideally, cancer patients should learn as much as they can about their condition and its treatments. It is better that they approach their physicians with questions or suggestions than that they remain passive and defer to whatever the physician chooses. Becoming involved with their treatment and learning about their disease gives cancer patients a feeling of having some control and power in a situation in which it is easy to feel powerless. Cancer patients should try to control whatever aspects of their care and treatment they can. Even a small thing such as scheduling treatments according to the patient's schedule can help the patient feel some control.

Although cancer is certainly anger provoking, patients should try to let go of their anger. Anger is a normal emotion, but it can escalate symptoms such as pain and stomach upset and can increase emotional pain.

Humor may seem impossible when facing cancer, but it can be helpful to the patient who is facing cancer. The cancer patient should try to see the humor in some of the situations in which they find themselves. There is absurdity in many of the situations that life presents, even cancer. Cancer patients may find that humorous movies or television programs can help cheer them up. Writer Norman Cousins describes using laughter therapy to treat his neurological disease in *Anatomy of an Illness* (1979).

Cancer patients should insist that they be treated with respect by their health care providers. They should find a physician who treats them as a peer and member of the treatment team. If patients encounter condescension on the part of their physician or the medical staff, they should find another physician. Cancer patients should tolerate nothing less than respect from their physicians.

Cancer patients should do whatever it takes to nourish their spirit. Many people find it helpful to speak with a spiritual leader, to attend religious services, and to pray. Many religions involve an afterlife, which can be quite comforting for cancer patients.

Alternative medicine—therapies such as acupuncture, reflexology, and Reiki—may decrease the level of stress and pain in cancer patients. Massage therapy can help cancer patients relax mentally and physically. Vitamin supplements, herbs, or herbal tea (taken with the permission and knowledge of the doctor treating the cancer) may comfort patients or help them feel more whole. Visualization and meditation can assist cancer patients in coping with the changes in their lives and give them strength to deal with their treatments or pain.

Cancer patients should not be reluctant to ask for help from family members, friends, or outside agencies. The goal for cancer patients should be to simplify their lives so that they can rest when necessary and make the most out of life.

BIBLIOGRAPHY

Bertero, Carina, and Margaret Chamberlain Wilmoth. "Breast Cancer Diagnosis and Its Treatment Affecting the Self: A Meta Analysis." *Cancer Nursing* 30.3 (2007): 194–202. Print.

Botti, Mari, et al. "Barriers in Providing Psychosocial Support for Patients with Cancer." *Cancer Nursing* 29.4 (2006): 309–16. Print.

Carr, Brian I., and Jennifer Steel, eds. *Psychological Aspects of Cancer.* New York: Springer, 2013. Print.

Healy, Bernadine. *Living Time: Faith and Facts to Transform Your Cancer Journey.* New York: Bantam, 2007. Print.

Galgut, Cordelia. *The Psychological Impact of Breast Cancer.* Abingdon: Radcliffe, 2010. Print.

Schnipper, Hester Hill. *After Breast Cancer: A Common Sense Guide to Life After Treatment.* New York: Bantam, 2003. Print.

Thiboldeaux, Kim, and Mitch Golant. *The Total Cancer Wellness Guide.* Dallas: Benbella, 2007. Print.

Wise, Thomas N., Massimo Biondi, and Anna Costantini, eds. *Psycho-Oncology.* Arlington: American Psychiatric Pub., 2013. Print.

Christine M. Carroll

See Also: Anger; Coping: Chronic illness; Coping: Terminal illness; Death and dying; Denial; Depression; Exercise and mental health; Grieving; Hope and mental health; Hospice; Kübler-Ross, Elisabeth; Pain; Pain management; Self-help groups; Social support and mental health; Spirituality and mental health; Support groups.

Cannon, Walter Bradford

Born: October 19, 1871, in Prairie du Chien, Wisconsin
Died: October 1, 1945, in Franklin, New Hampshire
Identity: American physiologist
Type of psychology: Biological basis of behavior

Cannon was an American physiologist, known for a series of experimental investigations into the process of digestion, the nervous system, and the body's self-regulating mechanisms.

Walter Bradford Cannon earned his bachelor's, master's, and medical degrees from Harvard University, where he became a professor of physiology. Cannon served as chair of Harvard's physiology department from 1906 to 1942.

Cannon began his investigations in 1896, one year after German physicist Wilhelm Conrad Röntgen discovered X rays. Cannon used X rays to observe the process of digestion in laboratory animals. Using an instrument called a fluoroscope, he watched the progress of food and waste through the body. During these experiments, he noticed that when an animal was under stress, its digestive processes halted. This led him to wonder about the body's response to danger, fear, and trauma.

Using mainly surgical and chemical means, Cannon investigated the response of the heart, the sympathetic nervous system, and the adrenal gland to unnatural circumstances. He also studied the body's self-regulating mechanisms, and especially the work of nineteenth century French physiologist Claude Bernard, who investigated carbohydrate metabolism in humans as well as the function of the autonomic nervous system. The basis of health, according to Bernard, is the organism's success in maintaining a dynamic internal equilibrium. Cannon named this dynamic state " homeostasis" and showed that the body could adjust to meet serious external danger through such processes of the human body as internal regulation of body heat and alkalinity of the blood and preparation of the body for defense by the secretion of epinephrine (also called adrenaline) in the adrenal gland.

Beginning in 1931, Cannon suffered from cancer associated with the X-ray exposures that he underwent early in his career. He remained active in national scientific circles, however, overseeing the organization of research for the effective treatment of shock and blood loss during World War II. He died in 1945.

BIBLIOGRAPHY

Benison, Saul, Elin L. Wolfe, and A. Clifford Barger. *Walter B. Cannon: The Life and Times of a Young Scientist*. Cambridge, Mass.: Belknap Press, 1987. The first volume of a biography of Cannon, covering his childhood, training, and early years as a scientist.

Wolfe, Elin L., Saul Benison, and A. Clifford Barger. *Walter B. Cannon: Science and Society*. Cambridge, Mass.: Harvard University Press, 2000. The second volume of Cannon's biography, taking up the story from World War I through the end of his life.

Mary E. Carey

See Also: Adrenal gland; Animal experimentation; Fight-or-flight response; General adaptation syndrome; Stress: Physiological responses; Stress-related diseases.

Career and personnel testing

Type of psychology: Personality

The popularity of career and personnel testing reflects the trend toward the utilization of interest surveys, ability and aptitude tests, and personality tests for the systematic development of personal careers.

Key Concepts

- Achievement tests
- Aptitude tests
- Intelligence tests
- Interest inventories
- Personality tests
- Value tests

INTRODUCTION

Psychologists have developed numerous testing devices for assessing human capabilities. The groups of tests that have been used most frequently for career and personnel purposes have been those measuring interests, abilities and aptitudes, personality, and values.

Inventories that survey interest patterns are useful in providing indications of the areas in which individuals might work. Research by psychologist Edward K. Strong Jr. has shown that people in the same line of work also tend to have similar hobbies, like the same types of books and magazines, and prefer the same types of entertainment.

Psychological research by John L. Holland concluded that most occupations can be grouped into six vocational themes reflecting certain employment preferences: "realistic," favoring technical and outdoor activities such as mechanical, agricultural, and nature jobs; "investigative," interested in the natural sciences, medicine, and the process of investigation; "artistic," favoring self-expression and dramatics such as the musical, literary, and graphic art occupations; "social," reflecting an interest in helping others, as in teaching and social service; "enterprising," interested in persuasion and political power, as in management, sales, politics, and other areas of leadership; and "conventional," including enjoyment of procedures and organization such as office practices, clerical, and quantitative interest areas.

Tests that measure ability include intelligence tests, achievement tests, and aptitude tests. Intelligence tests purport to measure objectively a person's potential to learn, independent of prior learning experiences. Attempting such objective measurement is a highly complex task; whether it can truly be achieved is open to debate. The very concept of "intelligence," in fact, has been controversial from its inception. The most highly developed tests of individual intelligence include updated versions of the Stanford-Binet test, a scale originally developed in 1916, and the Wechsler Adult Intelligence Scale, originally developed in 1939.

Achievement tests are designed to measure how much a person has learned of specific material to which he or she has been previously exposed. Aptitude tests measure a personal ability or quality (such as musical or mechanical aptitude) to predict some future performance. For example, the military would like to be able to predict the likelihood that a given candidate for pilot training will successfully complete the complicated and expensive course of training. Flying a plane requires good physical coordination and a good sense of mechanical matters, among other things. Therefore, candidates for flight training are given a battery of aptitude tests, which include tests of mechanical aptitude and eye-hand coordination, to estimate later performance in flight training. People who score poorly on such aptitude tests tend to fail pilot training.

Psychologists recognize that it is important to understand a person's interests and abilities—and personality tendencies—if a thorough appraisal of career potentials is to be made. Personality tests, also often known as personality rating scales, measure dispositions, traits, or tendencies to behave in a typical manner. Personality tests are described as either objective (a structured test) or subjective (a projective personality test). Objective tests are structured by providing a statement and then requiring two or more alternative responses, such as in true-or-false questions in the Woodworth Personal Data Sheet. In contrast, projective personality tests ask open-ended questions or provide ambiguous stimuli that require spontaneous responses (as in the Rorschach inkblot test). The two types of personality test reveal different information about the respondent.

The development of objective personality tests was greatly improved when studies showed that personality tests did not have to rely completely on face validity, or the apparent accuracy of each test question. Through empirical research, the accuracy of a question can be tied to the likelihood of a question being associated with certain behavior. Consequently, it does not matter whether a person answers the question "I am not aggressive" as either "true" or "false." What does matter is whether that question is accurately associated with aggressive or nonaggressive behavior for a significant number of people who answer it in a particular way. This approach is referred to as criterion keying: The items in a test are accurately associated with certain types of behavior regardless of the face validity of each question.

Beginning with Gordon Allport's study of values, psychologists have recognized that personal values affect individual career choices. Allport found six general values that are important to most individuals: theoretical, economic, aesthetic, social, political, and religious. Occupational values represent a grouping of needs, just as abilities represent a grouping of work skills. René Dawis and Lloyd Lofquist found that there are six occupational values: achievement, comfort, status, altruism, safety, and autonomy.

TESTING IN PRACTICE

For people to enter careers that will be satisfactory for them, it is desirable to make an effort to match their personal interests with the day-to-day activities of the careers they will eventually choose. Interest inventories are one method of helping people make career choices that compare their interest patterns with the activities of persons in the occupation they hope to enter.

The Strong Vocational Interest Blank (SVIB) was developed by Strong. It matches the interests of a person to the interests and values of a criterion group of employed people who were happy in the careers they have chosen. This procedure is an example of criterion keying. Strong revised the SVIB in 1966, using 399 items to relate to fifty-four occupations for men and a separate form for thirty-two occupations for women. The reliability of this test to measure interests is quite good, and validity studies indicate that the SVIB is effective in predicting job satisfaction.

The Strong-Campbell Interest Inventory (SCII) was developed by psychologist D. T. Campbell as a revision of the SVIB. In this test, items from the men's and women's forms were merged into a single scale, reducing the likelihood of gender bias, a complaint made about the SVIB. Campbell developed a theoretical explanation of why certain types of people like working in certain fields; he based it on Holland's theory of vocational choice. Holland postulated that interests are an expression of personality and that people can be classified into one or more of six categories according to their interests and personality. Campbell concluded that the six personality factors in Holland's theory were quite similar to the patterns of interest that had emerged from many years of research on the SVIB. Therefore, Holland's theory became incorporated into the SCII. The SCII places individuals into one of the six Holland categories, or groupings of occupations, with each group represented by a national sample.

The Kuder Occupational Interest Survey (KOIS) was first developed in 1939. This survey also examines the similarity between the respondent's interests and the interests of people employed in different occupations. It can provide direction in the selection of a college major. Studies on the predictive validity of the KOIS indicate that about half of a selected group of adults who had been given an early version of the inventory when they were in high school were working in fields that the inventory suggested they enter. The continuing development of this measure suggests that it may be quite useful for guidance decisions for high school and college students.

The Self-Directed Search (SDS) was developed by Holland as a means of matching the interests and abilities of individuals with occupations that have the same characteristics. Holland uses a typology that groups occupations in the categories of realistic, investigative, artistic, social, enterprising, and conventional. There are three forms of the SDS: Form E is designed for use with middle-school students or older individuals with limited reading ability; Form R is for use with high school students, college students, or adults; and Form CP is designed for use with college students and adults. The test is also available in other languages, such as Spanish.

Several ability and aptitude tests have been used in making decisions concerning employment, placement, and promotion. The Wonderlic Personnel Test (WPT), later renamed the Wonderlic Cognitive Ability Test, was based on the Otis Self-Administering Tests of Mental Ability. The Wonderlic Cognitive Ability Test is a quick test of mental ability in adults. Normative data are available for more than fifty thousand adults between twenty and seventy-five years of age. The Revised Minnesota Paper Form Board Test (RMPFBT) is a revision of a study in the measurement of mechanical ability. The RMPFBT is a twenty-minute speed test consisting of two-dimensional diagrams cut into separate parts. The test seems to measure those aspects of mechanical ability requiring the capacity to visualize and manipulate objects in space. It appears to be related to general intelligence.

The US Department of Labor developed an instrument to measure abilities known as the General Aptitude Test Battery (GATB). The GATB measures nine specific abilities: general learning, verbal ability, numerical ability, spatial ability, form perception, clerical perception, eye-hand coordination, finger dexterity, and manual dexterity. Another ability test that was developed by the US government is the Armed Services Vocational Aptitude Battery (ASVAB). The ASVAB is used by the Department of Defense to assist individuals in identifying occupations that match their personal characteristics.

Personality tests were developed in an effort to gain greater understanding about how an individual is likely to behave. As tests have been improved, specific traits and characteristics have been associated with career development, such as leadership propensities or control of impulses. Several personality tests have been used in career and personality development. The Minnesota Multiphasic Personality Inventory II Restructured Form (MMPI-2-RF) is the 2008 version of a scale developed in 1943 by S. R. Hathaway and J. C. McKinley. The test was designed to distinguish normal from abnormal behavior. It was derived from a pool of one thousand items selected from a wide variety of sources. The California Psychological Inventory (CPI) was developed by Harrison Gough in 1957 and was revised in 1987. The test is regarded as a good measure for assessing normal individuals for interpersonal effectiveness and internal controls.

The Sixteen Personality Factor Questionnaire (16PF) was developed by Raymond Cattell in 1949 and was revised in 1993. Considerable effort has been expended to provide a psychometrically sound instrument to measure personality, and it remains an exemplary illustration of the factor-analytic approach to measuring personality traits. The Personality Research Form (PRF) was developed by Douglas Jackson in 1967. It was based on Henry A. Murray's theory of needs. The PRF includes two validity scales and twenty multidimensional scales of personality traits. It has been favorably reviewed for its psychometric rigor and is useful in relating personality tendencies to strengths and weaknesses in working within a corporate or employment setting.

Tests to measure occupational values include the Minnesota Importance Questionnaire (MIQ), developed by David Weiss, René Dawis, and Lloyd Lofquist, and the Values Scale (VS), developed by Doris Nevill and

Donald Super. The MIQ compares individual needs with reinforcers found in occupations. The VS measures work values that are commonly sought by workers, such as personal development and achievement. The values in the test are also cross-referenced with the occupational groups found in Holland's typology.

An alternative to paper-and-pen tests is the use of computerized career guidance systems, which may consist of specialized software or web-based programs. The common elements of these systems include the use of an assessment instrument, the provision of an individualized detailed occupational profile, and instructions on how to use the information in career planning.

FUNCTIONS OF TESTING

These instruments are examples of tests that are frequently used for career and personnel assessment. The range of psychological assessment procedures includes not only standardized ability tests, interest surveys, personality inventories and projective instruments, and diagnostic and evaluative devices but also performance tests, biographical data forms, scored application blanks, interviews, experience requirement summaries, appraisals of job performance, and estimates of advancement potential. All these devices are used, and they are explicitly intended to aid employers who make hiring decisions to choose, select, develop, evaluate, and promote personnel. Donald N. Bersoff notes that the critical element in the use of any psychological test for career and employment purposes is that employers must use psychometrically sound and job-relevant selection devices. Such tests must be scientifically reliable (appropriate, meaningful, or useful for the inferences drawn from them) and valid (measuring what they claim to measure).

Each of the test procedures previously described would be used for different purposes. Ability tests can be used to determine whether a person has the potential ability to learn a certain job or specific skills. Ability tests are used for positions that do not have a minimum educational prerequisite (such as high school, college, or professional degree). They are also used to select already employed individuals for challenging new work assignments and for promotion to a more demanding employment level. The United States Supreme Court has held that the appropriate use of "professionally developed ability tests" is an acceptable employment practice; however, the employer must demonstrate a relationship between the relevance of the selection test procedure and job qualification. This requirement is to ensure that the ability test provides a fair basis for selection and is nondiscriminatory. The goal of Title VII of the Civil Rights Act of 1964 was to eliminate discrimination in employment based on race, color, religion, sex, or national origin in all of its forms. The use of a selection procedure or test must meet this standard.

Interest inventories have been developed to identify a relationship between the activities a person enjoys and the activities of a certain occupation. For example, a salesperson should enjoy meeting people and persuading others to accept his or her viewpoint. An interest inventory can validly link a person's preferences and interests with associated social activities and can thereby identify sales potential. Interest inventories are frequently given when an employer seeks more information that could lead to a good match between a prospective employee and a job's requirements. Interest inventories typically survey a person's interests in leisure or sports activities, types of friends, school subjects, and preferred reading material.

Personality, or behavior traits, can be identified by test inventories and related to requisite employment activities. Once again, these personality dimensions must be demonstrated to be job-related and must be assessed reliably from a performance appraisal of the specific position to be filled. For example, behavior traits such as "drive" or "dependability" could be validated for use in promoting individuals to supervisory bank teller positions if demonstrated to be job-related and assessed reliably from a performance appraisal.

The use of psychological tests has grown immensely since the mid-twentieth century. Increased public awareness, the proliferation of different tests, and the use of computer technology with tests indicate that continually improving career and personnel tests will emerge. Yet these developments should proceed only if testing can be conducted while protecting the human rights of consumers—including their right not to be tested and their right to know test scores and how test-based decisions will affect their lives. Psychological testing must also be nondiscriminatory and must protect the person's right to privacy. Psychologists are ethically and legally bound to maintain the confidentiality of their clients.

Making a selection among the many published psychological tests is a skill requiring experienced psychologists. In personnel selection, the psychologist must determine if the use of a psychological test will improve the selection process above what is referred to as the base rate, or the probability of an individual succeeding at a job without any selection procedure. Consequently, the use of a test must be based on its contributing something beyond chance alone. This requirement necessitates that a test be reasonably valid and reliable, in that it consistently tests what it was designed to test. Consequently, the use of a test is only justified when it can contribute to the greater likelihood of a successful decision than would be expected by existing base rates.

Existing theories of career selection have related career choices to personal preferences, developmental stages, and the type of relationship a person has had with his or her family during childhood. More extensive research will continue to assess other relationships between one's psychological makeup and successful career selection. This positive beginning should eventually result in more innovative, more objective, and more valid psychological tests that will greatly enhance future career and personnel selection.

BIBLIOGRAPHY

American Psychological Association. "Ethical Principles of Psychologists." *American Psychologist* 36 (1981): 633–38. Print.

Bersoff, Donald N., Laurel P. Malson, and Donald B. Verrilli. "In the Supreme Court of the United States: Clara Watson v. Fort Worth Bank and Trust." *American Psychologist* 43 (1988): 1019–28. Print.

Buros Institute of Mental Measurement. *The Fourteenth Mental Measurements Yearbook.* Lincoln: U of Nebraska P, 2001. Print.

Campbell, Donald Thomas. *Manual for the Strong-Campbell Interest Inventory.* Stanford: Stanford UP, 2001. Print.

Capuzzi, David, and Mark D. Stauffer, eds. *Career Counseling: Foundations, Perspectives, and Applications.* New York: Routledge, 2012. Print.

Committee to Develop Standards for Educational and Psychological Testing. *Standards for Educational and Psychological Testing.* Washington: American Psychological Association, 1999. Print.

Darley, John M., Samuel Glucksberg, and Ronald A. Kinchia. *Psychology.* 5th ed. Englewood Cliffs: Prentice-Hall, 1991. Print.

Holland, John L. *Manual for the Self-Directed Search.* Palo Alto: Consulting Psychologists, 1985. Print.

Kapes, Jerome T., Marjorie Moran Mastie, and Edwin A. Whitfeld. *A Counselor's Guide to Career Assessment Instruments.* Broken Arrow: National Career Development Association, 2008. Print.

Koppes, Laura L., ed. *Historical Perspectives in Industrial and Organizational Psychology.* New York: Psychology, 2014. Print.

Swanson, Jane L., and Nadya A. Fouad. *Career Theory and Practice: Learning through Case Studies.* Los Angeles: Sage, 2010. Print.

Zunker, Vernon. *Using Assessment Results for Career Development.* Belmont: Brooks, 2006. Print.

Robert A. Hock; updated by Debra S. Preston

See Also: Ability tests; Allport, Gordon; Assessment; Career Occupational Preference System (COPS); Creativity: Assessment; General Aptitude Test Battery (GATB); Human resource training and development; Intelligence tests; Interest inventories; Kuder Occupational Interest Survey (KOIS); Scientific methods; Stanford-Binet test; Strong Interest Inventory (SII); Survey research: Questionnaires and interviews; Testing: Historical Perspectives; Wechsler Intelligence Scale for Children-Third Edition (WISC-III).

Career occupational preference system (COPS)

Date: 1960s forward
Type of psychology: Intelligence and intelligence testing

Career interest inventories such as the COPS have been developed to assist people in making career-planning decisions. The COPS purports to assess certain abilities, interests, and other characteristics and matches them with characteristics of jobs, occupations, college majors, and careers. These selections imply that an individual can make better decisions with the help of an interest inventory.

Key Concepts

- Career
- Interest inventory
- Job choice

INTRODUCTION

The Career Occupational Preference System (COPS), an interest inventory, presents 168 job-related items that can be grouped into fourteen job-determinant areas: science, professional; science, skilled; technology, professional; technology, skilled; consumer economics; outdoor; business, professional; business, skilled; clerical; communication; arts, professional; arts, skilled; service, professional; and service, skilled. The descriptor professional can be best characterized as referring to those job choices that require at least four years of college education and lead to a career, as opposed to those that do not.

The person completing the inventory is asked to rate the 168 job-related items, noting whether these are things they like very much, like moderately, dislike moderately, or dislike very much. The person completing the inventory uses the scale to state preferences concerning a number of different job activities.

The COPS was first developed in the late 1960s and has undergone several editions and revisions. Editions in foreign languages are available. Although the test is untimed, most individuals who take the test finish in less than one hour. The scores recorded by the COPS can be used to enter most occupational information systems. Both professionals and nonprofessionals can benefit from information received from the COPS. However, like most reference or interest systems, the COPS should be used to guide exploration and not judge respondents. Given the reading level of the inventory and the types of information solicited, it would be appropriate for the COPS to be used in junior high schools, senior high schools, community colleges, and four-year colleges and universities.

TECHNICAL ASPECTS

The COPS has been developed and interpreted through the statistical procedure of multiple-factor analysis. The purpose of this type of analysis is to understand which sets of variables match up or correlate best with one another. For example, are the "professional" and "skilled" items the same or different? If the cluster of items is the same, reporting and interpreting the scores would be influenced one way; however, if the cluster of items is different, the way the scores are reported and interpreted would be very different. With that in mind, it is possible to suggest that all fourteen clusters present as "different" when using this statistical procedure.

In addition to the statistical procedure of multiple-factor analysis of the variables in the cluster, it is equally important to understand whether the items themselves are relevant to the world of work.

Additionally, the specific descriptions used in the clusters should match up, specifically, to the world of work. For example, descriptions of skills used in the clerical cluster should generally deal with clerical duties and specifically detail expected clerical duties. Without this type of matching, much of the usefulness of the COPS would be compromised. The 168 items used in the COPS match both the general and the specific nature of clusters. This provides further evidence that individual scores do match what might be expected during the accomplishment of the fourteen general clusters.

Of equal importance is whether the COPS can be considered statistically reliable, whether it is internally consistent (demonstrated by correlation studies), and whether it can be relied on to give the same results over time (demonstrated by time-sequential statistical correlation studies). It is difficult to place much confidence in a survey that does not hold together or that does not give the same results over time; therefore, these factors are extremely important to the usefulness of the COPS as an assessment.

The COPS does well on both counts of reliability considerations. Reports of internal consistency, parallel forms (different items for the same clusters from completely different, independent tests), and tests given after time periods ranging from one week to one year all point to the usefulness of the COPS. In fact, COPS scores do seem to point to a similarity between attained scores and choices of college major, actual job location, and actual job title.

CRITIQUE

For individuals to enter an appropriate career, they must begin to identify specific interests and examine the relative importance of those interests. Some individuals will need little guidance in making career choices, while others will need the guidance of a survey instrument such as the COPS interest inventory when beginning the process of career selection. In the decades since the introduction of the first interest inventory, millions of people have received important information to use in decision making. Caution is always expressed by the authors of these inventories that no decision should be made on the basis of the results determined by one inventory. The COPS interest inventory is only one of many inventories in use within the broad field of career and personnel testing.

BIBLIOGRAPHY

Bauernfeind, R. H. "COPSystem Interest Inventory." *Test Critiques*. Vol. 5. Austin: Pro-Ed, 1992. Print.

Brown, Steven D., and Robert W. Lent, eds. *Career Development and Counseling: Putting Theory and Research to Work.* Hoboken: Wiley, 2013. Print.

Capuzzi, David, and Mark D. Stauffer, eds. *Career Counseling: Foundations, Perspectives, and*

Applications. New York: Routledge, 2012. Print.

Murphy, L. L., and J. C. Conoley, eds. *Tests in Print* IV. Vol. 1. Lincoln: Buros Institute of Mental Measurements, 1994. Print.

Quinn, Barbara. *Snap, Crackle, or Stop: Change Your Career and Shape Your Own Destiny.* New York: Basic, 2003. Print.

Swanson, Jane L., and Nadya A. Fouad. *Career Theory and Practice: Learning through Case Studies.* Los Angeles: Sage, 2010. Print.

Daniel L. Yazak

See Also: Ability tests; Assessment; Career and personnel testing; College entrance examinations; Creativity: Assessment; General Aptitude Test Battery (GATB); Human resource training and development; Intelligence tests; Interest inventories; Kuder Occupational Interest Survey (KOIS); Peabody Individual Achievement Test (PIAT); Race and intelligence; Scientific methods; Stanford-Binet test; Strong Interest Inventory (SII); Survey research: Questionnaires and interviews; Testing: Historical Perspectives; Wechsler Intelligence Scale for Children-Third Edition (WISC-III)

Career selection, development, and change

Type of psychology: Developmental psychology

The world of work is changing at an increasingly rapid rate, and many working people find themselves forced to find new careers. By examining their personal interests and needs as well as the possibilities for financial rewards in a given field, those people selecting or changing careers can be more certain of career satisfaction and success.

Key Concepts

- Career
- Career choice
- Career development
- Career transition
- Re-careering
- Redirection

INTRODUCTION

A review of theories prominent in the psychology of career development points to their profound preoccupation with the idea that adults must work. The average adult spends more time working than performing any other waking activity. Satisfaction in one's career has been found empirically to have the potential for fulfilling such needs as productivity, competition, altruism, functioning as a team member, and independence. It is the most important avenue for fulfilling one's dreams. These studies also reveal that both personality traits and career interest change over time.

The definitions of career, career choice, and career development emphasize the idea that careers unfold throughout the life span and therefore require that individuals have the skills to adapt to these changes. According to Carl McDaniels in Rich Feller and Garry Walz's *Career Transitions in Turbulent Times* (1997), a career is defined as the totality of work and leisure experiences over a life span. Career choice refers to the decisions that individuals make at any point in their careers. Career development encompasses the total constellation of psychological, sociological, educational, physical, economic, and chance factors that combine to shape the career of any given individual over the life span. Thus, individuals are constantly in a state of career development that often results in career change.

CAREER CHOICE AND CHANGE

The reasons individuals select certain occupations are varied. Frank Parsons's trait factor model of the early 1900s matched personal traits to job characteristics. Its assumptions included the idea that people possess stable and persistent traits, among them interests, talents, and intelligence. A related assumption was that jobs could be differentiated in terms of their needs for differing skills and levels of ability. The person with certain traits could therefore be matched with certain job needs, and the individual would be satisfied forever. Psychological testing became prominently used to measure traits and to classify occupations.

Parsons's basic tenets were expanded by John L. Holland in 1959. Numerous studies have supported his contention that individuals in similar jobs have similar interests and abilities. His highly respected and useful research resulted in the development of six categories of persons and jobs: realistic (R), investigative (I), artistic (A), social (S), enterprising (E), and conventional (C). Holland assumes that most people have a dominant type and one or two other types of some, but lesser, importance. To reflect this belief, he arranged the typology in a clockwise order around a hexagon, as R, I, A, S, E, C. He argues empirically that some types are more compatible and some are less compatible. The closer they are on the hexagon, the more compatible. For instance, RI, AS, and EC are examples of consistent types and have higher job achievement and satisfaction and more stable choices and personalities. RS, AC, and IE would be examples of those, therefore, who would have lower job achievement and satisfaction and less stable choices and personalities.

Holland leaves room, however, for change to occur. His basic belief is that personality type stabilizes between ages eighteen and thirty and is thereafter rather difficult to change. The more consistent a person's type is, the more he or she will find a satisfactory job environment. Consistent types, he says, will more often deal with job dissatisfaction by altering the work environment rather than by changing their own personalities. The need for a new repertoire of skills, new training, and new credentialing when making drastic career changes tends to reduce the amount of personality change people must make. In other words, changing careers, even when this requires reeducation, may be preferred over major changes in personality.

DEVELOPMENT AND TRANSITION

McDaniels has converged the works of Parsons, Holland, and Donald Edwin Super into an approach called developmental trait factor. From this point of view, career development consists of a continuous interaction of work and leisure across the life span in a series of transitional situations. Career choices are made that reflect the individual's interests and abilities at a certain point in time, but the choices will need to be reevaluated periodically as the individual grows and the surrounding world changes.

Nancy Schlossberg states that individuals are more likely than not to experience a career transition at some point in their lives. She defines a transition as any event or nonevent that results in a change in relationships, routines, assumptions, or role within self, work, family, health, or economics. A unique aspect of transitions as defined by Schlossberg is that nonevents can result in life changes. Examples of nonevents are anticipated promotions that did not occur and unexpected job layoffs. Thus, transitions, whether anticipated or not, involve a process of continuing and changing reactions over time that are linked to the individual's continuous and changing appraisal of self in the situation.

An important contributor to the psychology of careers is Donald Super, who states that career choice develops in five stages: growth (birth through age fourteen), exploration (ages fourteen through twenty-five), establishment (ages twenty-five through forty-five), maintenance (ages forty-five through sixty-five), and decline or disengagement (age sixty-six and older). He refers to this long-term developmental process as the "maxicycle." He emphasizes, however, that as a person matures and becomes more realistic, the possibility of career change may direct the individual into a new job or even an entirely new career. The maxicycle may then be repeated from the beginning in a very brief time frame, in "minicycle" form. In changing to the new position, the person experiences growth, exploration, establishment, and maintenance, but they are focused into days, weeks, or months rather than years.

CAREER SATISFACTION

Major psychological theories of career development recognize the possibility, and even probability, of change. The change may be in job choices within a particular career, a process of redirecting one's energies with a minimum of reschooling. The change may, however, involve more than redirection and move into major recareering. The reasons for this shift are especially important to psychologists who believe that career satisfaction invades all facets of psychological wholeness. They believe that adults work for more than a livelihood. Otherwise, the rich would cease working and those who could perform high-paying jobs would not choose work that pays much less than their earnable income.

Super studied numerous lists of human motives, of reasons for working and of reasons people like or dislike jobs. These lists emanated from the research of a variety of students of human nature. His comparison and reduction of these lists pointed to three major needs for which satisfaction is sought: human relations, the work itself, and livelihood. Human relations involve the recognition of the person, independence, fair treatment, and status. Work means that the activity is interesting, is an opportunity for self-expression, and has a satisfying physical work situation and conditions. Livelihood refers to adequate earnings and security. Although Super's work is a product of the 1950s, it is regularly updated. He added self-realization to his motives for working, a common term used in humanistic psychology to emphasize the integration or wholeness that Carl R. Rogers believed achievable by the "fully functioning individual." Work has the potential for satisfying personal determinants that are psychological and biological, as well as satisfying situational determinants that are historical and socioeconomic.

From Super's lengthy and impressive research, the implications for change in careers are noteworthy. The frustration of any one or a combination of the three basic satisfactions sought in work (human relations, interesting work, and livelihood) that hinders one from achieving self-realization is sufficient motivation for change. To say it negatively, one may feel frustration in human relations because of lack of recognition, in work because tasks fail to maintain interest, or in livelihood because of insufficient earnings and security.

Super's work dealing with change based on changing interests and circumstances includes the idea that new careers emerge with changing times. The worker of the early twenty-first century has literally hundreds of new careers to consider. Scores of occupations are disappearing from the American scene and scores of new jobs are being added that did not exist twenty-five years ago. The shift from industrial jobs to high-tech jobs necessitates different job skills.

RE-CAREERING

The idea of changing careers, or recareering,is a contemporary phenomenon. Since the 1980s, hundreds of books have centered on the topic. A valuable asset to the reader of such books is a strong statistical message: People change jobs or careers several times during their tenure of work. One example of such a change might be a bank employee who moves to another bank but fills an entirely new position, with new requirements and job description (redirection). The job has actually changed. Redirection does not refer to the person who works in a bank and then moves to another bank in an identical position but at a higher salary. Career change includes both redirection and recareering. Another, more drastic example is of a social worker with a master's degree in social work. After nine years of listening to people's problems, she is burned out; she also finds the pay increments to be insufficient for her needs. She begins exploring the possibility of combining her interest in helping people with her developing interest in investment counseling (recareering).

Career change requires methodology. Self-help books on career change provide valuable advice as to the methods of recareering. They provide practical ideas on reassessing one's assets and liabilities, narrowing one's choices, determining one's career preferences, packaging or repackaging oneself, writing a resumé, and negotiating the career change. Such changes are often more easily executed within the same career. The individual, for example, who is in business marketing may, as he or she matures, decide that management rather than marketing would provide a greater challenge and better financial security. Such a career may not require reschooling as much as it does repackaging oneself as to interests, strengths, and desired goals. An actor who tires of acting may find new excitement in the areas of directing and producing.

One example of career change involves a man who began as a high school science teacher. He later became a high school principal. Still later, he changed to become a consultant for the Ohio State Board of Education. Finally, he took an administrative position at a liberal arts college. In his case, recareering involved additional graduate work and the meeting of certain requirements. He took all the suggested steps of reassessment, determining preferences, repackaging himself, interviewing, and negotiating the change. The necessary further education and meeting of certification requirements along the way seemed to be well worth the effort to him. The result is a professional educator with an obviously renewed zest for life because of the challenges of attaining desired goals. He was excited about his original job as high school science teacher, but as he changed, so did his interests and goals.

The literature, whether in the form of vocational guidance and career development, in the psychology of career counseling, or in the practical paperbacks that teach concrete steps to be taken, all carries the same theme: Career change is a skill that can be learned and applied with considerable success. Individuals are told in various ways, whether by noted theorists such as Super and Holland, or by practitioners such as McDaniels, Feingold, and others, to identify and communicate transferable skills or to acquire new job-related skills.

Ronald L. Krannich states that recareering is a process that means repeatedly acquiring marketable skills and then changing careers in response to one's own interests, needs, and goals, as well as in response to the changing needs and opportunities of a technological society. The standard careering process must be modified with three new careering emphases: acquiring new marketable skills through retraining on a regular basis, changing careers several times during a lifetime, and utilizing more efficient communication networks for finding employment. Sigmund Freud said very little about adulthood except that it is the time "to love and to work." A large segment of life's satisfaction derives from satisfaction in one's work and will, no doubt, carry over to enhance the chances of one's ability to love.

CAREER TESTING AND RESOURCES

Several tests have been developed to assist in the process of matching individual traits to comparable work environment traits. One example is Holland's Self-Directed Search (SDS). As a result of completing the SDS, users are assigned a two- or three-letter code (such as RI, AS, ECR) that will lead them to a list of occupations that should reflect their interests and abilities. Some tests have been developed that integrate matching traits with a developmental approach. An example is the Career Exploration Inventory (CEI) developed by John Liptak, which contains an interest inventory and also includes a career-planning component. The results of such career testing should not be the only factor in a person's decision to pursue a particular career, but aptitude tests and similar evaluations can provide valuable insights to those seeking direction.

Several career information resources have been developed to provide individuals with information on the world of work. One of the first of these resources was the *Dictionary of Occupational Titles* (DOT). The DOT was developed in 1972 by the US Employment Service and was regularly updated. It was a compendium of more than twelve thousand occupations, each one described and classified. The DOT was later superseded by the Occupational Information Network (O*NET), an online database of occupational requirements and worker attributes. The *Occupational Outlook Handbook*, managed by the US Bureau of Labor Statistics, is also available online and contains information on work environments, earnings, and job outlooks for specified occupations.

This theoretical emphasis on the complexity of human change had to be coupled with the societal phenomenon of dynamic technological change. More and greater changes are to come, as attested by the suggestions of researchers that future workers should be equipped with skills, flexibility, and the keen notion that their options should remain open throughout life.

BIBLIOGRAPHY

Alboher, Marci. *One Person/Multiple Careers: A New Model for Work/Life Success.* New York: Business Plus, 2007. Print.

Bolles, Richard. *What Color Is Your Parachute?* Rev. ed. Berkeley: Ten Speed, 2014. Print.

Brown, Steven D., and Robert W. Lent, eds. *Career Development and Counseling: Putting Theory and Research to Work.* 2nd ed. Hoboken: Wiley, 2013. Print.

Ducat, Diane Elizabeth. *Turning Points: Your Career Decision-Making Guide.* Upper Saddle River: Prentice Hall, 2002. Print.

Feller, Rich, and Garry Walz, eds. *Career Transitions in Turbulent Times.* Austin: Pro-Ed, 2007. Print.

Harvard Business Review, ed. *Harvard Business Review on Advancing Your Career.* Cambridge: Harvard Business School Pub., 2011. Print.

Krannich, Ronald L. *Re-Careering in Turbulent Times: Skills and Strategies for Success in Today's Job Market.* Manassas: Impact, 1983. Print.

Schlossberg, Nancy, and S. P. Robinson. *Going to Plan B: How You Can Cope, Regroup, and Start Your Life on a New Path.* New York: Simon, 1996. Print.

Super, Donald Edwin. *The Psychology of Careers: An Introduction to Vocational Development.* New York: Harper, 1957. Print.

US Dept. of Labor. *Dictionary of Occupational Titles.* Washington: Employment and Training Administration, 1991. Print.

US Dept. of Labor. *Occupational Outlook Handbook.* New York: McGraw-Hill, 2008. Print.

Vanderkam, Laura. *Grindhopping: Building a Rewarding Career without Paying Your Dues.* New York: McGraw-Hill, 2006. Print.

F. Wayne Reno; updated by Debra S. Preston

See Also: Ability tests; Career and personnel testing; Coaching; Human resource training and development; Interest inventories; Midlife crisis; Rogers, Carl R.; Self-actualization; Work motivation.

Case study methodologies

Type of psychology: Psychological methodologies

Case study methodologies examine a bounded system over time in detail, employing multiple sources of data found in that setting. The case may be a program, an event, an activity, or an individual. The researcher chooses the case and its boundary. A case can be selected because of its uniqueness or because of its typicality.

Key Concepts

- Anna O.
- Little Albert
- Little Hans
- Qualitative research
- Quantitative research

INTRODUCTION

In research using case study methodology, the researcher seeks to obtain a thorough knowledge and present a clear picture of an individual, a program, or a situation. Sometimes the researcher obtains this information over a long period of time. With the goal of investigating a contemporary phenomenon within its real-life context, case studies may include observations, interviews, anecdotes, vignettes, direct quotes, audiovisual materials, psychological testing, documents and reports, analysis, and naturalistic summaries. The richness of detail from these multiple sources makes case studies fascinating. In addition, the researcher typically provides key issues to illustrate the complexity of the situation. Often, the researcher ends with lessons learned or implications that might be applicable to similar cases.

Case study research has advantages and disadvantages. Advantages include being well-suited for the study of certain phenomena, particularly psychological disorders. Also, case studies can provide compelling illustrations to support a theory and can inspire new therapeutic techniques or unique applications of existing techniques. Disadvantages include depending on what observers choose to include, as their choices may be biased. Also, subjectivity makes it easy to see what one expects to see, and the person or phenomenon chosen for the case study may not be representative.

QUALITATIVE VERSUS QUANTITATIVE RESEARCH

Case study research is considered a qualitative experimental method. The term qualitative refers to the fact that researchers collect data in face-to-face situations by interacting with selected persons in a natural setting such as a school, a home, or a community.

A related type of qualitative research method is narrative research, but significant distinctions exist. Narrative research is chronological in focus and tells the story of an individual. Case studies, in contrast, focus on an issue, with the case selected to provide insight into that issue. Therefore, the focus in case study research is not predominantly on the whole person, as in narrative research, but on the issue illustrated by the case. Also, in case study research, the analytic approach involves a detailed description of the case, the setting within its environmental and cultural context, and a presentation that may or may not be chronological.

A contrasting type of research method is quantitative. Quantitative experimental designs typically study groups of individuals and rely on objective information. Correlation designs tell the association between two variables. Randomized, controlled experimental trials have control groups and can rule out the impact of extraneous factors that might account for findings. Case studies, in contrast, typically focus on the individual, rely on anecdotal information, and have no control groups. Case studies do not provide the arrangements that permit conclusions that are as clear as those available from experimentation. However, case studies can show the impact of treatment on one or a few individuals and can lead to scientific hypotheses. In case studies, researchers do not confine themselves to asking a limited number of questions as they would in a survey or randomized, controlled experimental study. Rather, researchers try to be open to learning from the individual or situation. Both qualitative research and quantitative research have value; which one a researcher uses depends on the specific research question.

For example, a researcher interested in studying do-not-resuscitate (DNR) orders may use different kinds of research designs, including correlation research, randomized experimental design research, narrative research, or case study research. An example of a correlation design would be a survey asking people how much they knew about DNR orders and how long they stayed in the hospital, to see if there is an association between length of hospitalization and knowledge of DNR orders. An example of a randomized experimental design could be a project in which the researcher randomly assigns people to one of two groups. One group would receive standard instructions about their upcoming elective surgery; the other group would receive the same standard instructions, plus additional information about DNR orders. After discharge, people in both groups might answer questions about their satisfaction with the hospital treatment. An example of narrative research could be for the experimenter to focus on one person who had experience with a DNR order, with the goal of telling this person's story, chronologically. The DNR order might be a part of this person's story. An example of case study research would be for the researcher to focus on one or several people who had experiences with DNR orders. The researcher would interview these people, asking specific and open-ended questions on the DNR aspects of their experience. The researcher might also, with permission, read the hospital charts and speak to hospital staff. The researcher might discern themes gleaned from reading transcripts of the interviews and other information, and develop theories or generalizations from these themes.

HISTORY

Modern social science case studies originated in the fields of anthropology and sociology. In the United States, case study methodology was most closely associated with the University of Chicago. In 1935, there was a public dispute between Columbia University scientists, who were championing quantitative experiments, and scientists at the University of Chicago. The outcome seemed to be in favor of Columbia University, and consequently, the use of case study methodology as a scientific research method declined. However, in the 1960s, researchers became increasingly concerned with the limitations of quantitative methods. Hence, there was a renewed interest in case studies.

Case study methodology is frequently used in the social sciences because of its popularity in psychology, medicine (case analysis of a problem), law (case law), political science (case reports), and education (instructional strategy). The fields of psychiatry and psychology have always depended on classical clinical cases to study different problems. Some important theories were developed from intensive one-on-one case studies of individuals.

EXAMPLES

Some famous case studies in psychology are Anna O., Little Hans, and Little Albert. Anna O. was the pseudonym given by Viennese physician Josef Breuer to Bertha Pappenheim, a patient he treated from 1880 to 1882 in Vienna. She suffered from severe complaints, including paralysis, memory loss, mental deterioration, nausea, and disturbances of vision and speech. The symptoms first appeared when she was nursing her dying father, who had always pampered her. Her symptoms had no physical or organic cause and thus were diagnosed as hysteria. Much to Breuer's surprise, Anna O.'s symptoms cleared up when she talked to Breuer about emotionally charged experiences from her past. Breuer and the Viennese psychoanalyst Sigmund Freud, thirteen years later, wrote a famous paper about her treatment. Since then, psychiatrists and psychoanalysts have included this information in discussions of hysteria, acknowledging that the case study of Anna O. is part of the prehistory of psychology and psychoanalysis.

Little Hans, a five-year-old boy, had phobias of horses, streets, and trucks. He feared leaving the house and abandoning his mother. Gathering information from detailed letters from Hans's father, a physician who had attended lectures on psychoanalysis, and from his own limited interviews with Hans, Freud wrote a case study on Hans, describing Hans's sexual oedipal desire for his mother. Freud believed that the case study of Little Hans demonstrated the therapeutic potential of a verbal approach for treating children as well as adults. This case study is also the first recorded instance of psychoanalytic supervision, because Freud treated Hans by advising Hans's father on steps to take.

Little Albert (his surname remains unknown) has been termed the most famous baby in the history of psychology. As an eleven-month-old boy, Albert liked to play with toys and initially showed no fear of a live white rat. To illustrate behavioral principles, John B. Watson, noted as the founder of behaviorism, on several occasions struck a loud gong while the baby was playing with a white rat. Soon, Little Albert reacted with fear whenever he saw the white rat. Further, his fearfulness and crying generalized so that he cried when he saw other white furry things, including a rabbit, a fur coat, and even a Santa Claus mask. Watson called Little Albert's fear a conditioned response and concluded that adult fears, anxieties, and phobias develop from similar conditioning experiences. The case study of Little Albert illustrates behavioral principles in action. The case studies of Anna O., Little Albert, and Little Hans are seminal in the field of psychology.

Some famous case studies about individuals receiving psychological treatment are described in Case Studies in *Psychotherapy* (1989), edited by Danny Wedding and Raymond J. Corsini. The editors include one example of psychoanalysis that involved more than eight hundred therapy sessions spanning more than seven years, illustrating how a skilled therapist managed problems such as personal vacations, sexual misbehavior, and suicide attempts. Among the other case studies in this volume are illustrations of cognitive therapy for a depressed professional woman and illustrations of existential therapy for an obese woman who was anxious about death.

Case studies occupy an important place in mental health. They are useful for developing hypotheses about clinical problems and exploring innovative treatments.

The problems for which case studies are appropriate are those related to exploratory studies (for example, generating new theories), or to critical and unusual cases. Case study methodology is less fit to test a theory.

BIBLIOGRAPHY

Breuer, Josef, and Sigmund Freud. "Fräulein Anna O." *Studies on Hysteria.* Vol. 2 in The Standard Edition of the Complete Psychological Works of Sigmund Freud. Ed. and trans. J. Strachey. London: Hogarth, 1955. Print.

Coolican, Hugh. Research *Methods and Statistics in Psychology.* 5th ed. New York: Routledge, 2013. Print.

Creswell, John W., et al. "Qualitative Research Designs: Selection and Implementation." *Counseling Psychologist* 35.2 (2007): 236–64. Print.

Franklin, Ronald D., David B. Allison, and Bernard S. Gorman, eds. *Design and Analysis of Single-Case Research.* New York: Psychology, 2014. Print.

Kazdin, Alan E. "Drawing Valid Inferences from Case Studies." *Methodological Issues and Strategies in Clinical Research.* Ed. Alan E. Kazdin. 3d ed. Washington: American Psychological Association, 2003. Print.

Sternberg, Robert J., Henry L. Roediger, and Diane F. Halpern. *Critical Thinking in Psychology.* New York: Cambridge UP, 2007. Print.

Wedding, Danny, and Raymond J. Corsini, eds. *Case Studies in Psychotherapy.* 5th ed. Belmont: Thomson, 2008. Print.

Willig, Carla. *Introducing Qualitative Research in Psychology.* 3rd ed. New York: McGraw-Hill, 2013. Print.

Wilson, Barbara A. "Single-Case Experimental Designs." *Choosing Methods in Mental Health Research: Mental Health Research from Theory to Practice.* Ed. Mike Slade and Stefan Priebe. New York: Routledge, 2006. Print.

Yin, Robert K. "Case Study Methods." *Handbook of Complementary Methods in Education Research.* Ed. Judith L. Green, Gregory Camilli, and Patricia B. Elmore. Mahwah: Erlbaum, 2006. Print.

Lillian M. Range

See Also: Conditioning; Experimental psychology; Experimentation: Independent, dependent, and control variables; Freud, Sigmund; Hysteria; Little Albert study; Psychology: Definition; Qualitative research; Scientific methods

Causal attribution

Type of psychology: Social psychology

Causal attribution concerns the explanations people offer about the causes of their own or other people's behavior. It has contributed to an understanding of emotions as well as people's reactions to failures and the reasons that they give for those failures.

Key Concepts

- Consensus information
- Consistency information
- Distinctiveness information
- External causes
- Internal causes
- Stable causes
- Unstable causes

INTRODUCTION

When an individual hears about the behavior of a serial killer, sees a person shoplift, or is rejected by a friend, that person may ask why such behaviors or events occurred. Identifying the causes of behaviors may help people learn what kind of behaviors they can expect. People speculate about the causes of positive behaviors as well. For example, one may want to understand why a great athlete has set a number of records, why someone received a job promotion, or why one did well on a test.

The study of causal attribution focuses on the explanations that people make about the causes of their own or other people's behavior. Researchers in this area have gone beyond identifying attributions to trying to understand why people make the attributions that they do. Research on causal attribution has contributed to an understanding of many other aspects of people's behavior, such as attitude change, interpersonal attraction, and helping behavior.

CLASSIFICATIONS

Attribution theories classify causal attributions in a number of ways. One of the most important classifications is whether the attribution is made to an internal state or an external force. Internal attributions are made to causes internal to the person, such as individual personality characteristics, moods, and abilities. For example, one may attribute the cause of a shoplifter's behavior to kleptomania, of a friend's rejection to one's own lack of social skills, and of an athlete's records to his or her ability. External attributions, on the other hand, are made to causes external to the person, such as characteristics of the environment. Thus, the shoplifter's behavior might be perceived to be caused by a broken home, a friend's rejection by some characteristic of the friend (for example, lack of loyalty), and the athlete's record to the efforts of the team.

Causal attributions are also classified according to their stability. Stable causes are relatively permanent and are consistent across time. Unstable causes fluctuate across time. Internal and external causes may be either stable or unstable. For example, a person's ability is usually considered internal and stable, whereas effort is internal and unstable. Laws are external and stable, whereas the weather is external and unstable. If shoplifting is attributed to kleptomania, the cause is internal and stable; if shoplifting is attributed to a dare from someone, the cause is external and unstable.

Bernard Weiner includes a third classification for causal attributions, that of controllability or uncontrollability: Some causes are within a person's control, whereas others are not. In this approach, controllability can exist with any combination of the internal/external and stable/unstable dimensions. Thus, ability—an internal, stable cause—is largely perceived as uncontrollable. For example, people have little control over whether they have the ability to distinguish green from red. On the other hand, effort—an internal, unstable cause—is perceived as controllable. A student can choose whether or not to study hard for a test.

KELLEY'S THEORY

Psychological research on causal attributions has gone beyond the classification of attributions. Psychologists have developed theories that help predict the circumstances under which people make various attributions. In this regard, Harold Kelley's theory has been extremely useful in making predictions about how people make internal and external attributions. From Kelley's perspective, attributions are made on the basis of three kinds of information: distinctiveness, consensus, and consistency.

Information about distinctiveness is derived from knowing the extent to which a person performs a certain behavior only in a certain situation. For example, the behavior of a person who only steals items from stores has higher distinctiveness than the behavior of a person who steals from stores, people's homes, and people on the street. According to Kelley, a behavior low in distinctiveness is likely to elicit an internal attribution. Thus, the behavior of a person who steals in a number of situations is more likely to be explained by an internal attribution (kleptomania) than by an external one.

Information about consensus is derived from knowing the way in which other people respond to the stimulus object. If the behavior is shared by a large number of people—if everyone steals items from stores, for example—the behavior has higher consensus than if few people steal from stores. A behavior high in consensus is likely to elicit an external attribution. If everyone steals from a certain store, there might be something about the store that elicits shoplifting.

Finally, information about consistency is derived from knowing how the person responds over time. If the person shoplifts most of the times that he or she shops, the behavior has higher consistency than if the person shoplifts occasionally. According to Kelley, behaviors high in consistency are likely to elicit internal attributions. Thus, the behavior of a person who shoplifts much of the time is likely to be explained by an internal attribution (kleptomania).

Kelley's theory has generated many more predictions than those described here. His theory, along with those of other attribution researchers, assumes that people have a need to predict behavior. If behavior is predictable, the world becomes a more controllable place in which to live.

ROLE OF EMOTIONS

One of the earlier applications of the research on causal attributions by social psychologists was in understanding emotions. Stanley Schachter and Jerome Singer proposed that perceptions of emotions are influenced by the physiological arousal that a person feels and by the cognitive label that the person uses (for example, "I'm jealous" or "I'm angry"). They argued that the physiological arousal is the same for all emotions. For example, a rapid heart rate can be the result of intense love or intense anger. According to Schachter and Singer, when someone feels physiologically aroused, the person looks to the situation to label his or her feelings. If someone is unaware of the true source of his or her arousal, it is possible for him or her to misattribute that arousal to a plausible cause.

An example can illustrate this approach. When "George" began drinking coffee as a teenager, he was unaware of the physiologically arousing effects of caffeine. He can recall drinking too much coffee one morning and getting in an argument about some issue. The caffeine created arousal; however, because George was in an argument, he attributed the cause of his arousal to his being angry. As a result of that attribution, he acted in an angry manner. Thus, George misattributed the physiological arousal produced by the caffeine to a feeling of anger.

Various psychological investigations have used this attributional approach. In an experiment on romantic attraction by Gregory White, Sanford Fishbein, and Jeffrey Rutsein, male subjects ran in place for 120 seconds (high physiological arousal) or 15 seconds (low physiological arousal) and were presented with a picture of an unattractive or attractive woman. Subsequently, the subjects were asked to evaluate the woman in terms of romantic attractiveness. Male subjects with high physiological arousal indicated that they were more romantically attracted to the attractive woman than did the male subjects with less physiological arousal. Similarly, in an experiment on crowding by Stephen Worchel and Charles Teddie, subjects sat close (high physiological arousal) or far apart (low physiological arousal). For some of the subjects, there were pictures on the wall; for other subjects, there were no pictures on the wall. Subsequently, subjects were asked how crowded they felt. For the subjects with high physiological arousal, those with no pictures on the wall indicated that they felt more crowded than did those with pictures on the wall. Without pictures on the wall, the subjects could only attribute their arousal to other people. In each of these examples, the subjects used an external cue to label their internal state (emotion).

LEARNED HELPLESSNESS

Causal attributions have also been used to understand the phenomenon of learned helplessness. Martin E. P. Seligman has demonstrated in a number of experiments that people take longer to solve soluble problems after they have tried and failed to solve a series of insoluble problems than if they had not been presented with the insoluble problems. Seligman initially proposed that people did not try harder on the soluble problems because they learned that their outcomes (failures on the insoluble problems) were independent of what they did. From an attributional perspective, however, the argument would be that people do not try harder on the soluble problems because it is less damaging to their self-esteem to attribute their failure on the insoluble problems to a lack of effort, an internal, unstable cause, rather than to an internal, stable cause, such as ability. People can then retain the belief that they can always do better next time if they try harder. Research favors the attributional interpretation of learned helplessness, as is indicated by the research of Arthur Frankel and Melvin Snyder.

EXCUSE THEORY

An area in which causal attribution has played a crucial role is in excuse theory as proposed by C. R. Snyder. People make excuses to protect themselves from their failure experiences, as excuses help them feel that they are not totally responsible for their failures. Kelley's attribution theory was influential in the development of Snyder's model of excuse making. People can excuse a poor performance by using consensus-raising excuses, consistency-lowering excuses, or distinctiveness-raising excuses.

When people employ distinctiveness-raising excuses, they claim that the poor performance is specific to one situation and not generalizable to others ("I performed poorly only in this class"). When people employ consistency-lowering excuses, they claim that they have a poor performance occasionally, not frequently ("This was the only time I performed poorly"). Finally, when people employ consensus-raising excuses, they claim that everyone performed as poorly as they did ("This test was so hard that everyone did poorly on it"). George Whitehead and Stephanie Smith have examined the impact of an audience on the use of consensus-raising excuses. They found that people are less likely to use consensus-raising excuses in public than in private. Thus, one is more likely to say, "This test was hard, and everyone did poorly on it," to oneself than to one's teacher, who knows how everyone else performed.

EVOLUTION OF RESEARCH

The basic ideas for causal attribution were presented by Fritz Heider in his 1958 book The Psychology of Interpersonal Relations. From the richness of Heider's writings, a number of social psychologists have generated different attributional theories. One problem with this research area, as with other research areas in social psychology, is that no single theory effectively encompasses all the different ideas proposed by causal attribution theorists. Nevertheless, causal attribution research has played an important role in the history of psychology because of its emphasis on cognition—that is, how people think.

In the late 1950s, when Heider published his book, and the early 1960s, when Schachter and Singer did their experiment regarding emotion, psychology was heavily influenced by behaviorism and had been for many years. From a behavioristic perspective, the study of thinking was in disrepute because it involved processes that were largely unobservable. Theorizing about causal attribution involved theorizing about how people think about the causes of behavior. Today, as can be seen from the amount of research on causal attribution and other cognitive processes, psychologists' interest in cognition has broadened.

Early research on causal attribution generally supported the theories being tested but often found that they had limitations as well. For example, research on Kelley's attribution theory found that people do use information about distinctiveness, consensus, and consistency when making attributions, and Kelley's theory further suggests that each type of information should be considered equally important in the attribution process. Subsequent research, however, indicated that consensus information may be underutilized in certain circumstances.

One important area of research is the influence of culture on causal attributions. Much of the theorizing and empirical research on causal attribution has been done in the United States. It is important to know whether the phenomena that psychologists have documented among people in the United States generalize to people from other cultures. Evidence from several sources has indicated that people from the United States attribute outcomes more to internal causes than do people from developing nations, which is believed to reflect different cultural traditions.

Once the causal attributions that people make are understood, research can focus on the consequences of these attributions. For example, when people excuse a poor performance, they should feel better about themselves. Also, when people attribute their positive outcomes to internal factors, their feelings about themselves should be better than when they attribute their positive outcomes to external factors. This area is one of many that is likely to receive more attention from social psychological researchers in the future.

BIBLIOGRAPHY

Bastounis, Marina, and Jale Minibas-Poussard. "Causal Attributions of Workplace Gender Equality, Just World Belief, and the Self/Other Distinction." *Social Behavior and Personality* 40.3 (2012): 433–52. Print.

Fiske, Susan T., and Shelley E. Taylor. *Social Cognition: From Brains to Culture*. 2nd ed. Thousand Oaks: Sage, 2013. Print.

Frankel, Arthur, and Melvin L. Snyder. "Poor Performance following Unsolvable Problems: Learned Helplessness or Egotism?" *Journal of Personality and Social Psychology* 36.12 (1978): 1415–23. Print.

Heider, Fritz. *The Psychology of Interpersonal Relations*. Hillsdale: Erlbaum, 1983. Print.

LaBelle, Sara, and Matthew M. Martin. "Attribution Theory in the College Classroom: Examining the Relationship of Student Attributions and Instructional Dissent." *Communication Research Reports* 31.1 (2014): 110–16. Print.

Savolainen, Reijo. "Approaching the Motivators for Information Seeking: The Viewpoint of Attribution Theories." *Library and Information Science Research* 35.1 (2013): 63–68. Print.

Schachter, Stanley, and Jerome Singer. "Cognitive, Social, and Physiological Determinants of Emotional State." *Psychological Review* 69.5 (1962): 379–99. Print.

Seligman, Martin E. P. *Helplessness: On Depression, Development, and Death*. San Francisco: Freeman, 1975. Print.

Snyder, C. R., Raymond L. Higgins, and Rita J. Stucky. *Excuses: Masquerades in Search of Grace*. 1983. New York: Percheron, 2005. Print.

White, Gregory L., Sanford Fishbein, and Jeffrey Rutsein. "Passionate Love and the Misattribution of Arousal." *Journal of Personality and Social Psychology* 41.1 (1981): 56–62. Print.

Whitehead, George I., III, and Stephanie Smith. "Competence and Excuse-Making as Self-Presentational Strategies." *Public Self and Private Self*. Ed. Roy F. Baumeister. New York: Springer, 1986. 161–77, Print.

Worchel, Stephen, and Charles Teddie. "The Experience of Crowding: A Two-Factor Theory." *Journal of Personality and Social Psychology* 34.1 (1976): 30–40. Print.

George I. Whitehead III and Stephanie Smith

See Also: Abnormality: Psychological models; Attributional biases; Cognitive dissonance; Cognitive maps; Emotions; Learned helplessness; Motivation; Motivation: Intrinsic and extrinsic.

Child abuse

Type of psychology: Developmental psychology

The experience of physical or psychological abuse in childhood can have profound, long-term, and deleterious effects on a person's social development and emotional well-being. Child abuse places individuals at increased risk for developing a variety of psychological problems, including low self-esteem, anxiety, depression, behavioral disorders, educational difficulties, and distorted relationships with peers and adults.

Key Concepts

- Neglect
- Physical abuse
- Psychological abuse
- Sexual abuse

INTRODUCTION

It is difficult to imagine anything more frightening to a child than being neglected, threatened, beaten, or molested by an adult who is supposed to be his or her primary source of care and protection. Yet throughout human history, children have been abandoned, incarcerated, battered, mutilated, exploited, and even murdered by their caregivers. Although the problem of child maltreatment is an old one, both the systematic study of child abuse and the legally sanctioned mechanisms for child protection are relatively new and have gained momentum in the last half of the twentieth century.

In the United States, child abuse and neglect are defined in both federal and state legislation. The federal legislation provides a foundation for states by identifying a minimum set of acts or behaviors that characterize maltreatment.

The Child Abuse Prevention and Treatment Act (CAPTA), passed in 1974 and amended in 2003 by the Keeping Children and Families Safe Act, defines child abuse and neglect as "any recent act or failure on the part of a parent or caretaker, which results in death, serious physical or emotional harm, sexual abuse or exploitation, or an act or failure to act which presents an imminent risk of serious harm."

When applied by legal and mental health professionals in real-world situations, however, the definition of abuse may vary according to the developmental age of the child victim, the frequency or intensity of the behaviors regarded as abusive, the degree of intentionality, and a consideration of extenuating circumstances. In general, however, child abuse includes any act or omission on the part of a parental figure that damages a child's physical or psychological well-being or development that is nonaccidental or the result of a habitual behavioral pattern. A broad spectrum of behaviors is considered to be abusive, ranging from the more easily recognizable physical abuse to more subtle forms of maltreatment, including neglect and emotional abuse.

TYPES OF ABUSE

Physical abuse is characterized by the nonaccidental infliction of physical injury as a result of punching, pushing, striking, kicking, biting, burning, shaking, or otherwise harming a child. The parent or caretaker may not have intended to badly hurt the child; rather, the injury may have resulted from overdiscipline or physical punishment. Child neglect is characterized by failure to provide for the child's basic needs. Neglect can be physical, educational, or emotional. Physical neglect includes refusal of, or delay in, seeking health care, food, clothing, or shelter; abandonment; expulsion from the home or refusal to allow a runaway to return home; and inadequate supervision. Educational neglect includes the allowance of chronic truancy, failure to enroll a child of mandatory school age in school, and failure to attend to a special educational needs. Emotional neglect includes such actions as marked inattention to the child's needs for affection; refusal of or failure to provide needed psychological care; spouse abuse in the child's presence; and permission of drug or alcohol use by the child. The assessment of child neglect requires consideration of cultural values and standards of care, as well as recognition that the failure to provide the necessities of life may be related to poverty.

Sexual abuse includes fondling a child's genitals, intercourse, incest, rape, sodomy, exhibitionism, and commercial exploitation through prostitution or the production of pornographic materials. Many experts believe that sexual abuse is the most underreported form of child maltreatment because of the secrecy or "conspiracy of silence" that so often characterizes these cases.

Emotional abuse (psychological or verbal abuse, or mental injury) includes acts or omissions by the parents or other caregivers that have caused behavioral, cognitive, emotional, or mental injury. In some cases of emotional abuse, the acts of parents or other caregivers alone, without any harm evident in the child's behavior or condition, are sufficient to warrant intervention and investigation by the Child Protective Services (CPS). For example, the parents or caregivers may use extreme or bizarre forms of punishment, such as confinement of a child in a dark closet. Less severe acts, such as habitual scapegoating, belittling, or rejecting treatment, are often difficult to prove. Therefore, CPS may not be able to intervene without evidence of harm to the child.

EXTENT OF ABUSE

According to data from the National Child Abuse and Neglect Data System of the Department of Health and Human Services, there were approximately 686,000 reports of child abuse or neglect in the United States in 2012, representing a 3.3 decrease in the number of reports from 2008 (716,000). Of these reports, approximately 78 percent indicated child neglect, 18 percent indicated physical abuse, 9 percent reported sexual abuse, and 8.5 percent reported psychological or emotional abuse. It is estimated that more than four children die every day in the United States as a result of child abuse, with 70 percent of these children being under the age of four years. It is important, when considering the actual magnitude of the problem of child maltreatment, to remember that the estimates given most likely underestimate the true incidence of child abuse, both because of the large number of cases that go unreported and because of the lack of agreement as to precisely which behaviors constitute "abuse" or "neglect." In addition, abusive treatment of children is rarely limited to a single episode, and it frequently occurs within the context of other forms of family violence.

Certain forms of maltreatment seem to appear with greater regularity within certain age groups. Neglect is most often reported for infants and toddlers, with incidence declining with age. Reports of sexual abuse and emotional maltreatment are most common among older school-aged children and adolescents. Physical abuse seems to be reported equally among all age groups; however, children less than five years old and adolescents have the highest rates of actual physical injury. Boys and girls are equally as likely to be victims of child abuse and neglect, but the rate of abuse-related fatality is slightly higher for boys.

Although research studies generally conclude that there is no "typical" child abuse case consisting of a typical abused child and a typical abusive parent or family type, certain characteristics occur with greater regularity than others. For example, there is considerable evidence that premature infants, low-birth-weight infants, and children with problems such as attention-deficit hyperactivity disorders, physical disabilities, and intellectual disabilities are at particularly high risk for being abused by their caregivers. Physical abuse and neglect are reported with approximately equal frequency for girls and boys, while sexual abuse against girls is reported four times more frequently than sexual abuse against boys.

Although female caregivers are the perpetrators in approximately 60 percent of all reported cases of child maltreatment, male caregivers are more likely to inflict serious physical injury, and men are the primary perpetrators in cases of sexual abuse of both male and female children. Although no single abusive personality type has been identified, research has revealed a number of areas of psychological functioning in which abusive parents often differ from nonabusive parents. Abusive parents tend to exhibit low frustration tolerance, have poor impulse control, and express negative emotions (for example, anger or disappointment) inappropriately. They are more socially isolated and are more likely to abuse alcohol or drugs than nonabusive parents. Abusive parents also tend to have unrealistic expectations of their children, to misinterpret their children's motivations for misbehaving, to utilize inconsistent and inflexible parenting skills, and to view themselves as inadequate or incompetent as parents.

Research also indicates that marital conflict, unemployment, large and closely spaced families, overcrowded living conditions, and extreme household disorientation are common in abusive homes. Statistics regarding race, education level, and socioeconomic status of abusive families are somewhat controversial in that there exists the possibility of an underreporting bias favoring white, middle- to upper-class families. However, like several other negative outcomes in childhood (for example, academic underachievement, criminality, teen pregnancy), child abuse is associated with family poverty, underemployment, insufficient education, and the increased experience of stress and social isolation that coexists with these sociodemographic variables.

CONSEQUENCES OF ABUSE

Children who have experienced abuse are believed to be at much greater risk of developing some form of pathology in childhood or in later life, most commonly depression, anxiety, eating disorders such as anorexia and bulimia, or suicide ideation. When considered as a group and compared to nonabused youngsters, abused children are at a higher risk of exhibiting a variety of psychological difficulties and behavioral problems. Yet no single emotional or behavioral reaction is consistently found in all abused children. It is important, when investigating the impact of child abuse, to view the abuse within a developmental perspective. Given a child's different developmental needs and capabilities over the course of a child's development, one might expect that both the psychological experience and the impact of the abuse would be quite different for an infant than if the same maltreatment involved an eight-year-old child or an adolescent. One should also note that, in some cases, the experience of the abuse per se may not be the singular, most powerful predictor of the psychological difficulties found in abused children. Rather, the child's daily exposure to other, more pervasive aspects of the psychological environment associated with an abusive family situation (for example, general environmental deprivation, impoverished parent-child interactions, or chronic family disruption and disorganization) may prove to be more psychologically damaging. Finally, it is important not to view the range of symptoms associated with abused children solely as deficits or pathology. These "symptoms" represent an abused child's best attempt at coping with an extremely stressful family environment given the limited psychological resources and skills he or she has available at that particular time in his or her development.

From the home environment, and from parents in particular, children learn their earliest and perhaps most influential lessons about how to evaluate themselves as valuable, lovable, and competent human beings. They learn about controlling their own actions and about successfully mastering their environment. They learn something about the goodness of their world and how to relate to the people in it. Growing up in an abusive home distorts these early lessons, often resulting in serious interference with the most important dimensions of a child's development: the development of a healthy sense of self, the development of self-control and a sense of mastery, the capacity to form satisfying relationships, and the ability to utilize one's cognitive capacities to solve problems.

In general, research has shown that abused children often suffer from low self-esteem, poor impulse control, aggressive and antisocial behaviors, fearfulness and anxiety, depression, poor relationships with peers and adults, difficulties with school adjustment, delays in cognitive development, lowered academic achievement, and deficits in social and moral judgment. The way in which these difficulties are expressed will vary according to a child's stage of development.

SIGNS OF ABUSE

In infancy, the earliest sign of abuse or neglect is an infant's failure to thrive. These infants show growth retardation (weight loss can be so severe as to be life-threatening) with no obvious physical explanation. To the observer, these infants appear to have "given up" on interacting with the outside world. They become passive, socially apathetic, and exhibit little smiling, vocalization, and curiosity. Other abused infants appear to be quite irritable, exhibiting frequent crying, feeding difficulties, and irregular sleep patterns. In either case, the resulting parent-child attachment bond is often inadequate and mutually unsatisfying.

Abused toddlers and preschoolers seem to lack the infectious love of life, fantasy, and play that is characteristic of that stage of development. They are typically anxious, fearful, and hypervigilant. Their emotions are blunted, lacking the range, the spontaneity, and the vivacity typical of a child that age. Abused toddlers' and preschoolers' ability to play, particularly their ability to engage in imaginative play, may be impaired; it is either deficient or preoccupied with themes of aggression. Abused children at this age can either be passive and overcompliant or oppositional, aggressive, and hyperactive.

School-aged children and adolescents exhibit the more recognizable signs of low self-esteem and depression in the form of a self-deprecating attitude and self-destructive behaviors. They may be lonely, withdrawn, and joyless.Behaviorally, some act in a compulsive, overcompliant, or pseudomature manner, while others are overly impulsive, oppositional, and aggressive. Problems with school adjustment and achievement are common. With the school-aged child's increased exposure to the larger social environment, deficits in social competence and interpersonal relationships become more apparent. Progressing through adolescence, the manifestations of low self-esteem, depression, and aggressive, acting-out behaviors may become more pronounced in the form of suicide attempts, delinquency, running away, promiscuity, and drug use.

These distortions in self-esteem, impulse control, and interpersonal relationships often persist into adulthood. There has been much concern expressed regarding the possibility of an intergenerational transmission of abuse—of the experience of abuse as a child predisposing a person to becoming an abusive parent. Research indicates that abused children are six times more likely to abuse their own children than are members of the general population. Approximately 30 percent of abuse and neglected children will abuse their own children in the future; however, the vast majority of people who experienced abuse and neglect as children will never neglect or abuse their own children.

EXPLANATIONS

Child maltreatment is a complex phenomenon that does not have a simple, discrete cause, nor does it affect each victim in a predictable or consistent manner.

Perhaps the most comprehensive and widely accepted explanation of child abuse is the ecological model, which examines both the risk factors for and protective factors against child abuse and neglect. This model views abuse as the final product of a set of interacting factors, including child-mediated stressors (for example, temperamental difficulties or intellectual or physical disabilities), parental predispositions (for example, the parent's history of abuse as a child, emotional immaturity, or substance abuse), and situational stresses (for example, marital conflict, insufficient social support, or financial stress) occurring within a cultural context that inadvertently supports the mistreatment of children by its acceptance of corporal punishment and tolerance for violence and its reluctance to interfere with family autonomy. Utilizing this ecological framework, one can imagine how an abusive situation can develop when, for example, an irritable, emotionally unresponsive infant is cared for by an inexperienced, socially isolated mother in a conflict-filled and financially strained household embedded within a larger cultural context in which the rights and privileges of childhood do not necessarily include freedom from violence.

Knowledge regarding the impact of child abuse has also changed over the years, from a view of maltreated children as almost doomed to develop some form of psychopathology to an acknowledgment that child abuse, like other major childhood stressors, can result in a broad spectrum of adaptive consequences, ranging from psychological resilience to severe psychiatric disorder. Some children actually do well in their development despite their experience with extreme stress and adversity. For example, while adults who were abused as children are more likely than nonabused individuals to become child abusers, nearly two-thirds of all abused children do not become abusive parents. The important questions to be answered are why and how this is so. Research on "stress-resistant" individuals such as these nonabusers has shifted the focus away from pathology to the identification of factors within the individual (for example, coping strategies) and within the environment (for example, social support) that appear to serve a protective function.

Finally, while the treatment of abused children and their abusive caregivers remains an important goal in the mental health field, a focus on the prevention of child abuse has also gained momentum. Many abused children and their families can be helped with proper treatment; however, the existing need for services far exceeds the mental health resources available. An increased understanding of the factors that protect families against engaging in abusive behaviors has resulted in the creation of successful preventive interventions. These prevention programs seek to reduce the incidence of new cases of child abuse by encouraging the identification and development of competencies, resources, and coping strategies that promote psychological well-being and positive change in parents, children, and families.

The problem of child abuse does not occur in isolation. It coexists with other abhorrent problems facing families such as poverty, lack of access to adequate medical care, insufficient quality child care, and unequal educational resources. Child abuse, like these other problems, can be prevented and eradicated.

BIBLIOGRAPHY

Bass, Ellen, and Laura Davis. *The Courage to Heal: A Guide for Women Survivors of Child Sexual Abuse*. New York: Collins Living, 2008. Print.

Briere, John N. *Child Abuse Trauma*. Newbury Park: Sage , 1992. Print.

Cicchetti, Dante, and Vicki Carlson, eds. *Child Maltreatment: Theory and Research on the Causes and Consequences of Child Abuse and Neglect*. New York: Cambridge UP, 1997. Print.

Clark, Robin E., and Judith Freeman Clark. *The Encyclopedia of Child Abuse*. 3rd ed. New York: Facts On File, 2007. Print.

Conte, Jon R., ed. *Critical Issues in Child Sexual Abuse: Historical, Legal, and Psychological Perspectives*. Newbury Park: Sage, 2002. Print.

Crosson-Tower, Cynthia. *Understanding Child Abuse and Neglect*. 7th ed. Boston: Allyn & Bacon, 2007. Print.

Garbarino, James, and Gwen Gilliam. *Understanding Abusive Families*. San Francisco: Jossey-Bass, 1997. Print.

Goodyear-Brown, Paris. *Handbook of Child Sexual Abuse: Identification, Assessment, and Treatment*. Hoboken: Wiley, 2012. Print.

Kantor, Glenda K., and Jana L. Jasinski, eds. *Out of the Darkness: Contemporary Perspectives on Family Violence*. Newbury Park: Sage, 1997.

McCoy, Monica L., and Stefanie M. Keen. *Child Abuse and Neglect*. New York: Routledge, 2014. Print.

Sargent, John, Rochelle F. Hanson, and Robert M. Reece. *Treatment of Child Abuse: Common Ground for Mental Health, Medical, and Legal Practitioners*. 2nd ed. Baltimore: John Hopkins UP, 2014. Print.

United States. Dept. of Health and Human Services. *Child Maltreatment 2012*. N.p.: n.p., 2013. PDF file.

Wolfe, David A. *Child Abuse: Implications for Child Development and Psychopathology*. 2nd ed. Newbury Park: Sage, 1999. Print.

Judith Primavera; updated by Shelley A. Jackson

SEE ALSO: Aggression; Attachment and bonding in infancy and childhood; Battered woman syndrome; Children's mental health; Depression; Domestic violence; Ego defense mechanisms; Elder abuse; Gender identity formation; Psychoanalytic psychology and personality: Sigmund Freud; Rape and sexual assault; Self-esteem; Separation and divorce: Children's issues; Teenagers' mental health; Violence and sexuality in the media; Violence: Psychological causes and effects.

Childhood disorders

TYPE OF PSYCHOLOGY: Psychopathology

Childhood disorders involve significant behavioral or psychological patterns that are associated with distress, disability, an important loss of independence, or significantly increased risk of dysfunction, disability, or death that affect infants, children, or adolescents.

KEY CONCEPTS

- Attention-deficit and disruptive disorders
- Communication disorders
- Elimination disorders
- Feeding and eating disorders
- Learning disorders
- Mental retardation
- Motor coordination disorders
- Pervasive development disorders
- tic disorders

INTRODUCTION

The concept of mental disorder, like many other concepts in science and medicine, lacks a consistent operational definition that covers all situations. A useful tool to evaluate mental disorders is the American Psychiatric Association's *Diagnostic and Statistical Manual of Mental Disorders* (DSM). The DSM is coordinated with the *International Statistical Classification of Diseases and Related Health Problems* (ICD), developed by the World Health Organization for all diseases. A comprehensive manual, the DSM conceptualizes a mental disorder as a syndrome characterized by clinically significant disturbance in an individual's cognition, emotional regulation, or behavior that reflects a dysfunction in the psychological, biological, or developmental processes underlying mental functioning. These disturbances must be more than expected and culturally sanctioned responses to a particular event, for example, the death of a loved one.

Mental disorders that are predominantly diagnosed during childhood or adolescence include intellectual disability, learning disorders, motor skills disorders, pervasive developmental disorders, attention-deficit disorders, feeding and eating disorders, tic disorders, and elimination disorders, among others. Other disorders are associated with adults, but children may have them as well. This second group includes neurocognitive disorders; mood disorders; anxiety disorders; somatic symptom disorders; factitious disorders; dissociative disorders; sleep-wake disorders; disruptive, impulse-control, and conduct disorders; and adjustment disorders. In the fifth edition of the DSM (DSM-5), each diagnostic chapter is organized by chronological order, with diagnoses most applicable to infancy and childhood listed first, followed by diagnoses more common to adolescence and early adulthood, and ending with diagnoses most relevant to adulthood.

INTELLECTUAL DISABILITY

Intellectual disability (also know as intellectual developmental disorder and formerly known as mental retardation) involves impairments of general mental abilities that affect adaptive functioning in three main areas: the conceptual domain, which includes skills in language, mathematics, reasoning, and memory; the social domain, which relates to empathy, interpersonal communication skills, and social judgment; and the practical domain, which involves self-management in areas such as personal care, job responsibilities, money management, and organization. On an intelligence quotient (IQ) test, intellectual disability is defined as two standard deviations or more below the mean, corresponding to an IQ score of 70 or below. A common misconception regarding intelligence tests is the assumption that these tests represent an absolute trait. A low score on an intelligence test might reflect below-average intellectual functioning, but it might also reflect illness, distraction, or a native language or sociocultural background that differs from that of the examiner or test creators, among other reasons. For this reason, the DSM-5 emphasizes both clinical assessment of impairments in adaptive functioning and standardized testing of intelligence when diagnosing intellectual disability. There are four degrees of intellectual disability: mild, moderate, severe, or profound. The severity of intellectual disability is determined by impairments in adaptive functioning rather than by IQ score. Mild intellectual disability characterizes more than 80 percent of individuals with intellectual disabilities.

By late adolescence, most individuals with mild intellectual disability can function up to about a sixth-grade academic level. As adults, these individuals typically live self-sufficiently in the community, although they may need assistance when they are in unusual, complex, or stressful situations. People with moderate intellectual disabilities have sufficient communication skills but may struggle with social cues. These individuals profit from vocational training and, with some support and instruction, can attend to personal care on their own.

Severe intellectual disability is characterized by limited communication skills and the need for assistance in most activities of daily living. Most individuals with several intellectual disabilities benefit from residence in supportive housing. Individuals with profound intellectual disability typically require twenty-four-hour care, have very limited communications skills, and often have co-occurring sensory or physical disabilities. Individuals in this range account for only 1 to 2 percent of persons with intellectual disabilities.

There are many causes of intellectual disabilities, but psychiatrists identify a specific cause in only about 25 percent of cases. Causes for intellectual disability include genetics, metabolic conditions such as phenylketonuria (PKU) and congenital hypothyroidism, early problems in embryonic or perinatal development, environmental influences such as nutritional deficiencies in infancy or exposure to toxins in utero, and trauma.

SPECIFIC LEARNING DISORDER

In specific learning disorders, a child's academic achievement is substantially below that expected for age, schooling, and level of intelligence. In children with learning disorders, the specific learning difficulty persists for at least six months despite intervention and instruction targeting the area of difficulty.

Approximately 5 to 15 percent of school-aged children worldwide have a learning disorder. Learning disorders are different from normal variations in academic achievement and from learning deficits caused by lack of opportunity, poor teaching, or cultural factors. Impaired vision or hearing may affect learning ability, so vision and hearing should be assessed by a health care provider if a learning disorder is suspected. In order for an individual to fit the diagnostic criteria for a specific learning disorders, the learning difficulties must occur in the absence of intellectual disability, visual or hearing impairments, mental disorders such as anxiety or depression, neurological disorder, psychosocial difficulties, language differences, and lack of access to quality instruction.

Learning disorders can involve problems with reading, mathematics, written expression, or some combination of these areas. In reading disorder, a family pattern is often present. In mathematics and written expression disorder, parents or teachers typically notice a problem as early as the second or third grade but not earlier, because few children are exposed to mathematics or formal writing instruction before then.

MOTOR DISORDERS

Motor coordination disorders include developmental coordination disorder, stereotypic movement disorder, Tourette syndrome, persistent (chronic) motor or vocal disorder, provisional tic disorder, other specified tic disorder, and unspecified tic disorder. Motor disorders are typically diagnosed in childhood. Motor disorders involve abnormal and involuntary movements and are often characterized by marked delays in motor development.

A tic is a sudden, rapid, recurrent, nonrhythmic, stereotyped motor movement or vocalization. For example, the person may have an eye tic that involves small, jerky, involuntary movement of the muscles surrounding the eye. All children and adults experience mild tics, but a tic disorder means that the tics are frequent, recurrent, and not due to substances or medical conditions.

COMMUNICATION DISORDERS

Communication disorders include problems with expressive or receptive language, phonology, stuttering, or some combination of these areas. Aspects of these problems vary depending on their severity and the child's age.

When the problem involves expressive language, the features may include limited speech, limited vocabulary, difficulty acquiring new words, and simplified sentences. Nonlinguistic functioning and comprehension, however, are within normal limits. When the problem involves difficulties with both expressive language and receptive language, the child also has difficulty understanding words, sentences, or specific types of words. When the problem involves phonology, the child fails to use developmentally expected speech sounds. Severity ranges from a limited vocabulary to completely unintelligible speech. Lisping may also be present. When the problem involves stuttering, the child has a disturbance in the normal fluency and time patterning of speech.

AUTISM SPECTRUM DISORDER

Autism spectrum disorder (ASD) is characterized by impaired social interactions or communication skills and by restricted or repetitive behaviors, interests, and activities. As of the DSM-5, ASD encompasses four diagnoses that were previously categorized as separate disorders in the fourth edition of the DSM: autistic disorder (autism), Asperger syndrome, Rett syndrome, and childhood disintegrative disorder. ASD is usually evident in the first years of life and may be associated with some degree of intellectual disability. ASD is sometimes observed with a diverse group of other general medical conditions, including chromosomal abnormalities, congenital infections, and structural central nervous system abnormalities.

Autism involves abnormal social interactions and communication and a restricted repertoire of activity and interests. The child may fail to maintain eye-to-eye contact or to share enjoyment, interests, or achievements spontaneously with others and may develop no age-appropriate peer relationships. The child also shows qualitative impairment in communication, such as delay in developing spoken language, inability to initiate or sustain a conversation, or repetitive use of language. Children with this disorder may be uninterested in other children, including siblings. In recent decades, major headway has been made in treating children with ASD through behavioral management therapy and cognitive behavioral therapy, particularly those children with ASD who benefit from early intervention.

ATTENTION-DEFICIT HYPERACTIVITY DISORDER

Attention-deficit hyperactivity disorder (ADHD) involves persistent inattention or hyperactivity and impulsivity that is more severe than is typical for the child's age. Several inattentive or hyperactive-impulsive symptoms must be present before the age of twelve, persist for at least six months, and be present in at least two settings, such as school and home. Most children with ADHD show a combined set of problems, including both inattention and hyperactivity. Symptoms of ADHD include failure to pay close attention to details, difficulty organizing tasks and activities, excessive talking, fidgeting, an inability to remain seated in appropriate situations, and frequent interruptions or intrusions.

FEEDING AND EATING DISORDERS

These disorders include persistent feeding and eating disturbances. They include pica, rumination, feeding disorder, anorexia, and bulimia.

Pica involves persistently eating one or more nonnutritive substances, such as paint or dirt. The behavior is developmentally inappropriate and not part of a culturally sanctioned practice.

Rumination involves repeated regurgitation and rechewing of food after feeding. Infants may develop rumination after a period of normal functioning, and it lasts for at least one month. The infant shows no apparent nausea, retching, disgust, or associated gastrointestinal disorder. Age of onset is between three months and twelve months.

Feeding disorder involves persistent failure to eat adequately without a gastrointestinal or other general medical explanation. Infants with this disorder may be more irritable and difficult to console during feeding than other infants. Age of onset is before six years.

Anorexia nervosa, often called simply anorexia, involves refusing to maintain a minimally normal body weight (85 percent less than expected), being intensely afraid of gaining weight, and having a distorted body image. Teenaged girls with anorexia may have such a low body weight that they stop having menstrual periods.

Bulimia nervosa, often called simply bulimia, involves binge eating and inappropriate compensatory methods to prevent weight gain, such as purging or using laxatives excessively. Episodes of binging and purging occur at least twice a week for at least three months. Individuals with this disorder experience a lack of control over eating, and their self-evaluation is unduly influenced by body shape and weight. Bulimia is also most typical of adolescent girls from industrialized societies.

ELIMINATION DISORDERS

Elimination disorders involve age-inappropriate soiling (encopresis) or wetting (enuresis). Most often the behavior is involuntary, but occasionally it may be intentional. The incontinence must not be due to substances or a general medical condition.

Encopresis involves passage of feces into inappropriate places such as clothing or the floor that occurs at least once a month for at least three months. The child must be at least four years old. Most commonly, there is evidence of constipation and feces are poorly formed. Less often, there is no evidence of constipation and feces are normal. Encopresis is more common with boys than with girls.

Enuresis involves repeated voiding of urine into bed sheets or clothes that occurs at least twice per week for at least three months or else causes clinically significant distress or impairment. The child must be at least five years old. Nocturnal enuresis occurs only at night and is most common. Diurnal enuresis occurs only during the day and more often with girls than with boys. It is uncommon after age nine.

OTHER CHILDHOOD DISORDERS

A few other disorders are more characteristic of children than adults. They include separation anxiety disorder, selective mutism, reactive attachment disorder, and stereotypic movement disorder.

Although most children experience some transient anxiety when separated from a loved one, children with separation anxiety disorder have excessive anxiety when separated from the home or from their attachment figures. The anxiety lasts for at least four weeks, begins before age eighteen years, and causes clinically significant distress or impairment.

Children with selective mutism persistently fail to speak in specific social situations (such as school or with playmates) where speaking is expected, despite speaking in other situations. The disturbance interferes with educational or occupational achievement or with social communication and bonding. Selective mutism lasts for at least one month and is not limited to the first month of school, when many children may be shy and reluctant to speak.

Reactive attachment disorder involves markedly disturbed and developmentally inappropriate social relatedness in most contexts. It begins before age five and is associated with grossly pathological care, such as child abuse or neglect. In inhibited attachment, the child persistently fails to initiate and respond to most social interactions in a developmentally appropriate way. In disinhibited attachment, the child shows indiscriminate sociability or a lack of selectivity in the choice of attachment figures. Thus, the child has diffuse attachments and shows excessive familiarity with relative strangers.

Stereotypic movement disorder involves motor behavior that is repetitive, seemingly driven, and nonfunctional. For example, the child may repeatedly strike a wall. The motor behavior markedly interferes with normal activities or results in self-inflicted bodily injury that would require medical treatment if unprotected.

ADULT DISORDERS IN CHILDREN

In addition to disorders associated with infancy, childhood, or adolescence, children may have behavioral or psychological disorders that are typically associated with adults. They include schizophrenia, mood disorders, anxiety, somatic symptom disorders, factitious disorders, dissociative disorders, sleep disorders, impulse-control disorders, and adjustment disorders.

Schizophrenia involves delusions, hallucinations, or disorganized speech and behavior, with symptoms lasting for at least six months. Onset is typically late teens to mid-thirties.

Depression involves loss of interest or pleasure in nearly all activities. Additional symptoms include changes in appetite, sleep, or activity; decreased energy; feelings of worthlessness or guilt; difficulty thinking, concentrating, or making decisions; and recurrent thoughts of death or suicide. Bipolar disorder involves at least one episode of mania as well as at least one episode of depression.

Anxiety disorders include panic disorder, agoraphobia, specific phobias, social anxiety disorder, and generalized anxiety disorder. Trauma- and stressor-related disorders include posttraumatic stress disorder and adjustment disorder. Obsessive-compulsive and related disorders include obsessive-compulsive disorder, body dysmorphic disorder, trichotillomania, and hoarding disorder.

Somatic symptom disorder is characterized by one or more chronic symptoms about which the patient is excessively concerned, preoccupied, or fearful, causing significant distress or dysfunction. Illness anxiety disorder is characterized by heightened bodily sensations and intense anxiety about the possibility of having an undiagnosed illness; patients with illness anxiety disorder may spend excessive amounts of time worrying about and researching health concerns, and they are not easily reassured about their health status.

Factitious disorders are characterized by intentionally produced physical or psychological symptoms. The motivation is to assume the sick role.

Dissociative disorders involve disruptions in consciousness, memory, identity, or perception that are more than ordinary forgetfulness. One dissociative disorder is psychogenic amnesia, which involves an inability to recall important personal information, usually of a traumatic or stressful nature. Another is dissociative identity disorder, formerly called multiple personality disorder, which is characterized by two or more distinct identities.

Sleep-wake disorders may be due to other mental disorders, medical conditions, or substances. Sleep-wake disorders arise from abnormalities in the ability to generate or maintain sleep-wake cycles. Symptoms of sleep disorder may include insomnia (difficulty initiating or maintaining sleep), hypersomnia (excessive sleepiness), narcolepsy (irresistible attacks of sleep), nightmares, sleep terror, or sleepwalking.

Disruptive, impulse-control, and conduct disorders are characterized by problems in emotional and behavioral self-control. The essential feature of impulse control disorders is a failure to resist an impulse, drive, or temptation to perform an act that is harmful to self or others.

Adjustment disorders involve a psychological response to an identifiable stressor that results in emotional or behavioral symptoms. As with other disorders, one must consider cultural setting in evaluating for the possibility of this disorder.

BIBLIOGRAPHY

Barkley, R. A. "Attention-Deficit Hyperactivity Disorder." *Scientific American* 279.3 (1998): 66–71. Print.

Costello, Charles G. *Symptoms of Schizophrenia*. New York: Wiley, 2000. Print.

Davis, Andrew S., ed. *Psychopathology of Childhood and Adolescence: A Neuropsychological Approach*. New York: Springer, 2012. Print.

Glasberg, Beth A. *Functional Behavior Assessment for People With Autism: Making Sense of Seemingly Senseless Behavior.* Bethesda: Woodbine House, 2000. Print.

Howlin, Patricia. *Autism: Preparing for Adulthood*. 2d ed. London: Routledge, 2004. Print.

Levy, Terry M., and Michael Orlans. *Attachment, Trauma, and Healing: Understanding and Treating Attachment Disorder in Children and Families.* Washington: Child Welfare League of America, 1998. Print.

Mash, Eric J., and Russell A. Barkley. *Child Psychopathology.* 3rd ed. New York: Guilford, 2014. Print.

Parritz, Robin Hornik, and Michael F. Troy. *Disorders of Childhood: Development and Psychopathology.* 2nd ed. Belmont: Wadsworth, 2012. Print.

Schwartz, S. *Abnormal Psychology: A Discovery Approach*. Mountain View: Mayfield, 2000. Print.

Lillian M. Range

See Also: Anxiety disorders; Asperger syndrome; Attachment and bonding in infancy and childhood; Attention-deficit hyperactivity disorder; Autism; Bed-wetting; Child abuse; Children's mental health; Conduct disorder; Depression; Dyslexia; Eating disorders; Family life: Children's issues; Father-child relationship; Hypochondriasis, conversion, and somatization; Impulse control disorders; Juvenile delinquency; Learning disorders; Mother-child relationship; Parental alienation syndrome; Piaget, Jean; Prenatal physical development; Psychotherapy: Children; Schizophrenia: High-risk children; Separation and divorce: Children's issues; Sibling relationships; Stepfamilies; Stuttering; Teenage suicide; Teenagers' mental health; Violence by children and teenagers.

Childhood obesity

Type of psychology: Addiction; Behavioral bases of human behavior; Behavioral medicine; Developmental; Family; Social

Childhood obesity is a nutritional and behavioral disorder that is quantifiably determined by having a body mass index (BMI) at or above the 95th percentile for children of the same age and sex. There are rapid changes from infant through adolescent development that are part of normal and expectable development. The norm used to identify obesity or how close to being obese a child is, must be corrected for that child's age and sex.

Key terms

- Adipose tissue
- Body mass index
- Hormones
- Metabolic syndrome

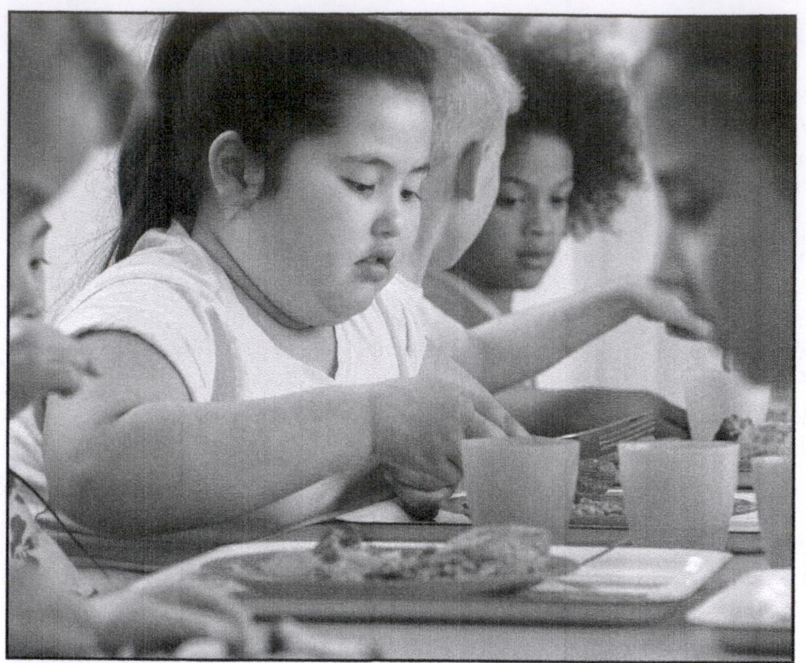

Photo: iStock

INTRODUCTION

Chronic or recurrent imbalance between energy expended (how active one is) and energy ingested (how much one eats and drinks) will promote ill health. When ingestion regularly exceeds expenditure, the unused energy is stored in adipose tissue, or "body fat." Animal species which developed the capacity to store fat had a better chance to survive times of scarcity. Chronic storage of excessive energy, as commonly occurs when high levels of physical activity are less and less necessary for survival, produces its own physical pathology. Almost everyone who eats and drinks more than he or she uses up in energy (usually calculated in calories) will produce adipose tissue to store the excess energy.

Peptide hormones like leptin and adiponectin regulate and balance energy expended with energy ingested. When leptin is absent (leptin-deficiency), massive obesity is present, and the condition improves when people are given leptin. Adiponectin, the most abundant hormone in fat cells, is also an insulin sensitizer and an anti-inflammatory signaler. Leptin and adiponectin, along with other peptide hormones, initiate a series of signaling processes that eventually lead to signaling hormones that turn on the food (energy) seeking abilities of organs and muscles.

The formal definition of obesity in children is a BMI greater than or equal to the 95th percentile. Children between the 85th and 95th percentiles are at risk for obesity; those less than the 85th percentile are generally considered to have normal weight when correlated with their height.

Childhood obesity has many detrimental effects and co-morbidities (other diseases and disorders) that often extend into adolescence and adulthood. It is simplistic to say that obese children will become obese adults. Still, childhood obesity often produces a metabolic syndrome that children easily bring into adolescence and adulthood. This syndrome has serious quality of life and length of life implications. It is a combination of high insulin levels (hypersinsulinemia), obesity, hypertension, and abnormal lipid levels (dyslipidemia), and over a million adolescents have it.

Metabolic syndrome initiates a process that leads to an excess of insulin production that, in turn, promotes high blood pressure and dyslipidemia. Together these produce aortic and coronary atherosclerosis—hardening of the arteries and clogging of heart values by fatty deposits in the blood.

Genetic factors play a fundamental role as genetically obese families illustrate. People cannot exchange the genes they have inherited. But, environmental factors are also important as they are the only ones where management is possible.

The psychosocial impact of obesity is no less serious than physical syndromes, leading to poor body image, low self-confidence, social isolation, recurrent anger, early forms of eating disorders, clinical depression, and negatively acting-out in school and other social settings. Obese children are more often than not underachieved, under-active, unpopular, and unhappy. Promoting physical activity is an important intervention to lessen obesity's psychological harm, no less than is controlling the amount and type of food and drink.

WHAT TO DO

The most effective treatment is prevention and it can begin shortly after birth. Research shows that breast fed children have significantly less obesity in later years. All children have to gain weight as they grow and having an adequate amount of fat cells during early ante-natal development is critically important for maximal growth of key organs. "Baby fat" is important; its absence problematic. As infants become toddlers and toddlers become children, the difference between healthy weight gains and weight gains that suggest the onset of obesity often require the expert eye of a pediatrician or family physician. A healthy five pound weight gain in one five-year-old child may not be healthy in another child of the same age.

It is not until adolescence that children play a significant role in choosing and purchasing food. Until then, whatever children eat is most likely what adults have purchased or provided. Preventing obesity and correcting it when it occurs requires thoughtful selection of food and beverage items at home and school. Fast and take-out foods are always an easy solution to busy, hectic family schedules, but are almost always obesity promoting. Junk food snacks, also a quick solution to the transient hunger pangs of youth, are similarly harmful.

Prevention and treatment are almost one and the same in dealing with child obesity. Parents control the food world of children and making available a variety of healthy choices becomes an important part of achieving and maintaining healthy bodies that have modest amounts of adipose tissue. Children with BMI's less than 20 are unhealthy and at risk. Obesity is much less likely to occur in families and schools that support healthy lifestyles: balanced nutritional consumption, physical activity and exercise, and sufficient sleep. (As a group, children who consistently sleep less than they need have far more obesity than children who sleep enough. The specific number of hours any child might need is a function of several factors including age.)

Successful school-based interventions in the management of obesity always include a prioritization of physical education classes, healthy choices on the student menu and in vending machines, proportional servings, encouraging water as the main beverage, and the ready availability of after-school activities which involve physical activity (e.g., intramural sports). When these elements are not present, effective obesity management for school-age children is just about impossible.

The key to successful long-term obesity prevention and treatment involves awareness of and respect for the individual child's personal preferences and enjoyments—nothing will enhance motivation more. Decreasing sitting time and the active encouragement of free play is far more effective than mandates to exercise or reduce food intake. Even in families where genetics play a major role in obesity, a healthy lifestyle will decrease the negative impact obesity can have on the children's overall health.

FINAL THOUGHTS

Childhood obesity is a still-growing epidemic that has achieved the status of a public health crisis. Obesity has profound impact on children's long term physical and psychological health and, much more often than not, leads to serious comorbidities in adulthood that are costly to treat and difficult to control. Focused strategies on modifying behavior and the slow but steady acquisition of healthy habits is the only way children will reliably manage the balance between calories consumed and calories burned. Adult habits, good and bad, are usually fostered during childhood. They reflect either the care, attention, and perseverance of caregivers, or caregivers' lack of care, attention, and perseverance. Childhood obesity can be a problem of adults' mismanagement much more than it is a problem of children's choices. Parents and teachers make a major contribution to children when they provide a health-oriented environment. In this environment, children are more likely to acquire the habits that promote wellness throughout their lives.

BIBLIOGRAPHY

Berg, Frances. (2005). *Underage & Overweight: America's Childhood Crisis—What Every Parent Needs to Know*. New York: Random House. A parent and guardian overview of how to practically manage children's obesity in their own homes. User-friendly, sensitive, and a reliable, scientifically-based guide.

Okie, Susan. (2005). *Fed Up! Winning the War Against Childhood Obesity.* Washington, DC, National Academies Press. Revolutionary when first published, this is a policy-oriented work that can also be adapted to local environments such as individual schools or school systems.

Sothern, Melinda S., Heidi Schumacher, and T. Kristian Von Almen (2003). *Trim Kids: The Proven 12-Week Plan That Has Helped Thousands of Children Achieve a Healthier Weight.* New York: Harper Collins. This is one of the more successful and effective plans for child and adolescent weight management. Provides for coordination among all the adults in children's and adolescents' lives.

Paul Moglia and Kenneth Dill

SEE ALSO: Binge eating; Childhood development; Eating behavior; Health; Nutrition; Obesity; Self esteem.

Children's depression inventory (CDI)

DATE: 1977 forward
TYPE OF PSYCHOLOGY: Psychopathology

The Children's Depression Inventory is a self-report questionnaire that allows children to report on their feelings of sadness and depression. This widely used questionnaire can be completed by children and adolescents themselves.

KEY CONCEPTS
- Multiple informants
- Norm
- Psychometric properties

INTRODUCTION

The Children's Depression Inventory (CDI) was first developed in 1977 by Maria Kovacs. It was based on the Beck Depression Inventory, which is a self-report measure for depression for adults. The CDI was designed to assess depression in children and adolescents from the ages of seven to seventeen. The second edition of the CDI was published in 2011. The measure has twenty-seven items that ask children to report on their possible depressive experiences, such as feeling sad, crying a lot, not having fun anymore, being tired, not wanting to live, having trouble sleeping, experiencing low self-esteem, and having difficulties with friends.

The CDI is worded so that children and adolescents can read the questions themselves and write down their own answers. Each item offers three statements that signify varying levels of severity (from no problems to severe problems). Children and adolescents are asked to choose the statement that is most reflective of how they have been feeling within the past two weeks.

For example, one item gives children the following three options: I am sad once in a while; I am sad many times; I am sad all the time. Children are asked to put a mark by the sentence that describes their feelings. The first sentence (I am sad once in a while) is something that even people who are not depressed would be likely to endorse, whereas the third sentence (I am sad all the time) is more reflective of depression.

There is no specific item that confirms a diagnosis of depression. Instead, all of the items on the CDI are added together to provide an overall picture of how the child feels. The measure has been normed so that a child's responses are compared against other children of that age and gender. The idea is that children's answers should be compared with what is average or normative for that age and gender. Through this norming process, professionals can be sure not to diagnose a child who is just feeling normal amounts of distress. Overall, the CDI can help professionals gain a better understanding of children's and adolescents' feelings of depression and related concerns.

STRENGTHS AND WEAKNESSES

One of the primary strengths of the CDI is that it is very widely used throughout many countries. This commonality allows easy communication between professionals. The norms and standardization sample of the CDI allow professionals to have confidence in their interpretations of children's and adolescents' depressive symptoms. The strong psychometric properties suggest that the CDI is reliable (that is, stable) and valid (that is, meaningful). In addition, the CDI is practical to use because it is easy to administer and to score, and it is not expensive for professionals to purchase.

Even with these strengths, the CDI has some limitations. Although it was originally meant to assess depression only, there is now research to suggest that it assesses other problems as well as depression. For example, children who have difficulty with school or who have problems with peers because of excessive fighting might receive high scores on the CDI. Thus, it is important for professionals to assess many aspects of the child's life rather than relying on the CDI alone to help diagnose depression.

OTHER METHODS TO ASSESS CHILDHOOD DEPRESSION

Even with a well-respected measure such as the CDI, it is standard practice for professionals to use a variety of measures before diagnosing depression in children and adolescents. In addition to using the CDI, professionals could conduct a structured diagnostic interview (such as the Diagnostic Interview Schedule for Children) with the child to assess for symptoms of depression and other psychological difficulties. Professionals may also want to observe the child (either in their office or in the classroom) to evaluate how the child interacts with others and to assess for depressive symptoms such as withdrawal or crying.

In addition to gathering information from the child directly, it is incumbent on professionals to use multiple informants (such as parents and teachers) to assess depression. The term "multiple informants" is used to suggest that other individuals in the child's life can provide useful information about the child's psychological symptoms. Structured diagnostic interviews can be conducted with parents about their child, and both parents and teachers can complete behavior checklists that might shed more light on the child's psychological functioning. Many widely used behavior checklists (such as the Child Behavior Checklist and the Teacher Report Form, both developed by Tom Achenbach) can be used in conjunction with the CDI. Professionals should try to get an overall view of the child's functioning and the family's functioning, rather than using the CDI by itself to diagnose depression.

BIBLIOGRAPHY

Abela, John R. Z., and Benjamin L. Hankin, eds. *Handbook of Depression in Children and Adolescents.* New York: Guilford, 2007. Print.

Allgaier, Antje-Kathrin, et al. "Is the Children's Depression Inventory Short Version a Valid Screening Tool in Pediatric Care? A Comparison to Its Full-Length Version." *Jour. of Psychosomatic Research* 73.5 (2012): 369–74. Print.

Cole, David A., Kit Hoffman, Jane M. Tram, and Scott E. Maxell. "Structural Differences in Parent and Child Reports of Children's Symptoms of Depression and Anxiety." *Psychological Assessment* 12.2 (2000): 174–85. Print.

Gladstone, Tracy R. G., and Nadine J. Kaslow. "Depression and Attributions in Children and Adolescents: A Meta-analytic Review." *Jour. of Abnormal Child Psychology* 23.5 (1995): 597–606. Print.

Gomez, Rapson, Alasdair Vance, and Andre Gomez. "Children's Depression Inventory: Invariance Across Children and Adolescents With and Without Depressive Disorders." *Psychological Assessment* 24.1 (2012): 1–10. Print.

Kovacs, Maria. *Children's Depression Inventory Manual.* North Tonawanda: Multi-health Systems, 2003. Print.

Liss, Heidi, Vicky Phares, and Laura Liljequist. "Symptom Endorsement Differences on the Children's Depression Inventory with Children and Adolescents on an Inpatient Unit." *Jour. of Personality Assessment* 76, no. 3 (2001): 396–411. Print.

Maughan, Barbara, et al. "Depression in Childhood and Adolescence." *Jour. of the Canadian Academy of Child & Adolescent Psychiatry* 22.1 (2013): 35–40. Print.

Petersen, Anne C., Bruce E. Compas, Jeanne Brooks-Gunn, Mark Stemmler, Sydney Ey, and Kathryn E. Grant. "Depression in Adolescence." *American Psychologist* 48.2 (1993): 155–68. Print.

Vicky Phares

See Also: Beck Depression Inventory (BDI); Childhood disorders; Children's mental health; Depression; Diagnosis

Children's mental health

Type of psychology: Biological bases of behavior; Developmental psychology; Intelligence and intelligence testing; Learning; Psychotherapy

According to the Centers for Disease Control and Prevention in 2009, an estimated 13 to 20 percent of children in the United States exhibit a mental health issue that, if not treated, could lead to functional impairment in activities of daily life and a failure to achieve the normal developmental stages of childhood. Satisfactory completion of the cognitive, emotional, and social phases of development is necessary for an enhanced quality of life and a healthy transition to adulthood. Parents, schools, and health care providers play a role in the recognition of the signs and symptoms of common childhood emotional and mental disorders so that children can receive the proper treatment.

Key Concepts

- Attention-deficit hyperactivity disorder (ADHD)
- Autism spectrum disorder
- Bipolar disorder
- Borderline personality disorder
- Depression
- Eating disorders
- Elimination disorders
- Schizophrenia

INTRODUCTION

Mental health may be defined as how people interact with others, handle stress related to life situations, work through problems, and cope with daily living in an appropriate manner. Children, just like adults, face these same issues in their daily lives. Mental health disorders in children are usually a result of environment, genetics, injuries to the central nervous system, and chemical imbalances. The effects of environment may include exposure to toxins such as lead or pesticides, exposure to violence, physical or sexual abuse, and stress related to poverty, bullying, or loss of a parent or significant family member through divorce or death. Genetic factors are evident in mental disorders such as depression, schizophrenia, and autism spectrum disorders. Traumatic brain injuries from abuse or falls, for example, may lead to both physical damage and changes in behavior, including depression, acting out, and aggression. Children may also exhibit signs of post-traumatic stress disorder caused by violence they have witnessed or experienced.

Mental health disorders are often overlooked in children unless the child's behavior is severely disruptive at home or school. If their disorder is untreated, children may experience school failure, conflicts with family and peers, and failure to achieve the developmental milestones of childhood that result in a healthy adulthood. Studies have reported that only one in five children with mental health issues receive needed services and intervention. Treatment for many disorders is effective; however, untreated disorders can have significant negative consequences.

The number of children in the United States being medicated for mental-health-related reasons is increasing at a rate higher than that of other countries, leading to the premise that mental health disorders in children are being overdiagnosed and overtreated with medications. Conversely, studies also show that some mental disorders are not being recognized and treated in an appropriate manner. Ways in which opportunities for children with mental health issues to be diagnosed and treated include increased awareness of mental health disorders in children due to media coverage; increased access to health care for children, which in turn leads to more physician-child observation; and programs designed to educate parents and educators on the mental health needs of children

PROMOTING GOOD MENTAL HEALTH

The physical needs of children for shelter and safety, adequate nutrition, play and rest, timely health care, and immunizations are easily recognized; however, understanding how to promote good mental health in children is not as obvious. Good mental health allows children to progress through expected developmental stages of life, allowing for age-appropriate learning and social development. Childhood is a time to develop self-esteem, self-confidence, and a sense of security. Family, school, and community all play a vital role in promoting children's mental health.

Children must feel a sense of love and security to try new skills and test the boundaries of their environment. Unconditional love from family allows children to experience both success and failure without feeling that love will be withdrawn if their accomplishments are not perfect. Attention, praise, and honesty in actions will promote self-esteem and support self-confidence. Providing a safe environment at home, day care, and school for play and learning will encourage exploration, leading to new skills. Positive verbal encouragement and realistic goal setting will reinforce desired behaviors. Negative or sarcastic comments may lead to discouragement and failure, if children perceive they are not good enough in the eyes of their caregivers. Negative comments should not be confused with teaching children when behaviors are unacceptable and when there are consequences to their actions. Criticizing the behavior, not the child, is central to the application of any needed discipline. When setting limits for acceptable behaviors, positive statements and unconditional love should guide the action.

Even with everyone surrounding the child providing unconditional love and respect, mental health disorders may still surface. Recognizing the need for early intervention is critical.

RECOGNIZING SIGNS OF DISORDERS

Parents, caregivers, teachers, and health care providers should all be sensitive to changes in children's capabilities, behavior, or mood. Babies who develop normally and then begin to regress or children who show a decline in school performance, exhibit hyperactivity, have temper tantrums, fight with siblings and peers, or withdraw from activities usually perceived as fun may be signs of a mental health disorder. Excessive or unreasonable fears, nightmares, hearing voices, killing animals, and changes in eating patterns are often evident in children with mental health issues that need immediate intervention.

Parents and caregivers should discuss any concerns about children's behavior in an open and honest manner without defensiveness. Recognizing that changes in behavior may be signs or symptoms of a mental health disorder is the first step in obtaining help for children in a timely manner. Discussing concerns about children with their pediatrician or school counselor will assist in determining if they need a referral for assessment or services from a mental health professional. Mental health organizations, libraries, the Internet, and hotlines are also resources for additional information.

Children's mental health problems should be recognized and addressed early. Many children have mental health issues, and problems can be real and painful to the child and the family. Recognizing that psychotherapy, behavioral intervention, and medications are effective therapies and can make a difference in the child's quality of life is essential to allowing a healthy and normal development.

Mental health disorders commonly seen in children include attention-deficit hyperactivity disorder (ADHD), attention-deficit disorder (ADD), anxiety disorders, autism spectrum disorders (ASD), depression, bipolar disorder, borderline personality disorder, eating disorders, and to a lesser degree, schizophrenia. Elimination disorders, when physical causes are ruled out, may also be considered a mental health disorder.

ADHD AND ADD

Two of the most common mental disorders in children, which often overlap, are attention-deficit hyperactivity disorder (ADHD) and attention deficit disorder (ADD). Children with these disorders have difficulty functioning at home, in daycare or school, and in relationships with others. Behaviors evident in ADHD and ADD include hyperactivity, impulsiveness, and inattention. Children with ADHD or ADD often act without thinking, cannot sit still or focused for any length of time, run instead of walk, talk incessantly or interrupt others, daydream, and are distracted by the environment, all of which lead to an inability to focus on the task at hand. The diagnosis must be made by a professional such as a child psychiatrist, psychologist, or physician with training in ADHD and ADD who also uses medical and school records, interviews caregivers and/or parents, and rules out other possible reasons for the exhibited behaviors. Treatment is generally effective and includes behavioral therapy and medications.

ANXIETY DISORDERS

Anxiety disorders in children are common and are evidenced by fears, unease, or unrealistic worry not associated with a recent event; panic attacks that include physical manifestations such as high heart rate and lightheadedness; and obsessive-compulsive disorder. Children who are victims of abuse or neglect, or who have been exposed to trauma such as a natural disaster may exhibit signs of post-traumatic stress disorder. Separation anxiety disorder, normally seen in infants and toddlers, becomes an issue when older children cannot separate from their parents, are afraid to sleep alone, or are unable to leave the home for school or other events. Obsessive-compulsive disorder involves recurrent, compulsive behaviors such as hand washing that become so time-consuming as to interfere with daily activities. There is some evidence that an increase in obsessive-compulsive disorder occurs after a bout of streptococcal infection, and obsessive-compulsive disorder is considered to have a strong familial influence. Social anxiety disorder is said to occur when the child is afraid of being embarrassed in social or performance settings. Treatment depends on the symptoms exhibited and is focused on behavior changes. Psychotherapy is used in some disorders, but its efficacy is not certain.

AUTISM SPECTRUM DISORDERS

Autism spectrum disorders are developmental disorders of brain function that range from autistic disorder in the most severe form, to pervasive developmental disorders not otherwise specified (PDD-NOS) in a less severe form, and to Asperger syndrome, a mild form. Two rare disorders include childhood disintegrative disorder and Rett syndrome. The disorder is usually diagnosed early in childhood, often when parents notice that their baby seems different or is not interacting with people. At times, the baby may develop normally to a point and then regress. A toddler who quits talking, does not interact with others, or becomes self-abusing may be exhibiting signs of autism spectrum disorders. The classic findings include impairments in social interactions and verbal and nonverbal communication; limitations in or severely restricted interests; repetitive movements such as hair twirling, rocking, or head banging; and heightened sensitivity to external stimuli. Diagnosis is made by assessing behavior based on a set of developed criteria that includes observation of play, social interactions, language, interests, rituals, and interaction with objects. Hearing and intelligence quotient (IQ) testing may also be part of the diagnostic procedure. Treatments are individualized and may include behavioral, educational, and medical interventions, but there is no cure.

DEPRESSION

A report from the Federal Interagency Forum on Child and Family Statistics indicated that in 2011, major depression occurred in approximately 8 percent of all children ages twelve to seventeen, with a major depressive episode occurring in girls more than twice than in boys. The percent of youths who reported a major depressive episode who were also receiving treatment in the form of therapy and/or medication was reported to be just under 40 percent in 2011. Causes of depression may include a variety of factors such as environment, life events, family changes, school problems, genetics, and biochemical disturbances. If a child seems sad or loses interest in activities normally of interest, withdraws from friends and family, or does poorly in school for an extended period of time, depression may be the cause. Depression is often overlooked, and changes in behavior are inappropriately blamed on emotional and hormonal changes as the child ages. Symptoms of depression in children may also include anger, changes in appetite or sleep patterns, fatigue, and thoughts of death and suicide. Although suicide in children is rare, it does occur. A diagnosis of depression is made by a physician or mental health professional based on duration and type of symptoms, interviews with family and others, and questionnaires and other nonmedical tests. Treatment may include psychotherapy and medications. The Food and Drug Administration (FDA) has determined that antidepressants in children may increase the risk of suicidal thoughts, so their use must be carefully monitored.

BIPOLAR DISORDER

Bipolar disorder, also known as manic-depressive disorder, is evidenced by sometimes rapid changes in mood, functioning, and activity or energy level. Dramatic shifts in mood from high or irritable to low or sad are classic symptoms of bipolar disorder and are called periods of mania or depression, respectively. These periods may occur multiple times in the same day in children. Differentiating mania episodes from ADHD may pose a challenge in diagnosis. Elated mood, lack of need for sleep, expansive or grandiose behaviors, and a feeling that rules do not apply are common in manic episodes and are not common in ADHD. Diagnosis is based on an assessment by a physician or mental health professional. Treatments are individualized and may include several medications in combination, accompanied by psychotherapy. Bipolar disorder in children is usually more severe than in adults, with shorter periods of time between manic and depressive periods. Adults may have longer periods of normal functioning between episodes.

BORDERLINE PERSONALITY DISORDER

Borderline personality disorder (BPD) causes instability in behavior, interactions with others, personal image, and mood, including emotional regulation of actions, lasting hours rather than days as in other disorders. Individuals diagnosed with borderline personality disorder often report physical or sexual abuse, neglect, or separation from a parent or significant person as a young child. Genetic factors are also thought to play a role in borderline personality disorder. The onset of the disease is usually the late teens or young adulthood, and the disorder is more prevalent in female adolescents and young women. Borderline personality disorder is thought to begin with childhood issues related to environment and stress factors. In some instances, younger children may be diagnosed. The disorder is often the cause for psychiatric hospital admissions. Treatment includes psychotherapy and medications, including antidepressants, antipsychotics, and mood stabilizers. Dialectical behavior therapy (DBT) was developed to treat borderline personality disorder and shows promise. Neuroscience research, including brain imaging and studies of alteration in brain chemicals, is also showing promise in treatment.

EATING DISORDERS

Eating disorders, including anorexia nervosa, bulimia nervosa, and binge eating, are being seen in younger children at increasing rates. Collectively, eating disorders in children are said to exist when a child is overly preoccupied with weight, food selection or avoidance, and body image. Causes of eating disorders may include struggles at mealtime with a parent, being a picky eater, seeing mealtime and meals as unpleasant because of conflict or disruptions, and other environmental factors. Children with eating problems at a young age are more likely to develop eating disorders later in childhood or in their teenage years. Obesity, changes in weight, and unusual behavior are clues to eating disorders. Treatment is based on the severity of the disorder and includes psychotherapy, behavioral therapy, and hospitalization and medical intervention, such as the giving of electrolytes and fluids in more severe cases.

SCHIZOPHRENIA

Schizophrenia is a disabling brain disorder most common in young adults eighteen years of age and older. Although rare, it does occur in children. Individuals with the disorder often hear voices that others do not hear and believe that others are listening in on their thoughts and that people are trying to hurt them. Children with schizophrenia withdraw and become shy over time, may exhibit a decline in personal hygiene, and may talk about fears, strange ideas, and death. Causes are thought to be brain changes, biochemical changes, genetics, and environment. Symptoms include delusional thoughts, hallucinations, disordered thoughts, social withdrawal, and flat affect. Treatment is based on medication management, individual and group therapy, family therapy, and often a structured program at school. Careful management may allow the child to grow into independent living.

ELIMINATION DISORDERS

Elimination disorders involve both defecation and urination. Encopresis is when a child passes feces in places other than the toilet, and enuresis is the passing of urine in places other than the toilet. Elimination disorders such as encopresis and enuresis are not to be confused with occasional accidents. When a child repeatedly demonstrates elimination disorders, especially if the child is over the age of five, and no physical reason exists, intervention may be needed. Encopresis is generally caused by constipation because of inadequate fluid and nutrition leading to poor nerve function in the anus, fear of using public toilets, and fear or frustration related to toilet training or stressful life events. Enuresis may be caused by a small bladder, urinary tract infection, severe stress, or developmental issues related to toilet training. Once all physical reasons for encopresis and enuresis are ruled out, treatment is focused on determining the influences on the child leading to the elimination disorder. Determining sources of anxiety and stress and eliminating or decreasing their influence is essential to treatment. Behavior therapy is usually successful in correcting mental-health-related reasons for elimination disorders. Diet modifications to prevent constipation and liquid restrictions to assist in bladder control support treatment success. Medications are available that may assist with encopresis (laxatives, stool softeners) and enuresis management (drugs that affect urine production in the kidney) but are generally used only if other methods of treatment fail. Early intervention will protect the child's self-esteem, as an elimination disorder may result in social isolation and increased anxiety and depression.

PROMPT RECOGNITION OF MENTAL HEALTH DISORDERS

The prompt recognition of children's mental health issues is essential to their health and well-being during childhood and leads to a healthy transition to adulthood. If children do not receive care for mental health disorders, they will experience recurring problems at home, school, and in relationships. Parents must also understand that mental disorders are not the fault of parenting in most situations and that a disorder is not something that the child can control. Treatment for mental health disorders may take months or years, but most disorders are manageable with appropriate interventions.

BIBLIOGRAPHY

Axelrad, M. E., J. S. Pendley, D. L. Miller, and W. D. Tynan. "Implementation of Effective Treatments of Preschool Behavior Problems in a Clinic Setting." *Journal of Clinical Psychology in Medical Settings* 15.2 (2008): 120–6. Print.

Barlow, Jane, and P. O. Svanberg, eds. *Keeping the Baby in Mind: Infant Mental Health in Practice.* New York: Routledge, 2010. Print.

Burgio, Maria R. *Is My Child Normal? When Behavior Is Okay, When It's Not, How to Tell the Difference, and What to Do Next.* Fort Lee: Barricade, 2008. Print.

Daviss, W. B. "A Review of Co-morbid Depression in Pediatric ADHD: Etiology, Phenomenology, and Treatment." *Journal of Child and Adolescent Psychopharmacology* 18.6 (2008): 565–71. Print.

Gnaulati, Enrico. *Back to Normal: Why Ordinary Childhood Behavior is Mistaken for ADHD, Bipolar Disorder, and Autism Spectrum Disorder.* Boston: Beacon, 2013. Print.

Kogan, M. D., et al. "A National Profile of the Health Care Experiences and Family Impact of Autism Spectrum Disorder Among Children in the United States, 2005–2006." *Pediatrics* 122.6 (2008): 1149–58. Print.

McDougall, Tim, and Andy Cotgrove. *Specialist Mental Healthcare for Children and Adolescents: Hospital, Intensive Community and Home-Based Services.* New York: Routledge, 2014. Print.

Mullers, E. S., and M. Dowling. "Mental Health Consequences of Child Sexual Abuse." *British Journal of Nursing* 17.22 (2008): 1428–33. Print.

Shannon, Scott M. *Mental Health for the Whole Child: Moving Young Clients from Disease & Disorder to Balance & Wellness.* New York: Norton, 2013. Print.

Vostanis, Panos, ed. *Mental Health Interventions and Services for Vulnerable Children and Young People.* Philadelphia: Jessica Kingsley, 2008. Print.

Patricia Stanfill Edens

SEE ALSO: Abnormality: Biomedical models; Abnormality: Psychological models; Anorexia nervosa and bulimia nervosa; Anxiety disorders; Asperger syndrome; Attachment and bonding in infancy and childhood; Attention-deficit hyperactivity disorder; Autism; Bipolar disorder; Borderline personality disorder; Bullying; Child abuse; Childhood disorders; Conduct disorder; Depression; Developmental disabilities; Eating disorders; Elimination disorders; Family life: Children's issues; Father-child relationship; Impulse control disorders; Misbehavior; Mother-child relationship; Personality disorders; Pervasive developmental disorders; Psychotherapy: Children; Schizophrenia: High-risk children; Separation and divorce: Children's issues; Tic disorders.

Christian counseling

TYPE OF PSYCHOLOGY: Clinical; Counseling; Psychology and Religion, Psychotherapy

Christian counseling is faith-based counseling typically utilizing the Bible and its teachings. Counselors may use examples from Scripture in their sessions with clients. There are many different types of Christian counselors including pastors, priests, and laymen. Other Christian counselors are licensed mental health professionals. A major issue within Christian counseling relates to how Christian counselors work with those who identify themselves as homosexual, bisexual, or transgender. Although conversion therapy is frowned upon in most psychological circles, it is still a technique used by some Christian counselors.

KEY CONCEPTS

- Christian counseling
- Neouthetic counseling
- Biblical or pastoral counseling
- Conversion therapy
- Cultural competence

INTRODUCTION

Christian counseling can be defined as a genre of faith or spirituality based counseling that adheres to biblical teachings, specifically, the teachings of Jesus Christ. Practitioners of Christian counseling generally believe that the Bible addresses all problems in life, and that talking and listening to the Word of God can be helpful in addressing mental, emotional, and personal issues. Christian counselors tend to see God as the ultimate agent of change.

JAY ADAMS AND NEOUTHETIC COUNSELING

Although religion has always been seen as a psychological comfort to many, the field of Christian counseling gained new energy in the 1970s when Dr. Jay Adams published his book *Competent to Counsel.* Adams calls Christians to shun modern psychological theory in the application of counseling and instead turn to the Bible and its teachings in order to heal people's emotional problems and relationship issues. Adams termed this type of counseling neouthetic counseling. Neouthetic counseling focuses on three basic tenets: confrontation, concern, and change.

Within neouthetic counseling, confrontation occurs when a counselor (which could be a pastor, layperson, or licensed mental health practitioner) instructs or gently confronts a counselee with Scripture or biblical advice regarding their personal issue. According to Adams, the counselor must always address the counselee with authentic concern, making sure that the counselee is the one benefitting from the spiritual counseling. Finally, Christian counselors must always focus on change, centering on deepening a client's relationship with Christ.

BASIC TENETS

Most Christian counselors believe that in prayerfully following Jesus Christ and His teachings, clients may find psychological and physical relief from the pain and emotional disharmony they may be experiencing. Suffering is purposeful, because it allows individuals to experience what Christ experienced in his own life. The role of the self is less important than in secular counseling, and clients are asked to meditate on God's call and what would be pleasing to God, instead of focusing on one's idea of happiness or self worth. The goal of Christian counseling is to lead individuals to a place where joyful living becomes dependent on their trust in God and their relationship with God. The emphasis is on repentance, confession, and the experience of divine forgiveness.

Christian counselors believe the root of most problems is sin, both the original sin that Christians believe individuals are born with, as well as sin individuals involve themselves with as citizens of the world. Most Christian counselors and laypeople will say that all humans are vulnerable to Satan's influence, but that the protective power of the Holy Spirit can help individuals resist the temptation of sin. Thus, a major goal of Christian counseling is to strengthen a client's relationship with Christ, therefore creating a protective buffer against the works of Satan.

The role of the counselor is to model the joy of having a Christ centered life. Counselors are asked to reflect the love, compassion, and kindness of Jesus Christ in their words and actions during sessions with clients. Most Christian counselors choose to focus on their personal and professional commitment to "soul care," or healing a client with a focus on the client's spiritual life. Similar to the counselor-client relationship in humanistic forms of therapy, Christian counselors do not see themselves as having a "one up, one down" relationship with clients. Instead, they see themselves on the same level as the client, seeking the wisdom and grace of God.

The New Testament includes a reference to Jesus as "wonderful counselor." Christian counselors aim to follow the path of Jesus while counseling others. They use the Bible frequently and quote verses. Christian counselors perceive the Bible as a sacred book that addresses feelings of anxiety, loneliness, discouragement, loss, relationships, marital issues, and grief.

TYPES OF CHRISTIAN COUNSELING

Researchers McMinn, Staley, Webb, and Seegobin (2010) discuss a variety of counseling approaches that may fall under the umbrella of Christian counseling. It is important for prospective clients as well as mental health practitioners to be aware of the differences in these approaches when choosing a counselor or referring a client.

Biblical counseling is most likely sought and given by those who identify themselves as conservative Christians. Biblical counselors function under the belief that the Word of God is superior to psychological science or evidence-based practice. Those who practice biblical counseling are usually not professional psychologists, mental health counselors, or social workers. Instead, they may be leaders, pastors, or elders within a church. The effectiveness of biblical counseling is not well researched.

Pastoral counseling is a type of Christian counseling done by religious leaders such as pastors, priests, or clergy. Pastoral counseling can also be done by non-Christian leaders such as rabbis or imams. There are two basic types of pastoral counselors. One has minimal experience with counseling but much spiritual experience as a church leader. The second may have equal experience in counseling and spiritual leading, perhaps because of formal education or having graduated from a dual degree program in ministry and psychotherapy/counseling.

The term Christian psychologist is also used on occasion. Some Christian psychologists are licensed mental health practitioners who are willing to integrate spirituality and tenets of Christianity into their work with clients. Other Christian psychologists are those who belong to the Society of Christian Psychology (SCP) and base their counseling practice on the Bible and other major Christian texts.

HOMOSEXUALITY AND CONVERSION THERAPY

One hot button issue that affects the field of Christian counseling is Christians' views on homosexuality and how it is applied within a clinical context. Although the American Psychiatric Association declassified homosexuality as a disorder in 1973, some Christians and Christian counselors believe that homosexuality is pathological in nature, and individuals who identify as gay or lesbian can be cured.

Conversion or reorientation therapy is a controversial process with the goal of changing an individual's sexual

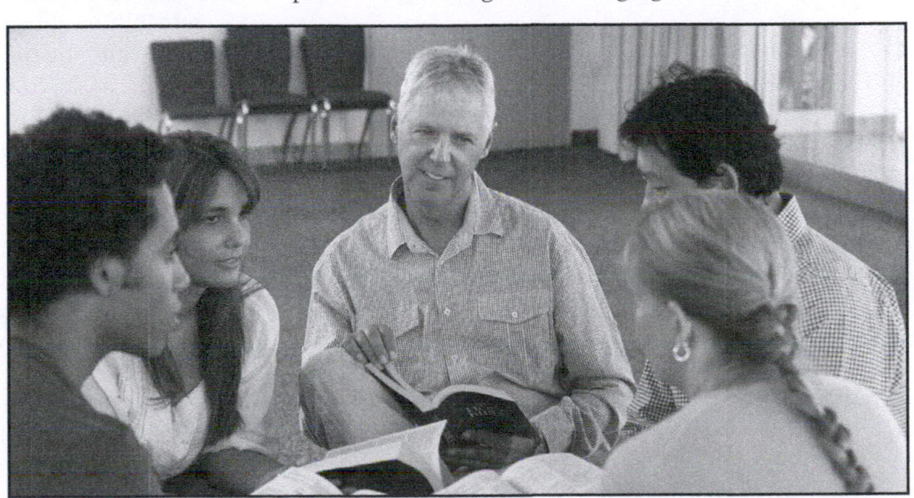

Photo: iStock

orientation from homosexual to heterosexual. Although it is ethically discouraged, conversion therapy is still practiced in some Christian circles, based on the biblical view that God designed sex to be practiced between a male and a female. Those who have been involved in conversion therapy have reported intense feelings of shame associated with their sexual orientation and have had negative outcomes with regards to mental health including depressive, anxious, and suicidal thoughts and feelings. The call to ban reorientation therapy was reignited in 2015, after transgender teen Leelah Alcorn committed suicide following several rounds of Christian based conversion therapy.

PROFESSIONAL ETHICS AND CULTURAL COMPETENCE

All major psychological and counseling ethical boards, including the American Psychological Association (APA) and American Counseling Association (ACA), warn against using conversion therapy as a "treatment" for homosexuality. However, they view conversion therapy as a religious, not psychological, practice,thereby releasing themselves from ethical responsibilities surrounding reorientation therapy.

Nevertheless, counselors who choose religious based interventions instead of evidence-based practices with regards to LGBT issues do present a serious ethical quandary to these professional boards. Culturally competent, licensed Christian counselors should be aware of both their Christian worldview as well as the role they play as counselors in the professional world when engaging in the therapeutic process with clients.

CONCLUSION

In recent years, professional associations such as the American Psychological Association and American Psychiatric Association have addressed the role of religion and spirituality within clinical practice. There is an acknowledgement that bringing spirituality into a counseling and psychotherapy practice may be helpful for those clients who already adhere to a particular religion. However, much more research must be done on the specific effectiveness of Christian counseling as well as the process of integrating religious and spiritual based practices into the mostly secular clinical psychology or psychiatry practice.

BIBLIOGRAPHY

Association of Biblical Counselors. (2014). *Philosophy of Ministry.* Retrieved from http://christiancounseling.com/content/philosophy-of-ministry. Outlines the basic tenets of biblical based counseling for licensed and non-licensed Christian counselors. Offers news, information, and support for Christian counselors.

Collins, G. R. (2007). *Christian Counseling: A Comprehensive Guide* (3rd ed.). Nashville, TN: Thomas Nelson.Provides an in-depth look at Christian counseling as a whole. Includes chapters on how to work with children, adults, and the elderly as well as how the Christian counselor may address a myriad of personal issues including homosexuality, anger, grief, anxiety, depression, and substance abuse.

Flentje, A., Heck, N.C., & Cochran, B.N. (2014). Experiences of ex-ex-gay individuals in sexual reorientation therapy: Reasons for seeking treatment, perceived helpfulness and harmfulness of treatment, and post treatment identification. *Journal of Homosexuality*, 61, 1242-1268. A qualitative study of 38 individuals who went through conversion therapy yet still identify as gay or lesbian. Mentions perceived helpful aspects of conversion therapy as well as hurtful aspects.

Interview with Dr. Mark McMinn, a professor of psychology who researches and writes about spirituality and Christian counseling.

Kersting, K. (2003). "Religion and Spirituality in The Treatment Room". *Monitor on Psychology*, 34, 40. Discusses issues of bringing aspects of spirituality or religion into a secular psychology practice. Reviews the American Psychological Association's call for more research on integrating spirituality and religious elements into the therapeutic process.

McMinn, M.R., Staley, R.C., Webb, K.C., & Seegobin, W. (2010). "Just What is Christian Counseling Anyway?" *Professional Psychology: Research and Practice,* 41, 39- 397. Outlines and provides explanation about the variety of approaches that fall within the realm of Christian counseling.

The varieties of religious therapy: Christian psychology (Interview by R. Howes) [Transcript]. (2011, November 16). Retrieved from Psychology Today website: http://www.psychologytoday.com/blog/in-therapy/201111/the-varieties-religious-therapy-christian-psychology

Whitman, J.S., Glosoff, H.L., Kocet, M.M., & Tarvydas, V. (2006). *Exploring Ethical Issues Related To Conversion or Reparative Therapy.* Retrieved from http://ct.counseling.org/2006/05/

exploring-ethical-issues-related-to-conversion-or-reparative-therapy/. Gives a clear definition of conversion therapy as well as the ethical issues surrounding conversion therapy. Outlines the American Counseling Association's official stance on conversion therapy.

Gina Riley

See Also: Christianity; Counseling; Religion; Religious beliefs; Theology.

Chronic pain management
Psychological impact

Type of psychology: Addiction; Behavioral medicine; Clinical; Counseling; Health; Psychopathology; Psychotherapy

Chronic pain can be defined as a pervasive health condition that impacts an individual's daily life, including episodes of increased pain which impacts ability to function physically and emotionally. Diagnosing and managing chronic pain can be a lifelong battle leading to psychological distress and physical disability.

Key concepts:

- Pain
- Chronic pain
- Depression
- Pain management
- Disability

INTRODUCTION

A pain free life is something that most of us take for granted. Pain is a phenomenon that we experience in episodes such as falling off a ladder, breaking an arm, or waking up with a headache from too much champagne the previous night. Most experiences of pain are short lived and diminish quickly over time. Our ideas of health and wellness often revolve around the absence of pain; therefore overall well-being can be quantified by the level of pain experienced on a daily basis.

With lack of pain topping the list of what defines a healthy life, those who suffer from chronic pain may struggle with even the most mundane of tasks. It has been estimated that 1.5 billion people suffer from chronic pain conditions in the world on a daily basis. In the United States, chronic pain has been suggested to be the top cause of people seeking medical attention, costing an annual average of $100 billion in health care. The magnitude of this problem is vast and can be extremely complicated due to the challenge in understanding the cause, diagnosis, and methods to treat chronic pain. It is necessary for knowledge to spread in order to support those around us who battle pain every day of their lives.

CHRONIC PAIN

Chronic pain can be described as mild to severe pain which has been present for six months or longer. This pain can be due to an injury, illness, or a specific chronic pain diagnosis such as fibromyalgia. It has been estimated that approximately 100 million American adults are living with chronic pain. The impact of chronic pain can vary as much as the severity from something as mild as a headache or as severe as debilitating, widespread pain. People dealing with these symptoms often experience an overall change or challenge to their abilities and functioning level. This impact also will vary with the severity and frequency that the person experiences the pain symptoms. Chronic headaches may occur once a month and require the person to take the day off work, while a person with fibromyalgia or lupus may be rendered disabled. Because pain is a non-tangible, subjective, and personal experience it can be challenging to determine the necessary treatment and level of disability. This is the reason that chronic pain is often undiagnosed, misdiagnosed, or ignored for long periods of time.

TYPES AND SOURCES OF CHRONIC PAIN

As previously stated, chronic pain ranges in severity, frequency, and duration. The source of pain may be known as in the instance of injury. It could be the result of an illness that was either cured or uncured. Diabetes is a common cause of chronic pain affecting 25 million Americans. In other instances such as chronic joint pain or headaches, the root of the pain may not be identified. Regardless of whether the cause of the chronic pain is known or unknown, it can be classified by the level of disturbance to one's overall functioning and ability to participate in previously enjoyable activities. People often seek medical attention when pain becomes overwhelming or negatively impacts their lives, such as difficulty performing work requirements or household tasks.

DIAGNOSIS

Because pain is a subjective experience, medical professionals often find it a challenge to accurately diagnosis chronic pain. Medical professionals must rely on the patient's self-description of pain to determine how to explore causes and treatments. Because each person will have different ways in which he or she experiences and describes pain, diagnosing chronic pain is often a difficult task. It may take many years to arrive at an accurate diagnosis and correct treatment. For patients suffering from widespread chronic pain like fibromyalgia, this is a common occurrence. These individuals often tell stories of many years of seeking out numerous doctors and specialists without any relief. Each doctor may have a different option or hypothesis of what is causing the pain which leads down different diagnostic and treatment paths. Exploring these different avenues can take months or even years to rule out specific disorders and may cause increased stress on the person who is experiencing chronic pain. Due to the burdenof searching for help, including the variety of interventions and treatments attempted, the person may even give up before finding any relief.

PSYCHOLOGICAL IMPACT

Chronic pain is linked to many psychological issues, especially depression and anxiety. People suffering from long lasting pain may experience intense emotional distress based on both physical and emotional impacts. The physical experience of pain links to the stress of a constant search for a cure, doctor's appointments, and the participation in both Western medicine and/or Eastern holistic treatments. The management of care can itself cause extensive emotional stress including time and financial burden. Even the least invasive of treatments can be pricey, leaving people with chronic pain constantly paying for care, and the cost of medical bills alone can put people into financial hardship, adding further stress and forcing the need to make difficult decisions regarding how to manage care.

Based on the severity and frequency of the chronic pain the person may have difficulty keeping regular employment, and chronic pain is a common reason people file for disability.

The emotional strife of dealing with chronic pain can lead to further and more severe mental struggles. Depression, anxiety, and long-lasting fatigue can decrease the body's ability to produce natural painkillers. Therefore, the experience of chronic pain coupled with psychological struggle can exacerbate pain's severity, frequency, and duration. As chronic pain adds to emotional turmoil, it also leads to a breakdown of the immune system needed to fight disease. Those suffering with chronic pain are more susceptible to other common illnesses such as cold or flu. As this negative cycle continues, the person dealing with chronic pain is apt to become even more depressed, anxious, angry, and fatigued. The psychological impact of chronic pain will vary for each person based on many biopsychosocial factors. Unfortunately for those experiencing chronic pain, the physical pain and emotional strife seem to influence the other, and as the physical pain worsens the psychological struggle may also worsen.

PSYCHOLOGICAL TREATMENT

Although chronic pain patients are often in search of a cure to their suffering, most treatment plans only have the ability to stabilize and manage the pain. As this news often comes with extreme disappointment and sadness, emotional support and mental health counseling can be very beneficial. Coping with the loss of living a pain-free life can put the chronic pain sufferer into an intense depression accompanied with anger and anxiety. Because chronic pain is an invisible ailment it is often overlooked or not understood by others. Even people closest to the individual experiencing chronic pain may not be able to understand the extent of struggle the person is experiencing. This may come across as invalidating or hurtful to the person suffering and may create further difficulties. On the other hand, even if family, friends, and employers are supportive they may still not have the ability to fully comprehend the limitations that the person is feeling. It can be hard to quantify the level of debilitation that chronic fatigue or headaches may cause. A person experiencing chronic pain may feel very alone in his or her suffering. Therefore, having a therapist, counselor, or support group is very important. Finding others to share the struggle greatly alleviates the emotional turmoil these people are feeling. Moreover, support groups are know to be beneficial because having the ability to discuss and process the challenge of managing chronic pain validates the chronic pain experience and serves as a source of pain management solutions. Thus, in addition to any medical or holistic treatment options offered, mental health support is also recommended as part of treatment. Taking an all-encompassing holistic approach is the most inclusive arena for helping the person suffering with chronic pain.

Because chronic pain is generally not a curable condition, the treatment goal revolves around helping the person return to a normal level of functioning. This includes being able to manage daily routines such as work, household management, and recreational activities.

Again this will vary for each person and will be measured by the individual experiencing the pain.

MEDICATIONS AND SURGERY

Common treatments of chronic pain include pain medications and nerve-blocking medications. eMdical professionals may recommend anything from aspirin to prescription narcotics. Nerve-blocking medications are often used to treat fibromyalgia which is known to cause overactive and oversensitive nerves resulting in chronic pain. Often people who experience migraines or suffer from diabetes are on a regiment of medications to manage symptoms. In some cases surgeries or electrical stimulations are used when medications do not prove to be effective. These more invasive options range in effectiveness and may leave the individual deeply disappointed if they do not alleviate symptoms. Surgery is a common option for those experiencing chronic back pain. These invasive surgeries can result in pain and long recoveries; however, the possibility of reduced pain motivates many individuals to choose this option.

HOLISTIC TREATMENTS

Many people in the United States begin their treatment with traditional Western medicine options. Along with medication or surgery, rehabilitation such as physical therapy are often the next prescribed treatment. Physical therapy is most common when suffering occurs from a known injury that precipitates the chronic pain. Physical therapy may include stretching, strengthening, muscle stimulation, and other types of rehabilitation.

Another avenue often explored by those suffering with chronic pain is Eastern or holistic medicine. Treatments include acupuncture, acupressure, biofeedback, chiropractic manipulation, massage therapy, and relaxation therapies. These alternative treatments are often used in conjunction with Western treatments. Other areas often explored are nutritional and exercise impacts and benefits. Meeting with nutritionists and exercise specialists can be extremely beneficial in managing chronic pain. Dietitians create diet plans for individuals experiencing chronic pain by including and excluding certain foods that may impact pain levels. Exercise is also suggested based on the person's mobility. Low impact exercise such as swimming, walking, or Thai Chi may be recommended.Overall, health care professionals agree that maintaining health, including a balanced body weight and nutrition, has a large impact on the management of chronic pain.

SELF-MANAGEMENT

As an individual journeys from being diagnosed with chronic pain to managing a treatment plan, he or she will need to take the driver's seat. It is very important for these individuals to self-manage care, because chronic pain is a unique and individual experience for each person. Doctors and health care professionals may have a variety of ideas to assist their patients, but a patient must be assertive in what has worked and what has not. Chronic pain sufferers also need to advocate for themselves through research and willingness to try different avenues of pain management. It is important to be educated in their unique issues and keep track of how different treatments, foods, exercise, and medication impact pain level. As their own self-care managers, patients have the ability to join a community of others who also experience and understand chronic pain, increase their knowledge of chronic pain, and find the best options for managing levels of pain and psychological distress.

BIBLIOGRAPHY

Bullington, J., Rolf, N., Nordemar, K., & Sjöström-Flanagan, C. (2003). "Meaning Out of Chaos: A Way To Understand Chronic Pain". *Scandinavian Journal of Caring Sciences*, 17(4), 325-331. DOI: 10.1046/j.0283-9318.2003.00244.x Explains the stress and difficulty surrounding the diagnosis and management of chronic pain.

Carlson, M. (2014). *CBT For Chronic Pain and Psychological Well-Being: A Skills Training Manual Integrating DBT, ACT, Behavioral Activation and Motivational Interviewing*. Minneapolis, MN: Wiley-Blackwell. Provides detailed information regarding different theoretical interventions used when working with chronic pain patients.

Greve, K. W., & Bianchini, K. J. (2012). *The Psychological Assessment of Pain-related Disability.* Coping with psychiatric and psychological testimony Based on the original work by Jay Ziskin (6th ed.). Faust, David (Ed); New York, NY: Oxford University Press. Focuses on how a diagnosis of chronic pain impacts and influences psychological issues and assessment.

Heverly, J. (2007). *Chronic Pain: Implications For Therapy. Dissertation Abstracts International: Section B: The Sciences and Engineering,* 68(6-B), 4132. While written in a doctoral dissertation format and presumes some academic familiarity on the part of readers, it includes an excellent exploration of how mental health professionals understand the impact of chronic pain on psychological issues and discusses how to handle these issues in therapy.

Lebovits, A. (2002). Psychological issues in the assessment and management of chronic pain. *Annals of the American Psychotherapy Association*, 5(3), 19-21. Discusses the process of assessing and managing chronic pain.

Kimberly Ortiz

See Also: Coping; Medication; Occupational therapy; Pain; Pain management; Physical therapy.

Circadian rhythms

Type of psychology: Biological bases of behavior; Consciousness; Stress

Circadian rhythms are cyclical variations in biological processes or behavior with duration of approximately one day. Most physiological, biochemical, and molecular events follow a circadian pattern, repeating themselves once in approximately twenty-four hours. Among the most studied physiological activities are the sleep-wake cycle and body temperature. The severity of many human diseases, such as asthma and hypertension, also fluctuates in a diurnal pattern. Shift-work problems, jet lag, and seasonal affective disorder (SAD) are examples of disorders caused by alterations in circadian rhythms.

Key Concepts

- Chronobiology
- Free-running rhythm
- Jet lag
- Melatonin
- Seasonal affective disorder
- Suprachiasmatic nucleus
- Zeitgeber

INTRODUCTION

Circadian rhythms are a fundamental characteristic of life. The term circadian was coined by Franz Halberg and refers to rhythms that are about a day in length (from the Latin *circa*, "about," and *dies*, "day"). Although historically many of the early observations were made on plants and animals, later research has shown a remarkable similarity in the structure and functioning of the circadian clock across different species. Circadian rhythms are ubiquitous and are exhibited by most physiological, biochemical, and molecular events that occur in organisms and share common mechanisms of operation.

The most obvious rhythm of human activity is the sleep-wake cycle. Human beings are most active during the daylight hours and sleep for much of the dark period. A species with this schedule is called diurnal (animals active during the dark period are termed nocturnal). Human beings are essentially diurnal except for the adaptations that come with work, travel, and other circumstances.

It is known that the sleep-wake cycle is not determined as rigidly as many other physiological rhythms. For example, one can choose not to sleep for several days and thereby temporarily abolish the pattern. A more fundamental and less easily modified rhythm is the circadian rhythm of core body temperature. In this case, there is a daily fluctuation of slightly more than 1 degree Celsius over the course of twenty-four hours, with the lowest body temperature occurring between 4:00 and 5:00 a.m., when a person is deep in sleep. The temperature rhythm continues its fluctuation, although somewhat dampened, even if a person stays awake for several days. This condition is called desynchronization of rhythms—in this case, the temperature rhythm and the sleep-wake rhythm are desynchronized from each other.

One of the first discoveries made on circadian rhythms is that they are endogenous in nature—the rhythmic activities are engendered and controlled from within the organism rather than being influenced or controlled by external agents such as the changing light and dark cycles or changes in temperature. Isolating human beings under constant conditions, where natural changes to day and night or fluctuations in temperature are absent, do not lead to abolition of rhythmicity. Even in the absence of external time cues, human beings are able to tell time because of the presence of an endogenous clock. The daily rhythmic occurrence of events (such as the time interval between the onset of sleep or the time interval between the occurrences of temperature minima) is measured by period. Under normal conditions, the period is close to twenty-four hours because the rhythms are synchronized or "entrained" by the light-dark cycles and other cues afforded by nature. However, if human beings are kept under constant conditions, they exhibit a period called a free-running rhythm that deviates slightly from twenty-four hours.

Free-running rhythms are observed in humans if the individual lives for many days or weeks in an isolated cave or bunker, where possible time cues such as the light-dark cycle or other factors have been eliminated. The famous cave explorer Michel Siffre found that he had a sleep-wake cycle of twenty-four hours and thirty-one minutes when he lived alone in a cave for two months without time cues. Similar studies in the more controlled environments of World War II bunkers were carried out by the German scientist Jürgen Aschoff. In each case, it was found that the body's rhythms gradually drifted out of phase with the actual time of day when watches and the natural cycle of light changes were eliminated. Aschoff termed factors that maintain a circadian periodicity Zeitgebers, or time givers. Individual subjects were found to have their own unique period, or length, for their free-running rhythms—for example, 24.3, 24.5, 24.7, or 24.9 hours. It has been well documented that various rhythms such as the sleep-wake cycle, body temperature, blood pressure, respiration rate, and urinary excretion of sodium, under constant conditions, will show slightly different period lengths and will therefore become desynchronized. Desynchronization, which may occur in the elderly under normal living conditions, is thought by some scientists to lead to various disease states. For example, episodes of mania in people with bipolar disorder can be triggered by travel to a geographical zone with increased sunlight.

Various mental abilities in humans have been shown to be subject to circadian variations. A person's ability to estimate time duration varies during the day inversely to the daily change in temperature. The ability to memorize numbers is better in the morning than in the afternoon, and the ability to add random numbers is better in the morning than in the afternoon. Eye-hand coordination changes with a circadian rhythm, with skills better during the day and performance reduced at night. The existence of these rhythms has many implications, and the further study of such rhythmic factors remains a vital common ground between physiology and psychology.

Two small nuclei, suprachiasmatic nuclei (SCN), situated just below the optic chiasma in the hypothalamus of the brain, are implicated to be crucial for the generation and sustenance of rhythmic behavior. They are called the core circadian clock, and their removal abolishes an array of rhythmic activities, including sleep-wake and temperature cycles. The hypothalamus, located just above the pituitary gland in the brain, is thought to regulate many human rhythms. Its cell clusters, or nuclei, receive input from various sense organs and brain areas. In response, they secrete releasing hormones, which travel to glands in the body and stimulate the release of second and third downstream hormonal systems that modulate body processes. These hypothalamic nuclei and secondary hormones are active in many cyclical patterns. For example, female sex hormones from the pituitary gland follow characteristic circadian patterns—monthly patterns that develop the female ovum (egg) and regulate each menstrual cycle—and lifetime patterns that initiate sexual maturation and menopause.

GENETIC AND MOLECULAR BASIS

In 1971, Ronald J. Konopka and Seymour Benzer isolated mutations in the fruit fly, *Drosophila melanogaster*, with consistent differences in their periods (such as short-period mutants and long-period mutants) and identified three alleles of the *Period* gene (*PER*) as being responsible for the changes. Understanding of the components and the functioning of circadian clocks at the molecular level has increased tremendously. More than ten genes have been shown to be responsible for proper functioning of the circadian clock (core clock genes) and several others have been indicated as clock-controlled genes. At least three period genes (*PER1*, *PER2*, and *PER3*) have been identified in mammals as components of the core clock. These, along with other identified circadian clock genes such as *Cryptochrome* 1 and 2 (*CRY* 1, *CRY* 2), *CLOCK*, *BMAL1*, and REV-ERB *alpha*, generate the twenty-four-hour rhythmicity of the circadian clock through a series of transcriptional and translational events. The mechanism of their action involves an interlocking positive and negative feedback loop (turning the expression of certain genes on and off at given intervals of time, while having their own expression turned on and off at given intervals of time). Such molecular oscillations are observed in the SCN as well as in several other peripheral organs like the liver and the brain. The molecular mechanism of the circadian clock function is remarkably similar among different species, including fungi, insects, rodents, and humans.

MANIPULATING CIRCADIAN RHYTHMS

The most familiar way humans apply their understanding of body clocks is to adjust to external changes in the sleep-wake cycle. A person can willfully avoid sleep for hours without a parallel increase in fatigue, as is attested by students who get a "second wind" once they study past 3:00 or 4:00 a.m. Some researchers envision an underlying circadian rhythm of alertness and fatigue that enhances a person's ability to awaken in the morning and to fall asleep in the late evening. In general, it is easier to awaken in the morning when the body temperature is increasing, and it is easier to fall asleep in the late evening when body temperature is falling. So-called owls and larks do exist in the human population; people who fall into these two groups differ as to when their body temperature peaks, with larks peaking earlier.

In human beings, such manipulations are a bit tricky because the sleep-wake cycle can be modified by alcohol, drugs, and social interactions, among other factors. However, studies on a specific population in Utah found people who have an inherently shifted period. Individuals in this population had their sleep phase advanced by about four to six hours a day. This is called familial advanced sleep phase syndrome (FASPS). FASPS manifests itself in early childhood as a dramatic advance in the sleep schedule, and with advances in age it gets even worse. This syndrome is in contrast to the delayed sleep phase syndrome (DSPS) observed in many adolescents. Extensive genetic studies identified alterations in *hPER2*, (human period 2), a critical core circadian clock gene, in the affected population. Several clock genes, including *hPER3*, *arylalkylamine N-acetyltransferase*, and *hCLOCK* have been linked to DSPS.

The detailed makeup of sleep also shows periodicity. Brain waves measured with an electroencephalograph (EEG) record four distinct waves, each associated with a type and depth of sleep that repeats two to five times each night. The pattern changes with age; children sleep most deeply on initiation of sleep, while adults sleep most deeply just before waking. Rapid eye movement (REM) sleep, associated with dreaming, occurs more frequently later during the sleep period. Most major cities now have sleep laboratories in which scientists monitor the sleep of patients and apply theories involving circadian rhythms to improve the type and timing of medications.

SHIFT WORK AND JET LAG

When people are forced to change their sleep-wake schedule for either work or travel, shift-work problems and jet lag can result. Shift work is required in circumstances in which around-the-clock services are either essential or economically beneficial. These include medical, police, military, utility, transportation, and other essential services, as well as tasks in the chemical, steel, petroleum, and various other manufacturing industries. Work is done and days off are given according to many different schedules. A number of catastrophic events, such as the Three Mile Island nuclear accident (1979), the chemical explosion in Bhopal, India (1984), and the Chernobyl nuclear accident (1986) happened during the late-evening or night shift, when fatigue of ill-adapted workers may have been a factor. Within the population, there are owls who can adapt to night shift work without the physical problems experienced by their peers. It is known that physiological and behavioral rhythms will shift to a new schedule only if the schedule is kept the same for a period of weeks. Shift workers who stay on their schedule of night work and day sleep will quickly shift their sleep-wake cycle and eventually shift their various behavioral and more fundamental physiological rhythms such as body temperature. Because the body's circadian rhythms are more than twenty-four hours in length, it is easier to start work later on successive days than it is to start work earlier.

What later became known as jet lag was first experienced by Wiley Post and Harold Gatty on their 1931 around-the-world airplane trip. By the 1950s, increasing numbers of tourists, diplomats, flight crews, and pilots were suffering from the general malaise, headaches, fatigue, disruptions of the sleep-wake cycle, and gastrointestinal disorders that can occur when people cross several time zones within a few hours. The effects are worse on eastward flights than on westward flights, perhaps because the circadian rhythms can undergo an adjustment to a lengthening in timing better than to a shortening. A night flight from New York to Paris results in a six-hour time shift, with breakfast coming six hours early according to nonshifted circadian rhythms. Within a few days, the sleep-wake cycle adjusts, but deeper physiological rhythms may take two or more weeks to shift to the new time zone.

There is mounting evidence to suggest that jet lag and shift-work sleep disorders are due to disturbances in the circadian phase of plasma melatonin levels. Melatonin, the so-called hormone of sleep, is available for shifting the phase of sleep (phase shifting) and to synchronize sleep patterns. Melatonin is widely used for treating problems related to jet lag and shift work. The hormone melatonin binds to its receptors—melatonin receptors 1 and 2, called MT1 and MT2. Both of these receptors are located in the SCN region of the brain. The administered dose of melatonin changes depending on the duration of the travel time. Longer travel requires starting of the treatment regimen a few days in advance of the travel, while shorter travel can bypass this step. Drugs that bind to the melatonin receptor and activate it are being tested in clinical settings.

SEASONAL AFFECTIVE DISORDER

Another application of chronobiology is in the study and treatment of seasonal affective disorder (SAD). People with SAD typically experience clinical depression in March and April, at the end of the winter months of shorter daylight. This depression is unlike the more common melancholic depression, which is characterized by loss of sleep and appetite, in that it is accompanied by increased eating, particularly of carbohydrates, and increased sleep, up to sixteen hours per day. It is also distinguished from the winter blues, which occur in one of four individuals, usually earlier in the winter. Although SAD is not considered a variant of bipolar disorder, it resembles bipolar disorder in the type of depressive symptoms and its relationship to sunlight. Many highly creative individuals, such as artist Vincent Van Gogh, writers Tennessee Williams and Edgar Allan Poe, President Abraham Lincoln, and many others have suffered either bipolar illness or SAD, describing the "seasons of the mind" in their work.

Circadian rhythms are fundamental to the pathophysiology and treatment of SAD. Response to daylight is modulated by the pineal gland, a pea-sized organ midline under the cerebral hemispheres of the brain. In darkness, the pineal gland secretes melatonin and possibly other substances. Information about light, transmitted along specific nerve pathways from the eyes, inhibits release of melatonin. Although it is not clear exactly how loss of daylight leads to seasonal depression, bright light therapy can reverse or prevent it, possibly by altering circadian rhythms such as those influencing mood, sleep, and appetite via secondary effects of melatonin. The standard light therapy involves exposure to approximately 1,500 lux (the unit of measurement for light) at a frequency that mimics sunlight. For mood disorders, patients are exposed to 10,000 lux light intensity daily for twenty to thirty minutes, preferably in the morning as nighttime treatments have been known to cause insomnia. Although the majority of light therapy products filter or completely block harmful UV light, individuals should not look directly at the light but instead have it nearby so that the light is absorbed through peripheral vision.

The severity of other illnesses also follows a circadian rhythm. Stomach acid secretion peaks in the late afternoon and just after midnight, leading to worsened symptoms of peptic ulcers at these times. Drugs that inhibit acid secretion are given at night to take advantage of this phenomenon. Similarly, asthma exacerbations tend to occur at night; predictably, oral medications for asthma produce better results if given before bedtime. Some types of high blood pressure peak at night, others in the morning; again, drugs should be given so that peak drug levels coincide with peak blood pressure readings.

There has been tremendous progress in the understanding of the cellular and molecular mechanisms dictating the functioning of a normal circadian clock. Associations of pathophysiology of diseases to disruptions in circadian clock functions are being investigated. Many clock genes have been implicated in complex mental illnesses such as major depression, bipolar, and schizophrenia, in addition to insomnia and SAD. Modifications of treatments based on the understanding of circadian rhythms have become a reality. For example, chemotherapy is given for cancer at more exact times to coincide with the most vulnerable period of cancer cell division, allowing for lower doses, fewer side effects, and better treatment results. As circadian rhythms are better understood, many aspects of health and daily life may be managed with greater ease.

CIRCADIAN RHYTHM RESEARCH

In 1729, French astronomer Jean Jacques d'Ortous de Mairan reported his observations on the leaf movements of a "sensitive" heliotrope plant that continued to open and close its leaves approximately every twenty-four hours even when it was kept in continuous dark. This was the first demonstration of a free-running rhythm. Studies on humans included those by Sanctorius, who in the seventeenth century constructed a huge balance on which he was seated in a chair and studied circadian rhythms in body weight. Julian-Joseph Virey, a Parisian pharmacist, postulated endogenous biological clocks modified by environmental input in his 1814 doctoral thesis and is credited with formally establishing the field of chronobiology. Yet despite these early studies, it was the 1950's before circadian rhythms were more widely studied and research on humans began to be more common.

In psychology, Nathaniel Kleitman and Eugene Aserinsky in the 1940's discovered rapid eye movement, or REM, sleep. The rhythmic patterns in REM sleep and their relation to the circadian sleep-wake cycle have remained an active area for research. The psychobiologist Curt Richter carried out work on the activity rhythms in rats. Richter also identified the general area in which the suprachiasmatic nuclei are found as a region of the hypothalamus important in controlling circadian rhythms. Simon Folkard and colleagues have studied various human performance tests and have found numerous circadian rhythms. They found that the circadian rhythms in memory tests peaked at different times, depending on the complexity of the number to be memorized. There remains a need for more research by psychologists who incorporate variation due to circadian rhythm into their research design.

The research on the genetics of circadian rhythms was initiated by Konopka and Benzer in 1971, using a forward genetic approach. The *Period* gene was first identified in *Drosophila*, and its orthologs in mammals were identified in 1997. Another important clock gene, *Clock* was identified through genetic studies in 1994 and was subsequently cloned in 1997. Two other important genes, the cryptochromes, *CRY1* and *CRY2* were identified in the same year, and the molecular mechanism involving the positive and negative feedback loops was uncovered subsequently. Research on this field focuses not only on further details and missing elements of the circadian clock, but also on how alterations in these identified genes could be related to various disease states.

BIBLIOGRAPHY

Foster, Russell G., and Leon Kreitzman. *Rhythms of Life: The Biological Clocks That Control the Daily Lives of Every Living Thing*. New Haven: Yale UP, 2004. Print.

Ko, C. H., and J. S. Takahashi. "Molecular Components of the Mammalian Circadian Clock." *Human Molecular Genetics* 15 (2006): R271–77. Print.

Konopka, R. J., and Benzer, S. "Clock Mutants of Drosophila Melanogaster." *Proceedings of National Academy of Sciences* USA 68 (1971): 2112–16. Print.

Kramer, Achim, and Martha Merrow. *Circadian Clocks*. New York: Springer, 2013. Print.

Lignelli, Alfredo V., ed. *Circadian Rhythms and Health Research Trends*. New York: Nova Biomedical, 2007. Print.

Murray, George Ward. *Seasonality, Personality, and the Circadian Regulation of Mood*. New York: Nova Science, 2006. Print.

Rosato, Ezio, ed. *Circadian Rhythms: Methods and Protocols*. Totowa: Humana, 2007. Print.

Shaw, Paul, Medhi Tafti, and Michael J. Thorpy. *The Genetic Basis of Sleep and Sleep Disorders*. New York: Cambridge UP, 2013. Print.

Terman, Michael, and Ian McMahan. *Chronotherapy: Resetting Your Inner Clock to Boost Mood, Alertness, and Quality Sleep*. New York: Penguin, 2012. Print.

Toh, K. L., et al. "An hPER2 Phosphorylation Site Mutation in Familial Advanced Sleep Phase Syndrome." *Science* 291 (2001): 1040-1043. This article showed that mutations in a single gene (hPER2) caused alterations in sleep behavior. The study was conducted in a small population in Utah. This is the first identification in humans of a single gene mutation affecting as complex a behavior as sleep.

John T. Burns; updated by Elizabeth Haase and Geetha Yadav

See Also: Abnormality: Biomedical models; Bipolar disorder; Dreams; Genetics and mental health; Insomnia; Seasonal affective disorder; Sleep; Workplace issues and mental health.

Clinical interviewing, testing, and observation

Date: Early 1900s forward

Type of psychology: Personality

Clinical interviewing, testing, and observation are the three major components of a comprehensive assessment used to develop a formulation of a person's personality, make a diagnosis, and develop a plan of treatment. Each of these components contributes to the development of an integrative view of the patient, which is focused on the referral question or why the assessment was requested.

Key Concepts

- Chief complaint
- Clinical formulation
- Clinical interviewing
- Cognitive assessment
- Compulsions
- Delusions
- Hallucinations
- Mental status exam
- Neuropsychological assessment
- Obsessions
- Personality assessment
- Phobias
- Psychological testing

INTRODUCTION

The purpose of clinical interviewing, testing, and observation is to obtain a clear, comprehensive, balanced view of the patient, which is termed a clinical formulation, and to develop a rational treatment plan to address the patient's difficulties. Clinical interviewing, in combination with observation, is the backbone of all mental health professions, a creative and dynamic process that represents a somewhat elusive set of complex skills, including integrating a large amount of information about a person into a clinically useful formulation, developing a diagnosis, and making recommendations for treatment based on the clinical assessment. Today the clinician is required to perform many types of interviews suited to the clinical task at hand, including assessments in settings as diverse as an inpatient psychiatric unit, an inpatient medical unit, a psychotherapy practice that includes either a consultation and/or a liaison setting, and an emergency room. Psychological testing may also be needed to gain additional information and to validate a diagnosis developed during the clinical interview and observations.

CLINICAL INTERVIEWING AND OBSERVATION

The clinical interview can be structured, semistructured, or unstructured. In the structured interview, the clinician covers the topics in a consistent way, using one of several published guidelines. In the semistructured interview, only part of the interview uses a published interview schedule. Most clinicians use a free-flowing, unstructured exchange between the clinician and patient. No matter what format is used, the clinician will work to develop rapport with the patient so that the essential information needed to help the patient can be obtained. Observation of the patient's verbal and nonverbal behavior is also noted during the interview.

Whether the interview is structured, semistructured, or unstructured, the clinician must produce a written record of the interview. This report is focused on the referral question, which is the reason the assessment was requested. Most clinicians begin by presenting identifying information such as the patient's name, age, marital status, sex, occupation, race or ethnicity, place of residence and circumstances of living, and referral information. The chief complaint or the problem for which the patient seeks professional help is usually described next, stated in the patient's own words. The intensity and the duration of the problem are noted, including any possible precipitating events, such as the loss of a loved one. Symptoms associated with the chief complaint are assessed and noted in the report.

Current and past health history, for both physical and psychological problems, is important to review. There are physical illnesses that may affect the patient's psychological state and vice versa. Prior episodes of emotional and mental disturbances should be described. The clinician needs to inquire about and report prescribed medication and alcohol and drug use.

Personal history may include information about the patient's parents and other family members and any family history of psychological or physical problems. The account of the patient's own childhood and noteworthy experiences can be very detailed. Educational and occupational history are outlined, along with social, military, legal, and marital experiences. The mental status exam is also part of the clinical interview and written report.

THE MENTAL STATUS EXAM

The mental status exam is simply the clinician's evaluation of the patient's current mental functioning. It is a staple of the initial mental health examination. The mental status exam may be viewed as consisting of two major parts: the behavioral observation aspects and the cognitive aspects.

The behavioral observation aspects include noting general appearance and behavior, mood, and flow of thought of the patient. General appearance and behavior are assessed by noting such things as the patient's apparent age in relation to stated age(for instance, does the patient look younger or older than he or she actually is?), body posture, degree of alertness, hygiene, motor activity, facial expressions, and voice quality. Anything that seems outside the general norm would be noted (for instance, agitation). The clinician should also note any physical difficulties such as the need to wear glasses. The basic quality of mood is closely monitored and noted during the interview. The basic moods can be boiled down to anger, anxiety, contentment, disgust, fear, guilt, irritation, joy, sadness, shame, and surprise. Finally, the flow of the patient's thoughts must be described if it is unusual in any way.

It is important to clearly delineate any noteworthy aspects of the person's appearance, behavior, mood, or thought content rather than just providing a summary statement. For example, the clinician may write in the report that the person had a sad face and appeared to be about to cry, yet claimed to be happy. Another patient may have jumped from topic to topic and seemed unaware that there appeared to be no connection between topics. Attitude toward the clinician is also important. For example, some patients might be openly hostile while others are very cooperative. All the findings made in this first portion of the mental status exam are generally discovered by observation alone.

The second part of the mental status exam, the cognitive aspect, is determined by asking the patient certain types of questions. Some clinicians fail to assess the cognitive aspects of the mental status exam, despite the critical importance of this information to the overall evaluation of the patient. These clinicians may believe that it may be insulting to ask obvious questions of a patient who appears unimpaired. The clinician can prepare the patient for such questions by explaining that these questions are just a routine part of the clinical interview. The initial questions assess the person's orientation to person, place, and time. That is, does the patient know who he or she is, where he or she is (city, state, facility), and what the date is? Then the patient is asked to memorize three common objects. Serial sevens are conducted, a task in which the patient is asked to subtract seven from one hundred, and then subtract seven from the result and so on toward zero. After that task is completed, the patient is asked to name the three objects memorized earlier. Other tasks may include naming objects the clinician points to, such as a pencil, following three-stage commands, and copying simple designs. These tasks assess attention, concentration, language, and short-term memory. Abstract thinking ability can be assessed by asking the patient to interpret proverbs (for instance, "What does it mean when someone says that people who live in glass houses shouldn't throw stones?") or explain likenesses and differences (such as, "How are an orange and an apple alike?").

In this part of the mental status exam, the patient's content of thought is noted, particularly bizarre ideas. A delusion is a fixed, false belief that cannot be explained by the patient's culture and education. Types of delusions include delusions of grandeur (such as believing that one is a musical virtuoso when one actually has little musical ability), body change (such as believing that one's insides are rotting), reference (such as believing that others are always talking about one), and thought broadcasting (such as believing that one's thoughts can be transmitted across the world). Hallucinations are false sensory perceptions that occur in the absence of a related sensory stimulus. Any of the five senses can be involved in hallucinations, but it is the auditory or visual modalities that are typically involved. For example, a patient may see someone who is not there. A phobia is an unreasonable and intense fear associated with some object (such as spiders) or some situation (such as closed spaces). Finally, the presence of obsessions and compulsions needs to be assessed. An obsession is a belief, idea, or thought that dominates the patient's thought content, while a compulsion is an impulse to perform an act repeatedly in a way that the patient realizes is neither appropriate nor useful.

INTERVIEWING INFORMANTS

While most patients will tell clinicians all they need to know, it is often useful to obtain information about the patient's present difficulties from other sources such as relatives, friends, and other mental health professionals. In some instances, verifying data or seeking additional information is essential. For example, information gained from children, adolescents, and adults who are psychotic or have limited cognitive ability may need to be verified and supplemented. Having a personality disorder may not particularly bother the patient, but family and friends suffer and can offer specific examples of problems involving the patient. Informants can also give information about cultural norms, childhood health history, and other relevant facts. Therefore, valuable information can be gained from people who know the patient well.

Interviewing informants will provide the opportunity to gain additional insight into the patient's interpersonal relationships. The extent and quality of emotional and tangible support available to the patient may also be determined. Emotional support is having someone to talk to about problems, everyday occurrences, and triumphs. Types of tangible support include financial assistance, a place to live, and transportation to work and doctor appointments.

PSYCHOLOGICAL TESTING

Testing may be requested by the mental health professional to clarify issues that came up in the clinical interview and to validate a diagnostic impression. Psychological testing is essentially assessing a sample of behavior using an objective and standardized measure. Although all mental health professionals are trained to conduct clinical interviews, typically, applied psychologists conduct and interpret the testing required. Applied psychologists include school, clinical, and counseling psychologists. The type of testing requested depends on what information is needed to answer the referral question or questions. For example, if there were some question about the patient's level of intelligence, cognitive testing would be needed. The types of testing requested may include personality assessment, cognitive assessment, and assessment of specific abilities or interests.

Personality assessment is the measurement of affective aspects of a person's behavior such as emotional states, motivation, attitudes, interests, and interpersonal relations using standardized instruments. Cognitive assessment includes intelligence, achievement, and neuropsychological testing. Neuropsychological testing is used to assess brain dysfunction. The measurements of specific abilities or interests include assessing multiple aptitudes such as the potential to do well in a certain type of job (such as mechanical skills) and the measurement of values and interests. Information gathered from the clinical interview, observations, and the results of the tests are integrated into a formal report usually written by a psychologist.

Although some instruments can be administered by those trained by a psychologist, others require rather extensive training. For example, most pencil and paper instruments such as the well-known Minnesota Multiphasic Personality Inventory II (MMPI-2), a comprehensive personality assessment instrument, require little training to administer. Others, such as individual intelligence tests and most projective instruments (such as the Rorschach inkblot test), require extensive advanced training to administer. Interpretation of psychological tests needs to be done by doctoral-level applied psychologists.

Behavioral observations are also done during the testing process. How does the patient approach the task? For example, one patient may approach a task in a careful, systemic way, while another patient may use a trial-and-error approach. Verbalizations during testing are noted and may reveal a pattern of behavior. Some patients, for example, may consistently make excuses for what they perceive as poor performance on tests. Signs of anxiety, restlessness, boredom, anger, or other noteworthy reactions are important data.

Information gleaned from various psychological tests, the clinical interview, and behavioral observations are formed into a comprehensive and useful report with a diagnosis and specific recommendations for treatment. Writing this type of psychological report is a highly developed skill formed in graduate-level coursework and during extensive supervised experience.

THE DSM

The results of the clinical interview, observations, and any psychological testing are used to develop a clinical formulation and to decide on a diagnosis. The American Psychiatric Association's (APA) *Diagnostic and Statistical Manual of Mental Disorders*, fifth edition (DSM-5), which was released in 2013, is the primary diagnostic system used by all mental health professionals. Whereas the previous edition of the DSM (*DSM-IV-TR*. Rev. 4th ed., 2000) summarized information according to five axes that organized, discussed, and evaluated syndromes, disorders, codes, assessments, and diagnoses, the DSM-5 utilizes a nonaxial documentation of diagnosis (formerly Axes I–III in the DSM-IV) with separate notations for significant psychosocial and contextual factors (formerly Axis IV) and disability (formerly Axis V). Psychosocial and contextual factors covered in the DSM-5 are provided in an expanded set of V codes, which allow clinicians to note other conditions affecting diagnosis, prognosis, or the course of treatment of a primary disorder. The GAF (Global Assessment of Functioning) and C-GAS (Children's Global Assessment Scale for children ages four through sixteen), which were covered under Axis V in the DSM-IV and provided a scoring system to help clinicians assess and diagnose the severity of a psychiatric illness, were also changed in the DSM-5: separate measures of the severity of symptoms and disability are now listed for individual disorders. The DSM-5 also provides what it calls a "crosswalk," which serves to help clinicians match DSM-5 diagnosis codes with the codes used by insurance companies for billing purposes. Insurance companies only accept ICD-9 codes (International Classification of Diseases, ninth revision) when submitting invoices, and the ICD-9 codes do not always match the codes provided in the DSM. One of the APA's goals in revising the DSM-5 was to bring it more in-line with approaches and terminology consistent with the World Health Organization (WHO) and the Centers for Disease Control and Prevention's (CDC) *International Classification of Diseases*.

BIBLIOGRAPHY

American Psychiatric Association. *Diagnostic and Statistical Manual of Mental Disorders: DSM-5*. Washington: American Psychiatric Association, 2013. Print.

Diagnostic and Statistical Manual of Mental Disorders: DSM-IV-TR. Rev. 4th ed. Washington, DC: American Psychiatric Association, 2000. Print.

Barlow, David H. *The Oxford Handbook of Clinical Psychology.* New York: Oxford UP, 2011. Print.

Gladding, Samuel T. *Counseling: A Comprehensive Profession*. 4th ed. Upper Saddle River, N.J.: Prentice Hall, 2008. Print.

Goldstein, Gerald, and Michel Hersen. *Handbook of Psychological Assessment*. 3d ed. New York: Pergamon, 2000. Print.

McConaughy, Stephanie H. *Clinical Interviews for Children and Adolescents*. 2nd ed. New York: Guilford, 2013. Print.

Morrison, James. *The First Interview*. 3d ed. New York: Guilford, 2008. Print.

Reik, Theodore. *Listening with the Third Ear*. 1948. Reprint. New York: Farrar, Straus and Giroux, 1983. Print.

Silverstein, Marshall L. *Personality Assessment in Depth: A Casebook*. New York: Routledge, 2013. Print.Sommers-Flanagan, John, and Rita Sommers-Flanagan. Clinical Interviewing. 5th ed. Hoboken: John Wiley, 2014. Print.

Karen D. Multon

See Also: Beck Depression Inventory (BDI); California Psychological Inventory (CPI); Children's Depression Inventory (CDI); Diagnosis; Minnesota Multiphasic Personality Inventory (MMPI); Personality interviewing strategies; Personality: Psychophysiological measures; Personality rating scales; Qualitative research; Rorschach inkblots; State-Trait Anxiety Inventory (STAI); Thematic Apperception Test (TAT).

Coaching

Date: 1970's forward

Type of psychology: Social psychology

Coaching is a strategy, most commonly used in business-related organizations, to help executives increase their personal effectiveness and manage their careers.

Key Concepts

- Coaching practice
- Content coaching
- Developmental coaching
- External versus internal coaching
- Feedback coaching

INTRODUCTION

Executives in most organizations, regardless of their levels of responsibility, are challenged with the impact of technology, competitive markets, consumer demands, the expectations of a diverse workforce, and the problems associated with leadership. The practice of executive coaching, as an intervention, has been used in business settings since the 1970s. During this period, executives were enrolled in short-term programs to learn skills such as business etiquette and employee relations. In the 1980s, more sophisticated programs were developed that also focused on personal effectiveness. By the late 1990s, executive coaching was considered one of the fastest growing areas in consulting, with the number of coaches estimated in the tens of thousands.

The increased popularity of coaching is linked to its efficiency and cost-effectiveness. It is intended to be a goal-focused, personal plan for managers to improve performance, enhance a career, or work through organizational issues. The one-on-one, targeted approach of coaching adds to its appeal.

MODELS OF COACHING

Coaching can be categorized into three areas: feedback coaching, developmental coaching, and content coaching. Each is delivered differently, and variations are based on company needs. However, all types of coaching are designed to help managers enhance their skills or improve in a specific area. Feedback coaching involves helping managers create a plan that addresses a particular need and giving them a responsive evaluation. An assessment instrument is used to identify strengths and areas needing improvement. Coaching usually occurs through several in-person conversations over a one- to six-month period. It begins with a planning meeting and is followed by subsequent sessions that assess progress and challenges and provide encouragement. The final meeting is used to conduct a mini-assessment and update the development plan. At this point, there also may be an option to continue coaching.

In-depth coaching generally lasts between six months and one year. This type of coaching is characterized as a close, intimate relationship between the executive and the coach. The information collection and analysis phases are extensive, and they typically involve interviews with the executive's staff, colleagues, and, in some instances, clients, vendors, and family members. Multiple assessment tools are used to measure competencies, interests, and strengths. The coach may even observe the executive at work.

These data are reviewed during an intensive feedback session, which may last up to two days and results in the creation of a development plan. The coach continues to be involved during the implementation phase of the plan to determine progress, discuss roadblocks, and offer support. This work continues until the development plan has been completely implemented and the executive has made noticeable improvements.

Content coaching distinguishes itself from the other types of coaching because its goal is to help managers learn about specific areas of knowledge or develop a certain skill. For example, a manager may need to know more about global marketing or how to improve presentation skills. Content coaches, as experts in specialized fields, may require managers to read books to increase their content knowledge about a topic and participate in follow-up discussions. Other forms of coaching may involve analyzing videotaped role-playing or demonstrations and attending seminars or one-on-one meetings. The manager's skill level and the desired outcome determine the duration of the coaching.

EXTERNAL VERSUS INTERNAL COACHES

The cornerstones of the coaching relationship are trust and confidentiality. The degree of a coach's involvement with the organization whose members are being coached is the source of debate, especially regarding whether a coach should be external or internal. External coaches offer a safe place for the coaching process. As outside resources, they have no appearance of a conflict of interest. Since they have no company-related interest in the outcome, the managers can speak freely without fear of reprisal.

Internal coaches have the dual role of serving both the company and the employee. An advantage is that the internal coach knows the organization's policies and people. This knowledge can serve to benefit the overall organizational and individual goals. However, the sense of anonymity is lost, which could result in a compromise of the coaching relationship. In either instance, the integrity of the coaching relationship contributes to its success.

THE FUTURE OF COACHING

Although coaching is characterized by the individual nature of the relationship between the executive and the coach, it occurs within the context of an organization. Many coaches believe that merely helping executives to change is insufficient, because these executives have created organizations that reflect their own personalities and inadequacies. Therefore, the responsibilities of the coach must broaden to encourage the executive to implement changes in a way that will benefit the entire organization. The notion of coaching can then be extended to that of coaching organizations. In this way, team building and performance-support techniques enable employees to manage themselves and their own behavior with increasing competence.

BIBLIOGRAPHY

Cook, Marshall. *Effective Coaching*. New York: McGraw-Hill, 1999. Print.

Flaherty, James. *Coaching: Evoking Excellence in Others*. Boston: Butterworth-Heinemann, 2005. Print.

Gilley, J. W. *Stop Managing, Start Coaching: How Performance Coaching Can Enhance Commitment and Improve Productivity*. New York: McGraw-Hill, 1997. Print.

Goldsmith, M., L. Lyons, and A. Freas, eds. *Coaching for Leadership: How the World's Greatest Coaches Help Leaders Learn*. San Francisco: Jossey-Bass/Pfeiffer, 2000. Print.

Markle, G. L. *Catalytic Coaching: The End of the Performance Review*. Westport, Conn.: Quorum Books, 2000. Print.

McCarthy, Grace, and Julia Milner. "Managerial Coaching: Challenges, Opportunities, and Training." *Journal of Management Development* 32.7 (2013): 768–79. Print.

O'Neill, M. *Executive Coaching with Backbone and Heart: A Systems Approach to Engaging Leaders with Their Challenges*. San Francisco: Jossey-Bass, 2007. Print.

Passmore, Jonathan, David B. Peterson, and Tereza Freire. *The Wiley-Blackwell Handbook of the Psychology of Coaching and Mentoring*. Hoboken: Wiley, 2013. Print.

Reilly, Edward T. *AMA Business Boot Camp: Management and Leadership Fundamentals That Will See You Successfully Through Your Career*. Toronto: American Management Association, 2013. Print.

Rostron, Sunny Stout, Daniel Marques Sampaio, and Marti Janse Van Rensburg. *Business Coaching International: Transforming Individuals and Organizations*. 2nd ed. London: Karnac, 2014. Print.

Whitworth, Laura, Karen Kimsey-House, Henry Kimsey-House, and Phillip Sandahl. *Co-active Coaching: New Skills for Coaching People Toward Success in Work and Life*. Mountain View, Calif.: Davies-Black, 2007. Print.

Anna Lowe

See Also: Achievement motivation; Career selection, development, and change; Motivation; Motivation: Intrinsic and extrinsic; Sports psychology; Work motivation.

Codependency

Date: Late 1970's forward
Type of psychology: Personality; Psychopathology

Codependency is a set of behaviors that people living with alcoholics, drug addicts, or troubled persons tend to develop. Codependents engage in excessive caretaking of the alcoholic, drug addict, or troubled person, and little or no caretaking of themselves. Although the caretaking is intended to control the behavior of the alcoholic, drug addict, or troubled person, it actually enables the person to stay addicted and to remain blameless for the addiction.

Key Concepts

- Alcoholism
- Caretaking
- Co-Dependents Anonymous
- Dysfunctional family
- Hypervigilance
- Low self-esteem
- Perfectionism
- Spousal abuse
- Twelve-step program

INTRODUCTION

Codependency is a behavioral pattern that has been identified as existing in pathological relationships. These behaviors can develop in childhood and are a response to living in a dysfunctional family or relationship. Typically these families have "rules" that prohibit dealing with family issues and feelings in a direct way. These families usually have an alcoholic, drug-addicted, mentally ill, or chronically ill member. Family members focus their attention on this troubled member to the exclusion of other family members. Family members are taught to care for the "ill" member and to do what is necessary to keep this person content. They learn to repress their feelings, to try to be perfect, and to ignore their own needs. The family attempts to keep the problems of the "ill" member a secret.

Codependent people tend to be caretakers of others and typically ignore their own needs and feelings. They have difficulty trusting other people and attempt to control others by their behavior, often by trying to be perfect or by taking over the care of the other person. Codependents are attracted to people who cannot be counted on to meet their needs and who are inconsistent and unreliable. Typically, codependent people are unable to nurture and care for their own emotional needs. Codependency tends to be passed on from one generation to the next.

Codependent behavior is based on a need to control others and to change their behavior. Codependents attempt to control others by being perfect and loving all the time; always responding to requests for assistance even when they do not want to help; trying to be in control of things all the time; and trying to do what the other person wants them to do, not what they actually want to do. Because they make little attempt to meet their own needs and are often abused by another or simply overwhelmed with all that they have to do, codependents tend to be anxious and depressed. Often, this is why they seek treatment. Initially, they are usually treated for depression.

Although codependent people appear to be taking responsibility for another person, they are actually wishing that the other person would take care of them. They are unable to ask for what they want, but they expect the other person to make them feel cared for and happy. Because the other person is incapable of making them feel cared for and happy, codependents never have their wants met.

Codependents become attached to other people to the point that they are willing to suppress their own feelings to maintain the relationship. Some codependent behavior is considered to enable people who are alcoholic, drug addicted, or sick to avoid taking responsibility for their behavior and for changing this behavior. It is thought that most alcoholics and drug addicts have an enabler to make excuses for their addiction or alcoholism. The lives of the codependent and the alcoholic or drug addict become pathologically intertwined. Codependents tend to be attracted to people who are alcoholic, drug addicted, or troubled, so they tend to have relationship after relationship with such people.

Some groups feel that what is deemed codependent behavior is actually normal spousal or relationship behavior, in which one person cares for the other. Certainly wives and mothers engage in much caretaking. However, it is the degree of caretaking and attachment that differentiates the codependent from the normal wife or mother. Healthy spousal and parental relationships do not enable cared-for persons to avoid responsibility for

CHARACTERISTICS OF CODEPENDENT PEOPLE

According to the National Mental Health Association, the following are characteristics of codependent individuals:

- an exaggerated sense of responsibility for the actions of others
- a tendency to confuse love and pity, with the tendency to "love" people they can pity and rescue
- a tendency to do more than their share, all of the time
- a tendency to become hurt when people do not recognize their efforts
- an unhealthy dependence on relationships; the codependent will do anything to hold on to a relationship, to avoid a feeling of abandonment
- an extreme need for approval and recognition
- a sense of guilt when asserting themselves
- a compelling need to control others
- lack of trust in self and/or others
- fear of being abandoned or alone
- difficulty identifying feelings
- rigidity/difficulty adjusting to change
- problems with intimacy/boundaries
- chronic anger
- lying/dishonesty
- poor communication
- difficulty making decisions

their behaviors, nor do they force the family members to deny their own needs.

POSSIBLE CAUSES

Codependency behaviors were initially identified in the families of alcoholics and drug addicts. These same behaviors have more recently been identified in pathological family situations, including families in which spousal or child abuse is occurring, families with poor communication patterns, and families with a mentally or chronically ill member. Codependency does not develop in all families with mentally or chronically ill members; rather it will develop only in those families in which the sick person is controlling the family and in which the parents exhibit codependent behaviors. It is possible for families to function normally in this situation. However, in homes with alcoholics, drug addicts, or abusers, it is much harder to avoid codependency.

DIAGNOSING

Codependent behavior is diagnosed by the identification of codependent behavior patterns. Codependent people often experience anxiety, depression, or both. The symptoms that are seen in the codependent person are controlling behavior, distrust of others, perfectionism, repression of feelings, problems with intimacy, caretaking, hypervigilance, stress-related illnesses, insomnia, low self-esteem, dependency, denial, weak boundaries, anger, sexual problems, and poor communication skills. Once people learn codependent patterns, they are likely to apply these behaviors to other relationships, even though the new relationships are unlike the one that spawned these behaviors. They may establish codependent relationships with their counselor, physicians, friends, bosses, and other authority figures. Codependency becomes the only way they know to establish relationships with other people.

People of all ages can demonstrate symptoms of codependency, although typically the symptoms appear in childhood. This behavioral pattern usually continues for the rest of people's lives unless they have long-term counseling to identify their behaviors and assist them in changing these behaviors.

TREATMENT OPTIONS

The treatments for codependency include long-term counseling and support groups. In counseling, codependent people are taught to identify their own needs, to deal with their feelings, to be assertive, to refuse when they do not want to do something, to communicate their needs to others, and to care for and nurture themselves. Sometimes during treatment, a person forms a codependent relationship with his or her counselor and tries to appear perfect to this person. At this point, counseling ceases to be effective because the patient has stopped working on problem behaviors. This negates the purpose of counseling, which is to learn to change codependent behavior patterns. Consequently, it may be helpful for codependents to periodically change counselors.

Codependency support groups such as Co-Dependents Anonymous, based on the twelve-step program of Alcoholics Anonymous, have developed. The twelve steps involve accepting that one's life is out of control and asking a higher power for assistance, but some people are repelled by references to a higher power. Some codependency groups are geared toward specific codependency issues, such as living with an alcoholic or in a dysfunctional family. Usually they deal with general issues of codependency without consideration of the attractive behavior. Groups vary in their effectiveness, so codependents may have to try several groups before they find one that is helpful to them.

THE HISTORY OF TREATMENT

Codependency was first discussed in the late 1970's. At this time, it was noticed that people addicted to drugs or alcohol tended to have relationships with people with a particular set of behaviors. However, as early as the 1940's, spouses, particularly wives, of alcoholics met and formed support groups to deal with the behavior of their spouses. At first, these groups were called Al-Anon, in reference to the Alcoholics Anonymous groups for alcoholics. As mental health professionals became more familiar with these behavior patterns, they realized that the behaviors occurred not only in people in relationships with alcoholics and drug addicts but also in people in relationships with people with other compulsive behaviors such as gambling, overeating, and some sexual behaviors. These same behavior patterns were discovered in adult children of alcoholics, people in relationships with emotionally disturbed or chronically ill people, and in professionals in helping professions, such as nurses and social workers.

BIBLIOGRAPHY

Babcock, Marguerite, and Christine McKay, eds. *Challenging Codependency: A Feminist Critique.* Toronto, Ont.: University of Toronto Press, 1995. This collection of essays criticizes the label of codependency as damaging to women and challenges some of codependency's tenets.

Beattie, Melody. *Beyond Codependency: And Getting Better All the Time.* New York: Harper & Row, 1989. Beattie focuses on recovery from codependency in this book. She uses frequent examples of codependents to demonstrate her points.

_______. *Codependent No More: How to Stop Controlling Others and Start Caring for Yourself.* Center City, Minn.: Hazelton, 1992. This classic work defines codependent behavior and gives examples of codependents and their lives. The main focus of the book is to assist readers in identifying their codependent behaviors and changing their lives.

_______. *The New Codependency: Help and Guidance for Today's Generation.* New York: Simon & Schuster, 2009. In this self-help book, Beattie clears up misconceptions about codependency and provides self-assessments regarding various codependent behaviors.

Lewis, Rebekah. *Doormats and Control Freaks: How to Recognize, Heal, or End Codependent Relationships.* Far Hills, N.J.: New Horizon, 2005. Lewis provides a twelve-step plan for increasing self-esteem and creating healthy relationships.

Weinhold, Barry K., and Janae B. Weinhold. *Breaking Free of the Codependency Trap.* Rev. ed. Novato, Calif.: New World Library, 2008. Two clinicians provide step-by-step tools that people can follow to end codependent behavior.

Christine M. Carroll

SEE ALSO: Addictive personality and behaviors; Alcohol dependence and abuse; Coping: Chronic illness; Self-esteem; Self-help groups; Substance use disorders; Support groups.

Cognitive abilities test (CogAT)

DATE: 1954 forward

TYPE OF PSYCHOLOGY: Intelligence and intelligence testing

The Cognitive Abilities Test (CogAT) is a group-administered, ability test battery designed for children in kindergarten through twelfth grades. Coauthored by David F. Lohman and Elizabeth P. Hagen, its purpose is to measure children's reasoning and problem-solving abilities with regard to verbal, quantitative, and nonverbal (spatial) symbols.

KEY CONCEPTS

- Cognitive abilities
- Crystallized and fluid intelligence
- Gifted student
- Intelligence test
- Norms
- Reliability
- Standardized test scores

- Test battery
- Validity

INTRODUCTION

The first version of the Cognitive Abilities Test (CogAT) was published in 1954 by Irving Lorge and Robert L. Thorndike. Then called the Lorge-Thorndike Intelligence Tests, its purpose was to measure general abstract reasoning skills that were important for students in educational settings (grades three through twelve). This first version yielded verbal and nonverbal scores, as well as an overall intelligence score. In subsequent revisions, the far-reaching term "intelligence" was removed, and the title was changed to the Cognitive Abilities Test (CogAT) to emphasize cognitive theory. The 2001 edition, Form 6, was said to measure developed abilities, as opposed to innate ones. In terms of its theory base, early versions of the test relied on Philip E. Vernon's notion of hierarchical abilities and Raymond B. Cattell's theory of crystallized and fluid intelligence. In addition, John B. Carroll's hierarchical model also contributed to the CogAT, Form 6. CogAT Form 7, featuring several major revisions intended to make the test fairer for English language learners while retaining much of the successful components of Form 6—was released in 2011.

DESCRIPTION

Form 7 is divided into the primary edition (ages five and six through eight) and the multilevel edition (ages nine through seventeen and eighteen). The primary edition consists of three test batteries—verbal, quantitative, and nonverbal (each of these consisting of three tests)—provided in three levels, kindergarten through second grade. In the primary edition, the test directions and items are read to students. In Form 7, the primary edition uses the same nine subtests as the multilevel edition, with the exception of two verbal subtests which use picture-based items in place of a teacher reading questions aloud. Untimed, this edition reportedly takes 140 to 170 minutes to administer.

The multilevel edition is made up of three batteries—verbal, quantitative, and nonverbal—each battery consisting of three tests. Although teachers read the directions for these tests, students are required to read the test items themselves. The nine subtests of the multilevel edition are verbal classification, sentence completion (optional in the primary edition), verbal analogies, number series, number analogies, number puzzles, figure classification, figure analogies, and paper folding. A composite score is also provided. The multilevel edition takes about 145 minutes to administer.

Scoring can be done either by hand, by computer software, or via submission to the publisher. Three primary uses of the test are recommended by the test authors: to guide instruction to ensure that it matches the abilities of each student; to serve as an alternative measure of cognitive development, versus the familiar measures represented by grades and standardized achievement test scores; and to identify students who have achievement or ability discrepancies. It has also been found to be helpful in identifying giftedness.

NORMS, SCORES PROVIDED, RELIABILITY, AND VALIDITY

The CogAT was standardized on a very large, stratified national norm group. In the process, the test was also standardized with the Iowa Test of Basic Skills (grades kindergarten through eight) and the Iowa Test of Educational Development (grades nine through twelve). Age norms (ages five to eighteen) and grade norms (kindergarten through twelve, or K–12) are reported, and the publisher can also produce local norms if desired.

The test yields several scores for each of the three batteries (verbal, quantitative, and nonverbal) and an overall composite score. Stanines, percentile ranks, and standard age scores (SAS) are reported. Stanines represent a "standard nine" scale, wherein students receive a score from 1 to 9. Percentile rank gives the number of students who scored below a certain score. The standard age score is a standard score with a mean of 100 and a standard deviation of 16. Finally, the composite universal scale score (USS) places the student on a continuous growth scale across all levels (K–12). Also, profiles (graphs) of student performance (including confidence intervals based on standard errors of measurement) are provided. The profile narrative report interprets the graphed profile.

Generally, Kuder-Richardson Formula 20 (KR-20) reliabilities, which measure internal consistency, run in the high 0.90s for the verbal and nonverbal scores, and low 0.90s for the quantitative score. Validity is supported through confirmatory factor analysis and convergent validity evidence—specifically, correlations with the Wechsler Intelligence Scale for Children (third edition) and the Woodcock-Johnson Tests of Cognitive Abilities (third edition). The test correlates well with the Iowa Test of Basic Skills and Iowa Test of Educational Development, with which it was conormed.

In conclusion, the CogAT is an excellent K–12 ability test battery. Its strengths include a very large, representative normative sample, efficient group administration, a sound theory base, good evidence for reliability and validity, and the fact that it was conormed with the Iowa Test of Basic Skills and the Iowa Test of Educational Development.

BIBLIOGRAPHY

Cognitive Abilities Test (CogAT), Form 6. http://www.riverpub.com/products/cogAt.

DiPerna, James C. "Review of the Cognitive Abilities Test, Form 6." *The Sixteenth Mental Measurements Yearbook*. Ed. Robert A. Spies and Barbara S. Plake. Lincoln: Buros Institute of Mental Measurements, 2005. Print.

Fernandez-Ballesteros, Rocio, ed. *Encyclopedia of Psychological Assessment*. Thousand Oaks: Sage Publications, 2003. Print.

Lakin, Joni, M. "Assessing the Cognitive Abilities of Culturally and Linguistically Diverse Students: Predictive Validity of Verbal, Quantitative, and Nonverbal Tests." *Psychology in the Schools* 49.8 (2012): 756–68. Print.

Lohman, David F. "Introducing CogAT Form 7." *Cognitively Speaking* 7 (2011): 1–9. Print.

Lohman, David F., and J. Gambrell. "Use of Nonverbal Measures in Gifted Identification." *Jour. of Psychoeducational Assessment* 30 (2012): 25–44. Print.

Lohman, David F., Katrina A. Korb, and Joni M. Lakin. "Identifying Academically Gifted English Language Learners Using Nonverbal Tests: A Comparison of the Raven, NNAT, and CogAT." *Gifted Child Quarterly* 52 (2008): 275–96. Print.

Naglieri, Jack A., and Sam Goldstein, eds. *Practitioner's Guide to Assessing Intelligence and Achievement*. Hoboken: Wiley, 2009. Print.

Rogers, Bruce G. "Review of the Cognitive Abilities Test, Form 6." *The Sixteenth Mental Measurements Yearbook*. Ed. Robert A. Spies and Barbara S. Plake. Lincoln: Buros Institute of Mental Measurements, 2005. Print.

Mary Moore Vandendorpe; updated by Cathy J. Bogart and Ursula Goldsmith

See Also: Assessment; Cognitive ability: Gender differences; Intelligence; Intelligence quotient (IQ); Intelligence tests; Stanford-Binet test.

Cognitive ability
Gender differences

Type of psychology: Cognition; Developmental psychology

Cognitive differences between men and women have been attributed to both biological and social learning differences. Most differences are quite small; others can be reduced by educational and social intervention. Different cognitive styles may encourage diverse solutions to important problems.

Key Concepts

- Academic achievement
- Adolescence
- Cognition
- Gender
- Sociocultural contexts

INTRODUCTION

The study of differences between men and women includes biological, emotional, social, and cognitive variables. Cognitive psychologists study the ways in which people process information, including perceiving, attending, learning and memory, and thinking and language. A pioneer review of all the studies concerning gender differences by Eleanor Maccoby and Carol Jacklin, published in 1974, concluded that men and women are more alike than different. Published studies note that there is considerable overlap between men's and women's performances, no matter what is being measured. An individual man or woman may be much better than most of the opposite gender on any characteristic that is studied. The term "gender differences" refers to differences between groups, rather than between particular individuals. The degree of difference necessary to be considered significant does not have to be great, but the observed differences must be reliable.

Studies of cognitive abilities typically include assessments of verbal skills, including the ability to use and understand words and sentences; mathematical skills, including the ability to manipulate abstract symbols; and spatial skills or the ability to manipulate objects in space. Psychologists Janet Shibley Hyde, Nita McKinley, Paula and Jeremy Caplan, Mary Crawford, and Roger Chaffin have done extensive reviews of published studies on gender differences in cognition and have reported the following overall findings: there are no consistent gender differences in verbal abilities, except that women tend to perform better than men in speech production. Men tend to perform better on spatial abilities, but the sizes of these observed differences are highly dependent on what is required on each specific test. There are no consistent differences in mathematical abilities, with the exception that male adolescents tend to perform better than female adolescents on tests of mathematical problem solving. Finally, differences between men and women in science achievement are minute, and the sizes of such differences vary depending on the specific area of science being tested.

Many attempts have been made to determine whether gender differences are caused by biological or environmental factors. Traditionally, psychologists have referred to attempts to separate these causal factors as the "nature versus nurture" debate. However, biologist Anne Fausto-Sterling says that biological and environmental influences on human development are inseparable. Attempting to separate these effects "both oversimplify biological development and downplay the interactions between an organism and its environment."

EDUCATIONAL SETTINGS

In educational settings, infants and preschool children are typically tested and observed in the areas of verbal development and spatial ability. Differences before age six are relatively minor, but girls do have a slight advantage in verbal development. By age three, boys generally have somewhat better visual-spatial abilities than girls do. Differing rates of central nervous system maturation, differing prenatal exposures to sex hormones, and other theories to have been proposed to explain these phenomena. While it is accepted that girls' nervous systems mature earlier than boys' do, the role of sex hormones in cognitive development is not well understood and remains the subject of ongoing research.

In grade school, girls typically outperform boys. Girls do at least as well at mathematics and usually better in verbal activities, such as reading, writing, and spelling. Boys' relatively poorer performance has been attributed to the predominantly feminine atmosphere of the early school years and to their somewhat slower rate of neurological development. Boys may also be more vulnerable to conditions such as attention-deficit hyperactivity disorder (ADHD) that may interfere with their academic achievement.

In adolescence, gender differences are at their most extreme. Girls who did quite well in school before adolescence often show a drop in grades as well as in standardized test performance. Boys seem to do much better, particularly in the areas of mathematics and science. A few researchers have suggested that increased amounts of testosterone, a male sex hormone, may be related to the teenage boy performing better. Hyde has emphasized that cultural pressure to conform to traditional gender roles becomes stronger in adolescence. The female adolescent is socialized to believe that achievement, particularly in male-dominated disciplines such as math and science, is gender inappropriate. This culturally imposed belief in "femininity-achievement incompatibility" puts girls "in a situation in which two equally important systems of value are in conflict." Thus, for girls to continue to achieve in traditionally masculine disciplines is unfeminine. When they are younger, girls may be encouraged to get good grades and excel academically in all subjects, but this reward system may change abruptly when they reach adolescence and societal pressure to conform to the traditional feminine role gets stronger.

In adulthood, test-score differences tend to diminish. Hyde concluded that there are no verbal differences between the genders. There seems to be a difference in performance rather than ability, which is caused by social expectations of appropriate gender roles.

Sex differences in cognitive ability can reemerge in late adulthood, as women tend to be at greater risk for cognitive impairment and dementia. Estrogen decline in postmenopausal women appears to be linked to diminished cognitive ability. In studies done in the late 1990s, women receiving estrogen replacement therapy (ERT) tested better for short-term memory and visual perception than those who were not receiving ERT. Preliminary data also appeared to show a decreased risk for Alzheimer disease among ERT users; however, a controversial 2003 study by the Women's Health Initiative suggested the reverse, spurring further study of estrogen and Alzheimer disease development. Estradiol, produced from testosterone, may play a similar protective function in the male brain, but the research lags.

Cognitive style, or the way in which people solve problems, represents another area of gender differences. Jean Piaget studied cognitive development in children and noted that male adolescents used more formal operational thinking than did female adolescents. In formal operational thinking, people approach problems in a precisely logical way. In 1970, William Perry published a study of the cognitive development of undergraduates at Harvard, beginning at the time they entered college until graduation. Although his study included few women, he found the intellectual development of both genders was fairly similar. In the mid-1980s, Mary Field Belenky, Blythe McVicker Clinchy, Nancy Rule Goldberger, and Jill Mattuck Tarule did a similar study based on personal interviews with 135 women, 90 of whom were college students. These researchers were able to identify five "ways of knowing" among these women; however, they were careful to point out that these categories are not necessarily fixed, exhaustive, or universal and that they are similar to categories seen in men's thinking. They concluded that any gender differences observed were due to socialization and experiences in traditional educational institutions.

TESTING DIFFERENCES

Male and female differences have been noted in achievement tests such as the SAT Reasoning Test and the ACT. The tests are designed not to benefit one gender more than the other, but gender differences are still found. Men are more likely to have extremely high scores and to do better in mathematics. For example, a study of mathematically precocious youths surveyed forty thousand seventh-graders who scored extremely well on the SAT, a test usually taken by college-bound eleventh- and twelfth-graders. Of the 280 children who scored above 700, only twenty were female. However, some researchers have found that, when the number of advanced math classes taken in high school is taken into account, such differences diminish. In 1991, the American Association of University Women released a report titled Shortchanging Girls, Shortchanging America, which stated that gender inequities in the classroom contribute to gender differences in academic achievement. For example, in male-dominated disciplines, such as math and science, girls were often discouraged from taking advanced courses. Teachers called on boys to answer questions more often and challenged them more in class.

Differences in mathematics ability have been used to explain why some occupations are male dominated and others female dominated. Both men and women are largely unaware of the many accomplishments of high-achieving women in traditionally male-dominated fields. An example of such invisible contributions include those of scientist Rosalind Franklin to the discovery of the structure of deoxyribonucleic acid (DNA), which is widely associated with Francis Crick and James Watson. Educators and school counselors should emphasize the merits of all career opportunities. For example, boys can be encouraged to explore traditionally female professions, such as nursing and elementary education, while girls can be encouraged to pursue careers in traditionally male professions, such as engineering and computer science.

Differences in male and female abilities have interested educators as they try to maximize the potential of all their students. It is vitally important that both boys and girls receive encouragement to excel in all areas. For example, in grade school, boys need male teachers to imitate, and girls need to have contact with female scientists, engineers, and mathematicians. Counselors should be especially aware of the need to allow adolescents to explore various careers. Training is an important factor in gender differences. Mathematics scores are directly related to the number of mathematics classes a person has taken. Gender differences on tests of spatial perception can also be eliminated by training. Paul Tobin used the embedded figures test, which requires people to pick out a drawing hidden within another drawing. He gave the test to teenage boys and girls, finding that boys performed better. After one practice session, however, the gender differences were eliminated.

Family and sociocultural contexts also influence cognitive abilities. In their study of women's cognitive styles, Belenky and associates did intensive interviews with women of various backgrounds and ages. They found that some women did not believe that they could think things out. One group of women was called "silent" and had typically been physically or emotionally abused. These "silent" women did not believe that they could understand anything. In addition, both Perry, who studied mostly male undergraduates, and Belenky and her colleagues observed a stage in which some young women and men look to external sources, such as experts and authorities, for "right answers" and "truth." However, many of the men seemed to identify with the experts and authorities in a way that women did not. It was as though the men saw themselves as "potential future experts."

CONCLUSIONS

Interest in gender differences is common to most societies, but only recently have scientists begun to ask about the origins of such differences. Many researchers are questioning the usefulness of the study of group comparisons in general. Such studies of "difference" are often based on a dominant "standard" group that is then used as a frame of reference to assess how other groups deviate from this standard.

An increased demand for social justice arose during the 1960s and renewed interest in the question of gender differences. Maccoby and Jacklin surveyed every research report on male and female cognitive differences up to 1970 and concluded that the research supported very few real differences. Further studies have suggested that social influences are at least as important as biological influences.

One reason that women have been judged to be inferior to men is that male success has traditionally been used as the standard by which women are measured. If women behaved differently from men, they were thought to be inferior. In the area of personality, Sigmund Freud came to the mistaken conclusion that women are innately psychologically inferior. Karen Horney's psychology of women considers the role of culture in shaping perceptions of women, pointing out that women's perceived weaknesses were based on the experiences of men.

Overall, research shows that there is much more variability in cognitive performance within each gender. All social groups, such as men and women, are heterogeneous. Individual differences within such groups are caused by the continuous interplay between the biology of the organism and its experiences with its environment.

BIBLIOGRAPHY

Belenky, Mary Field, et al. *Women's Ways of Knowing: The Development of Self, Voice, and Mind.* Rev. ed. New York: Basic, 1997. Print.

Bleier, Ruth. *Science and Gender.* New York: Pergamon, 1984. Print.

Eagly, Alice H., Anne E. Beall, and Robert J. Sternberg, eds. *The Psychology of Gender.* 2nd ed. New York: Guilford, 2005. Print.

Fausto-Sterling, Anne. *Myths of Gender: Biological Theories about Women and Men.* Rev. ed. New York: Basic, 1992. Print.

Halpern, Diane F. *Sex Differences in Cognitive Abilities.* 4th ed. New York: Psychology, 2012. Print.

Halpern, Diance F., Anna S. Beninger, and Carli A. Straight. "Sex Differences in Intelligence." *The Cambridge Handbook of Intelligence*. Ed. Scott Barry Kaufman and Robert J. Sternberg. New York: Cambridge UP, 2011. 253–72. Print.

Hare-Mursten, Rachel T., and Jeanne Marecek. "The Meaning of Difference: Gender Theory, Post-Modernism, and Psychology." *American Psychologist* 43 (1988): 455–64. Print.

Hyde, Janet Shibley. *Half the Human Experience.* 8th ed. Belmont: Wadsworth, 2013. Print.

Hyde, Janet Shibley, and Marcia C. Linn, eds. *The Psychology of Gender: Advances through Meta-Analysis.* Baltimore: Johns Hopkins UP, 1986. Print.

Jacklin, Carol. "Female and Male: Issues of Gender." *American Psychologist* 44 (1989): 127–33. Print.

"FAQ's on the Brain." *Zero to Three.* National Center for Infants, Toddlers, and Families, 2012. Web. 27 Mar. 2014.

Mary Moore Vandendorpe; updated by Cathy J. Bogart and Ursula Goldsmith

See Also: Ability tests; Achievement motivation; Cognitive development: Jean Piaget; College entrance examinations; Femininity; Gender identity formation; Gender roles and gender role conflicts; Gilligan, Carol; Horney, Karen; Intelligence; Intelligence tests; Masculinity; Men's mental health; Moral development; Sexism; Women's mental health; Women's psychology: Carol Gilligan; Women's psychology: Karen Horney; Women's psychology: Sigmund Freud

Cognitive behavior therapy (CBT)

Type of psychology: Psychotherapy

A number of approaches to therapy fall within the scope of cognitive behavior therapy. These approaches all share a theoretical perspective that assumes that internal cognitive processes, called thinking or cognition, affect behavior; that this cognitive activity may be monitored; and that desired behavior change may be effected through cognitive change.

Key Concepts

- Behavior therapy
- Cognition
- Cognitive restructuring
- Cognitive therapy
- Depression

INTRODUCTION

The cognitive behavior therapies are not a single therapeutic approach, but rather a loosely organized collection of therapeutic approaches that share a similar set of assumptions. At their core, cognitive behavior therapies share three fundamental propositions: Cognitive activity affects behavior; cognitive activity may be monitored and altered; and desired behavior change may be effected through cognitive change.

The first of the three fundamental propositions of cognitive behavior therapy suggests that it is not the external situation that determines feelings and behavior, but rather the person's view or perception of that external situation that determines feelings and behavior. For example, if a person has failed the first examination of a course, that individual could appraise it as a temporary setback to be overcome or as a horrible loss. Although the situation remains the same, the thinking about that situation is radically different in the two examples cited. Each of these views will lead to significantly different emotions and behaviors.

The third cognitive behavioral assumption suggests that desired behavior change may be effected through cognitive change. Therefore, although cognitive behavior theorists do not reject the notion that rewards and punishment (reinforcement contingencies) can alter behavior, they are more likely to emphasize that there are alternative methods for behavior change, one in particular being cognitive change. Many approaches to therapy fall within the scope of cognitive behavior therapy as it is defined here. Although these approaches share the theoretical assumptions described, a review of the major therapeutic procedures subsumed under the heading of cognitive behavior therapy reveals a diverse amalgam of principles and procedures, representing a variety of theoretical and philosophical perspectives.

Rational emotive therapy, developed by psychologist Albert Ellis, is regarded by many as one of the premier examples of the cognitive behavioral approach; it was introduced in the early 1960s. Ellis proposed that many people are made unhappy by their faulty, irrational beliefs, which influence the way they interpret events. The therapist interacts with patients, attempting to direct patients to more positive and realistic views. Cognitive therapy, pioneered by Aaron T. Beck, has been applied to such problems as depression and stress. For stress reduction, ideas and thoughts that are producing stress in the patient are identified, and the therapist then gets the patient to examine the validity of these thoughts. Working together, they restructure thought processes so that the situations seem less stressful. Cognitive therapy has been found to be quite effective in treating depression, as compared with other therapeutic methods. Beck held that depression is caused by certain types of negative thoughts, such as devaluing the self or viewing the future in a consistently pessimistic way.

Rational behavior therapy, developed by psychiatrist Maxie Maultsby, is a close relative of Ellis's rational emotive therapy. In this approach, Maultsby combines several approaches to include rational emotive therapy, neuropsychology, classical and operant conditioning, and psychosomatic research; however, Maultsby was primarily influenced by his association with Ellis. In this approach, Maultsby attempts to couch his theory of emotional disturbance in terms of neuropsychophysiology and learning theory. Rational behavior therapy assumes that repeated pairings of a perception with evaluative thoughts lead to rational or irrational emotive and behavioral reactions. Maultsby suggests that self-talk, which originates in the left hemisphere of the brain, triggers corresponding right-hemisphere emotional equivalents. Therefore, to maintain a state of psychological health, individuals must practice rational self-talk that will, in turn, cause the right brain to convert left-brain language into appropriate emotional and behavioral reactions.

Rational behavior therapy techniques are quite similar to those of rational emotive therapy. Both therapies stress the importance of monitoring one's thoughts to become aware of the elements of the emotional disturbance. In addition, Maultsby advocates the use of rational emotive imagery, behavioral practice, and relaxation methods to minimize emotional distress.

SELF-INSTRUCTIONAL TRAINING

Self-instructional training was developed by psychologist Donald Meichenbaum in the early 1970s. In contrast to Ellis and Beck, whose prior training was in psychoanalysis, Meichenbaum's roots were in behaviorism and the behavioral therapies. Therefore, Meichenbaum's approach is heavily couched in behavioral terminology and procedures. Meichenbaum's work stems from his earlier research in training schizophrenic patients to emit "healthy speech." By chance, Meichenbaum observed that patients who engaged in spontaneous self-instruction were less distracted and demonstrated superior task performance on a variety of tasks. As a result, Meichenbaum emphasizes the critical role of "self-instructions"—simple instructions such as "Relax . . . Just attend to the task"—and their noticeable effect on subsequent behavior.

Meichenbaum developed self-instructional training to treat the deficits in self-instructions manifested in impulsive children. The ultimate goal of this program was to decrease impulsive behavior. The way to accomplish this goal, as hypothesized by Meichenbaum, was to train impulsive children to generate verbal self-commands and to respond to their verbal self-commands and to encourage the children to self-reinforce their behavior appropriately.

The specific procedures employed in self-instructional training involve having the child observe a model performing a task. While the model is performing the task, he or she is talking aloud. The child then performs the same task while the model gives verbal instructions. Subsequently, the child performs the task while instructing himself or herself aloud, then while whispering the instructions. Finally, the child performs the task while silently thinking the instructions. The self-instructions employed in the program included questions about the nature and demands of the task, answers to these questions in the form of cognitive rehearsal, self-instructions in the form of self-guidance while performing the task, and self-reinforcement. Meichenbaum and his associates have found that this self-instructional training program significantly improves the task performance of impulsive children across a number of measures.

SYSTEMATIC RATIONAL RESTRUCTURING

Systematic rational restructuring is a cognitive behavioral procedure developed by psychologist Marvin Goldfried in the mid-1970s. This procedure is a variation on Ellis's rational emotive therapy; however, it is more clearly structured than Ellis's method. In systematic rational restructuring, Goldfried suggests that early social learning experiences teach individuals to label situations in different ways. Further, Goldfried suggests that emotional reactions may be understood as responses to the way individuals label situations, as opposed to responses to the situations themselves. The goal of systematic rational restructuring is to train clients to perceive situational cues more accurately.

The process of systematic rational restructuring is similar to systematic desensitization, in which a subject is to imagine fearful scenes in a graduated order from the least fear-provoking to the most fear-provoking scenes. In systematic rational restructuring, the client is asked to imagine a hierarchy of anxiety-eliciting situations. At each step, the client is instructed to identify irrational thoughts associated with the specific situation, to dispute them, and to reevaluate the situation more rationally. In addition, clients are instructed to practice rational restructuring in specific real-life situations.

STRESS INOCULATION

Stress inoculation training incorporates several of the specific therapies already described. This procedure was developed by Meichenbaum. Stress inoculation training is analogous to being inoculated against disease. That is, it prepares clients to deal with stress-inducing events by teaching them to use coping skills at low levels of the stressful situation and then gradually to cope with more and more stressful situations. Stress inoculation training involves three phases: conceptualization, skill acquisition and rehearsal, and application and follow-through.

In the conceptualization phase of stress inoculation training, clients are given an adaptive way of viewing and understanding their negative reactions to stressful events. In the skills-acquisition and rehearsal phase, clients learn coping skills appropriate to the type of stress they are experiencing. With interpersonal anxiety, the client might develop skills that would make the feared situation less threatening (for example, learning to initiate and maintain conversations). The client might also learn deep muscle relaxation to lessen tension. In the case of anger, clients learn to view potential provocations as problems that require a solution rather than as threats that require an attack. Clients are also taught to rehearse alternative strategies for solving the problem at hand.

The application and follow-through phase of stress inoculation training involves the clients practicing and applying the coping skills. Initially, clients are exposed to low levels of stressful situations in imagery. They practice applying their coping skills to handle the stressful events, and they overtly role-play dealing with stressful events. Next, clients are given homework assignments that involve gradual exposure to actual stressful events in their everyday life. Stress inoculation training has been effectively applied to many types of problems. It has been used to help people cope with anger, anxiety, fear, pain, and health-related problems (for example, cancer and hypertension). It appears to be suitable for all age levels.

PROBLEM-SOLVING THERAPY

Problem-solving therapy, as developed by psychologists Thomas D'Zurilla and Goldfried, is also considered one of the cognitive behavioral approaches. In essence, problem-solving therapy is the application of problem-solving theory and research to the domain of personal and emotional problems. Indeed, the authors see the ability to solve problems as the necessary and sufficient condition for emotional and behavioral stability. Problem solving is, in one way or another, a part of all psychotherapies.

Cognitive behavior therapists have taught general problem-solving skills to clients with two specific aims: to alleviate the particular personal problems for which clients have sought therapy and to provide clients with a general coping strategy for personal problems.

Clients are given steps of problem solving that they are taught to carry out systematically. First, clients need to define the dilemma as a problem to be solved. Next, they must select a goal that reflects the ultimate outcome they desire. Clients then generate a list of many different possible solutions, without evaluating their potential merit (a kind of brainstorming). They then evaluate the pros and cons of each alternative in terms of the probability that it will meet the goal selected and its practicality, which involves considering the potential consequences of each solution to themselves and to others. They rank the alternative solutions in terms of desirability and practicality and select the highest one. Next, they try to implement the chosen solution. Finally, clients evaluate the therapy, assessing whether the solution alleviated the problem and met the goal, and if not, what went wrong—in other words, which of the steps in problem solving needs to be redone.

Problem-solving therapies have been used to treat a variety of target behaviors with a wide range of clients. Examples include peer relationship difficulties among children and adolescents, examination and interpersonal anxiety among college students, relapse following a program to reduce smoking, harmony among family members, and the ability of chronic psychiatric patients to cope with interpersonal problems.

SELF-CONTROL THERAPY

Self-control therapy for depression, developed by psychologist Lynn Rehm, is an approach to treating depression that combines the self-regulatory notions of behavior therapy and the cognitive focus of the cognitive behavioral approaches. Essentially, Rehm believes that depressed people show deficits in one or some combination of the following areas: monitoring (selectively attending to negative events), self-evaluation (setting unrealistically high goals), and self-reinforcement (emitting high rates of self-punishment and low rates of self-reward). These three components are further broken down into a total of six functional areas.

According to Rehm, the varied symptom picture in clinically depressed clients is a function of different subsets of these deficits. Over the course of therapy with clients, each of the six self-control deficits is described, with emphasis on how a particular deficit is causally related to depression, and on what can be done to remedy the deficit. A variety of clinical strategies are employed to teach clients self-control skills, including group discussion, overt and covert reinforcement, behavioral assignments, self-monitoring, and modeling.

STRUCTURAL PSYCHOTHERAPY

Structural psychotherapy is a cognitive behavioral approach that derives from the work of two Italian mental health professionals, psychiatrist Vittorio Guidano and psychologist Gianni Liotti. These authors are strongly influenced by cognitive psychology, social learning theory, evolutionary epistemology, psychodynamic theory, and cognitive therapy. Guidano and Liotti suggest that for an understanding of the full complexity of an emotional disorder and subsequent development of an adequate model of psychotherapy, an appreciation of the development and the active role of an individual's knowledge of self and the world is critical. In short, to understand a patient, one must understand the structure of that person's world.

Guidano and Liotti's therapeutic process uses the empirical problem-solving approach of the scientist. Indeed, the authors suggest that therapists should assist clients in disengaging themselves from certain ingrained beliefs and judgments, and in considering them as hypotheses and theories subject to disproof, confirmation, and logical challenge. A variety of behavioral experiments and cognitive techniques are used to assist patients in assessing and critically evaluating their beliefs.

OTHER THERAPIES

The area of cognitive behavior therapy involves a wide collection of therapeutic approaches and techniques. Other cognitive behavioral approaches include anxiety management training, which comes from the work of psychologist Richard Suinn, and personal science, from the work of psychologist Michael Mahoney.

The cognitive behavioral approaches are derived from a variety of perspectives, including cognitive theory, classical and operant conditioning approaches, problem-solving theory, and developmental theory. All these approaches share the perspective that internal cognitive processes, called thinking or cognition, affect behavior, and that behavior change may be effected through cognitive change.

These approaches have several other similarities. One is that all the approaches see therapy as time limited. This is in sharp distinction to the traditional psychoanalytic therapies, which are generally open-ended. The cognitive behavior therapies attempt to effect change rapidly, often with specific, preset lengths of therapeutic contact. Another similarity among the cognitive behavior therapies is that their target of change is also limited. For example, in the treatment of depression, the target of change is the symptoms of depression. Therefore, in the cognitive behavioral approaches to treatment, one sees a time-limited focus and a limited target of change.

EVOLUTION

Cognitive behavior therapy evolved from two lines of clinical and research activity: First, it derives from the work of the early cognitive therapists (Ellis and Beck); second, it was strongly influenced by the careful empirical work of the early behaviorists.

Within the domain of behaviorism, cognitive processes were not always seen as a legitimate focus of attention. In behavior therapy, there has always been a strong commitment to an applied science of clinical treatment. In the behavior therapy of the 1950s and 1960s, this emphasis on scientific methods and procedures meant that behavior therapists focused on events that were directly observable and measurable. Within this framework, behavior was seen as a function of external stimuli that determined or were reliably associated with observable responses. Also during this period, there was a deliberate avoidance of such "nebulous" concepts as thoughts, cognitions, or images. It was believed that these processes were by their very nature vague, and one could never be confident that one was reliably observing or measuring these processes.

It is important to note that by following scientific principles, researchers developed major new treatment approaches that in many ways revolutionized clinical practice (among them are systematic desensitization and the use of a token economy). Yet during the 1960s, several developments within behavior therapy had emphasized the limitations of a strict conditioning model to understanding human behavior.

In 1969, psychologist Albert Bandura published his influential volume Principles of Behavior Modification. In this volume, Bandura emphasized the role of internal or cognitive factors in the causation and maintenance of behavior. In response, behavior therapists who were dissatisfied with the radical behavioral approaches to understanding complex human behavior began actively to seek and study the role of cognitive processes in human behavior.

CRITICISMS AND QUESTIONS

In the case of depression, cognitive behavior therapy holds that patients' excessive self-criticism and self-rejection are the causes of their depression. However, other psychologists argue that the patients' negative thoughts are the result of their depression, and that these patients are better helped through pharmacological means. Other criticisms are that cognitive behavior therapy, because it holds that people's perceptions of events, rather than events cause their emotions and feelings, does not delve deeply enough when causes of mental illness are deeply rooted in childhood abuse or trauma.

Cognitive behavior therapy has been used in combination with drug therapy in the treatment of schizophrenia and bipolar disorder, with some success. It has been suggested by some psychologists that the best use of cognitive behavior therapy is in combination with other therapies.

BIBLIOGRAPHY

Beck, Judith S. *Cognitive Behavior Therapy: Basics and Beyond.* New York: Guildford, 2011. Print.

Brodsky, Beth B., and Barbara B. Stanley. *The Dialectical Behavior Therapy Primer: How DBT Can Inform Clinical Practice.* Hoboken: J. J. Wiley, 2013. Print.

D'Zurilla, Thomas J., and Arthur M. Nezu. *Problem-Solving Therapy: A Positive Approach to Clinical Intervention.* 3d ed. New York: Springer, 2006. Print.

Herbert, James D., and Evan M. Forman. *Acceptance and Mindfulness in Cognitive Behavoir Therapy: Understanding and Applying the New Therapies.* Hoboken: J. J. Wiley, 2011. Print.

Maultsby, Maxie C., Jr. *Rational Behavior Therapy.* Englewood Cliffs, N.J.: Prentice-Hall, 1984. Print.

Meichenbaum, Donald. *Cognitive Behavior Modification.* New York: Plenum, 1979. Print.

Meichenbaum, Donald. *Stress Inoculation Training.* New York: Pergamon, 1985. Print.

Norcross, John C., and Marvin R. Goldfried, eds. *Handbook of Psychotherapy Integration.* 2d ed. New York: Oxford University Press, 2005. Print.

O'Donohue, William, and Jane E. Fisher, eds. *Cognitive Behavior Therapy: Applying Empirically Supported Techniques in Your Practice.* 2d ed. Hoboken, N.J.: John Wiley & Sons, 2009. Print.

Donald G. Beal

See Also: Behavior therapy; Behavioral family therapy; Cognitive social learning: Walter Mischel; Cognitive therapy; Dialectical behavioral therapy; Existential psychology; Rational emotive therapy; Transactional analysis.

Cognitive development
Jean Piaget

Type of psychology: Developmental psychology

Piaget, in one of the twentieth century's most influential development theories, proposed a sequence of maturational changes in thinking. From the sensorimotor responses of infancy, the child acquires symbols. Later, the child begins relating these symbols in such logical operations as categorizing and quantifying. In adolescence, abstract and hypothetical mental manipulations become possible.

Key Concepts

- Concrete operations stage
- Conservation
- Egocentric
- Formal operations stage
- Operations
- Preoperational stage
- Schema (*pl.* schemata)
- Sensorimotor stage

INTRODUCTION

Jean Piaget, a Swiss psychologist, generated the twentieth century's most influential and comprehensive theory of cognitive development. Piaget's theory describes how the maturing child's interactions with the environment result in predictable sequences of changes in certain crucial understandings of the world about him or her. Such changes occur in the child's comprehension of time and space, quantitative relationships, cause and effect, and even right and wrong. The child is always treated as an actor in his or her own development. Advances result from the active desire to develop concepts or schemata that are sufficiently similar to the real world that this real world can be fitted or assimilated into these schemata. Schemata can be defined as any process of interpreting an object or event, including habitual responses, symbols, or mental manipulations. When a schema ("Cats smell nice") is sufficiently discrepant from reality ("That cat stinks"), the schema itself must be accommodated or altered ("That catlike creature is a skunk"). For children everywhere, neurologically based advances in mental capacity introduce new perceptions that make the old ways of construing reality unsatisfactory and compel a fundamentally new construction of reality—a new stage of development. Piaget conceptualizes four such stages: sensorimotor (in infancy), preoperational (the preschool child), concrete operational (the school-age child), and formal operational (adolescence and adulthood).

SENSORIMOTOR STAGE

In the sensorimotor stage, the infant orients himself or herself to objects in the world by consistent physical (motor) movements in response to those sensory stimuli that represent the same object (for example, the sight of a face, the sound of footsteps, or a voice all represent "mother"). The relationship between motor responses and reappearing objects becomes progressively more complex and varied in the normal course of development. First, reflexes such as sucking become more efficient; then sequences of learned actions that bring pleasure are repeated (circular reactions). These learned reactions are directed first toward the infant's own body (thumb sucking), then toward objects in the environment (the infant's stuffed toy).

The baby seems to lack an awareness that objects continue to exist when they are outside the range of his or her senses. When the familiar toy of an infant is hidden, he or she does not search for it; it is as if it has disappeared from reality. As the sensorimotor infant matures, the infant becomes convinced of the continuing existence of objects that disappear in less obvious ways for longer intervals of time. By eighteen months of age, most toddlers have achieved such a conviction of continuing existence, or object permanence.

PREOPERATIONAL STAGE

In the preoperational stage, the preschool child begins to represent these permanent objects by internal processes or mental representations. Now the development of mental representations of useful objects proceeds at an astounding pace. In symbolic play, blocks may represent cars and trains. Capable of deferred imitation, the child may pretend to be a cowboy according to his memory image of a motion-picture cowboy. The most important of all representations are the hundreds of new words the child learns to speak.

As one might infer from the word "preoperational," this period, lasting from about age two through ages six or seven, is transitional. The preschool child still lacks the attention, memory capacity, and mental flexibility to employ his or her increasing supply of symbolic representations in logical reasoning (operations). It is as if the child remains so focused on the individual frames of a motion picture that he or she fails to comprehend the underlying plot. Piaget calls this narrow focusing on a single object or salient dimension centration. The child may say, for example, that a quart of milk he or she has just seen transferred into two pint containers is now "less milk" because the child focuses on the smaller size of the new containers. Fido is seen as a dog, not as an animal or a mammal. The child uncritically assumes that other people, regardless of their situation, share his or her own tastes and perspectives. A two-year-old closes his eyes and says, "Now you don't see me, Daddy." Piaget calls this egocentrism.

CONCRETE OPERATIONS STAGE

The concrete operations stage begins at age six or seven, when the school-age child becomes capable of keeping in mind and logically manipulating several concrete objects at the same time. The child is no longer the prisoner of the momentary appearance of things. In no case is the change more evident than in the sort of problem in which a number of objects (such as twelve black checkers) are spread out into four groups of three. While the four-year-old, preoperational child would be likely to say that now there are more checkers because they take up a larger area, to the eight-year-old it is obvious that this transformation could easily be reversed by regrouping the checkers. Piaget describes the capacity to visualize the reversibility of such transformations as " conservation." This understanding is fundamental to the comprehension of simple arithmetical manipulations. It is also fundamental to a second operational skill: categorization. To the concrete-operational child, it seems obvious that while Rover the dog can for other purposes be classified as a household pet, an animal, or a living organism, he will still be a "dog" and still be "Rover." A related skill is seriation: keeping in mind that an entire series of objects can be arranged along a single dimension, such as size (from smallest to largest). The child now is also capable of role-taking, of understanding the different perspective of a parent or teacher. No longer egocentric (the assumption that everyone shares one's own perspective and the cognitive inability to understand the different perspective of another), the child becomes able to see himself as others see him and to temper the harshness of absolute rules with a comprehension of the viewpoints of others.

FORMAL OPERATIONS STAGE

The formal operations stage begins in early adolescence. In childhood, logical operations are concrete ones, limited to objects that can be visualized, touched, or directly experienced. The advance of the early adolescent into formal operational thinking involves the capacity to deal with possibilities that are purely speculative. This permits coping with new classes of problems: those involving relationships that are purely abstract or hypothetical, or that involve the higher-level analysis of a problem by the systematic consideration of every logical (sometimes fanciful) possibility. The logical adequacy of an argument can be examined apart from the truth or falsity of its conclusions.

Concepts such as "forces," "infinity," or "justice," nowhere directly experienced, can now be comprehended. Formal operational thought permits the midadolescent or adult to hold abstract ideals and to initiate scientific investigations.

ILLUSTRATING STAGE DEVELOPMENT

Piaget was particularly clever in the invention of problems that illustrate the underlying premises of the child's thought. The crucial capability that signals the end of the sensorimotor period is object permanence, the child's conviction of the continuing existence of objects that are outside the range of his or her senses. Piaget established the gradual emergence of object permanence by hiding from the child familiar toys for progressively longer periods of time, with the act of hiding progressively less obvious to the child. Full object permanence is not considered achieved until the child will search for a familiar missing object even when he or she could not have observed its being hidden.

The fundamental test of concrete operational thought is conservation. In a typical conservation task, the child is shown two identical balls of putty. The child generally affirms their obvious equivalence. Then one of the balls of putty is reworked into an elongated, wormlike shape while the child watches. The child is again asked about their relative size. Younger children are likely to say that the wormlike shape is smaller, but the child who has attained conservation of mass will state that the size must still be the same. Inquiries concerning whether the weights of the differently shaped material (conservation of weight) are the same and whether they would displace the same amount of water (conservation of volume) are more difficult questions, generally not answerable until the child is older.

STANDARDIZED TESTS

Since Piaget's original demonstrations, further progress has necessitated the standardization of these problems with materials, questions, procedures, and scoring so clearly specified that examiners can replicate one another's results.Such standardization permits the explanation of the general applicability of Piaget's concepts. Standardized tests have been developed for measuring object permanence, egocentricity, and role-taking skills. The Concept Assessment Kit: Conservation, for example, provides six standard conservation tasks for which comparison data (norms) are available for children in several widely diverse cultures. The relative conceptual attainments of an individual child (or culture) can be measured. It is encouraging that those who attain such basic skills as conservation early have been shown to be advanced in many other educational and cognitive achievements.

IMPLICATIONS FOR EDUCATION

Piaget's views of cognitive development have broad implications for educational institutions charged with fostering such development. The child is viewed as an active seeker of knowledge. This pursuit is advanced by his or her experimental engagement with problems that are slightly more complex than those problems successfully worked through in the past. The teacher is a facilitator of the opportunities for such cognitive growth, not a lecturer or a drillmaster. The teacher provides physical materials that can be experimentally manipulated. Such materials can be simple: Blocks, stones, bottle caps, and plastic containers all can be classified, immersed in water, thrown into fire, dropped, thrown, or balanced. Facilitating peer relationships and cooperation in playing games are also helpful in encouraging social role-taking and moral development.

Since each student pursues knowledge at his or her own pace and in his or her own idiom, great freedom and variety may be permitted in an essentially open classroom. The teacher may nudge the student toward cognitive advancement by presenting a problem slightly more complex than that already comprehended by the student. A student who understands conservation of number may be ready for problems involving the conservation of length, for example. Yet the teacher does not reinforce correct answers or criticize incorrect ones. Sequencing is crucial. The presentation of knowledge or skill before the child is ready can result in superficial, uncomprehended verbalisms. Piaget does not totally reject the necessity of the inculcation of social and cultural niceties (social-arbitrary knowledge), the focus of traditional education. He would maintain, however, that an experimentally based understanding of physical and social relationships is crucial for a creative, thoughtful society.

FINESSING PIAGET'S RESEARCH

Piaget hypothesized sequences of age-related changes in ways of dealing with reality. His conclusions were based on the careful observation of a few selected cases. The voluminous research since Piaget's time overwhelmingly supports the sequence he outlined. The process almost never reverses. Once a child understands the conservation of substance, for example, his or her former conclusion that "Now there is more" seems to the child not simply wrong but absurd. Even within a stage, there is a sequence. Conservation of mass, for example, precedes conservation of volume.

Post-Piagetian research has nevertheless led to a fine-tuning of some of his conclusions and a modification of others. Piaget believed that transitions to more advanced cognitive levels awaited neurological maturation and the child's spontaneous discoveries. Several researchers have found that specific training in simplified and graded conservation and categorization tasks can lead to an early ripening of these skills. Other research has called into question Piaget's timetable. The fact that, within a few months of birth, infants show subtle differences in their reactions to familiar versus unfamiliar objects suggests that recognition memory for objects may begin earlier than Piaget's age for object permanence. If conservation tasks are simplified—if all distraction is avoided, and simple language and familiar materials are used—it can be shown that concrete operations also may begin earlier than Piaget thought. Formal operations, on the other hand, may not begin as early or be applied as universally in adult problem solving as suggested by Piaget's thesis. A significant percentage of older adolescents and adults fail tests for formal operations, particularly in new problem areas.

More basic than readjustments of his developmental scheduling is the reinterpretation of Piaget's stages. The stage concept implies not only an invariant sequence of age-related changes but also developmental discontinuities involving global and fairly abrupt shifts in an entire pattern or structure. Yet the prolonged development and domain-specific nature of many operational skills, cited above, suggest a process that is neither abrupt nor global. An alternative view is that Piaget's sequences can also be understood as the results of continuous improvements in attention, concentration, and memory. Stages represent only transition points on this continuous dimension. They are more like the points of a scale on a thermometer than the stages of the metamorphosis of a caterpillar into a moth.

PIAGET'S IMPACT

Even with the caveat that his stages may reflect, at a more fundamental level, an underlying continuum, Piaget's contributions can be seen as a great leap forward in approximate answers to one of humankind's oldest questions: how human beings know their world. The eighteenth century philosopher Immanuel Kant described certain core assumptions, such as quantity, quality, and cause and effect, which he called "categories of the understanding." Human beings make these assumptions when they relate specific objects and events to one another—when they reason. Piaget's work became known to a 1960's-era American psychology that was dominated by B. F. Skinner's behavioral view of a passive child whose plastic nature was simply molded by the rewards and punishments of parents and culture. The impact of Piaget's work shifted psychology's focus back to a Kantian perspective of the child as an active reasoner who selectively responds to aspects of culture he or she finds relevant. Piaget himself outlined the sequence, the pace, and some of the dynamics of the maturing child's development of major Kantian categories. Such subsequent contributions as Lawrence Kohlberg's work on moral development and Robert Selman's work on role-taking can be viewed as an elaboration and extension of Piaget's unfinished work. Piaget, like Sigmund Freud, was one of psychology's pivotal thinkers. Without him, the entire field of developmental psychology would be radically different.

BIBLIOGRAPHY

Barrouillet, Pierre, and Vinciane Gaillard. *Cognitive Development and Working Memory: A Dialogue Between Neo-Piagetian and Cognitive Approaches.* Hove: Psychology, 2012. Print.

Herman, William E. "The Ideas of Jean Piaget: Using Theory to Better Understand Theory and Improve Learning." *Swiss American Historical Society Review* 48.3 (2012): 18–31. America: History and Life with Full Text. Web. 24 Apr. 2014.

Perret-Clermont, Anne Nelly, and Jean-Marc Barrelet. *Jean Piaget and Neuchâtel: The Learner and the Scholar.* New York: Psychology Press, 2008. Print

Piaget, Jean. *The Psychology of the Child.* Translated by Helen Weaver. New York: Basic Books, 2000. Print.

Rogers, Anissa. *Human Behavior in the Social Environment.* 3rd ed. New York: Wiley-Blackwell, 2013. Print.

Scholnik, Ellin Kofsky, ed. *Conceptual Development: Piaget's Legacy.* Hillsdale, N.J.: Lawrence Erlbaum, 1999. Print.

Serulnikov, Adriana. *Piaget for Beginners.* New York: Writers and Readers, 2000. Print.

Singer, Dorothy G., and Tracey A. Robinson. *A Piaget Primer: How a Child Thinks.* Madison, Conn.: International Universities Press, 1998. Print.

Smith, Lesley M., ed. *Critical Readings on Piaget.* New York: Routledge, 1996. A collection of essays assessing Piaget's theories and their impact, all originally published between 1990 and 1995. Print

Derived from: "Cognitive development: Jean Piaget." *Psychology and Mental Health.* Salem Press. 2009.

Thomas E. DeWolfe

See Also: Adolescence: Cognitive skills; Cognitive ability: Gender differences; Cognitive psychology; Development; Language; Moral development; Piaget, Jean.

Cognitive dissonance

Type of psychology: Social psychology

Cognitive dissonance theory examines the effects of inconsistencies between attitudes and behaviors. It has evolved into an important theory of attitude change and has offered insights into diverse topics, including the effects of rewards, punishment, and choice on attitudes.

Key Concepts

- Attitude
- Cognition
- Consonance
- Dissonance
- External justification

INTRODUCTION

Cognitive dissonance theory, developed by social psychologist Leon Festinger, suggests that there is a basic human tendency to strive for consistency between and among cognitions. Cognitions are defined as what people know about their attitudes and behaviors. An attitude is defined as one's positive or negative evaluations of a person, place, or thing. If an inconsistency does arise—for example, if an individual does something that is discrepant with his or her attitudes—cognitive dissonance is said to occur. Dissonance is an uncomfortable state of physiological and psychological tension. It is so uncomfortable, in fact, that when individuals are in such a state, they become motivated to rid themselves of the feeling. This can be done by restoring consistency to the cognitions in some way.

What exactly does dissonance feel like? Although it is difficult to describe any kind of internal state, the reactions one has when one hurts the feelings of a loved one or breaks something belonging to someone else are probably what Festinger meant by dissonance.

RESTORING CONSONANCE

When in a state of dissonance, there are three ways a person can restore consistency or, in the language of the theory, consonance. Consonance is defined as the psychological state in which cognitions are not in conflict. One way to create consonance is to reduce the importance of the conflicting cognitions. The theory states that the amount of dissonance experienced is a direct function of the importance of the conflicting cognitions. Consider, for example, a person who actively pursues a suntan. The potential for dissonance exists with such behavior, because the cognition "I am doing something that is increasing my chances for skin cancer" may be in conflict with the cognition "I would like to remain healthy and live a long life." To reduce dissonance, this person may convince him- or herself that he or she would rather live a shorter life filled with doing enjoyable and exciting things than live a longer, but perhaps not so exciting, life. The inconsistency still exists, but the importance of the inconsistency has been reduced.

A second way to reduce dissonance is to add numerous consonant cognitions, thus making the discrepancy seem less great. The suntanner may begin to believe he or she needs to be tan to be socially accepted because all of his or her friends have tans. The tanner may also begin to believe that suntanning makes him or her look healthier and more attractive and, indeed, may even come to believe that suntanning does promote health.

The last method Festinger proposed for reducing dissonance is the simplest, and it is the one that caught the attention of many social psychologists. It is simply to change one of the discrepant cognitions. The suntanner could either stop suntanning or convince him- or herself that suntanning is not associated with an increased risk of skin cancer. In either case, the inconsistency would be eliminated.

This latter possibility intrigued social psychologists because it offered the possibility that people's behaviors could influence their attitudes. In particular, it suggested that if someone does something that is inconsistent with his or her attitudes, those attitudes may change to become more consistent with the behavior. For example, imagine that a person wanted a friend to favor a particular candidate in an upcoming election, and the friend favored the opposing candidate. What would happen if this person convinced the friend to accompany him or her to a rally for the candidate the friend did not support? According to the theory, the friend should experience some degree of dissonance, as the behavior of attending a rally for candidate X is inconsistent with the attitude "I do not favor candidate X." To resolve the inconsistency, the friend may well begin to convince him- or herself that candidate X is not so bad and actually has some good points. Thus, in an effort to restore consonance, the friend's attitudes have changed to be more consistent with behavior.

DISSONANCE-INDUCED ATTITUDE CHANGE

Changes in behavior cannot always be expected to lead to changes in attitudes. Dissonance-induced attitude change—that is, the adjustment of one's attitude in an effort to be consistent with a behavior—is likely to happen only under certain conditions. For one, there must not be any external justification for the behavior. An external justification is an environmental cause that might explain the inconsistency. If the friend was paid a hundred dollars to attend the rally for the candidate or was promised a dinner at a fancy restaurant, he or she most likely would not have experienced dissonance, because he or she had a sufficient external justification. Dissonance is most likely to occur when no external justification is present for a behavior.

Second, dissonance is most likely to occur when individuals believe that the behavior was done of their own free will—that is, when they feel some sort of personal responsibility for the behavior. If the friend had been simply told that he or she was being taken out for an exciting evening and was not told that they were going to this candidate's rally until they got there, the friend most likely would not have experienced dissonance.

Third, dissonance is more likely to occur when the behavior has some sort of foreseeable negative consequences. If the friend knew that each person who attended the rally was required to pay a donation or hand out pamphlets for the candidate and yet still elected to go, he or she would probably have experienced considerable dissonance; now the friend is not only attending a rally for a candidate he or she opposes but also actively campaigning against his or her preferred candidate.

EFFECT OF REWARDS

Perhaps the most-researched application of dissonance theory concerns how attitudes are affected by rewarding people for doing things in which they do not believe. In one study, Festinger and J. M. Carlsmith had students perform a boring screw-turning task for one hour. They then asked the students to tell another student waiting to do the same task that the task was very interesting. In other words, they asked the students to lie. Half the students were offered twenty dollars to do this; the other half were offered one dollar. After the students told the waiting student that the task was enjoyable, the researchers asked them what they really thought about the screw-turning task. The students who were paid twenty dollars said they thought the screw-turning task was quite boring. The students who were paid only one dollar, however, said that they thought the task was interesting and enjoyable.

Although surprising, these findings are precisely what dissonance theory predicts. When a student informed a waiting student that the task was enjoyable, the possibility for dissonance arose. The cognition "This task was really boring" is inconsistent with the cognition "I just told someone that this task was quite enjoyable." The students paid twenty dollars, however, had a sufficient external justification for the inconsistency, so there was no dissonance and no need to resolve any inconsistency. The students paid one dollar, however, did not have the same external justification; most people would not consider a dollar to be sufficient justification for telling a lie, so these students were in a real state of dissonance. To resolve the inconsistency, they changed their attitudes about the task and convinced themselves that the task was indeed enjoyable, thereby achieving consonance between attitudes and behavior. Thus, the less people are rewarded for doing things they might not like, the more likely it is that they will begin to like them.

EFFECT OF PUNISHMENT

Dissonance theory makes equally interesting predictions about the effects of punishment. In a study by Elliot Aronson and Carlsmith, a researcher asked preschool children to rate the attractiveness of toys. The researcher then left the room, but, before leaving, he instructed the children not to play with one of the toys they had rated highly attractive. This became the "forbidden" toy. The researcher varied the severity of the punishment with which he threatened the children if they played with the forbidden toy. For some children, the threat was relatively mild: the researcher said he would be upset. For others, the threat was more severe: the researcher said that he would be angry, would pack up the toys and leave, and would consider the child a baby.

Both threats of punishment seemed to work, as no children played with the forbidden toy. When the researcher asked the children later to rerate the attractiveness of the toys, however, it was apparent that the severity of the threat did make a difference. For children who were severely threatened, the forbidden toy was still rated as quite attractive. For the mildly threatened children, however, the forbidden toy was rated as much less attractive.

By not playing with the forbidden toy, children were potentially in a state of dissonance. The cognition "I think this is an attractive toy" is inconsistent with the cognition "I am not playing with the toy." Those in the severe-threat condition had a sufficient external justification for the discrepancy. Hence, there was no dissonance and no motivation to resolve the inconsistency. Those in the mild-threat condition had no such external justification for the inconsistency, so they most likely felt dissonance, and they resolved it by convincing themselves that the toy was not so attractive. Thus, perhaps surprisingly, the more mild the threats used to get children not to do something, the more likely it is that they will come to believe that it is not something they even want to do.

ROLE OF DECISION MAKING

A last type of everyday behavior for which dissonance theory has implications is decision making. According to the theory, many times when one makes a decision, particularly between attractive alternatives, dissonance is likely to occur. Before making a decision, there are probably some features of each alternative that are attractive and some that are not so attractive. When the decision is made, two sets of dissonant cognitions result: "I chose something that has unattractive qualities" and "I did not choose something that has attractive qualities." To resolve this dissonance, people tend to convince themselves that the chosen alternative is clearly superior to the unchosen alternative. Because of this, although each alternative was seen as equally attractive before the decision was made, after the decision, the chosen alternative is seen as much more attractive. For example, Robert Knox and James Inkster went to a racetrack and asked a sample of people who were waiting in line to place their bets how confident they were that their horse was going to win. They then asked a sample of people who were leaving the betting window the same question. As might have been predicted by now, a bettor was much more confident about a horse's chances after having placed the bet. Before placing a bet, there is no dissonance. After actually placing money on the horse, the potential for dissonance ("I placed money on a horse that might lose and I did not bet on a horse that might win") arises. To avoid or resolve this dissonance, bettors become much more confident that their horse will win and, by default, more confident that other horses will not.

PROMINENT INFLUENCE IN PSYCHOLOGY

Cognitive dissonance theory was introduced in 1957, at a time when social psychologists' interest in the motives underlying people's attitudes and behaviors was at a peak. Although dissonance theory has emerged as perhaps the best-known and most-researched theory in social psychology, when it was first developed it was one of a handful of theories, now collectively known as cognitive consistency theories, that proposed that people are motivated to seek consistency among and between thoughts, feelings, and behaviors.

There are numerous explanations for why cognitive dissonance theory has become as important as it has, but two seem particularly intriguing. One concerns the intellectual climate in psychology during the time the theory was introduced. At the time, research in most fields of psychology, including social psychological research on attitude change, was influenced by learning theory. Learning theory suggests that behavior is a function of its consequences: people do those things for which they are rewarded and do not do those things for which they are not rewarded or for which they are punished. Therefore, according to this perspective, to significantly change any form of behavior, from overt actions to attitudes and beliefs, some kind of reward or incentive needs to be offered. The bigger the incentive (or the stronger the punishment), the more change can be expected. Research on attitude change, therefore, also focused on the role of rewards and punishment. What made dissonance theory stand out was its prediction that sometimes less reward or incentive will lead to more change. This counterintuitive prediction, standing in stark contrast to the generally accepted ideas about the roles of reward and punishment, brought immediate attention to dissonance theory not only from the social-psychological community but also from the psychological community in general, and it quickly vaulted the theory to a position of prominence.

A second reason dissonance has become such an important theory has to do with its particular influence on the field of social psychology. Before the theory was introduced, social psychology was identified with the study of groups and intergroup relations. Dissonance theory was one of the first social psychological theories to emphasize the cognitive processes occurring within the individual as an important area of inquiry. As a result, interest in the individual waxed in social psychology, and interest in groups waned. Indeed, the study of groups and intergroup relations began, in part, to be considered the province of sociologists, and the study of the individual in social settings began to define social psychology. Thus, dissonance theory can be credited with significantly changing the focus of research and theory in social psychology.

BIBLIOGRAPHY

Allahyani, Mariam Hameed Ahmed. "The Relationship between Cognitive Dissonance and Decision-Making Styles in a Sample of Female Students at the University of Umm Al Qura." *Education* 132.3 (2012): 641–63. Print.

Aronson, Elliot. "The Theory of Cognitive Dissonance: A Current Perspective." *Advances in Experimental Social Psychology.* Vol. 4. Ed. Leonard Berkowitz. New York: Academic, 1969. 2–34. Print.

Cooper, Joel. *Cognitive Dissonance: Fifty Years of a Classic Theory.* Newbury Park: Sage, 2007. Print.

Festinger, Leon. *A Theory of Cognitive Dissonance.* Stanford: Stanford UP, 1957. Print.

Gawronski, Bertram. "Back to the Future of Dissonance Theory: Cognitive Consistency as a Core Motive." *Social Cognition* 30.6 (2012): 652–68. Print.

Harmon-Jones, Eddie, and Judson Mills, eds. *Cognitive Dissonance: Progress on a Pivotal Theory in Social Psychology.* Washington: APA, 1999. Print.

Martinie, Marie-Amélie, Laurent Milland, and Thierry Olive. "Some Theoretical Considerations on Attitude, Arousal and Affect during Cognitive Dissonance." *Social and Personality Psychology Compass* 7.9 (2013): 680–88. Print.

McClure, John. Explanations, Accounts, and Illusions: *A Critical Analysis.* Cambridge: Cambridge UP, 1991.

Print.

Tavris, Carol, and Elliot Aronson. *Mistakes Were Made (but Not by Me): Why We Justify Foolish Beliefs, Bad Decisions, and Hurtful Acts.* Orlando: Harcourt, 2007. Print.

Kenneth G. DeBono

See Also: Attitude-behavior consistency; Attitude formation and change; Attributional biases; Causal attribution; Motivation; Motivation: Intrinsic and extrinsic; Self-perception theory; Social perception.

Cognitive maps

Type of psychology: Cognition; Learning; Memory; Social psychology

A cognitive map is a representation of one's social and cultural environment. Individuals from different cultures may have different perceptions of the world due to their cognitive maps. These differences can influence how people interact with their surrounding environment. In a more specific sense, a cognitive map is the development of an internal representation of spatial relationships between items, allowing for navigation through an environment, acquired through actual experience or through other means.

Key Concepts

- Cognition
- Competence
- Context
- Culture
- Expectancy
- Latent learning
- Performance

INTRODUCTION

Edward C. Tolman first identified what he later named cognitive maps as a result of a series of experiments conducted in the 1920s and 1930s. In these experiments, Tolman sought to discover whether learning occurred that might not be immediately reflected in performance—what he came to term "latent learning."

In a typical experiment, Tolman constructed an intricate maze. Three groups of hungry rats ran the maze once a day for twelve days. The first group, the rewarded control group, received food for successfully completing the maze. The second group, the nonrewarded control group, received no food; its members investigated the maze. The third group, the experimental group, also received no food for the first ten days of the experiment, and its members simply surveyed the maze. On the eleventh day, the experimental group was provided with food; on the twelfth day, this group performed as well as the rewarded control group.

Tolman concluded that latent learning had taken place and that under the appropriate conditions, the experimental group reflected this learning through its performance—the successful completion of the maze. He asserted that the rats had formed "cognitive maps" that enabled them to solve the maze. Therefore, learning—defined here as the construction of cognitive maps—is not the same as performance. Although learning is reflected in performance, Tolman's work strongly suggests that the appropriate context is necessary to elicit that performance. In the case of the experimental group, the context was the food the experimenters provided on the eleventh day of a twelve-day experiment. The rats, Tolman inferred, anticipated that successful completion of the maze on the next attempt would result in their receiving the desired food.

Research has supported Tolman's pioneering work. In 1978, Emil W. Menzel used chimpanzees to illustrate the spatial dimensions of cognitive maps. He hid food in a field and then carried a chimpanzee around the field with him. He did not allow the ape either to eat or approach the food, preventing both instrumental conditioning and primary reinforcement from taking place. Later, the chimpanzee that had been shown the food's hiding places and five experimental chimpanzees that had not seen them were released in the field. Invariably, the first chimpanzee went directly to the food. The experimental animals found their food through scrutinizing the area near the chimpanzee that had been shown the hidden supply of food or begging food from this chimpanzee.

In 1976, David S. Olton and Robert J. Samuelson demonstrated spatial memory (cognitive maps) in rats through employment of a radial maze. Each arm of the maze had food at the end of it. Through a series of manipulations, the experimenters demonstrated that the rats remembered which arms they had explored and at which arms they had been fed. They eliminated the possibility that the animals used smell to locate the food through altering the animals' sense of smell. Furthermore, other researchers moved the maze to note whether other factors, such as tactile clues, influenced the rats. In each variation of the experiment, the rats behaved as if they were responding to spatial location and not tactile clues. In 1985, William Roberts and Nelly Van Veldhuizen demonstrated that pigeons, as well as rats, can work the radial maze.

LEARNING THEORIES

Cognitive theories in learning have gained in popularity. Tolman's groundbreaking work established the concepts of cognitive maps, internal spatial memories of the animal's relevant environment, and expectancy, an animal's anticipation of a sequence of events in time. Tolman's work, supported and developed through additional research, further established the distinction between learning and performance. Linguists such as Noam Chomsky express this distinction as one between competence and performance.

Cognitive anthropologists, influenced by Tolman's work, have applied the concept of the cognitive map to the learning of individuals within sociocultural systems. Cognitive maps, in the anthropologists' view, provide guides to cultural behavior by organizing psychological, social, and cultural landscapes in terms of their relevant characteristics for members of any given society. Two famous covers of the New Yorker magazine illustrate this point. One cover is a New Yorker's view of the West. In that view, the entire center of the United States comprises an area smaller than Midtown Manhattan. The view to the east is little better: the Atlantic Ocean becomes a puddle, and the geography of Europe is greatly distorted. The point is not that New Yorkers are more ethnocentric than other people; it is that all people exaggerate those aspects of their landscapes or environments that are most important to them, and they neglect those features that they consider unimportant.

A number of factors enter into perceptions of what is most relevant and what is not. Some of these are personal, such as age, gender, likes, and dislikes; others are social, such as class, ethnic group, and occupation. All factors, however, fit into a cultural context and take on meanings within that context. Anyone attempting to understand the manner in which people learn and demonstrate that learning through adequate and appropriate performance must take into account these factors and how they help shape an individual's cognitive map.

In education, the prior-learning approach has sought to come to grips with these issues and to apply them to instructional ends. Essentially, this perspective maintains that it cannot be assumed that learning has not taken place merely because a student does not demonstrate the desired performance. William Labov demonstrated, for example, that the presumed inarticulateness of African American street youths was a function of the setting in which people had tested them. In more natural settings, Labov determined that they were, in fact, highly articulate.

Tolman's insight that rats in a maze will demonstrate latent learning through performance when an appropriate stimulus is present has influenced cognitive therapy. This therapy is based on the hypothesis that people base their behavior on cognitive maps and expectancies. These internal representations of spatial relationships and anticipated sequences of events, based on past experiences—psychological, social, and cultural—form individuals' perceptions of reality, even when these stimuli are not materially present.

Cognitive motivation theory is a "pull" theory of motivation, based on the hypothesis that people's expectancies provide incentives for behavior. There are positive-incentive and negative-incentive motivations. Working for a promotion along paths anticipated to achieve that desired goal is an example of positive-incentive motivation. In contrast, a youngster who is developing his or her martial arts skills to deal with bullies who frequently beat him or her provides an example of negative-incentive motivation.

Values enter intimately into cognitive motivation theory. To motivate people, incentives must be valued. If people do not value an incentive, such as a promotion, they are less likely to perform the actions they associate with receiving that incentive. If they receive the goal without performing the behavior—for example, if someone receives a promotion undeservedly—they are less likely to value the goal. In sum, there is an intrinsic relationship between expectancies and value.

Moreover, relief and frustration enter the picture. Relief refers to not receiving an expected negative result (a person does not fail a test for which he or she did not study). Frustration involves failure to attain a goal for which a person has prepared. Failure to receive a promotion to which a person is entitled is an example of frustration. Relief is an example of positive-incentive motivation, and frustration is an example of negative-incentive motivation.

Albert Bandura and others have advocated cognitive behavior therapy based on the application of positive and negative incentives. Such therapy seeks to alter the expectancies and relational maps of clients. Thus, clients can relearn their environment through redrawing cognitive maps and altering their expectancies. There are many techniques employed to bring about these changes in spatial and event expectations. Therapists who employ Albert Ellis's rational emotive therapy believe that the therapist should take a strong interventionist role in the therapy, aggressively confronting the client whenever he or she exhibits examples of irrational thought. These confrontations seek to force clients to learn new, more rational ways of thinking and, therefore, behaving.

Cognitive behavioral therapists seek to change a person's inappropriate thoughts to more effective ones. They first learn what their clients are thinking and then relate these thoughts to inappropriate behavior. They seek to help their clients learn new thoughts that will result in more appropriate behavior. Patients are taught to "talk to themselves," substituting good thoughts for bad. Rather than dwelling on failure, patients concentrate on success or positive aspects of their lives. A student taking an examination, for example, would stop thoughts of failure and remind him- or herself about how well test preparation had gone. Self-encouragement would replace self-disparagement.

Each of these applications is based on the theory that people's behavior is based on internal representations of the world. Each person's representations differ in some way from those of others. These representations influence both the way in which one learns about the world and the manner in which one represents that world. The application of Tolman's work on cognitive maps and their related internal representations, or expectancies, has led to a deeper understanding of learning.

RELEVANCE OF COGNITIVE MAPS TO PSYCHOLOGY

One of the important issues for the field of cognitive psychology is that of representation. In general terms, how do humans store information in the brain? In 1969, Allen Paivio presented the dual code theory, which suggests that both analogical and verbal codes are used for representing information. Some information maybe stored in an imagelike form (analogue), while other information is stored in a verbal format. In 1973, Zenon Phylyshyn advocated the propositional hypothesis, which suggests that concepts are stored in an abstract form that captures the underlying relationship between ideas. People may experience images, but this experience is simply a by-product, an epiphenomenon, of the retrieval of information. Research into cognitive maps may provide some insight into the issue of representation.

SOURCES OF INFORMATION FOR A COGNITIVE MAP

The development of a cognitive map may include in the representation information from a variety of sources, including landmarks, route information, and survey information. This information may be incorporated into a cognitive map over time and is not necessarily mutually exclusive. Salient features such as landmarks, distinctive objects that stand out from the rest of the environment, provide a point of reference for orientation and navigation within an environment. Route knowledge is specific information regarding how to navigate from one location to another. The directions one gives to allow another to navigate from one location to another would be similar to route information. Survey knowledge provides an overview of the relationships between locations; this perspective has a better grasp of the global relationship between various locations. This type of knowledge is acquired from maps by traversing the environment from a number of different perspectives.

In addition to the type of information available, a number of other factors can influence the development of a cognitive map, such as angle, shape, and orientation. These factors may lead to distortions in generating a map. For example, streets that cross each other at an odd angle tend to be drawn closer to a ninety-degree angle than they really are. Still other factors that are not spatial in nature may affect the retrieval of information. In 1991, Keith Clayton and Ali Habibi discussed the confounding of time and space. Locations experienced close together in space are often experienced close together in time. Retrieval of information, in some cases, may be due to temporal proximity versus spatial proximity. Other such factors in this category may include semantic clustering (grouping together of similar items) and route knowledge (grouping of items spatially and temporally).

METHODS FOR ASSESSING COGNITIVE MAPS

A variety of methods have been used to test spatial knowledge, including location judgment (whether a location is closer to one reference point or another), recognition (whether the item is part of the map or not), distance estimations (how far it is between two locations), map drawing, providing directions, and pointing (what direction would one travel from a given location to another specific location). In a 1986 study, Timothy

McNamara discussed the merits of using tasks such as location judgment and recognition that allow one to look at priming, which taps into automatic processes. These tasks may be informative in terms of how spatial information is organized in long-term memory. Other tasks, such as pointing, may be more informative in terms of strategies that are used to answer spatial questions.

In 1978, Albert Stevens and Patty Coupe asked subjects which is farther west, Reno, Nevada, or San Diego, California. Many incorrectly inferred that San Diego is farther west than Reno, since California is farther west than Nevada. In actuality, the state of California curves under the state of Nevada, making Reno farther west. This implies the use of information such as relative position within categories (states) rather than actual spatial information between the two locations.

OTHER AREAS OF RESEARCH IN COGNITIVE MAPS

Research suggests that the ability to form and use a cognitive map begins to develop around the age of three. Judy DeLoache, in her 1987 experiments, used a scaled model of a larger room to test children's spatial knowledge. Children of various ages were asked to find a small hidden toy in the model. After finding the small toy, children were then asked to find the larger toy, which was hidden in the same location in the larger room. This task required the child to use the information from the scaled model to find the object in the larger environment. DeLoache suggested that the younger children had a difficult time using the scaled model of a room as a basis for a representation of the larger room. Research in this area continues to look at the application and development of these skills over time.

Studies on gender differences in spatial knowledge have focused on strategies such as wayfinding and direction pointing. The use of such spatial strategies tends to be gender specific. It appears that women prefer to use a strategy of wayfinding based on the use of landmarks, while men tend to prefer using more of a global or survey strategy. Studies suggest, however, that these differences may be due to preferred strategies versus actual differences in acquisition of spatial knowledge.

REALITY REPRESENTATION AND BEHAVIOR

Tolman's concept of the cognitive map grew out of a recognition that internal representations of reality influence behavior. Moreover, learning is not indistinguishable from performance—the two processes are analytically distinct. An organism may have learned behavior without demonstrating that behavior through performance. This latent learning can be elicited through the presentation of adequate incentives.

Tolman's work in the 1920s and 1930s did much to advance the field of cognitive psychology at a time when behavioral psychology dominated the schools. It provided an additional dimension to learning, advancing the position of internal representations of reality. The empirical evidence offered to support cognitive theory has been impressive, and its status in psychology has advanced accordingly; it is often combined with behavioral concepts, as in the work of Bandura.

That combination has enabled educators and therapists to bring about behavioral changes based on changes in the manner in which students and patients perceive their worlds. New internal representations of the external environment can be brought about through changes in cognitive maps and expectancies. In turn, these changes alter the bases of decisions that influence an individual's future behavior.

Tolman's work has influenced linguistics, anthropology, sociology, and other social and behavioral sciences. Scholars in these areas have applied the concept of the cognitive map cross-culturally and within cultures to members of subgroups. Future work will apply it to the manner in which each individual negotiates his or her way within cultural and social systems. Continuing work in anthropology and sociology in the negotiated nature of sociocultural systems draws heavily on cognitive maps. Prior-learning theory is based on the idea of latent learning, and future work will continue to extract applications of significant value to education.

Future advances will likely occur in studies that investigate field dependence and independence in cognition as related to other aspects of culture, such as child-rearing patterns and subsistence practices. The continuing interest in the relationship between language and the cultural organization of reality holds promise for further advances in understanding and applying cognitive maps. The role of choice in the individual's construction of these maps is also an area of intensive investigation.

BIBLIOGRAPHY

Bandura, Albert. *Social Foundations of Thought and Action: A Social Cognitive Theory.* Englewood Cliffs: Prentice, 1986. Print.

Bukatko, Danuta, and Marvin W. Daehler. *Child Development: A Thematic Approach.* 5th ed. Boston:

Houghton, 2004. Print.

Carbon, Claus-Christian, and Vera M. Hesslinger. "Attitudes and Cognitive Distances: On the Non-Unitary and Flexible Nature of Cognitive Maps." *Advances in Cognitive Psychology* 9.3 (2013): 121–29. Print.

Chomsky, Noam. *Language and Mind*. 3rd ed. New York: Cambridge UP, 2006. Print.

Fromkin, Victoria, Robert Rodman, and Nina Hyams. *An Introduction to Language*. 10th ed. Boston: Wadsworth, 2014. Print.

Gallistel, C. R. *The Organization of Learning*. Cambridge: MIT P, 1990. Print.

Labov, William. *The Social Stratification of English in New York City.* 2nd ed. New York: Cambridge UP, 2006. Print.

Matlin, Margaret W. *Cognition*. 8th ed. Hoboken: Wiley, 2013. Print.

Menzel, Emil W. "Cognitive Mapping in Chimpanzees." *Cognitive Processes in Animal Behavior.* Ed. Stewart H. Hulse, Harry Fowler, and Werner K. Honig. Hillsdale: Erlbaum, 1978. 375–422. Print.

Olton, David S., and Robert J. Samuelson. "Remembrance of Places Passed: Spatial Memory in Rats." *Journal of Experimental Psychology: Animal Behavior Processes* 2.2 (1976): 97–116. Print.

Pazzaglia, Francesca, and Angelica Moe. "Cognitive Styles and Mental Rotation Ability in Map Learning." *Cognitive Processing* 14.4 (2013): 391–99. Print.

Roberts, William A., and Nelly Van Veldhuizen. "Spatial Memory in Rats on the Radial Maze." *Journal of Experimental Psychology: Animal Behavior Processes* 11.2 (1985): 241–60. Print.

Suzuki, Ikuo. "Effects of Sense of Direction on Internet Skill and Cognitive Maps of the Web." *Computers in Human Behavior* 28.1 (2012): 120–28. Print.

Tolman, Edward C. "Cognitive Maps in Rats and Men." *Psychological Review* 55.4 (1948): 189–208. Print.

Tolman, Edward C. *Purposive Behavior in Animals and Men.* New York: Century, 1932. Print.

Zhu, Qing, Rubin Wang, and Ziyin Wang. "A Cognitive Map Model Based on Spatial and Goal-Oriented Mental Exploration in Rodents." *Behavioural Brain Research* 256 (2013): 128–39. Print.

Frank A. Salamone; updated by Michael S. Bendele

See Also: Bandura, Albert; Cognitive behavior therapy; Cognitive psychology; Cognitive social learning: Walter Mischel; Cognitive therapy; Concept formation; Decision making; Incentive motivation; Learning; Mischel, Walter; Motivation; Motivation: Intrinsic and extrinsic; Tolman, Edward C.

Cognitive psychology

Type of psychology: Cognition

Cognitive psychology is concerned with the scientific study of human mental activities involved in the acquisition, storage, retrieval, and utilization of information. Among its wide concerns are perception, memory, reasoning, problem solving, intelligence, language, and creativity; research in these areas has widespread practical applications.

Key Concepts

- Artificial intelligence
- Cognitive behavioral therapy
- Cognitive science
- Episodiac memory
- Long-term memory
- Metamemory
- Prospective memory
- Semantic memory
- Short-term memory
- Working memory

INTRODUCTION

Cognitive psychology is that branch of psychology concerned with human mental activities. A staggering array of topics fits under such a general heading. In fact, it sometimes seems that there is no clear place to end the catalog of cognitive topics, as mental operations intrude into virtually all human endeavors. As a general guideline, one might consider the subject matter of cognitive psychology as those mental processes involved in the acquisition, storage, retrieval, and utilization of information.

Among the more specific concerns of cognitive psychologists are perception, attention, memory, and imagery. Studies of perception and attention might be concerned with how much of people's vast sensory experience they can further process and make sense of, and how they recognize incoming information as forming familiar patterns. Questions regarding the quality of memory include how much information can be maintained, for how long, and under what conditions; how information is organized in memory and how is it retrieved or lost; and how accurate the memory is, as well as what can be done to facilitate a person's recall skills. Cognitive researchers concerned with imagery are interested in people's ability to "see" in their minds a picture or image of an object, person, or scene that is not physically present; cognitive researchers are interested in the properties of such images and how they can be manipulated.

In addition to these concerns, there is great interest in the higher-order processes of planning, reasoning, problem solving, intelligence, language, and creativity. Cognitive psychologists want to know, for example, what steps are involved in planning a route to a destination or a solution to a problem, and what factors influence people's more abstract ability to reason. They seek to understand the importance of prior knowledge or experience, to discover which strategies are effective, and to see what obstacles typically impede a person's thinking. They are interested in the relationships between language and thought and between creativity and intelligence.

The following exchange is useful in illustrating some of the topics important to cognitive psychologists. Imagine that "Jacob" and "Janet" are two children on a busy playground:

Jacob: Do you want to play some football?
Janet: Sure! Tell me where the ball is and I'll go get it.
Jacob: The football's in my locker in the equipment room. Go back in the building. Go past our classroom, turn right at the water fountain, and it's the second door on your left. My locker is number 12, and the combination is 6-21-13.
Janet: Okay, it'll just take me a couple of minutes. [As she runs to get the ball, Janet repeats over and over to herself, "12; 6, 21, 13. . . . "]
Jacob: [shouting] The football field's being watered; meet me in the gym.

Even such a simple encounter involves and depends on a rich assortment of cognitive skills. At a basic level, Jacob and Janet have to be aware of each other. Their sensory systems allow the detection of each other, and their brains work on the raw data (information) from the senses to perceive or interpret the incoming information. In this case, the data are recognized as the familiar patterns labeled "Jacob" and "Janet." During the course of the brief conversation, the children must also attend to (concentrate on) each other, and in doing so they may be less attentive to other detectable sights and sounds of their environment.

This scenario illustrates the use of more than one type of memory. Janet stores the locker number and combination in short-term memory (STM), and she maintains the information by rehearsing it. After Janet retrieves the ball and redirects her attention to choosing teams for the football game, she may forget this information. Jacob does not need to rehearse his combination continually to maintain it; rather, his frequent use of his combination and the meaningfulness of this information have helped him to store it in long-term memory (LTM). If someone later asks Janet where she got the football, she will retrieve that information from her episodic LTM. Episodic memory holds information about how things appeared and when they occurred; it stores things that depend on context. The language comprehension of the children also illustrates another type of LTM. Semantic LTM, or absolute threshold, holds all the information they need to use language; it includes not only words and the symbols for them, their meaning and what they represent, but also the rules for manipulating them. When Janet hears the words "football," "water fountain," and "locker," she effortlessly retrieves their meanings from LTM. Furthermore, metamemory, an understanding of the attributes of one's own memories, is demonstrated. Janet knows to rehearse the combination to prevent forgetting it. Jacob probably employed mental imagery and relied on a cognitive map to direct Janet to the equipment room. From his substantial mental representation of the school environment, Jacob retrieved a specific route, guided by a particular sequence of meaningful landmarks. In addition to their language capabilities and their abilities to form and follow routes, a number of other higher-level mental processes suggest something of the intelligence of these children. They appear to be following a plan that will result in a football game. Simple problem solving is demonstrated by Janet's calculation of how long it will take to retrieve the football and in Jacob's decision to use the gym floor as a substitute for the football field.

THEORETICAL AND METHODOLOGICAL APPROACHES

To understand cognitive psychology, one must be familiar not only with the relevant questions—the topic matter of the discipline—but also with the approach taken to answer these questions. Cognitive psychologists typically employ an information-processing model to help them better understand mental events. An assumption of this model is that mental activities (the processing of information) can be broken down into a series of interrelated stages and scientifically studied. A general comparison can be made between the information processing of a human and a computer. For example, both have data input into the system, humans through their sense organs and computers through the keyboard. Both systems then translate and encode (store) the data. The computer translates the keyboard input into electromagnetic signals for storage on a disk. People often translate the raw data from their senses to a linguistic code that is retained in some unique human storage device (for example, a piercing, rising-and-falling pitch may be stored in memory as "baby's cry"). Both humans and computers can manipulate the stored information in virtually limitless ways, and both can later retrieve information from storage for output. Although there are many dissimilarities between how computers and humans function, this comparison accurately imparts the flavor of the information-processing model.

In addition to constructing computational models that specify the stages and processes involved in human thought, cognitive psychologists use a variety of observational and experimental methods to determine how the mind works. Much can be learned, for example, from the study of patients with neuropsychological disorders such as the progressive dementias, including Alzheimer's disease. The "lesion," or brain injury, study is the oldest and most widely used technique to study brain function. Examining what happens when one aspect of cognition is disrupted can reveal much about the operation of the remaining mechanisms.

Behavioral studies—in contrast to "lesion" studies—examine cognitive function in healthy subjects, using a variety of experimental methods developed throughout the twentieth century. One of the continuing challenges of cognitive psychology is the construction of experiments in which observable behaviors accurately reveal mental processes. Researchers bring volunteers into the laboratory and measure, for example, the time it takes for subjects to judge whether a word they are shown had appeared in a list of words they had earlier studied.

Other researchers study human cognition in more naturalistic settings called field studies. In one such study, the average score of grocery shoppers on a paper-and-pencil arithmetic test was 59 percent, but their proficiency in the supermarket on analogous tasks reached ceiling level (98 percent). Much of what is done in the laboratory could be thought of as basic research, whereas field approaches to the study of cognition could be characterized as applied research.

APPLIED RESEARCH IN COGNITIVE PSYCHOLOGY

For many psychologists, the desire to "know about knowing" is sufficient reason to study human cognition; however, there are more tangible benefits. Examples of these widespread practical applications may be found in the fields of artificial intelligence and law and in the everyday world of decision making.

Artificial intelligence (AI) is a branch of computer science that strives to create a computer capable of reasoning, processing language, and, in short, mimicking human intelligence. While this goal has yet to be obtained in full, research in this area has made important contributions. The search for AI has improved the understanding of human cognition; it has also produced applied benefits such as expert systems. Expert systems are computer programs that simulate human expertise in specific domains. Such programs have been painstakingly developed by computer scientists who have essentially extracted knowledge in a subject area from a human expert and built it into a computer system designed to apply that knowledge. Expert systems do not qualify as true artificial intelligence, because, while they can think, they can only do so very narrowly and on one particular topic.

A familiar expert system is the "chess computer." A computerized chess game is driven by a program that has a vast storehouse of chess knowledge and the capability of interacting with a human player and "thinking" about each game in which it is involved. Expert systems are also employed to solve problems in law, computer programming, and various facets of industry. A medical expert system has even been developed to consult interactively with patients and to diagnose and recommend a course of treatment for infectious diseases.

There are legal implications for the cognitive research of Elizabeth F. Loftus and her colleagues at the University of Washington. Some of their experiments demonstrate the shortcomings of human long-term memory, research relevant to the interpretation of eyewitness testimony in the courtroom. In one study, Loftus and John Palmer showed their subjects films of automobile accidents and asked them to estimate the speeds of the cars involved. The critical variable was the verb used in the question to the subjects. That is, they were asked how fast the cars were going when they "smashed," "collided," "bumped," "hit," or "contacted" each other. Interestingly, the stronger the verb, the greater was the speed estimated. One interpretation of these findings is that the nature of the "leading question" biased the answers of subjects who were not really positive of the cars' speeds. Hence, if the question employed the verb "smashed," the subject was led to estimate that the cars were going fast. Any astute attorney would have no trouble capitalizing on this phenomenon when questioning witnesses to a crime or accident.

In a second experiment, Loftus and Palmer considered a different explanation for their findings. Again, subjects saw filmed car accidents and were questioned as to the speeds of the cars, with the key verb being varied as previously described. As before, those exposed to the verb "smashed" estimated the fastest speeds. In the second part of the experiment, conducted a week later, the subjects were asked additional questions about the accident, including, "Did you see any broken glass?" Twenty percent of the subjects reported seeing broken glass, though none was in the film. Of particular interest was that the majority of those who made this error were in the group that had been exposed to the strongest verb, "smashed."

Loftus and Palmer reasoned that the subjects were melding actual information that they had witnessed with information from another source encountered after the fact (the verb "smashed" presented by the questioner). The result was a mental representation of an event that was partly truth and partly fiction. This interpretation also has implications for the evaluation of eyewitness testimony. Before testifying in court, a witness will likely have been questioned numerous times (and received many suggestions as to what may have taken place) and may even have "compared notes" with other witnesses. This process is likely to distort the originally experienced information.

Consider next the topic of decision making, an area of research in cognitive psychology loaded with practical implications. Everyone makes scores of decisions on a daily basis, from choosing clothing to match the weather, to selecting a college or a career objective. Psychologists Amos Tversky and Daniel Kahneman are well known for their research on decision making and, in particular, on the use of heuristics. Heuristics are shortcuts or rules of thumb that are likely, but not guaranteed, to produce a correct decision. It would seem beneficial for everyone to appreciate the limitations of such strategies. For example, the availability heuristic often leads people astray when their decisions involve the estimating of probabilities, as when faced with questions such as, Which produces more fatalities, breast cancer or diabetes? Which are more numerous in the English language, words that begin with k or words that have k as the third letter? Experimental subjects typically, and incorrectly, choose the first alternative. Kahneman and Tversky's research indicates that people rely heavily on examples that come most easily to mind—that is, the information most available in memory. Hence, people overestimate the incidence of breast-cancer fatalities because such tragedies get more media attention relative to diabetes, a more prolific but less exotic killer. In a similar vein, words that begin with k come to mind more easily (probably because people are more likely to organize their vocabularies by the initial sounds of the words) than words with k as the third letter, although the latter in fact outnumbers the former. One's decision making will doubtless be improved if one is aware of the potential drawbacks associated with the available heuristic and if one is able to resist the tendency to estimate probabilities based on the most easily imagined examples.

COGNITIVE CONTEXTS

The workings of the human mind have been pondered throughout recorded history. The science of psychology, however, only dates back to 1879, when Wilhelm Wundt established the first laboratory for the study of psychology in Leipzig, Germany. Although the term was not yet popular, Wundt's primary interest was clearly in cognition. His students laboriously practiced the technique of introspection (the careful attention to and the objective reporting of one's own sensations, experiences, and thoughts), as Wundt hoped to identify through this method the basic elements of human thought. Wundt's interests remained fairly popular until around 1920 when John B. Watson, a noted American psychologist and behaviorist, spearheaded a campaign to redefine the agenda of psychology. Watson was convinced that the workings of the mind could not be objectively studied through introspection and hence mandated that the proper subject matter for psychologists should be overt, observable behaviors exclusively. In this way, dissatisfaction with a method of research (introspection) led to the abandonment of an important psychological topic (mental activity).

In the 1950s, a number of forces came into play that led to the reemergence of cognitive psychology in the United States. First, during World War II, considerable research had been devoted to human-factor issues such as human skills and performance within, for example, the confines of a tank or cockpit. After the war, researchers showed continued interest in human attention, perception, decision making, and so on, and they were influenced by a branch of communication science known as information theory, which dealt abstractly with questions of information processing. The integration of these two topics resulted eventually in the modern information-processing model.

Second, explosive gains were made in the field of computer science. Of particular interest to psychology were advances in the area of artificial intelligence. It was a natural progression for psychologists to begin comparing computer and brain processes, and this analogy served to facilitate cognitive research.

Third, there was growing dissatisfaction with behavioral psychology as defined by Watson and with its seeming inability to explain complex psychological phenomena. In particular, Noam Chomsky, a well-known linguist, proposed that the structure of language was too complicated to be acquired via the principles of behaviorism. It became apparent to many psychologists that to understand truly the diversity of human behavior, internal mental processes would have to be accepted and scientifically studied.

Working memory , or short-term memory, emerged as an important theoretical construct in the 1980s and 1990s. Everyday cognitive tasks—such as reading a newspaper article or calculating the appropriate amount to tip in a restaurant—often involve multiple steps with intermediate results that need to be kept in mind temporarily to successfully accomplish the task at hand. Working memory refers to the system or mechanism underlying the maintenance of task-relevant information during the performance of a cognitive task. As the "hub of cognition," working memory has been called "perhaps the most significant achievement of human mental evolution." According to Alan Baddeley, working memory comprises a visuospatial sketchpad; a phonological loop, concerned with acoustic and verbal information; a central executive that is involved in the control and regulation of the system; and an episodic buffer that combines information from long-term memory with that from the visuospatial sketchpad and the phonological loop. Prospective memory has also emerged as an important domain of research in cognitive psychology. This type of memory involves the intention to carry out an action in the future: for instance, to pick up dry cleaning after work.

Cognitive psychology is now a vibrant subdiscipline that has attracted some of the finest scientific minds. It is a standard component in most undergraduate and graduate psychology programs. More than half a dozen academic journals are devoted to its research, and it continues to pursue answers to questions that are important to psychology and other disciplines as well. The cognitive perspective has heavily influenced other subfields of psychology. For example, many social psychologists are interested in social cognition, the reasoning underlying such phenomena as prejudice, altruism, and persuasion. Some clinical psychologists are interested in understanding the abnormal thought processes underlying problems such as depression and anorexia nervosa; a subspecialty—cognitive behavioral therapy—treats mental illness using methods that attempt to directly treat these abnormal thoughts.

The burgeoning field of cognitive science represents a contemporary union of cognitive psychology, neuroscience, computer science, linguistics, and philosophy. Cognitive scientists are concerned with mental processes but are particularly interested in establishing general, fundamental principles of information processing as they may be applied by humans or machines. Their research is often heavily dependent on complex computer models rather than experimentation with humans. With fast-paced advances in computer technology, and the exciting potential of expertise shared in an interdisciplinary fashion, the field of cognitive science holds considerable promise for answering questions about human cognition.

BIBLIOGRAPHY

Ashcraft, Mark H. *Human Memory and Cognition*. 4th ed. Upper Saddle River, N.J.: Pearson Prentice Hall, 2006. Print.

Baddeley, Alan D. "The Cognitive Psychology of Everyday Life." *British Journal of Psychology* 72, no. 2 (1981): 257-269. Print.

Berger, Dale E., Kathy Pezdek, and William P. Banks, eds. *Applications of Cognitive Psychology.* Hillsdale, N.J.: Lawrence Erlbaum, 1987. Print.

Cialdini, Robert B. *Influence: Science and Practice*. 5th ed. Boston: Pearson Education, 2009. Print.

Hughes, Brian M. *Conceptual and Historical Issues in Psychology.* New York: Pearson, 2012. Print.

Kahneman, Daniel, Paul Slovic, and Amos Tversky, eds. *Judgment Under Uncertainty: Heuristics and Biases.* New York: Cambridge University Press, 2007. Print.

Kendler, Howard H. *Historical Foundations of Modern*

Psychology. Chicago: Dorsey Press, 1987. Print.

Manktelow, K. I. *Thinking and Reasoning: An Introduction to the Psychology of Reason, Judgement, and Decision Making*. New York: Psychology P, 2012. Print.

Miyake, Akira, and Priti Shah, eds. *Models of Working Memory: Mechanisms of Active Maintenance and Executive Control.* New York: Cambridge University Press, 1999. Print.

Pinker, Steven. *How the Mind Works.* London: Penguin, 2005. Print.

Siegal, Michael, and Luca Surian. *Access to Language and Cognitive Development*. New York: Oxford UP, 2012. Print.

Sternberg, Robert J., and Talia Ben-Zeev. *Complex Cognition: The Psychology of Human Thought*. New York: Oxford University Press, 2001. Print.

Wells, Gary L., and Elizabeth F. Loftus, eds. *Eyewitness Testimony: Psychological Perspectives*. New York: Cambridge University Press, 1987. Print.

Mark B. Alcorn; updated by Allyson Washburn

SEE ALSO: Alzheimer's disease; Artificial intelligence; Attention; Cognitive ability: Gender differences; Cognitive behavior therapy; Cognitive development: Jean Piaget; Cognitive maps; Cognitive therapy; Computer models of cognition; Decision making; Language; Logic and reasoning; Memory; Pattern recognition; Piaget, Jean; Short-term memory.

Cognitive social learning
Walter Mischel

TYPE OF PSYCHOLOGY: Personality

Walter Mischel's social learning theory presents a cognitive-social alternative to traditional personality theories. He posits that behavior is determined by a complex interaction of situational and cognitive variables and cannot be predicted from a few widely generalized traits. Consistent features in behavior result from cognitive person variables, defined as acquired and relatively stable modes of information processing.

KEY CONCEPTS

- Construction competencies
- Enconding strategy
- Expectancies
- Person variable
- Personal construct
- Personality trait
- Prototype
- Stimulus value

INTRODUCTION

Psychologist Walter Mischel developed a cognitive social learning approach to personality that presents a serious challenge to traditional theories and their central tenet that behavior can be predicted from a few widely generalized traits. In his influential book *Personality and Assessment* (1968), Mischel reviewed the literature on personality traits. Personality traits can be defined as a stable disposition to behave in a given way over time and across situations. Although Mischel found impressive consistencies for some attributes such as intelligence, the vast majority of behavior patterns were not consistent, even in highly similar situations. Mischel concluded that behavior is largely determined by situational variables that interact in complex ways with individual modes of information processing. Stable features in behavior result from acquired cognitive person variables (relatively stable individual differences that influence how people interact with their world).

PERSON VARIABLES

Cognitive and behavioral construction competencies represent the first of the person variables. Mischel terms them "competencies" to emphasize that they represent potentials—that is, what people can do, rather than what they do. Referring to their "constructive" quality implies that people do not passively store but actively construct their experiences by transforming and synthesizing incoming information in novel ways. Another of these person variables involves encoding strategies and personal constructs. People encode information and classify events in personalized, unique ways. For different individuals, traitlike constructs such as intelligence or honesty may therefore have some overlapping features but may also have many idiosyncratic ones. This explains why two people can witness and process the same event but interpret it differently. Both people only attend to stimuli consistent with their own personal construct systems and ignore discrepant information.

Mischel maintains that besides knowing people's potentials and how they construct events, to predict behavior people must also know their expectations. One type, termed stimulus-outcome expectancies, develops when people form associations between two events and begin to expect the second event as soon as the first occurs. For example, if a child learns to associate parental frowning with being scolded or spanked, any angry face alone may soon instill anxiety.

A second type, termed response-outcome expectancies, refers to learned "if-then rules," in which specific actions will result in certain outcomes. Outcome expectancies can have a significant influence on what people do. When expectations are inconsistent with reality, they can lead to dysfunctional behavior. Expecting relief from alcohol, when drinking actually leads to multiple problems, illustrates this point.

Subjective stimulus values—subjective values or worth that a person attributes to an object or event—are another type of person variable. In spite of holding identical outcome expectancies, people may behave differently if they do not attribute equal value to this outcome. For example, many believe that practice makes perfect, but not everyone values achievement. Furthermore, the worth of a given outcome often depends on its context. Even an avid skier might cancel a ski trip on an icy, stormy winter day.

Self-regulatory systems and plans are yet another kind of person variable. Besides being affected by external rewards and punishments, people are capable of regulating their own behavior. They set goals and mediate self-imposed consequences, depending on whether they meet their own standards. These self-regulatory processes produce individual differences in behavior independently from the effects of extrinsically imposed conditions.

In addition, Mischel and his colleagues have proposed that people also classify events based on cognitive prototypes. These are analogous to templates, and they contain only the best or most typical features of a concept. Although prototypes facilitate the classification of input information, they carry with them the danger of stereotyping. Anyone who, for example, has mistaken a female business executive for the secretary can appreciate the problem resulting from inaccurate classification.

In summary, with the concept of person variables, Mischel can explain behavioral consistency and at the same time take into account the environment as an important determinant of human actions. In psychologically strong situations, person variables play a minimal role (at a church service, for example, all people behave similarly). In psychologically weak situations (such as a cocktail party), however, individual differences are pronounced, because there are no consistent cues to signal what behaviors are deemed appropriate. Therefore, whether or how much cognitive dispositions influence behavior varies with the specific situation.

DISPOSITIONAL AND SITUATIONAL VARIABLES

Despite a widespread tendency among people to describe themselves and others in traitlike terms (intelligent, friendly, aggressive, domineering, and so forth), research has shown that a person's behavior cannot be predicted from a few broadly generalized personality traits. This does not mean that behavior is totally inconsistent, but that dispositions alone are insufficient to explain consistency and that dispositional, as well as situational, variables need to be taken into account for a complete analysis.

To separate the effects of person and situation variables on behavior, Mischel and his colleagues conducted a series of experiments. In one study, the experimenters assessed adolescents' dispositions toward success or failure. Weeks later they had them solve skill-related tasks and, regardless of their actual performance, gave one group success, a second group failure, and a third group no feedback on their performance. Then the adolescents had to choose between a less desirable reward, one for which attainment was independent of performance on similar tasks, and a preferred reward, for which attainment was performance-dependent. In both bogus feedback conditions, the situational variables had a powerful effect and completely overrode preexisting dispositions toward success or failure. Adolescents who believed they had failed the tasks more often selected the noncontingent reward, while those who believed they had succeeded chose the contingent reward. For subjects in the no-feedback condition, however, the preexisting expectancy scores were highly accurate predictors of their reward choices. This study illustrates how dispositions emerge under weak situational cues but play a trivial role when the setting provides strong cues for behavior (1973). Therefore, Mischel considers it more meaningful to analyze "behavior-contingency units" that link specific behavior patterns to those conditions in which they are likely to occur, rather than looking only at behavior. In other words, instead of labeling people "aggressive," it would be more useful to specify under what conditions these people display aggressive behaviors. Such precise specifications would guard against an oversimplified trait approach and highlight the complexities and idiosyncrasies of behavior as well as its interdependence with specific stimulus conditions.

389

SELF-CONTROL

Mischel and his colleagues also have conducted extensive research on self-control. Their work has been summarized in an article published in 1989 in the journal Science. In several experiments, the researchers attempted to clarify why some people are capable of self-regulation, at least in some areas of their lives, while others fail in such attempts. They found enduring differences in self-control as early as the preschool years. In one study, for example, they showed young children pairs of treats, one less and one more desirable (for example, two versus five cookies or one versus two marshmallows). The children were told that the experimenter would leave the room and that they could obtain the more valuable treat if they waited until he or she returned. They could also ring the bell to bring the experimenter back sooner, but then they would receive the lesser treat. During the waiting period, which lasted a maximum of fifteen minutes, the children were unobtrusively observed. Later, the children's strategies to bridge the waiting period were analyzed. It became apparent that self-control increased when the children used behavioral or cognitive strategies to bridge the delay, such as avoiding looking at the rewards, distracting themselves with singing, playing with their fingers, or cognitively transforming the rewards (for example, thinking of marshmallows as clouds). Interestingly, a follow-up study more than ten years later revealed that those preschool children who had displayed more self-control early were socially and academically more competent, more attentive, more verbal, and better able to cope with stress than their peers as adolescents. In a related study, the length of delay time in preschool proved to be correlated with the adolescents' SAT Reasoning Test scores, suggesting that greater self-control is related to superior academic achievement.

These studies provide an excellent illustration of how cognitive person variables sometimes can have very stable and generalized effects on behavior. The early acquisition of effective cognitive and behavioral strategies to delay gratification had a positive influence on the children's long-term adjustment. Thus, self-control fulfills the requirements of a "personality disposition" in Mischel's sense, because it constitutes an important mediating mechanism for adaptive social behavior throughout the life cycle.

Although the examples presented above lend support to Mischel's theory, one might argue that children's behavior under the constraints of a research setting is artificial and may not reflect what they normally do in their natural environment. While this argument is plausible, it was not supported in a later study with six- to twelve-year-old children in a summer residential treatment facility. Observing children under naturalistic circumstances in this facility led to comparable results. Children who spontaneously used effective cognitive-attentional strategies for self-regulation showed greater self-control in delay situations and were better adjusted than their peers.

An unanswered question is how best to teach children effective information-processing skills. If these skills acquire dispositional character and influence overall adjustment, their attainment would indeed be of vital importance to healthy development.

EVOLUTION OF RESEARCH

Until the late 1960s, the field of personality psychology was dominated by trait and state theories. Their central assumption, that people have traits that produce enduring consistencies in their behavior, went unchallenged for many years. The widespread appeal of these trait assumptions notwithstanding, since the late 1960s personality and social psychologists have been entangled in the "person-situation debate," a controversy over whether the presumed stability in behavior might be based more on illusion than reality. While doubts about the existence of traits were already raised in the middle of the twentieth century, the work of Mischel was instrumental in bringing the controversy into the forefront of academic psychology. In reviewing a voluminous body of literature, Mischel showed in 1968 that virtually all so-called trait measures, except intelligence, change substantially over time and even more dramatically across situations. Traits such as honesty, assertiveness, or attitudes toward authority typically showed reliability across situations of 0.20 to 0.30. This means that if the correlation of behavior presumably reflecting a trait in two different situations is 0.30, less than one-tenth (0.30 0.30 = 0.09, or 9 percent) of the variability in the behavior can be attributed to the trait. Mischel therefore concluded that perceptions of behavioral stability, while not arbitrary, are often only weakly related to the phenomenon in question.

FUNCTIONAL ANALYSIS

There is consensus, however, that human actions show at least some degree of consistency, which is evidenced most strongly by the sense of continuity people experience in their own selves. How can people reconcile the inconsistency between their own impressions and the empirical data? Mischel's cognitive social learning perspective presents one possible solution to this dilemma. Rather than trying to explain behavior by a few generalized traits, Mischel has shifted the emphasis to a thorough examination of the relationship between behavior patterns and the context in which they occur, as the following example illustrates. Assume that parents are complaining about their child's demanding behavior and the child's many tantrums. After observing this behavior in various situations, a traditional personality theorist might conclude that it manifests an underlying "aggressive drive." In contrast, a social learning theorist might seek to identify the specific conditions under which the tantrums occur and then change these conditions to see if the tantrums increase or decrease. This technique, termed "functional analysis" (as described by Mischel in 1968), systematically introduces and withdraws stimuli in the situation to examine how the behavior of interest changes as a function of situational constraints.

The controversy sparked by Mischel's work has not been completely resolved. Few psychologists today, however, would assume an extreme position and either argue that human actions are completely determined by traits or advocate a total situation-specificity of behavior. As with so many controversies, the truth probably lies somewhere in the middle.

BIBLIOGRAPHY

Lieber, Robert M., and Michael D. Spiegler. *Personality: Strategies and Issues*. 8th ed. Pacific Grove: Brooks/Cole, 1998. Print.

Mischel, Harriet N., and Walter Mischel, eds. *Readings in Personality*. New York: Holt, 1973. Print.

Mischel, Walter. *Personality and Assessment*. 1968. Reprint. Mahwah: Lawrence Erlbaum, 1996. Print.

Mischel, Walter. "Toward a Cognitive Social Learning Reconceptualization of Personality." *Psychological Review* 80.4 (1973): 252–83. Print.

Mischel, Walter, Yuichi Shoda, and Monica L. Rodriguez. "Delay of Gratification in Children." *Science* 244.4907 (1989): 933–38. Print.

Olson, Matthew H., and B. R. Hergenhahn. *An Introduction to Theories of Personality. Upper Saddle River:* Prentice Hall, 2011. Print.

Plaks, Jason. *The Social Psychology of Motivation*. New York: Oxford UP, 2011. Print.

Vohs, Kathleen D., and Roy F. Baumeister. *Handbook of Self-Regulation: Research, Theory, and Applications*. New York: Guilford, 2011. Print.

Edelgard Wulfert

See Also: Bandura, Albert; Cognitive behavior therapy; Cognitive psychology; Cognitive therapy; Kelly, George A.; Learning; Mischel, Walter; Personal constructs: George A. Kelly; Social learning: Albert Bandura.

Cognitive therapy (CT)

Type of psychology: Psychotherapy

Cognitive therapy holds that emotional disorders are largely determined by cognition or thinking, that cognitive activity can take the form of language or images, and that emotional disorders can be treated by helping patients modify their cognitive distortions. Treatment programs based on this model have been highly successful with depression, panic disorder, generalized anxiety disorder, and other emotional problems.

Key Concepts

- Arbitrary inference
- Automatic thoughts
- Cognitive specificity hypothesis
- Cognitive triad
- Schemata
- Selective abstraction

INTRODUCTION

Cognitive therapy, originally developed by Aaron T. Beck, is based on the view that cognition (the process of acquiring knowledge and forming beliefs) is a primary determinant of mood and behavior. Beck developed his theory while treating depressed patients. He noticed that these patients tended to distort whatever happened to them in the direction of self-blame and catastrophes. Thus, an event interpreted by a normal person as irritating and inconvenient (for example, the malfunctioning of an automobile) would be interpreted by the depressed patient as another example of the utter hopelessness of life. Beck's central point is that depressives draw illogical conclusions and come to evaluate negatively themselves, their immediate world, and their future. They see only personal failings, present misfortunes, and overwhelming difficulties ahead. It is from these cognitions that all the other symptoms of depression derive.

It was from Beck's early work with depressed patients that cognitive therapy was developed. Shortly thereafter, the concepts and procedures were applied to other psychological problems, with notable success.

AUTOMATIC THOUGHTS AND SCHEMATA

Two concepts of particular relevance to cognitive therapy are the concepts of automatic thoughts and schemata. Automatic thoughts are thoughts that appear to be going on all the time. These thoughts are quite brief—only the essential words in a sentence seem to occur, as in a telegraphic style. Further, they seem to be autonomous, in that the person made no effort to initiate them, and they seem plausible or reasonable to the person (although they may seem far-fetched to somebody else). Thus, as a depressed person is giving a talk to a group of business colleagues, he or she will have a variety of thoughts. There will be thoughts about the content of the material. There is also a second stream of thoughts occurring. In this second channel, the person may experience such thoughts as: "This is a waste of time," or "They think I'm dumb." These are automatic thoughts.

Beck has suggested that although automatic thoughts are occurring all the time, the person is likely to overlook these thoughts when asked what he or she is thinking. Thus, it is necessary to train the person to attend to these automatic thoughts. Beck pointed out that when people are depressed, these automatic thoughts are filled with negative thoughts of the self, the world, and the future. Further, these automatic thoughts are quite distorted, and finally, when these thoughts are carefully examined and modified to be more in keeping with reality, the depression subsides.

The concept of schemata, or core beliefs, becomes critical in understanding why some people are prone to having emotional difficulties and others are not. The schema appears to be the root from which the automatic thoughts derive. Beck suggests that people develop a propensity to think crookedly as a result of early life experiences. He theorizes that in early life, an individual forms concepts—realistic as well as unrealistic—from experiences. Of particular importance are individuals' attitudes toward themselves, their environment, and their future. These deeply held core beliefs about oneself are seen by Beck as critical in the causation of emotional disorders. According to cognitive theory, the reason these early beliefs are so critical is that once they are formed, the person has a tendency to distort or view subsequent experiences to be consistent with these core beliefs. Thus, an individual who, as a child, was subjected to severe, unprovoked punishment from a disturbed parent may conclude "I am weak" or "I am inferior." Once this conclusion has been formulated, it would appear to be strongly reinforced over years and years of experiences at the hands of the parent. Thus, when this individual becomes an adult, he or she tends to interpret even normal frustrations as more proof of the original belief: "See, I really am inferior." Examples of these negative schemata or core beliefs are: "I am weak," "I am inferior," "I am unlovable," and "I cannot do anything right." People holding such core beliefs about themselves would differ strongly in their views of a frustrating experience from those people who hold a core belief such as "I am capable."

Another major contribution of cognitive therapy is Beck's cognitive specificity hypothesis. Specifically, Beck has suggested that each of the emotional disorders is characterized by its own patterns of thinking. In the case of depression, the thought content is concerned with ideas of personal deficiency, impossible environmental demands and obstacles, and nihilistic expectations. For example, a depressed patient might interpret a frustrating situation, such as a malfunctioning automobile, as evidence of his or her own inadequacy: "If I were really competent, I would have anticipated this problem and been able to avoid it." Additionally, the depressed patient might react to the malfunctioning automobile with: "This is too much, I cannot take it anymore." To the depressed patient, this would simply be another example of the utter hopelessness of life.

PATTERNS OF THOUGHT

While the cognitive content of depression emphasizes the negative view of the self, the world, and the future, anxiety disorders are characterized by fears of physical and psychological danger. The anxious patient's thoughts are filled with themes of danger. These people anticipate detrimental occurrences to themselves, their family, their property, their status, and other intangibles that they value.

In phobias, as in anxiety, there is the cognitive theme of danger; however, the "danger" is confined to definable situations. As long as phobic sufferers are able to avoid these situations, they do not feel threatened and may be relatively calm. The cognitive content of panic disorder is characterized by a catastrophic interpretation of bodily or mental experiences. Thus, patients with panic disorder are prone to regard any unexplained symptom or sensation as a sign of some impending catastrophe. As a result, their cognitive processing system focuses their attention on bodily or psychological experience. For example, one patient saw discomfort in the chest as evidence of an impending heart attack.

The cognitive feature of the paranoid reaction is the misinterpretation of experience in terms of mistreatment, abuse, or persecution. The cognitive theme of the conversion disorder (a disorder characterized by physical complaints such as paralysis or blindness, where no underlying physical basis can be determined) is the conviction that one has a physical disorder. As a result of this belief, the patient experiences sensory and/or motor abnormalities that are consistent with the patient's faulty conception of organic pathology.

CHANGING THE PATIENT'S MIND

The goal of cognitive therapy is to help patients evaluate their thought processes carefully, to identify cognitive errors, and to substitute more adaptive, realistic cognitions. This goal is accomplished by therapists helping patients to see their thinking about themselves (or their situation) as similar to the activity of a scientist—that they are engaged in the activity of developing hypotheses (or theories) about their world. Like a scientist, patients need to "test" their theories carefully. Thus, patients who have concluded that they are "worthless" people would be encouraged to test their "theories" rigorously to determine if this is indeed accurate. Further, in the event that the theories are not accurate, patients would be encouraged to change their theories to make them more consistent with reality (what they find in their experience).

A slightly different intervention developed by Beck and his colleagues is to help the patient identify common cognitive distortions. Beck originally identified four cognitive distortions frequently found in emotional disorders: arbitrary inference, selective abstraction, overgeneralization, and magnification or minimization. These were later expanded to ten or more by Beck's colleagues and students.

Arbitrary inference is defined as the process of drawing a conclusion from a situation, event, or experience when there is no evidence to support the conclusion or when the conclusion is contrary to the evidence. For example, a depressed patient on a shopping trip had the thought, "The salesclerk thinks I am a nobody." The patient then felt sad. On being questioned by the psychologist, the patient realized that there was no factual basis for this thought. Selective abstraction refers to the process of focusing on a detail taken out of context, ignoring other, more salient features of the situation, and conceptualizing the whole experience on the basis of this element. For example, a patient was praised by friends about the patient's child-care activities. Through an oversight, however, the patient failed to have her child vaccinated during the appropriate week. Her immediate thought was, "I am a failure as a mother." This idea became paramount despite all the other evidence of her competence.

Overgeneralization refers to patients' patterns of drawing a general conclusion about their ability, their performance, or their worth on the basis of a single incident. For example, a student regards his poor performance on the first examination of the semester as final proof that he "will never make it in college." Magnification and minimization refer to gross errors in evaluation. For example, a person, believing that he has completely ruined his car (magnification) when he sees that there is a slight scratch on the rear fender, regards himself as "good for nothing." In contrast, minimization refers to minimizing one's achievements, protesting that these achievements do not mean anything. For example, a highly successful businesswoman who was depressed concluded that her many prior successes "were nothing . . . simply luck." Using the cognitive distortions, people are taught to examine their thoughts, to identify any distortions, and then to modify their thoughts to eliminate the distortions.

THERAPEUTIC TECHNIQUES

In terms of the therapeutic process, the focus is initially on the automatic thoughts of patients. Once patients are relatively adept at identifying and modifying their maladaptive automatic thoughts, the therapy begins to focus on the maladaptive underlying beliefs or schemata. As previously noted, these beliefs are fundamental beliefs that people hold about themselves. These beliefs are not as easy to identify as the automatic thoughts. Rather, they are identified in an inferential process. Common patterns are observed; for example, the person may seem to be operating by the rule: "If I am not the best _____, then I am a failure," or "If I am not loved by my spouse or mate, then I am worthless." As in the case of the earlier cognitive work with automatic thoughts, these beliefs are carefully evaluated for their adaptability or rationality. Maladaptive beliefs are then modified to more adaptive, realistic beliefs.

A variety of techniques have been developed by cognitive therapists for modifying maladaptive cognitions. One example of these techniques is self-monitoring. This involves the patients keeping a careful hour-by-hour record of their activities, associated moods, or other pertinent phenomena. One useful variant is to have patients record their moods on a simple zero-to-one-hundred scale, where zero represents the worst they have ever felt and one hundred represents the best. In addition, patients can record the degree of mastery or pleasure associated with each recorded activity.

A number of hypotheses can be tested using self-monitoring, such as: "It does not do any good for me to get out of bed," "I am always miserable; it never lets up," and "My schedule is too full for me to accomplish what I must." By simply checking the self-monitoring log, people can easily determine if their miserable moods ever cease. A careful examination of the completed record is a far better basis for judging such hypotheses than are memories of recent events, because their recollections are almost always tainted by the depression.

As therapy progresses and patients begin to experience more elevated moods, the focus of treatment becomes more cognitive. Patients are instructed to observe and record automatic thoughts, perhaps at a specific time each evening, as well as recording when they become aware of increased dysphoria. Typically, the thoughts are negative self-referents ("I am worthless"; "I will never amount to anything"), and initially, the therapist points out their unreasonable and self-defeating nature. With practice, patients learn "distancing," that is, dealing with such thoughts objectively and evaluating them rather than blindly accepting them. Homework assignments can facilitate distancing: Patients record each automatic thought, and next to it they write down a thought that counters the automatic thought, as the therapist might have done. According to Beck, certain basic themes soon emerge, such as being abandoned, as well as stylistic patterns of thinking, such as overgeneralization. The themes reflect the aforementioned rules, and the ultimate goal of therapy is to assist patients to modify them.

Finally, cognitive therapy has been applied to a variety of psychological disorders with striking success. For example, studies from seven independent centers have compared the efficacy of cognitive therapy to antidepressant medication, a treatment of established efficacy. Comparisons of cognitive therapy to drugs have found cognitive therapy to be superior or equal to antidepressant medication. Further, follow-up studies indicate that cognitive therapy has greater long-term effects than drug therapy. Of special significance is the evidence of greater sustained improvement over time with cognitive therapy.

Cognitive therapy has been successfully applied to panic disorder, resulting in practically complete reduction of panic attacks after twelve to sixteen weeks of treatment. Additionally, cognitive therapy has been successfully applied to generalized anxiety disorder, eating disorders, and inpatient depression.

DEPRESSION AND COGNITIVE THERAPY

Cognitive theory and cognitive therapy originated in Beck's observation and treatment of depressed patients. Originally trained in psychoanalysis, Beck observed that his patients experienced specific types of thoughts, of which they were only dimly aware, that they did not report during their free associations. Beck noticed that these thoughts were frequently followed by an unpleasant effect. Further, he noted that as the patients examined and modified their thoughts, their moods began to improve.

At the time of the emergence of the cognitive model, the treatment world was dominated primarily by the psychoanalytic model (with its heavy emphasis on the unconscious processes) and to a lesser extent by the behavioral model (with its emphasis on the behavioral processes, to the exclusion of thought). The psychoanalytic model was under attack, primarily because of a lack of careful empirical support. In contrast, behavior therapists were actively demonstrating the efficacy of their approaches in carefully designed studies. Beck and his students began to develop and test cognitive procedures systematically, and they have developed an impressive body of research support for the approach.

BIBLIOGRAPHY

Beck, Aaron T. *Cognitive Therapy and the Emotional Disorders*. 1976. Reprint. London: Penguin, 1991. Print.

Beck, Aaron T., and Gary Emery. *Anxiety Disorders and Phobias: A Cognitive Perspective*. Reprint. Cambridge, Mass.: Basic Books, 2005. Print.

Beck, Aaron T., A. J. Rush, B. F. Shaw, and Gary Emery. *Cognitive Therapy of Depression*. Reprint. New York: Guilford, 1987. Print.

Burns, David D. *Feeling Good: The New Mood Therapy*. Rev. ed. New York: William Morrow, 2002.Print.

Emery, Gary, Steven D. Hollom, and Richard C. Bedrosian, eds. *New Directions in Cognitive Therapy: A Casebook*. New York: Guilford, 1981. Print.

Ryan, Frank. *Cognitive Therapy for Addiction: Motivation and Change*. Malden: Wiley, 2013. Print.

Sanders, Diana, and Frank Wills. *Cognitive Behaviour Therapy: Foundations for Practice*. 3rd ed. London: Sage, 2013. Print.

Segal, Zindel V., J. Mark G. Williams, and John D. Teasdale. *Mindfulness-Based Cognitive Therapy for Depression.* 2nd ed. New York: Guilford, 2013. Print.

Wenzel, Amy. *Strategic Decision Making in Cognitive Behavioral Therapy.* Washington: American Psychological Association, 2013. Print.

Donald G. Beal

See Also: Anxiety disorders; Beck, Aaron T.; Behavior therapy; Cognitive behavior therapy; Cognitive social learning: Walter Mischel; Depression; Kelly, George A.; Mischel, Walter; Panic attacks; Personal constructs: George A. Kelly; Rational emotive therapy; Reality therapy; Transactional analysis.

Collectivism

Type of psychology: Developmental psychology; Social psychology

Collectivism subordinates personal goals to preserve group values. Value is placed on harmonious relationships and the interdependence of the members of the group. Values that serve the group are primary. This contrasts with individualism, which gives priority to personal goals. Collectivism is more typical of Eastern cultures, whereas individualism is more typical of Western cultures.

Key Concepts

- Cultural competence
- Culture
- Diverse populations
- Group goals
- Identity
- Individual goals
- Individualism
- Worldview

INTRODUCTION

The construct of collectivism is traditionally compared with individualism when considered in the literature of social psychology. The dual constructs are powerful in their ability to identify general differences in cultural perspective or worldview. The danger that accompanies the constructs is the tendency to overgeneralize. Nevertheless, when painting with a broad sweep, the two categories provide a helpful model for understanding foundational differences in cultural groups.

Social psychologists attempt to both define and measure collectivism but are not unified in what they propose. A definition developed by Harry C. Triandis describes collectivism as a "social pattern consisting of closely linked individuals who see themselves as parts of one or more collectives (family, co-workers, tribe, nation)." A definition that includes a functional aspect identifies collectivism as being a cultural syndrome of norms, values, and a way to engage in the world that is embedded in practices, artifacts, and institutions. In collectivism, members give priority to the goals of the collective rather than personal goals. Norms and duties of the collective motivate members, and value is placed on connection with members of the group. Countries known for their highly collectivist natures are Pakistan, Venezuela, Colombia, Peru, Taiwan, Thailand, Japan, and China.

INDIVIDUALISM AND COLLECTIVISM

In contrast to collectivism, individualism gives priority to personal goals and to values that serve the self such as personal distinction, achievement, and independence. The individual is the most basic unit. Countries that represent individualistic societies include Canada, Great Britain, Belgium, France, the Scandinavian countries, and the Netherlands. The majority group in the United States represents individualism.

Several contrasts between individualism and collectivism can be drawn relative to the functioning and perception of group members. Collectivism values the public self. Achievement includes cooperation for the benefit of the in-group. Individualism places importance on the private self, personal achievement, competition, and power. Collectivism values obedience, in-group harmony, and a few close relationships. Individualism values pleasure and freedom and is more likely to represent many casual relationships. Collectivism stresses saving face for both self and others, and favors people who are modest and self-effacing. Individualism emphasizes saving one's own face and favors people who are self-assured.

DIVERSE GROUPS AND COLLECTIVISM

Although the majority population in the United States tends to represent individualism, diverse cultural groups are more likely to have a collective worldview. Within such groups, high priority is placed on loyalty to family and culture.

Many immigrants come from countries with collectivist narratives for self and family. A primary component of such collectivist narratives is the internalized obligation to help extended family members, regardless of whether there was a strong relationship with the member. Depending on the ethnic group, this sense of family obligation and support often continues to exist as an enduring psychosocial feature.

In Middle Eastern societies, the development of an individual identity that separates one from the family or ethnic community is not valued or encouraged. The enhancement of family honor and status is a primary goal. Family members are expected to control their individual behavior because it reflects on the family's reputation.

In Asian cultures, the group often takes precedence over the needs of the individual. The activities of the individual may be more directly related to the status and wealth of the family as a whole, rather than to the advancement of the individual. This group focus tends to emphasize dependency and respect for authority rather than independence and egalitarian relationships more common in northern European countries.

American Indians view the focus on the solitary individual to the exclusion of the group as meaningless. They question the concentration on the individual in Western philosophy, law, and the religious thinking of modern society. For the American Indian, concepts about religion and spirituality have a communal rather than an individual basis. Because all things are perceived as interconnected, relationships among people are critically important. Indian tribes would view individuals without loyalty to anyone else as people who are exceedingly dangerous. Relationships within the family and clan are valued so highly that banishment, refusal of the tribe to recognize the wrongdoer as a member, has traditionally served as punishment for heinous crimes.

COLLECTIVISM AND THE FAMILY UNIT

In collectivist cultures, marriages link families rather than individuals and may be arranged. Group boundaries are explicit, and great value is placed on shared activities, solidarity, and family/group loyalty. In contrast, individualist cultures reflect relationships that are loosely connected and autonomous, with flexible boundaries. Relationship goals include personal fulfillment and romance as important components in the pursuit of life.

Collectivist cultures have traditionally viewed marriage as a vehicle for maintaining social order and for forming links between families rather than as a means of fulfilling personal desires. In traditional Hindu societies, marriage is one of the most important events in a person's life and is perceived as a social and cultural duty. Individualist cultures follow a love-based approach to marriage, which values feelings of personal compatibility and mutual attraction, rather than a duty to meet the needs of family or society.

As diverse families are served by mental health professionals, they are often placed within the Western value systems of psychology and counseling, in which individuation is expected to place boundaries on cohesion and individual goals. On one commonly used family scale, families identified as unbalanced have the following characteristics: high dependence, very high togetherness, very high closeness, high loyalty, and mainly shared activities.

RESEARCH AND APPLICATION

Collectivism appears to be a variable associated with romantic partner preferences. Although universal values for a core group of dispositional features have been identified in research, cultural differences exist. Adults in collectivist cultures such as China and India tend to value "practical" characteristics(such as being a good housekeeper) and demographic similarity (such as sharing the same religion or caste) in a potential spouse more than do adults from individualist cultures. This would seem consistent with cultures that have a history of arranged marriage.

Individuals from collectivist cultures tend to view chastity as a relatively important attribute in a potential mate, whereas it appears to be a dispensable or even undesirable trait for men and women in many Western countries. An overview of research finds that young adults in collectivist cultures are more likely to disapprove of premarital sex as compared with young adults from individualist cultures, who typically hold more permissive attitudes.

Low-income families are more likely than higher-income families to have a collective worldview relative to financial style and spending practices. Individuals from groups reflecting a collective worldview value helping family members, friends, or neighbors when assistance is needed. Consequently, money is more often shared than used to better the individual in purchasing houses, furthering education, or investments. Mental health professionals and financial advisers from European American, middle-class groups may view this as being irresponsible.

CONCLUSION

Cultural competence refers to the expertise and information needed by those who work with diverse populations. Culture is defined as the behavior, patterns, beliefs, and all other products of a particular group of people that are passed on from generation to generation. If members of diverse populations do try to implement practices that are in conflict with strengths of their own cultural group, members of the helping profession may actually cause harm to the family because they encourage a "cultural clash" that negatively affects family life. Mental health workers and agencies should carefully assess their cultural competence.

Proponents of the collectivist worldview argue that the Western emphasis on individualism devalues the role that groups play in the survival of human beings and may undermine the basic need for relatedness. Comparison of collectivist and individualist cultures reveal that individualistic cultures have higher rates of suicide, drug abuse, crime, divorce, and mental disorders.

All individuals incorporate both individualism and collectivism in their patterns of living. When comparing the two, the focus is more one of preference and degree. Some of the more common contrasts between individualism and collectivism involve self-descriptions and contextual information. In collectivism, the social group is incorporated into self-descriptions, context is used to describe the self, and contextual information is used for decision making. A balance between collectivism and individualism may be the optimal position. Either in its extremity will result in undesirable consequences. The point of agreement is the need to have both a positive sense of self and a sense of connectedness to others.

BIBLIOGRAPHY

Al-Deen, N. "Understanding Arab Americans: A Matter of Diversities." *In Cross-Communications and Aging in the U.S.* Mahwah, N.J.: Lawrence Erlbaum, 1991. Provides comprehensive information on the values of Arab Americans. Illustrates their collective identity in a number of characteristics.

Kagitcibasi, C. *Family, Self, and Human Development Across Cultures.* Mahwah, N.J.: Lawrence Erlbaum, 2007. Focuses on diversity of cultures in areas such as human development. Notes the tendency of developmental psychology to use individualism as its standard and identifies the disadvantages of this approach.

Khallad, Y. "Mate Selection in Jordan: Effects of Sex, Socio-economic Status, and Culture." *Journal of Social and Personal Relationships* 22 (April 1, 2005): 155-168. Examines mate preferences of individuals from a collectivist culture in the Middle East to note the strength of the traditional social values.

McAuliffe, Garrett, et al., eds. *Culturally Alert Counseling.* Thousand Oaks, Calif.: Sage Publications, 2008. Provides an excellent background for mental health professionals working with diverse groups. The influence of varying worldviews is obvious.

McGoldrick, M., et al., eds. *Ethnicity and Family Therapy.* 3d ed. New York: Guilford Press, 2005. Almost all cultural groups are included, making the distinctions between collectivism and individualism evident.

Reis, H. T., and S. K. Sprecher, eds. *Encyclopedia of Human Relationships.* Thousand Oaks, Calif.: Sage Publications, 2009. A three-volume set that provides a vast amount of information about how people think, feel, and act toward others with whom they have relationships. Includes an article on the effect of collectivism on relationships.

Robins, Kikanza Nuri, et al. *Cultural Proficiency Instructions: A Guide for People Who Teach.* 2d ed. Thousand Oaks, Calif.: Sage Publications, 2006. Written for educational institutions, but its principles apply for mental health institutions.

Skogrand, L., D. Hatch, and A. Singh. *Strengths and Challenges of New Immigrant Families: Implications for Research, Policy, Education, and Service.* Lanham, Md.: Lexington Books, 2008. Interviews of many families from diverse cultural backgrounds provided data to make culturally relevant provisions in mental health policies and service. Includes differences relative to collectivistic and individualistic worldviews.

Thomas, Anita Jones, and Sara Schwarzbaum Thomas. *Culture and Identity: Life Stories for Counselors and Therapists.* Thousand Oaks, Calif.: Sage Publications, 2006. Each chapter describes the experience of individuals from diverse cultures who are attempting to navigate the many challenges of developing a cultural identity. A number of cultures are considered, helping the reader understand the importance of cultural identity within the larger framework of human development. Various activities are suggested as a means to apply the cultural setting to the mental health practitioner.

Triandis, H. C. *Individualism and Collectivism: New Directions in Social Psychology.* Boulder, Colo.: Westview Press, 1995. One of only a few sources that provides scholarly theoretical information on the distinctive aspects of collectivism.

Lillian J. Breckenridge

See Also: Community psychology; Cross-cultural psychology; Cultural competence; Culture and diagnosis; Culture-bound syndromes; Groups; Identity crises; Love; Multicultural psychology.

College entrance examinations and cultural biases

Date: 1920s forward
Type of psychology: Learning

College entrance examinations have been used since the 1920s in the United States to assist college administrators in making admissions decisions. The two most widely used exams are the ACT and the SAT. Although college entrance exams are useful in predicting first-year college grades, some critics of the tests have argued that the score gaps between racial and ethnic groups may be more reflective of cultural bias in the assessments than actual differences in cognitive ability.

Key Concepts

- Achievement gap
- Achievement tests
- ACT
- Aptitude tests
- College Board
- Grade point average (GPA)
- Racial and ethnic bias
- SAT Reasoning Test
- Standardized tests

INTRODUCTION

College entrance exams are standardized tests designed to predict student grades in the first year of college. Because research has shown that students' scores on these assessments are related to their grade point averages as college freshmen, many US colleges and universities use these scores as a source of information for selection and admissions decisions. In addition, college entrance exam scores are used for decisions about financial aid, scholarships, and placement into remedial course work.

The most commonly used college entrance exams in the United States are the SAT Reasoning Test and the ACT. In 2012, about 1.6 million high school students completed the ACT, and 1.6 million completed the SAT. ACT test takers are largely residents of the Midwest and the South, while SAT test takers tend to be residents of the Northeast and West, although most institutions will accept scores from either assessment.

THE SAT

Before the development of the SAT Reasoning Test, information used to make college admissions decisions varied widely. Many elite institutions selected the children of alumni or graduates from highly ranked preparatory schools for admission. Some colleges did have entrance exams; however, these differed from college to college, so students interested in multiple institutions had to take multiple exams. The aim of the SAT as designed by its developers, the College Entrance Examination Board (later the College Board), was to provide a standardized way to assess students' aptitude for college-level work, regardless of previous education or family lineage and, consequently, to select students for admittance on the basis of their own merits.

The SAT Reasoning Test, developed in the 1920s and originally called the Scholastic Aptitude Test, has evolved over the years. It was originally designed to measure aptitude, or an individual's innate ability to perform well in school. Critics of the test argued that the SAT favored students from middle- and upper-income families, and that tests designed to measure curriculum-based learning were likely to be more egalitarian and better predictors of college grade point average. In response to this criticism and to the rising number of higher education institutions who dropped the SAT as an application requirement, the College Board added a writing component to the SAT in 2005 and revised the existing test to more closely match content covered in high school curricula. In 2014, the College Board announced that in all forthcoming rounds of testing, the essay portion of the SAT would be optional.

The SAT is a three-hour test—three hour and fifty-minutes when including the essay—with three sections: critical reading (formerly verbal), mathematics, and writing. Both the critical reading and mathematics sections consist of multiple-choice and fill-in-the-blank questions. In the critical reading section, students complete sentences, read, and assess written passages, and in the math section, they apply mathematical concepts and interpret data. The writing section, is made up of an essay-writing portion and multiple-choice questions requiring students to recognize writing errors and improve sentences and paragraphs.

Scores on each section of the SAT range from 200 to 800. The average score varies slightly from year to year, but is relatively stable at approximately 500 on each of the sections with a standard deviation of about 100.

THE ACT

In the 1950s, E. F. Lindquist developed the American College Test (later known as the ACT) and founded the testing and measurement company ACT, Inc., in Iowa City, Iowa. Lindquist believed that although tests of aptitude such as the SAT measured an individual's innate ability, such tests failed to recognize achievement, or what individuals had done with their ability. The ACT, therefore, was designed to measure what students had learned in core college-preparatory curriculum areas. ACT regularly conducts a survey of high school and college faculty to ensure that the assessment stays consistent with high school curricula.

The ACT is a two-hour, fifty-five-minute test. The writing section of the ACT is optional and takes an additional thirty minutes to complete. Besides writing, the ACT has four sections—English, mathematics, reading and science—consisting entirely of multiple-choice questions. The English test measures knowledge of punctuation, grammar, sentence structure, organization, and style. Mathematics measures algebra, geometry, and trigonometry skills. Reading measures skills in reading college-level material, and the science section measures scientific reasoning skills, assuming that students have completed three years of science, including biology. The optional writing test is a single thirty-minute essay.

Scores on each of the four ACT scales range from 1 to 36. A composite score, which is the mean, or average, of the scores on all four scales, is also provided on a range from 1 to 36. The mean score varies slightly from year to year but remains relatively stable at approximately 20 on each of the scales and the composite, with a standard deviation of about 5. Scores on the writing section range from 2 to 12 and are reported in combination with the English subscale on a scale of 1 to 36.

Although the ACT is used for college admissions decisions, it is also designed to provide feedback to teachers and students on academic areas of strength and areas for development. Students can use ACT subscale scores to plan what courses to take and where to focus their studies to improve their achievement and, consequently, their level of preparation for college. In addition, teachers and high school administrators can use ACT scores to evaluate the effectiveness of their teaching and of the curriculum. Because the ACT is linked to high school course content, several states have also mandated its use as a high school exit exam.

ADVANTAGES OF THE TESTS

The recent revisions to the SAT have made it more similar in content to the ACT, although it still assesses critical thinking and problem-solving skills to a greater degree than does the ACT, which focuses on assessing acquired academic knowledge and skills. Regardless, both have been shown to be good predictors of college grade point average and, when considered in combination with high school grade point average, have proven to be better predictors than either the test score or grade point average alone. Some college admissions officials contend that looking at the tests in combination with a student's high school performance allows for more efficient and effective selection of those students most likely to succeed in a college environment.

Test scores provide a uniform scale for the comparison of applicants. High school grade point averages and class rank vary widely depending on the school attended and the courses taken. A student might perform very well in remedial courses and poorly in honors courses, so the student's choice of classes might result in significantly different grade point averages. In addition, a 3.0 at one high school might reflect a very different level of performance than a 3.0 at another high school. For this reason, supporters of college entrance exams have argued that test scores allow for more accurate comparisons of students from diverse schools, or of students with different course work at the same schools.

CRITICISMS OF THE TESTS

The ACT and SAT tests have been criticized for a number of reasons, but the two common criticisms are that the tests are biased against certain racial and ethnic groups and ignore other key characteristics of applicants that may be useful in predicting college success.

Research has consistently shown that African Americans, Latinos, and Native Americans have lower mean scores on college entrance exams and other tests of achievement such as the National Assessment of Educational Progress than whites and Asian Americans. This difference is referred to as the achievement gap. Critics of entrance exams have argued that the difference is caused by the culture-specific nature of the tests, with items written to favor students from a white background and to put minorities at a disadvantage. Although there is evidence that such items once existed, the tests have been rewritten, researched, and extensively scrutinized by writers and consultants from diverse backgrounds so as to eliminate such bias. Researchers largely agree that this effort has met the educational standard for ensuring fairness. The achievement gap, however, continues to exist.

Some researchers have asserted that the achievement gap reflects differences that bear a relationship to race and ethnicity. These may include differences in quality and preparedness of teachers, rigor of the curriculum, quality and safety of the school, parental involvement and emphasis on school-related activities, socioeconomic status, and hunger and nutrition. Regardless of the reason, many institutions place greater emphasis on an applicant's high school grade point average, courses taken, and involvement in extracurricular activities, so as to address the concern that differences between racial and ethnic groups on test scores might result in the underselection of minorities for entry into college.

Critics have also suggested that college entrance exams measure only one determinant of success in college and ignore other influential variables. For example, the motivation to perform well, feelings of connection to the college, and study skills have all been shown to predict college performance and are marginally related, if at all, to performance on the SAT and ACT. The use of these noncognitive factors could help predict college performance better than SAT or ACT scores alone and would give a fuller picture of an applicant.

Both of these criticisms have led institutions to not use SAT or ACT scores as the sole basis of admissions decisions. In the absence of another uniform and standardized measure, it is unlikely that college entrance exams will disappear entirely. Instead, it is likely that exam results, along with other information such as students' personal statements, essays, extracurricular activities, high school coursework and grades, and letters of recommendations will continue to be used to make admissions decisions.

BIBLIOGRAPHY

ACT, Inc. *The ACT Technical Manual.* Iowa City, Iowa: Author, 2007. Print.

ACT, Inc. *ACT Writing Test: Preliminary Technical Report.* Iowa City, Iowa: Author, 2007. Print.

Adams, Caralee. "College Board Begins Redesign of SAT Exam." *Education Week* 6 Mar. 2013: 4. Print.

Barton, P. E., and R. J. Coley. "Windows on Achievement and Inequality." *Policy Information Report, PIC-WINDOWS.* Princeton, N.J.: Educational Testing Service, 2008. Print.

Lewin, Tamar. "A New SAT Aims to Realign with Schoolwork." *New York Times* 6 Mar. 2014: A1. Print.

Mattern, K., W. Camara, and J. L. Kobrin. *SAT Writing: An Overview of Research and Psychometrics to Date.* College Board Research Report no. RN-32. New York: The College Board, 2007. Print.

Noble, J., M. Davenport, J. Schiel, and M. Pommerich. *Relationships Between the Noncognitive Characteristics, High School Course Work and Grades, and Test Scores of ACT-Tested Students.* ACT Research Report No. 99-4. Iowa City, Iowa: ACT, Inc., 1999. Print.

Sackett, P. R., M. J. Borneman, and B. S. Connelly. "High-Stakes Testing in Higher Education and Employment: Appraising the Evidence for Validity and Fairness." *American Psychologist* 63, no. 4 (May/June, 2008): 215-227. Print.

Young, J. W. "The Past, Present, and Future of the SAT: Implications for College Admissions." *College & University* 78, no. 3 (March, 2003): 21-24. Print.

Zoroya, Gregg. "Sharpen Those Pencils, Kids: The SAT is Getting Harder." *USA Today* 6 Mar. 2014: 3a. Print.

Christina Hamme Peterson

SEE ALSO: Ability tests; Assessment; Emotional intelligence; Intelligence; Intelligence quotient (IQ); Intelligence tests; Learning; Multiple intelligences; Race and intelligence.

Community psychology

TYPE OF PSYCHOLOGY: Social psychology

Community psychology is dedicated to the development of a knowledge base that can be used to implement and evaluate culturally congruent human-services programs. Community psychology is associated with the community mental health movement, and community psychologists have a particular interest in research and services that focus on prevention.

KEY CONCEPTS

- Action-oriented research
- Culturally congruent services
- Ecology
- Epidemiology
- Incidence
- Person-environment fit
- Prevalence
- Primary prevention

- Secondary prevention
- Tertiary prevention

INTRODUCTION

Community psychology is founded on the following precepts: an emphasis on the competence of persons and communities; an appreciation of personal and cultural diversity; an orientation that promotes prevention; a preference for organizational, community- and systems-level intervention; and a belief in the need for an ecologically valid database with which to determine the appropriateness and value of human-service interventions.

Community psychology emphasizes social, environmental, and cultural factors as significant elements influencing the development and expression of behaviors commonly identified as signs of maladjustment. Community psychology demands a respect for human diversity—people have a right to be different. Requiring that people fit into a particular mold or conform to a particular standard increases the probability that some will be considered failures or maladjusted individuals. Instead of focusing on how to motivate "deviant" people to adjust, the community psychologist attempts to increase behavioral options, expand cultural and environmental choices, redistribute resources, and foster the acceptance of variability.

From a community-psychology perspective, it is not the weakness of the individual that causes psychopathology, but a lack of person-environment fit. The concept of person-environment fit is founded in ecology. Ecology posits that each organism is in constant interaction with all aspects of its environment, including all things animate and inanimate. From the ecological perspective, it is the unique interaction of species with the environmental milieu that dictates survival. In relation to people, ecology requires an appreciation not only for the ambient environment but also for social, psychological, personal, and cultural factors that interact and influence an individual's adjustment and survival.

Community psychologists use their knowledge of ecological principles to create culturally congruent interventions that maximize service effectiveness. To develop services that are culturally congruent requires an appreciation for the history, aspirations, belief systems, and environmental circumstances of the community or group with which one is to work. Knowing that interactions and the fit between persons and environments are of primary importance, community psychologists work to promote changes at a systems level rather than only working to change the individual. Community psychologists know, however, that even systems-level changes will be of little value—and will perhaps even lead to harm—if they are not personally and culturally relevant to the persons they are designed to help.

There is considerable diversity in the training and orientation of community psychologists. Still, as a general rule, community psychologists can be expected to have knowledge and expertise in the following areas: program development, resource utilization, community organization, consultation, community mental health programming, preventive interventions, program evaluation, grant writing, needs assessment, advocacy, crisis intervention, direct service delivery, manpower training, systems analysis, and the political ramifications of social change. Community psychologists use their knowledge of these areas as they work within the framework of one of the following models: clinical/community, community/clinical, community activist, academic/research, prevention, social ecology, evaluation/policy analysis, or consultation.

COMMUNITY MODELS

Psychologists trained in the clinical/community model have expertise in individual assessment and psychotherapy. They are likely to work within community mental health centers or other human-services programs as direct service providers. They differ from traditionally trained clinical psychologists in having an orientation that is directed toward crisis intervention, public health, and prevention.

The community/clinical model leads to a primary emphasis of working with community groups to enable the development, implementation, and administration of human-services initiatives. This model is similar to the community-activist model; persons with a community/clinical orientation, however, are more likely to work within the system than outside it.

Persons following the community-activist model draw on their training in psychology to enable them to confront social injustice and misallocation of resources. These individuals are versed in grass-roots community organization, the realities of social confrontation, and advocacy.

The academic/research model of community psychology is founded on the principles of action-oriented research. Here the researcher is directed to work on real-world problems using ecologically valid methods. Furthermore, action-oriented research requires that recommendations that follow from the researcher's findings be implemented.

Psychologists who advocate the prevention model use epidemiological data information concerning the rates and distribution of disorders—to enable the development of programs designed to prevent mental health problems. Primary prevention programs—undertakings that attempt to keep problems from forming—are the preferred initiatives.

Persons trained in the social-ecology model participate in the development of research and interventions based on an ecological perspective. Here, an appreciation of the complexities and of the myriad interactions of communities and social organizations is paramount.

The evaluation/policy-analysis model requires that adherents be versed in program-evaluation methods—techniques related to the assessment of the quality, efficiency, and effectiveness of service initiatives. This model dictates that information obtained from program evaluation be fed back into the system in the form of policy recommendations.

The consultation model provides a framework for the dissemination of knowledge. To be an effective consultant, the community psychologist must be cognizant of various consultation methods. Furthermore, she or he must have specialized expertise founded in one of the preceding models.

Regardless of the model followed, community psychology demands a commitment to the community, group, or individual served. The job of the community psychologist is to foster competence and independence. The ideal client, whether the client is an individual or a community, is the client who no longer needs the psychologist.

PREVENTION PROGRAMS

Community psychology has played a major role in sensitizing human-services professionals to the need for services oriented toward prevention. Many of the assumptions and principles of prevention are taken from the field of public health medicine. Public health officials know that disease cannot be eradicated by treatment alone. Furthermore, the significant gains in life expectancy that have occurred over the last one hundred years are not primarily the result of wonder drugs, transplants, or other marvels of modern medicine. Instead, improved sanitation, immunizations, and access to an adequate food supply have been the key factors in conquering diseases and increasing the human life span.

To design and implement effective prevention-oriented programs, one must have an understanding of epidemiology, incidence, and prevalence. Epidemiology is the study of the rates and distributions of disorders as these data pertain to causes and prevention. Incidence is the number of new cases of a disorder that occur in a given population in a specific period. Prevalence is either the total number of cases of a disorder in a given population at a specific point in time or the average number of cases during a specific period. By combining information concerning epidemiology, incidence, and prevalence, it is possible to arrive at insights into the causes of a disorder, likely methods of transmission, prognosis, and intervention methods that may prove fruitful.

Community psychologists identify prevention activities as falling into one of three classifications: primary prevention, secondary prevention, and tertiary prevention. Although some have argued that only primary prevention activities should be recognized as prevention, all three classifications have a place.

In tertiary prevention, the underlying disorder is not directly treated or eliminated; instead, tertiary prevention focuses on mitigating the consequences of a disorder. Tertiary prevention has no effect on incidence rates and little or no effect on prevalence rates. Reducing the stigma associated with the label"mental illness," increasing the self-help skills of persons who have mental retardation, promoting the independence of persons with chronic mental disorders, and developing programs to provide cognitive retraining for persons who have suffered head injuries are examples of tertiary-prevention activities.

An example of a tertiary-prevention program is the community lodge program developed by George Fairweather, which has come to be known as the Fairweather Lodge Program. The program was begun as an attempt to solve a problem that arose in an experiment in giving psychiatric patients the power to direct their treatment by means of self-governing groups. Although it was quite effective, the program suffered because many of its gains did not carry over after patients were discharged. The community lodge program was developed to deal with this problem. During their hospital stays, patients were encouraged to form small support groups. Prior to discharge, members of these support groups would be introduced to the lodge concept. The lodge concept called for former patients to live together, pool their resources, and work as a team in a lodge-owned enterprise. This program, which began in the early 1960s, has been replicated on numerous occasions. Data show that patients discharged to a community lodge are more likely to maintain gainful employment and are less likely to be readmitted to the hospital than are patients discharged to a traditional community mental health program.

Secondary prevention has its basis in the belief that prevalence rates can be reduced if disorders are identified and treated as early as possible. Diversion programs for youths who manifest predelinquent behavior, acute care for persons with mental disorders, employee assistance programs, and psychological screenings for schoolchildren are examples of secondary prevention.

An example of a secondary-prevention program is the Primary Mental Health Project (PMHP) developed by Emory Cowen in the late 1950s. The PMHP was founded on the basis of the idea that maladjustment in early school grades is associated with the development of behavioral and emotional problems later in life. The program was designed to provide early detection so that interventions could be introduced before significant dysfunction had an opportunity to develop. Furthermore, consultation and competency building—rather than traditional therapeutic techniques—were viewed as the most effective interventions. Although the PMHP has not had a demonstrated effect in reducing later psychiatric disorders, the program has been shown to have other beneficial effects.

Primary prevention is aimed at the eradication of the causes of disorders and the development of interventions that can be initiated before pathology develops. Primary prevention results in a lowering of both incidence and prevalence rates. Psychological services for disaster victims, genetic screening, parenting classes, reducing exposure to toxins, immunization for rubella, and maternal nutrition programs are examples of primary-prevention activities. Another example of primary prevention is community education programs designed to teach safe sex and to reduce the sharing of contaminated needles. To the extent that these programs reduce the spread of acquired immunodeficiency syndrome (AIDS), they will also decrease the incidence of AIDS dementia complex.

Community psychologists are involved in many service activities besides prevention-oriented enterprises. These initiatives include the training and utilization of paraprofessionals, the promotion of self-help groups and natural helping networks, advocacy, community consultation, program evaluation, the planning and implementation of new human-services programs, crisis intervention, and mental health education.

AN EMERGING FIELD

Community psychology had its origins in the 1960s, a time of radical ideas, antiestablishment attitudes, and a belief in the perfectibility of humankind. In 1965, in Swampscott, Massachusetts, a meeting was called to ascertain how psychology could most effectively contribute to the emerging community mental health movement.

A transformation in treatment focus was taking place at the time of the Swampscott meeting. This change had been provided with a blueprint for its development in a report by the Joint Commission on Mental Illness and Health written in 1961. The Joint Commission report, Action for Mental Health, called for a shift from treating psychiatric patients in large state mental hospitals to the provision of care through outpatient community mental health clinics and smaller inpatient units located in general hospitals. Additionally, the report included the following recommendations: increasing support for research, developing "aftercare," providing partial hospitalization and rehabilitation services, and expanding mental health education to ensure that the public became more aware of mental disorders and to reduce the stigmatization associated with mental illness.

On February 5, 1963, President John F. Kennedy became the first US president to address Congress regarding the needs of the mentally ill and the mentally retarded. President Kennedy called for a "bold new approach" that would include funding for prevention, expanding the knowledge base regarding causes of disorders and treatment alternatives, and creating a new type of treatment facility that, independent of the ability to pay, would provide high-quality comprehensive care in the local community—the creation of community mental health centers.

In October of 1963, President Kennedy signed into law the Community Mental Health Act. The law required that programs funded through the act provide five essential services: inpatient care, outpatient treatment, emergency services, partial hospitalization, and consultation and education.

Although the initial purpose for convening the Swampscott meeting had been to determine how psychology could contribute to the staffing needs of community mental health centers, the conferees took a broader perspective and chose to view the community mental health movement as addressing a limited aspect of a larger set of social problems. As a consequence, the meeting failed to address adequately the training needs of psychologists who would be working in the new community mental health centers; instead, the most significant result of the meeting was the birth of community psychology.

In the ensuing years, community psychology and community psychology training programs have varied in the degree to which they involve the educational needs of psychologists employed by community mental health centers. Still, there is no doubt that the research and service initiatives that community psychologists have developed in regard to crisis intervention, consultation, prevention, empowerment, the use of paraprofessionals, program planning, resource development, and program evaluation serve as valuable models and contribute to the successful operation of community mental health programs and a variety of other human-services activities.

BIBLIOGRAPHY

Boyd, Neil M. "A 10-Year Retrospective of Organization Studies in Community Psychology: Content, Theory, and Impact." *Jour. of Community Psychology* 42.2 (2014): 237–54. Print.

Caplan, Gerald. *Principles of Preventive Psychiatry.* New York: Basic, 1964. Print.

Dalton James H., Maurice J. Elias, and Abraham Wandersman. *Community Psychology: Linking Individuals and Communities.* 2d ed. Belmont: Wadsworth, 2007. Print.

Heller, Kenneth, et al. *Psychology and Community Change: Challenges of the Future*. 2d ed. Homewood: Dorsey, 1984. Print.

Levine, Murray, and David V. Perkins. *Principles of Community Psychology: Perspectives and Applications.* 3d ed. New York: Oxford UP, 2005. Print.

Mann, Philip A. *Community Psychology: Concepts and Applications*. New York: Free Press, 1978. Print.

Neal, Jennifer Watling, et al. "Is Community Psychology 'Too Insular'? A Network Analysis of Journal Citations." *Jour. of Community Psychology* 41.5 (2013): 549–64. Print.

Nelson, Geoffrey, and Scot D. Evans. "Critical Community Psychology and Qualitative Research: A Conversation." *Qualitative Inquiry* 20.2 (2014): 158–66. Print.

Rappaport, Julian. *Community Psychology: Values, Research, and Action.* New York: Holt, 1977. Print.

Rappaport, Julian, and Edward Seidman, eds. Handbook of Community Psychology. New York: Plenum, 2000. Print.

Scileppi, John A., Robin Diller Torres, and Elizabeth Lee Tead. *Community Psychology: A Common Sense Approach to Mental Health.* Upper Saddle River: Prentice Hall, 1999. Print.

Bruce E. Bailey

See Also: Crisis intervention; Cross-cultural psychology; Ecological psychology; Environmental psychology; Human resource training and development; Juvenile delinquency; Mental health practitioners; Multicultural psychology; Psychology: Fields of specialization; Testing: Historical Perspectives.